Sybase® 15 Replication Server® Administration

Saroj Kapoor Bagai
Jagan Bandi Reddy
with Jeff Tallman

Wordware Publishing, Inc.

Library of Congress Cataloging-in-Publication Data

Bagai, Saroj Kapoor.
    Sybase 15.0 replication server administration / by Saroj Kapoor Bagai and Jagan Bandi Reddy, with Jeff Tallman.
        p. cm.
    Includes index.
    ISBN-13: 978-1-59822-045-2 (pbk.)
    ISBN-10: 1-59822-045-4
    1. Data recovery (Computer science) 2. Sybase. 3. Web servers.
    I. Reddy, Jagan Bandi. II. Tallman, Jeff. III. Title.
    QA76.9.D348B35 2008
    005.8'6--dc22   2008041833
                                                            CIP

ISBN-13: 978-1-59822-045-2
ISBN-10: 1-59822-045-4
10 9 8 7 6 5 4 3 2 1
0811

All inquiries for volume purchases of this book should be addressed to Wordware
Publishing, Inc., at the above address. Telephone inquiries may be made by calling:

(972) 423-0090

This book is dedicated to my loving mother, who is always a candle whenever I stumble into darkness and has been always there for me as a friend, teacher, and role model.

Saroj Bagui

Dedicated to my father, Narasimha Reddy, and mother, Lakshmamma, who have worked hard to give me the education that allowed me to write this book and to my wife, Swarna Reddy, and my sons, Gireesh and Aneesh, who have supported me throughout writing this book.

Jagan Reddy

Contents

Contents

Contents

Contents

Contents

Contents

Contents

Contents

Acknowledgments

I have had the privilege to work with very talented, experienced, and supportive colleagues at Sybase. The work culture has always encouraged teamwork, and the supportive atmosphere at Sybase has helped me achieve my potential in serving my clients to the best of my abilities. I would like to thank Annette Kirkpatrick and Russ Bradley for reviewing the material for this book.

Saroj Bagui

My special thanks are due to our editors, Tim McEvoy and Beth Kohler. My thanks to Saroj Kapoor Bagai and Jeff Tallman who graciously accepted my request to join me in writing this book. Saroj also reviewed many of my chapters. I would also like to thank my colleagues Zhang Lu and Chuck Fox, who took time to review my writing. My sincere thanks to my manager, Michele Kontaxes, and to my vice president, Brian Sullivan, for their constant encouragement.

Jagan Reddy

Introduction

The success of a business often depends on the successful execution of the business's information systems in general and its continuity planning and disaster recovery plans in particular. A business can face severe penalties, customer rejection, and often total failure should it not adequately safeguard its critical data, and especially if it fails to recover sensitive business data in a disaster scenario. The agility of business, the quality of service, and the reduction in costs often lead information technology organizations to re-engineer their operational processes and to invest in automation. Sybase Replication Server is an industry standard product that helps businesses create extremely agile, highly scalable, and, most importantly, easily recovered database systems for both Sybase and non-Sybase databases.

Database management systems like Sybase's Adaptive Server Enterprise play a pivotal role in the accessibility, safety, and security of business-critical data. Sybase Replication Server, a part of the database management industry for more than a decade, provides highly available database solutions. This book discusses administering Sybase Replication Server in a manner that will help recover data in a disaster, and to provide additional functionality as described shortly. This book also addresses many enhancements included in Replication Server 15.0.

An effective Sybase Replication Server system administrator needs a good working knowledge of the database management systems, such as Oracle, Sybase, etc., that manage the replicated data. The Replication Server administrator should know how the Sybase Replication Server interacts with database management systems in maintaining data redundancy for recovery of business-critical data. Detailed explanations of individual database management systems is beyond the scope of this book. Please consult the individual vendor documentation for more information.

Administering the Sybase Replication Server requires knowledge of a number of topics. The following list details the topics in this book and indicates the chapters in which they are covered.

- ▶ Understanding the need for data replication (Chapter 1).

- ▶ Understanding the basic architecture of the Replication Server in order to become an effective Replication Server administrator (Chapter 2).

- ▶ Designing a replication model that suits your business needs (Chapter 3).

- ▶ Installation and upgrade issues. Installing a product is the first step a product administrator encounters after understanding the basic concepts of the product. The success of a product often depends on how easy it is to install and provide a minimal configuration. Chapter 4 covers the details of several alternative installation methods. The companion files, which can be downloaded from www.wordware.com/files/SybaseRS, include some additional help. The installation may be as simple as executing one of the resource templates included in the chapter or in the companion files, after changing appropriate values.

- ▶ Advanced configuration options are discussed in detail in Chapter 5. These configuration options will help achieve better performance. To get a complete understanding of performance and tuning, you may want to read this chapter in conjunction with Chapter 14, "Performance Monitoring and Tuning."

- ▶ Replication Server system disaster and recovery issues are discussed in Chapter 15. A successful Replication Server administrator must understand how to recover from system disasters. This includes disasters related to various components of the replication system and recovery techniques.

- ▶ Data replication often involves heterogeneous data. You may need to replicate data from Sybase to non-Sybase database management systems. Regardless, you need an understanding of the Replication Agent for the respective platform, discussed in Chapter 6, "Replication Agent." Chapter 16 will discuss more details about Sybase data replication to Oracle and vice versa.

▶ Connection management is discussed in Chapter 7.

▶ Administering routes between replication servers and data servers is discussed in Chapter 8.

▶ Establishing a replication for tables, the stored procedures, and using the function strings for manipulating replication is described in detail in Chapters 9-11. The Sybase Replication Server is very powerful in manipulating the replicated data via function strings. For example, what may be a delete operation on the primary database may be either completely ignored on the replicate database or may just be recorded in a log table to archive how many delete attempts occurred on the sensitive data. It can even capture who is attempting to delete such data and many more details.

▶ Multi-site availability (MSA) is replication at a database level. It is similar to the warm standby but easier to establish, especially where there are many tables in the database. If your application needs more control at the table or column level, you may consider table-level replication. Warm standby is discussed in greater detail in Chapter 12 and MSA is discussed in Chapter 13.

▶ The Replication Server needs a system database to store metadata related to the replication process management. Using the Embedded Replication Server System Database (ERSSD) is an alternative to using the traditional RSSD. An ERSSD is based on Adaptive Server Anywhere, which requires minimal system administration, whereas the RSSD is based on Adaptive Server Enterprise, which requires standard database management expertise and may actually become a point of failure. Chapter 19 discusses the ERSSD in detail.

▶ Security, internationalization, and troubleshooting of the Replication Server are discussed in Chapters 17, 18, and 20, respectively.

Sybase Replication Server is a versatile product. This book discusses in detail how to install and manage the Sybase Replication Server to enhance operational data availability.

You will find some convenient tools for managing replication and some screenshots for the installation demonstration in the companion files, available at www.wordware.com/files/SybaseRS.

Chapter 1

Data Replication

Why Replicate Data?

Businesses replicate data to provide better fault tolerance and enable disaster recovery as a part of business continuity planning. Replicating the data allows for either the decentralization or the consolidation of data. This gives businesses the ability to continue in the face of planned or unplanned outages and allows for data recovery in case of disasters. Disaster recovery in the context of the Sybase Replication Server is described in Chapter 15.

A disaster can strike an information systems database management system in many ways. The lowest level of a disaster is the loss of one or more specific database records. Higher levels of data loss progressively include loss of an entire database, loss of an entire instance or data server, and finally loss of an entire data processing center. Whether the disaster is natural or manmade, the recovery process often remains the same. The ease of recovery is contingent upon a well-planned recovery mechanism that the business enforces as part of its continuity planning. In an increasingly customer-sensitive business climate, the downtime required to recover the data in its entirety must be minimal. Because the Internet has made communications borderless and 24x7, the concept of downtime is elusive. For instance, a maintenance window of 4 a.m. to 7 a.m. EST will cause havoc if you have customers in Europe, while American customers are generally snoozing away. Thus, downtime must be minimized as much as possible and scheduled maintenance performed when it makes the most sense and has the least impact on the customer.

Fault tolerance is the ability of an information system to continue normal operations despite the presence of a software or hardware fault. Typically this means an online copy of the sensitive data that is available all the time and is as close as possible to the actual data. It also means that a process is in place for an easy, seamless, and instantaneous failover to the copy of the data that provides the data processing continuity. The failover mechanism may or may not require human involvement. The process of maintaining a current copy of the data in such a manner as to facilitate business continuity is often achieved by replicating the data.

Advantages of Data Replication

Data replication provides many benefits including but not limited to the following:

▶ Business process continuity — The main purpose of database replication is to provide business process continuity in case of a disaster resulting in the loss of a copy of the data. The simplest scheme of replicating the primary copy of the data is to replicate the data to a replicate site, typically one that is geographically separate. This ensures the continuity of business processing. Depending on the criticality of the data, different configurations of data replication may be adopted to derive the maximum protection. Several data replication designs are provided in Chapter 3. Sybase Replication Server replicates the transactions rather than the data.

▶ Fault tolerance – A good data replication scheme should provide tolerance against common mistakes including both system and human errors. If a disk drive is corrupted on the primary host, resulting in a severe loss of data, a replicated copy of the same data should be isolated from such corruption. Data replication should also offer methods to protect against common human errors. Since Sybase Replication Server replicates the transactions, the hardware issues are not replicated to the replicate copy.

▶ Load balancing — Every business wants to utilize its resources optimally. In the real data replication world, the processing load on the replicate is minimal. So, a true replication configuration should offer to balance the load on the primary as well as on the replicate. This will ensure optimal utilization of hardware and software resources and provide the best experience to the customers. However, utilizing both the primary and the replicate data processing sites simultaneously may pose some data integrity issues. Chapter 3 discusses the update conflicts when both the primary and replicate sites are used for load balancing.

▶ Data verification at will — A good replication mechanism should allow frequent verification of the replicated data. The replicated data should closely resemble the primary copy of the data. The latency of data replication should meet the business processing requirements. Data verification may include generating reports off of the replicated copy of the data, leaving the primary copy for customer transaction processing.

▶ Heterogeneous data replication — A standard replication mechanism should offer a means to replicate data between heterogeneous database management systems. Replicating Oracle data to Sybase and vice versa is discussed in Chapter 16.

▶ Report generation or a decision support system — The replicated online copy of the current production data offers an opportunity to run reports against it, reducing the report running load on the primary production server. Many businesses run reports daily or at regular intervals. Isolating very high I/O intensive report generating to a replicate copy allows the primary server to provide the best possible customer transaction processing experience.

Thus, the best replication system would offer site autonomy as well as the performance gains realized when both the primary and the replicate are used for data processing.

Data Replication and Failover Methods

Data can be replicated by several means to provide high availability. Data replication methods can be divided into three major categories: hardware data replication, software data replication, and a combination of hardware and software replication.

Hardware Data Replication

In hardware data replication, systems use some hardware component to copy data. RAID technology combined with some kind of SRDF (Symmetrix Remote Data Facility) can provide a high-availability solution. The advantage of such a method is ease of the replication. The disadvantages are that such a method does not provide online data verification of the replicate copy of the data, it may require some downtime to activate the mirror copy of the data, and it does not allow for load balancing. Another issue is data corruption. This method copies disk records in their entirety, meaning that any corruption in the data will be copied. In hardware data replication all data corruptions due to hardware faults will be replicated onto the secondary. In Sybase replication server, data corruptions due to hardware faults are rarely copied to the replicate.

In a hardware-only replication, failover is accomplished by bringing up the replicate host and performing a complete recovery of the database. Typically the recovery of a Sybase database does not take a long time. However, there is an inherent risk of losing the database if the recovery fails, and one cannot ensure the success of the database recovery until the recovery is complete. Hardware-only replication lacks many other replication advantages including load balancing, report generation, and data verification.

Software Data Replication

Software data replication is typically accomplished by using an industry standard replication management system such as Sybase Replication Server. Sybase replication provides all of the benefits of a replication system as detailed above. Software data replication is the primary focus of this book.

Software/Hardware Replication System

In the combination model, the hardware continues to replicate the data, and the software validates the data and keeps it ready for recovery. This solution usually assures data integrity and availability; however, the data is not online, which means functions like load balancing and report generation cannot be accomplished. Most hardware vendors provide this kind of solution.

Chapter 2

The Replication Server Architecture

Replication Server is an Open Client/Server application. Replication Server uses many asynchronous threads to communicate with and transfer data to and from the target and source data servers. Replication occurs in a typical publish and subscribe model with confirmed delivery. Source database users publish the data, while target database users subscribe to the data. Various connections and routes help transfer data from the source to the target. In this chapter we highlight the overall Replication Server architecture and briefly discuss individual sub-components or threads. Detailed discussion of connections and routes is provided in Chapters 7 and 8, respectively.

Replication Server is a complex system with multiple components running on different hosts.

ID Server

The Replication Server architecture includes the ID Server, an important component that assigns globally unique IDs to replication objects and connections. ID Server is a replication server that registers all the replication servers and databases in a replication system. Typically, this will be the first Replication Server installed. Note that the ID Server does not have to be a dedicated RS, it can also perform data distribution. The ID Server must be running when Replication Server is installed, a route is created, or a database connection is created. The ID Server user login is used only when a Replication Server logs into an ID Server, such as when databases, routes, or Replication Servers are added to the replication system domain. There is only one ID Server user for the entire replication system domain. When Replication Server is added to the replication system domain, the ID Server user login is added in its configuration file by rs_init.

ID Server configuration file:

```
cat prs.cfg
#
# Configuration file for Replication Server 'prs'. Created by rs_init.
#
RSSD_embedded=no
RSSD_server=pds
RSSD_database=prs_RSSD
RSSD_primary_user=prs_RSSD_prim
RSSD_primary_pw=prs_RSSD_prim_ps
RSSD_maint_user=prs_RSSD_maint
RSSD_maint_pw=prs_RSSD_maint_ps
RSSD_ha_failover=no
ID_server=prs
ID_user=prs_id_user
ID_pw=prs_id_passwd
RS_charset=iso_1
RS_language=us_english
RS_sortorder=binary
```

Replicate Replication Server configuration file:

```
cat rrs1.cfg
#
# Configuration file for Replication Server 'rrs1'. Created by rs_init.
#
RSSD_embedded=no
RSSD_server=rds
RSSD_database=rrs1_RSSD
RSSD_primary_user=rrs1_RSSD_prim
RSSD_primary_pw=rrs1_RSSD_prim_ps
RSSD_maint_user=rrs1_RSSD_maint
RSSD_maint_pw=rrs1_RSSD_maint_ps
RSSD_ha_failover=no
```

```
ID_server=prs
ID_user=prs_id_user
ID_pw=prs_id_passwd
RS_charset=iso_1
RS_language=us_english
RS_sortorder=binary
```

Replication System Domain

All Replication Servers that are registered under one ID Server constitute a replication system domain. While it is possible to set up cross-domain replication, it requires careful planning to ensure that database IDs and other identifiers are not duplicated between the domains. All the applications that belong to a business unit should belong to one replication system domain, so that they can exchange data between them. You can have as many domains as you need, and you can have as many Replication Servers as you want per replication system domain.

Excerpt from sample resource file ($SYBASE/REP-15_0/init/rs/install.rs) (where $SYBASE is Sybase release directory):

```
# The next two attributes should be set only when installing an ID Server
# and there are multiple ID Server domains

# First ID used for Replication Servers in this ID Server domain
rs.rs_start_rs_id: USE_DEFAULT

# First ID used for databases in this ID Server domain
rs.rs_start_db_id: USE_DEFAULT
```

The replication system utilizes the RepAgent or Log Transfer Manager (LTM) to scan the Adaptive Enterprise transaction log. The Replication Server uses many additional threads, or queues, to organize data in commit order. Replication Server even allows facilities to change the way a transaction is applied at the target site using function strings. Many of these details are discussed in this chapter from the architecture perspective. Installation and configuration aspects of some of the threads are discussed in appropriate chapters.

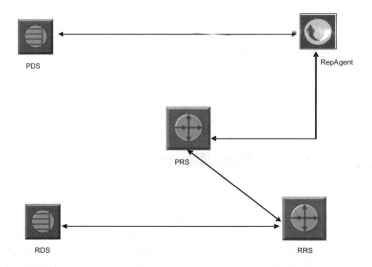

Figure 2-1

Figure 2-1 shows a replication system that contains the following components:

▶ Replication Server (primary (PRS) and replicate (RRS))

▶ RepAgent

▶ Adaptive Server Enterprise (primary (PDS) and replicate (RDS)) or other non-Sybase databases

Figure 2-2 shows Replication Server data flow.

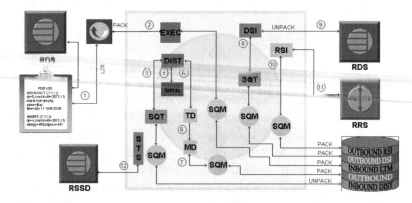

Figure 2-2

The data flow is as follows:

1. Replication Server transfers completed transactions from a primary (source) database to a replicate (target). RepAgent scans the primary database transaction log and generates LTL (Log Transfer Language) output. Replication Server uses the LTL proprietary language to process and distribute replicated transactions throughout the replication system.

2. The RepAgent log transfers the interface thread, then passes the LTL output to the Replication Server. The EXEC (Executor) thread or RepAgent user thread writes packed LTL into the inbound queue.

3. The DIST thread associated with the primary database waits for the SQT (Stable Queue Transaction) thread to read from the inbound queue by calling SQM (Stable Queue Manager) and collates all the commands of the transactions in commit order.

4. Once a complete transaction is seen, the DIST (Distributor) calls the SRE (Subscription Resolution Engine) to determine which command should be sent to which site. The SRE appends a destination database ID (DBID) to each row of the transaction.

5. DIST then calls the Transaction Delivery (TD) module to pack commands and place a begin transaction record in each outbound queue. TD also appends a two-byte counter to ensure the uniqueness of the origin queue ID (OQID) generated by RepAgent.

6. The MD (Message Delivery) module optimizes delivery by grouping messages bound for multiple sites that are governed by the same route. DSI (Data Server Interface) gets a callback from SQT when the closed queue has committed the transaction.

7. The DSI (Data Server Interface) scheduler attempts to group the transactions and then dispatches them to an available EXEC thread.

8. The EXEC performs function string mapping and error handling.

9. If messages are destined for another site, RSI sender will deliver messages to RRS (Replicate Replication Server).

10. The RSI user at RRS calls MD (Message Delivery) to read from the network and resolve the delivery instructions by reading the RSI_MESSAGE header.

11. RSI truncation point is passed to sending Replication Server when a route secondary truncation point message is received. The STS (System Table Services) interface is used to access all RSSD/ERSSD (Replication Server System Database/Embedded Replication Server System Database).

Inbound Queue

The scanned transaction log records for objects marked for replication are stored in the inbound queue of the stable device until the transactions are committed.

Outbound Queue

Subscribed transactions in the inbound queue are moved to the appropriate outbound queue in commit order.

Connection

Replication Server communicates with the database using appropriate connections. It then uses the connections for distributing transactions received from the primary database to the replicate database managed by the Replication Server. Replication Server can have connections to more than one database, but each database can have only one connection to the Replication Server. Function strings are retrieved from RSSD/ERSSD and outbound transactions are formatted into SQL statements. Replication Server makes client connections to the databases and applies transactions in commit order to the replicate database by the maintenance user. All integrity enforcements occur when Replication Server applies transactions. SQL errors cause the connection to suspend. Outbound queues can't drain until suspended connections are resumed by resolving SQL errors. Details about connections can be found in Chapter 7.

Route

Two Replication Servers communicate using routes. After delivering messages to the replicate Replication Server, the route uses a connection to apply transactions to the replicate database. Please refer to Chapter 8 for more information on routes.

Replication Server Threads

Replication Server threads are running processes that perform specific tasks in the data servers and Replication Server.

RepAgent

RepAgent scans the primary database transaction log. Log records for marked objects (tables and stored procedures marked with sp_setreptable) are sent to the primary Replication Server's (PRS) inbound queue. The Replication Server maintains a secondary truncation point within the primary database. The secondary truncation point is a pointer to the oldest active transaction that has not been completely read by RepAgent. The RSSD system table rs_locater is used by RepAgent to maintain a scan point between the secondary truncation point and the last page of the transaction log.

```
1> admin who
2> go
  Spid Name        State                  Info
  ---- ----------  --------------------   ---------------------------------
    41 DSI EXEC    Awaiting Command       101(1) pds.prs_RSSD
    34 DSI         Awaiting Message       101 pds.prs_RSSD
    37 DIST        Awaiting Wakeup        101 pds.prs_RSSD
    40 SQT         Awaiting Wakeup        101:1  DIST pds.prs_RSSD
    29 SQM         Awaiting Message       101:1 pds.prs_RSSD
    18 SQM         Awaiting Message       101:0 pds.prs_RSSD
    36 REP AGENT   Awaiting Command       pds.prs_RSSD
     .
     .
     .
```

Stable Queue Manager (SQM)

Replication Server utilizes stable storage to save messages. Stable storage is provided by one or more partitions (raw or file system devices). Replication Server has one SQM for each queue in stable storage, and uses a "store and forward" technique to increase availability and recovery in a distributed environment. Transactions travel from the primary (source) to one or more replicate (destination) sites. If a transaction is unable to be forwarded to a destination site, then messages are stored in the stable queue, and reapplied when the component is available (this is governed by the save interval). SQM detects duplicate messages. The physical I/O is performed by dAIO, not SQM. Messages read from the queues are not automatically deleted. Deletion is done only when SQM is requested to delete messages. Messages can be reread from the undeleted message in the queue. Duplicate messages from the origin queue ID (OQID) are recognized and ignored. SQM supports multiple writers and one reader of the stable queue.

```
1> admin who
2> go
 Spid Name        State                Info
 ---- ----------  -------------------- ---------------------------------
   41 DSI EXEC    Awaiting Command     101(1) pds.prs_RSSD
   34 DSI         Awaiting Message     101 pds.prs_RSSD
   37 DIST        Awaiting Wakeup      101 pds.prs_RSSD
   40 SQT         Awaiting Wakeup      101:1  DIST pds.prs_RSSD
   29 SQM         Awaiting Message     101:1 pds.prs_RSSD
   18 SQM         Awaiting Message     101:0 pds.prs_RSSD
   36 REP AGENT   Awaiting Command     pds.prs_RSSD
   32 RSI         Sleeping             rrs1
   30 SQM         Awaiting Message     16777318:0 rrs1
   33 RSI         Sleeping             rrs3
   31 SQM         Awaiting Message     16777320:0 rrs3
   35 dSUB        Sleeping
   15 dCM         Awaiting Message
   17 dAIO        Awaiting Message
   38 dREC        Sleeping             dREC
   42 USER        Active               sa
   14 dALARM      Awaiting Wakeup
   39 dSYSAM      Sleeping
```

Stable Queue Transaction (SQT)

SQT reads messages from the inbound queue and then sorts them in commit order:

```
begin transaction [tran]
[tran]
commit transaction
```

SQT also manages the outbound queue. The DIST thread is notified by SQT when the COMMIT record is scanned. DIST, DSI, and Standby DSI are SQT clients. The SQT cache is configured with:

```
configure replication server set "sqt_max_cache_size" to "size in bytes"
```

The default is 131,072 bytes.

The "Removed" column returned by the admin who,sqt command is frequently non-zero, which means sqt_max_cache_size is undersized, and it should be increased.

```
1> admin who,sqt
2> go
Spid State                Info                                        Closed
       Read       Open       Trunc      Removed    Full
       SQM Blocked First Trans                                         Parsed
       SQM Reader  Change Oqids Detect Orphans
---- -------------------- ---------------------------------------- -----------
     ----------- ----------- ----------- ----------- -----------
     ----------- ---------------------------------------- -----------
     ----------- ------------ --------------
  40 Awaiting Wakeup      101:1  DIST pds.prs_RSSD                         0
               0          0           0          0          0
               1                                                          0
               0          0           0
  34 Awaiting Message     101 pds.prs_RSSD                                 0
               0          0           0          0          0
               0                                                          0
               0          0           1
```

If the SQT cache is full, SQT selects transactions with the largest number of commands in the open queue and flushes them to disk to free space, which can slow down the transfer from the inbound queue to the outbound queue.

```
1> admin who
2> go
   Spid Name       State                Info
   ---- ---------- -------------------- ----------------------------------
     41 DSI EXEC   Awaiting Command     101(1) pds_prs_RSSD
     34 DSI        Awaiting Message     101 pds.prs_RSSD
     37 DIST       Awaiting Wakeup      101 pds,prs RSSD
     40 SQT        Awaiting Wakeup      101:1  DIST pds.prs_RSSD
     29 SQM        Awaiting Message     101:1 pds.prs_RSSD
     18 SQM        Awaiting Message     101:0 pds.prs_RSSD
     36 REP AGENT  Awaiting Command     pds.prs_RSSD
     32 RSI        Sleeping             rrs1
     30 SQM        Awaiting Message     16777318:0 rrs1
     33 RSI        Sleeping             rrs3
     31 SQM        Awaiting Message     16777320:0 rrs3
```

```
35 dSUB      Sleeping
15 dCM       Awaiting Message
17 dAIO      Awaiting Message
.
.
.
```

Executor (EXEC)

Every primary database has one EXEC thread for the RepAgent user to handle incoming connections. There are two types of EXEC threads: RA-USER and RSI USER.

Replication Server differentiates between these two threads with the connect source command.

Distributor (DIST)

Each primary database/inbound queue has one DIST thread. The DIST thread calls SQT and SQM to read the inbound queue in commit order. It makes calls to Subscription Resolution Engine (SRE), Transaction Delivery (TD), and Message Delivery (MD) to determine the destination of the transaction. The destination could be the outbound queue corresponding to replicate databases and/or RSI (route) outbound queues corresponding to downstream Replication Servers.

```
1> admin who
2> go
Spid Name        State              Info
---- ----------  ------------------ -----------------------------------
  41 DSI EXEC    Awaiting Command   101(1) pds.prs_RSSD
  34 DSI         Awaiting Message   101 pds.prs_RSSD
  37 DIST        Awaiting Wakeup    101 pds.prs_RSSD
  40 SQT         Awaiting Wakeup    101:1  DIST pds.prs_RSSD
  29 SQM         Awaiting Message   101:1 pds.prs_RSSD
  18 SQM         Awaiting Message   101:0 pds.prs_RSSD
  36 REP AGENT   Awaiting Command   pds.prs_RSSD
  32 RSI         Sleeping           rrs1
   .
   .
   .
```

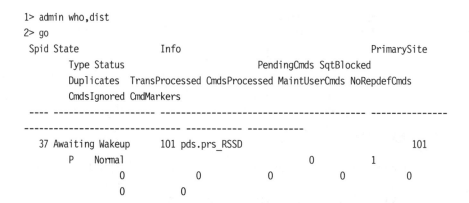

```
1> admin who,dist
2> go
 Spid State               Info                            PrimarySite
       Type Status                      PendingCmds SqtBlocked
       Duplicates  TransProcessed CmdsProcessed MaintUserCmds NoRepdefCmds
       CmdsIgnored CmdMarkers
 ---- -------------------- ---------------------------------------- ---------------
-------------------------------- ----------- -----------
   37 Awaiting Wakeup     101 pds.prs_RSSD                              101
        P    Normal                                   0         1
                0              0            0            0          0
                0              0
```

Subscription Resolution Engine (SRE)

SRE determines which transactions have subscriptions and their
destinations and then it appends a destination database ID to each
transaction row. Only transaction rows that match some subscription are marked to be sent. If the transaction row doesn't have
any subscription, then DIST is informed to delete that transaction
row.

Transaction Delivery Module (TD)

The Transaction Delivery module is called by DIST to deliver
transaction rows to data servers and other Replication Servers.
TD packs commands into binary or ASCII, depending on queue
and version, before requesting delivery to the outbound queue.
TD sends the BEGIN command to all sites before sending other
transaction commands and calls the MD (Message Delivery)
module for delivery to outbound queues.

Message Delivery Module (MD)

MD is called by the TD inside of DIST to optimize routing of
transactions to data servers and Replication Servers. DIST passes
the transaction row and the destination ID to the MD module.
The RSI_USER of RRS (replicate Replication Server) also calls
MD to read packets from the network.

Data Server Interface (DSI)

There can be one or many (parallel) DSI threads per database. DSI reads transactions from outbound queues using SQT and SQM and executes these transactions on Adaptive Server Enterprise/non-Sybase data servers. The DSI thread is composed of a DSI Scheduler (DSI-S) thread and n DSI Executor (DSI EXEC) threads.

DSI Scheduler (DSI-S) reads transactions from the outbound queue, sorts them into commit order using SQL Library and grouping logic, and submits them to DSI Executor for delivery. Several transaction commands can be grouped into one transaction and then applied at the data server. This reduces last page contention on the replicate database transaction log. (Actually the ULC at the replicate should do that; the real reason for transaction grouping is to reduce the overhead of maintaining rs_lastcommit — especially in online transaction processing systems/short transaction environments.) The transaction group is executed as one transaction using the begin tran of the first transaction and the commit transaction of the last transaction in the group. Not all transactions can be grouped. Transactions may be grouped together only if they are in memory (SQT closed transactions that are present in memory), have the same origin, and have the same username and password (transactions that are applied to the replicate data server are applied with the maintenance user and password except for DDL and request functions). Orphan, aborted routing, subscription, and dump/load transactions cannot be part of any transaction group. The maximum number of bytes placed into a command batch by Replication Server is controlled by dsi_cmd_batch_size (default: 8192 bytes) and the maximum number of transactions in a group is specified by dsi_max_xacts_in_group (default: 20). Performance can be improved by setting this parameter to a larger number.

DSI Executor (DSI EXEC) reads transactions from the DSI SQT cache, performs function string mapping, batches the transactions, and then executes them on the replicate data server. It also checks for errors (maps data server errors into Replication Server errors and error actions) before sending commits. Each parallel thread has one DSI EXEC.

It also checks for failed, duplicate, lost, and orphan transactions. When using parallel DSI threads, the serialization method should be chosen very carefully.

Duplicate Detection

DSI doesn't execute the transactions that are already applied against the replicate data server. There is a delay between the time the transaction is committed to the data server and the time the messages are actually deleted from the outbound queue. If Replication Server were to crash during this delay and then was restarted, it could result in messages being reapplied. Duplicate detection by DSI is performed during the interval when the Replication Server is restarted and the DSI connection is resumed after being suspended.

Loss Detection

Loss detection is also performed by DSI. DSI checks for loss detection when the rebuild queue is executed. If a loss is detected, it needs to be resolved by using:

```
ignore loss
    from data_server.database
    [to {data_server.database | replication_server}]
```

data_server.database

> The primary data server and database whose message loss is to be ignored.

data server.database

> The replicate data server and database for the lost messages.

replication_server

> The replicate Replication Server for the lost messages.

Replication Server Interface (RSI)

There can be only one RSI per route. RSI is composed of two components: the RSI sender thread and the RSI user thread.

If the route is not suspended, an RSI sender thread is started for each direct Replication Server (listed in rssd..rs_routes). The RSI sender thread establishes connection with the replicate Replication Server after reading all the route-specific parameters:

rsi_batch_size

> The number of bytes sent to the destination Replication Server before a truncation point is requested.

rsi_fadeout_time

> The number of seconds of idle time before the source Replication Server closes its connection to the destination Replication Server.

rsi_packet_size

> The packet size in bytes for communication with other Replication Servers.

rsi_sync_interval

> The interval in seconds between RSI sync messages.

rsi_xact_with_large_msg

> This parameter governs the route behavior if a large message is encountered. This is applicable to direct routes in which the site version at the replicate site is 12.1 or earlier.

The primary Replication Server establishes a connection to the replicate Replication Server by executing the connect source RSI *siteid version* command. The replicate Replication Server acknowledges this connection request and verifies that it is an actual RSI user, then it internally marks the EXEC thread as RSI USER.

The RSI user at the replicate Replication Server calls MD to read from the network, and then it copies messages to the outbound queue of the database connection (local subscriber) or of the route (if this Replication Server is an intermediate Replication Server). Note that the DIST.MD may distribute the same transactions to multiple outbound queues at once, if there are multiple destinations within that RS. Once the messages are copied to the replicate Replication Server outbound queue by MD, MD instructs the replicate Replication Server to delete the messages. Messages are written to the outbound queue not in receive order but in commit order. Delete requests may get delayed until all the transactions are applied in received order. Delete requests are then forwarded to the originating outbound queue. When the primary Replication Server receives the delete request from the replicate Replication Server, it calls the SQM for the outbound queue. Deletion of messages may be delayed by the configuration parameter save_interval.

Replication Server Daemons

Daemons are not configurable.

Alarm Daemon (dAlarm)

dAlarm tracks asynchronous I/O and callback completions and incompletions.

```
1> admin who
2> go
 Spid Name       State                 Info
 ---- ---------- --------------------- -----------------------------------
   41 DSI EXEC   Awaiting Command      101(1) pds.prs_RSSD
   34 DSI        Awaiting Message      101 pds.prs_RSSD
   37 DIST       Awaiting Wakeup       101 pds.prs_RSSD
    .
    .
    .
   35 dSUB       Sleeping
```

```
15 dCM       Awaiting Message
17 dAIO      Awaiting Message
38 dREC      Sleeping              dREC
43 USER      Active                sa
14 dALARM    Awaiting Wakeup
39 dSYSAM    Sleeping
```

Async I/O Daemon (dAIO)

This daemon handles physical I/O.

```
1> admin who
2> go
Spid Name        State                Info
---- ---------- -------------------- ------------------------------------
  41 DSI EXEC    Awaiting Command     101(1) pds.prs_RSSD
  34 DSI         Awaiting Message     101 pds.prs_RSSD
   .
   .
   .
  35 dSUB        Sleeping
  15 dCM         Awaiting Message
  17 dAIO        Awaiting Message
  38 dREC        Sleeping             dREC
  43 USER        Active               sa
  14 dALARM      Awaiting Wakeup
  39 dSYSAM      Sleeping
```

Connection Manager Daemon (dCM)

This daemon coordinates incoming connections.

```
1> admin who
2> go
Spid Name        State                Info
---- ---------- -------------------- ------------------------------------
  41 DSI EXEC    Awaiting Command     101(1) pds.prs_RSSD
  34 DSI         Awaiting Message     101 pds.prs_RSSD
   .
   .
   .
  35 dSUB        Sleeping
```

```
15 dCM        Awaiting Message
17 dAIO       Awaiting Message
38 dREC       Sleeping              dREC
43 USER       Active                sa
14 dALARM     Awaiting Wakeup
39 dSYSAM     Sleeping
```

SySAM Daemon (dSYSAM)

This license manager daemon keeps track of checked out licenses.

```
1> admin who
2> go
Spid Name        State                Info
---- ---------- -------------------- ------------------------------------
  41 DSI EXEC   Awaiting Command     101(1) pds.prs_RSSD
  34 DSI        Awaiting Message     101 pds.prs_RSSD
   .
   .
   .
  35 dSUB       Sleeping
  15 dCM        Awaiting Message
  17 dAIO       Awaiting Message
  38 dREC       Sleeping             dREC
  43 USER       Active               sa
  14 dALARM     Awaiting Wakeup
  39 dSYSAM     Sleeping
```

Subscription Retry Daemon (dSUB)

This daemon retries subscriptions.

```
1> admin who
2> go
Spid Name        State                Info
---- ---------- -------------------- ------------------------------------
  41 DSI EXEC   Awaiting Command     101(1) pds.prs_RSSD
  34 DSI        Awaiting Message     101 pds.prs_RSSD
   .
   .
   .
```

```
35 dSUB      Sleeping
15 dCM       Awaiting Message
17 dAIO      Awaiting Message
38 dREC      Sleeping              dREC
43 USER      Active                sa
14 dALARM    Awaiting Wakeup
39 dSYSAM    Sleeping
```

Recovery Daemon (dREC)

This daemon performs the recovery process.

```
1> admin who
2> go
Spid Name        State                 Info
---- ---------- -------------------- ------------------------------------
  41 DSI EXEC   Awaiting Command     101(1) pds.prs_RSSD
  34 DSI        Awaiting Message     101 pds.prs_RSSD
     .
     .
     .
  35 dSUB       Sleeping
  15 dCM        Awaiting Message
  17 dAIO       Awaiting Message
  38 dREC       Sleeping             dREC
  43 USER       Active               sa
  14 dALARM     Awaiting Wakeup
  39 dSYSAM     Sleeping
```

In summary, replication is an ongoing process of transferring completed transactions from the primary database, inbound queue, outbound queue, and replicate database connection. In replication:

▶ The RepAgent of the primary database forwards transactions to the inbound queue of the primary Replication Server.

▶ The inbound queue of the primary Replication Server filters transactions and passes them to the replicate Replication Server (via route) or the replicate database's outbound queue.

▶ The outbound queue of the replicate Replication Server sends batches over a route to the replicate database's outbound queue.

▶ Transactions in the replicate database's outbound queue are scheduled.

▶ Transactions are applied to the replicate database by the maintenance user.

Chapter 3

Replication Design and Implementation Strategies

In this chapter, we will discuss some basic replication terminology, application architecture, and different replication designs, and lay the groundwork for understanding the replication process. More details on each of the components discussed in this chapter can be found in their appropriate chapters. Also, be sure to read Chapter 14, "Performance Monitoring and Tuning," for an in-depth discussion on various components of Replication Server from the perspective of monitoring and tuning.

Replication Design Terminology

Before we consider what types of applications are suitable for replication and the application architecture for successful replication, we need to know some basic terminology related to replicating data.

Distributed Data vs. Replicated Data

Data can be replicated in two ways. One method is as simple as a copy and paste of data to a remote site to increase data availability. The second method is replicating transactions to remote site(s) so that an exact playback of transactions creates a redundant copy of data at one or more remote sites. Sybase Replication Server replicates committed transactions, not data.

Data must be duplicated to ensure recovery in the event one copy is compromised or becomes otherwise unavailable. If the data is just distributed over physical sites, you will achieve site autonomy, but not reliability. In a distributed database management system, data is fragmented and a piece of data is relocated to another site for ease of processing or departmentalized consumption. Such data distribution does not qualify as replication, as it does not provide a disaster recovery facility. Replication servers do not manage distributed data. Replicated data differs from distributed data in that the replicated data is an exact and full copy of the original data. Both copies of the data are available for production usage at any time.

Simple data distribution is typically achieved by a two-phase commit. A two-phase commit works on the principle of *pessimistic concurrency control*, wherein transaction failures are allowed to occur and are corrected later. This requires an inordinate amount of locking and network communications to maintain data integrity. Replication Server works on the principle of *optimistic concurrency control*, in which the system needs fewer resources and transactions are not allowed to continue if they are likely to fail.

Latency

Latency is the time required to replicate changes to data at one location to the subscribing or target location(s). The amount of time to replicate changes differs from application to application. For extremely critical business applications, latency must be as close to zero seconds as possible.

Tight Consistency vs. Loose Consistency

Consistency refers to the state of data at any given point in time. A promising database management system should maintain data consistent with the application at any given time. The same rule applies to the replication system as well. However, as the replication system encounters many layers of processing before reaching the target, consistency is not always guaranteed. Latency differs depending on the consistency type. With tight consistency, operations are synchronous; a transaction must commit at both primary and replicate in order to be completed. A typical two-phase commit is the best example of this. Either the transaction commits at both ends or it rolls back at both ends. With loose consistency, operations are asynchronous and there always exists a possibility that the primary and replicate are not consistent. Only committed transactions are replicated and there is no concept of rolling back. However, once applied at the replicate site, replicate data is always *state consistent with its primary data.*

Sybase Replication Server uses the loose consistency model. It is the responsibility of the application designer and replication server administrator to attempt to minimize latency.

It is also very important to decide if an application can use the replicate site for data processing. As previously stated, there is always the likelihood that the replicate site may lag behind the primary. A financially sensitive application like a banking withdrawal application may tolerate some conditional latency. For example, it may allow withdrawal of $100 each time, but when a withdrawal of thousands of dollars is attempted, it may block the transaction or will attempt to wait for data to be replicated from the primary before allowing the transaction.

Asynchronous Replication

In any database management system, asynchronous replication can be achieved by either using Replication Server or not using Replication Server.

Effect of asynchronous replication via Replication Server:

▶ Transactional consistency

▶ Sequential consistency

▶ High availability

▶ Fault tolerance

- ▶ Load balance
- ▶ Application transparency
- ▶ Database management system transparency

The Sybase replication system can also be used to replicate between heterogeneous database management systems.
Other asynchronous methods of replication:

- ▶ Dump the primary database and load at the replicate site.

    This method does not offer fault tolerance or load balancing. It is near high availability and includes latency equal to the transactional dump time delay plus the time required to load the transaction log. You never know if the replicate will be able to service the application until all the data is recovered and the replicate data server is up and running.

- ▶ Bulk load transfer the primary copy.

    This method suffers from almost all of the disadvantages. The best it offers is a snapshot of the production data at a point in time.

- ▶ Row flagging or store and forward tables.

    Changes to rows are saved in a separate table. Then some custom scripts or methods are used to constantly forward and apply those changes to the replicate site. This method involves too many manual or semi-automated methods and is prone to failure, and thus does not offer many Replication Server benefits.

- ▶ Use Component Integration Services (CIS).

    Proxy tables in conjunction with triggers may help replicate data changes. This is especially suitable for low transaction rate applications that use fewer tables so as to minimize CIS complexity.

- ▶ Use occasionally connected replication.

    Most mobile applications fit into this category, where clients are occasionally connected to the server. Servers are there to save the data. The client application must be able to utilize the data that it has at its disposal.

Replication Server Process Flow

As you may notice in the replication production process flow diagram in Figure 3-1, production transactions can flow in either direction, depending on the replication setup and configuration. In the case of either node (primary or replicate) failing, the application can point to the surviving node and production continues. Many of the later chapters will give more details on the configuration, tuning, and management aspects of the processes in the diagram.

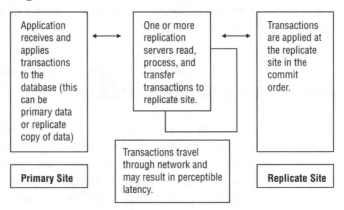

Figure 3-1

Another type of replication called warm standby works in a slightly different manner, but serves the same purpose. Please refer to Chapter 12 for details on warm standby functionality and management.

A Simplified Replication Model

In a simplified replication, typically there will be one Replication Server, replicating transactions from one or more primary databases to one or more replicate databases. This model may spread over a wide area network or may be confined to a single office location or may exist entirely on the same computer. Even though a replication system can be implemented on the same computer where the primary data server runs, it should be noted that this does not offer failover capability in the event of disaster. Such implementations, however, may be suitable for development and quality assurance testing.

Application Types for Replication

The type of replication design (see the "Replication Designs" section in this chapter for more information) chosen for an application depends on the type of application. Sybase's replication system can replicate transactions for a variety of applications. The major application types that we come across when we think of replicating transactions are the following:

▶ Decision support systems (DSS) — Applications that are primarily used for report generation purposes. These applications consist mostly of reads and fewer writes or updates. Writes in general are batched and executed in large volumes over a short span of time in order to load the warehouse with the latest data.

▶ Online transaction processing systems (OLTP) — These are primarily the transaction processing databases. Frequent reads and writes are common in this type of application, which is the most common type of business application. We implement replication for OLTP applications most of the time. OLTP applications benefit the most from a robust replication system.

▶ Warm standby applications — These can be either DSS or OLTP applications, both of which require a copy of the primary data to be available in a remote location. The standby database can easily be switched to take the role of primary production database in the event the production database becomes unavailable.

Replication Server can service replicating transactions for all of the above types of applications. However, depending on the nature of the application and application load, Replication Server may need to be evaluated to verify if it can meet the application's requirements. The nature and intensity of reads and writes differ between types of applications; consequently, so will the implementation strategy selected to replicate data. It is very important to select an appropriate replication implementation strategy to achieve efficient replication.

Replication Server allows maintaining a mixed workload in an information processing system. For example, multiple OLTP primary databases can be replicated to a single DSS database. All the reads associated with DSS reporting (i.e., long queries with greater numbers of locks obtained) can then be directed to the DSS database, offloading the OLTP server(s) to provide optimal performance in the processing of transactions while satisfying the business's need for timely reporting.

Replication Designs

Implementing a promising business continuity process using replication usually starts with designing a replication system suitable to the data processing requirements. Once your business organization has determined its latency requirements, you now need to figure out which replication design to use to achieve your goals.

Remember, the replication system works like a newspaper publication. A newspaper is created by the publisher, and many readers subscribe to the newspaper. Thus, there is one publisher with many subscribers. Even with one primary copy of data, multiple editions of the newspaper with different combinations of the primary data can be published as different editions. That is true of replication systems as well. Each publication can have its own subscribers.

Sybase replication is transaction log based. In a transaction log-based replication, transaction logs (redo logs in the case of Oracle) record changes to the database. Replication Server simply reads the transaction log and sends the changes to the replicate site. If the replication is based on request functions or stored procedures (please refer to Chapter 9 for a complete discussion on procedure or function-based replication), only the functions or procedures along with their associated arguments are replicated.

One-to-Many Regular Replication Model

This type of replication model or implementation strategy is the simplest form of replication. In this model there is one primary site. Application transactions update data at the primary site. Transactions then get transmitted to multiple replicate sites via Replication Server. There is a one-way route from the primary Replication Server to each of the replicate Replication Servers.

This type of design is especially suitable for separating an OLTP primary from DSS replicates. Customer transactions can continue on the primary with optimal performance and the read-intensive reporting functions can be directed to the replicate sites. This is a centralized data processing model, where there is just one central location and all changes take place at the central location. Multiple replicate sites can then use the replicated local copies to act upon and generate reports or perform any kind of read operations. Updates at the remote site are typically not allowed in this model.

The disadvantages in this model include the lack of failover capability. If the primary database becomes unavailable, there will be an application interruption.

Multi-Site Availability Model with Warm Standby

This type of replication model is similar to the one-to-many regular replication model, except we introduce the warm standby component here. For more information on how to set up and administer a warm standby, please refer to Chapter 12.

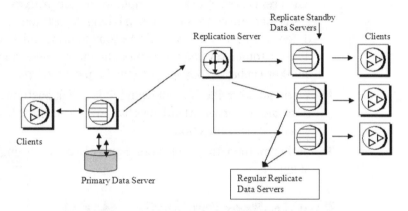

Figure 3-2

Figure 3-2 shows a one-to-many multi-site availability and warm standby setup. The significant advantages include ease of installation, configuration, and administration. In addition, this design allows adding a failover capability. In case the primary OLTP server goes down, the application can switch to the warm standby copy for continuous processing. Depending on the implementation of the warm standby, a warm standby can take read or read/write operations. One Replication Server manages the active (or primary) and standby (replicate) databases. Multi-site availability allows easy replication setup at the database level.

There are several factors to consider when choosing this design, including the following:

▶ Use this method if a database-level replication is all you need. However, warm standby replication does allow object-level replication.

▶ This is a quick and easy replication setup.

▶ Use this design when multiple functional processes can each use a replicate copy. For example, while the primary copy resides at one central location, a billing department located at a different site may use a replicate copy to print and send bills. The customer service department at another site can use another replicate copy to view and help customers.

▶ Warm standby does not allow function string customization. Replication Server provides `rs_default_function_class` for the standby DSI connection.

▶ In this method, the Replication Server becomes a single point of failure.

Peer-to-Peer Replication Model

The most popular replication design, peer-to-peer replication is also called bidirectional replication. In this implementation, both the primaries and replicates are equal, and both primaries and replicates can take any type of load. This replication model has the potential to introduce intersite update conflicts, however. Please refer to the section titled "Managing Intersite Update Conflicts" later in this chapter for more information on how to prevent and resolve update conflicts.

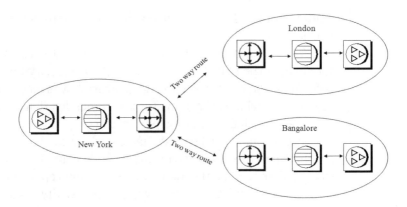

Figure 3-3: Peer-to-peer replication

Figure 3-3 shows a peer-to-peer replication model. Peer-to-peer replication works at the object level and is highly extensible. This replication model can involve many data servers, many databases per server, and many tables per database. Full support of function-based replication and unrestricted control of function strings are provided in this model. This model can get very complicated to administer if many tables from many databases per data server are replicated to multiple locations. Streamlined administration policies, procedures, and tools will ease the management of the multiple connections, routes, and other replication components. The number of replication definitions, subscriptions, and publications can also become overwhelming when many tables from many databases are involved in a replication system. Before you decide to use this replication model, consider if a warm standby model is better suited to your processing situation.

The peer-to-peer replication model also allows column-level replication. For example, modifications to columns from a table can be replicated to a different location where additional processing on those columns can be accomplished. Performance-related improvements can be accomplished in this model. All sites can update data simultaneously, subject to intersite update conflicts. This model is the best for a load balancing scheme where certain applications can use the primary copy and other applications can use a replicate copy. This model also allows multiple hops with multiple routes. Route installation and configuration is discussed in Chapter 8.

When replicating tables, triggers for replicated transactions should be turned off. Additionally, a suitable primary key must be defined for the table. Even though primary key is all that is required for table replication, it is recommended that a unique index be provided to improve performance.

Also, exclude local or static tables, which can be loaded at startup when the primary database is loaded onto the remote sites. Either exclude the identity column from replication, as the remote server will automatically generate identity columns for replicated transactions, or use the appropriate replication definition clauses to allow identity datatype replication. Better yet, avoid the identity datatype and use the newid() function to create a GUID (globally unique identifier) for row identification purposes. The advantage here is newid() will generate a unique value across any given domain.

When choosing this design keep the following factors in mind:

▶ Recovery granularity required: As replication is the best choice for recovery of business-critical data, it is important to define the granularity of data recovery. If you need object-level or sub-object-level recovery, consider this replication model.

▶ Load balancing: If your environment can handle the intersite conflicts with appropriate application design, then this model offers excellent load balancing. If a primary copy is replicated to three different replicates, then all the replicates can simultaneously work on a different segment of the data for both reads and writes. The data segmentation is the key to avoid intersite conflicts. More advanced and complicated intersite conflict resolution techniques are also available. Please refer to the end of this chapter for more details on conflict resolution techniques.

▶ This model is equally effective at replicating within the same primary data server, whereas warm standby is not recommended.

▶ If replication performance is critical to your environment, this model offers opportunities to tune many performance parameters. Extensive and advanced discussion of performance tuning is offered in Chapter 14.

▶ As part of the disaster recovery, often you need to recover the Replication Server System Database (RSSD). This model offers full replication and recovery of RSSD.

▶ Parallel DSI connections are possible only in this kind of replication model.

▶ Consider using function strings when you need to replicate across time zones. For example, if data is replicating from the U.S. to England and you want to preserve the transaction commit time, it is a good idea to use function strings to insert local times.

Latency is an important factor in this type of replication as well. As previously stated, this replication model can become very complex based on the replication components involved, since each component can influence latency. By following important design considerations described throughout this book, it is possible to minimize latency. The tools and configuration solutions offered in Chapter 14 are essential to maintaining optimal performance.

Some of the factors that contribute to latency in this type of replication are:

▶ Replication definitions (see Chapter 9)

▶ Subscriptions (see Chapter 10)

▶ Stable queue design issues (see Chapter 2)

▶ Overall Replication Server tuning (see Chapter 14)

Network efficiency also plays an important role in this type of replication. You want to achieve the fastest possible data transmission. The larger the transaction rate, the larger the data transfer volume, and consequently the greater the impact on network resources.

Latency can become significant in this model depending on the following:

▶ The number of intermediate replication servers used. Between every pair of replication servers, a route has to be defined. Routes are discussed in Chapter 8. A route can span across a wide area network wide enough to constrain network transmission rate. The more routes in the replication model, the more the network hops, and the more network hops there are, the longer it takes to transmit the data from the primary database to the replicate database.

▶ Since Replication Server is host independent, there exists a potential that the replication servers may be housed on different types of hosts, which can cause problems specific to the host operating system, stability, and performance.

▶ If text or image datatypes are being replicated and proper performance measures have not been applied, latency can be a significant problem.

▶ Heterogeneous data replication. When replicating transactions between heterogeneous database management systems, problems specific to target or source database management systems can constrain the smooth flow of data, affecting the latency. Chapter 16 provides a detailed discussion on to how to replicate Oracle data to Sybase and vice versa. Similar concepts apply in replicating to other heterogeneous database management systems that Sybase Replication Server supports.

In all of these cases, proper implementation considerations must be exercised, tested, and verified to reduce latency.

Additionally, replication definitions define data components to be published. Refer to Chapter 9 for more details on replication definitions. A bundled form of replication definitions called publications are also described in Chapter 9.

Subscriptions define the data to be applied at the replicate. Details on subscription definitions, subscription materialization, and error handling are discussed in Chapter 10.

A platform-specific replication agent reads committed transactions from the transaction log and forwards them to the Replication Server. Chapter 6 describes the installation and configuration of RepAgent. Chapter 14 describes the performance tuning measures and monitoring counters for RepAgent.

After transactions are transferred to the Replication Server, transactions are massaged in the various components of the replication system. These components are described in Chapter 2. Stable queue implementation considerations, and monitoring and tuning of various replication threads affect replication server performance. Please refer to Chapter 14 for more details on each of these components and tuning them for best performance.

There are several variations of the peer-to-peer replication model. Some of the popular peer-to-peer replication models include the one-to-many peer-to-peer replication model and the many-to-many peer-to-peer replication model.

One-to-Many Peer-to-Peer Replication Model

This is a replication model that serves one source database to many replicate databases. This model can get very complicated as well. Just as with any peer-to-peer replication model, in this model every sub-component of a source database can become a different component of a different database. For example, all columns from a selected table can be replicated to different sites with different databases having different tables each with one or more source columns. The columns can be renamed. The only restriction is the target column datatype must match the source datatype or should be implicitly convertible. Please check Chapter 9 for more details on the column datatype restrictions during replication.

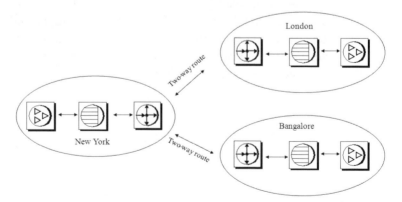

Figure 3-4: One-to-many peer-to-peer replication

Figure 3-4 shows the one-to-many peer-to-peer replication model. In this type of replication, you can have multiple primary databases, and each database can be both primary and replicate. The application can update data on both the primary and replicate, but must take into consideration the problems with data inconsistency and conflict resolution when updates happen at both the primary and the replicate databases.

This type of peer-to-peer replication can span across the WAN to any distance. Of course, you will need to be cognizant of latency if the number of replication hops increase and the total distance increases. Also, the more naming changes and automatic datatype conversions that you include, the more likely that latency will increase. The concept of replicating minimal columns is one of the methods in this model to increase replication efficiency. Replication definitions created with the minimal columns clause will only transfer the primary key and the changed columns. If this clause is not used, then the entire row is transmitted for each change in a transaction.

Many-to-Many Peer-to-Peer Replication Model

If you think the one-to-many peer-to-peer replication model is complicated, this model certainly is more complicated. In this model many source databases can be permutated and combined into many databases in the target. The target, of course, can be many targets. The number of replication definitions and subscriptions can get very complicated, and management becomes an overwhelming challenge. But as a model, it can service any type of business replication requirement.

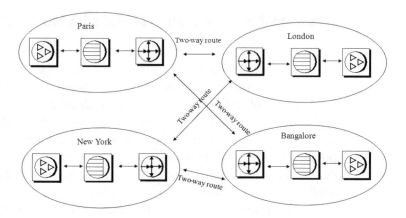

Figure 3-5: Many-to-many peer-to-peer replication

Figure 3-5 shows the many-to-many peer-to-peer replication model. A source business table can be split into many target tables and replicated to many locations where each column becomes a business unit. For example, a student registration source table can be replicated to multiple sites, where course load can be in one table at one location, student names can be directed to a different location, and the fee paid can be directed to yet another location.

Typically many production environments adopt one or more types of peer-to-peer replication models. In many cases, the final model of an information processing department may include a combination of one or more peer-to-peer replication models. It is also possible to combine a typical peer-to-peer replication with direct updates to the primary without using the replication system. In this case, the replicate system is used mainly for reads. Updates to any tables are directed to the primary, directly bypassing the replication system.

A Peer-to-Peer Replication Model with Warm Standby

In this model, shown in Figure 3-6, a peer-to-peer replication model can be combined with a warm standby. For example, some tables at the replicate site can be set up to warm standby to a local domain of an information processing department. The same replicate site can also have a peer-to-peer replication, extending far beyond the local domain. The primary updates then will be propagated to the warm standby. Both the warm standby copy and peer-to-peer replication copy offer a failover in the event of an application or host failure. However, failover using peer-to-peer replication is more convenient. In such an event, the warm standby may not get updated if the primary copy is down. If the latency is tolerable, the warm standby will resume updates once the failed primary become available and latency between the peer-to-peer replicates disappear.

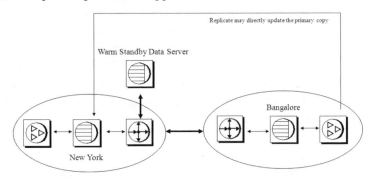

Figure 3-6: Peer-to-peer replication with warm standby

In this model, the update to the replicate can skip the replication system and be directed to the primary, though such configurations are rare. The convenience of such a model includes the complete elimination of update conflict.

Keep the following factors in mind when choosing this replication model:

▶ A local or near local copy is required for additional read processing, typically for report generation. Because this is typically achieved in this model with a warm standby addition to the replication model, be aware of performance requirements. If the database is complex enough, warm standby may not scale up unless special replication definitions are included in the replication model. More details on warm standby implementation and replication definitions to improve the performance are provided in Chapter 12.

► A regular peer-to-peer or bidirectional replication is also required to replicate data for easy failover and load balancing, and to accomplish any complexities in the replication of data.

► Different processing requirements need different types of copies of data. One copy is of the entire database as delivered under warm standby, and multiple copies of fragments of data are delivered to distant locations.

► Function strings are required to modify the behavior of data replication at one end while the warm standby is unaltered.

► Function-based replication is required for some of the data.

Replication Design Strategies

As you might have gleaned by this time, there are multiple replication design combinations possible. When it comes to choosing which design fits your application, the choice is mostly dependent on the nature of the application and your processing requirements. The sensitivity of the application to legal compliance may also play a role in choosing a replication design. If you are a global player, a crosscontinental replication model may need to be implemented for effective protection or performance. In such a case, a local save and forward may be attractive so that a copy of the data is available locally (or near locally) and a copy is forwarded to a distant location. A local warm standby (peer-to-peer replication with warm standby) along with a full replication to a distant location may be desirable here.

In this section, we will discuss some important considerations that may help you choose the appropriate replication design. As every application is different, be sure to experiment in a non-production environment to make sure your selection fits your requirements before going to production.

Replication Strategy for Backup

Figure 3-7 shows the replication strategy for backup. This provides a redundant copy of the data as well as an opportunity to back up the replicated copy. In this scenario, the primary server typically does not have enough cycles to execute a backup, the production environment does not offer the opportunity to back up, or you just want a redundant offsite copy of the data with a facility to back up. The entire primary database or selectively the *changing* data is replicated to the replicate site. Data is regularly backed up off of the secondary data server. In addition to the backup, the secondary source also offers the opportunity to implement regular database consistency checks (DBCC), which may prove to be too expensive on the primary. If any problems are found on the replicate, a fix is attempted on the replicate. Once a successful fix has been executed at the replicate, the same fix may be applied to the primary site.

In case of emergency, the offsite standby database can be activated to take the processing load. Another permutation of the same design may be to use a full peer-to-peer replication offsite, in place of the warm standby. Using that model, you will have a full load balancing opportunity as well.

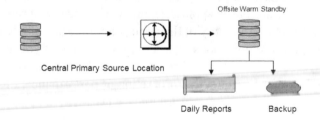

Figure 3-7: Replication strategy for backup

Replication for Application Partitioning

Figure 3-8 shows a replication design for application partitioning. This strategy uses one or more combinations of replication designs to achieve application partitioning and locate partitioned applications in this global information world. Information systems are critical for today's economy, and today's economy is global, so the information system's application or parts of applications are distributed all over the world.

Application and business rules should allow such physical and logical application partitioning. All the data can be coalesced at the central location. The centralized repository can be useful for business intelligence and other reporting needs. The distributed data across the globe serves as a redundant copy and isolates data processing views.

In the following example we can see that a big financial firm can distribute functionally partitioned data across the globe.

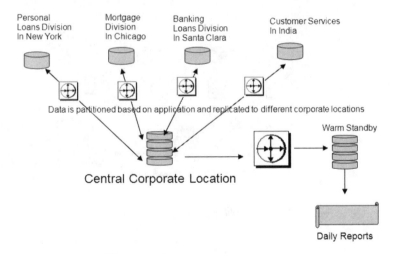

Figure 3-8: Application partitioning strategy

Business Intelligence

A typical business intelligence processing database should be able to handle massive decision support queries. Figure 3-9 shows a replication model for business intelligence processing. Notice that it includes a data warehouse. Replication can copy data from multiple primary sources to a centralized data warehouse. The target database can have different indexing schemes such as those enforced by multidimensional databases like Sybase IQ.

Such a model alleviates query processing response time issues on a typical OLTP database. In addition to being the business intelligence repository, the target database can also serve as redundant data. However, this model does not help in failover or in load balancing. As said earlier, by combining a peer-to-peer replication or warm standby with multisource replication to warehousing, the failover and load balancing is achieved independently.

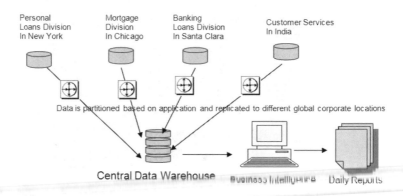

Figure 3-9: Business intelligence strategy

With Sybase replication, you may combine one or more of the designs discussed in this chapter to meet your business requirements and achieve maximum return on investment.

The strategies discussed here are based on combinations of models discussed in this chapter. You are not limited to the designs or models discussed in this chapter, as many combinations can be achieved. But as with anything else, it is better to keep the design simple. The more databases that you use in conjunction with more combinations of replication designs, the more likely it is that the replication definitions, subscription definitions, routes, and so on will become extremely complex. Though it is not a problem for the Replication Server, it can become overwhelming to the administrator. It may be a good idea to explore publications in place of individual replication definitions, or use warm standby in place of peer-to-peer replication if you do not need table-level replication granularity. It may be also be worth exploring if multi-site availability (MSA) is suitable to your application. Multi-site availability is discussed in detail in Chapter 13.

Managing Intersite Update Conflicts

Intersite update conflicts are a major concern in a bidirectional or peer-to-peer replication system where updates to a fragment of the data can be performed either at the primary site or at the replicate site. It is possible an update at a replicate site can overwrite a legitimate update performed at the primary site. Due to intersite update conflicts, it becomes tough to determine which dataset is accurate when performing recovery.

To maintain the integrity of the data due to intersite update conflicts, always choose one site to perform a specific update that does not conflict with others. For example, the replicate site may be allowed to perform updates on columns that are not likely to be updated by the primary. Both primary and replicate should use the same primary key to perform updates. Avoid updates to the primary key itself.

Similarly, restrict one site to update a particular set of rows based on site identification. For example, if a table holds data for multiple departments, allow updates to the table for some departments at the true primary and for different departments at the replicate primary.

Location	Reserved range for the primary key column
London	1-200,000
Bangalore	200,001-300,000
MakaMambaPuram	300,001-1,000,000

There is yet another less favorable alternative of using version control as a parameter to a stored procedure to update the table at multiple sites. Based on the version number passed to the stored procedure, the stored procedure will either continue to update the table or roll back the update. This process is more involved and requires careful planning.

Chapter 4

Replication Server Installation and Upgrade

In this chapter, we will discuss the installation process in detail and briefly discuss the configuration process. Additional configuration details are covered in Chapter 5. This chapter also includes important points regarding upgrading an existing replication system. While this chapter focuses on installing Replication Server on the Linux operating system, the process is similar in other operating environments.

During the installation process, isolating operating system issues from actual Replication Server issues is very important. It is highly recommended that you read the release bulletins that come with the product you are trying to install. Be sure to note the minimum requirements for the operating system patch level, amount of memory, and any specific libraries required. Also make sure you write down the environment variables that need to be set before embarking on the installation process.

The Sybase Replication Server installation process entails the following:

▶ Pre-installation

▶ Installation

▶ Post-installation, including basic configuration

The examples cited in this chapter are for the Linux operating system. The installation process is similar in other operating environments except for some minor differences. Again, we suggest you read the release bulletin for the platform you intend to use to see if there are any platform-specific requirements.

Pre-installation

Preparation for Replication Server installation includes obtaining the Replication Server software from the distribution media. This is primarily achieved by running the InstallShield program that comes with the software. Replication Server 15.0 can be installed along with other Sybase products including Replication Server 12.6. Do not install Replication Server 15.0 on a replication installation directory with Sybase product releases earlier than 12.5. Some Replication Server 15.0 components conflict with products earlier than 12.5. That may incapacitate all of the Sybase products including Replication Server. Even uninstall may not work properly at that time.

Take the following into consideration before installing Replication Server:

1. Back up your existing Replication Server system files and data files.

2. Install SySAM software for licensing and configure licenses.

3. Decide if you would like to use an external Replication Server System Database (RSSD) in an ASE or an Embedded RSSD. If you choose to use an ASE to hold RSSD, you should install an ASE or use an existing ASE. If you are going to use an ASE just to support the Replication Server RSSD, then the ASE default minimal configuration is enough. In any case, a repository for RSSD or ERSSD must be available to complete the installation process.

4. If you chose to use Embedded RSSD, you do not need to access an ASE during the Replication Server initialization phase. Chapter 19 contains an overview of ERSSD and its components. Approximately 200 MB of disk space is required for RSSD.

5. Replication Server is light on memory requirements. However, some memory structures within Replication Server constrain the Replication Server performance. At the end of installation, Replication Server will have the default configuration. Advanced configuration issues based on monitoring

counters for specific performance problems are discussed in Chapters 5 and 14.

Replication Server Installation

The first step in Replication Server installation is to extract the Replication Server software from the distribution media.

Software Extraction Using InstallShield

InstallShield is a Java-based process and the installation process is the same for both Windows and UNIX environments.

1. Use InstallShield to extract the software files from the distribution media to the installation directory. When you run the setup program on the Replication Server CD-ROM, the InstallShield program will start with the welcome screen as shown in Figure 4-1.

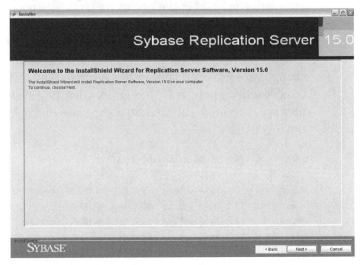

Figure 4-1

2. InstallShield provides an option to install a sample Replication Server with the default configuration. Continue to

provide responses to the InstallShield screens to complete downloading the Replication Server to a desired directory location.

3. We will use rs_init, the installation utility provided by Sybase, to initialize Replication Server. rs_init can be run in either console mode or it can be executed with a resource file.

Upon successful installation the following message will be displayed:

```
The InstallShield Wizard has successfully installed
Replication Server Software, Version 15.0. Choose
next to continue the wizard.
```

Replication Server Installation Using Console Mode

The installation of Replication Server using console mode is done in a command shell. The console method is a character-based interactive method at the end of which the responses can be saved into a response file. Thereafter, rs_init can be executed with the response file as an argument. The response file can be suitably changed for further installations. Details of response file changes are provided later in this chapter. The installation process described here is for the Linux operating system. Once the files are extracted, the directory structure under Linux looks like the following:

```
sybase@host:/apps/sybase/REP_150_1>ls -lrt
total 88
drwxr-xr-x    7 sybase sybase   4096 Sep  6 09:58 shared
drwxr-xr-x   12 sybase sybase   4096 Sep  6 09:58 OCS-15_0
drwxrwxr-x   14 sybase sybase   4096 Sep  6 09:58 locales
drwxr-xr-x   58 sybase sybase   4096 Sep  6 09:58 charsets
drwxr-xr-x    3 sybase sybase   4096 Sep  6 09:58 collate
drwxr-xr-x   14 sybase sybase   4096 Sep  6 09:58 ua
drwxr-xr-x    5 sybase sybase   4096 Sep  6 09:58 SYSAM-2_0
drwxrwxr-x   13 sybase sybase   4096 Sep  6 09:58 REP-15_0
drwxr-xr-x    2 sybase sybase   4096 Sep  6 09:58 config
drwxrwxr-x    3 sybase sybase   4096 Sep  6 09:58 uninstall
```

```
-rw-rw-r--   1 sybase sybase    805 Sep  6 09:58 SYBASE.sh
-rw-rw-r--   1 sybase sybase    807 Sep  6 09:58 SYBASE.env
-rw-rw-r--   1 sybase sybase    998 Sep  6 09:58 SYBASE.csh
drwxrwxr-x   7 sybase sybase   4096 Sep  6 09:58 REP-15_0
-rw-rw-r--   1 sybase sybase    708 Sep  6 10:02 log.txt
drwxrwxr-x   5 sybase sybase   4096 Sep  6 10:02 _jvmrep
-rw-rw-r--   1 sybase sybase  23644 Sep  6 10:02 vpd.properties
```

Start **rs_init** from the install directory off of REP-15_0.

There are two sections in this installation topic:

1. Installing a replication server

2. Adding a database to the replication system

In this example installation we are using an existing ASE to manage a Replication Server System Database (RSSD) database. Please refer to Chapter 19 for more information on using Embedded RSSD as the Replication Server System Database.

Step 1: Make sure you execute the shell environment setup script. It may be SYBASE.sh or SYBASE.csh, depending on your shell. Also, be sure you have this script adjusted to your environment.

On UNIX platforms, make sure the interfaces file is accessible at the Replication Server install directory. The Replication Server install directory is the $SYBASE variable defined in the SYBASE.[c]sh script discussed above. This variable may be different from the $SYBASE variable defined in the Adaptive Server Enterprise environment script, which means the $SYBASE variable may be different for Replication Server and ASE if both are located on the same host.

If the interfaces file is not accessible, you will notice that during the process of rs_init you will be prompted to enter the dsedit or dscp program to complete the interfaces information. If the interfaces file is accessible and you have already entered the interfaces entries for Replication Server and for ERSSD server (if you plan to use ERSSD), then the system will recognize that during the rs_init and will show the status as complete; you do not need to use the dsedit or dcsp programs. Add Replication Server and ERSSD server interface entries ahead of installation to avoid using dsedit or dscp.

Step 2: Use cd to switch to the Replication Server software installation directory, then source the environment script.

```
Sybase@host>cd /usr/sybase/REP_150_1
Sybase@host> ./SYBASE.sh
Sybase@host>cd REP-15_0/install
Sybase@host> ./rs_init
```

In the script above, /SYBASE.sh is used to source the environment shell script to set the Sybase variables. Once you enter the initialization command, /rs_init, you should see the first screen as shown below.

Follow each of the menu items and enter your responses. Press Ctrl-a, to accept, whenever you enter some input data. For menu item selections, just enter the menu item number and press Return to continue. If the menu item that you enter is a switch, then pressing Return toggles the switch and presents the screen for your next entry.

```
RS_INIT

1.  Release directory:  /usr/sybase/REP_150_1

2.  Configure a Server product




Ctrl-a Accept and Continue, Ctrl-x Exit Screen, ? Help.

Enter the number of your choice and press return  ▊
```

Enter option **2**.

```
CONFIGURE SERVER PRODUCTS

Products:
Product                  Date Installed    Date Configured
1.  Replication Server                       Feb 22 107 09:03




Ctrl-a Accept and Continue, Ctrl-x Exit Screen, ? Help.

Enter the number of your choice and press return: 1
```

Enter **1** to choose the Replication Server Configuration (includes installation).

```
CONFIGURE REPLICATION SYSTEM

1.  Install a new Replication Server
2.  Add a database to the replication system
3.  Upgrade an existing Replication Server
4.  Downgrade RSSD for an existing Replication Server
5.  Upgrade an existing database in the replication system
6.  Enable password encryption for a Replication Server
7.  Alter a Replication Server configuration file password


Ctrl-a Accept and Continue, Ctrl-x Exit Screen, ? Help.

Enter the number of your choice and press return: 1
```

Enter **1** to choose to install a new Replication Server.

```
NEW REPLICATION SERVER

1.  Replication Server Information              Incomplete
2.  ID Server Information                       Incomplete
3.  Replication Server System Database          Incomplete
4.  Disk Partition                              Incomplete
5.  Remote Site Connections                     Incomplete



Ctrl-a Accept and Continue, Ctrl-x Exit Screen, ? Help.

Enter the number of your choice and press return: 1
```

Enter **1** and the Replication Server name.

```
REPLICATION SERVER NAME

1.  Replication Server Name:




Ctrl-a Accept and Continue, Ctrl-x Exit Screen, ? Help.

Enter the number of your choice and press return: 1
Enter the name for the Replication Server:
NYRS
```

```
REPLICATION SERVER NAME

1.  Replication Server Name:  NYRS





Ctrl-a Accept and Continue, Ctrl-x Exit Screen, ? Help.

Enter the number of your choice and press return: <Ctrl-a>
```

As some input has been entered (here the Replication Server name), press **Ctrl-a** to accept and continue. In the next screen you will set up the ID Server. Because this is the first Replication Server in this domain, you will set this Replication Server to serve as the ID Server as well.

```
REPLICATION SERVER INFORMATION

1.  Is this Replication Server the ID Server?  no
2.  Replication Server error log:
        /usr/sybase/REP_150_1/REP-15_0/install/NYRS.log
3.  Replication Server configuration file:
        /usr/sybase/REP_150_1/REP-15_0/install/NYRS.cfg
4.  Replication Server password encryption:  no
5.  Replication Server character set:  iso_1
6.  Replication Server language:  us english
7.  Replication Server sort order:  binary
8.  Replication Server Interfaces Information           Complete
9.  Use SSL Service:  no




Ctrl-a Accept and Continue, Ctrl-x Exit Screen, ? Help.
```

When you enter **1** as your response, the first item related to the ID Server will toggle to "yes". Select menu item **2** to change the error log location if you want.

Continue by choosing **4** to change the Replication Server password option to encrypt the password and **5** to change the default character set. We used utf8 as the default character set. Because our Adaptive Server uses utf8, we use utf8 here to avoid character set conversion. Character set conversions can reduce performance. This is discussed further in Chapter 18.

```
REPLICATION SERVER CHARACTER SET

Current language:  us_english
Current character set:  iso_1
Current sort order:  binary

1.  ascii_8: ASCII, for use with unspecified 8-bit data.
2.  iso_1: ISO 8859-1 (Latin-1) - Western European 8-bit characters
3.  roman9: Hewlett-Packard proprietary character set for European l
4.  iso15: ISO_8859-15:1998, Latin9, Western Europe
5.  deckanji: DEC Kanji Code for JIS-X0208.
6.  mac: Macintosh default character set for Western European locale
7.  eucjis: Extended Unix Code for JIS-X0201 and JIS-X0208
8.  utf8: Unicode 3.1 UTF-8 Character Set
9.  eucgb: Extended Unix Code for GB2312-80 (Simplified Chinese)
10. gb18030: Character set for P.R.C. standard GB 18030-2000
11. roman8: Hewlett-Packard proprietary character set for European l
12. eucksc: Extended Unix Code for KSC-5601
13. cp437: Code Page 437 (United States) character set
14. sjis: IBM/Microsoft Code for JIS-X0201 and JIS-X0208


<More>
Ctrl-f Scroll Forward, Ctrl-b Scroll Backward.  <Ctrl-f><Ctrl-a>
```

Press **Ctrl-a** to accept the following display of inputs.

```
REPLICATION SERVER INFORMATION

1.  Is this Replication Server the ID Server?  yes
2.  Replication Server error log:  /usr/sybase/logs/NYRS.log
3.  Replication Server configuration file:
        /usr/sybase/REP_160_1/REP-15_0/install/NYRS.cfg
4.  Replication Server password encryption;  yes
5.  Replication Server character set: utf8
6.  Replication Server language: us_english
7.  Replication Server sort order:  binary
8.  Replication Server Interfaces Information          Complete
9.  Use SSL Service:  no



Ctrl-a Accept and Continue, Ctrl-x Exit Screen, ? Help.


Enter the number of your choice and press return: <Ctrl-a>
```

The Replication Server Interfaces Information will be listed as "Complete" if the interfaces entry has already been added to the interfaces file. Make sure the interfaces file is accessible to the Replication Server install directory. You may define symbolic links to the original location of the interfaces file. This is particularly true when the Adaptive Server and Replication Server are co-located in the same host.

In the next screen you will select to set up the Replication Server System Database (RSSD). RSSD can either be located in an Adaptive Server or embedded. Embedded RSSD, or ERSSD, is discussed in more detail in Chapter 19. In this example, we are using an Adaptive Server Enterprise to host the RSSD database.

```
NEW REPLICATION SERVER

1.  Replication Server Information           Complete
2.  ID Server Information                    Complete
3.  Replication Server System Database       Incomplete
4.  Disk Partition                           Incomplete
5.  Remote Site Connections                  Complete




Ctrl-a Accept and Continue, Ctrl-x Exit Screen, ? Help.

Enter the number of your choice and press return: 3
```

```
REPLICATION SERVER SYSTEM DATABASE CHOICE

1.  Do you want Replication Server System Database embedded: no

2.  Replication Server System Database on ASE          Incomplete




Ctrl-a Accept and Continue, Ctrl-x Exit Screen, ? Help.

Enter the number of your choice and press return: 2
```

You are going to enter information regarding the ASE, which will host RSSD and other RSSD information.

```
REPLICATION SERVER SYSTEM DATABASE

1.  RSSD SQL Server name:
2.  RSSD name:  NYRS_RSSD
3.  RSSD will be replicated:  yes
4.  Allow HA Failover for RSSD connections:  no
5.  Create RSSD:  no
6.  SA user:  sa
7.  SA password:
8.  Primary user:  NYRS_RSSD_prim
9.  Primary password:  NYRS_RSSD_prim_ps
10. Maintenance login:  NYRS_RSSD_maint
11. Maintenance password:  NYRS_RSSD_maint_ps




Ctrl-a Accept and Continue, Ctrl-x Exit Screen, ? Help.

Enter the number of your choice and press return: ???
```

Although you can change the names and passwords for the primary and maintenance users, we are leaving them set to the default in the example installation. You can also change them in the resource file that you can generate at the end of this installation process. Later in this chapter we'll discuss how to save the responses into a resource file that can be used for repeated installations later on.

 IMPORTANT: Make sure you add the interfaces entries for the ASE that you are likely to use to create the RSSD. If you are going to use ERSSD, be sure to add the ERSSD interfaces entry as well.

Enter **NYDS** as the data server for RSSD, select menu **5** item to change the Create RSSD item to "yes", and select the option to enter the RSSD data server sa password. The screen will look like the following. In the case of warm standby setup, as there is only one replication server, and thus one RSSD, the RSSD need not be replicated.

```
REPLICATION SERVER SYSTEM DATABASE

1.  RSSD SQL Server name:  NYDS
2.  RSSD name:  NYRS_RSSD
3.  RSSD will be replicated:  yes
4.  Allow HA Failover for RSSD connections:  no
5.  Create RSSD:  yes
6.  SA user:  sa
7.  SA password:  reptest
8.  Primary user:  NYRS_RSSD_prim
9.  Primary password:  NYRS_RSSD_prim_ps
10. Maintenance login:  NYRS_RSSD_maint
11. Maintenance password:  NYRS_RSSD_maint_ps


Ctrl-a Accept and Continue, Ctrl-x Exit Screen, ? Help.

Enter the number of your choice and press return: <Ctrl-a>
```

Once you accept and continue, you will be taken to a previous window where you need to select another option to continue setting up the details. In the following screens, you will first complete the RSSD device information and then complete the disk partition details for a stable queue device.

```
REPLICATION SERVER SYSTEM DATABASE CHOICE

1.  Do you want Replication Server System Database embedded: no

2.  Replication Server System Database on ASE            Complete




Ctrl-a Accept and Continue, Ctrl-x Exit Screen, ? Help.

Enter the number of your choice and press return: <Ctrl-a>
```

```
NEW REPLICATION SERVER

1.  Replication Server Information              Complete
2.  ID Server Information                       Complete
3.  Replication Server System Database          Complete
4.  RSSD Device Information                     Incomplete
5.  Disk Partition                             Incomplete
6.  Remote Site Connections                     Complete



Ctrl-a Accept and Continue, Ctrl-x Exit Screen, ? Help.

Enter the number of your choice and press return: 4
```

Be sure to find the device names that you are going to use to create the RSSD database. It is also suggested to use **disk_init** on these devices ahead of time, especially if the ASE is located on a different host than Replication Server.

In the example, we initialized the RSSD data and log devices ahead of time in the ASE that will host RSSD, so we picked "no" to create the devices. Our ASE is located on a different host. If you toggle the option Create RSSD to "yes", you will be prompted to enter the RSSD device physical name and size. You can also instruct rs_init to initialize the RSSD log device.

```
RSSD DEVICE INFORMATION

1.  Size of the RSSD database:  100
2.  RSSD device name:  dbdev_RSSD
3.  Create the RSSD device:  no
4.  Size of the RSSD log:  50
5.  RSSD log device name:  logdev_RSSD
6.  Create the RSSD log device:  no



Ctrl-a Accept and Continue, Ctrl-x Exit Screen, ? Help.

Enter the number of your choice and press return: <Ctrl-a>
```

The last part of the configuration before installing the Replication Server is to first initialize the stable queue disk partition. This partition is a temporary partition that serves the purpose of installing Replication Server. Depending on your application requirements, you may need to add more stable device partitions after installing Replication Server. After adding additional stable device partitions, you should drop the initial partition added during the installation process. The typical rule is to add stable devices at least three times the size of the replicating database's transaction log. This partition should be local to the host where Replication Server is being created. You can use any method to create an empty OS file for the first partition, which is typically specified to be 20 MB or larger. If proper operating system libraries, such as asynchronous I/O libraries, are missing at the OS level, you may experience difficulty in adding the disk partition. If there are problems in initializing the first partition, you will notice that a 16 KB file is created irrespective of the size of the partition you specified. Most of the time the problem may be related to operating system patches or Replication Server environment variables for libraries. Unfortunately, during the rs_init execution process, rs_init may simply fail to initialize the disk to the extent configured, but does not provide any message why it cannot complete disk initialization. Sometimes, the rs_init gets hung up during the disk partition initialization. This is also a symptom of missing libraries or some OS-level missing pieces.

```
sybase@host:/home/sybase/devices> pwd
/home/sybase/devices
sybase@host:/home/sybase/devices> ls
sybase@host:/home/sybase/devices> touch P2
sybase@host:/home/sybase/devices> ls
P2
sybase@host:/home/sybase/devices>
```

The logical identifier is just a logical name. Enter any name you like for this partition; in this example we use **P2**. Leave the size at **20** and the vstart value for this file at **0**. Once you are done entering inputs to install a Replication Server, accept the entries with **Ctrl-a**.

```
DISK PARTITION INFORMATION


1.  Disk Partition path:   /home/sybase/devices/P2
2.  Logical Identifier for Disk Partition:   P2
3.  Size of Disk Partition:   20
4.  Vstart value for partition:   0




Ctrl-a Accept and Continue, Ctrl-x Exit Screen, ? Help.

Enter the number of your choice and press return: <Ctrl-a>
```

Generating a Reusable Resource File

When prompted with "Execute the Replication Server tasks now?n," select no or accept the default value no and be sure to press **Ctrl-w**. You will be prompted with: "Enter the number of your choice and press return: Dump out current attributes?y."

Press **Return** to accept the default file name and create the file.

```
Enter the number of your choice and press return: Dump out current
        attributes?y
Enter an attribute resource filename (default is '/usr/sybase/REP_150_1/
        REP-15_0/init/logs/resource.dmp'):
```

After entering the fully qualified file name, the program confirms the dump of the resource file as:

```
Enter the number of your choice and press return: Dump out current
        attributes?y
Enter an attribute resource filename (default is '/usr/sybase/REP_150_1/
        REP-15_0/init/logs/resource.dmp'):
        /usr/sybase/REP_150_1/REP-15_0/install/NYRS.rs

Attributes successfully dumped to '/usr/sybase/REP_150_1/
        REP-15_0/install/NYRS.rs'.
Press <return> to continue.
```

The resource file that you save here can serve as a template file for future automated installations. You can use any shell script or editor to change responses related to the new installation and use the response file with rs_init for future installations. Please refer to the following section titled "Preparing a Resource File or Response File" for more information on preparing files for future installations. If you press Ctrl-a (instead of Ctrl-w) to accept the fully completed inputs and continue, rs_init will start executing the inputs to install the instance of Replication Server.

```
NEW REPLICATION SERVER

1.  Replication Server Information              Complete
2.  ID Server Information                       Complete
3.  Replication Server System Database          Complete
4.  RSSD Device Information                     Complete
5.  Disk Partition                             Complete
6.  Remote Site Connections                     Complete


Ctrl-a Accept and Continue, Ctrl-x Exit Screen, ? Help.

Enter the number of your choice and press return: Ctrl-a
```

Following is the rs_init run-time output:

```
Enter the number of your choice and press return:
Execute the Replication Server tasks now? y
Running task: check the RSSD SQL Server.
Task succeeded: check the RSSD SQL Server.
Running task: configure the Replication Server System Database.
Creating the Replication Server System Database 'NYRS_RSSD'.
The database 'NYRS_RSSD' already exists. It will be dropped and recreated.
SQL Server message: msg 1805, level 10, state 2
"CREATE DATABASE: allocating 25600 logical pages (100.0 megabytes) on disk
'dbdev_RSSD'.
"
SQL Server message: msg 1805, level 10, state 2
"CREATE DATABASE: allocating 12800 logical pages (50.0 megabytes) on disk
'logdev_RSSD'.
"
Created database 'NYRS_RSSD'.
SQL Server message: msg 0, level 10, state 1
"New user added."
Added primary login 'NYRS_RSSD_prim' to database 'NYRS_RSSD' as a user.
SQL Server message: msg 0, level 10, state 1
"New user added."
Added maintenance user login 'NYRS_RSSD_maint' to database 'NYRS_RSSD'.
Loading Replication Server System Database in 'NYDS'. This will take a few
minutes.
..Done
...Done
Done
......SQL Server message: msg 0, level 10, state 1
"Type added."
...............SQL Server message: msg 0, level 10, state 1
"The replication status for 'rs_marker' is set to true."
SQL Server message: msg 0, level 10, state 1
"New group added."
......................SQL Server message: msg 0, level 10, state 1
"The replication status for 'rs_classes' is set to true."
SQL Server message: msg 0, level 10, state 1
"The replication status for 'rs_columns' is set to true."
SQL Server message: msg 0, level 10, state 1
"The replication status for 'rs_databases' is set to true."
SQL Server message: msg 0, level 10, state 1
"The replication status for 'rs_erroractions' is set to true."
```

```
SQL Server message: msg 0, level 10, state 1
"The replication status for 'rs_functions' is set to true."
SQL Server message: msg 0, level 10, state 1
"The replication status for 'rs_objects' is set to true."
SQL Server message: msg 0, level 10, state 1
"The replication status for 'rs_routes' is set to true."
SQL Server message: msg 0, level 10, state 1
"The replication status for 'rs_funcstrings' is set to true."
SQL Server message: msg 0, level 10, state 1
"The replication status for 'rs_systext' is set to true."
SQL Server message: msg 0, level 10, state 1
"The replication status for 'rs_dbreps' is set to true."
SQL Server message: msg 0, level 10, state 1
"The replication status for 'rs_dbsubsets' is set to true."
.SQL Server message: msg 0, level 10, state 1
"The replication status for 'rs_cmd_marker' is set to function."
SQL Server message: msg 0, level 10, state 1
"The log mode is set to log_sproc."
SQL Server message: msg 0, level 10, state 1
"The replication status for 'rs_section_marker' is set to function."
SQL Server message: msg 0, level 10, state 1
"The log mode is set to log_sproc."
.SQL Server message: msg 0, level 10, state 1
"Installing rs_get_sitename"
SQL Server message: msg 0, level 10, state 1
"Installing rs_get_classname"
.SQL Server message: msg 0, level 10, state 1
"Installing rs_helpdb"
SQL Server message: msg 0, level 10, state 1
"Installing rs_helprepdb"
SQL Server message: msg 0, level 10, state 1
"Installing rs_helproute"
.Done
Done
Loading Replication Server stored procedures in RSSD 'NYDS'.
Loading script 'rsprocs_ase.sql' into database 'NYRS_RSSD'.
.......Done
Loaded script 'rsprocs_ase.sql' successfully.
Replication Server System Database loaded successfully in 'NYDS'.
Successfully truncated the log of database 'NYRS_RSSD'.
Successfully set the truncation point to IGNORE because the Replication
Server will not hold primary data.
Adding maintenance and primary users to group rs_systabgroup.
```

Successfully added maintenance and primary users to group rs_systabgroup.
Task succeeded: configure the Replication Server System Database.
Running task: create the Replication Server configuration file.
Existing Configuration file
'/usr/sybase/REP_150_1/REP-15_0/install/NYRS.bak' renamed to
'/usr/sybase/REP_150_1/REP-15_0/install/NYRS.005'.
Existing Configuration file
'/usr/sybase/REP_150_1/REP-15_0/install/NYRS.cfg' renamed to
'/usr/sybase/REP_150_1/REP-15_0/install/NYRS.bak'.
Task succeeded: create the Replication Server configuration file.
Running task: create the Replication Server runserver file.
Task succeeded: create the Replication Server runserver file.
Running task: start the Replication Server.
waiting for server 'NYRS' to boot...
Task succeeded: start the Replication Server.
Running task: configure the Replication Server.
SQL Server message: msg 14125, level 11, state 0

WARNING: "Application 'sybinit' is using character set 'iso_1', but the
Replication Server is using character set 'utf8'. Because the character
sets are different, character set conversion problems may occur."
Press <return> to continue. **<Press Return>**

Adding partition 'P2'.
Successfully added partition 'P2'.
Connecting to Replication Server and defining users for LTM/Replication
Agent and other Replication Servers.
Successfully defined users in Replication Server.
Task succeeded: configure the Replication Server.
Running task: configure the Replication Agent.
Task succeeded: configure the Replication Agent.
Running task: start the Replication Agent.
Task succeeded: start the Replication Agent.
Configuration completed successfully.
Press <return> to continue. **<Press Return>**

Upon pressing **Return**, the main menu appears again, giving you
the opportunity to add databases to the replication system. At this
time the password for the sa user to the Replication Server is
null.

```
CONFIGURE REPLICATION SYSTEM

1.  Install a new Replication Server
2.  Add a database to the replication system
3.  Upgrade an existing Replication Server
4.  Downgrade RSSD for an existing Replication Server
5.  Upgrade an existing database in the replication system
6.  Enable password encryption for a Replication Server
7.  Alter a Replication Server configuration file password




Ctrl-a Accept and Continue, Ctrl-x Exit Screen, ? Help.

Enter the number of your choice and press return: Ctrl-x
```

Let's log in to the Replication Server and try out some commands.

```
sybase@host>isql -Usa -SNYRS -w899 -Jutf8    <
Password:
1> admin who
2> go
Spid  Name        State                Info
----  ----------  -------------------- -----------------------------------
  13  DSI EXEC    Awaiting Command     101(1) NYDS.NYRS_RSSD
   8  DSI         Awaiting Message     101 NYDS.NYRS_RSSD
  12  SQM         Awaiting Message     101:0 NYDS.NYRS_RSSD
   9  dSUB        Sleeping
   6  dCM         Awaiting Message
   7  dAIO        Awaiting Message
  10  dREC        Sleeping             dREC
  17  USER        Active               sa
   5  dALARM      Awaiting Wakeup
  11  dSYSAM      Sleeping
1>
```

For more information on these threads, please see Chapter 5, "Configuration Parameters," and Chapter 2, "The Replication Server Architecture."

Check to see if any of the connections are down by entering the admin who_is_down command.

```
1> admin who_is_down
2> go
Spid  Name      State               Info
----  --------- ------------------- -----------------------------------
1>
```

As shown above, none of the threads are down. You now have a running Replication Server. You need to configure the server to your application requirements; add databases, routes, replication definitions, and subscriptions; and materialize the data before it can be production ready.

Check the stable queue partition disk space with the admin disk_space command. You need to add more partitions before actually replicating the production data as this small stable queue may not be enough.

Now change the sa password to a valid password:

```
1> alter user sa set password 'reptest'
2> go
User 'sa' is altered.
1>
```

A utility tool to automatically generate reusable resource files for installing Replication Server and adding databases can be downloaded from www.wordware.com/files/SybaseRS.

Preparing a Resource File or Response File

A resource file or response file can be obtained by using one of the following methods:

▶ Copy the file from $SYBASE/REP-15_0/init/rs, where $SYBASE is the Replication Server installation directory.

▶ Use **rs_init** in the console (interactive mode) as described in the section titled "Replication Server Installation Using Console Mode." At the end of the configuration process, save the responses to a response file by pressing Ctrl-w.

▶ Copy the file from a prior installation setup.

You can customize the resource file as follows:

`sybinit.release_directory: /usr/sybase/REP_150_1`

> Change the release directory to the directory where you copied the files from the distribution medium.

`sybinit.product: rs`

> Do not change.

`rs.rs_operation: rs_install`

> Do not change.

`rs.rs_idserver_name: NYRS`

> If this is the first replication server, then set this equal to the Replication Server being installed. If you later add additional replication servers, you may want to use this replication server as the ID Server.

`rs.rs_id_server_is_rs_server: yes`

> Yes means that you want to use this replication server as the ID Server as well.

`rs.rs_idserver_user: sa`

> Login that other Replication Servers will use to connect with the ID Server. Change this to a user of your preference.

`rs.rs_idserver_pass: xxxxx`

> Password for the ID Server user. Default is *rs_idserver_name*_id_passwd. Provide your preferred password.

`rs.rs_start_rs_id: USE_DEFAULT`

> First ID used for Replication Servers in this ID Server domain.

`rs.rs_start_db_id: USE_DEFAULT`

> First ID used for databases in this ID Server domain.

rs.rs_name: **NYRS**

> Set the Replication Server name to the name of the replication server installing.

rs.rs_needs_repagent: **yes**

> Set this parameter to "yes" so that rs_init will configure and enable a RepAgent thread on the Adaptive Server for RSSD. Please note that you can add RepAgent to the Sybase primary server in this method using rs_init. For other database sources like Oracle, UDB, or MS SQL server, the method needs additional setup and configuration. Please note the Replication Agents for user databases will be created when user databases are added to the replication system.

rs.rs_rs_errorlog: **/db/logs/errorlog/NYRS.log**

> The error log location for the replication server. The directory should exist and the Sybase user should have write permissions to the directory.

rs.rs_rs_cfg_file: **USE_DEFAULT**

> You may want to change this to your site-specific naming convention. Include the full path. Installing users must have write permission to the directory. The default location is $SYBASE_REP/install and the default file name is *rep server*.cfg.

rs.rs_charset: **utf8**

> Set the character set to an appropriate value. This needs to be set to the same as your replicated ASE servers.

rs.rs_language: **us_english**

> If you leave this at the default, make sure you get the correct language installed. The default depends on locales.

rs.rs_sortorder: **binary**

> If you leave this at the default, make sure you get the correct sort order installed, which should be the same as the ASE sort order. The default is binary sort order.

`rs.rs_rssd_sqlsrvr:` **NYDS**

If you are considering using ERSSD, then you need to set up ERSSD parameters in the resource file. For more information, please refer to Chapter 19, "ERSSD." In this example installation we are using RSSD on ASE server. If you are not using ERSSD, then set the RSSD data server name.

`rs.rs_rssd_db:` **USE_DEFAULT**

The default name will be *rs name*_RSSD.

`rs.rs_create_rssd:` **yes**

Set this parameter so that rs_init will create the RSSD database. Please note that after setting this resource value, each time you execute rs_init again, it will drop and recreate the RSSD database.

This option controls if rs_init creates the RSSD database every time it is invoked, even if the previous invocation of rs_init created the RSSD. This option assumes the RSSD data and log devices are ready to use. These devices can either be left to rs_init to initialize or manually initialized ahead of execution of rs_init. More information on options related to data and log devices are provided below. It is convenient to initialize the data and log devices in the ASE manually as part of the data server installation process. Setting this option also expects data and log device names specified for rs.rs_rssd_db_device_name and rs.rs_rssd_log_device_name.

`rs.rs_rssd_ha_failover:` **no**

High availability option. Typically set to no unless you have the Sybase high availability option chosen. Please consult the Sybase documentation for more information on Sybase high availability.

`rs.rs_rssd_sa_login:` **sa**

`rs.rs_rssd_sa_pass:` **xxxxxx**

Be consistent with passwords and logins.

The following parameters are best left as defaults unless you want to customize user names and passwords:

rs.rs_rssd_prim_user: USE_DEFAULT

Name of the RSSD primary user. Default is rs_rssd_db_prim.

rs.rs_rssd_prim_pass: USE_DEFAULT

Password for the RSSD primary user. Default is rs_rssd_db_prim_ps.

rs.rs_rssd_maint_user: USE_DEFAULT

Name of the RSSD maintenance user. Default is rs_rssd_db_maint.

rs.rs_rssd_maint_pass: USE_DEFAULT

Password for the RSSD maintenance user. Default is rs_rssd_db_maint_ps.

rs.rs_rssd_dbo_user: USE_DEFAULT

Scanned by someone other than rs_rssd_sa_login. Use this only if you need the Log Transfer Manager (LTM).

rs.rs_rssd_dbo_pass: USE_DEFAULT

Use this only if you need the Log Transfer Manager.

rs_init will use the rs_rssd_sa_login to access the RSSD database. But if you either use LTM or want some other user to scan the RSSD, then change the last two values related to rs_rssd_db_[user|pass].

REPLICATION SERVER SYSTEM DATABASE DEVICE INFORMATION

Leave the device creation options set to "no" but specify the following:

```
rs.rs_rssd_db_device_path
rs.rs_rssd_log_device_path
rs.rs_rssd_db_device_name
rs.rs_rssd_log_device_name
```

Rs_init will use these device names to create the RSSD if the rs.rs_create_rssd option is set to yes. It is better to create the database devices before installing Replication Server. This way we can customize the sizes and naming standards and locate ASE with RSSD and Replication Server on different hosts.

STABLE QUEUE DISK PARTITION INFORMATION

```
rs.rs_diskp_name: /home/sybase/devices/P2
rs.rs_diskp_lname: P2
rs.rs_diskp_size: 20
rs.rs_diskp_vstart: 0
```

This is the first disk partition that the Replication Server initializes. This stable queue partition is required during setup. Once the Replication Server is up and running, you can add more partitions and drop this partition. The rs.rs_diskp_ name should point to a file with a full path definition. Make sure you use the touch command in the location specified. If the operating system patches are not up to date, it is likely the stable queue partition initialization will not succeed. When the stable queue partition initialization fails, the messages may not point to the correct problem. You will need to verify host related problems like file system permissions, operating system patches, and Sybase library lookup path variables like $LD_LIBRARY_PATH, etc., to resolve the issue.

REMOTE SITE CONNECTION INFORMATION

The connection thread called RSI (Replication Server Interface) is how remote replication servers connect to the replication server you are installing. If you are installing just one replication server, then you do not need RSI connection. Similarly, if you are installing a warm standby, you do not need the RSI thread. For more information on routes (RSI threads), please refer to Chapter 8.

You can leave the following two options at the default or customize them.

```
rs.rs_rs_user: USE_DEFAULT
```

Default is rs_name_rsi.

```
rs.rs_rs_pass: USE_DEFAULT
```

Password for the Replication Server login name. Default is rs_name_rsi_ps.

SYSTEM DATABASE LOG TRANSFER MANAGER INFORMATION

Change these parameters only if you need LTM instead of RepAgent for the Replication Server System Database. In general, a RepAgent is preferred over LTM. In many cases, the LTM option may not even be available. Verify the release bulletin for your platform to see if you need an LTM instead of Replication Agent.

```
rs.ltm_name: NY_LTM
rs.rs_ltm_rs_user: USE_DEFAULT — for the LTM to login to RSSD
rs.rs_ltm_rs_pass: USE_DEFAULT — for the LTM to login to RSSD
rs.rs_ltm_admin_user: USE_DEFAULT — the user who can start and stop LTM
rs.rs_ltm_admin_pass: USE_DEFAULT
```

ID SERVER SETUP INFORMATION

Unless there is a specific reason, it is not necessary to change any of these parameters. If you set rs.rs_id_server_is_rs_server to "yes", then this section of information is not required. The rs_init will use all the information related to the Replication Server being installed for ID_SERVER as well. ID Server is a Replication Server that registers the Replication Servers in a domain. ID Server is the first Replication Server that you start in a replication system.

```
rs.do_add_id_server: USE_DEFAULT
```

The interface's entry for ID Server. This is by default "no" on UNIX systems. On Windows, an interfaces entry cannot be added using the resource file. Leave it set to the default.

```
rs.rs_id_server_connect_retry_delay_time: USE_DEFAULT
```

Amount of time in seconds the ID Server entry connection waits before attempting to connect again. This follows the typical Sybase client library timeout rules.

```
rs.rs_id_server_notes: Default Sybase Configuration
```

Additional information about ID Server.

```
rs.rs_id_server_network_protocol_list: tcp
```

Specify if this Replication Server is not the ID Server.

```
rs.rs_idserver_hostname: hostname
```

Specify if this Replication Server is not the ID Server

```
rs.rs_idserver_port: port number
```

Specify if this Replication Server is not the ID Server.

REPLICATION SERVER INTERFACES INFORMATION

It is generally suggested that the Replication Server interfaces information be added before rs_init and this entire section left at the defaults. Please refer to the interfaces information provided at the beginning of this chapter in the section titled "Replication Server Installation Using Console Mode."

LOG TRANSFER MANAGER INTERFACES INFORMATION FOR RSSD

If a LTM is required this section should be completed. In most cases, this section should be left at the defaults as a RepAgent is a better alternative to LTM.

REPLICATION SERVER SECURITY INFORMATION

Security issues are discussed in detail in Chapter 17. During the installation process, we will leave this entire section at its defaults.

Once a response file is prepared, you are ready to install a Replication Server.

Installing Replication Server Using rs_init Utility with the Response File

If the response file is ready, you can start installation with the rs_init command:

```
%SYBASE/REP-15_0/install/rs_init -r SAMPLE_RS.res
```

A complete installation log on RH4.0 Linux is shown on pages 68-70. That log shows what you can expect in a successful installation process. If your installation fails in any one of the steps, please look through what may be required for the installation to continue to the next step.

Configuration File

After a successful installation, a default configuration file is typically created in the $SYBASE_REP/install directory, where $SYBASE_REP is the directory where the replication software is located. This configuration file is named *rs name*.cfg. Please see the detailed configuration parameters in Chapter 5 for more configuration options, and refer to Chapter 14 for advanced monitoring and tuning options.

```
#
# Configuration file for Replication Server 'NYRS'. Created by rs_init.
#
RSSD_embedded=no
RSSD_server=NYDS
RSSD_database=NYRS_RSSD
RSSD_primary_user=spam_rs_prim
RSSD_primary_pw_enc=0x02c19ac500dccf689634552a94679cdf8e2af540f3753906eb6deab8fce302eb
RSSD_maint_user=spam_rs_maint
RSSD_maint_pw_enc=0x02c19ac500dccf689634552a94679cdf8e2af540f3753906eb6deab8fce302e6
RSSD_ha_failover=no
ID_server=NYRS
ID_user=NYRS_id_user
ID_pw_enc=0x02c494a43192096fb901d87c509bb638a343d62ebf77677fa278bfd278d2cac6
RS_charset=iso_1
CONFIG_charset=utf8
```

```
RS_language=us_english
RS_sortorder=binary
```

Typical RUN File

At the end of a successful installation, rs_init creates a RUN file. This RUN file is used to start the Replication Server. This file is also located in the $SYBASE_REP/install directory, where $SYBASE_REP is the directory where the replication software is located.

```
sybase@host:/usr/sybase/REP_150_1/REP-15_0/install>cat RUN_NYRS

#
# Runserver file for Replication Server 'NYRS'. Created by rs_init.
#
export SYBASE=/usr/sybase/REP_150_1

/usr/sybase/REP_150_1/REP-15_0/bin/repserver -SNYRS \
-C/usr/sybase/REP_150_1/REP-15_0/install/NYRS.cfg
-E/usr/sybase/logs/NYRS.log \
-I/usr/sybase/REP_150_1/interfaces
```

If you have not specified the correct error log location in rs_init resource, you can change it now. Note that the RUN file points to the configuration file that we already discussed. You may also notice that we purposely exported the $SYBASE variable in this RUN file. This line is added after the installation. It is required if an ASE is also installed on this host and at a different location. It sets the SYBASE environment variable to the Replication Server installation directory, not the ASE installation directory. Depending on your environment, the startup may not work if this line is not included.

You may also create symbolic links for the startserver and showserver programs that come with the ASE installation to this Replication Server installation directory, as shown below.

```
sybase@host:/usr/sybase/REP_150_1/REP-15_0/install> ls -lrt
total 22108
-rwxr-x---  1 sybase sybase  1615303 Jul 26 2006 rs_init*
drwxr-x---  2 sybase sybase     4096 Sep  6 09:58 SPR/
```

```
-rw-------  1 sybase sybase    580 Feb  7 11:49 NYRS.bak
-rw-------  1 sybase sybase    580 Feb  7 14:08 NYRS.cfg
-rwxr-xr-x  1 sybase sybase    281 Feb 12 11:01 RUN_NYRS*
lrwxrwxrwx  1 sybase sybase     52 Feb 12 11:02 startserver ->
/db/sybase/ASE64_1501_0/ASE-15_0/install/startserver*
lrwxrwxrwx  1 sybase sybase     51 Feb 12 11:03 showserver ->
/db/sybase/ASE64_1501_0/ASE-15_0/install/showserver*
```

Now the Replication Server is installed and you can log in to the Replication Server. As usual with Sybase products, the initial password is null.

```
sybase@host:/usr/sybase/REP_150_1/REP-15_0/install> isql -Usa -SNYRS -w999
Password:
1>
```

Check the Replication Server components as of now:

```
sybase@host:/home/sybase> isql -Usa -SNYRS -w899
Password:
1> admin who
2> go
```

Spid	Name	State	Info
16	DSI EXEC	Awaiting Command	101(1) NYDS.NYRS_RSSD
10	DSI	Awaiting Message	101 NYDS.NYRS_RSSD
12	DIST	Awaiting Wakeup	101 NYDS.NYRS_RSSD
15	SQT	Awaiting Wakeup	101:1 DIST NYDS.NYRS_RSSD
9	SQM	Awaiting Message	101:1 NYDS.NYRS_RSSD
8	SQM	Awaiting Message	101:0 NYDS.NYRS_RSSD
21	REP AGENT	Awaiting Command	NYDS.NYRS_RSSD
11	dSUB	Sleeping	
6	dCM	Awaiting Message	
7	dAIO	Awaiting Message	
13	dREC	Sleeping	dREC
23	USER	Active	sa
5	dALARM	Awaiting Wakeup	
14	dSYSAM	Sleeping	

```
1>
```

The Name column in the above output refers to the Replication Server thread name. These names and their roles are described in Chapter 2.

Check if one or more threads are down:

```
1> admin who_is_down
2> go
 Spid Name       State                Info
 ---- ---------- -------------------- -----------------------------------
1>
```

This completes the basic Replication Server installation process. If you are installing warm standby replication, the Replication Server will be installed exactly as described above except that you will not replicate the RSSD database as there will be only one Replication Server.

The next step in the installation process is to add the databases to the replication system. This is covered in the section titled "Adding a Database to the Replication System." Any user database can be added to the replication system, either for regular replication or for setting up a warm standby application.

Post Installation

After one Replication Server is installed and configured, the next steps depend on your application requirements. If the installation was for a warm standby application, then one Replication Server installation is all you need.

The following are typically performed after successfully installing one Replication Server:

▶ Install the Replicate Replication Server (RRS) and configure it. If additional Replication Servers are needed to establish an indirect route, you will need to install those Replication Servers as well.

▶ Configure a route (direct or indirect, depending on your application requirements) to RRS. Please see Chapter 8 for more information on configuring a route.

▶ Add one or more databases. Adding a database to a bidirectional replication system is covered in the following section. Adding active and standby databases to a warm standby setup is described in Chapter 12.

▶ Establish table or stored procedure replication. Please refer to Chapter 9 for more information.

▶ Set up multi-site availability (MSA), yet another way of replicating data at higher granularity. This is described in Chapter 13.

Replication Server Initial Configuration

The initial Replication Server configuration is normally done via the rs_init configuration program. Please see Chapter 14 for information on performance monitoring, and Chapter 5 for advanced configuration options. Based on the monitoring counters, it is possible to tune the Replication Server for better performance.

Adding a Database to the Replication System

The following steps describe how to add a database to the replication system.

1. Execute **rs_init** at the command level.

2. Follow the menu items to go to the Configure Replication System window.

```
CONFIGURE REPLICATION SYSTEM

1.  Install a new Replication Server
2.  Add a database to the replication system
3.  Upgrade an existing Replication Server
4.  Downgrade RSSD for an existing Replication Server
5.  Upgrade an existing database in the replication system
6.  Enable password encryption for a Replication Server
7.  Alter a Replication Server configuration file password



Ctrl-a Accept and Continue, Ctrl-x Exit Screen, ? Help.

Enter the number of your choice and press return: 2
```

Select option **2** to add a database to the replication system.

3. In the Add Database to Replication System window, select option **1** to specify Replication Server information. In the windows that follow, continue entering Replication Server information.

4. Then select option **2** to enter database information. This is the database that you are planning to add to the replication system.

```
ADD DATABASE TO REPLICATION SYSTEM

1.  Replication Server Information              Complete
2.  Database Information                        Incomplete




Ctrl-a Accept and Continue, Ctrl-x Exit Screen, ? Help.

Enter the number of your choice and press return: 2
```

In the Database Information window, enter all the information for the data server and database that is being added to the replication system. The final option here, "Is this a Physical Connection for Existing Logical Connection," relates to warm standby setup. When you toggle this to "yes", logical connection information for warm standby active or standby database will be entered. In this example, we are adding a database for a potential bidirectional replication, so we leave this switch set to "no". We left the maintenance user and maintenance password to the system default, although you may consider changing this if your environment requires additional security.

```
DATABASE INFORMATION

1.  SQL Server name:  MYDB_SYB
2.  SA user:  sa
3.  SA password:  x873j7
4.  Database name:
5.  Will the database be replicated:  no
6.  Maintenance user:
7.  Maintenance password:
8.  Is this a Physical Connection for Existing Logical Connection: no



Ctrl-a Accept and Continue, Ctrl-x Exit Screen, ? Help.

Enter the number of your choice and press return: 4
Enter the name of the database:
```

After filling in all the information, the Database Information window will look as follows:

```
DATABASE INFORMATION

1.  SQL Server name:  MYDB_SYB
2.  SA user:  sa
3.  SA password:  x873j7
4.  Database name:  mydba1_db
5.  Will the database be replicated:  yes
6.  Maintenance user:  mydba1_db_maint
7.  Maintenance password:  mydba1_db_maint_ps
8.  Is this a Physical Connection for Existing Logical Connection: no



Ctrl-a Accept and Continue, Ctrl-x Exit Screen, ? Help.

Enter the number of your choice and press return:
```

5. Accept the entries with **Ctrl-a**. The terminal will go back to the main window, where you can press **Ctrl-w** to save the response file as described in the "Replication Server Installation Using Console Mode" section earlier in this chapter. After saving the response file, you can accept it by pressing

Ctrl-a one more time, then you will be prompted with "Execute the Replication Server tasks now?" Once you answer "y" to this question, rs_init will start adding the database.

```
Execute the Replication Server tasks now? n/y
Running task: check the SQL Server.
Task succeeded: check the SQL Server.
Running task: verify users and their passwords.
Verified that 'NYRS_ra' can log into Replication Server 'NYRS'.

Verified that 'sa' can log into Replication Server 'NYRS'.
Task succeeded: verify users and their passwords.
Running task: check the database.
Verified that database 'ny_db' exists.
Verified that SQL Server 'NRDS' supports replication.
Added maintenance user login 'ny_db_maint' to database 'ny_db'.
Verified that maintenance user 'ny_db_maint' can log into SQL Server NYDS'.
Task succeeded: check the database.
Running task: configure database for primary data.
Loading script 'rs_install_primary.sql' into database 'ny_db'.
..Done
Loaded script 'rs_install_primary.sql' successfully.
Done
Granting permissions on the lastcommit functions and rs_marker.
Granting permissions on the lastcommit functions.
Granted maintenance user permissions on the lastcommit functions and
rs_marker.

Granted replication role to maintenance user
Task succeeded: configure database for primary data.
Running task: configure the Replication Agent.
Task succeeded: configure the Replication Agent.
Running task: set connection to the database.
Adding database 'ny_db' to the replication system.
Successfully executed 'create connection'. Database 'ny_db' is now managed
by Replication Server 'NYRS'.
Task succeeded: set connection to the database.
Running task: start the Replication Agent.
Task succeeded: start the Replication Agent.

Configuration completed successfully.
Press <return> to continue.
```

Replication Server Upgrade

There are two methods of upgrading the Replication Server:

▶ A fresh Replication Server installation and replication setup. In this approach, a new Replication Server is installed with the desired version level.

All the steps in the Replication Server installation, setup, and configuration, including adding user databases, creating replication definitions, creating subscriptions, and using materialization methods, are followed to establish a fresh replication.

This approach is time-consuming but straightforward. This method is not discussed further, because it includes everything discussed earlier in this chapter as part of Replication Server installation. By following proper standards and scripting the procedures, this method becomes easy and repeatable.

▶ An in-place upgrade. The rest of the Replication Server upgrade discussion in this chapter refers to in-place upgrade. If the in-place upgrade fails for any reason, then the full installation method may be the only alternative.

The process of upgrading Replication Server in-place from Replication Server 12.6 or earlier includes multiple steps:

1. Installing the new Replication Server software. You may need to run InstallShield to install the software from the distribution media.

2. Upgrading the RSSD using rs_init.

3. Upgrading the user databases using rs_init if there are any and if this is required.

4. Upgrading the route (this is discussed in Chapter 8).

Installing the New Replication Server Software

It is recommended that the newer Replication Server software be installed in a different directory than the existing Replication Server install directory. In a UNIX environment, for example, it would be convenient to create a symbolic link to the new directory structure.

Upgrading the Replication Server RSSD

The procedure to upgrade the Replication Server RSSD includes backing up the current installation and upgrading the RSSD using rs_init.

Upgrading the RSSD may add new RSSD tables, rows, stored procedures, and columns and may change any of the existing RSSD data values. To upgrade the RSSD in-place, follow these steps:

1. Verify that the Replication Server and all of the components of the Replication Server to be upgraded are working properly.

2. If the RSSD is controlled by an Adaptive Server Enterprise, be sure to grant the replication role to the primary user at the RSSD server. You can find the primary user name in the Replication Server configuration file.

3. Invoke **rs_init** and follow the menus to select the options for upgrading an existing replication server.

Before attempting to upgrade an existing Replication Server to Replication Server 15.0, please check the Sybase Replication Server release guide to verify that the current Replication Server can be upgraded to Replication Server 15.0.

The upgrade process may need to create new system tables in the RSSD database. It may be better to make the RSSD primary user the dbo of the RSSD database to grant the permission required during upgrade.

1. Start **rs_init**. Follow through the screens to select option **3** from the Configure Replication System window.

```
CONFIGURE REPLICATION SYSTEM

1.  Install a new Replication Server
2.  Add a database to the replication system
3.  Upgrade an existing Replication Server
4.  Downgrade RSSD for an existing Replication Server
5.  Upgrade an existing database in the replication system
6.  Enable password encryption for a Replication Server
7.  Enable password encryption for an LTM
8.  Alter a Replication Server configuration file password
9.  Alter a password in an LTM configuration file


Ctrl-a Accept and Continue, Ctrl-x Exit Screen, ? Help.

Enter the number of your choice and press return: 3
```

2. Fill in the information as required in the window. Make sure the Replication Server configuration file location is correct and points to the current Replication Server configuration file.

```
UPGRADE EXISTING REPLICATION SERVER

1.  Replication Server name:  R1250RRS
2.  RS SA user:  R1250RRS_RSSD_prim
3.  RS SA password:  R1250RRS_RSSD_prim_ps
4.  Replication Server configuration file:
        /apps/sybase/REP_1250_2/REP-12_5/install/R1250RRS.cfg




Ctrl-a Accept and Continue, Ctrl-x Exit Screen, ? Help. <Ctrl-a>
```

3. Complete the Upgrade Existing Replication Server screen input and press **Ctrl-a** to continue. Answer yes to the message from rs_init, "Execute the Replication Server tasks now?" If the Replication Server is running, rs_init will shut

down Replication Server and will complete upgrading the RSSD. At the end of a successful upgrade, rs_init will display the message, "Upgraded from *old_rel_no* to *new_rel_no*. Replication Server '*rs_name*' can now be restarted. Task succeeded: upgrade the RSSD. Configuration completed successfully."

4. If you have installed the new Replication Server software in a different directory, update the RUN_*server* file with the new directory name.

5. If you want to save your inputs for a future Replication Server upgrade, you may want to save the upgrade configuration by pressing **Ctrl-w** before exiting the rs_init.

You need to run rs_init in the new release directory, for example, in the Replication Server 15.x directory. You can now start the upgraded Replication Server.

If the upgrade fails, you can repeat the same process multiple times by correcting any problems until you succeed. But you cannot start the Replication Server with an incomplete RSSD upgrade.

When you accept the input in the Upgrade Existing Replication Server window by pressing **Ctrl-a**, the Replication Server upgrade process starts.

```
Running task: check the RSSD SQL Server.
Task succeeded: check the RSSD SQL Server.
Running task: upgrade the RSSD.
..Done
...Done
Done
Loading script 'rsupgr1260.sql' into database 'LONDON_DS'.
...SQL Server message: msg 0, level 10, state 1
"Column name has been changed."
SQL Server message: msg 0, level 10, state 1
"The replication status for 'rs_objects' is set to false."
.SQL Server message: msg 0, level 10, state 1
"Default bound to column."
SQL Server message: msg 0, level 10, state 1
"Object name has been changed."
SQL Server message: msg 0, level 10, state 1
"Object name has been changed."
```

```
.SQL Server message: msg 0, level 10, state 1
"Object name has been changed."
SQL Server message: msg 0, level 10, state 1
"Object name has been changed."
.........SQL Server message: msg 0, level 10, state 1
"The replication status for 'rs_objects' is set to true."
SQL Server message: msg 0, level 10, state 1
"Object name has been changed."
SQL Server message: msg 0, level 10, state 1
"Object name has been changed."
SQL Server message: msg 0, level 10, state 1
"Object name has been changed."
.SQL Server message: msg 0, level 10, state 1
"Object name has been changed."
SQL Server message: msg 0, level 10, state 1
"Object name has been changed."
SQL Server message: msg 0, level 10, state 1
"Object name has been changed."
SQL Server message: msg 0, level 10, state 1
"Object name has been changed."
.SQL Server message: msg 0, level 10, state 1
"Object name has been changed."
......SQL Server message: msg 0, level 10, state 1
"The replication status for 'rs_objects' is set to false."
SQL Server message: msg 0, level 10, state 1
"The replication status for 'rs_columns' is set to false."
SQL Server message: msg 0, level 10, state 1
"The replication status for 'rs_functions' is set to false."
..SQL Server message: msg 0, level 10, state 1
"The replication status for 'rs_objects' is set to true."
.SQL Server message: msg 0, level 10, state 1
"The replication status for 'rs_columns' is set to true."
SQL Server message: msg 0, level 10, state 1
"The replication status for 'rs functions' is set to true."
.Done
Loading script 'rsupgr_ase.sql' into database 'LONDON_DS'.
....SQL Server message: msg 0, level 10, state 1
"Object name has been changed."
SQL Server message: msg 0, level 10, state 1
"The replication status for 'rs_objects' is set to true."
.SQL Server message: msg 0, level 10, state 1
"Object name has been changed."
```

```
SQL Server message: msg 0, level 10, state 1
"The replication status for 'rs_columns' is set to true."
.SQL Server message: msg 0, level 10, state 1
"Object name has been changed."
SQL Server message: msg 0, level 10, state 1
"The replication status for 'rs_functions' is set to true."
.SQL Server message: msg 0, level 10, state 1
"Object name has been changed."
SQL Server message: msg 0, level 10, state 1
"The replication status for 'rs_funcstrings' is set to true."
.SQL Server message: msg 0, level 10, state 1
"Object name has been changed."
SQL Server message: msg 0, level 10, state 1
"Object name has been changed."
.SQL Server message: msg 0, level 10, state 1
"Object name has been changed."
SQL Server message: msg 0, level 10, state 1
"The replication status for 'rs_dbreps' is set to true."
.SQL Server message: msg 0, level 10, state 1
"Object name has been changed."
SQL Server message: msg 0, level 10, state 1
"The replication status for 'rs_dbsubsets' is set to true."
.SQL Server message: msg 0, level 10, state 1
"Object name has been changed."
.SQL Server message: msg 0, level 10, state 1
"Object name has been changed."
SQL Server message: msg 0, level 10, state 1
"Object name has been changed."
.SQL Server message: msg 0, level 10, state 1
"Object name has been changed."
....Done
Loading Replication Server stored procedures in RSSD 'LONDON_DS'.
Loading script 'rsprocs_ase.sql' into database 'R1250RRS_RSSD'.
.......Done
Loaded script 'rsprocs_ase.sql' successfully.
Upgraded from '12.5.0' to '15.0.0'..
Replication Server 'R1250RRS' can now be restarted.
Task succeeded: upgrade the RSSD.

Configuration completed successfully.
Press <return> to continue.
```

You may see the following message during the upgrade process:

```
WARNING: "Please complete your pending subscriptions create/drop before
upgrading."
Press <return> to continue.
```

If you get this message, one or more of the subscriptions have not been materialized properly. Please complete the materialization process before upgrading. If you believe there is no problem with materialization and every component is working properly, you may want to update the rs_subscriptions table to set the column's materialization and dematerialization equal to 0, as shown below.

```
use RSSD
go
begin tran
2> go
1> update rs_subscriptions set materializing=0 where materializing<> 0
2> go
(1 row affected)
1> commit
```

Post RSSD Upgrade Process

After the successful upgrade of the RSSD to release level 15.x, keep the following in mind:

▶ You must start the server using Replication Server 15.x binaries. Otherwise, you may encounter the following message:

```
I. 2007/06/20 08:56:33. Reading 'LONDON_DS.R1250RRS_RSSD..rs_config'
for system configuration parameters.
F. 2007/06/20 08:56:33. FATAL ERROR #31132 GLOBAL RS(GLOBAL RS)
/cfginit.c(1854)
        The RSSD version level required by the repserver is '1250'
while the current RSSD version level is '1500'. This repserver execut-
able cannot run against this RSSD. Please use the newer version of
repserver executable.
F. 2007/06/20 08:56:33. FATAL ERROR #18028 GLOBAL RS(GLOBAL RS) -
servmain.c(286)
        Initialization failed. Server is shutting down.
```

▶ The RUN file and the configuration file may need to be moved to the new destination.

▶ You need to edit the RUN file to refer to the new directory structure.

Current RUN file copied to the new directory:

```
#
# Runserver file for Replication Server 'R1250RRS'. Created by rs_init.
#
. /apps/sybase/REP_1250_2/SYBASE.sh

/apps/sybase/REP_1250_2/REP-12_5/bin/repserver -SR1250RRS \
-C/apps/sybase/REP_1250_2/REP-12_5/install/R1250RRS.cfg \
-E/usr/sybase/logs/errorlog_R1250RRS -I/apps/sybase/REP_1250_2/interfaces
```

Updated RUN file in the new directory:

```
#
# Runserver file for Replication Server 'R1250RRS'. Created by rs_init.
#
. /apps/sybase/REP_150_1/SYBASE.sh

/apps/sybase/REP_150_1/REP-15_0/bin/repserver -SR1250RRS \
-C/apps/sybase/REP_150_1/REP-15_0/install/R1250RRS.cfg \
-E/usr/sybase/logs/errorlog_R1250RRS -I/apps/sybase/REP_150_1/interfaces
```

▶ Before starting the new Replication Server, you need to complete upgrading the user database(s) and the route version. Otherwise, you may see the following message in the error log. Note that invalid routing can result in replication problems.

```
I. 2007/06/20 09:30:40. RSI: connection to R1250RRS' is established and the
route is active.
I. 2007/06/20 09:30:48. RSI version (126) for 'R1250RRS' does not match the
default RSI version for this Replication Server 125 using version 125.
```

Upgrading a User Database

Upgrading a user database for a newly upgraded Replication Server is very similar to upgrading the Replication Server RSSD. It may add special tables to RSSD.

1. Start **rs_init** and follow the steps to get to the Configure Replication System window, then choose option 5, "Upgrade an existing database in the replication system."

2. Complete the input screen as required.

3. Press **Ctrl-a** to allow the rs_init to complete upgrading the user database. Upon a successful upgrade, rs_init will display success status messages.

4. If you have more user databases to upgrade to Replication Server 15.x, repeat the process for each of the databases to be upgraded.

```
UPGRADE A DATABASE IN A REPLICATION SYSTEM


1.  SQL Server name:  LONDON_DS
2.  Database name:  pubs2
3.  SA user:  sa
4.  SA password:  reptest
5.  Maintenance user:  pubs2_maint




Ctrl-a Accept and Continue, Ctrl-x Exit Screen, ? Help.  Ctrl-a
```

When you accept the inputs in the Upgrade a Database in a Replication System window by pressing **Ctrl-a**, the Replication Server upgrade process starts.

```
Running task: load a SQL script into a database.
Loading script 'upgrade/rsupgrdb.sql' into database 'pubs2'.
.Done
Loaded script 'upgrade/rsupgrdb.sql' successfully.
SQL Server message: msg 11107, level 10, state 1
"All the roles specified to be granted in the grant role statement have
already been granted to grantee 'pubs2_maint'.
```

```
"
Granted replication role to maintenance user
Task succeeded: load a SQL script into a database.

Configuration completed successfully.
Press <return> to continue.
```

Setting the Site Version

Replication Server 15.x requires the site version to be at least
1200 or higher. You cannot create, alter, or drop replication definitions until the Replication Server system version is set to 1200
or higher. Use admin show_site_version to find out the current
Replication Server site version in the newly upgraded Replication
Server.

```
sybase@host:/apps/sybase/REP_1250_2/REP-12_5/install>isql -Usa -S R1250RRS
-w899
Password:
1> admin show_site_version
2> go
 Site Version
 ------------
         1250
```

You can also use the sysadmin site_version command to check
the current site version.

```
1> sysadmin site_version
2> go
The current site version is '1250'.
1>
```

To find out the system version, use the sysadmin system_version
command:

```
1> sysadmin system_version
2> go
The current system version is 1102
1>

1> admin version
2> go
```

97

```
Version
-------------------------------------------------------------------------
Replication Server/12.5/EBF 11678/Linux Intel/Linux 2.4.7-10enterprise
i686/1/OPT/Mon Jan 12 11:02:12 2004
1>
```

Set the site version equal to the lower of the site versions of connecting
Replication Servers via this route. In this example upgrade we have two
Replication Servers involved; one is the Primary Replication Server and the
other Replicate Replication Server. One Replication Server is version 15.0
and the other Replication Server is version 12.6. So, the site version for
the newly upgraded Replication Server 15.0.1 is set to 1500.

```
1> sysadmin site_version, 1500
2> go
The site version has been set to '1500'.
```

A site version cannot be higher than the software version or the
release level of the Replication Server.

Chapter 5

Configuration Parameters

In this chapter we will discuss Replication Server configuration parameters. Configuration parameters are options that the user can set, using the configure replication server, alter connection, and alter route commands. Configuration parameters are stored in the rs_config system table, and config file parameters are stored in the Replication Server configuration file. These parameters can only be modified by users with "sa" permissions. Note that Replication Server release 15.0.1 and above supports dynamic configuration.

`admin config`

`admin config` is a new Replication Server command that can be used to display Replication Server command-line parameters and configuration file parameters. Server parameters that affect Replication Server globally are set with the `configure replication server` (rs_config) command, connection parameters are set using the `alter connection` command, logical connection configuration parameters, are set with the `alter logical connection` command, and route configuration parameters are set using the `alter route` command.

Syntax:

```
admin config [, "connection" | , "logical connection" | , "route"]
[, "server" [, "database"]] [, configuration_name]
```

Example:

```
1> admin config, 'server'
2> go
 Configuration    Config Value   Run Value   Default Value   Legal Values
 Datatype       Status
 ---------------  -------------  ----------  --------------  ------------
 ------------   ------
  id_server        prs            prs         N/A             NULL
 string       Restart required
  oserver          prs            prs         N/A             NULL
 string       Restart required
  RSSD_server      pds            pds         N/A             NULL
 String       Restart required
```

To retrieve connection configuration information:

```
1> admin config, 'connection', 'pds', 'prs_RSSD', 'dynamic_sql'
2> go
 Configuration                    Config Value   Run Value   Default Value
 Legal Values      Datatype       Status
 ----------------------------   -------------  ----------  -------------
 -----------------  ------------   ------
  dynamic_sql                     on             on          off
 list: on,off     string       Restart not required
  dynamic_sql_cache_management    mru            mru         mru
 list: mru,fixed    string       Restart not required
  dynamic_sql_cache_size          20             20          20
 range: 1,65535    integer      Restart not required
```

The admin config command only works with isql 12.5 and above.
Replication Server configuration parameters can be changed
using any of the following alternatives:

▶ The configure replication server command
▶ The alter connection/alter route commands
▶ Sybase Central
▶ Replication Monitoring Services

Some of the configuration changes are static and need Replication
Server to be restarted or the connection/route to be suspended
and resumed. Please note that Replication Server 12.6 and above
no longer support the rs_configure system procedure.

Configuring Replication Server

Replication parameters specify default configuration values that are relevant to the local server. The `configure replication server` command can be used to customize and tune Replication Server configuration parameters, including network-based security and Embedded RSSD configuration parameters.

```
configure replication server
```

Syntax:

```
configure replication server
    {set repserver_param to 'value' |
    set route_param to 'value' |
    set database_param to 'value' |
    set logical_database_param to 'value' |
    set security_param to 'value' |
    set id_security_param to 'value' |
    set security_services [to] 'default'}
```

repserver_param

The Replication Server parameter's values for the local replication server. `repserver_param` can be configured with the `configure replication server` command. These parameters are static. Replication Server must be restarted after changing these parameters.

```
configure replication server set repserver_param to 'value'
```

route_param

Route parameters can be set with the `configure replication server` or the `alter route` command. The route must be suspended and restarted for changes to take effect.

```
configure replication server set route_param to 'value'
```

or

```
alter route to destination_replicationserver
set route_param to 'value'
```

database_param

> Database parameters indicate the value for the database connection. These parameters can be set with the `configure replication server` or `alter connection` commands. The connection must be suspended and resumed for changes to take effect.
>
> `configure replication server set `*`database_param`*` to '`*`value`*`'`
>
> or
>
> `alter connection to `*`dataserver.database`*` set `*`database_param`*` to '`*`value`*`'`

logical_database_param

> `logical_database_param` specifies the default value for the logical connection originating from the source replication server. Logical connections are used in warm standby replication setup. Changes made to these parameters are dynamic.
>
> `configure replication server set `*`logical_database_param`*` to '`*`value`*`'`

security_param

> `security_param` sets network security related parameters. Except for `use_security_services` and `use_ssl`, all other security parameters set with `configure replication server` are dynamic.
>
> `configure replication server set `*`security_param`*` to '`*`value`*`'`

id_security_param

> `id_security_param` specifies network security parameters for the ID Replication Server.
>
> `configure replication server set `*`id_security_param`*` to '`*`value`*`'`

security_services

> This parameter sets network security parameters for connections to match the global settings of the Replication Server. Sybase supported security mechanisms are listed under

SECURITY in $SYBASE/OCS-15_0/libtcl.cfg. The default
security mechanism is the first mechanism listed.

```
configure replication server set security_services to 'value'
```

batch

Specifies how Replication Server sends commands to data servers. When batch is "on", Replication Server may send multiple
commands to the data server as a single command batch. When
batch is "off", Replication Server sends commands to the data
server one at a time.

Default: "on"

Example:

```
1> configure replication server
2> set batch to 'off'
3> go
Config parameter 'batch' is modified. This change will not take effect on
existing connections/routes until they are restarted. Use suspend and
resume commands to restart a connection/route.
```

batch_begin

Indicates whether a begin transaction can be sent in the same
batch as other commands (such as insert, delete, and so on).

Default: "on"

Example:

```
1> configure replication server
2> set batch_begin to 'off'
3> go
Config parameter 'batch_begin' is modified. This change will not take
effect on existing connections/routes until they are restarted. A connec-
tion/route can be restarted with the suspend and resume commands.
```

byte_order

Indicator of Replication Server's byte order. This is machine dependent.

cm_fadeout_time

Default outbound RSSD connection fadeout time.

Unit: seconds
Minimum: 1
Maximum: 2,147,483,648
Default: 300

Example:

If cm_fadeout_time is set to –1, Replication Server will never close a connection with the RSSD database.

```
1> configure replication server
2> set cm_fadeout_time to '-1'
3> go
Config parameter 'cm_fadeout_time' is modified. This change will not take
effect until the Replication Server is restarted.
```

cm_max_connections

Maximum number of outgoing connections available. The value for cm_max_connections must be greater than 0.

Default: 64

Example:

```
1>configure replication server
2>set cm_max_connections to '32'
3> go
Config parameter 'cm_max_connections' is modified. This change will not
take effect until the Replication Server is restarted.
```

ha_failover

Enables or disables HA (Sybase) failover support for non-RSSD connections from Replication Server to Adaptive Server Enterprise. To enable ha_failover support, set ha_failover to "on".

Default: "off" (failover is disabled)

Example:

```
1> configure replication server
2> set ha_failover to 'on'
3> go
Config parameter 'ha_failover' is modified. This change will not take
effect on existing connections/routes until they are restarted. A connec-
tion/route can be restarted with the suspend and resume commands.
```

Full details of the Sybase high availability component is beyond the scope of this book. Please refer to the Sybase documentation on how to use high availability in conjunction with Sybase Replication Server.

memory_limit

Max memory in megabytes that can be used by Replication Server.

Unit: megabytes (M)
Maximum: 2048
Default: 40
Status: Dynamic

Example:

```
1> configure replication server set 'memory_limit' to '100'
2> go
Config parameter 'memory_limit' is modified.
```

num_concurrent_subs

Maximum number of subscription materialization or dematerialization requests that can be processed at any given time. This limit only applies to atomic and nonatomic materialization. It does not apply to bulk materialization. If the maximum number of subscription materialization or dematerialization requests exceed the configured value, then requests over the maximum are fulfilled after previous requests have been fulfilled.

Minimum: 1
Default: 10
Status: Dynamic

num_msgqueues

Maximum number of Open Server message queues allowed. num_msgqueues should be set higher than the num_threads parameter.

Default: 178

num_msgs

Maximum number of Open Server messages allowed.

Default: 45,568

num_mutexes

Maximum number of Open Server mutexes allowed. The value for num_mutexes should be set higher than the num_threads value. The following formula should be used to estimate the value for num_mutexes:

num_mutexes = 200 + 3*IBQ + OBQ

where IBQ is the number of inbound queues including RepAgent and RSIUSER, and OBQ is the number of outbound queues including DSI warm standby (1 IBQ + 1 OBQ), DSI Subscription, and RSI.

Default: 1024

num_stable_queues

The maximum number of stable queues allowed. This parameter is relevant only for HP9000.

Default: 32

num_threads

Maximum number of Open Server threads allowed. The following formula can be used to estimate num_threads:

$$num\_threads = 30 + 4*IBQ + 2*RSIQ + DSIQ*(3 + max(DSIE))$$

where IBQ is the number of inbound queues including RepAgent and RSIUSER, RSIQ is the number of RSI (route) queues, DSIQ is the number of DSI queues including warm standby (1 IBQ + 1 DSIQ), and max (DSIE) is the maximum setting of the dsi_num_threads configuration among all your active DSIs.

Minimum: 20
Default: 50

oserver

The name of the current RepServer, specified while installing the current Replication Server with rs_init.

password_encryption

Indicates whether or not the password encryption option is enabled. A value of 1 means the password encryption option is enabled, and a value of 0 means the password encryption option is disabled.

Default: 0 (disabled)

rec_daemon_sleep_time

Amount of time that the recovery daemon sleeps before waking up to handle a strict save_interval message.

Unit: Seconds
Default: 120

rssd_error_class

The error class for RSSD.

Default: "rs_sqlserver_error_class"

smp_enable

This parameter enables symmetric multiple processing for Replication Server, which enables it to take advantage of all the CPU resources available on the host machine. There is no mechanism within Replication Server for controlling which processors its threads will use or how much time its threads get on the processors it does use. The components of process administration are completely under the control of the operating system. As such, system administrators must rely on the operating system mechanism for establishing process to processor affinities and process priorities. You can estimate a base of two CPUs plus one for every four queues. A value of 1 is on, and a value of 0 is off.

Default: 0 (off)

sqm_recover_segs

The number of stable queue segments a Replication Server scans during initialization. For better performance this parameter should be tuned (i.e., start with 100 stable queue segments, and monitor performance with monitor counter).

Minimum: 1
Maximum: 2,147,483,648
Default: 1
Status: Dynamic

sqm_warning_thr1

Logs first SQM threshold (stable queue space) warning to the Replication Server error log.

Unit: Percent
Range: 1-100
Default: 75
Status: Dynamic

sqm_warning_thr2

Logs second SQM threshold (stable queue space) warning to the Replication Server error log.

Unit: Percent
Range: 1-100
Default: 90
Status: Dynamic

sqm_warning_thr_ind

Logs SQM threshold warnings per stable queue to the Replication Server error log.

Unit: Percent
Range: 51-100

Default: 70
Status: Dynamic

sqm_write_flush

This parameter governs whether partitions should be opened with DSYNC flag.

Default: "on"

sqt_init_read_delay

The length of time an SQT (Stable Queue Transaction) thread sleeps while waiting for a stable queue read to complete before checking to see if it has been given new instructions in its command queue. At expiration of sqt_init_read_delay, if the command queue is empty, SQT doubles its sleep time up to the value set for sqt_max_read_delay.

Unit: Milliseconds
Minimum: 1000
Maximum: 86,400,000
Default: 2000
Status: Dynamic

sqt_max_cache_size

Maximum SQT (Stable Queue Transaction) cache size in bytes. This Replication Server configuration parameter should not be configured too big. sqt_max_cache_size usage should be monitored with monitor counter 24005 (CacheMemUsed), which may sometimes indicate that sqt_max_cache_size is full. You should also check monitor counter 24009 (TransRemoved); if Trans-Removed remains zero, which means that transactions are not being flushed from cache to make room for other transactions, you don't have to increase sqt_max_cache_size. During heavy load you should also check monitor counter 24019 (SQTCacheLow-Bnd) to check the minimum sqt_max_cache_size required before transactions are flushed. You should add 10 to 20 percent to the size reported by SQTCacheLowBnd. Occasionally you may notice a few transactions have been removed from the cache, but a frequency of no more than one transaction every five minutes doesn't indicate any significant latency. (See Chapter 14 for detailed information about monitor counters.)

Unit: Bytes
Default: 1,048,576
Status: Dynamic

sqt_max_prs_size

Maximum SQT memory size for command parsing. This configuration parameter is obsolete.

sqt_max_read_delay

The maximum length of time an SQT thread sleeps while waiting for a stable queue read to complete before checking to see if it has been given new instructions in its command queue. For low-volume systems, sqt_max_read_delay should be set lower to reduce latency.

Unit: Milliseconds
Minimum: 1000
Maximum: 86,400,000
Default: 10000
Status: Dynamic

sre_reserve

This parameter specifies how much space (as a percentage) to preallocate for new subscriptions (e.g., sre_reserve 100% means double the space it currently needs). This parameter should be updated by updating the rs_config system table directly.

Unit: Percent
Minimum: 0

Maximum: 500
Default: 0

sub_daemon_sleep_time

Duration in seconds the subscription daemon sleeps before waking up to recover subscriptions.

Unit: Seconds
Minimum: 1
Maximum: 31,536,000
Default: 120

sts_cachesize

The total number of rows for each RSSD system table cached. Increasing the value for this configuration parameter to the number of active replication definitions prevents Replication Server from executing expensive system table lookups.

Default: 100
Status: Dynamic

sts_full_cache_*rssd_system_table*

This parameter specifies an RSSD system table that is to be fully cached. Depending on the number of replication definitions and subscriptions used, fully caching rs_objects, rs_columns, and rs_functions tables may significantly reduce RSSD access requirements. However, if the number of unique rows in rs_objects is approximately equal to the value for sts_cachesize, these tables may already be fully cached.

Status: Dynamic

Example:

```
1> configure replication server
2> set sts_full_cache_rs_columns to "on"
3> go
```

Config parameter 'sts_full_cache_rs_columns' is modified.

sts_full_cache_rs_articles: Default: "off"
sts_full_cache_rs_classes: Default: "off"
sts_full_cache_rs_columns: Default: "off"
sts_full_cache_rs_config: Default: "off"
sts_full_cache_rs_databases: Default: "off"
sts_full_cache_rs_datatype: Default: "off"
sts_full_cache_rs_diskaffinity: Default: "off"
sts_full_cache_rs_diskpartitions: Default: "off"
sts_full_cache_rs_erroractions: Default: "off"
sts_full_cache_rs_exceptscmd: Default: "off"
sts_full_cache_rs_exceptshdr: Default: "off"
sts_full_cache_rs_exceptslast: Default: "off"
sts_full_cache_rs_funcstrings: Default: "off"
sts_full_cache_rs_functions: Default: "off"
sts_full_cache_rs_idnames: Default: "off"
sts_full_cache_rs_ids: Default: "off"
sts_full_cache_rs_maintusers: Default: "off"
sts_full_cache_rs_objects: Default: "off"
sts_full_cache_rs_oqid: Default: "off"
sts_full_cache_rs_publications: Default: "off"
sts_full_cache_rs_queuemsg: Default: "off"
sts_full_cache_rs_queuemsgtxt: Default: "off"
sts_full_cache_rs_queues: Default: "off"
sts_full_cache_rs_recovery: Default: "off"
sts_full_cache_rs_repdbs: Default: "off"
sts_full_cache_rs_repobjs: Default: "on"
sts_full_cache_rs_routes: Default: "off"
sts_full_cache_rs_routeversion: Default: "off"
sts_full_cache_rs_rules: Default: "off"
sts_full_cache_rs_segments: Default: "off"
sts_full_cache_rs_sites: Default: "off"
sts_full_cache_rs_statcounters: Default: "off"
sts_full_cache_rs_statdetail: Default: "off"
sts_full_cache_rs_statrun: Default: "off"
sts_full_cache_rs_subscription: Default: "off"
sts_full_cache_rs_systext: Default: "off"
sts_full_cache_rs_translation: Default: "off"
sts_full_cache_rs_users: Default: "on"
sts_full_cache_rs_version: Default: "off"
sts_full_cache_rs_whereclauses: Default: "off"

The following system tables can be fully cached: rs_classes, rs_databases, rs_objects, rs_sites, rs_repobjs, rs_dbsubsets, rs_columns, rs_diskaffinity, rs_queues, rs_systext, rs_version, rs_config, rs_functions, rs_repdbs, rs_publications, rs_datatype, rs_routes, rs_users, and rs_dbreps.

stats_sampling

Enables sampling counters.

Default: "on"

stats_show_zero_counters

Indicates whether counters reported with the admin stats command reports counters with zero observations for a specified sample period. A value of "on" means counters with zero observations are reported, and a value of "off" means counters with zero observations are not reported.

Default: "off"

use_security_services

This configuration parameter tells Replication Server whether or not security features should be used.

Default: "off"

use_ssl

Indicates if Replication Server is enabled for session-level SSL security service. A value of "on" means Replication Server is enabled for SSL, and a value of "off" means Replication Server is not enabled for SSL.

varchar_truncation

Enabling `varchar_truncation` allows truncation of varchar columns at the primary or replicate Replication Server.

Default: "off"

Configuration Parameters for Both Database Connection and Route

In this section we will cover Replication Server configuration parameters that are common to both database connections and routes.

disk_affinity

Specifies an allocation hint for assigning the next partition. Enter the logical name of the partition to which the next segment should be allocated when the current partition is full.

Default: "off"

msg_confidentiality

This parameter indicates if Replication Server should send and receive encrypted messages.

Values:

"not required": Replication Server will accept incoming data whether it is encrypted or not encrypted.

"required": Incoming and outgoing data must be encrypted

Default: "not_required"

msg_integrity

Network messages are checked for integrity.

Values:

"not_required": Network messages are not checked for integrity.

"required": Network messages are checked for integrity.

Default: "not_required"

msg_origin_check

When set to required, the origin of the network message is checked. When set to not_required, it is not checked.

Default: "not_required"

msg_replay_detection

Indicates whether a network message should be checked to make sure it has not been intercepted and then resent.

Default: "not_required"

msg_sequence_check

Indicates whether data should be checked to make sure it has been received in the same order it was sent.

Default: "not_required"

mutual_auth

Indicates whether the remote server must provide proof of identity before a connection is established.

Values:

"not_required": Do not use mutual authentication for outbound connections and accept inbound connections without mutual authentication.

"required": Use mutual authentication.

Default: "not_required"

save_interval

The number of minutes that the Replication Server saves messages after they have been successfully passed to the destination data server. See the section titled "Queues Are Full, They Are Not Getting Truncated" in Chapter 20 for details about save_interval.

Unit: Minutes
Default: 0

security_mechanism

The name of the security mechanism to use. An empty string means no security mechanism is used.

Default: First mechanism listed in the SECURITY section of $SYBASE/OCS-15_0/libtcl.cfg

unified_login

Indicates how Replication Server seeks to log in to remote data servers and accept incoming logins.

Values:

"not_required": Do not use unified login for outbound connections and accept inbound connections with or without unified login.

"required": Always log in to remote server with credentials.

Default: "not_required"

Configuration Parameters Unique to Database Connection (DSI)

Database connection configuration parameters specify default values for all database connections that originate from this source Replication Server. Values for these parameters can be set with the alter connection or configure replication server commands. The database connection must be suspended and resumed for changes to take effect.

command retry

The number of times to retry a failed transaction. The value must be greater than or equal to 0.

Default: 3

db_packet_size

The maximum size of a network packet. During database communication, the network packet value must be within the range accepted by the database.

Unit: Bytes
Maximum: 16,384
Default: 512

dist_sqt_max_cache_size

The maximum SQT cache size of the inbound queue of the DIST thread is controlled by the global parameter sqt_max_cache_size, which means that the maximum SQT cache size for the inbound queues must be the same. This configuration parameter can be tuned to set the inbound queue maximum SQT cache size of the DIST thread individually.

Unit: Bytes
Default: 0 (A charvalue of 0 means that it uses the sqt_max_cache_size. Any other value is the override.)

```
alter connection to data_server.database set
    dist_sqt_max_cache_size to 'value'
```

```
1> alter connection to pds.prs_RSSD
2> set dist_sqt_max_cache_size to '2000000'
3> go
Config parameter 'dist_sqt_max_cache_size' is modified. This change will
not take effect until the Replication Server is restarted.
```

After restarting the RepServer, you can check the newly configured value from the RSSD database with the following:

```
1> select objid, optionname, charvalue=substring(charvalue, 1,25) from
rs_config
2> where optionname like 'dist%'
3> go
objid              optionname                    charvalue
------------------ ----------------------------- -------------------------
0x0000006500000000 dist_sqt_max_cache_size       2000000
```

dsi_charset_convert

The specification for handling character set conversion on data
and identifiers between the primary Replication Server and the
replicate Replication Server. This parameter applies to all data
and identifiers to be applied at the DSI in question.

Values:

"on": Convert from the primary Replication Server character
set to the replicate Replication Server character set; if the
character sets are incompatible, shut down the DSI with an
error.

"allow": Convert where character sets are compatible; apply
any unconverted updates to the database as well.

"off": Do not attempt conversion. This option is useful if you
have different but compatible character sets and do not want
any conversion to take place. During subscription materialization, a setting of "off" behaves as if it were "allow".

Default: "on"

dsi_cmd_batch_size

The maximum number of bytes that Replication Server places
into a command batch.

Unit: Bytes
Default: 8192

dsi_cmd_separator

The character that separates commands in a command batch.

Default: newline (\n)

 Note: You must update this parameter in an interactive mode, not by executing a DDL-generated script or any other script. You cannot reset dsi_cmd_separator by running a script.

---

dsi_commit_check_locks_intrvl

The number of milliseconds (ms) the DSI Executor thread waits between executions of the rs_dsi_check_thread_lock function string. This parameter should be set to an optimal value that balances the cost of executing the function string versus waiting too long before checking if rollback is necessary.

Unit: Milliseconds
Minimum: 0
Maximum: 86,400,000
Default: 1000

dsi_commit_check_locks_log

Specifies the maximum number of times a DSI Executor thread will execute the rs_dsi_check_thread_lock function string and get a 0 in return before logging a warning message. This parameter should be set to an optimal value, as the higher the number of iterations, the longer the wait times. For example, the default of 200 equals about 16 minutes of processor time.

Unit: Iterations
Minimum: 1
Maximum: 1,000,000
Default: 200

dsi_commit_check_locks_max

The maximum number of times a DSI Executor thread checks whether it is blocking other transactions in the replicate database before rolling back its transaction and retrying it. This parameter should be set to an optimal value, as the higher the number of iterations, the longer the wait time.

Minimum: 1
Maximum: 1,000,000
Default: 400

dsi_commit_control

Specifies whether commit control processing is handled internally by Replication Server using internal system tables (on) or externally using the rs_threads system table (off).

Default: "on"

dsi_exec_request_sproc

Turns on or off request stored procedures and request functions at the DSI of the primary Replication Server.

Default: "on"

dsi_fadeout_time

The number of seconds of idle time before a DSI connection is closed. A value of "–1" indicates that a connection will not close.

Unit: Seconds
Default: 600

dsi_ignore_underscore_name

When the transaction partitioning rule is set to "name", this parameter specifies whether or not Replication Server ignores transaction names that begin with an underscore. Values are "on" and "off".

Default: "on"

dsi_isolation_level

Specifies the isolation level for transactions. The ANSI standard and Adaptive Server supported values are:

0: Ensures the data written by one transaction represents the actual data.

1: Prevents dirty reads and ensures that data written by one transaction represents the actual data.

2: Prevents nonrepeatable reads and dirty reads, and ensures that data written by one transaction represents the actual data.

3: Prevents phantom rows, nonrepeatable reads, and dirty reads, and ensures that data written by one transaction represents the actual data.

Note: Data servers supporting other isolation levels are supported as well through the use of the rs_set_isolation_level function string. Replication Server supports all values for replicate data servers.

The default value is the current transaction isolation level for the target data server.

Example:

```
Alter connection to dataserver.database
Set dsi_isolation_level to '3'
```

Isolation level 3 is equivalent to the dsi_serialization_method "wait_for_start" option.

dsi_keep_triggers

Specifies whether triggers should fire for replicated transactions in the database. Set to "off" to cause Replication Server to turn triggers off in the Adaptive Server database, so that triggers do not fire when transactions are executed on the connection. Set to "on" for all databases except standby databases.

Default: "on" (except standby databases)

dsi_large_xact_size

The number of commands allowed in a transaction before the transaction is considered to be large. Large transactions can cause performance difficulties. To improve performance, dsi_large_xact_size should be set to the maximum.

Minimum: 4
Maximum: 4,294,967,295
Default: 100

dsi_max_cmds_to_log

The number of commands to write into the exceptions log for a transaction.

Default: –1 (all commands)

dsi_max_text_to_log

The number of bytes to write into the exceptions log for each rs_writetext function in a failed transaction. Change this parameter to prevent transactions with large text, unitext, image, or rawobject columns from filling the RSSD or its log.

Default: –1 (all text, unitext, image, or rawobject columns)

dsi_max_xacts_in_group

Specifies the maximum number of transactions in a group. Larger numbers may improve data latency at the replicate database.

Values: 1-100
Default: 20

dsi_num_large_xact_threads

The number of parallel DSI threads to be reserved for use with large transactions. The maximum value is one less than the value of dsi_num_threads.

Default: 0

dsi_num_threads

The number of parallel DSI threads to be used. The maximum value is 255.

Default: 1

dsi_partitioning_rule

Specifies the partitioning rules (one or more) the DSI uses to partition transactions among available parallel DSI threads. Values are origin, ignore_origin, origin_sessid, time, user, name, and none.

Default: none

dsi_replication

Specifies whether or not transactions applied by the DSI are marked in the transaction log as being replicated.

When dsi_replication is set to "off", the DSI executes set replication off in the Adaptive Server database, preventing Adaptive Server from adding replication information to log records for transactions that the DSI executes. Since these transactions are executed by the maintenance user and, therefore, not usually replicated further (unless there is a standby database), setting this parameter to "off" avoids writing unnecessary information into the transaction log.

dsi_replication must be set to "on" for the active database in a warm standby application for a replicate database, and for applications that use the replicated consolidated replicate application model.

Default: "on" ("off" for standby database in a warm standby application)

dsi_replication_ddl

Supports bidirectional replication by specifying whether or not transactions are to be replicated back to the original database.

When dsi_replication_ddl is set to "on", DSI sends set replication off to the replicate database, which instructs it to mark the succeeding DDL transactions available in the system log not to be replicated. Therefore, these DDL transactions are not replicated back to the original database, which enables DDL transaction replication in a bidirectional MSA replication environment.

Default: "off"

dsi_rs_ticket_report

Determines whether or not to call function string
`rs_ticket_report`. The `rs_ticket_report` function string is
invoked when `dsi_rs_ticket_report` is set to "on".

Default: "off"

dsi_serialization_method

Specifies the method used to determine when a transaction can
start, while still maintaining consistency. In all cases, commit
order is preserved.

These option methods are ordered from most to least amount
of parallelism. Greater parallelism can lead to more contention
between parallel transactions as they are applied to the replicate
database. To reduce contention, use the `dsi_partitioning_rule`
option.

Values:

"no_wait": Specifies that a transaction can start as soon as it
is ready — without regard to the state of other transactions.

"wait_for_start": Specifies that a transaction can start as soon
as the transaction scheduled to commit immediately before it
has started.

"wait_for_commit": Specifies that a transaction cannot start
until the transaction scheduled to commit immediately preceding it is ready to commit.

These options are retained only for backward compatibility:

"none": Same as "wait_for_start"

"single_transaction_per_origin": Same as "wait_for_start"
with `dsi_partitioning_rule` set to origin.

Example:

```
Alter connection to dataserver.database
Set dsi_serialization_method to 'wait_for_start'
```

Default: "wait_for_commit"

dsi_sql_data_style

Formats datatypes (particularly date/time, binary, bit, and money) to be compatible with the following:

- ▶ DB2 ("db2")
- ▶ Lotus Notes ("notes")
- ▶ SQL Anywhere, formerly Watcom SQL ("watcom")
- ▶ SQL Remote ("sqlremote")

To support Transact-SQL instead, set this parameter to any value other than those listed above.

When you configure a connection to DB2, specify the name of the NetGateway using the data_server parameter in the main clause of alter connection.

When you configure a connection to Lotus Notes, SQL Anywhere, or any other ODBC data source, specify the connection as replication_driver_name.odbc_data_source_name. Refer to the ODBC Driver Reference Guide, which is part of the Open Client/Server version 11.1.1 collection, for more information.

Note: This is obsolete for Replication Server version 12.0 and later.

Default: " " (blank space)

dsi_sqt_max_cache_size

Maximum SQT (Stable Queue Transaction interface) cache memory for the database connection, in bytes.

The default of 0 means that the current setting of sqt_max_cache_size is used as the maximum cache size for the connection.

Default: 0

dsi_text_convert_multiplier

Changes the width of text or unitext datatype columns at the replicate site. Use dsi_text_convert_multiplier when text or unitext datatype columns must expand or contract due to character set conversion. Replication Server multiplies the length of primary text or unitext data by the value of dsi_text_convert_multiplier to determine the length of the text or data at the replicate site. Its type is float.

If the character set conversion involves expanding text or unitext datatype columns, set dsi_text_convert_multiplier equal to or greater than 1.0. If the character set conversion involves contracting text or unitext datatype columns, set dsi_text_convert_multiplier equal to or less than 1.0.

Default: 1

dsi_xact_group_size

The maximum number of bytes, including stable queue overhead, to place into one grouped transaction. A grouped transaction is composed of multiple transactions that the DSI applies as a single transaction. A value of –1 means no grouping.

Sybase recommends that you set dsi_xact_group_size to the maximum value and use dsi_max_xacts_in_group to control the number of transactions in a group.

Note: This is obsolete for Replication Server version 15.0 and later.

Unit: Bytes
Maximum: 2,147,483,647
Default: 65,536

dump_load

Set to "on" at replicate sites only to enable coordinated dump.

Default: "off"

dynamic_sql

This parameter is only available in Replication Server releases 15.0.1 and above. To use the dynamic SQL feature for the connection, this parameter should be set to "on". When enabled, DSI applies commands to the replicate in dynamic SQL instead of language command. Dynamic SQL commands are prepared once and executed many times. DSI will apply commands in dynamic SQL, if the command is insert, update, or delete, it doesn't have any text, image, or java columns, and it doesn't have more than 255 parameters. It cannot be used with customized function strings. If the command includes user-defined datatypes with the delimiter, the delimiters must be single or double quotes.

Default: "off"

```
1> alter connection to pds.prs_RSSD set dynamic_sql 'on'
2> go
Config parameter 'dynamic_sql' is modified.
```

dynamic_sql_cache_management

This parameter manages the dynamic SQL cache for the DSI executor thread. When dynamic_sql_cache_management is set to "mru", the most recently used statements are allocated and the rest of the statements are deallocated to allocate new dynamic statements when dynamic_sql_cache_size is reached. When dynamic_sql_cache_management is set to "fixed", no new statements are allocated by Replication Server once dynamic_sql_cache_size is reached.

Unit: String
Values: "mru" and "fixed"
Default: "mru"

Connection level example:

```
1> alter connection to pds.prs_RSSD
2> set dynamic_sql_cache_management 'fixed'
3> go
Config parameter 'dynamic_sql_cache_management' is modified.
```

Server level example:

```
1> configure replication server
2> set dynamic_sql_cache_management to 'fixed'
3> go
Config parameter 'dynamic_sql_cache_management' is modified. This change
will not take effect on existing connections or routes until they are
restarted. A connection or route can be restarted with the suspend and
resume commands.
```

dynamic_sql_cache_size

This parameter tells Replication Server how many tables will be using dynamic SQL commands.

Unit: Integer
Values: 1-65,535
Default: 20
Status: Dynamic

Replication Server sets the cache size to three times the configured value because each table may have three commands — insert, delete, and update.

For example, if dynamic_sql_cache_size is set to 20, the actual cache used by Replication Server will be set to 60.

Connection level example:

```
1> alter connection to pds.prs_RSSD
2> set dynamic_sql_cache_size '25'
3> go
Config parameter 'dynamic_sql_cache_size' is modified.
```

Server level example:

```
1> configure replication server
2> set dynamic_sql_cache_size to '25'
3> go
Config parameter 'dynamic_sql_cache_size' is modified. This change will not
take effect on existing connections/routes until they are restarted. A con-
nection/route can be restarted with the suspend and resume commands.
```

exec_cmds_per_timeslice

Specifies the number of LTL commands an LTI or RepAgent
Executor thread can possess before it must yield the CPU to
other threads. Set it to 20 for better performance

Minimum: 1
Maximum: 2,147,483,647
Default: 5

exec_sqm_write_request_limit

Specifies the amount of memory available to the LTI or RepAgent
Executor thread for messages waiting to be written to the
inbound queue. For a performance boost, set it to 4194304.

Unit: Bytes
Maximum: 2,147,483,647
Default: 1,048,576

md_sqm_write_request_limit

Specifies the amount of memory available to the distributor for
messages waiting to be written to the outbound queue.

Unit: Bytes
Maximum: 2,147,483,647
Default: 1,048,576

parallel_dsi

Provides a shorthand method for configuring parallel DSI threads. A setting of "on" configures these values:

▶ `dsi_num_threads` to 5

▶ `dsi_num_large_xact_threads` to 2

▶ `dsi_serialization_method` to `'wait_for_commit'`

▶ `dsi_sqt_max_cache_size` to 1 million bytes.

A setting of "off" configures these parallel DSI values to their defaults.

You can set this parameter to "on" and then set individual parallel DSI configuration parameters to fine-tune your configuration.

Default: "off"

rep_as_standby

Replicate standby only commands through table subscription.

Default: "off"

sub_sqm_write_request_limit

Specifies the memory available to the subscription materialization or dematerialization thread for messages waiting to be written to the outbound queue.

Unit: Bytes
Maximum: 2,147,483,647
Default: 1,048,576

Configuration Parameters Unique to Replication Server Route

These parameters can be changed with the `configure replication server` or `alter route` commands.

```
configure replication server set route_parameter to 'value'

  suspend route to destination Replication Server

    alter route to destination Replication Server
    set route_parameter to 'value'

    resume route to 'value'
```

rsi_batch_size

The number of bytes sent to the destination Replication Server before requesting a truncation point, which allows Replication Server to delete the message in the source RSI queue.

Unit: Bytes
Minimum: 1024
Maximum: 134,317,728
Default: 262,144

rsi_fadeout_time

The amount of idle time in seconds before an RSI connection is closed. When this parameter is set to –1, the RSI connection never fades out.

Example:

```
1> suspend route to rrs1
2> go
Route to 'rrs1' is suspended.

1> alter route to rrs1
2> set rsi_fadeout_time to '-1'
3> go
Config parameter 'rsi_fadeout_time' is modified. This change will not take
effect until the connection/route is restarted. A connection/route can be
restarted with the suspend and resume commands.

1> resume route to rrs1
2> go
Route to 'rrs1' is resumed.
```

rsi_packet_size

Network packet size for communication with other Replication Servers.

Unit: Bytes
Default: 2048

rsi_sync_interval

The amount of time between RSI sync messages.

Unit: Seconds
Default: 60

Security Configuration Parameters for Connecting to the ID Server

These configuration parameters govern network-based security for the ID Server. They can be set with the `configure replication server` command.

Example:

```
configure replication server set id_security_param, 'value'

configure replication server set id_msg_confidentiality to 'required'
```

id_msg_confidentiality

Indicates whether or not network messages for ID Server connections should be encrypted. `'not_required'` means do not encrypt outgoing messages and accept incoming messages with or without encryption.

Default: "not_required"

id_msg_integrity

Check network message integrity for ID Server connections.

Default: "not_required"

id_msg_origin_check

This configuration parameter governs whether the origin of the data packets should be verified.

Default: "not_required"

id_msg_replay_detection

Detect replayed network messages for ID Server connections. `'not_required'` means do not detect replayed messages.

Default: "not_required"

id_msg_sequence_check

Detect out-of-sequence network messages for ID Server connections. "not_required" means do not detect out-of-sequence messages.

Default: "not_required"

id_mutual_auth

Use mutual authentication for ID Server connections. "not_required" means do not use mutual authentication for ID Server connections.

Default: "not_required"

id_security_mechanism

Name of security mechanism to use for ID Server connections. An empty string means do not use a security mechanism. Sybase supported security mechanisms are listed under the SECURITY section in $SYBASE/OCS-15_0/libtcl.cfg.

Default: The first mechanism listed in the SECURITY section in the libtcl.cfg

id_server

Name of the ID Server.

id_unified_login

Use unified login for ID Server connections. "not_required" means do not use unified login for ID Server connections.

Default: "not_required"

Other Valid Replication Server Configuration Parameters

This section lists both configuration parameters that the user should not change and parameters that are obsolete.

current_rssd_version

The Replication Server version supported by this RSSD. Replication Server checks this parameter at startup. This parameter is only changed by the rs_init program when Replication Server is upgraded or downgraded.

minimum_rssd_version

The RSSD can only support Replication Servers that require RSSD versions greater than or equal to this version. At startup, Replication Server checks the value of this parameter when current_rssd_version is higher than minimum_rssd_version. This parameter is only modified by the rs_init program when Replication Server is upgraded or downgraded.

md_source_memory_pool

Memory available to MD (message delivery module) for holding pending writes for each distributor, in bytes. This parameter is replaced by md_sqm_write_request_limit in Replication Server 12.1. md_source_memory_pool is ignored if md_sqm_write_request_limit is used.

Unit: Bytes
Default: 100,000

memory_max

Maximum memory used by the memory manager in megabytes. This parameter is obsolete.

Embedded RSSD Configuration Parameters

Embedded RSSD configuration parameters can be configured to set the backup directory location, backup start date and time, and the interval between backups.

erssd_backup_interval

This parameter is set to schedule the interval between backups of the database and transaction log. It can be specified as "nn hours", "nn minutes", or "nn seconds".

Default: 24 hours

erssd_backup_path

This parameter can be configured to set the full directory path of stored backup files.

Default: The directory path for storing backup files can be specified in rs_init. The default location is same as the transaction log mirror.

erssd_backup_start_time

This parameter can be set to schedule a backup time. It can be specified as "hh:mm:AM/PM" or "hh:mm".

Default: 01:00AM

erssd_backup_start_date

This parameter can be set to schedule a backup start date. It can be specified as "MM/DD/YYYY".

Default: Current date

erssd_ra

This parameter can be configured to set the Replication Agent name, in order to create a route from the current source Replication Server to the destination Replication Server. The destination Replication Server must be listed in the interfaces file.

Default: erssd_name_ra

Chapter 6

Replication Agent

Replication Agent for Adaptive Server Enterprise is an internal thread to the data server. Replication Agent for a non-Sybase database is an external program that logs into the primary database. Replication Agent scans the transaction log of the primary database for transactions or stored procedure executions for objects that are marked for replication. It then forwards those transactions to the primary Replication Server using Log Transfer Language (LTL). Each primary database can only have one Replication Agent thread. The Replication Agent maintains the secondary truncation point in the primary database transaction log, which prevents the transaction log from being truncated until transactions marked for replication are forwarded and stored in the Replication Server's stable device.

This chapter's primary focus is on Sybase Replication Agent, although support and requirements for heterogeneous RepAgents are also discussed in this chapter. Replication Agent installation and configuration issues for Oracle are discussed in Chapter 16.

Replication Agent can be configured during installation using rs_init. Please refer to Chapter 4 for more information on using rs_init.

When it comes to replicating non-Sybase databases, the Replication Agent must be capable of understanding non-Sybase database components and of reading and forwarding committed transactions. The installation, configuration, and execution processes differ significantly between different database systems. A comprehensive discussion of heterogeneous data replication of Oracle data and models using Sybase Adaptive Server is included in Chapter 16.

Replication Agent 15.0

Replication Agent 15.0 supports replicating transaction log records from Sybase and non-Sybase databases. Replication Agent 15.0 offers support for:

- ▶ Oracle
- ▶ UDB
- ▶ Microsoft SQL Server 2005
- ▶ Sybase Adaptive Server Enterprise 15.0

Oracle Support

Replication Agent 15.0 supports replication from Oracle 10g, including two new binary datatypes: BINARY_FLOAT and BINARY_DOUBLE. It also supports reading from Oracle archive logs as well as online redo logs for both Oracle 9i and 10g.

Three new configuration parameters have been added to support archive log management:

pdb_archive_path

Specifies the fully qualified path to the Oracle archive logs.

pdb_archive_remove

Enables removing the archive redo logs.

pdb_include_archive

Enables reading archived redo logs as well as online redo log files.

UDB Support

Replication Agent 15.0 supports Universal Database 8.x. For more details, see the Replication Agent Primary Database Guide.

Microsoft SQL Server 2005 Support

Replication Agent 15.0 now supports the Microsoft SQL Server 2005 JDBC driver. This means Replication Agent 15.0 can support both Microsoft SQL Server 2000 and Microsoft SQL Server 2005. In addition to this extended support, Replication Agent 15.0 also supports Windows authentication. For additional information, please see the Sybase Replication Agent Primary Database Guide.

Sybase Adaptive Server Enterprise 15.0 Support

In order to support Sybase Replication Server 15.0, a new configuration parameter called pdb_support_large_identifier has been introduced, which either enables or disables replicating large identifiers up to 255 characters in length.

In addition to large identifier support, four new unsigned datatypes are supported as well. These datatypes are: *unsigned bigint* — numeric (20), *unsigned int* — numeric (10), *unsigned smallint* — int, and *unsigned tinyint* — tinyint.

Common Installation Requirements for Replication Agent 15.0

The following items must be taken into consideration when installing Replication Agent 15.0:

▶ Be aware of SySAM licensing requirements, and make sure you have proper licensing in place. Please refer to the Sybase documentation for SySAM administration and licensing requirements.

▶ Replication Agent needs JDBC/ODBC libraries to connect to the primary database of your choice. Please verify the Replication Agent release bulletin for the most recent driver compatibility list.

▶ Sybase Replication Agent for heterogeneous replication is a Java-based application, which means an appropriate JRE (Java Run-time Environment) is required. A matching JRE is automatically installed when the Replication Agent is installed. However, some specific libraries and environment variables may need to be set for proper functioning.

▶ Make sure your operating system is updated with necessary patches to support the JRE installed during the Replication Agent installation. Operating system patches must support Java 1.4.2. Please check the operating system vendor's web sites for appropriate patch information.

▶ Sybase Replication Agent is available for HP UX (11i, 1iR2), IBM AIX (5.2, 5.3), RedHat Linux (AS 3.0, ES 4.0), Solaris (8, 9), and Microsoft Windows (2000, 2003). Check the Sybase Replication Agent Installation Guide for current updates on the availability.

▶ A minimum of 128 MB of memory and 300 MB of disk space is required. More disk space may be required for different platforms.

▶ Check the Sybase documentation and especially the Replication Agent installation guide for more details on product compatibility. As of this writing, the Sybase Replication Agent Installation Guide lists product compatibility as follows:

Table 6-1: Product compatibility with Replication Agent 15.0

Database	Version
IBM DB2 Universal Database	Enterprise Edition 8.?.?
Oracle Server	9i (9.2.0), 10g (10.1, 10.2)
Microsoft SQL Server	2000, 2005
Sybase Replication Server	12.5, 12.6, 15.x
Sybase Software Asset Management (SySAM)	SySAM 2.0

Proper JDBC-compliant drivers are very important for primary
database connectivity. Replication Agent 15.0 requires JDBC 2.0
compliant drivers. The Replication Agent release bulletin contains the most recent driver compatibility list as well as
up-to-date platform and operating system compatibility
information.

Replication Agent Configuration

These are the basic steps for configuring RepAgent:
1.   Enable the RepAgent feature on Adaptive Server using
     `sp_configure`.
2.   Configure a Replication Agent for a database using
     `sp_config_rep_agent`.
3.   Enable log transfer on Replication Server using `alter
     connection`.
4.   Start the RepAgent on Adaptive Server using
     `sp_start_rep_agent`.
5.   If you need to stop the RepAgent, use `sp_stop_rep_agent`.

First, use `sp_configure` to enable the RepAgent for the Adaptive
Server. Then, to check if the configuration parameter is enabled,
execute `sp_configure 'enable rep agent threads'` without
arguments.

```
1> sp_configure 'enable rep agent threads'
2> go
 Parameter Name                   Default     Memory Used Config Value
Run Value    Unit                 Type
 ------------------------------ ----------- ----------- ------------
------------ -------------------- ----------
 enable rep agent threads               0           0            0
          0 switch               dynamic
```

You can also enable the RepAgent using the same procedure with an argument of 1. This will allow adding Replication Agents to the databases on the Adaptive Server Enterprise instance:

```
1> sp_configure 'enable rep agent threads', 1
2> go
 Parameter Name                       Default     Memory Used Config Value
Run Value    Unit                     Type
 ----------------------------- ----------- ----------- ------------
------------ -------------------- ----------
 enable rep agent threads                     0           0             1
          1 switch               dynamic
```

Now use sp_config_rep_agent to configure Replication Agent.

Execute sp_config_rep_agent once for each configuration parameter. See Table 6-2 for some important Replication Agent configuration parameters. The number of log records that the Replication Agent sends to the Replication Server is configurable. To change the number of log records sent to the Replication Server in each batch, log in to Adaptive Server and enter:

```
use dbname
go
sp_config_rep_agent dbname, 'scan batch size', '2000'
go
```

Then (re)start the replication agent. You may need to stop and restart.

```
sp_start_rep_agent dbname
go
```

Table 6-2: Replication Agent configuration parameters

Configuration Parameter	Description
batch ltl	Sets Replication Agents to send LTL commands either in a batch or one at a time. The default is true, which sends a batch.
connect server name	Name of the data server that Replication Agent connects to or the name of the temporary data server that Replication Agent connects to in recovery mode.

Configuration Parameter	Description
connect database name	Name of the database that Replication Agent connects to or the name of the temporary database that Replication Agent connects to in recovery mode.

data limits filter mode	Replication Agent takes different actions when it encounters log records that exceed maximum allowed sizes.
	
	The limits are column counts greater than 250, column lengths greater than 255 bytes, and parameter lengths greater than 255 bytes.
	
	off
	
	    Replication Server 12.5 and above: RepAgent allows records to pass through.
	
	    Replication Server 12.1 and earlier: May result in undesirable effects.
	
	stop
	
	    RepAgent stops in Replication Server 12.1 or earlier.
	
	skip
	
	    RepAgent skips the record in Replication Server 12.1 or earlier.
	
	truncate
	
	    RepAgent truncates the data to allowable sizes before sending to the Replication Server.

rs_name rs_username rs_password	How RepAgent connects to Replication Server.
ha_failover	RepAgent will be Sybase failover aware.
priority	Priority values range from 4 to 6, with 4 being the highest priority, 5 medium priority, and 6 low priority. Increase the priority when you suspect RepAgent is slow in the overall replication process.
retry timeout	Number of seconds that RepAgent remains inactive before attempting to connect to the Replication Server after a recoverable error or when the Replication Server is unreachable.
scan batch size	Sets the number of log records in each batch sent to Replication Server. After sending the batch size of records, RepAgent asks for a new secondary truncation point. The default is 1000 records. See the scan timeout parameter.

Configuration Parameter	Description
scan timeout	The length of time in seconds that the RepAgent times out after sending the batch and before querying the Replication Server for a new secondary truncation point. If there are no more log records to send, RepAgent times out for this time also. The default is 15 seconds.
send maint xacts to replicate	Sets whether or not to send the maintenance user transactions to the subscribing sites. The default is false, which means don't send. This is how DBAs execute some transactions that do not affect regular processing. For example, if you want to run a large update and you want to update the data outside the Replication Server, you may want to update the data as the maintenance user on the primary and secondary independently.
send warm standby xacts	When set to true, enables some DDL commands, system transactions, and transactions by the maintenance user to be sent to the standby databases. The default is false. When setting up a warm standby application replication, you need to set this to true.

For additional configuration parameters not listed in Table 6-2, please refer to the Sybase Replication Server documentation.

Replication Agent Installation for Sybase Databases

Sybase Replication Agent installation is the easiest of the Replication Agent installations since it's one of the steps of Replication Server installation. The process of adding Sybase Replication Agent includes the following steps:

1. Install the primary Replication Server first by following any of the methods presented in Chapter 4.

2. Prepare a resource file or use the console to invoke rs_init to add a primary database. A sample resource file can be found in the downloadable files, along with a sample shell script to dynamically change this resource file.

Once the primary database is added to the replication system, a Replication Agent thread will be created for you to read and transfer the Adaptive Server Enterprise transaction log to the Replication Server.

The rs_init process adds a Replication Agent for RSSD if you chose the option rs.rs_needs_repagent: yes. You need a Replication Agent for the RSSD for system table replication.

Add Replication Agent for Sybase Databases

Use rs_init to add the Sybase ASE database to the replication system. This creates and activates a Replication Agent thread. The process of creating a Replication Agent for other database management systems differs from the process with Sybase ASE Replication Agent. Detailed procedures to add Replication Agent for Oracle replication are provided in Chapter 16.

The example below adds the active Sybase ASE database to the warm standby logical connection. The syntax is similar for adding a primary database to the replication system; you just remove the as active for server.db clause. Similarly, you will add the standby database to the logical connection in the next section. Execute the create connection command in the Replication Server. For more information on create connection, please refer to Chapter 7.

```
create connection to NYDS.reptest_db1
set error class to rs_sqlserver_error_class
set function string class to rs_sqlserver_function_class
set username to spam_rs_maint
set password to spam_rs_maint_ps
with log transfer on
as active for ACTIVE_SERVER.jagandb
Active connection to 'NYDS.reptest_db1' is created.
```

Configure RepAgent for the Database

Configure Replication Agent in the Adaptive Server:

```
exec sp_config_rep_agent "reptest_db1", "enable", "NYRS", "NYRS_ra",
"NYRS_ra_ps"
go
exec sp_config_rep_agent "reptest_db1", "send warm standby xacts", true
go
exec sp_setreplicate rs_marker, "true"
go
exec sp_setreplicate rs_update_lastcommit, "true"
go
exec sp_start_rep_agent "reptest_db1"
go
```

Mark the active database for replication:

```
1> exec sp_reptostandby reptest_db1, "all"
2> go
The replication status for database 'reptest_db1' has been set to 'ALL'.
(return status = 0)
```

Add the standby database to the replication system:

```
create connection to LONDON_DS.reptest_standby
set error class to rs_sqlserver_error_class
set function string class to rs_sqlserver_function_class
set username to spam_rs_maint
set password to spam_rs_maint_ps
with log transfer on
as standby for ACTIVE_SERVER.jaqandb
use dump marker
go
Standby connection to 'LONDON_DS.reptest_standby' is created.
```

When the standby database is added with a dump marker, the DSI
thread for the standby database will go down.

```
1> admin who_is_down
2> go
```

```
Spid Name       State               Info
---- ---------- ------------------- ------------------------------------
     DSI EXEC   Suspended           104(1) LONDON_DS.reptest_standby
     DSI        Suspended           104 LONDON_DS.reptest_standby
     DSI EXEC   Down                103(1) NYDS.reptest_db1
     DSI        Down                103 NYDS.reptest_db1
```

The DSI thread for NYDS.reptest_db1 in this case is down because it is not required at this stage. The DSI connection to LONDON_DS.reptest_standby will be resumed a little later when the dump from the active database is loaded onto the standby database, because we are using the dump marker for materializing. More details on materialization are available in Chapter 10.

Replication Agent Installation for Non-Sybase Databases

Pre-installation Requirements

▶ When using Replication Agent for Oracle, the Replication Agent system database will be created on Adaptive Server Anywhere. This database can grow in size pretty rapidly if Oracle replicates DDL, as each DDL replicated is copied to this database before replicating. Allow enough space for such unexpected growth. If there is not enough space, Replication Agent will shut down and the entire replication process will stop.

▶ Install recommended JDBC drivers as listed in the Sybase Replication Agent release bulletin. Please consult the web pages suggested in the bulletin to find out which up-to-date JDBC drivers are compatible with your operating environment.

▶ The Sybase Replication Server release bulletin also lists some known issues for Replication Agent installation, which may change from time to time. These known issues may have a workaround or other solution.

▶ Replicating Oracle sequences is of special interest. If you are using Oracle sequences in your application, be sure to read the information on how to replicate them. Oracle caches sequence numbers, but the sequence numbers in the sys.seq$ table do not increment sequentially. Instead, the number in that column tells what the next sequence number would be once the Oracle uses all the sequences cached.

Installation Process

Following is a detailed worksheet that will aid in the procedure to install and configure Replication Agent so as to replicate transactions to and from Oracle databases as described in Chapter 16.

Step	Description	Value
1	Replication Agent (RA) information 1. Replication Agent instance type. For example, oracle or ibmdb. This identifies what type of RA instance you are installing. 2. RA instance name. Give a name to this installation. For example, ora_ra_*hostname*. 3. Admin port number for RA. For Oracle the installation will add two ports. Make sure two consecutive port numbers are available. For example, 1011 and 1012. 4. Specify the interfaces file location. This is typically $SYBASE on UNIX and %SYBASE% on Windows. 5. Decide the administrative user and password.	
2	Replication Server related information 1. Replication Server source data server/instance name. For example, ora_adm1. 2. Replication Server source database name. For example, oradb1. 3. Replication Server maintenance user and password. If you leave them at the default, the user name is typically *rep server*_maint and the password is *rep servermaint_pw*.	

Step	Description	Value
3	Replication Agent related information for Replication Server 1. Replication Server host name and port number. 2. Replication Server user name and password. This is the login that RA will use to connect to the primary Replication Server and should not be the same as the maintenance user listed in step 2.3. This user will need the connect_resource privilege in the Replication Server. 3. Specify the RA character set equal to the Replication Server character set. This will enable RA to convert the data to proper LTL.	
4	Replication Agent information for RSSD 1. RSSD host name, which is the data server host where RSSD is located. 2. RSSD port number, which is the port of the data server. 3. RSSD database name. 4. RSSD login and password.	
5	Primary data server information for Replication Agent 1. Some of the parameters you want to list here are the primary data server host name, port number, primary data server name, and primary database name. 2. Primary data source name (DSN), which is the ODBC driver that is required for DB2 Replication Agent. 3. Login information to the primary data server (primary data server login and primary data server password). 4. Replication Agent JVM compliant character set. Please refer to the Sybase Replication Agent Installation Guide for more details on the Java character set.	
6	Replication Server information for replicate database The replicate database information is platform dependent. If you are replicating from Sybase to Oracle, for example, you will need to collect Oracle information for this part of the worksheet. Some of the parameters you might want to list here are the replicate database host, replicate database user name, replicate database password, and replicate database name.	

The information you collect with this worksheet will help you organize the information for various parameters during installation. The proper JDBC driver is required to establish connectivity to the primary data source. Make sure there is just one JDBC driver in the CLASSPATH variable. Otherwise, the RepAgent connectivity may not be smooth. Since the DB2 connectivity is in reality a JDBC/ODBC bridge, an ODBC data source name should be defined in the DB2 client software. The ODBC information is specified via two Replication Agent configuration parameters. The pds_database_name parameter is the database name and the pds_datasource_name parameter is the datasource name.

Set the CLASSPATH variable that will include the path and name of JDBC driver. For example:

```
export CLASSPATH=/path_name/driver:$CLASSPATH
```

Where path_name is the path where the JDBC driver file is located and driver is the driver file name. The driver file for Replication Agent 15.0 for Oracle is called ojdbc14.jar and the driver file for SQL Server is called sqljdbc.jar. For Oracle, make sure the Oracle primary server is running the TNS service.

The Replication Agent software can be installed by using a response file either in console mode or in silent mode. A template resource file can be found in the software resource directory. The template file can be updated with the parameters that were recorded in the installation worksheet.

On UNIX, mount the software distribution CD-ROM or go to the directory where the setup program is located and enter:

```
./setup_type -silent -options RAX.resp -W SybaseLicense.agreeToLicense=true
```

For example, the setup_type for Linux is called setuplinux.

Post-installation Administration

The Replication Agent administration is as simple as connection management for replicating Sybase Adaptive Server databases. Connections and connection management are discussed in detail in Chapter 7. Replication Agent administration for Oracle data replication is discussed in Chapter 16. The concepts described for Oracle data replication also apply to replicating other heterogeneous data sources.

Chapter 7

Connections

Sybase Replication Server establishes various connections to databases that it supports. A database connection defines a database to the Replication Server. The Replication Server in which the database connection is defined manages the replication for that database. If the database is a replicate database, the connection distributes the data. The connection attributes can be modified to suit application and performance needs. This chapter describes the connections and the maintenance of those connections.

Use admin who or admin show_connections to display connection information in the Replication Server.

```
1> admin show_connections
2> go
Server            User                    Database          State     Owner       Spid
----------------  ----------------------  ----------------  --------  ----------  ----
NYDSA_SYB         db01_maint              db01              idle      DSI EXEC    178
NYDSA_SYB         NYDSA1_RS_RSSD_maint    NYDSA1_RS_RSSD    idle      DSI EXEC    16
LONDONDSA1_RS     LONDONA1_RS_rsi         NULL              active    RSI         39
NYDSA_SYB         db02_maint              db02              idle      DSI EXEC    181
NYDSA_SYB         NYDSA1_RS_RSSD          NYDSA1_RS_RSSD    free
NYDSA_SYB         NYDSA1_RS_RSSD          NYDSA1_RS_RSSD    free
connection state   number  comments
----------------   ------  --------------------------------------------------
connecting         0       in the process of connecting to a server
active             1       established connections owned and used by threads
idle               3       established connections owned but not being used
being_faded_out    0       idle connections that are being closed
already_faded_out  0       idle connections that have been closed
free               2       established connections not owned by any threads
closed             114     closed connections not owned by any threads
```

```
limbo            0      connection handles in state transition
total          120      total number of connection handlers available

1> admin who
2> go
Spid Name        State                Info
---- ----------  -------------------- ------------------------------------
 16  DSI EXEC    Awaiting Command     101(1) NYDSA_SYB.NYDSA1_RS_RSSD
 10  DSI         Awaiting Message     101 NYDSA_SYB.NYDSA1_RS_RSSD
 12  DIST        Awaiting Wakeup      101 NYDSA_SYB.NYDSA1_RS_RSSD
 15  SQT         Awaiting Wakeup      101:1  DIST NYDSA_SYB.NYDSA1_RS_RS
  9  SQM         Awaiting Message     101:1 NYDSA_SYB.NYDSA1_RS_RSSD
  8  SQM         Awaiting Message     101:0 NYDSA_SYB.NYDSA1_RS_RSSD
140  REP AGENT   Awaiting Command     NYDSA_SYB.NYDSA1_RS_RSSD
178  DSI EXEC    Awaiting Command     111(1) NYDSA_SYB.rsys_db01
177  DSI         Awaiting Message     111 NYDSA_SYB.rsys_db01
102  DIST        Awaiting Wakeup      111 NYDSA_SYB.rsys_db01
103  SQT         Awaiting Wakeup      111:1  DIST NYDSA_SYB.rsys_db01
101  SQM         Awaiting Message     111:1 NYDSA_SYB.rsys_db01
 99  SQM         Awaiting Message     111:0 NYDSA_SYB.rsys_db01
141  REP AGENT   Awaiting Command     NYDSA_SYB.rsys_db01
181  DSI EXEC    Awaiting Command     112(1) NYDSA_SYB.rsys_db02
180  DSI         Awaiting Message     112 NYDSA_SYB.rsys_db02
115  DIST        Awaiting Wakeup      112 NYDSA_SYB.rsys_db02
117  SQT         Awaiting Wakeup      112:1  DIST NYDSA_SYB.rsys_db02
114  SQM         Awaiting Message     112:1 NYDSA_SYB.rsys_db02
112  SQM         Awaiting Message     112:0 NYDSA_SYB.rsys_db02
142  REP AGENT   Awaiting Command     NYDSA_SYB.rsys_db02
 39  RSI         Awaiting Wakeup      BMSAMUDRAM6A1_RS
 38  SQM         Awaiting Message     16777322:0 BMSAMUDRAM6A1_RS
227  RSI USER    Awaiting Command     BMSAMUDRAM6A1_RS
 11  dSUB        Sleeping
  6  dCM         Awaiting Message
  7  dAIO        Awaiting Message
 13  dREC        Sleeping             dREC
246  USER        Active               sa
  5  dALARM      Awaiting Wakeup
 14  dSYSAM      Sleeping
```

Connections provide Replication Server the information necessary to properly manage the database. The information may
include error classes, function strings, performance attributes,
the maintenance user login name and password, and standby or

active database information. Connections can be created using either rs_init or Sybase Central. For example, connections for the databases are created when you use rs_init to add databases to a Replication Server. Connections can also be created within a Replication Server using the create connection Replication Server command.

Creating Connections Using Create Connection

The create connection command is a Replication Server command used to add non-Sybase databases to the replication system. To add Sybase databases to the replication system, use either Sybase Central or rs_init. If you use create connection to add Sybase databases, you must prepare the database for replication by enabling log transfer.

The syntax for create connection is:

```
create connection to data_server.database
set error class [to] error_class
set function string class [to] function_class
set username [to] user
[set password [to] passwd]
[set database_param [to] 'value']
[set security_param [to] 'value']
[with {log transfer on, dsi_suspended}]
[as active for logical_ds.logical_db |
as standby for logical_ds.logical_db
[use dump marker]
```

Where:

data_server.database

This refers to the data server and the database combination of the connection. This also serves as the connection name.

set error class [to] *error_class*

For some data server errors, for example, duplicate key on unique index, you can create an error class and assign actions to the error class. Each database connection is automatically

157

assigned a default error class. You may create a new error class or modify an existing one and assign it to a database connection.

An error class is a group of defined errors and associated actions. Assigning an action to an error class instructs Replication Server on how to respond when such an error occurs. For example, error messages 2601 and 3621 occur when a DSI thread receives an attempt to insert a duplicate key. (As a side note, error 3621 occurs in conjunction with just about every non-fatal error thrown by the data server and needs to be added to any created error class.) The default action of Replication Server is to stop replication as defined in the rs_sqlserver_error_class. However, you can instruct the Replication Server to ignore the error and continue. The result and the consequence of ignoring an error depend on the context of the error.

As an example of altering a connection, the procedure to assign the ignore action to the duplicate key in index error (2601) is described in Table 7-1. The point of such action in this case is to prevent the DSI thread from going down due to duplicate rows during materialization. When you use bulk materialization without stopping the application from making changes to your primary database, there is a possibility that some transactions will already be in the queue, depending on the sequence of your materialization process. At the end of bulk materialization, when you resume the DSI connection, the duplicate transactions in the queue will result in the duplicate key in unique index violation. Ignoring such errors is fine to prevent replication from stopping, as the duplicate row already exists due to materialization. Another alternative to avoid a unique index violation is to use the set autocorrection command. There are pros and cons associated with doing this. Autocorrection is explained in detail in Chapter 10.

Table 7-1: Error class management

Where to execute	Command	Description
Replication Server	create error class ASEallowdupsErrorClass	syntax: create error class *error class name* The error class name can be any acceptable name.
RSSD for the same Replication Server	rs_init_erroractions ASEallowdupsErrorClass, rs_sqlserver_error_class	This initializes the newly created error class with the components of the default error class rs_sqlserver_error_class. rs_init_erroractions is a stored procedure.
Replication Server	assign action ignore for ASEallowdupsErrorClass to 2601, 3621	Assign a particular action to the error message number in this error class. The action can be ignore, warn, retry_log, or log. The log referred to is the exceptions log table in the RSSD. Only the warning messages are posted to the error log file. For both retry_log and log, the transaction is rolled back and the next transaction is executed after the initial attempt fails.
Replication Server	alter connection to MYSERVER.MYDB set error class to ASEallowdupsErrorClass	Alter the connection to take the new error class assignment.
Replication Server	suspend connection to MYSERVER.MYDB resume connection to MYSERVER.MYDB	If the connection is not already suspended, it must be suspended and resumed for any new configuration parameter to take effect.

Where to execute	Command	Description

Other Replication Servers that are routed with the Replication Server where the error class is defined	`assign action ignore for ASEallowdupsErrorClass to 2601, 3621`
	
	`alter connection to MYSERVER.MYDB set error class to ASEallowdupsErrorClass`
	
	`suspend connection to MYSERVER.MYDB`
	
	`resume connection to MYSERVER.MYDB`
		A route must exist for the error class definition to be propagated to all the Replication Servers routed.
		
		There is no need to create and initialize the class, as the initialization is propagated to all the Replication Servers routed with Replication Server where the error class is created and initialized the first time.

Additional information on creating and assigning error classes is also available in Chapter 20.

```
set function string class [to] function_class
```

Set the function strings to be used for this connection.

Syntax:

```
alter connection to data_server.database
set function string class [to] function_class
```

Example:

```
1> alter connection to LONDON_DS.pubs2
set function string class to repbook_function_class
2> go
Connection to 'LONDON_DS.pubs2' is altered.
```

```
set username [to] user
[set password [to] passwd]
```

These set clauses are used to set the connection authentication parameters. Connections use the maintenance user to connect to the defined databases and perform operations. If you change the connection authentication parameters in the Replication Server, be sure to change the password in the associated data server as well.

[set *database_param* [to] *'value'*]

Setting database_param to a connection alters the connection. Remember to stop and restart the connection for the new value to take effect. The possible values to modify the connection attributes are provided in Table 7-2.

Table 7-2: Parameters to modify database connections

Parameter	Description
batch	One of the most important parameters affecting database connections and replication performance. When set to "on", Replication Server sends multiple commands in each batch; otherwise, it will send single commands to the data server. The default is "on".
batch_begin	Specifies whether a begin transaction command can be sent in the same batch as other commands.
db_packet_size	The maximum size of the network packet. This parameter may not exceed the data server's maximum network packet size. The default is 512 bytes, and the maximum is 16 KB.
dsi_charset_convert	This option specifies whether a character set conversion should take place between primary and replicate Replication Servers. If set to "on", the primary Replication Server character set will be converted to the replicate Replication Server character set. If the character sets are incompatible, the DSI will shut down. If set to "allow", the character sets will be converted where compatible. Apply any unconverted character sets directly to the data server. If set to "off", the character sets are not converted. If the primary and replicate character sets are compatible, this option may be acceptable. During materialization an option of "off" is equal to "allow". The default is "on".
dsi_cmd_batch_size	Maximum number of bytes a Replication Server places in a command batch.
dsi_fadeout_time	The number of seconds of idle time after which the DSI connection will fade out. The default is 600 seconds. A value of -1 will cause the DSI thread to never fade out. This reduces overhead and can improve performance as the connection is not constantly destroyed and recreated.

Parameter	Description
dsi_keep_triggers	Specifies whether triggers should fire for replicated transactions. Set "off" to disable firing triggers. The default is "on", except for standby databases in a warm standby application setup.
dsi_large_xact_size	The number of commands in a transaction before a transaction is considered large. The minimum is 4, and the default is 100.
dsi_max_cmds_to_log	When the commands fail, Replication Server writes the commands to the rs_exceptions table in RSSD. This parameter specifies the number of commands in a transaction to be written to the exceptions log. The default is -1, which indicates all commands.
	For larger transactions, this can fill the RSSD database. See the dsi_max_text_to_log parameter, which also affects the RSSD.
dsi_max_text_to_log	This specifies the number of bytes of failed transaction text to be written to the exceptions log for each rs_writetext function. For larger text datatypes like unitext, image, or rawobject, setting this parameter to a particular value will prevent filling RSSD or its log. The default is -1, which indicates all text.
dsi_max_xacts_in_group	This parameter specifies the maximum number of transactions in a group. Larger groups will improve performance at the replicate database. The default is 20, with a range of 1 to 100.
dsi_num_threads	The number of parallel DSI threads to be used. The default is 1, and the maximum value is 255. See the parallel_dsi parameter for a simpler way of setting parallel DSI.
dsi_partitioning_rule	Specifies the rules to apply while partitioning the transactions among the available parallel DSI threads. For more details refer to Chapter 14. The default is none.

Parameter	Description
dsi_replication	Transactions that are applied at the replicate database by the maintenance user are not logged at the replicate database. This parameter instructs the Replication Server to log the transactions at the replicate database for further replication. However, the logged replicate transactions will not be returned to the primary database in a bidirectional replication setup. The default is "on" ("off" for a standby database in a warm standby application setup).
dsi_serialization_method	This parameter works in conjunction with setting up parallel DSI. It controls when a transaction can be started on an available parallel DSI thread with respect to the previous transaction in the commit order. "no_wait" — Specifies that the next transaction can start without regard to the state of the other transactions. "wait_for_start" — Specifies that a transaction can start as long as the transaction before it has started. "wait_for_commit" — Specifies that a transaction cannot start until the transaction scheduled to commit immediately preceding it is ready to commit.
dsi_sqt_max_cache_size	This is the cache that the SQT interface uses for the connection, in bytes. If left at the default of "0", the DSI connection will use the size set in the sqt_max_cache_size parameter as the max size.
dsi_xact_group_size	Obsolete for Replication Server 15.0 and later, but retained for backward compatibility. Specifies the maximum size in bytes for a grouped transaction. Replication Server DSI connection applies the grouped transaction (with many transactions) as a single transaction to the target database. Use the dsi_max_xacts_in_group parameter to control the number of transactions in a group.
dump_load	Can only be set at the replicate site. The default is "off". If set to "on", coordinated dumps are enabled, meaning that a database dump or transaction log dump command at the primary is also replicated so that a matching dump operation takes place at the replicate. This ensures the replicate database recoverability.

Parameter	Description
exec_sqm_write_request_limit	The amount of memory that a RepAgent or LTI Exec thread uses for the messages waiting to be written to the inbound queue. The default is 1 MB, with a range of 16 KB to 2 GB.
md_sqm_write_request_limit	This affects the outbound queue. This parameter specifies the amount of memory available for the Distributor (DIST) for messages waiting to be written to the outbound queue. The memory setting limits for this parameter are like those for exec_sqm_write_request_limit. The default is 1 MB, with a range of 16 KB to 2 GB.
parallel_dsi	This is the easiest way to set up for parallel DSI threads. Please refer to Chapter 14 for more information on parallel DSI. This parameter affects multiple parameters: • dsi_num_threads to 5 • dsi_num_large_xact_threads to 2 • dsi_serialization_method to wait_for_commit • dsi_sqt_max_cache_size to 1 million bytes. The default setting of "off" will set the above parameters to their defaults. You can also change the above parameters individually to suit your application requirements.
save_interval	This is another important parameter, though in most cases it is left at the default. This parameter specifies the number of minutes that the Replication Server saves messages after they have been successfully passed to the destination data server. The longer the save interval, the larger the stable queue usage. Larger stable sizes may affect the performance. By default, the save interval is set to 0 (minutes). For a low-volume replication setup, the default setting may be fine, since Replication Server does not delete messages immediately after receiving acknowledgment from destination servers. Transactions are deleted periodically in large chunks. For a large-volume replication setup, save_interval should be increased to accommodate the recovery in case of partition failure. Save_interval can be configured for physical connections, logical connections, and routes.

Parameter	Description
sub_sqm_write_request_limit	This parameter specifies the amount of memory available for materialization and dematerialization threads for messages to be written to outbound queue.

```
set security_param [to] 'value'
```

security_param comprises a set of network-based security options that a connection can be set to. Connection parameters related to security are listed in Table 7-3. Connections can be set to accept only encrypted data or to check that data is not tampered with or intercepted in the network transfer. Of all the network security parameters, security_mechanism, unified_login, and use_security_services are of particular interest. The security_mechanism parameter specifies the name of the third-party security mechanism to use, such as Kerberos security.

Table 7-3: Connection parameters affecting security

Security Parameter Value	Description
msg_confidentiality	Specifies whether the data is transferred encrypted through Replication Server. If set to "required", data is encrypted. Otherwise Replication Server accepts data either encrypted or unencrypted. Default: "not_required"
msg_integrity	Replication Server checks for data integrity. Default: "not_required"
msg_origin_check	Requires the Replication Server to check the data's origin. Default: "not_required"
msg_replay_detection	Indicates whether data should be read or intercepted. Default: "not_required"
msg_sequence_check	Indicates how the data packages should be checked. The possible values are "required" and "not_required". If the value is "required", the data packages should be checked to see if they have been received in the order sent. Default: "not_required"

Please refer to the Sybase Replication Server documentation for additional connection parameters.

Altering a Connection

While create connection is used to instantiate a connection, alter connection is used to modify the parameters of existing connections. The configure replication server command can be used to modify the connection parameters of all of the connections of a Replication Server. The syntax and usage of alter connection is similar to the create connection command. Please refer to Table 7-2 for a list of connection parameters that can be altered for physical connections. For parameters that can affect the logical connections in a standby application setup, please refer to Chapter 12. Parameters affecting parallel DSI and replication performance are listed in Chapter 14.

Syntax:

```
alter connection to data_server.database {
    set function string class [to] function_class |
    set error class [to] error_class |
    set password [to] passwd |
    set log transfer [to] {on | off} |
    set database_param [to] 'value'} |
    set security_param to {'required' | 'not_required'} |
    set security_services [to] 'default'
}
```

To alter an existing connection, suspend the connection first, alter the connection, and then resume the connection, thus allowing the modification to take effect.

```
suspend connection to dataserver.database [with nowait]
```

When the connection is suspended, use the alter connection command to alter the connection parameter(s). Then resume the connection using the resume connection command. Use the "with nowait" option if you want to suspend the connection immediately. The default is to wait until the current transactions complete before suspending the connections. "with nowait" may be appropriate if a large transaction is affecting the replication process and the connection needs to be modified.

```
resume connection to dataserver.database [skip transaction] [execute
transaction]
```

The "skip transaction" clause option is typically used when the replication is stopped because of an error that is mapped to stop the replication. If one or more transactions are skipped using the "skip transaction" clause, it is possible the replicated database can become inconsistent. Please refer to Chapter 20 for more information on how to capture skipped transactions and how to apply them to the replicate site if necessary. The "execute transaction" clause is used when a system transaction failed and it is the first transaction in the queue when the connection is resumed. Please refer to Chapter 20 for more information on loss detection.

Dropping Connections

Use drop connection to remove a database from the replication system. If the connections are dropped from the replicate Replication Server, all subscriptions or any other references to the connections must be dropped first. To drop a database connection from the primary database, all of the replication definitions must be dropped as well. In the primary database, RepAgent should also be stopped and disabled. Additional information on enabling and disabling the RepAgent as well as RepAgent thread configuration is included in Chapter 6. You can use Sybase Central, rs_init, or any interactive client to drop connections.

The syntax is:

```
drop connection to dataserver.database
```

To view a list of existing database connections use admin who or admin show_connections.

To drop a logical connection to a standby database in a warm standby application setup, use drop logical connection to *dataserver.database.*

In order to drop a logical connection while dismantling a warm standby setup, you must drop the standby database before attempting to drop the logical connection. Warm standby application setup is discussed in Chapter 12.

When a connection to a database is dropped, any data already replicated is retained.

Finally, if you want all the references to this database to be removed from the replication system, you need to remove the database references from the ID Server. The system table rs_idnames holds information about Replication Servers, databases, and ID Servers.

To remove an entry from the rs_idnames system table, issue the sysadmin dropdb command in the Replication ID Server:

```
sysadmin dropdb, dataserver, database
```

To remove a logical database name entry from the rs_idnames system table, issue the sysadmin dropldb command in the Replication ID Server:

```
sysadmin dropldb, dataserver, database
```

Monitoring Connections

Connections and connection status can be monitored using Sybase Central, any other Replication Server supporting GUI tools, or interactive tools like isql. Use the admin show_connections, admin who, or admin who_is_down commands to check the status of available connections in a Replication Server. In the RSSD database, you can also find a list of the databases managed by the corresponding Replication Server by using rs_helpdb. Additional admin commands like admin who,dsi, admin who,sqm, or admin who,sqt may be helpful to find out the status connections. To determine the status of RepAgent, use the sp_help_rep_agent Adaptive Server stored procedure. Inside the RSSD there are tables that can be queried. Specifically, rs_oqids and rs_exceptslast may contain information about stopped DSI threads that is not available elsewhere.

While admin commands can provide some information on the connection status, for detailed analysis you'll need to use additional monitoring tools such as rs_ticket, Replication Server monitoring counters, and DBMS metrics. Monitoring Replication Server using these tools is discussed in detail in Chapter 14.

Chapter 8

Routes

Routes are the logical connections used by the Replication Servers to send messages to other Replication Servers within the same domain. (The replication system domain refers to all Replication Servers that use the same ID Server.) A route is a one-way message stream that sends requests from the source Replication Server to the destination Replication Server. Between any two Replication Servers, there can be either unidirectional or bidirectional routes.

In a distributed environment, routes are needed when Replication Servers at each site manage local databases. Source and destination Replication Servers should be identified, as well as direct and indirect routes from each source to its corresponding destination.

Replication Servers that manage primary databases require routes to Replication Servers that manage subscribing (replicate) databases. A route from a replicate Replication Server to a primary Replication Server is not needed if no request stored procedures are executed from the replicate database. Intermediate Replication Servers, which use indirect routes, require routes to the destination Replication Servers. Using indirect routes can lead to better performance in systems with a large number of replicate sites.

Routes carry data modifications and applied stored procedures from the primary database to one or more replicate databases that are not controlled by the same Replication Server. Routes also carry system table modification commands from a source Replication Server's RSSD to a destination Replication Server's RSSD and the request stored procedures from replicate databases to the primary databases.

Types of Routes

Direct Route

A direct route is a route between two Replication Servers without any intermediate sites (see Figure 8-1). When a row is updated at the primary site, messages are distributed by the primary Replication Server through a wide area network to each remote site that has a subscription for the row. When a direct route is created between the source and the destination Replication Servers, the source Replication Server creates an RSI outbound stable queue to hold messages to the destination site and starts an RSI thread that logs into the destination or the next Replication Server in the route.

In Figure 8-1, prs can send identical data through six different routes. If replicated stored procedures are executed from rds1 (replicated database) to update the primary database (pds), then a route must be created from rrs1 to prs.

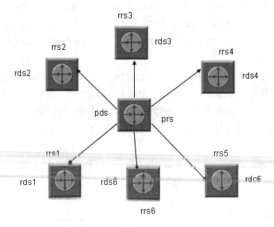

Figure 8-1

Indirect Route

Figure 8-2 shows a route that has intermediate sites. The prerequisite for creating an indirect route is successful creation of direct routes between each successive Replication Server along the intended indirect route.

Figure 8-2

The routes from prs to rrs1 and rrs1 to rrs2 are direct routes. The route prs to rrs2 is an indirect route, and the intermediate Replication Server is rrs1. In an indirect route prs sends messages for rrs2 to the intermediate Replication Server rrs1, which has a route (direct or indirect) to rrs2. By setting up an indirect route, the amount of processing at the primary site is reduced and the load is distributed among intermediate Replication Servers. Messages stored at intermediate sites can be used to recover from partition failure at remote sites. Partition failure and recovery is discussed in Chapter 15.

With indirect routes, the primary Replication Server can route subscriptions that are common to destination sites through the same intermediate Replication Server. When subscriptions overlap, Replication Server sends only one message per row modification, which is common to all destination sites, to the intermediate Replication Server, thus improving the overall replication performance to multiple sites.

In Figure 8-3, the primary Replication Server (prs) has indirect routes to rrs2 and rrs3 through rrs1 (intermediate Replication Server). Whenever data is updated at the primary site, one copy of each update is sent to rrs2 and rrs3 via the intermediate Replication Server rrs1.

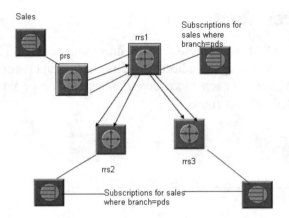

Figure 8-3

Unsupported Routes

In Figure 8-4, the route from prs to rrs1 and prs to rrs2 is supported, but rrs1 to rrs2 is not supported. A route cannot diverge
from the source Replication Server and then converge at the
same intermediate or destination Replication Server. Such a
route is superfluous and not supported.

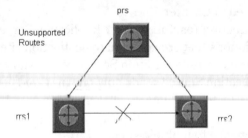

Figure 8-4

Creating Routes

Routes for Replication Server 15.x can only be created with Replication Server 11.0.3 and later. Before creating a direct route, the interfaces file entries for source and destination Replication Servers should be added at the source and destination sites, respectively. RepAgent for the RSSD database should be running. ID Replication Server, the destination Replication Server, and any intermediate Replication Servers in the route should also be running.

Syntax:

```
create route to destination_replication_server
     (set next site [to] intermediate_replication_server
     [set username [to] user]
     [set password [to] password]
     [set route_param to 'value']
     [set security_param to 'value'])
```

The login name and passwords are usually added during installation using rs_init. If this login name and password do not exist or if you chose to use a different login name and password, then they should be created in the destination Replication Server before you create the route.

```
create user username set password password
```

The default login name is RS_name_rsi and the default password is RS_name_rsi_ps, where RS_name is the Replication Server name. The rsi_user created with the rs_init utility is stored in the rs_users system table. When a route is created, the destination Replication Server's username and password (specified with the create route command) are stored in the source Replication Server's rs_maintusers system table. Passwords can be stored in cleartext or encrypted.

Refer to Chapter 17 for more details.

The username and password are optional when network-based security and unified login are enabled. The source Replication Server logs into the destination Replication Server as

principal user name. (The principal user name is specified using
the -S flag in Replication Server's runserver file.) Refer to Chapter 17 for more information about security.

The next site clause is used only for creating an indirect
route.

You can either accept the default values for the route parameters or customize them with create route or alter route
commands. These parameters include disk_affinity, rsi_batch_
size, rsi_fadeout_time, rsi_packet_size, rsi_sync_interval,
rsi_xact_with_large_msg, and save_interval. Refer to Chapter 14
for more details.

Let's create direct routes from prs to rrs1 and rrs1 to rrs2
and then create an indirect route from prs to rrs2.

At primary Replication Server (prs):

```
isql -Usa -P -Sprs
1> create route to rrs1              -> direct route from prs to rrs1
2> set username rrs1_rsi
3> set password rrs1_rsi_ps
4> go
Route to 'rrs1' is being created.
```

Primary Replication Server RSSD:

```
1> use prs_RSSD
2> go
1> rs_helproute
2> go
 route                                 route_status
 -------------------------------- ---- ---------------------------------
 prs ---------> rrs1

     Route is being created. Source RS has not yet attempted to send the protocol
message to the destination RS.

(return status = 0)
1> rs_helproute
2> go
 route                                 route_status
 ---------------------------- ---- ---------------------------------
 prs ---------> rrs1
```

Route is being created. Destination has not yet finished creating system table subscriptions.

```
Systable Subs to be created       (11 RSSD system tables are replicated)
-----------------------------
rs_objects0_at_16777317           (16777317 is site id of prs)
rs_columns1_at_16777317
rs_classes2_at_16777317
rs_functions3_at_16777317
rs_funcstrings4_at_16777317
rs_routes5_at_16777317
rs_databases6_at_16777317
rs_systext7_at_16777317
rs_systext8_at_16777317
rs_erroractions9_at_16777317
rs_dbreps10_at_16777317
rs_dbsubsets11_at_16777317
(return status = 0)
1>


1> rs_helproute
2> go
route                              route_status
------------------------------     -----------------------------------
prs --------> rrs1                  Active

(return status = 0)
```

Row is inserted to rs_routes:

```
1> select * from rs_routes
2> go
 dest_rsid    through_rsid source_rsid status suspended src_version
-----------  ------------ ----------- ------ --------- -----------
  16777318     16777318    16777317     2        0        1500

(1 row affected)
```

Destination Replication Server (rrs1) is added to rs_sites:

```
1> select * from rs_sites
2> go
name                               id           status
------------------------------     -----------  ------
 prs                               16777317       0
 rrs1                              16777318       0

(2 rows affected)
```

rsi user is added to rs_maintusers:

```
1> select * from rs_maintusers
2> go
 destid   username          password            use_enc_password  enc_password
--------  ---------------   -----------------   ----------------  ------------
     101  prs_RSSD_maint    prs_RSSD_maint_ps                  0  NULL
16777318  rrs1_rsi          rrs1_rsi_ps                        0  NULL

(2 rows affected)
```

From primary Replication Server (prs):

```
1> admin who
2> go
Spid Name         State                 Info
---- ----------   --------------------  ------------------------------------
  28 DSI EXEC     Awaiting Command      101(1) pds.prs_RSSD
  19 DSI          Awaiting Message      101 pds.prs_RSSD
  26 DIST         Awaiting Wakeup       101 pds.prs_RSSD
  27 SQT          Awaiting Wakeup       101.1  DIST pds.prs_RSSD
  25 SQM          Awaiting Message      101:1 pds.prs_RSSD
  23 SQM          Awaiting Message      101:0 pds.prs_RSSD
  29 REP AGENT    Awaiting Command      pds.prs_RSSD
  57 RSI          Awaiting Wakeup       rrs1 -- RSI sender thread is started
  56 SQM          Awaiting Message      16777318:0 rrs1 -- SQM queue is
                                        created and started
  20 dSUB         Sleeping
  15 dCM          Awaiting Message
  18 dAIO         Awaiting Message
  21 dREC         Sleeping              dREC
  55 USER         Active                sa
```

```
14 dALARM      Awaiting Wakeup
22 dSYSAM      Sleeping
```

Create direct route from rrs1 to rrs2:

```
isql -Usa -P -Srrs1
1> create route to rrs2
2> set username rrs2_rsi
3> set password rrs2_rsi_ps
4> set rsi_fadeout_time '-1'      -> Source Replication Server (rrs1)
doesn't close connection with destination Replication Server (rrs2)
5> go
Route to 'rrs2' is being created.


1> admin who
2> go
Spid Name        State                  Info
---- ----------  --------------------   -----------------------------------
  29 DSI EXEC    Awaiting Command       102(1) rds.rrs1_RSSD
  20 DSI         Awaiting Message       102 rds.rrs1_RSSD
  27 DIST        Awaiting Wakeup        102 rds.rrs1_RSSD
  28 SQT         Awaiting Wakeup        102:1  DIST rds.rrs1_RSSD
  26 SQM         Awaiting Message       102:1 rds.rrs1_RSSD
  24 SQM         Awaiting Message       102:0 rds.rrs1_RSSD
  30 REP AGENT   Awaiting Command       rds.rrs1_RSSD
  69 RSI         Awaiting Wakeup        rrs2 -> RSI sender thread is started
  68 SQM         Awaiting Message       16777319:0 rrs2 -> SQM queue is
                                        created and started
  42 RSI USER    Awaiting Command       prs
  21 dSUB        Sleeping
  15 dCM         Awaiting Message
  19 dAIO        Awaiting Message

  22 dREC        Sleeping               dREC
  67 USER        Active                 sa
  14 dALARM      Awaiting Wakeup
  23 dSYSAM      Sleeping
```

At rrs1_RSSD:

```
1> rs_helproute
2> go
 route                                route_status
 ------------------------------       ------------------------------
 prs --------> rrs1                   Active


 route                                route_status
 ------------------------------       ------------------------------
 rrs1 --------> rrs2
```

Route is being created. Destination has not yet finished creating system table subscriptions.

```
Systable Subs to be created
------------------------------
rs_objects0_at_16777318      -- siteid of rrs1
rs_columns1_at_16777318
rs_classes2_at_16777318
rs_functions3_at_16777318
rs_funcstrings4_at_16777318
rs_routes5_at_16777318
rs_databases6_at_16777318
rs_systext7_at_16777318
rs_systext8_at_16777318
rs_erroractions9_at_16777318
rs_dbreps10_at_16777318
rs_dbsubsets11_at_16777318
```

```
1> rs_helproute
2> go
 route                                route_status
 ------------------------------       ------------------------------
 prs --------> rrs1                   Active


 route                                route_status
 ------------------------------       ------------------------------
 rrs1 --------> rrs2                   Active
```

Row is inserted to rs_routes

```
1> select * from rs_routes
2> go
 dest_rsid   through_rsid source_rsid status suspended src_version
 ----------- ------------ ----------- ------ --------- -----------
    16777318    16777318    16777317     2         0        1500
    16777319    16777319    16777318     2         0        1500

(2 rows affected)

Destination Replication Server (rrs2) is added to rs_sites
1> select * from rs_sites
2> go
name                            id          status
------------------------------- ----------- ------
prs                                16777317  0
rrs1                               16777318  0
rrs2                               16777319  0

(3 rows affected)

Rrs2_rsi user is added to rs_maintusers

1> select * from rs_maintusers
2> go
 destid   username        password           use_enc_password enc_password
 -------- --------------- ------------------ ----------------- ------------
    102   rrs1_RSSD_maint rrs1_RSSD_maint_ps                0 NULL
16777319 rrs2_rsi        rrs2_rsi_ps                       0 NULL

(2 rows affected)
```

Create indirect route from prs to rrs2:

```
isql -Usa -P -Sprs
1>  create route to rrs2
2> set next site rrs1
3> go
Route to 'rrs2' is being created.
```

No RSI Sender and SQM queue is started for indirect route:

```
1> admin who
2> go
Spid Name        State              Info
---- ----------  -----------------  ------------------------------------
  28 DSI EXEC    Awaiting Command   101(1) pds.prs_RSSD
  19 DSI         Awaiting Message   101 pds.prs_RSSD
  26 DIST        Awaiting Wakeup    101 pds.prs_RSSD
  27 SQT         Awaiting Wakeup    101:1  DIST pds.prs_RSSD
  25 SQM         Awaiting Message   101:1 pds.prs_RSSD
  23 SQM         Awaiting Message   101:0 pds.prs_RSSD
  29 REP AGENT   Awaiting Command   pds.prs_RSSD
  57 RSI         Awaiting Wakeup    rrs1
  56 SQM         Awaiting Message   16777318:0 rrs1
  20 dSUB        Sleeping
  15 dCM         Awaiting Message
  18 dAIO        Awaiting Message
  21 dREC        Sleeping           dREC
  78 USER        Active             sa
  14 dALARM      Awaiting Wakeup
  22 dSYSAM      Sleeping
```

At prs_RSSD:

```
1> use prs_RSSD
2> go
```

Row for indirect Route is inserted
```
1> select * from rs_routes
2> go
```

dest_rsid	through_rsid	source_rsid	status	suspended	src_version
16777318	16777318	16777317	2	0	1500
16777319	**16777318**	**16777317**	**2**	**0**	**1500**

```
(2 rows affected)
```

Destination Replication Server (rrs2) is added to rs_sites

```
1> select * from rs_sites
2> go
```

```
name                            id          status
-----------------------------   ----------  ------
prs                             16777317    0
rrs1                            16777318    0
rrs2                            16777319    0
```

Altering Routes

Routes can be altered to change direct routes to indirect routes, indirect routes to direct routes, or the next intermediate site for an indirect route. Additionally, the username and password and route parameters can be changed. The following shows some ways to alter routes:

▶ At each Replication Server that manages a database with Replication Agent, suspend log transfer:

```
suspend log transfer from all
```

▶ Quiesce the Replication Server so that all queued messages are delivered to other Replication Servers:

```
admin quiesce_force_rsi
admin quiesce_check
```

▶ Execute suspend route first if changing a password for a direct route or changing a direct route to an indirect route or an intermediate site in an indirect route:

```
suspend route to destination_replication_server
```

▶ If a route is altered to use a new or existing intermediate site, then you should already have a direct route to the next site and it must have a direct or indirect route to the destination Replication Server.

▶ If a direct route is altered to an indirect route, then you should already have a direct route to the intermediate Replication Server and the intermediate Replication Server should have a direct route to the destination Replication Server.

▶ The alter route command should be executed at the source
Replication Server.

```
alter route to dest_replication_server
    {set next site [to] thru_replication_server |
     set username [to] 'user' set password [to] 'passwd' |
     set password [to] 'passwd' |
     set route_param [to] 'value' |
     set security_param [to] 'value' |
     set security_services [to] 'default'}
```

▶ After altering the route, execute resume log transfer followed
by resume route at each Replication Server where log transfer
was suspended.

```
resume log transfer from all
resume route to destination_replication_server
```

Altering RSI User Password

The RSI user's password can only be changed for direct routes, as
detailed in the following steps:

1. Suspend log transfer from each Replication Server:

```
1> suspend log transfer from all
2> go
Suspending LogTransfer for pds.prs_RSSD
```

2. Quiesce the replication system. At each Replication Server:

```
1> admin quiesce_force_rsi
2> go
Replication Server prs is Quiesced
```

```
1> admin quiesce_check
2> go
Replication Server prs is Quiesced
```

If flow is from prs to rrs1 and rrs1 to rrs2, then quiesce the
Replication Servers in that order.

3. Suspend the route to the destination Replication Server:

```
1> suspend route to rrs1
2> go
Route to 'rrs1' is suspended.
```

4. Alter the RSI user's password at the destination Replication Server:

```
1> alter user rrs1_rsi
2> set password newpass
3> go
User 'rrs1_rsi' is altered.
```

5. Alter the user's password at the source Replication Server:

```
1> alter route to rrs1
2> set password newpass
3> go
Password on the route to rrs1 is changed.
```

6. Resume log transfer at each Replication Server:

```
1> resume log transfer from all
2> go
Resuming LogTransfer for pds.prs_RSSD
```

7. Resume the route to the destination Replication Server:

```
1> resume route to rrs1
2> go
Route to 'rrs1' is resumed.
```

Changing an Indirect Route to a Direct Route

In the source Replication Server from which the route will originate, issue the alter route command and specify the RSI username and password.

Prs has an indirect route to rrs2; let's change it to a direct route.

```
1> alter route to rrs2
2> set username rrs2_rsi
3> set password rrs2_rsi_ps
4> go
Route to rrs2 is altered at this site.
```

Changing a Direct Route to an Indirect Route

There should be a direct route to the intermediate (through) Replication Server and it must have a direct route to the destination Replication Server. First, suspend log transfer at each Replication Server in the replication system that manages databases with Replication Agent. Then quiesce the source Replication Server. In the following example, let's change the direct route from prs to rss2 to an indirect route:

1. Suspend log transfer from each Replication Server that manages Replication Agent:

    ```
    1> suspend log transfer from all
    2> go
    Suspending LogTransfer for pds.prs_RSSD
    ```

2. Quiesce the replication system:

    ```
    1> admin quiesce_force_rsi
    2> go
    Replication Server prs is Quiesced
    1> admin quiesce_check
    2> go
    Replication Server prs is Quiesced
    ```

3. Change the direct route from prs to rrs2 to an indirect route:

    ```
    1> alter route to rrs2 set next site rrs1
    2> go
    Route to rrs2 is altered at this site.
    ```

4. Resume log transfer from each Replication Server that manages RepAgent:

    ```
    1> resume log transfer from all
    2> go
    Resuming LogTransfer for pds.prs_RSSD
    ```

Changing the Next Site (Intermediate Site) for an Indirect Route

There should be a direct route to the new next site and it must have a direct or indirect route to the destination Replication Server.

From each Replication Server that manages a database with Replication Agent, suspend log transfer, quiesce the Replication Servers, and then alter the route to change the next site for an indirect route.

The current route topology looks like this:

```
(prs ---- (Next site: rrs1) ----> rrs2
```

To change the intermediate site (rrs1) to rrs3, follow these steps:

1. Create a direct route from prs to rrs3 (new site):

   ```
   1> create route to rrs3
   2> set username rrs3_rsi
   3> set password rrs3_rsi_ps
   4> go
   Route to 'rrs3' is being created.
   ```

2. Create a direct route from rrs3 to rrs2:

   ```
   1> create route to rrs2
   2> set username rrs2_rsi
   3> set password rrs2_rsi_ps
   4> go
   Route to 'rrs2' is being created.
   ```

3. Suspend log transfer from each Replication Server that manages a database with RepAgent:

   ```
   1> suspend log transfer from all
   2> go
   Suspending LogTransfer for pds.prs_RSSD
   ```

4. Quiesce the replication system:

   ```
   Admin quiesce_force_rsi
   Admin quiesce_check
   ```

5. Alter the route to change the new next site:

   ```
   1> alter route to rrs2 set next site rrs3
   2> go
   Route to rrs2 is altered at this site.
   ```

6. Resume log transfer from all. The route topology should now look like this:

   ```
   prs ---- (Next site: rrs3) ----> rrs2
   ```

Changing Route Parameters

Route parameters for individual routes can be changed with the alter route or configure repserver commands for all the routes originating at the source Replication Server.

To change route configuration parameters for an individual route:

1. Suspend the route at the source Replication Server (prs):

   ```
   1> suspend route to rrs1
   2> go
   Route to 'rrs1' is suspended.
   ```

2. Alter the route to the destination Replication Server at the source Replication Server to change the default rsi_batch_size:

   ```
   1> alter route to rrs2
   2> set rsi_batch_size '4096'
   3> go
   Config parameter 'rsi_batch_size' is modified. This change will not
   take effect until the connection/route is restarted. A connection/
   route can be restarted with the suspend and resume commands.
   ```

3. Resume the route to the destination Replication Server:

   ```
   1> resume route to rrs1
   2> go
   Route to 'rrs1' is resumed.
   ```

To change route configuration parameters for all routes originating from the source Replication Server:

1. Suspend routes to all Replication Servers originating from the source Replication Server (prs):

   ```
   1> suspend route to rrs1
   2> go
   Route to 'rrs1' is suspended.
   1> suspend route to rrs3
   2> go
   Route to 'rrs3' is suspended.
   ```

2. Alter the route configuration parameter rsi_batch_size with the configure replication server command:

   ```
   1> configure replication server
   2> set rsi_batch_size to '4096'
   ```

```
3> go
Config parameter 'rsi_batch_size' is modified. This change will not
take effect on existing connections/routes until they are restarted. A
connection/route can be restarted with suspend and resume commands.
```

3. Resume the route to the destination Replication Server:

```
1> resume route to rrs1
2> go
Route to 'rrs1' is resumed.
1> resume route to rrs3
2> go
Route to 'rrs3' is resumed.
```

Suspending and Resuming Routes

The suspend route and resume route RCL (Replication Command
Language) commands can be used to suspend a route and then
restart it. Routes can be suspended in order to alter route topology or configuration or to perform maintenance.

Syntax:

```
suspend route to destination_replication_server

resume route to destination_replication_server
```

To suspend a route at the source Replication Server:

```
1> suspend route to rrs3
2> go
Route to 'rrs3' is suspended.
```

When a route is suspended, the messages will not be sent over
the route but will be stored in the outbound queue until the route
is resumed.

To resume a route that was suspended for topology/configu-
ration changes or for maintenance or was down due to some
error, issue the resume route command at the source Replication
Server:

```
1> resume route to rrs3
2> go
Route to 'rrs3' is resumed.
```

Dropping Routes

The drop route command closes the route to the specified destination Replication Server from the source Replication Server.

drop route to *destination_replication_server* [with nowait]

Executing the drop route command does the following:

▶ Deletes system table subscriptions from the rs_subscriptions
  table

▶ Deletes route information from the rs_config table

▶ Stops RSI Sender and deletes the outbound stable queue

▶ Deletes route entry from rs_routes

▶ Deletes the prs_RSSD entry from rs_databases

▶ Deletes rs_users for this site's primary user

▶ Deletes rs_maintusers for rsi_user entry

▶ Deletes entry in the rs_locater table associated with the RSI
  receiver thread for this route

▶ Deletes entry from rs_sites if this Replication Server has no
  route to the source Replication Server.

Routes cannot be dropped if the Replication Server whose route
is to be dropped is part of another direct or indirect route, the
source Replication Server has replication definitions subscribed
to by the destination Replication Server, or the source Replication Server is designated as the owning site/primary of a
function-string class or error class. The progress of the drop
route command can be monitored by executing the rs_helproute
stored procedure from the RSSD database.

Example:

```
1> drop route to rrs3
2> go
Route to 'rrs3' is being dropped.


1> use rrs2_RSSD
2> go
1> rs_helproute
2> go
route                             route_status
--------------------------------  ----------------------------------------
rrs2 --------> rrs3

    Route is being dropped. Entries from system table subscriptions are
being dropped.

System table Subs to be dropped
-------------------------------
rs_databases6_at_16777319

route                             route_status
--------------------------------  ----------------------------------------
rrs2 --------> rrs3               Being dropped.
```

The drop route protocol message should be either in the RSSD Replication Agent queue or in the inbound queue.

```
1> rs_helproute
2> go
There are no routes.
(return status = 1)
```

The route is now dropped. You may have to repeatedly check the route status until you get a message that there are no routes.

Routes can be dropped with the "with nowait" clause. This should be used only if that destination Replication Server will not ever be used, if the route must be dropped because the destination Replication Server is not available, or if login names and passwords for direct routes need to be changed. Avoid using the "with nowait" clause whenever possible. A route cannot be dropped when there are active subscriptions. After using drop route with the "with nowait" clause, issue the sysadmin purge_ route_at_replicate command to remove all references to a source (primary) Replication Server from the replication RepServer at the destination (replicate) site.

From the replicate RepServer:

```
sysadmin purge_route_at_replicate, primary_replication_server
```

This command removes all the subscriptions and route information originating from a specified source (primary) Replication Server after a route is dropped from that server. This command will work only if there is no route from the destination (replicate) Replication Server to the source (primary) Replication Server. If a route exists from the destination Replication Server to the source Replication Server, then it has to be dropped before executing the sysadmin purge_route_at_replicate command.

Example:

From source Replication Server (prs):

```
1> drop route to rrs1 with nowait
2> go
```

From replicate Replication Server (rrs1):

```
1> sysadmin purge_route_at_replicate,prs
2> go
```

Monitoring Routes

The create route and drop route commands and route status can be monitored from Sybase Central or with the rs_helproute stored procedure.

rs_helproute should be executed from the RSSD database. It returns information on route status (active, being created, being dropped, being dropped with nowait) for all the routes from or to that Replication Server. When the route is being dropped or created, rs_helproute lists all system table subscriptions that are being created or dropped. If rs_helproute at both sites (primary and replicate RSSDs) reports a status of "Active", that route is valid.

```
1> rs_helproute          →(no parameters)
2> go
route                                    route_status
---------------------------------------- ------------------------------
prs --------> rrs1                        Active

route                                    route_status
---------------------------------------- ------------------------------
prs ---- (Next site: rrs3) ----> rrs2    Active
prs --------> rrs3

route                                    route_status
---------------------------------------- ------------------------------
prs --------> rrs3                        Active

route                                    route_status
---------------------------------------- ------------------------------
rrs1 --------> rrs2                       Active

route                                    route_status
---------------------------------------- ------------------------------
rrs1 --------> rrs3                       Active

route                                    route_status
---------------------------------------- ------------------------------
rrs2 --------> rrs1                       Active

1> rs_helproute rrs3
2> go
route                                    route_status
---------------------------------------- ------------------------------
prs --------> rrs3                        Active

route                                    route_status
---------------------------------------- ------------------------------
rrs1 --------> rrs3                       Active
```

admin who displays the status for all Replication Server threads, and admin who,rsi returns information about RSI threads:

```
1> admin who
2> go
Spid Name        State               Info
---- ----------  ------------------- ------------------------------------
 259 DSI EXEC    Awaiting Command    101(1) pds.prs_RSSD
 258 DSI         Awaiting Message    101 pds.prs_RSSD
 335 DIST        Awaiting Wakeup     101 pds.prs_RSSD
 336 SQT         Awaiting Wakeup     101:1  DIST pds.prs_RSSD
 160 SQM         Awaiting Message    101:1 pds.prs_RSSD
  18 SQM         Awaiting Message    101:0 pds.prs_RSSD
 358 REP AGENT   Awaiting Command    pds.prs_RSSD
 360 RSI         Awaiting Wakeup     rrs1
 254 SQM         Awaiting Message    16777318:0 rrs1
 361 RSI         Awaiting Wakeup     rrs3
 315 SQM         Awaiting Message    16777320:0 rrs3
  33 dSUB        Sleeping
  15 dCM         Awaiting Message
  17 dAIO        Awaiting Message
  35 dREC        Sleeping            dREC
 304 USER        Active              sa
  14 dALARM      Awaiting Wakeup
  36 dSYSAM      Sleeping

1> admin who,rsi
2> go
Spid State          Info  Packets Sent  Bytes Sent     Blocking Reads
  Locater Sent
    Locater Deleted
---------- ----- ---                 ----------- ----------
    ----------------------                ---------------------------------------
    -------------------------------------------------------------------
360  Awaiting Wakeup rrs1 4220.000000   187926.000000            88
    0x000000000000000000000000000000000000000000000000000000000000090002
    0x000000000000000000000000000000000000000000000000000000000000090002
361  Awaiting Wakeup rrs3 220.000000    13434.000000             20
    0x000000000000000000000000000000000000000000000000000000000000130005
    0x000000000000000000000000000000000000000000000000000000000000130005
```

Upgrading Routes

After upgrading to Replication Server 15.0 and setting the site version to 1500, routes must be upgraded in order to use 15.0 features. Upgrading the route rematerializes data in system tables.

To check the route version of source and destination replication servers:

```
1> admin show_route_versions
2> go
```

Source RepServer	Dest. RepServer	Route Version
prs	rrs1	1500
prs	rrs2	1500
prs	rrs3	1500

In mixed version replication server systems, if the source replication server site version is 1500 and the destination replication server site version is 1260, the route version will be 1260 and each replication server will be able to use features of 1260.

Site version of source replication server (prs):

```
1> admin show_site_version
2> go
Site Version
------------
      1500
```

```
1> admin show_route_versions
2> go
```

Source RepServer	Dest. RepServer	**Route Version**
prs	rrs	**1260**

```
1> select * from rs_routeversions
2> go
```

| dest_rsid | source_rsid | dest_rssd_id | route_version | min_path_version |
marker_serial_no		status	proposed_version	
-----------------	-----------	----------------		
16777318	16777317	102	**1260**	0
0		0	**1260**	

If the primary replication server has not used any new features, then the route can be upgraded with sysadmin fast_route_ upgrade:

```
sysadmin fast_route_upgrade, destination_replication_server
```

sysadmin fast_route_upgrade rematerialize the data in system tables, and information related to new features is available to the upgraded replication server.

In all other cases, routes should be upgraded with Replication Server manager from Sybase Central's Replication Manager plug-in.

The Replication Manager provides a route upgrade process. The upgrade process is only available in a two-tier environment.

To upgrade a route:

1. Right-click the Replication Server in the left pane to display the context menu.
2. Select **Upgrade Route**. The Upgrade Route dialog displays.
3. Select a route and press the **Upgrade** button.

Upgrading the route will:

▶ Load the route upgrade script files.

▶ Identify all the required upgrade scripts

▶ Test the primary site to determine if any data needs to be replicated to the replicate site

▶ Execute the pass through to update the route version.

▶ Print a message if the route upgrade process completed.

After upgrading, check the route version from the source replication server (prs):

```
1> admin show_route_versions
2> go
Source RepServer              Dest. RepServer            Route Version
-----------------------------  --------------------------  -------------
prs                            rrs                                  1500
```

For information about setting up a RMS domain, please check the Sybase Central online help.

All route commands can be executed from the command line, Sybase Central, and Replication Monitoring Services.

Chapter 9

Managing Replicated Tables and Stored Procedures

Replicating transactions using Replication Server includes installing one or more Replication Servers, adding routes, managing replication connections, and managing replicated tables. After making sure all the Replication Server components are properly set up, databases can be added to the replication system.

Managing replicated tables may include defining replication definitions, defining publications, defining function definitions, defining subscriptions, and materializing subscriptions. Subscription definitions and materialization methods are discussed in Chapter 10.

Make sure the following Replication Server components are properly installed and configured before defining replication definitions:

1. One or more Replication Servers are successfully installed.

    Replication Server installation using rs_init is described in detail in Chapter 4.

2. Proper routing is defined and created.

    Creating routes is discussed in Chapter 8.

3. One or more databases are added to the replication system.

   Chapter 4 also includes instructions on using rs_init to add a database to the replication system. Some resource files to add a database to the replication system are also included in the downloadable files for this book (at www.wordware.com/files/SybaseRS). You may want to modify these resource files to your requirements and use them with the rs_init -r *resource file* option to add databases to your replication system.

   When a database is added to the replication system, you will notice that rs_init adds a secondary truncation point. A *secondary truncation point* is a marker in the transaction log of the replicated database beyond which the transaction log will not be truncated even if you try to truncate it. The transactions up to this point have been successfully replicated to the replicate site. If you ever need to disable replication, you can use dbcc settrunc('ltm', 'ignore'); to enable replication again, use dbcc settrunc('ltm', 'valid'). To check if a database has a valid secondary truncation point, use dbcc gettrunc. A "1" in the ltm_trunc_state column indicates the secondary truncation point is turned on and valid.

When the Replication Server is ready for defining one or more replication definitions, the Replication Server components may look like the following:

```
1> admin who
2> go
Spid Name        State                  Info
---- ----------  -------------------    ----------------------------------
  14 DSI EXEC    Awaiting Command       110(1) LONDON_DS.SYBRRS_RSSD
   9 DSI         Awaiting Message       110 LONDON_DS_SYBRRS_RSSD
  18 DIST        Awaiting Wakeup        110 LONDON_DS.SYBRRS_RSSD
  19 SQT         Awaiting Wakeup        110:1  DIST LONDON_DS.SYBRRS_RSSD
  17 SQM         Awaiting Message       110:1 LONDON_DS.SYBRRS_RSSD
  13 SQM         Awaiting Message       110:0 LONDON_DS.SYBRRS_RSSD
  20 REP AGENT   Awaiting Command       LONDON_DS.SYBRRS_RSSD
  77 DSI EXEC    Awaiting Command       112(1) LONDON_DS.reptest_db2
  72 DSI         Awaiting Message       112 LONDON_DS.reptest_db2
  74 DIST        Awaiting Wakeup        112 LONDON_DS.reptest_db2
```

```
76 SQT         Awaiting Wakeup    112:1  DIST LONDON_DS.reptest_db2
73 SQM         Awaiting Message   112:1 LONDON_DS.reptest_db2
71 SQM         Awaiting Message   112:0 LONDON_DS.reptest_db2
75 REP AGENT   Awaiting Command   LONDON_DS.reptest_db2
50 RSI         Awaiting Wakeup    MMPRRS
49 SQM         Awaiting Message   16777320:0 MMPRRS
23 RSI USER    Awaiting Command   MMPRRS
10 dSUB        Sleeping
 6 dCM         Awaiting Message
 8 dAIO        Awaiting Message
11 dREC        Sleeping           dREC
78 USER        Active             sa
 5 dALARM      Awaiting Wakeup
12 dSYSAM      Sleeping
```

You will notice the database to be replicated is already active in the replication system. There will be a Replication Agent up and running for that database. If it is a bidirectional replication, then a DSI thread will be active on this database as well. This DSI thread will apply transactions to the replicate site. If there is a route, an RSI thread will be running to the replicate site. If you have a route, there will be a Replication Agent thread and a DSI thread running for the RSSD database. A similar type of connection setup may be found in a replicate Replication Server.

Replication Definitions and Subscription Definitions

Replication definitions are used to describe a primary table and primary data that will be available for replication. The primary data defined by replication definitions can be used in a warm standby application where no subscription definitions are required, or can be used by subscriptions in a regular replication. A replication definition lists all the columns that need to be replicated and the datatypes of the columns. The replication definition also specifies the columns that will constitute the primary key, and the columns that can be used in the where clause of the subscription definition. Having a unique index on the primary key column is highly recommended for performance improvements and for maintaining data consistency.

There can be multiple replication definitions per table. Similarly, more than one subscription definition can subscribe to a replication definition, just like a person can subscribe to more than one newspaper. Additional replication definitions can define a subset of columns of the first replication definition. A subsequent replication definition can be as simple as a new replication definition name for the first replication definition.

Making tables or stored procedures ready for replication is a multistep process involving the following:

1. Create a replication definition for a table or stored procedure using `create replication definition` or `create function replication`, respectively.

2. Mark a table or stored procedure for replication using the `sp_reptable` or `sp_setrepproc` Adaptive Server stored procedures, respectively.

Once a table is marked for replication, whether or not a replication definition exists, the replication agents will begin forwarding the table. If a matching replication definition does not exist on the table when marking the table for replication, Replication Server may report message 32032 and its error log file may fill up.

Create a Replication Definition

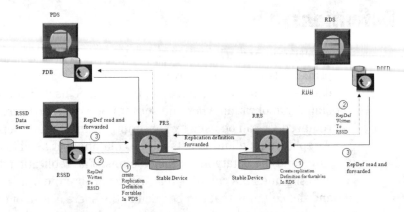

Figure 9-1: Creating a replication definition

Syntax:

```
create replication definition replication_definition
    with primary at data_server.database
    [with all tables named [table_owner.] 'table_name' |
    [with primary table named [table_owner.]'table_name']
    with replicate table named [table_owner.]'table_name']]
    (column_name datatype [, column_name datatype]...)
    primary key (column_name [, column_name]...)
    [searchable columns (column_name [, column_name]...)]
    [send standby [{all | replication definition} columns]]
    [replicate {minimal | all} columns]
    [replicate_if_changed (column_name [, column_name]...)]
    [always_replicate (column_name [, column_name]...)]
    [do_not_replicate (column [, column]...)]
```

For the complete syntax, please refer to the Sybase Replication Server Reference Manual.

Some of the most frequently used keywords are described below.

replication_definition

> By default the replication definition name is the combination of the primary and replicate table names. If either the primary or the replicate table name is omitted from the replication definition syntax, the other will constitute the name of the replication definition. However, it is suggested that the replication definition name always be included and that the name include as much information as possible to identify the replication components involved. For example, it is a good practice to use an abbreviated form such as PDS_PDB_ptbl_repdef for the naming convention. This identifies the primary data server, primary database, and primary table to which the replication definition belongs. In this convention, we assume the primary and replicate tables have the same name. A subscription to such a replication definition might look like this: RDS_RDB_rtbl_subdef. Please refer to Chapter 10 for more information about subscriptions.

`with all tables named`

> This specifies that both the primary and replicate table names and table owners are the same.

`primary key`

> This specifies a list of one or more columns that form the primary key for the table. You cannot include text, unitext, image, rawobject, rawobject in row, or rs_address columns as part of the primary key.

`with primary table named`
`with replicate table named`

> These two optional parameters specify the different table names at the primary and replicate sites. The combination of these two parameters constitutes the replication definition name if the name is not specified. If one of these parameters is omitted, the other parameter is assumed to be the same as the replication definition name. If you omit both of these parameters, you must provide the replication definition name.

column_name datatype

> This clause includes one or more of the columns from the primary table. Use the extended clause `'as replicate_column_name'` to specify a different column name at the replicate site. The datatypes must be the same or compatible. The rules for converting datatypes are discussed in Chapter 18. There may be a performance impact with datatype conversions. It is suggested that the datatypes be the same at both the primary and replicate sites.

> Specifying a datatype is optional if another replication definition already exists that includes the datatype of the column. Also, the attribute null or not null apply only to text, unitext, image, and rawobject datatypes. More information on special considerations required to replicate these special datatypes can be found later in this chapter.

searchable columns

A list of columns used in the where clause of the correspond-ing create subscription, define subscription, and create article commands for this replication definition. Columns containing text, unitext, image, and rawobject datatypes can-not be searchable columns.

Searchable column values take extra space in the stable device as these values are parsed and stored separately from the regular data. Specifying unnecessary searchable columns can impact stable queue usage. Searchable columns are used to restrict data to be replicated from a table.

For example, if the primary table has data from many departments in an organization and if a replicate site wants to subscribe to data belonging to the "legal" department only, you would do the following:

Replication Definition	Corresponding Subscription Definition
create replication definition repdef_name <rest of the syntax> **searchable columns 'department', 'city'** <rest of the syntax>	create subscription *subdef name* <rest of syntax> **where department = 'legal'**

This combination of replication definition and subscription defini-tion will allow only the "legal" department data to be replicated to this replicate site. For another replicate site, a subscription defi-nition may include where city = 'DWARAKA'. This site will monitor the resources available to different departments located in the city Dwaraka.

While Replication Server does not check if a column included in the searchable column list is nullable or not, null columns cause problems when Replication Server receives the data. It is recommended that you use non-nullable columns or default or dummy values for searchable columns.

send standby

A replication for a warm standby application setup does not need replication definitions. But to improve warm standby performance, it is recommended that you define replication definitions. Replication definition clauses like primary key and minimal columns will be useful for restricting the data. Please refer to Chapter 12 for more information on setting up warm standby applications and replication definitions for warm standby applications.

replicate minimal columns

By default Replication Server sends all columns for every subscribed table. If replicate minimal columns is used in the replication definition, only the columns required to satisfy the data manipulation statements are sent to the target Replication Server. If replicate minimal columns is specified, autocorrection cannot be used for subscriptions. Autocorrection helps when index conflicts occur during replication due to duplicate key rows. Please refer to Chapter 10 for more information on autocorrection.

replicate_if_changed
always_replicate

These two parameters control how text, unitext, image, or rawobject columns are replicated. These datatypes will have a performance impact as they are large objects. If replicate_if_changed is specified, Replication Server will send data of these datatypes only when data changes.

Automating replication definition creation is the best method. Sybase provides a set of stored procedures to create many different types of replication objects including replication definitions. You can find other utility tools in the codeXchange program available at www.sybase.com. You will also find a simple automation tool, a shell script, to generate replication definitions for multiple tables, and necessary documentation from our web site at www.wordware.com/files/SybaseRS. Please read the instructions and exceptions provided with the tool. You may customize it, if necessary, before using it in your production environment.

Please download the script gen_repdef.ksh from Sybase's codeXchange site at https://repserver.codexchange.sybase.com/files/documents/10/2887/genrepdefs.ksh.

The script can be excuted as gen_repdefs - Uusername - Ppassword [- Sservername] [- Ddatabase] [table_name…]. It will generate multiple files with RCL commands for create-repdefs, droprepdefs, and setrep. Please refer to the script documentation for more options and a detailed description.

Check the output files to see if any of the Sybase reserved words are used in the definitions. If you notice any reserved words, it may be possible to create the definitions by enclosing those words in double quotation marks.

Once the replication definitions are created using the script, you may need to modify them for your application preferences. Make sure a primary key is defined for each table for which you are creating a replication definition. Though an index on the table is not necessary for the replication to function, a unique index on the table helps improve replication performance.

When you are ready to create replication definitions, do so using isql at the primary replication server:

```
sybase@host:/usr/sybase/REP_150_1/REP-15_0/install/tools isql -Usa -SMMPRRS
-iNYDS_rep_defs -oNYDS_rep_defs.out
password

sybase@host:/usr/sybase/REP_150_1/REP-15_0/install/tools> cat
NYDS_rep_defs.out
Replication definition 'NYDS_majorCourses_rep' is created.
Replication definition 'NYDS_teachingStaff_rep' is created.
Replication definition 'NYDS_student_rep' is created.
```

Verify the replication definitions in the RSSD database. Connect to the RSSD for the Replication Server where you defined the replication definitions and either execute rs_helprep without arguments to get a full list of all the replication definitions or use rs_helprep *replication_definition* to get full details of that replication definition. If a route is already defined to a replicate Replication Server, you can find the replication definitions replicated in the replicate Replication Server RSSD database.

```
sybase@host> isql -Usa -SNYDS -DMMPRRS_RSSD -w899
Password:
1> rs_helprep
2> go
Replication Definition Name  PRS      Primary DS.DB     Primary Table
  Replicate Table   Type
---------------------------- ------- ----------------- --------------
  --------------- ----
NYDS_majorCourses_rep        MMPRRS  NYDS.reptest_db2  majorCourses
  majorCourses    Tbl
```

To get full details of a replication definition, execute rs_helprep
with the replication definition name. The details include each column in the replication definition. Because the column name in the
table and the column name as replicated can be different, you will
notice the column name repeated twice in the following output as
this example uses the same name for the replicated column as
well.

```
sybase@host> isql -Usa -SNYDS -DMMPRRS_RSSD -w899
Password:
1> rs_helprep NYDS_student_rep
2> go
Replication Definition Name  PRS      Type   Creation Date
---------------------------- -------- ------ -------------------
NYDS_student_rep             MMPRRS   Tbl    Mar 25 2007  9:10AM


PDS.DB                Primary Owner  Primary Table
------------------    -------------- ------------------------------
NYDS.reptest_db2      student


Replicate Owner                Replicate Table
-----------------------------  ------------------------------------
                               student


Send Min Cols.  Used by Standby  Min Vers
--------------- ---------------- --------
No              No               1000
```

```
Col. Name  Rep. Col. Name  Datatype  Len.  Pri. Col.  Searchable
---------- ---------------  --------  ----- ---------- ----------
studentId  studentId       int       4     1          1
fname      fname           varchar   30    0          0
```

< Rest of the column definition list omitted to save space here>

```
Function Name        FString Class                  FString Source   FString Name
-------------------- -----------------------------  ---------------  --------------------
rs_delete            rs_sqlserver_function_class    Class Default    rs_delete
rs_insert            rs_sqlserver_function_class    Class Default    rs_insert
rs_select            rs_sqlserver_function_class    Class Default    rs_select
rs_select_with_lock  rs_sqlserver_function_class    Class Default    rs_select_with_lock
rs_truncate          rs_sqlserver_function_class    Class Default    rs_truncate
rs_update            rs_sqlserver_function_class    Class Default    rs_update
```

Subscriptions known at this Site 'MMPRRS'.
```
Subscription Name    Replicate DS.DB     Owner              Creation Date
-------------------- ------------------  ------------------ ----------------
```
(return status = 0)

You will notice this particular replication definition does not
define minimal columns (Send Min Cols.). You will also notice
that there are no subscriptions for this replication definition for
now. We will add subscriptions in Chapter 10. The syntax for
creating replication definitions includes many options to meet
your application requirements. You'll notice the default function-
string classes and the default function strings are assigned for the
functions for this replication definition. It is possible to change
the default function behavior for the replication definition by modifying the function strings. For example, the rs_delete function
for this replication definition can be modified so that a delete
operation on the primary table may not delete the row in the replicate. Instead, it can just record who is trying to delete the record
and when. For more details on function strings, please refer to
Chapter 11. This replication definition, to be effective, requires a
Replication Server version of at least 10.0.

Altering a Replication Definition

The syntax for altering a replication definition is as robust as the syntax for creating the replication definition.

```
alter replication definition replication_definition
    {with replicate table named
    [table_owner.]'table_name' |
add colum_name [as replicate_column_name]
    [datatype [null | not null]]
    [map to published_datatype],... |
alter columns with column_name
    [as replicate_column_name],... |
alter columns with column_name
    datatype [null | not null]
    [map to published_datatype],... |
add primary key column_name [, column_name]... |
drop primary key column_name [, column_name]... |
add searchable columns column_name [, column_name]... |
drop searchable columns column_name [, column_name]... |
send standby [off | {all | replication definition} columns] |
replicate {minimal | all} columns |
replicate_if_changed column_name [, column_name]... |
always_replicate column_name [, column_name]...}
```

To alter a replication definition, connect to the Replication Server where the replication definition was originally created and execute the alter replication definition command.

```
sybase@host > isql -Usa -SMMPRRS -w899
Password:
1> alter replication definition NYDS student rep
2> replicate minimal columns
3> go
Replication definition 'NYDS_student_rep' is altered.
1>
```

If you check the rs_helprep now you will notice the following change:

Send Min Cols.	Used by Standby	Min Vers
Yes	No	1000

Marking Tables for Replication

Even if a table replication definition exists, the data from any table will not be replicated unless the table is marked for replication. If a matching replication definition does not exist on the table when marking the table for replication, Replication Server may report message 32032 and the error log file may fill up. Warm standby applications, in which replication definitions are optional, are not affected by this condition.

In the sequence of operations in setting up table replication, marking the table for replication can be thought of as a last step. It is possible to mark the table for replication after subscriptions are defined but before data changes take place.

The system stored procedure sp_setreptable is used to mark or unmark an entire table for replication. You can check the current replication status of a table with sp_setreptable and the table name. To activate or deactivate replication for the table, you log in to the Adaptive Server managing the table being replicated and execute sp_setreptable *table* [, true|false] in the database where the table exists.

```
sybase@host> isql -Usa -SNYDS -w899 -Dreptest_db2 -w899          <
Password:
1> sp_setreptable student
2> go
The replication status for 'student' is currently false, owner_off.
(return status = 0)
1>
```

A status of false indicates replication is not active for this table even though a replication definition is already created on this table. You can verify the replication status of all the tables in the database if you enter sp_setreptable with no arguments.

Use sp_setreptable to verify whether the replication status is active on all of the replicated tables. The transactions up to the secondary truncation point for an object when marked for replication with sp_setreptable will be forwarded to the Replication Server irrespective of whether a replication definition or subscription exists for that table. The data from the table will be lost during the subscription resolution phase if there is no subscription for a table replication definition. An incorrect sequence of operations during the replication setup often will result in a loss of data before the replicate site ever gets the opportunity to pick up the transactions.

The syntax to activate replication on the student table is:

```
sp_setreptable student, 'true'
```

Replicating Tables with text, unitext, image, and rawobject Datatypes

At the column level you can use the sp_setrepcol stored procedure to include or exclude a column in the replication. Also, replicating text, unitext, image, and rawobject datatypes may be controlled by the attributes replicate_if_changed or replicate_always. By default, sp_setreptable sets the replication status of text, unitext, image, or rawobject columns to always_replicate. Use sp_setrepcol to change the replication status of these columns individually. You can update a table with text, unitext, image, or rawobject columns along with regular base datatypes in a single operation. However, the replication server issues two updates at the target database, one for base datatype columns and one for text, unitext, image, or rawobject columns. Because of this behavior, it is possible for the target database to become inconsistent if certain Replication Server errors are ignored manually.

```
create replication definition NYDS_majorCourses_rep
    with primary at NYDS_reptest_db2
    with all tables named 'majorCourses'
        (courseId          tinyint,
         courseName         varchar(50),
         instructorId       smallint,
         courseDescription  text null)
        primary key (courseId)
        searchable columns (courseId)
        replicate_if_changed (courseDescription)
```

The courseDescription column has a replication status (replicate_if_changed) and a null status (null). Only columns containing

text, unitext, image, or rawobject datatypes can have both a replication status and null status in the replication definition. They
cannot be part of the primary key and searchable columns. The
replicate_if_changed parameter can be modified using the
sp_setrepcol stored procedure.

```
sp_setrepcol table, column, replicate_if_changed | always_replicate
```

Replicating Tables with Computed Columns

Computed columns allow you to create an expression and place
the result of the expression in a table column. There are two
types of computed columns:

▶ Materialized — The values are evaluated when the data row is
  inserted or updated.

▶ Virtual — The values are evaluated when they are queried.

Both materialized and virtual computed columns can be either
deterministic or non-deterministic. When a value is deterministic,
the value remains the same each time it is evaluated; when a
value is non-deterministic, the value changes each time it is evaluated. A datetime datatype column, for example, is
non-deterministic as the datetime column changes every time it
is evaluated. For more information on computed columns, refer to
the Sybase Adaptive Server Enterprise documentation.

Replication Server replicates deterministic columns similar
to any other replicated column. Replication Server does not replicate virtual columns. Support for computed column replication is
provided by function strings. For Replication Server 15.0 or later,
when a DSI connection is established to the replicate site, a
class-level function string called rs_set_dml_on_computed is
applied. It issues set dml_on_computed "on" after the use database
statement. This statement is ignored for Replication Server
releases prior to 15.0.

When creating replication definition, you do not need to
include deterministic columns, as they can be evaluated as part of
the DML statement at the replicate site. However, it is required
that non-deterministic columns be included in the replication definition to keep primary and replicate data synchronized.

Replicating Tables with Encryptod Columns

Replication Server 15.0 and later support replication of encrypted columns and encryption keys.

Replicating Tables with Different Ownership

It is possible to replicate tables owned by two different owners at the primary and replicate sites. If the replicate table is owned by a different owner, the owner_on option should be used when activating the replication status of a table with sp_setreptable. The replication definitions on that table should also include owner information. Please refer to the Replication Agent documentation for your platform to verify that the Replication Agent supports replicating tables with different ownership.

To mark the table for replication with owner_on, log in to Adaptive Server, specify use *database*, and enter:

```
sp_setreptable table_name, 'true', 'owner_on'
```

In the replication definition, use the table_*owner* option to provide owner information at the primary and the replicate:

```
create replication definition replication_definition
    with primary at data_server.database
    [with all tables named [table_owner.] 'table_name' |
    [with primary table named [table_owner.]'table_name']
    with replicate table named [table_owner.]'table_name']]
```

To change the owner status of a table previously marked for replication, use the sp_setrepdefmode system stored procedure.

```
sp_setrepdefmode table_name, ['owner_on' | 'owner_off']
```

Creating Replication Definition for Java Columns

You can create replication definitions for Java columns using the rawobject and rawobject in row datatypes. These Replication Server datatypes are stored in the same manner as the base datatypes image and varbinary(255), respectively. Similarly, if a stored procedure has Java objects as parameters, it cannot be replicated as part of the stored procedure, but the effect of such an object can be accomplished using table-level replication. Note that there are additional restrictions on replicating Java columns.

Because rawobject and rawobject in row datatypes should be used to represent Java objects, all the rules related to these datatypes apply for replication definition and subscription definition. They cannot be part of the replication definition primary key nor can they be part of searchable columns.

Java objects pass through the replication system in a serialized format that allows the Replication Server to update Java columns directly. To replicate Java columns, Replication Server uses the `rs_raw_object_serialization` function string to pass Java columns. Whenever a rawobject is included, Replication Server treats it as image data and creates the `rs_get_textptr`, `rs_textptr_init`, `rs_datarow_for_writetext`, and `rs_writetext` function strings.

The following example creates a replication definition for a table that contains Java columns.

```
create replication definition NYDS_pictures_repdef
    with primary at NYDS.reptest_db2
    with all tables name pictures
        (pictureId int,
        thumbnail rawobject null,
        picture rawobject not null,
        frame rawobject in row)
    primary key (pictureId)
    replicate_if_changed (thumbnail)
    always_replicate (picture)
```

Notice in the above example that the frame column that is rawobject in row does not have replication or null status. The other two rawobject columns do have replication and null status. For rawobject columns, replication status attributes like replicate_if_changed and always_replicate can be used. For the purpose of replication, the rawobject columns follow the rules of image datatype, and rawobject in row follow the rules of varbinary(255).

If the column datatype allows, you can change the replication status attributes of a column using the sp_setrepcol stored procedure.

Managing Replicated Stored Procedures

The execution of a stored procedure is replicated to the replicate site via use of function replication. When you use function replication, the Replication Server copies the execution of a stored procedure at the primary to the replicate site. Function replication, in general, is best suited for a primary copy model where a single primary source of transactions is copied to multiple destination sites. For more information on the one-to-many regular replication model, please refer to Chapter 3.

The method of replicating stored procedure execution depends on whether or not the underlying tables addressed in the stored procedures have table-level replication definitions. If the table-level replication and function replication replicate transactions to the destination site, there will be duplicate data at the destination site.

If a stored procedure is associated with a table replication definition, use asynchronous procedures. If a stored procedure is associated with a function replication definition, use function replication. Function replication is recommended for replicating stored procedures.

Function Replication

The execution of a stored procedure at the primary site invokes an associated stored procedure at the replicate site. The names of the two stored procedures and the results of the two stored procedures need not be the same. This requires a route to the destination Replication Server and assumes there are no table-level replication definitions replicating the same transactions affected by these replicated stored procedures.

There are two ways to implement the replicate functions:

▶ Applied function: To replicate a transaction that occurred first at the primary database to the replicate database.

▶ Request function: To replicate transactions initiated first at the replicate database to the primary database. Typically this model is useful where a client application receives data changes, but always changes the master copy at the primary site.

Asynchronous Procedures

Asynchronous procedures are used for replicating stored procedures that are associated with table replication definitions. Asynchronous procedures marked for replication can be executed at either primary or replicate sites. The stored procedures replicated as asynchronous procedures are marked for replication with sp_setreplicate or sp_setrepproc.

There are two types of asynchronous procedure delivery methods:

▶ Applied stored procedures — Replicated stored procedures that deliver from the primary database to the replicate database.

▶ Request stored procedures — Replicated stored procedures that deliver from the replicate database to the primary database. Do not execute the request stored procedure in the primary database, as that will create a looping effect where the replicate Replication Server causes the same stored procedure to be executed circularly. It is possible to avoid such looping by giving the stored procedures different names in the primary and the replicate sites.

Replicated Adaptive Server stored procedures may not contain parameters with the text, unitext, or image datatypes.

Adaptive Server logs the stored procedure where the enclosing transaction is executed. If the user does not explicitly start a transaction, Adaptive Server starts a transaction in the user's current database before executing the replicated stored procedure.

If the user explicitly starts a transaction before executing the replicated stored procedure, the stored procedure is logged in the database where the transaction is executed irrespective of the database where the stored procedure gets executed. If table-type stored procedure replication execution is logged in one database and it affects the replicated tables in another database, there is the possibility of duplicate data replicating to the destination site(s). The replication system needs to be implemented so that such duplicate data replication is avoided.

In a mixed mode transaction, where a transaction includes execution of applied stored procedures, request stored procedures, and other data modification operations, the Replication Server will process all request stored procedures as a single operation after processing all of the other operations. This situation is likely to occur where primary and replicate data is managed by a single Replication Server.

Do not execute request stored procedures in the primary database. Doing so can create a looping problem where the replicate Replication Server may try to invoke the same stored procedure or related stored procedure in the primary database. Executing the request stored procedures at the replicate Replication Server keeps the primary data copy model safe. Request stored procedures always make data changes to the primary data copy. The changes will then be propagated to replicate sites later.

Setting Up Function Replication

The following sections explain how to set up applied function replication and request function replication.

Setting Up Applied Function Replication

1. Create a stored procedure to meet your requirements:

```
2> create proc update_student
3> @studentId int, @registrationStatus char(1), @gradePointAvg
numeric(4,2)
4> as
5> update student
6> set registrationStatus='R', gradePointAvg = 0.0
```

```
7> where studentId = @studentId
8> go
```

2. Create a function replication definition. Log in to the Replica-
    tion Server that manages the database where the stored
    procedure is defined.

    The syntax for creating a function replication definition to
    replicate a stored procedure as a function replication is shown
    here:

```
create function replication definition
function_rep_def
with primary at data_server.database
[deliver as 'proc_name']
([@param_name datatype [, @param_name datatype]...])
[searchable parameters (@param_name
[, @param_name]...)]
[send standby {all | replication definition}
parameters]
```

    If deliver as is not used, then the function is delivered as a
    stored procedure with the same name as the function replica-
    tion definition.

    send standby all is the default, where all parameters in
    the function are sent to the standby database in a warm
    standby application. If you want to limit the parameters to the
    replication definition parameters, use send standby replica-
    tion definition.

```
1> create function replication definition update_student_frep
2> with primary at NYDS.reptest_db2
3> (@studentId int, @registrationStatus char(1), @gradePointAvg
numeric)
4> searchable parameters (@studentId)
5>
6> go
Function replication definition 'update_student_frep' is created.
1>
```

3. In the Adaptive Server Enterprise, mark the stored proce-
    dure for replication using the system procedure
    sp_setrepproc.

```
sp_setrepproc stored procedure name, 'function'
```

By specifying the keyword function, the stored procedure is marked for function replication.

The complete syntax is:

```
sp_setrepproc [proc_name [, {'function' | 'table' | 'false'},
[{log_current | log_sproc}]]]
```

where:

function

Marks the stored procedure for replication associated with the function replication definition.

table

Enables replication for a stored procedure associated with a table replication definition. For more information about replicating stored procedures associated with a table replication definition, please refer to the section in this chapter titled "Asynchronous Procedures."

false

Disables an active stored procedure replication definition.

{log_current | log_sproc}

Controls where the execution of the stored procedure is logged. By default the execution is logged where the transaction executing the stored procedure is initiated, irrespective of where the stored procedures effects data changes.

sp_setrepproc can be used to check the status of stored procedure replication. To list the replication status of all the stored procedures in the database, use sp_setrepproc without any arguments.

```
1> sp_setrepproc
2> go
Name                                      Type            Log Mode
----------------------------------------- --------------- ---------------
rs_marker                                 table           log_current
```

```
(1 row affected)
(return status = 0)
```

To get the status of a particular stored procedure, include the stored procedure name as an argument.

4. If you are using the default function string, Replication Server automatically creates the function with the default function-string class. If you want to customize the function strings, please refer to the Sybase Replication Server documentation or to Chapter 11.

5. Create a subscription definition and materialize the data for the subscription. This topic is discussed in Chapter 10.

Setting Up Request Function Replication

The process of setting up request function replication is the same as setting up applied function replication except for a few minor differences. In request function replication, the transaction is initiated at the replicate site, but the data changes happen at the primary copy by executing the matching stored procedure at the primary data source.

Follow these steps:

1. Create the actual stored procedure to make data changes in the primary database.

2. Grant the execute permissions to the same login that will execute the request function in the replicate database. Please note the permissions are granted to the login who executes the stored procedure in the replicate database, not the maintenance user.

3. Do not mark this stored procedure created in the primary database for replication. In a request function delivery, only the stored procedure in the replicate database is marked as replicated. However, in a warm standby application, if you need the primary stored procedure replicated, you may mark the primary database stored procedure as replicated.

4. Create a stored procedure, typically with a different name, in the replicate database with the same parameters and datatypes. This stored procedure in the replicate database

should do nothing or should just print an informative message.

```
create proc update_student_request
@studentId int, @registrationStatus char(1), @gradePointAvg numeric)
as
print "Transaction accepted."
```

5. In the replicate database, mark the stored procedure as replicated.

```
sp_setrepproc update_student_request, 'function'
```

6. In the replicate database, grant the execute permission to the user who will execute it. This user should be the same user in the primary database as well.

7. In the primary Replication Server, create a function replication definition for the stored procedure in the replicate database.

```
create function replication definition update_student_request
with primary at RDS.reptest_db2
deliver as 'update_student'
(@studentId int, @registrationStatus char(1), @gradePointAvg numeric)
```

This definition will request execution of a stored procedure called update_student at the primary data server whenever a request stored procedure called update_student_request is executed at the replicate site.

If you are going to replicate a stored procedure for the same purpose as the request function delivery in the primary database, then give the stored procedure a different name for request function delivery. In this example, we called the stored procedure update_student_request for request function delivery, and update_student in the primary database. Even if update_student in the primary database is replicated as an applied stored procedure, a matching stored procedure with the same name will be executed in the replicate database, avoiding circular reference.

8. Verify that the stored procedures and function replication definitions are properly propagated to the expected destinations. You should now be able to execute the request function in the replicate site.

Creating Publications

Publications are the next higher level of abstraction for replication definitions. With publications, many replication definitions for the same or related tables and/or stored procedures can be grouped as one entity to subscribe to. If there are lots of replication definitions, it may be inconvenient to create and manage that many subscriptions. You may consider creating a publication and subscribing to that publication. With publications, you can monitor the replication status for one publication subscription rather than multiple subscriptions for replication definitions.

The following are the most important steps in replicating data using publications:

1. Create replication definitions on the same or related tables or stored procedures if they do not already exist. Select replication definitions to include in the publication.

```
2> create replication definition "LN_titles_rep"
3> with primary at LONDON_DS.pubs2
4> with all tables named "titles"
5> (
6>      "title_id" varchar(6),
7>      "title" varchar(80),
8>      "type" char(12),
9>      "pub_id" char(4),
10>     "price" money,
11>     "advance" money,
12>     "total_sales" int,
13>     "notes" varchar(200),
14>     "pubdate" datetime,
15>     "contract" bit
16> )
17> primary key ("title_id")
18> searchable columns ("title_id")
19>
20> go
Replication definition 'LN_titles_rep' is created.
```

2. Create the publication definitions.

```
1> create publication LONDON_pubs2_pub
2> with primary at LONDON_DS.pubs2
```

```
3> go
Publication 'LONDON_pubs2_pub' for LONDON_DS.pubs2 is created.
```

3. Create articles referencing the selected replication definition.

   Articles are replication definition extensions that let you
   group replication definitions in a publication. Articles can
   have where clause(s) much like subscription definitions. Just
   like subscription definitions, articles need to be validated at
   the replicate site. Not all of the logical operators are available
   in the where clause, however. The columns in the where
   clause should be part of the searchable columns of the replication definitions referred to in the article. You may use the
   OR clause to join multiple where clauses in the article. The &
   operator is only available with the rs_address datatype.

```
1> create article LONDON_pubs_art
2>      for LONDON_pubs2_pub with primary at LONDON_DS.pubs2
3>      with replication definition LN_titles_rep
4>      where title_id <= 'P%'
5>
6> go
Article 'LONDON_pubs_art' is created for publication LONDON_pubs2_pub
with primary at LONDON_DS.pubs2.
```

There cannot be more than one article referencing the same
primary replicated object in a publication. One alternative is
to create a new publication that can include an article referencing the same replicated object.

```
1> create article LONDON_pubs_art
2>      for LONDON_pubs2_pub with primary at LONDON_DS.pubs2
3>      with replication definition LN_titles_rep
4>      where title_id <= 'T%'
5>
6> go
Msg 15403, Level 12, State 0:
Server 'R1250RRS':
Article LONDON_pubs_art already exists for publication
LONDON_pubs2_pub with primary at LONDON_DS.pubs2.
```

The following is also possible:

a. Create a new replication definition referencing the same primary table that has already been added to a publication.

b. Create a new publication.

c. Create an article including the new replication definition.

```
1> create replication definition NYDS_student_2_rep
2>     with primary at NYDS.reptest_db2
3>     with all tables named 'student'
4>        (studentId           int,
5>         gradePointAvg        numeric)
6>     primary key (studentId)
7>     searchable columns (studentId)
8>
9> go
Replication definition 'NYDS_student_2_rep' is created.


1> create publication nyds_reptest_db2_pub2
2>     with primary at NYDS.reptest_db2
3>
4> go
Publication 'nyds_reptest_db2_pub2' for NYDS.reptest_db2 is created.


1> create article student_2_art
2>     for nyds_reptest_db2_pub2 with primary at NYDS.reptest_db2
3>     with replication definition NYDS_student_2_rep
4>     where studentId >= 1000
5>
6> go
Article 'student_2_art' is created for publication
nyds_reptest_db2_pub2 with primary at NYDS.reptest_db2.
```

4. Validate the publication.

When a new publication is created or when an article is dropped or added to a publication, the publication has to be validated to be ready for subscription.

Check the publication status in the RSSD database with the rs_helppub Adaptive Server stored procedure.

```
1> rs_helppub
2> go
```

Publication Name	PRS	Primary DS.DB	Num Articles	Status	Request Date
LONDON_pubs2_pub	R1250RRS	LONDON_DS.pubs2	1	Invalid	Nov 18 2007 9:17PM

Article Name	Replication Definition	Type	Primary Object Name
Replicate Object Name	Request Date		

LONDON_pubs_art	LN_titles_rep	Table	titles
titles	Nov 18 2007 9:16PM		

Subscription Name	Replicate DS.DB	Owner	Request Date

```
(return status = 0)
```

Note that the newly created publication is invalid, as indicated by the 0 return status. All publications need to be validated.

Log in to the Replication Server where you created the publications, and execute the `validate publication` command.

```
1> validate publication LONDON_pubs2_pub
2> with primary at LONDON_DS.pubs2
3>
4> go
Publication 'LONDON_pubs2_pub' for LONDON_DS.pubs2 is validated.
```

Now verify the status again in the RSSD. You can use rs_helppub, select the data from the rs_publications system table, or use the Replication Server command `check publication`. If the status is 1, then the publications are valid.

```
1> select pubname, status from rs_publications
2> go
pubname                          status
-------------------------------- -----------
LONDON_pubs2_pub                       1
```

The following shows how to use `check publication`:

```
1> check publication LONDON_pubs2_pub
2> with primary at LONDON_DS.pubs2
3>
```

```
4> go
Publication LONDON_pubs2_pub for LONDON_DS.pubs2 is valid. The number
of articles in the publication is 1.
```

This is the best method as you just need to change the word "validate" to "check" and it can be easily scripted.

Create a subscription at the replicate Replication Server for the publication.

```
2>  create subscription "LONDON_titles_sub"
3>  for publication "LONDON_pubs2_pub"
4>  with primary at LONDON_DS.pubs2
5>  with replicate at JDBCD05A_SYB.pubs2
6>
7> go
Subscription 'LONDON_titles_sub' is in the process of being created.
```

And use check subscription to verify its status:

```
2>  check subscription "LONDON_titles_sub"
3>  for publication "LONDON_pubs2_pub"
4>  with primary at LONDON_DS.pubs2
5>  with replicate at JDBCD05A_SYB.pubs2
6>
7> go
Subscription LONDON_titles_sub for publication LONDON_pubs2_pub has
been defined at the replicate.
Materialization queue for subscription LONDON_titles_sub for article
LONDON_pubs_art has been completed.
```

If the permissions for the maintenance user are correct, and if the table is marked for replication with sp_setreptable, then the replication will work properly.

Dropping Publications

You cannot drop a publication when there are referencing subscriptions. You must first drop all the subscriptions at the replicate Replication Server. You do not need to drop the articles added to the publication before dropping the publication.

```
1> drop publication nyds_reptest_db2_pub2 with primary at NYDS.reptest_db2
2> go
Publication 'nyds_reptest_db2_pub2' for NYDS.reptest_db2 is dropped.
```

You can also drop all the replication definitions referenced in all of the articles of the publication by adding the drop_repdef clause to the drop publication command. Please note that this will drop all of the replication definitions in that publication.

Dropping Articles

Execute the drop article command at the Replication Server where the article is defined to drop an article. You can also drop the replication definition associated with the article by including the drop_repdef clause in the drop article command.

The following example drops the teachingStaff_art article for the db2_pub2 publication.

```
drop article teachingStaff_art
for nyds_reptest_db2_pub2 with primary at NYDS.reptest_db2
drop_repdef
```

Disabling Replication for a User Object

To disable replication at the table level, use sp_setreptable and unmark the table.

```
sp_setreptable table_name, 'false'
```

Even after creating the publications for a group of replication definitions, subscriptions from the replicate database can directly reference individual replication definitions if required. Publication creation and publication subscriptions are supported with Replication Server version 11.0 and above

Dropping Replication Definitions

You cannot drop a replication definition if it is referenced by a subscription or an article. You must first drop the referencing subscription or article, and then drop the replication definition using drop replication definition.

```
1> drop replication definition LONDON_DS_titles_rep
2> go
Msg 15101, Level 12, State 0:
Server 'R1250RRS':
Cannot drop replication definition LONDON_DS_titles_rep, because it is in
use by some subscriptions.
1>
```

```
1> drop replication definition LN_titles_rep
2> go
Msg 15368, Level 12, State 0:
Server 'R1250RRS':
Cannot drop replication definition LN_titles_rep, because it is in use by
some articles.
```

The syntax to drop a replication definition is:

```
drop replication definition replication_definition
```

Replication definitions, articles, and publications are different methods of publishing the data ready for subscriptions. Articles and publications group replication definitions into an abstract object and offer ease of handling and maintenance. A subscription defined at the replicate Replication Server can then refer to a publication.

Chapter 10

Subscriptions

Subscriptions serve the purpose of subscribing to the data published by replication definitions. There will always be a subscription for every type of replication definition or for a group of replication definitions in the form of a publication, and more than one subscription can subscribe to a replication definition. Note that subscription definitions are not required in the warm standby setup. Subscriptions resemble a SQL select statement with a where clause to specify a subset of data. The method of initializing the data from the primary site to the destination site is called *materialization*. After materialization, normal replication process resumes.

In Chapter 9, we discussed creating and managing replication definitions for tables and stored procedures. In this chapter, we will discuss subscriptions and materialization methods.

At the database level, a subscription to a database replication definition allows Replication Server to replicate database transactions from the primary to the replicate databases. For more information on multi-site availability, please refer to Chapter 13. With MSA, much of the complexity of setting up replication at the individual object level is abstracted. A subscription to a replication definition instructs Replication Server to replicate transactions from the primary database to the replicate database. Subscriptions resemble SQL statements and identify the replication definition (a table replication definition or a function replication definition, or a database replication definition or a publication) and other parameters to identify the information to be replicated to the target database. The object names, ownership, and column datatypes need not be the same in both the primary and replicate sites. With the use of the select statement either in the subscription definition or in a publication definition, a subset of data from the primary table can be replicated to the replicate object. Please note that the subscriptions to a publication definition will not have the select statement. Instead, the publication definition itself will have the select statement. (Publication definitions are discussed in Chapter 9.) Subscriptions are defined at the replicate Replication Server that manages the replicate databases. Once subscriptions are defined they must be known at the primary Replication Server before a replication can be active. See Figure 10-1 for the subscription creation sequence.

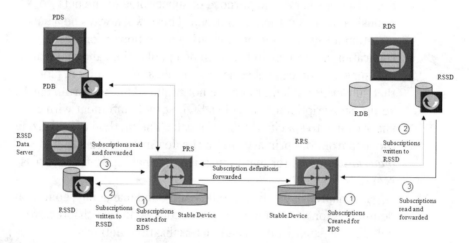

Figure 10-1

Subscription Coordination Process

The major subscription coordination process steps are included in Figure 10-2.

1. Clients apply transactions to the primary database.

2. The primary database is added to the replication system.

3. Replication definitions are defined. Publications may be defined to group replication definitions. The replication definitions or publication definitions with articles are defined at the primary Replication Server.

4. Subscriptions are defined to subscribe to replication or publication definitions. Subscriptions are defined at the replicate Replication Server.

5. Replication, publication, and subscription definitions must be recorded in the target Replication Server before a replication process can become active.

6. Objects must be marked for replication at the primary site. Until the objects are marked for replication, no data is transmitted to the Replication Server.

7. Initial data is applied to the replicate site or also called as "materialized at the replicate site" using an appropriate materialization technique. Materialization methods are discussed later in this chapter. After materializing the initial data, subscriptions are activated to resume normal subscription. Proper *subscription coordination* is essential for proper functioning of the replication system. If replication becomes active before transaction T5 (see Figure 10-2) reaches the destination via materialization, then duplicate transactions will reach the destination. Duplicate transactions can be handled at the replicate site by the use of *autocorrection*. (Autocorrection is discussed later in this chapter.) However, if replication becomes active after transaction T7, then transactions T6 and T7 will not reach the replicate site. Missing transactions are a problem because the primary and replicate will be out of sync. Missing transactions may be synced up using the rs_subcmp Replication Server utility. Depending on the data volume, rs_subcmp may take substantial time.

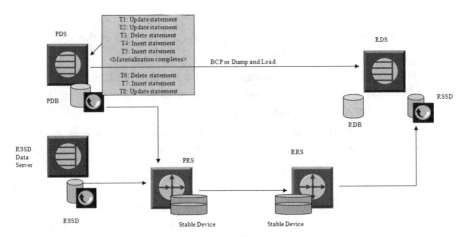

Figure 10-2

Materialization

Materializing a subscription copies the initial data to the destination before the replication becomes active. Subscription creation depends on the materialization method, and the materialization method depends on the application status. Since materialization is the initial data copy, the materialization method will have an impact on the application, network, and success of the replication process.

There are four materialization methods:

▶ Atomic materialization (default)

▶ Nonatomic materialization

▶ No materialization

▶ Bulk materialization

Based on whether or not data changes are allowed in the primary during the materialization process, the materialization is characterized as atomic or nonatomic.

Atomic Materialization

Atomic materialization is the default materialization method. In atomic materialization, no modifications are allowed in the primary while copying table data to the replicate. Replication Server coordinates the select from the primary and the insert into the replicate. Replication Server logs into the primary data server and the replicate data server with the same login that defined subscription definitions. Replication Server performs repeatable reads with the `select with holdlock` operation by issuing the `rs_select_with_lock` function to select the data in one atomic operation. This prevents data updates at the primary site until the select operation is completed. Data is copied to the replicate via network in one atomic operation. Since all the data is copied to the replicate before transactions are allowed in the primary, the replicate data will be consistent with primary data. This materialization method is not suggested if the subscription involves large data to be materialized, as the production processing may be affected for longer durations. The default form of the `create subscription` command provides atomic materialization.

Nonatomic Materialization

Nonatomic materialization is the same as atomic materialization except for the following:

▶ The data is selected from the primary site using `without holdlock` in the `create subscription` command.

▶ The data is incrementally applied at the replicate site.

▶ The transactions are allowed to continue at the primary site.

▶ The nonatomic method of data materialization is not allowed if `replicate minimal columns` is enabled in the replication definitions.

Since the subscription is activated even before the materialization is complete, the data may be applied twice at the replicate site. Duplicate data can be handled using autocorrection. Any queries run on the replicate tables may result in missing data as the primary data is applied incrementally.

No Materialization

If the primary database tables being replicated do not have any data, then you can activate the subscription with no materialization. To create subscriptions with no materialization, use create subscription with the without materialization clause.

Bulk Materialization

The DBA coordinates the data copy to the replicate. Data is copied using any of the bulk copy methods, including bcp or dump/load. This materialization method is appropriate where large amounts of data need to be copied to replicate through the network. This method includes sequence of subscription operations like define, activate, and validate subscription. If you cannot stop activity at the primary database, you can add the with suspension clause to the subscription definition; this will suspend the DSI thread at the replicate site. The bulk data is applied at the replicate data server using methods like dump database and load database. bcp is another bulk materialization method. After applying the data using bulk methods, the DSI can be resumed. Although duplicate transactions are likely to occur at the replicate site, autocorrection can be used to handle the duplicate transactions.

The sequence of operations in bulk materialization is as follows:

1. Define a subscription on one or more table replication or function replication definitions using the define subscription command.

2. If it is possible, you may stop updates on the primary database.

3. Use the activate subscription command to activate one or more subscriptions defined in step 1 above. The last active subscription will include the with suspension clause if updates on the primary are not stopped. This option leaves the DSI for the replicate database suspended.

4. Check the subscription status using the check subscription command. Subscriptions must be active at both the primary and replicate sites before you can continue to the next step.

5. Turn on replication for tables using sp_setreptable. Use sp_setrepfunction for function replication. This makes Replication Agent send the committed transactions to Replication Server. Because there will be matching subscriptions, the data will be forwarded to the destination replication server. Because the replicate database DSI thread is down, the data will not be applied to the replicate database.

6. Take one or more database or transaction log dumps and apply the dumps at the replicate. Continue applying the transaction logs dumps until all transaction log dumps are applied.

7. Resume the DSI connection to resume replication via network.

8. Validate the subscriptions with the validate subscription command.

9. If the processing on the primary data is stopped during subscription materialization, there is no duplicate data problem and autocorrection may not be necessary. Otherwise, autocorrection may be necessary.

Subscription Dematerialization

Materialized subscriptions can be dematerialized. Subscription dematerialization removes subscriptions and the information related to the subscription in the RSSD, both at primary and replicate sites. The materialized data can also be removed.

Subscription dematerialization is achieved by executing the drop subscription command using the with purge or without purge keywords, depending on whether or not you want to remove all the data from the replicate tables. Data materialized via function replication definitions cannot be dematerialized. Function replication data has to be removed manually. Also, if a subscription is materialized using any type of column or class level translations, the data cannot be removed with the drop sub-scription command.

The general syntax for dematerialization is as follows:

```
drop subscription sub_name
for {table_rep_def | function_rep_def |
{article article_name in pub_name |
publication pub_name | database replication definition db_repdef
with primary at data_server.database}
with replicate at data_server.database
[without purge [with suspension
[at active replicate only]] |
[incrementally] with purge]
```

Creating Subscriptions Using Atomic Materialization

Use the create subscription command with or without the where clause to create a subscription for atomic materialization. The create subscription command creates and initializes a subscription and materializes subscription data for a database replication definition, table replication definition, function replication definition, or publication.

The syntax is:

```
create subscription sub_name
for { table_repdef | func_repdef | { publication pub |
    database replication definition db_repdef }
    with primary at server_name.db }
with replicate at data_server.database
    [where {column_name | @param_name}
    {< | > | >= | <= | = | &} value
    [and {column_name | @param_name}
    {< | > | >= | <= | = | &} value]...]
[without holdlock | incrementally | without materialization]
[subscribe to truncate table]
[for new articles]
```

The syntax includes the replication definition name, and the primary and replicate site names.

`without holdlock`

> Data selected from the primary without holding locks for nonatomic materialization. Data is applied at the replicate in increments of 10 row inserts per transaction.

`incrementally`

> Data is applied in increments of 10 row inserts per transaction. A holdlock is used in case of atomic materialization. When you use `create subscription` to create atomic materialization, a holdlock is applied on the primary, and updates to the primary may not be possible.

`without materialization`

> Use this option if your application can suspend updates during materialization and you would like to materialize the data using any other materialization methods such as dump and load.

`subscribe to truncate table`

> With this option the `truncate table` command is also replicated. If a `truncate table` command is issued at the primary, data will be truncated both at primary and at replicate. The maintenance user must be aliased to dbo for the `truncate table` command to be replicated.

`for new articles`

> Refreshes an existing subscription to include newly created articles of a publication for which this subscription was originally created.

Here is an example:

```
create subscription students_sub
  for students_rep
  with replicate at LONDON_DS.reptest1
```

This creates a subscription with atomic materialization. Since it does not use the where clause, it will materialize all of the data in that table using atomic materialization.

```
create subscription students_sub
  for students_rep
  with replicate at LONDON_DS.reptest1
where zipcode = '20171'
```

Since this subscription includes a where clause, only qualified transaction data will be materialized.

In this example, the subscription will be created for the replication definition students_rep. The materialization has to be done manually. This is typically suitable when the primary table is empty or data already exists at the replicate.

```
create subscription students_sub
  for students_rep
  with replicate at LONDON_DS.reptest1
  without materialization
```

Here a subscription is dropped for the replication definition students_rep. The rows materialized with this subscription will be purged.

```
drop subscription students_sub
  for students_rep
  with replicate at LONDON_DS.reptest1
  with purge
```

In this example, a subscription is dropped for the replication definition students_rep. The rows materialized with this subscription will not be purged.

```
drop subscription students_sub
  for students_rep
  with replicate at LONDON_DS.reptest1
  without purge
```

In the example below, a subscription is dropped for the function replication definition update_student_frep. The rows materialized with this subscription will not be purged. When you drop a subscription for a function replication definition, you do not need to specify the with purge or without purge clause.

```
drop subscription students_sub
  for update_student_frep
  with replicate at LONDON_DS.reptest1
```

The following example creates a subscription for a publication definition.

```
create subscription students_sub
  for publication students_pub
  with primary at NYRS_DS.reptest1
  with replicate at LONDON_DS.reptest1
```

The following example drops a subscription for publication without purging the data.

```
drop subscription students_sub
  for publication students_pub
  with primary at NYRS_DS.reptest1
  with replicate at LONDON_DS.reptest1
  without purge
```

The following example is useful for creating a subscription for a replication definition at the database level using multi-site availability (MSA).

```
create subscription students_sub
  for database replication definition students_rep
    with primary at NYRS_DS.reptest1
    with replicate at LONDON_DS.reptest1
  without materialization
  subscribe to truncate table
```

Creating Subscriptions Using Bulk Materialization

The define subscription, activate subscription, and validate subscription commands are used to create bulk materialization subscriptions. Use the check subscription command to verify the status of the subscription process.

The define subscription command always creates a subscription using bulk materialization. There are five steps involved in creating a subscription using bulk materialization:

1. Defining a subscription
2. Activating the subscription
3. Completing the bulk materialization
4. Validating the subscription
5. Verifying the status of the subscription process

Step 1: Define a subscription.

The syntax for defining a subscription is:

```
define subscription sub_name
for { table_rep_def | function_rep_def |
     publication pub_name | database replication definition db_repdef
     with primary at data_server.database } |
with replicate at data_server.database
     [where {column_name | @param_name}
     {< | > | >= | <= | = | &} value
     [and {column_name | @param_name}
     {< | > | >= | <= | = | &} value] ]
[subscribe to truncate table]
[for new articles]
[use dump marker]
```

Where:

sub_name

The subscription name, which must conform to the standard naming conventions for any identifiers.

table_rep_def

> The name of the table replication definition the subscription is for.

function_rep_def

> The name of the function replication definition the subscription is for.

pub_name

> The name of the publication the subscription is for. When a subscription is defined for a publication, the where clause cannot be used. A where clause can be used in the publication definition.

db_repdef

> The name of the database replication definition the subscription is for. Please refer to Chapter 13 for more information on database replication definitions as part of multi-site availability.

with primary at/with replicate at

> These specify the location of the primary and replicate databases.

where

> Specifies the criteria to select qualifying column values or parameter values to replicate. If the where clause is not included, all rows or parameters are replicated. If the minimal columns clause is included in the table replication definition referred to by the subscription definition, only the minimal columns required for replicating the row will be replicated. Please see Chapter 9 for more information on minimal columns.

subscribe to truncate table

> For a table or publication replication definition, this option enables the subscribe to truncate table command. When you create the first subscription for a table replication, this

command is optional. However, any additional subscription definitions referring to the same table must include subscribe to truncate table. Otherwise, new subscription definitions will be rejected. You can use sysadmin apply_truncate_table to turn the option "on" or "off" for all of the subscriptions to a table. It is not necessary for warm standby databases to subscribe to the truncate table. The truncate table command is automatically replicated to standby databases.

use dump marker

This parameter activates and validates a database subscription automatically. If this option is not used, you need to manually activate and validate database subscriptions. Please refer to Chapters 12 and 13 for how to use the dump marker.

Some of the parameters described above also apply to the parameter descriptions for the activate subscription, validate subscription, and check subscription commands.

Here is an example of a subscription definition:

```
define subscription students_sub
  for students_rep
    with primary at NYRS_DS.reptest1
    with replicate at LONDON_DS.reptest1
  subscribe to truncate table
```

This subscription definition subscribes to the truncate table and does not include any materialization. It is expected that the user will use one of the bulk materialization methods to materialize the data from the primary to the replicate database. Subscribing to the truncate table should be carefully considered, as the truncate table will be replicated to the replicate database. After a subscription is defined for a replication definition, you need to activate the subscription.

When a subscription is defined, the subscription status changes to DEFINED. Make sure the status is DEFINED at both the primary and replicate Replication Servers by using the check subscription command. The check subscription command syntax is provided later in this section.

Step 2: Activate the subscription.

The syntax for activating a subscription is:

```
activate subscription sub_name
for { table_rep_def | function_rep_def |
    publication pub_name | database replication definition db_repdef
    with primary at data_server.database }
 with replicate at data_server.database
[with suspension [at active replicate only]]
```

Here is an example:

```
activate subscription students_sub
  for students_rep
    with primary at NYRS_DS.reptest1
    with replicate at LONDON_DS.reptest1
with suspension
```

When a subscription is activated the subscription status changes to ACTIVE. Make sure the status is ACTIVE at both the primary and replicate Replication Servers by using the check subscription command. If you include the with suspension clause, the DSI thread will be suspended upon activating the subscription. This is useful when a manual bulk materialization is required. In order to first apply transactions via bulk copy or dump/load, you can suspend the DSI connection on the replicate side. Thus, the transactions in the replication queues will not be applied until the bulk materialization is completed. If you do not use with suspension, you should consider stopping updates to the primary database.

Step 3: Complete bulk materialization.

If the data to be materialized is small enough, you can define a subscription with materialization. If the subscription is defined with materialization, then data is materialized in the subscription definition process. Otherwise, if the data is large enough that it would take a long time to materialize, you can use one of the bulk materialization techniques like bcp or the dump/load process. If you choose to use bulk materialization techniques, the subscription is defined without materialization and subscription is

activated with suspension. However, autocorrection can be used
to avoid the problem of duplicate row insertion and its associated
Replication Server issues.

Step 4: Validate the subscription.

The next step in the bulk materialization process is to validate
the subscription with the validate subscription command. This
command changes the subscription status to VALID. Use the
check subscription command to verify that the subscription status changes to VALID.

The syntax is:

```
validate subscription sub_name
for { table_ref_def | function_rep_def | publication pub_name |
      database replication definition db_repdef
      with primary at data_server.db }
with replicate at data_server.db
```

Here is an example:

```
validate subscription students_sub
  for students_rep
    with primary at NYRS_DS.reptest1
    with replicate at LONDON_DS.reptest1
```

Step 5: Check the status of the subscription process.

Check the status of the subscription at the Replication Server
where it is defined. You may need to wait a few minutes for the
status to propagate to both the primary and replicate Replication
Servers. You can use the check subscription command at any
step of the subscription creation process.

The syntax is:

```
check subscription sub_name
for { table_rep_def | function_rep_def | publication pub_name |
      database replication definition db_repdef
      with primary at data_server.db }
with replicate at data_server.db
```

For example:

```
check subscription students_sub
   for students_rep
      with primary at NYRS_DS.reptest1
      with replicate at LONDON_DS.reptest1
```

Subscriptions and Autocorrection

As described in the "Subscription Coordination Process" section earlier in this chapter, when transactions arrive at the replicate site while nonatomic materialization is still in process, any updates or inserts to the data at the primary site can result in duplicate rows at the replicate. Autocorrection instructs the Replication Server to delete the previous record and insert the new record. This avoids the duplicate row problem. Use the set autocorrection on option for every one of the replication definitions for which there will be data subscriptions.

The syntax to turn autocorrection on or off is:

```
set autocorrection {on | off}
for replication_definition
with replicate at data_server.database
```

Autocorrection cannot be used when minimal columns is specified in the replication definitions, as a full delete followed by an insert is not possible with minimal columns.

There may be a small performance impact when autocorrection is on. After the data is fully validated and the replication is stable, you may want to turn off autocorrection to improve performance. When autocorrection is turned off, it is possible to add the minimal columns clause to the replication definitions.

Materializing text, unitext, image, and rawobject Data

In general you can use any of the materialization methods to materialize data with text, unitext, image, and rawobject datatypes. However, the preferred method of materialization for these datatypes is bulk materialization. The data for these datatypes tend to be large. If you use atomic materialization, the queue should be big enough to hold a large dataset, but it can take a long time to materialize with this method. If the data row size is larger than 32K, you must use bulk materialization.

If the replication definitions include the `replicate_if_changed` option for these datatypes and if you use nonatomic materialization, Replication Server may generate a warning message. You can use the rs_subcmp utility to identify and optionally reconcile data inconsistencies. Please refer to Chapter 15 for more information on how to use rs_subcmp, and to Chapter 9 for more information on the `replicate_if_changed` option in the replication definitions.

Chapter 11

Functions and Function Strings

Sybase Replication Server is capable of replicating transactions heterogeneously. It provides a set of Replication Server functions that map to data server operations such as insert, delete, update, etc. Replication Server translates the data server operations from the primary data server to the Replication Server functions and transmits these functions to the remote Replication Servers.

Replication Server 15.0 supports the ASE truncate table command with the truncate partition clause. When using rs_truncate, a new function-string variable, ?n!parm?, is available to name the partition. The replicate data server is expected to have a matching portioning scheme with the primary data server. More details on function-string variables are presented later in this chapter.

The remote Replication Server converts Replication Server functions to commands specific to the destination data servers where they are ultimately executed. A *function string* contains the database-specific instructions for executing a function. The replicate Replication Server managing a database uses an appropriate function string to map the function to a set of instructions for the data server. For example, the function string for the rs_insert function provides the actual language to be applied in a replicate database. It is possible to redefine a Replication Server command to a set of SQL commands so that an application-specific result can be achieved. For example, a delete DML operation on the primary can be redefined on the replicate using the rs_delete Replication Server function to simply log the delete command into another table, and then it may either delete the row or perform any another action. It can also log such information as who is attempting to delete the row and the date and time of each delete attempt. In this way Replication Server function strings extend the functionality of the Replication Server. The following shows the Replication Server function strings created as part of the Replication Server 15.0.1 installation.

To list the function strings, use this command:

```
1> select distinct convert(varchar(30), name) from rs_funcstrings
2> go
------------------------------
rs_begin
rs_commit
rs_rollback
rs_setuser
rs_dump
rs_load
rs_get_lastcommit
rs_usedb
rs_marker
rs_get_sortorder
rs_trunc_set
rs_trunc_reset
rs_get_charset
rs_repl_off
rs_triggers_reset
rs_check_repl
rs_get_thread_seq
rs_set_isolation_level
rs_initialize_threads
rs_get_thread_seq_noholdlock
rs_update_threads
rs_setproxy
rs_raw_object_serialization
rs_dsi_check_thread_lock
rs_ticket_report
rs_set_ciphertext
rs_set_dml_on_computed
rs_batch_start
rs_batch_end
rs_repl_on
```

```
rs_update
rs_select
rs_truncate
rs_select_with_lock
rs_insert
rs_delete
pic
rs_datarow_for_writetext
copy

(39 rows affected)
```

A set of function strings grouped together forms a *function-string class*. Replication Server comes with a default set of function-string classes for each of the supported data server types. For example, default function-string classes are available for Sybase ASE, Oracle, DB2, and Informix. The following example shows the default function-string classes installed by Replication Server 15.0.1. You can create derived function-string classes where only a portion of the function strings are inherited from these default function-string classes. The remaining function strings will be either created new or modified from one of the existing function strings.

Use this query to list the default function-string classes:

```
1> select classname from rs_classes
2> go
classname
------------------------------
rs_asa_dt_class
rs_asa_function_class
rs_db2_dt_class
rs_db2_function_class
rs_default_function_class
rs_ims_dt_class
rs_ims_function_class
rs_informix_dt_class
rs_informix_function_class
rs_msss_dt_class
rs_msss_function_class
rs_oracle_dt_class
rs_oracle_function_class
```

```
rs_rs_dt_class
rs_sqlserver_dt_class
rs_sqlserver_error_class
rs_sqlserver_function_class
rs_udb_dt_class
rs_udb_function_class
rs_vsam_dt_class
rs_vsam_function_class

(21 rows affected)
```

You need a function string to manipulate data in the replicate database, including executing stored procedures. If a default function string is not available for an intended operation in the destination data server, a function string has to be created and appropriately instantiated. When a replication system is set up or a database is added to an existing replication system, a default set of function strings is applied by the Replication Server. Depending on the application requirements you may need to customize some of the default function strings or you may need to add new function strings to customize the operations on the replicate database.

Many function strings are included in each of the default function-string classes. The following query gets the number of function strings in the default function-string classes.

```
2> select classname, count(name) from rs_classes c, rs_funcstrings f
3> where c.classid = f.classid
4> group by classname
5>
6> go
classname

----------------------------- -----------
rs_sqlserver_function_class        2/14
rs_db2_function_class               28
rs_default_function_class           30

(3 rows affected)
```

The default Replication Server installation for Sybase ASE comes with function-string classes populated with function strings for

ASE. The following query produces no rows for the Oracle function-string class.

```
1> select * from rs_funcstrings r, rs_classes c
2> where r.classid = c.classid
3> and c.classname = "rs_oracle_function_class"
4> go
```

prsid	classid	funcid	name	fstringid
attributes	parameters	param_hash	expiredate	rowtype	minvers	classname
classid	classtype	prsid	attributes	parent_classid

```
----------- ------------------ ------------------ -------------- ------------------
--------------------- ----------- ----------- ---------------- --------------------
-------- ---------------- ----------- --------------
```

(0 rows affected)

The following query lists the function strings included in the
default function-string classes:

```
1>
2> select convert(varchar(30),classname),
3> convert(varchar(30),name),count(*) from rs_classes c, rs_funcstrings f
4> where c.classid = f.classid
5> group by classname, name
6> order by name
7> go
```

```
------------------------------ ------------------------------- -----------
rs_sqlserver_function_class     copy                                      6
rs_sqlserver_function_class     pic                                       6
rs_db2_function_class           rs_batch_end                              1
rs_default_function_class       rs_batch_end                              1
rs_sqlserver_function_class     rs_batch_end                              1
rs_db2_function_class           rs_batch_start                            1
rs_default_function_class       rs_batch_start                            1
rs_sqlserver_function_class     rs_batch_start                            1
rs_db2_function_class           rs_begin                                  1
rs_default_function_class       rs_begin                                  1
rs_sqlserver_function_class     rs_begin                                  1
rs_db2_function_class           rs_check_repl                             1
rs_default_function_class       rs_check_repl                             1
rs_sqlserver_function_class     rs_check_repl                             1
rs_db2_function_class           rs_commit                                 1
rs_default_function_class       rs_commit                                 1
```

253

rs_sqlserver_function_class	rs_commit	1
rs_sqlserver_function_class	rs_datarow_for_writetext	4
rs_sqlserver_function_class	rs_delete	33
rs_default_function_class	rs_dsi_check_thread_lock	1
rs_sqlserver_function_class	rs_dsi_check_thread_lock	1
rs_db2_function_class	rs_dump	1
rs_default_function_class	rs_dump	1
rs_sqlserver_function_class	rs_dump	1
rs_db2_function_class	rs_get_charset	1
rs_default_function_class	rs_get_charset	1
rs_sqlserver_function_class	rs_get_charset	1
rs_db2_function_class	rs_get_lastcommit	1
rs_default_function_class	rs_get_lastcommit	1
rs_sqlserver_function_class	rs_get_lastcommit	1
rs_db2_function_class	rs_get_sortorder	1
rs_default_function_class	rs_get_sortorder	1
rs_sqlserver_function_class	rs_get_sortorder	1
rs_db2_function_class	rs_get_thread_seq	1
rs_default_function_class	rs_get_thread_seq	1
rs_sqlserver_function_class	rs_get_thread_seq	1
rs_db2_function_class	rs_get_thread_seq_noholdlock	1
rs_default_function_class	rs_get_thread_seq_noholdlock	1
rs_sqlserver_function_class	rs_get_thread_seq_noholdlock	1
rs_db2_function_class	rs_initialize_threads	1
rs_default_function_class	rs_initialize_threads	1
rs_sqlserver_function_class	rs_initialize_threads	1
rs_sqlserver_function_class	rs_insert	33
rs_db2_function_class	rs_load	1
rs_default_function_class	rs_load	1
rs_sqlserver_function_class	rs_load	1
rs_db2_function_class	rs_marker	1
rs_default_function_class	rs_marker	1
rs_sqlserver_function_class	rs_marker	1
rs_db2_function_class	rs_raw_object_serialization	1
rs_default_function_class	rs_raw_object_serialization	1
rs_sqlserver_function_class	rs_raw_object_serialization	1
rs_db2_function_class	rs_repl_off	1
rs_default_function_class	rs_repl_off	1
rs_sqlserver_function_class	rs_repl_off	1
rs_db2_function_class	rs_repl_on	1
rs_default_function_class	rs_repl_on	1
rs_sqlserver_function_class	rs_repl_on	1
rs_db2_function_class	rs_rollback	1

rs_default_function_class	rs_rollback	1
rs_sqlserver_function_class	rs_rollback	1
rs_sqlserver_function_class	rs_select	33
rs_sqlserver_function_class	rs_select_with_lock	33
rs_db2_function_class	rs_set_ciphertext	1
rs_default_function_class	rs_set_ciphertext	1
rs_sqlserver_function_class	rs_set_ciphertext	1
rs_db2_function_class	rs_set_dml_on_computed	1
rs_default_function_class	rs_set_dml_on_computed	1
rs_sqlserver_function_class	rs_set_dml_on_computed	1
rs_db2_function_class	rs_set_isolation_level	1
rs_default_function_class	rs_set_isolation_level	1
rs_sqlserver_function_class	rs_set_isolation_level	1
rs_db2_function_class	rs_setproxy	1
rs_default_function_class	rs_setproxy	1
rs_sqlserver_function_class	rs_setproxy	1
rs_db2_function_class	rs_setuser	1
rs_default_function_class	rs_setuser	1
rs_sqlserver_function_class	rs_setuser	1
rs_default_function_class	rs_ticket_report	1
rs_sqlserver_function_class	rs_ticket_report	1
rs_db2_function_class	rs_triggers_reset	1
rs_default_function_class	rs_triggers_reset	1
rs_sqlserver_function_class	rs_triggers_reset	1
rs_db2_function_class	rs_trunc_reset	1
rs_default_function_class	rs_trunc_reset	1
rs_sqlserver_function_class	rs_trunc_reset	1
rs_db2_function_class	rs_trunc_set	1
rs_default_function_class	rs_trunc_set	1
rs_sqlserver_function_class	rs_trunc_set	1
rs_sqlserver_function_class	rs_truncate	33
rs_sqlserver_function_class	rs_update	33
rs_db2_function_class	rs_update_threads	1
rs_default_function_class	rs_update_threads	1
rs_sqlserver_function_class	rs_update_threads	1
rs_db2_function_class	rs_usedb	1
rs_default_function_class	rs_usedb	1
rs_sqlserver_function_class	rs_usedb	1

(97 rows affected)

DSI Thread and Function Strings

The DSI thread performs many actions. One of the more important actions is handling function strings appropriately based on
the destination data server type and the function string definition.
Following are the actions that the DSI thread performs:

▶ Groups small transactions by commit order.

▶ Maps replication server functions to function strings according
to the function-string class assigned to the data server database connection. The function-string class assigned to the
database connection depends on the destination data server
type. For example, a DB2 data server connection may get
DB2-specific function strings.

▶ Executes the transactions in the replicate database.

▶ Handles errors:

   ▶ Takes action on any errors returned by the data server
   depending on the assigned error actions.

   ▶ Logs errors in the error log and exception log depending
   on the error.

   ▶ Takes a default or mapped action for the errors returned
   by the data server.

Managing Function Strings

Every replication definition has its own set of inherited function
strings. These function strings have replication definition scope,
which means that the default data modification functions like
rs_insert, rs_delete, and rs_update will only affect the table referenced by the replication definition. Transaction controlling
function strings like rs_begin, rs_commit, and rs_rollback have
function-string class scope. Function strings with class scope can
be manipulated directly and have nothing to do with replication
definitions or data modifications. They are typically a single command. For example, rs_begin maps to begin tran.

The sequence of operations in managing function strings with replication definition scope is as follows:

1. Create a replication definition for a table.

2. Create a user-defined function for a function replication definition, if required.

3. Modify a function string. As every replication definition is automatically provided with a set of system-defined function strings, you can modify them with appropriate output language.

4. You can customize a function string either in the system-provided default function-string class `rs_sqlserver_function_class` by using the `alter function string` command, or by modifying the function string in a derived function-string class using the `create function string` command.

5. For each of the base or derived function-string classes, you must alter the function string to change the behavior of the inherited or newly added function strings.

6. Assign the function-string class to the destination data server connection.

Creating a User-defined Function

A user-defined function is mapped to a function replication definition and is automatically created. You do not need to create a user-defined function unless specific action is required for your application beyond the scope of what the Replication Server provides when you create a function replication definition. However, if you plan to use asynchronously delivered stored procedures associated with table replication definitions, you may need to create a user-defined function. Use the `create function replication_definition` command to create a function replication definition that also creates a user-defined function. Please refer to Chapter 9 for more information on creating function replication definitions and stored procedure replication.

Creating a Function-String Class

The Replication Server command create function string class creates a new, empty function-string class. Function-string classes are groups of function strings and are applied for a database. All of the function strings in a function-string class are assigned to a database connection using the create connection or alter connection command.

```
create function string class function_class
    [set parent to parent_class]
```

Where:

function_class

is the function string class name. The function-string class name must be unique to the replication system.

set parent to *parent_class*

Use this clause to inherit the function strings from one of the system-provided default function-string classes. For example, for Adaptive Server Enterprise the system-provided function-string classes are rs_sqlserver_function_class and rs_default_function_class. These function-string classes are the same, except that rs_sqlserver_function_class, unlike rs_defailt_function_class, cannot be used as a parent class. If you need to customize function strings, use only rs_sqlserver_function_class. Function strings in the rs_default_function_class cannot be customized.

If you omit the set parent to clause, you will be creating a base function-string class that will not inherit any function strings from any parent function-string class. You will need to add all of the system function strings to this newly created empty base function-string class. You can also add more customized function strings, and you can use this base function-string class as a parent class for future derived classes.

Here is an example:

```
1> create function string class reptest_fs
2> set parent to rs_sqlserver_function_class
3> go
Msg 15326, Level 12, State 0:
Server 'JDBCD05A_REP':
rs_sqlserver_function_class cannot be a parent class

1> create function string class repbook_function_class
2>  set parent to rs_default_function_class
3>
4> go
Function string class 'repbook_function_class' is created.
```

Function strings can only be modified in the rs_sqlserver_function_class. Create this function-string class in the primary Replication Server, then use the move primary command to move this function class to the Replication Server in the same domain where you want to modify the function strings belonging to rs_sqlserver_function_class. The site where you create this function class is the primary site by default.

```
1> create function string class rs_sqlserver_function_class
2> go
Function string class 'rs_sqlserver_function_class' is created.
```

If you try to use the move command in the same Replication Server where you created the function-string class, you will get an error message.

```
1> move primary of function string class rs_sqlserver_function_class to
JDBCD05A_REP
2> go
Msg 15181, Level 12, State 0:
Server 'JDBCD05A_REP':
This site is already the primary site for 'rs_sqlserver_function_class'.
```

By using a system-generated function-string class as parent, the derived function-string class can inherit as many function strings from the parent as you want. You may then modify some of them as you like or add new function strings.

Creating a Function String

Use the create function string command to create and add a function string to a function-string class.

The syntax of the create function string command is:

```
create function string
    [replication_definition.]function[;function_string]
    for function_class [with overwrite]
    [scan 'input_template']
    [output
    {language 'lang_output_template' |
    rpc 'execute procedure
    [@param_name=]{constant | ?variable!mod?}
        [, [@param_name=]
            {constant | ?variable!mod?}]...' |
    writetext [use primary log | with log |
        no log] |
    none}]
```

Where:

replication_definition

> The function string named by *function* operates on the specified replication definition name. The replication definition name is required only for the function strings with replication definition scope. Function strings can have either replication-definition scope or function-string class scope. Transaction control functions such as rs_begin and rs_commit have function-string class scope. User-defined functions and functions that perform data modifications such as DML statements like rs_insert, rs_update, and rs_delete have replication-definition scope.

function

> Name of either user-defined or system-defined function.

function_string

> The function string name. A function string is required for
> every one of the text or image datatype columns in the repli-
> cation definition.

function_class

> The name of the function-string class (a group). The function
> string is associated with this function class.

with overwrite

> This is equivalent to alter function string. It drops the
> function string, if one exists, and recreates it.

scan and *input template*

> The scan directive is used with input templates to associate
> the where clause in the create subscription command to the
> Replication Server function strings rs_select and
> rs_select_with_lock. The input template can be modified to
> create additional user-defined variables that can be used in
> the output template.

output, language, and *lang_output_template*

> These refer to the output template and suggest which lan-
> guage to use to develop a string of output sequence enclosed
> by a single quote and how the command would be modified if
> required before submitting it to the data server for execution.
> The output template is executable SQL code provided to the
> destination data server. You can modify the behavior of the
> system-defined or user-defined function string in the output
> template. For example, the rs_delete function can be modi-
> fied to simply ignore all the delete operations belonging to
> the entire replication system if the default rs_delete function
> string is modified in the system-provided function-string
> class. Likewise, it can ignore delete operations in a particular
> replication definition or user-defined function if the rs_delete
> function string is modified in a derived or in a new base func-
> tion-string class. If you have created a base function-string

class, then you must have manually added all of the system and user-defined function strings to it.

See the following examples:

Whenever a delete is performed in the primary database employee table, you can ignore the delete.

```
alter function string employee_rep.rs_delete
for sqlserver_derived_class
output ''
```

Whenever a delete is performed in the primary database employee table, you can execute a stored procedure in the replicate database that records who is attempting to delete and any other details available in the input template of this function. You can also use global variables.

```
alter function string employee_rep.rs_delete
for sqlserver_derived_class
output rpc
'execute record_emp_delete
@employee_id=?employee_id!old?'
```

Execute the `create function string` command to create a modified rs_delete function string at the primary Replication Server where the function-string class repbook_function_class was originally created.

```
1> create function string JDBCD05A_SYB_titles_rep.rs_delete for
repbook_function_class
2> output rpc
3> 'execute record delete
4> @who_deleted = ?rs_origin user!sys?,
5> @what table = "titles",
6> @what_deleted = ?title_id!old?'
7>
8> go
Function string 'rs_delete' is created.
1>
```

To determine the function strings mapped to a function class and assigned to a connection, query the RSSD system tables, as shown.

```
1> select t.textval from rs_classes c, rs_funcstrings s, rs_systext t,
rs_databases d
2> where c.classname = 'repbook_function_class'
3> and c.classid = s.classid
4> and s.fstringid = t.parentid
5> and d.dsname = 'LONDON_DS'
6> and d.dbname = 'pubs2'
7> and d.prsid = t.prsid
8> go
textval

 --------------------------------------------------------------------------
 --------------------------------------------------------------------------
 --------------------------------------------------------------------------
 ------------------------------
execute record_deletes
   @who_deleted = ?rs_origin_user!sys?,
   @what_table = "rep_test",
   @what_deleted = ?id!old?
```

The output template of the above function string provides the "old" value (before image) of the employee_id to the stored procedure as an argument. In the case of a delete, the new and old values will be the same. In the case of an update operation, the old and new values will be different and only the old value will be useful in identifying the original record.

On the primary database:

```
1> select * from rep_test
2> go
 id         name
 ----------- -----------------------------
         2 Sam
         3 Gerry
         4 Jay
         9 Anita

1> insert into rep_test values (10, 'Smith')
2> go

1> select * from rep_test
2> go
```

```
id          name
----------- -----------------------------
          2 Sam
          3 Gerry
          4 Jay
          9 Anita
         10 Smith

1> delete from rep_test where id = 10
2> go
(1 row affected)

1> select * from rep_test
2> go
 id          name
 ----------- -----------------------------
           2 Sam
           3 Gerry
           4 Jay
           9 Anita

(4 rows affected)
```

Check on the replicate. The record with ID 10 should not be deleted, but the attempt must be recorded in the table delete_history via the record_deletes stored procedure, which in turn is mapped to the JDBCD05A_SYB.pubs2 connection. This connection is altered to set the function class with the modified function string. This function string executes the record_deletes stored procedure as an output string.

```
1> select * from rep_test
2> go
 id          name
 ----------- -----------------------------
           2 Sam
           3 Gerry
           4 Jay
           9 Anita
          10 Smith

(5 rows affected)
```

264

```
1> select * from delete_history
2> go
id            who_deleted    what_table    what_deleted   when_deleted
------------- -------------- ------------- -------------- -----------------------
            1 sa             rep_test                 10  Nov 4 2007 10:41PM
(1 row affected)
1>
```

As you may notice, the delete attempt is recorded in the delete_history table.

Here is an example of inserting a record in a history table as well as in the replicate table:

```
create function string employee_rep.rs_insert
for sqlserver2_function_class
output language
''insert student values (?employee_id!new?,
?employee_name!new?, ?dept_name!new?, ?pay_day!new?,
?advance!new?, ?gross_salary!new?, ?net_salary!new?)';

create function string employee_rep.rs_insert
for sqlserver2_function_class
output language
'insert student_history values (?employee_id!new?,
?employee_name!new?, ?dept_name!new?, ?pay_day!new?,
?advance!new?, ?gross_salary!new?, ?net_salary!new?)'';
```

When multiple commands are batched, the DSI connection must be altered to allow command batching. The default is "on".

```
alter connection to ASE01_DS.emp_db
set batch to 'on'
```

Function strings limitlessly extend the possibilities with Replication Server.

Assigning a Function-String Class to a Connection

After creating a function string and adding that function string to a function-string class, the function-string class needs to be associated to a database connection. If you have created a derived or new base function-string class and have modified certain function strings in that class, you need to associate that class with a database connection for the modified function string translations to occur. This is shown in the following code:

```
alter connection to data_server.database
set function string class [to] function_class
```

```
1> alter connection to LONDON_DS.pubs2 set function string class to
repbook_function_class
2> go
Connection to 'LONDON_DS.pubs2' is altered.
```

You must suspend the connection, alter the connection, and resume the connection in sequence for changes to the connection to take effect.

Dropping a Function String

Dropping a function string can have a cascading effect. For example, if you drop a customized function string from rs_sqlserver_function_class, Replication Server drops not only the customized function string but also the default function string. To revert the customized function string to the default function string for a function in the rs_sqlserver_function_class, use alter function string with the without output clause. To modify an existing function string, use the alter function string command with required parameters.

If you drop the function itself, all function strings associated with that function will be dropped from all of the function classes.

See drop `function` in the Sybase Replication Server Reference Manual for more details.

The general syntax to drop a function string is:

```
drop function string
[replication_definition.]function[;function_string | all]
for function_class
```

Where:

replication_definition

> The name of the replication definition on which the function operates.

function

> The system- or user-defined function, such as rs_delete.

function_string

> The name of the function string to drop. By default the function name is the function string name as well.

all

> The keyword all drops all the function strings associated with this function. Even though a function will typically have just one function string, except for the functions rs_select, rs_select_with_lock, rs_datarow_for_writetext, rs_get_textptr, rs_textptr_init, and rs_writetext. However, all can be used as shorthand for the function string name.

function_class

> The function string to drop belongs to this function-string class.

Example 1:

Drop the rs_insert function string from the function-string class sqlserver2_function_class. The sqlserver2_function_class is a derived function-string class or a user-created base class.

Dropping the function string `rs_insert` from `sqlserver2_function_class` will not have any impact on its parent function class.

```
drop function string
employee_rep.rs_insert
for sqlserver2_function_class
```

Dropping a customized function string from a derived function class will restore the default function string from its parent function class.

Example 2:

Drop all of the function strings for a function.

```
drop function string
employee_rep.rs_select_with_lock; all
for sqlserver2_function_class
```

In the above case, `rs_select_with_lock` has more than one function string to drop, which is why `all` is used. Keep in mind that you can use `all` to drop any function, whether it has one or more than one function string.

Dropping a Function

Only user-defined functions can be dropped. Note that you cannot drop system-provided functions. Dropping a function drops related function strings from all of the function classes. Also, a function will be dropped from all of the replication definitions for that table if you a drop a function for a replication definition.

```
drop function [replication_definition.]function
```

Where:

```
replication_definition
```

Replication definition name a function is dropped for.

268

function

> User-defined function name.

Use this syntax to drop functions for table replication definitions. If you want to drop replicated functions, use `drop function replication definition` instead.

Dropping a Function-String Class

You can drop an entire function-string class. Dropping a function-string class drops all the function strings associated with the function class. You cannot drop the system-provided function classes for ASE — `rs_sqlserver_function_class`, `rs_default_function_class`, and `rs_db2_function_class`. Also, a function class that is still in use cannot be dropped. Use the `alter connection` command to disassociate the function class from all database connections before you drop the function-string class. A parent class cannot be dropped unless all of the derived function classes from this parent class are dropped.

The general syntax to drop the function-string class is:

```
drop function string class function_class
```

Here's an example:

```
drop function string class sqlserver2_function_class
```

Function strings extend the abilities of the Sybase Replication Server. Sybase Replication Server is a unique product with a modular design where instructions from the primary site can be modified at the replicate site.

Chapter 12

Warm Standby

Replication Server may be used to maintain a backup copy (warm standby) of an Adaptive Server database that applications can switch to in the event of a hardware crash, software error, or maintenance to the primary database. The warm standby system consists of state-consistent active and standby Adaptive Server databases connected by a single Replication Server. Latency between the active and standby databases is the difference in time between when transactions were applied at the active database and when they reach the standby database. During the latency period, transactions may be waiting in the transaction log to be read by Replication Agent, traversing the network, waiting for processing in the Replication Server stable queue, or waiting to be applied at the standby. Warm standby setup is only supported for Sybase Adaptive Server Enterprise databases; it is not supported for non-Sybase (heterogeneous databases).

Warm Standby vs. Hot Standby System

In a hot standby system, both copies of the database are in synchronization at all times. There is no data loss when a hardware crash or other failure occurs. Client applications can be switched over to the standby database transparently or with minimal delay. The hot standby system can be a hardware solution or can be implemented with software using the two-phase commit protocol.

Although there is no latency with a hot standby solution, it does have some limitations. For example, both the active and standby databases should be in close proximity, which makes the system susceptible to site failures. In addition, disk structure corruption will most likely be duplicated to a hardware maintained standby database, and performance of the application can degrade substantially as locks may have to be held in both the active and standby databases during the entire transaction. This is inherently costly due to the number of messages and components that must work together synchronously.

The warm standby system involves some latency. Warm standby solutions allow the primary and standby to be in geographically different locations, so that the system can survive site failures. Since the standby is updated asynchronously, the warm standby system can perform better than the two-phase commit system. Warm standby can be maintained using Replication Server or by dumping the transaction log on the active database and then loading it at the standby database.

The dumping and loading of transaction logs implies latency greater than that of Replication Server. Latency when applied to transaction logs with dump/load can be in minutes or hours, which means there will be more data loss when the active database fails. There is also a risk of copying software errors (page chain corruption) with a dump/load transaction log dump. Additionally, when the transaction log is applied at the standby database, the database is undergoing recovery and therefore is not available for access.

Replication Server applies logical connections and doesn't propagate corrupt page chains. It can also provide minimal latency because Replication Server applies transactions as soon as they commit. Thus, the average amount of data that is lost will tend to be less.

Hardware-implemented hot standby and Replication Server maintained warm standby can coexist and will provide more fault tolerance than either option alone.

Warm Standby Components

In Figure 12-1, the active primary pds_a.pdb and standby primary pds_b.pdb are primary logical connections. The active replicate rds_a.rdb and standby replicate rds_b.rdb are replicate logical connections.

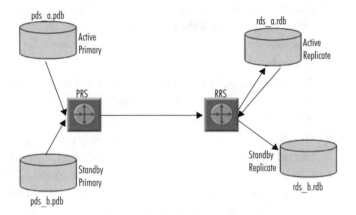

Figure 12-1

In this warm standby setup, clients execute a transaction in the active (primary) database, RepAgent in the primary database scans and forwards transactions from the primary database trans-action log to the primary Replication Server (PRS), and PRS executes these transactions in the standby (primary). PRS also copies these transactions to the replicate Replication Server (RRS), which executes transactions in the active replicate and also gets transactions from the active replicate and executes them in the standby replicate.

A warm standby system consists of a pair of Adaptive Server Enterprise databases controlled by a single Replication Server. The following are components of the warm standby system:

▶ **Active database:** Clients connect to this Adaptive Server Enterprise database.

▶ **Standby database:** An online copy of the active database on a separate Adaptive Server Enterprise on a different host machine. It is not required that the active and standby databases be separate host machines, but it reduces the likelihood of a single point of failure.

▶ **Database connections:** Physical connection for active database, physical connection for standby database, and logical connection for the active and standby databases. The logical connection is mapped by Replication Server to the active database and copies transactions from the active to the standby database.

▶ **Replication Server:** RepAgent from the active database forwards all the transactions to Replication Server, and then Replication Server forwards them to the standby database.

▶ **RepAgent:** Each database can have only one RepAgent thread. RepAgent scans the active database transaction log to find transactions that are marked for replication and forwards them to the Replication Server using LTL (Log Transfer Language). RepAgent also maintains a secondary truncation point in the transaction log; transactions before the secondary truncation point are not truncated until they are transferred to the Replication Server stable device. On the standby database, RepAgent is enabled for switchover but is not started. During switchover, RepAgent is stopped on the active database and started on the standby database.

▶ **Switchover** is a process in which the direction of replication is changed between the active and standby databases. During switchover, all remaining transactions from the active database are executed in the standby database by Replication Server. The old standby database becomes the new active, and the old active becomes the new standby database. As switchover is not automatic, manual intervention is needed in switching client connections. Switchover is covered in detail at the end of this chapter.

Keep in mind that warm standby is not the same as physical backup. You need to test your backup and recovery procedures. The standby database is closely consistent with the active database, but it may not be identical at any given point of time. If the active fails, you can lose some transactions, depending on how far behind RepAgent was in reading the transaction log. You will need to reconnect the application to standby, depending on your switchover method. You need to code your application carefully to check whether the most recent transactions are already being applied successfully before continuing.

Regular Replication vs. Warm Standby

The following table points out the differences between regular replication and warm standby.

Table 12-1

Regular Replication	Warm Standby
Complex setup; should be designed carefully for performance and maintenance.	Easy to set up and easy to maintain.
Primary and replicate databases can be non-Sybase (heterogeneous replication).	Both primary and replicate databases should be Adaptive Server Enterprise databases.
Primary and replicate databases can be managed by the same or different Replication Servers.	Both active and standby databases should be managed by the same Replication Server.
Data can replicate one way or both ways (should be planned carefully).	Data can only replicate from the active database to the standby database.
Table-level replication definitions and subscriptions are required.	No need for table-level replication definitions, but they can be created to improve performance. Subscriptions are not required.
Supports routes, function strings, and split workload/peer-to-peer replication. Function-string classes can be used by the connection to the replicate database, in which customized function-string classes can be used. For example, the derived class that inherits function strings from rs_default_function_class can be used.	Doesn't support routes, function strings, or split workload/peer-to-peer replication. The function-string class rs_default_function_class can be used by the connection to the standby database.
Logical connection not required.	Logical connection required.
Replicates only DML.	Replicates both DML and DDL.

Regular Replication	Warm Standby
Maintenance user transactions are not replicated, meaning RepAgent does not forward maintenance user transactions to the Replication Server to be executed in the replicate Replication Server.	All user transactions including maintenance user transactions are forwarded by RepAgent in the active database to the Replication Server to be executed in the standby database.

Data Modification Language (DML)

The insert, update, delete, and truncate table commands are replicated to standby. You can alter the logical connection to disable replication of the truncate table command.

```
alter logical connection to logical_DS.logical_DB
set send_truncate_table to 'off'
```

The default is "on".

Although select into is also an unlogged command like truncate table, it is not replicated, because row values are not logged in the transaction log. Therefore, RepAgent has no means for forwarding these changes to Replication Server. The truncate table command is replicated because data from the entire table is deleted without regard to row values.

Data Definition Language (DDL)

As mentioned earlier, warm standby supports replication of both DML and DDL. When a database object's schema is changed, the schema changes are logged in a process called schema versioning to ensure that each replicated data record uses the correct object schema. Schema versioning is automatic. When an object's schema is modified, its schema is logged in the database transaction log. When RepAgent encounters a row that uses the old schema, it reads the schema from the database transaction log to determine the row format.

If the master database is set up for replication, then only login, password, and role changes are replicated to the standby master database. For master database replication, both the source and the target Adaptive Server should be 15.0 ESD2 or later. Both the source and the target Adaptive Servers must have the same operating system and hardware architecture (32-bit and 64-bit versions are compatible).

Table 12-2 lists the supported Transact SQL commands and the system stored procedures from the master database. Only these system commands and system stored procedures can be replicated from the master database.

Table 12-2

alter role	create role
drop role	grant role
revoke role	sp_displaylogin
sp_addlogin	sp_droplogin
sp_locklogin	sp_modifylogin
sp_password	sp_passwordpolicy
sp_role	

For user databases, all system commands and system stored procedures that create, alter, or drop database objects are supported. System stored procedures related to user and group information are replicated.

Table 12-3 lists the replicated Transact SQL commands and the system stored procedures from user databases.

Table 12-3

alter key	alter table	create default	create index
create key	create plan	create procedure	create rule
create schema	create table	create trigger	create view
drop default	drop index	drop procedure	drop rule
drop table	drop trigger	drop view	grant
installjava	remove java	revoke	
sp_addalias	sp_addgroup	sp_addmessage	sp_addqpgroup
sp_addtype	sp_adduser	sp_bindefault	sp_bindmsg
sp_bindrule	sp_changegroup	sp_chgattribute	sp_commonkey
sp_config_rep_agent	sp_dropalias	sp_drop_all_qpplans	sp_dropuser
sp_encryption	sp_export_qpgroup	sp_foreignkey	sp_import_qpgroup
sp_primarykey	sp_procxmode	sp_recompile	sp_rename
sp_renameqpgroup	sp_setrepcol	sp_setrepdefmode	sp_setrepproc
sp_setreptable	sp_unbindefault	sp_unbindmsg	sp_unbindrule

Table 12-4 lists the system commands and the system stored procedures that are not replicated.

Table 12-4

select into	update statistics
fast bcp	reorg rebuild
sp_addlogin (if master database is not set up for replication)	sp_droplogin (if master database is not set up for replication)
sp_modifylogin (if master database is not set up for replication)	sp_configure

Minimally logged commands are not replicated, with the only exception being the truncate table command, which is replicated by default. Manual DML statements against the system tables are not replicated.

Table 12-5 lists the default users and the default passwords.

Table 12-5

User	Login Name	Password
ID Server user	idservername_id_user	idservername_id_user_passwd
RSSD primary user	rsname_rssdname_prim	rsname_rssdname_prim_ps
RSSD maintenance user	rssdname_maint	rssdname_maint_ps
RSSD RepAgent user	rssdname_ra	rssdname_ra_ps
Active database RepAgent user	rsname_ra	rsname_ra_ps
Active/standy maintenance user	dbname_maint	dbname_maint_ps

Enabling Replication to Standby Database

Replication to standby databases can be enabled in two ways — with `sp_reptostandby` and with `sp_setreptable`.

▶ **sp_reptostandby:** This system stored procedure can be used to mark the warm standby database for replication. It enables replication of DDL (Data Definition Language) commands, system stored procedures, and DML (Data Modification Language) commands to the standby database. Once the database has been marked with `sp_reptostandby`, replication for individual database objects cannot be turned off, but `set replication` can be used on the session level to control replication of individual database objects. When a database is marked for replication with `sp_reptostandby`, text/image/unitext columns are set to `replicate_if_changed`. Note that their replication cannot be changed to `always_replicate` or `do_not_replicate`. For databases with large tables holding text/image/unitext columns, marking with `sp_reptostandby` takes exclusive-table lock and can take a long time. To speed up the process, the `use_index` clause of `sp_reptostandby` should be used, which creates an internal non-clustered index on each text/image/unitext column of the table. An index is created on the text pointer in the data row. A shared-table lock is held while the index is created. These internal non-clustered indexes cannot be dropped with the `drop index` command; they are dropped automatically when tables and text/image/unitext columns are unmarked for replication.

```
sp_reptostandby dbname [,'L1' | 'all' | 'none'][, 'use_index']
```

L1

This option sets the schema replication feature to the support level introduced in Adaptive Server version 12.0.

All

The schema replication feature support level is set to the current Adaptive Server. If Adaptive Server is upgraded,

the support level implemented by the later version of
Adaptive Server is enabled automatically.

The database is unmarked for replication.

use_index

The database is marked to use a non-clustered index for
replication of text, image, unitext, and rawobject
columns.

▶ **sp_setreptable:** You can also mark individual tables for replication with sp_setreptable instead of sp_reptostandby. When
tables are marked with sp_setreptable, only DML commands
can be replicated. By default, the replication status for text/
image/unitext columns is set to always_replicate. It can be set
to replicate_if_changed or do_not_replicate with the
sp_setrepcol system stored procedure. To speed up this process, the use_index option of sp_setreptable/sp_setrepcol
should be used. Please refer to Chapter 9 for more information
on replicating text/image/unitext columns.

You can also replicate user stored procedures to the standby database. To replicate stored procedures, mark them with
sp_setrepproc. Only the execution of stored procedures and their
parameters are replicated to the standby database.

Syntax:

```
sp_setrepproc procname, 'function'
```

User stored procedures that perform DML changes should be
marked for replication. If you are creating an object in the stored
procedure that is marked for replication and then inserting/delet-
ing/updating data in that newly created object in the same stored
procedure, inserts/updates/deletes done on that object may fail
with the error message because the newly created object doesn't
exist on the standby database.

If the DML changes these stored procedures refer to are
objects that are created by these procedures, then errors are
raised by Replication Server because the objects do not exist in

the standby. User stored procedures from the master database are not replicated. If stored procedures are not marked for replication, then results of the execution (DML changes) of these stored procedures can be replicated to the standby database if the affected tables are marked for replication. User stored procedures should be marked for replication in the active database, and then the active database dump should be loaded into the standby database; this way, the stored procedure should be marked for replication in both the active and standby databases. If the stored procedure is created after materialization, then sp_setrepproc is replicated to the standby database when it is executed in the active database. If the stored procedure calls other stored procedures, then all stored procedures should be marked for replication with sp_setreproc. When a stored procedure is marked for replication, begin transaction and end transaction are wrapped around each stored procedure execution by Adaptive Server. Stored procedures should be coded to use savepoints instead of nested begin transaction and end transaction commands to ensure that commit and rollback are processed correctly.

For example:

```
if @@trancount=0
begin transaction  myproc
else
save transaction myproc
```

The Adaptive Server system variable @@trancount is incremented by each begin transaction and decremented by each save transaction. Stored procedures are executed by the maintenance user on the standby site. Table names used in stored procedure code should be fully qualified (e.g., dbname.dbo.tabname). Tables should be created by the dbo, and the maintenance user should be aliased to the dbo. As mentioned earlier, Adaptive Server wraps begin transaction and end transaction commands around execution of replicated stored procedures. For replication of stored procedures that perform DDL changes, the database option ddl_in_tran should be set to "true" in the active database, as shown below:

```
sp_dboption dbname,'ddl_in_tran', true
```

Setting Up Warm Standby

Warm standby can be set up with rs_init or Sybase Central. Before setting up warm standby, a single Replication Server that is going to manage both the active and standby databases should be installed and running. Please refer to Chapter 4 for information on installing a Replication Server. Active and standby databases should also be installed on Adaptive Servers managed by two different host machines.

Creating a Logical Connection

A logical connection is a symbolic specification for *dataserver.database*. Replication Server maps logical connections to the current active database. If a logical connection is for an existing physical connection from the Replication Server to the active database, then *dataserver.database* specified in the logical connection should be the same as the data server and database names of the existing connection (see Figure 12-2).

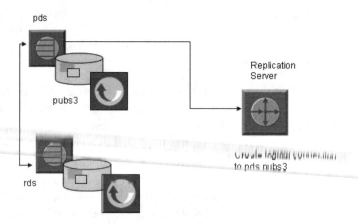

Figure 12-2

If the active database does not exist in the replication system, then the logical connection name can be different from the active or standby databases. It is recommended that the logical connection name be different.

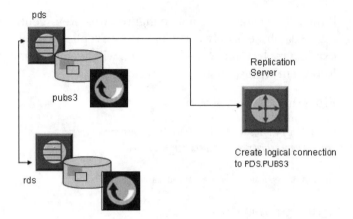

Figure 12-3

Here is the syntax:

```
create logical connection to dataserver.database
```

Example:

```
1> create logical connection to PDS.PUBS3
2> go
Logical connection to 'PDS.PUBS3' is created.
```

Adding the Active Database

If the active database already exists in the replication system, i.e., it is already replicating to another database, then creating a logical connection stops the RepAgent. You will need to reconfigure RepAgent for sending warm standby transactions.

From the active database:

```
sp_config_rep_agent dbname, 'send_warm_standby_xacts', 'true'
```

Then start RepAgent:

```
sp_start_rep_agent dbname
```

If the active database is not configured with RepAgent, i.e., the active database is only participating as a replicate database in an existing replication system, then you will need to configure RepAgent with `sp_config_rep_agent`.

From the active database:

```
sp_config_rep_agent dbname, 'enable', 'repserver_name',
'repserver_username', 'repserver_password'

sp_config_rep_agent dbname, 'send_warm_standby_xacts', 'true'

sp_start_rep_agent dbname
```

Example:

```
1> sp_config_rep_agent 'pubs3', 'enable', 'prs', 'prs_ra', 'prs_ra_ps'
2> go

1> sp_config_rep_agent pubs3, 'send_warm_send_xacts', 'true'
2> go

1> sp_start_rep_agent pubs3
2> go
```

For the complete `sp_config_rep_agent` syntax, refer to Chapter 6.

If an active database is not part of an existing replication system, then the database can be added to the replication system with rs_init or Sybase Central. If you add a database for warm standby setup using rs_init, the rs_init automatically configures the RepAgent for sending warm standby transactions. The rs_init Database Information window with the user inputs for a logical database setup is shown below.

```
DATABASE INFORMATION

1.  SQL Server name:  pds
2.  SA user:  sa
3.  SA password:
4.  Database name:  pubs3
5.  Will the database be replicated:  yes

6.  Maintenance user:  pubs3_maint
7.  Maintenance password:  pubs3_maint_ps
8.  Is this a Physical Connection for Existing Logical Connection: yes
9.  Logical DB Setup                                      Complete
        1.  Is this an Active Connection or Standby Connection: active
        2.  Logical DS Name: PDS
        3.  Logical DB Name: PUBS3




Ctrl-a Accept and Continue, Ctrl-x Exit Screen, ? Help.

Enter the number of your choice and press return:
```

Database Information:

▶ **SQL Server name:** Name of Adaptive Server Enterprise on which the active database resides.

▶ **SA user:** sa login

▶ **SA password:** Password for SA

▶ **Database name:** Active database name. For the warm standby replication system, both the active and standby databases should have the same name.

▶ **Will the database be replicated:** For configuring RepAgent, select "yes".

▶ **Maintenance user:** Default is databasename_maint.

▶ **Maintenance password:** Default is databasename_maint_ps. It is recommended that you change the password and encrypt it for production.

▶ **Is this a physical Connection for Existing Logical Connection:** A logical connection should be created before adding
the active database to the replication system.

Logical Connection Information:

▶ **Is this an Active Connection or Standby Connection:** For
an active database connection, enter "active".

▶ **Logical DS Name:** Logical data server name, defined with
the create logical connection command.

▶ **Logical DB Name:** Logical database name, defined with the
create logical connection command.

Enabling Replication in Active Database

You can enable replication in the active database for the warm
standby replication system in either of two ways — with
sp_reptostandby or sp_setreptable. Additionally, you can replicate
stored procedure executions with sp_setrepproc.

▶ **sp_reptostandby:** sp_reptostandby marks the entire database
for replication, and both DML and DDL replication is enabled.
Only user tables are replicated. Owner information is automatically replicated.

```
use active_db

sp_reptostandby dbname [, 'L1' | 'all' | 'none'][, 'use_index']
```

L1

This option sets the schema replication feature to the
support level introduced in Adaptive Server version 12.0.

all

The schema replication feature support level is set to the
current Adaptive Server. If Adaptive Server is upgraded,
the support level implemented by the later version of
Adaptive Server is enabled automatically.

This option unmarks the database for replication.

use_index

When use_index is used to mark the database, an internal index is created and used for replication on text, unitext, image, and rawobject columns.

```
1> use pubs3
2> go
1> sp_reptostandby pubs3, 'all', 'use_index'
2> go
(1 row affected)

The replication status for database 'pubs3' has been set to 'ALL'.
(return status = 0)
```

▶ **sp_setreptable**: Individual tables can be marked for replication with sp_setreptable. You will need to mark each individual table. This only enables DML replication. DDL for a particular table can be replicated only on the session level by using the set replication command (set replication needs sa_role and dbo permissions and replication_role).

set replication force_ddl

To turn off DDL replication:

set replication default

If tables with the same name exist in the active and standby databases but are owned by different owners, then the owner_on clause should be used to mark the table for replication.

sp_setreptable *tabname*, 'true', owner_on

```
1> use pubs3
2> go
1> sp_setreptable titles, 'true', 'owner_on'
2> go
```

- **sp_setrepproc:** To replicate stored procedure executions, each stored procedure should be marked for replication.

  ```
  sp_setrepproc proc_name, 'function'
  ```

  If stored procedures are associated with table replication definitions, then each stored procedure whose execution you want to replicate to standby should be marked with sp_setrepproc. For more information on stored procedure replication, please refer to Chapter 9.

  ```
  sp_setrepproc proc_name, 'table'
  ```

  If a database was marked with sp_reptostandby, then all new objects added after enabling replication are automatically marked for replication. If individual tables were marked for replication, then new tables added after enabling replication should be marked for replication with sp_setreptable. Similarly, each new stored procedure that is added should also be marked for replication with sp_setrepproc.

Adding the Standby Database

The standby database should be created before it is added to the warm standby replication system. Logical device and segment names should be the same as in the active database; otherwise, the on clause of create table and create index will fail on standby. The cache name and size must also be identical in both the active and standby servers. You cannot use the for load clause to create the standby database. Only the alter database for load, drop database, and load database commands are allowed on a database that is created with for load. rs_init will fail to create a connection to a standby database created with the for load clause. If the database is very large and creating it will take a long time, you can create a small database, add it to the replication system, then drop it, recreate it with for load, and then load dump from the active database.

On both active and standby Adaptive Servers, the suid (server user ID) of each login name must be the same as in the master..syslogins tables and the sysusers table in each user database. For warm standby, the uid (user ID) associated with a name in sysusers must map to the suid for the same login name in syslogins. The uids should be the same in both active and standby. Suid and role settings must also be the same in the syslogins and sysloginroles tables in the master database.

Mapping SUIDs

You can add all login names, including maintenance user logins, to both the active and the standby Adaptive Servers in exactly the same order. Server user IDs (suids) are sequentially assigned by the Adaptive Server, so the suids of all login names will match.

You can also maintain one Adaptive Server Enterprise as the "master" server with all the login names and copy the master..syslogins table from the master Adaptive Server Enterprise to all the newly created Adaptive Server Enterprise.

If the suids don't match in your system, then you can reconcile the sysusers table in the standby database with the master..syslogins table after loading the dump. You can do this by generating a script containing all the active database users, drop all users with the sp_dropuser *username* command and then add them using the script generated from the active database.

Adding the Maintenance User to the Standby Database

If you are going to use the dump and load materialization method with or without the dump marker option, then the maintenance user login name for the standby database should be added to both the active and the standby Adaptive Server, before adding the standby database to the warm standby system. The maintenance user is automatically added to the active database by rs_init or by Sybase Central when it is added to the warm standby system. When the standby database is initialized with dump and load, the sysusers table is loaded into the standby database along with the other data from the active database. If the maintenance user's suid doesn't map correctly to the uid in the sysusers table in the standby database, then the maintenance user should be dropped (sp_dropuser) and then added (sp_adduser). The maintenance user should be granted all the necessary permissions on all the objects.

```
grant all on tabname to maintuser
```

Table creation DDL in an active database is replicated to the standby database in a warm standby setup. If the maintenance user doesn't have the necessary permissions, replication will be suspended. You can do the following to resolve this issue:

1. If you are going to use the dump/load materialization method to initialize the standby database, you can grant permissions on all the tables to the maintenance user in the active database.

2. After creating each object, you can grant permissions to the maintenance user.

3. You can alias the maintenance user to dbo after the standby database has been added to the replication system. If you are planning to replicate identity columns, the maintenance user should be aliased to dbo.

```
use db
go
sp_dropuser maintuser
go
sp_addalias maintuser, dbo
go
```

Initializing the Standby Database

You can use one of the following methods to materialize the standby database:

► Use Adaptive Server dump and load commands, either without suspending writes (nonatomic) or by suspending writes (atomic) against the active database.

► Use bcp while writes are suspended against active (atomic).

► Use quiesce database ... to manifest_file and mount.

When a standby database is added to the replication system, the replication server writes an enable replication marker into the active database transaction log. The dump marker is written to the active database transaction log by Adaptive Server when the dump database or dump transaction is performed.

If the destination (standby) database is the master database, the destination database cannot be materialized with dump and load. You can use bcp for materialization, with some changes, to manipulate data to resolve inconsistencies.

Materializing using dump/load: If client connections to the active database cannot be suspended during materialization, you should use the dump marker option in rs_init or Sybase Central when adding the standby database. When the dump marker option is used, Adaptive Server writes dump marker to the transaction log of the active database when you dump the active database. Replication Server starts replicating only after it receives both an enable replication marker and a subsequent dump marker. Figure 12-4 shows an active database transaction log with enable replication and dump markers. The enable replication marker is written in the transaction log when:

▶ A logical connection for an existing physical connection to the active is created.

▶ A physical connection to the active database is created after creating a logical connection with a different name.

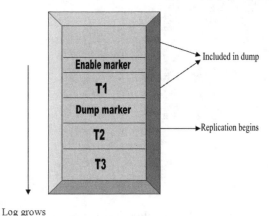

Log grows

Figure 12-4

In Figure 12-4, transaction T1 is executed after adding the standby database, included in the database dump, and then discarded by Replication Server when it is received from the RepAgent in order to avoid duplicates. Transactions T2 and T3 are executed after enabling dump marker and are not included in the dump. These transactions are sent to Replication Server by RepAgent, where they are accumulated in the inbound queue. The database connection (DSI) to the standby database is automatically suspended. After loading the standby database from the active database, the DSI connection can be resumed. Replication Server starts replicating transactions from the active database to the standby database only after it has received both the enable replication marker and the subsequent first dump marker.

Materializing database without dump marker: When you can suspend activity in the active database, you should not choose the dump marker option when adding the standby database. The standby database can be initialized by using dump/load, bcp, or mount.

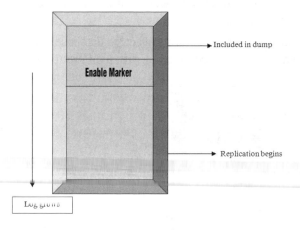

Figure 12-5

As shown in Figure 12-5, Replication Server starts replicating from the active database to the standby database beginning at the enable replication marker in the active database transaction log. Since activity is suspended in the active database, no transactions occur after the enable replication marker is written to the active database transaction log. You can use bcp to copy each of the tables (including the rs_lastcommit table) from the active database into the standby database, or load the active database dump until the enable replication marker is received by the standby database. Replication Server starts replicating transactions after receiving this enable replication marker.

Adding the Standby Database to the Replication System

Depending on the materialization method chosen, you may or may not need to suspend activities on the active database. If you don't suspend client connections from the active database, then use the dump marker option method.

Use rs_init or Sybase Central to add the standby database. The rs_init screens displayed during the add standby database process are shown below.

```
DATABASE INFORMATION

1.  SQL Server name:  rds
2.  SA user:  sa
3.  SA password:
4.  Database name:  pubs3
5.  Will the database be replicated:  yes
6.  Maintenance user:  pubs3_maint
7.  Maintenance password:  pubs3_maint_ps
8.  Is this a Physical Connection for Existing Logical Connection: yes
9.  Logical DB Setup                                        Incomplete


Ctrl-a Accept and Continue, Ctrl-x Exit Screen, ? Help.

Enter the number of your choice and press return:
```

After entering "yes" for item 8, rs_init prompts for the logical database connection. Once this information is entered, item 9 will display the setup as "complete".

```
DATABASE INFORMATION

1.  SQL Server name:  rds
2.  SA user:  sa
3.  SA password:
4.  Database name:  pubs3
5.  Will the database be replicated:  yes

6.  Maintenance user:  pubs3_maint
7.  Maintenance password:  pubs3_maint_ps
8.  Is this a Physical Connection for Existing Logical Connection: yes
9.  Logical DB Setup                                          Complete


Ctrl-a Accept and Continue, Ctrl-x Exit Screen, ? Help.

Enter the number of your choice and press return:
```

Since we are initializing the standby database with dump and load, use the dump command to dump the active database:

```
1> dump database pubs3 to '/tmp/pubsdmp'
2> go
```

Load the standby database from the active database dump:

```
1> load database pubs3 from '/tmp/pubsdmp'
2> go
```

If you have performed subsequent transaction log dumps, then load them in sequence before using the online database command.

```
1> online database pubs3
2> go
```

If you are using the bcp command to initialize the standby database, suspend activity on the active database and then bcp out each table from the active database including the rs_lastcommit table, and bcp in each of the replicated tables on the standby database.

Initialize the standby database using quiesce... to *manifest_file*:

```
1> quiesce database pubs3_tat hold pubs3 for external dump to
"/dumps/mpubs3_file", with override
2> go
```

Load using the mount command:

```
mount database all from "/dumps/mpubs3_file"
```

You can check the logical connection at any time by using admin logical_status:

```
1> admin logical_status
2> go
```

| Logical Connection Name | Active Connection Name | Active Conn State |
| Standby Connection Name | Standby Conn State | Controller RS |
Operation in Progress	State of Operation in Progress	Spid
[106] PDS.PUBS3	[107] pds.pubs3	Active/
[108] rds.pubs3	**Suspended/Waiting for Enable Marker**	[16777317] prs
None	None	

If you have initialized the standby database using bcp, quiesce database... to manifest_file and mount, or dump and load without the dump marker, Replication Server suspends the connection to the active database. You can resume the connection to the active database by using the following command from Replication Server:

```
resume connection to active_ds.active_db
```

Regardless of the materialization method used for initialization, Replication Server suspends the database connection to the standby database.

From Replication Server:

```
1> admin who_is_down
2> go
```

```
Spid Name        State                 Info
---- ---------- --------------------  -----------------------------------
DSI  EXEC        Suspended            108(1) rds.pubs3
DSI              Suspended            108 rds.pubs3
```

Resume the physical connection to standby:

```
1> resume connection to rds.pubs3
2> go
Connection to 'rds.pubs3' is resumed.
```

```
1> admin logical_status
2> go
Logical Connection Name  Active Connection Name  Active Conn State
  Standby Connection Name  Standby Conn State    Controller RS
    Operation in Progress  State of Operation in Progress    Spid
----------------------- -----------------------  -----------------
----------------------- -------------------- --------------
----------------------- ------------------------------- -----
[106] PDS.PUBS3         [107] pds.pubs3          Active/
  [108] rds.pubs3         Active/                [16777317] prs
    None                  None
```

Resume activity in the active database if you suspended it earlier.
You can also execute the wait for create standby blocking command in Replication Server. This command allows the client
session in Replication Server to wait for the standby process to
complete.

```
wait for create standby for logical_ds.logical_db
```

Maintenance User Permissions

After adding the standby database to the replication system, you
should grant replication_role and all necessary permissions on all
the user objects to the maintenance user.

```
1> use pubs3
2> go
```

```
1> sp_role "grant", replication_role, pubs3_maint
2> go
grant all on table_name to maint_user
```

```
1> grant all on authors to pubs3_maint
2> go
```

Or you can alias the maintenance user to dbo:

```
1> sp_dropuser pubs3_maint
2> go
```

```
1> sp_addalias pubs3_maint, dbo
2> go
Alias user added.
```

Enabling Replication in the Standby Database

For the switchover event, you must enable replication for tables and stored procedures in the standby database that you want to replicate in the new standby database after the switch. If the standby database was materialized with dump and load or quiesce database... to manifest_file and mount, then all replication settings from the active database are copied over to the standby database, but if you used bcp to materialize the standby database, you must enable replication in the standby database with sp_reptostandby, sp_setreptable, or sp_setrepproc. If you don't want to enable replication now, you must enable it after switchover.

Altering the Warm Standby Connections

Most of the time the default settings of warm standby work efficiently. If required, you can alter the logical and physical connections to modify connection configuration parameters.

Altering the Logical Connection

You can alter the logical connection to customize Replication Server parameters that affect logical connections, disable or enable the distributor, and enable or disable replication of the truncate table command to standby databases.

To modify parameters that affect the logical connection, you can log in to the Replication Server and issue the alter logical connection command to change parameter settings.

```
alter logical connection to logical_ds.logical_db
set distributor {on | off} |
set logical_database_param to 'value'
```

Changing the logical database parameter doesn't require restarting Replication Server. The parameter can be one of the following:

▶ **materialization_save_interval**: This parameter is only applicable for standby databases in a warm standby database. Default is "strict".

▶ **save_interval**: This parameter is set to "strict" when the logical connection is created. This ensures that transactions are not deleted from DSI queues before they are applied to standby databases.

Both materialization_save_interval and save_interval should be reset (from "strict" to a given number of minutes) only under rare circumstances, such as when you don't have enough space in stable queues to hold messages for a longer period. There might be risk of data loss at the standby database if these parameters are reset from "strict". As Replication Server cannot detect this type of loss, you will need to verify the integrity of the standby database.

Examples:

```
1> alter logical connection to PDS.PUBS3
2> set save interval to '60'
3> go
```

```
1> alter logical connection to PDS.PUBS3
2> set materialization_save_interval to '60'
3> go
```

▶ **replicate_minimal_columns**: This parameter specifies whether Replication Server should send all replication definition columns for all transactions or only those needed to perform DML (data modification language) operations at the standby database. This value is used by Replication Server in warm standby applications when a replication definition does not contain the send standby clause with any parameter. Otherwise, Replication Server uses the value of this parameter or replicate all columns. Default is "on".

Example:

```
1> alter logical connection to PDS.PUB3
2> set replicate_minimal_columns to 'off'
3> go
```

▶ **set_standby_repdef_cols**: This parameter specifies which columns Replication Server should send to the standby database for a logical connection. set_standby_repdef_cols overrides the send standby clause in the replication definition that tells Replication Server which table columns to send to the standby database. The following values can be used:

"on": Send only the table columns that appear in the matching replication definition. The send standby clause in the replication definition is ignored.

"off": Send only the table columns to the standby database. The send standby clause in the replication definition is ignored.

"check_repdef": All table columns based on the send standby option are sent to the standby database.

If you are not going to replicate data from the active database into replicate databases other than the standby database, you can disable the distributor thread to improve performance.

Example:

```
1> alter logical connection to PDS.pubs3
2> set distributor 'off'
3> go
```

Before disabling the distributor thread, be sure to drop any subscriptions for the data on the logical database. For replicating out of the active database to the regular replicate database, you can enable the distributor.

Example:

```
1> alter logical connection to PDS.pubs3
2> set distributor 'on'
3> go
```

Keep in mind that after disabling the distributor, if you drop the standby database from the replication system, no Replication Server thread will be left to read the inbound queue from the active database. The inbound queue keeps on filling until you create another standby database, enable the distributor thread, or drop the active database from the replication system.

Replicating truncate table to the Standby Database

The send_truncate_table command specifies whether or not to replicate the truncate table command to the standby database.

Example:

```
1> alter logical connection to PDS.pubs3
2> set send_truncate_table to 'off'
3> go
```

The value can be one of the following:

"on": Replication of the truncate table command is enabled for the standby database. This is the default for warm standby applications created in Adaptive Server 11.5 or later.

"off": Replication of the truncate table command is disabled for the standby database. This is the default for warm standby applications in which active/and or standby databases were created in pre-11.5 SQL Server and then upgraded to Adaptive Server 11.5 or later.

Altering the Physical Connections

The alter connection command can be executed at the source Replication Server to change parameters affecting physical connections for warm standby.

Syntax:

```
alter connection to dataserver.database
set database_param to 'value'
```

Example:

```
suspend connection to rds.pubs3

alter connection to rds.pubs3
set db_packet_size to '4096'

resume connection to rds.pubs3
```

Warm Standby as Primary

In this type of warm standby application, the logical database
serves as the primary in the replication system. The active database, the standby database, and the replicated database are
managed by a single Replication Server. If the replicated database
is not managed by the same primary Replication Server (prs),
then the primary Replication Server (prs) sends transactions to
the replicate Replication Server (rrs), which applies transactions
to the replicate database. Both the active and the standby databases are logical primary databases for the replicated database.
When creating a replication definition, you should provide the logical connection name as *dataserver.database*. As illustrated in
Figure 12-6, the active primary database is updated by the client's
transactions executed in the active primary Adaptive Server. The
primary active database RepAgent reads transactions flagged for
replication, including the maintenance user transactions, and forwards them to the inbound queue. Transactions from the inbound
queue are read and processed against subscriptions by the distributor and written into an outbound queue. Maintenance user
transactions are sent to the standby database but not to the replicated database unless you have configured the RepAgent
parameter send_maint_xacts_
to_replicate to "true". Transactions are then read by DSI from
the outbound queue and executed in the replicated Adaptive

Server. Adaptive Server then updates the replicate database. The standby DSI also reads transactions from the inbound queue and executes them in the standby Adaptive Server, and then Adaptive Server updates the standby database. Both the standby DSI and the distributor concurrently read transactions from the inbound queue. Messages are not deleted from the inbound queue until they have been read by both the standby DSI and the distributor and delivered to the target databases (replicate and standby databases).

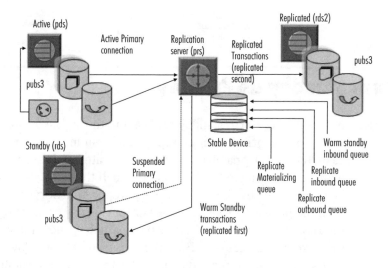

Figure 12-6

If the switch active command is issued, the materialization queue is dropped while the subscription is being materialized and is recreated by selecting data from the now active database.

Warm Standby as Replicate Database

Figure12-7 illustrates a single Replication Server managing the primary database, the active database for a logical replicate database, and the standby database for a logical replicate database. You can also have a primary Replication Server and a replicate Replication Server managing the primary and the replicate databases, respectively. You must create active and logical connections and materialize the standby database before creating subscriptions. When creating subscriptions, you should use the logical connection name in the *dataserver.database* clause. You cannot create subscriptions when the switch active command is being processed. Transactions from the primary database are replicated to both the active and the standby databases.

You can materialize subscriptions using the bulk nonatomic materialization method. You need to make sure that you are using the activate subscription command's with suspension clause, which suspends both the database DSI and the standby DSI. When the DSI is suspended, you will have to insert data into the standby database. The with suspension at active replicate only clause should be used when a slow bcp or a simple insert method is being used for materializing. This clause suspends the active database DSI but not the standby DSI, hence allowing data to be replicated to the standby database using the standby DSI.

```
activate subscription subname
for {repdef_name | publication pub_name with primary
at dataserver.database}
with replicate at dataserver.database
{with suspension [at active replicate only]}
```

Transactions from the regular primary are replicated to the active (replicate) and are executed as maintenance user transactions. In regular replication, maintenance user transactions are not replicated. In order to replicate maintenance user transactions to the standby database, the RepAgent for the active database should be configured to send maintenance user transactions to the standby database.

Syntax:

```
sp_config_rep_agent active_db, 'send_maint_user_xacts', 'true'
```

After switchover, RepAgent in the new active database (old standby) should have send_maint_user_xacts set to "true" and in the new standby (old active) it should be set to "false".

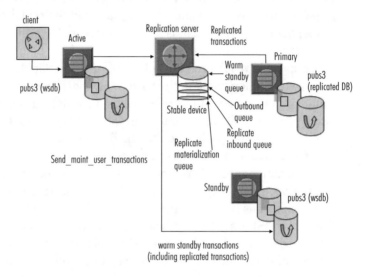

Figure 12-7

Figure 12-7 illustrates warm standby as replicate. The client executes transactions and updates data at the primary database on the primary data server; transactions marked for replication are read by the primary RepAgent from the primary database transaction log, forwarded to Replication Server, and written into an inbound queue. These transactions in the inbound queue are read by the distributor, processed by the distributor against subscriptions, and written into an outbound queue. If the primary database and the warm standby application for the replicated database are not managed by the same Replication Server, then the transactions received from the primary Replication Server are directly written to the outbound queue. Transactions in the outbound queue are read by DSI and executed by the DSI in the replicate Adaptive Server, which is the active Adaptive Server for the warm standby application. The active database is updated by the active Adaptive Server. If the primary database is managed by a different Replication Server, then transactions originating in the primary database are written into a primary Replication Server RSI outbound queue by the distributor. They are copied to a DSI outbound queue in the replicate Replication Server in order to be applied to an active database for the logical replicate database. These transactions are then read by RepAgent from the transaction log of the active database, forwarded to the Replication Server, and written into an inbound queue by the Replication Server. All the transactions marked for replication, including the maintenance user transactions, are forwarded to the Replication Server for application in the standby database. Transactions in the inbound queue are read by the standby DSI and then executed by the standby DSI in the standby database.

Save interval: By default, the save interval for logical connections is set to "strict". This guarantees that the transactions from the DSI queues are not deleted before they are applied to the standby database. The save interval setting of "strict" should be changed to a specific number of minutes only in rare circumstances, as setting it to a specific number of minutes may lead to data loss at the standby database. This kind of data loss cannot be detected by Replication Server, so you should verify data integrity of the standby database with rs_subcmp or some other method. When the standby database is not available for a long time and you don't have stable queue space, you can set save interval to "0", which allows Replication Server to delete messages from the queue.

DSI queue save interval: When a standby database is created, the DSI queue save interval for the logical connection is set to "strict". This ensures that messages in the DSI queue will not be deleted until they are delivered to the standby database. The DSI queue save interval can be changed with the configure logical connection command.

Example:

```
1> configure logical connection to PDS.PUBS3
2> set save_interval to '60'
3> go
Msg 15302, Level 11, State 0:
Server 'prs':
You have just reset strict save_interval for PDS.PUBS3. Consistency of
Standby data is not guaranteed any longer.
Config parameter 'save_interval' is modified. This change will not take
effect until the connection/route is restarted. A connection/route can be
restarted with the suspend and resume commands.
```

To set save_interval back to "strict":

```
1> configure logical connection to PDS.PUBS3
2> set save_interval to 'strict'
3> go
Config parameter 'save_interval' is modified. This change will not take
effect until the connection/route is restarted. A connection/route can be
restarted with the suspend and resume commands.
```

materialization_save_interval: This configuration parameter for logical connection is set to "strict" by default when a subscription is created. This ensures that messages are not deleted from the materialization queue until they are applied to the standby database. The materialization_save_interval parameter can be changed with the configure logical connection command. To save messages in materialization for 60 minutes:

```
1> configure logical connection to PDS.PUBS3
2> set materialization_save_interval to '60'
3> go
Msg 15302, Level 11, State 0:
Server 'prs':
You have just reset strict save_interval for PDS.PUBS3. Consistency of
Standby data is not guaranteed any longer.
```

You can reset to "strict" with the following:

```
1> configure logical connection to PDS.PUBS3
2> set materialization_save_interval to 'strict'
```

System Tables and System Stored Procedures for Warm Standby Setup

In this section, we will discuss the functionality of the rs_databases, rs_locator, and rs_lastcommit tables and the rs_helpdb stored procedure as related to warm standby replication.

rs_databases

You can query the rs_databases system table in RSSD or ERSSD to get information about which databases are active and standby.

Example:

```
1> select * from rs_databases
2> go
```

dsname	dbname	dbid	dist_status	src_status	attributes	errorclassid					
funcclassid		prsid		rowtype	sorto_status	ltype	ptype	ldbid	enable_seq		
PDS	**PUBS3**	106	65	1	0		0x0000000000000000				
0x0000000000000000		16777317		1	0	**L**	**L**	106	0		
pds	prs_RSSD	101	1	1	0		0x0000000001000002				
0x0000000001000001		16777317		0	0	P	A	101	0		
pds	**pubs3**	**107**	1	1	0		0x0000000001000002				
0x0000000001000001		16777317		1	0	**P**	**A**	106	0		
rds	**pubs3**	108	1	1	0		0x0000000001000002				
0x0000000001000001		16777317		1	0	**P**	**S**	106	0		

Take note of the following fields:

dsname

The data server name

dbname

The database name

dbid

The unique identifier for the database

dist_status

The connection status, which can be one of the following:

▶ 0x1 – valid

▶ 0x2 – suspended

▶ 0x4 – suspended by a standby-related action

▶ 0x8 – waiting for a marker

▶ 0x10 – will issue dbcc ('ltm', 'ignore')

▶ 0x20 – waiting for dump marker to initialize a standby database

▶ 0x40 – switching related duplicate detection when ltype is set to "P"

▶ 0x40 – allow switching when ltype is set to "L"

▶ 0x80 – temporarily not doing any grouping

ltype

Type of database, which can be one of the following values:

▶ P – physical database

▶ L – logical database connection

ptype

Type of database in warm standby application, which can be one of the following values:

▶ A – active database

▶ S – standby database

▶ L – logical database connection

ldbid

The dbid for the logical connection the database is associated with. If there is no logical connection, then ldbid is the same as dbid.

enable_seq

The sequence number used during an active database switch or the creation of a standby database.

rs_helpdb

rs_helpdb provides information about all the databases known to that Replication Server. If rs_helpdb is executed without parameters, it provides information about all the databases listed in the rs_databases system table.

```
1> rs_helpdb    ----------->(executed without parameters)
2> go
dsname    dbname     dbid   controlling_prs      errorclass
   funcclass                   status
-------- ---------- ------ -------------------- -----------------------
 ----------- ------------------ ---------------------------------------
pds       prs_RSSD   101    prs                  rs_sqlserver_error_class
   rs_sqlserver_function_class  Log Transfer is ON, Distribution is ON
PDS       PUBS3      106    prs                  No entry in rs_classes
   No entry in rs_classes       Log Transfer is ON,
pds       pubs3      107    prs                  rs_sqlserver_error_class
   rs_sqlserver_function_class  Log Transfer is ON, Distribution is ON
rds       pubs3      108    prs                  rs_sqlserver_error_class
   rs_sqlserver_function_class  Log Transfer is ON, Distribution is ON

1> rs_helpdb pds, pubs3
2> go
dsname    dbname     dbid   controlling_prs      errorclass
   funcclass                   status
-------- ---------- ------ -------------------- -----------------------
 --------------------------- ---------------------------------------
pds       pubs3      107    prs                  rs_sqlserver_error_class
   rs_sqlserver_function_class  Log Transfer is ON, Distribution is ON
(return status = 0)
```

rs_lastcommit

The rs_lastcommit table is created in the user database when the database is added to the replication system with rs_init. The rs_lastcommit table keeps track of the last committed transaction from each primary database. In the warm standby system, rs_lastcommit tracks the last transaction from the active database that was committed in the standby database.

```
1> select * from rs_lastcommit
2> go
origin   origin_qid
   secondary_qid
     origin_time          dest_commit_time     pad1 pad2 pad3 pad4 pad5 pad6 pad7 pad8
--------  ----------------------------------------------------------------------------
          ----------------------------------------------------------------------------
------------------  ------------------- ---- ---- ---- ---- ---- ---- ---- ----
0        0x00000000000000000000000000000000000000000000000000000000000000000000
 0x00000000000000000000000000000000000000000000000000000000000000000000
    Apr 8 2007 4:21PM   Apr 8 2007 4:21PM   0x00 0x00 0x00 0x00 0x00 0x00 0x00 0x00
```

Take note of the following fields:

origin

> Active/primary database ID

origin_quid

> The last committed transaction in the stable queue for the
> origin database. origin_quid is used by Replication Server to
> ensure that no duplicate transactions are processed.

origin_time

> Time the transaction occurred at the active database.

dest_commit_time

> Time the transaction was committed at the standby.

rs_locater

This table tracks information about the latest log transaction
record received by stable queues from each of their senders.

Using Replication Definitions and Subscriptions

Warm standby applications don't require replication definitions, but using replication definitions and function replication definitions can improve performance. You should use the logical connection name as the primary (*dataserver.database*) when creating replication definitions for the warm standby.

Adaptive Server limits the number of columns in the where clause to 1024. Replication Server builds the where clause with the columns listed in the primary key, so the primary key of the replication definition cannot have more than 1024 columns. You can replicate more than 1024 columns but you cannot have more than 1024 columns in the primary key; otherwise, error 15460 will be generated:

```
The number of columns exceeds the maximum of %d.
```

Replication definitions, internal replication definitions, function replication definitions, and functions can have a maximum of 1024 columns or parameters.

Using the primary key: Replication Server uses the columns specified in the primary key to generate the where clause for update and delete operations. If you do not have a replication definition for a table, the generated where clause will include all table columns except text, image, rawobject, and unitext columns, which can result in table scan on the standby database. For tables with replication definitions where the primary key is specified, the primary key is used as the where clause for the update and the deletes to standby. Replication Server uses indexes on the standby database to apply updates and deletes. Performance is improved by just sending key columns during updates and deletes, which reduces network traffic, requires less space usage in stable queues, and puts less load on Adaptive Server.

Send standby all columns: The send standby clause governs the way replication definition is used for replicating into the standby database. The send standby all columns clause instructs

Replication Server to send all columns with their original column names and datatypes to the standby database. The replication definition is only used for finding the primary key to build the where clause.

Example:

```
1> create replication definition titles_repdef
2> with primary at PDS.PUBS3
3> with all tables named titles
4> (title_id varchar(6))
5> primary key (title_id)
6> send standby all columns
```

In the above example, all the columns in the titles table are replicated to the standby, even though only title_id is listed in the column definition. If more than one replication definition is created with the send standby all columns clause, the most recently created replication definition is used.

Send standby replication definition columns: When a replication definition is created with the send standby replication definition columns clause, only columns listed in the column definition of the replication definition are sent to the standby. The primary key listed in the replication definition is used to build the where clause.

```
1> create replication definition titles_repdef
2> with primary at PDS.PUBS3
3> with all tables named titles
4> (title_id varchar(6), title varchar(80), price money)
5> primary key (title_id)
6> send standby replication definition columns
```

In the above example, only the title_id, title, and price columns of the titles table are replicated to the standby database.

Send standby parameters: The send standby parameters clause can be used in the function replication definition to replicate only selected parameters to the standby. send standby all parameters is used to replicate all the parameters in the function to the standby. send standby replication definition parameters tells

Replication Server to replicate only those parameters that are defined in the function replication definition to the standby. The default is `send standby all parameters`.

You should keep in mind that there can be only one function replication definition per stored procedure. If you are planning to replicate the stored procedure to both the regular replicate site and the standby, be sure to include all the parameters required by both function replication definitions.

Replicate minimal columns: If using replication definition for replicating into a standby database, you can improve performance by using `replicate minimal columns`. When you use this clause in replication definition, Replication Server sends only required columns to perform updates or deletes at standby (i.e., unchanged columns are omitted from update commands). Using the `replicate minimal columns` clause improves performance by reducing the size of transactions replicated through the replication system and placing less load on Adaptive Server.

Subscriptions: Subscriptions are not used in warm standby replication. You can however, create subscriptions for the data in a logical primary database or for replicating data from other databases into a logical database. Create and define subscriptions using the logical connection name (*dataserver.database*) instead of the physical data server and database names.

Please refer to the "Warm Standby as Primary" and "Warm Standby as Replicated Database" sections earlier in this chapter for more information. For subscription materialization details, see Chapter 10.

Restrictions on using subscriptions: All forms of materialization and dematerialization are supported by Replication Server for warm standby applications. Restrictions only apply when subscriptions are created for replicating data into warm standby databases:

▶ Subscriptions cannot be created on physical active or standby databases. To replicate subscription data into or from active and standby databases, a subscription should be created for a logical database.

▶ Subscriptions should be created only after the standby database has been added to replication system, not while adding the standby database.

▶ The standby database cannot be added to the replication system while you are creating subscriptions.

▶ No new subscriptions should be created while the switch active command is being executed.

Subscription materialization for logical primary database: Materialization is a process of creating and activating subscriptions and copying data from the primary database into a materializing queue and then applying the data to a replicate database. When the switch active command is executed, RSSD database information is replicated by the primary Replication Server to notify replicate sites that the old standby database is now the new active database. When this information is received by the replicate Replication Server with materializing queues, these queues are dropped and subscription data is reselected from the new active primary database to build a new queue.

Subscription materialization for logical replicate database:

▶ **Atomic materialization:** When atomic materialization is used, the save interval clause for the materialization queue is set to "strict" by Replication Server. Messages are not deleted from the materialization queue until all the data has been copied to the active database and replicated to the standby database. In the primary database, rs_marker is executed by Replication Server to mark the start of transactions that execute after the materialization queue is applied, and an information message is written to the Replication Server error log:

```
2007/04/21 12:51:58. rrs2: Created atomic subscription testws_sub for
replication definition testws_rep at active replicate for <PDS.PUBS3>
```

An informational message is again written to the Replication Server error log when the marker arrives at the standby database:

```
2007/04/21 12:51:58. rrs2: Created atomic subscription testws_sub for
replication definition testws_rep at standby replicate for <PDS.PUBS3>
```

After this, the materialization queue is dropped by Replication Server and the subscription status is marked as VALID at both the active and standby replicate databases.

If the `switch active` command is executed while the materialization queue is being processed, the materialization queue is reapplied to the new active database by Replication Server. If the `incrementally` option is used to create the subscription, then only the subscription data that was not already replicated into the new active database is executed.

▶ **Nonatomic materialization:** When data is materialized using nonatomic materialization and the save interval is set to "0", Replication Server deletes messages from the materialization queue after they are applied to the active database.

If the `switch active` command is executed while the subscription is being materialized, Replication Server marks the subscription as suspect after processing the materialization queue. You can execute the `check subscription` command to check the subscription status and then drop and recreate subscriptions with suspect status.

▶ **Bulk materialization:** When the bulk materialization method is used for materializing the data, you need to load into both active and standby databases. If you are going to use non-logged bcp, you will load data into the standby database because log records are not logged in the active database transaction log. If you are using logged bcp, then data inserted into the active database is replicated to the standby database.

When using bulk materialization, the subscription should be activated with the `activate with suspension` clause before loading data into the replicate database. Using this clause in a warm standby setup suspends both the active database DSI and the standby database DSI, allowing you to load the subscription data into both the active and the standby databases.

If you are going to load data using logged bcp or another method that logs log records, then you should activate the subscription using the `with suspension at active replicate only` clause. This clause suspends the active database DSI, not the standby database DSI; hence transactions are replicated from the active database into the standby database.

Checking subscription status: You can check subscription status for the logical database with the check subscription command. This command returns one status message if the status is the same on both the active and standby databases, or two status messages if the subscription status is different on the active and standby databases. For example, the subscription status can be VALID at the active database and ACTIVATING at the standby database.

```
check subscription subname for repdef
with replicate at dataserver.database
```

Dropping subscriptions: Use the drop subscription command with the with purge option to drop a subscription for the logical replicate database. The drop subscription command marker follows dematerialization messages in the active database DSI queue and proceeds to the standby database. Subscription data is deleted from both the active and standby databases after the drop subscription marker is received at the databases.

The switch active command can be executed at the replicate Replication Server while the subscription is being dropped using the with purge option. The DSI connection is suspended and dematerialization is temporarily suspended by Replication Server. Both the DSI connection and dematerialization queues are resumed after switch active completes.

Alter table support: The alter table command allows you to add non-nullable columns, drop columns, and modify column datatypes. Replication Server support for the alter table command in a warm standby application depends on whether or not the replication definition is used and the replication definition options. For details on the alter replication definition command, please refer to Chapter 9.

Alter table with no replication definition: If your warm standby application is not using replication definitions, then the alter table command executed at the active database is replicated to the standby replication.

Alter table with replication definition:

▶ **No send standby clause:** If the replication definition doesn't have the send standby clause, then data received from the primary table is replicated by Replication Server without any reference to replication definition. Original column names and datatypes are used by Replication Server to send transactions received from RepAgent. Replication definition is only used to find the primary key. The primary keys are the union of primary keys in all replication definitions for the table.

The replication definition can be altered to drop primary keys or add new primary key columns to the replication definitions before altering the primary table. You should drop the primary key only after quiescing the replication system; otherwise, the DSI thread will shut down and you will have to take corrective active.

▶ **Send standby all columns:** If the replication definition is created with send standby all columns, Replication Server uses the original column names and datatypes of the active database received from RepAgent to send them to the standby database. Replication definition is only used to find the primary key. If you are just going to make schema changes that do not involve dropping primary key columns, you don't have to take any special steps. To drop all primary key columns in a table:

1. Quiesce the replication system (drain stable queues), i.e., make sure that all existing data in stable queues is applied to the standby database.

2. Use the alter replication definition command to drop and add primary key columns.

3. Alter the primary table.

▶ **Send standby replication definition columns:** If the replication definition is created with send standby replication definition columns, Replication Server uses the original column names and datatypes defined in the replication definition. All options of alter table are supported unless primary keys in the table are dropped. To drop all primary key columns in a table, follow the steps above.

To add or alter columns in the primary database, all activities should be stopped on the primary. To ensure that all the previous commands have been applied to the standby database, issue a dummy update against the primary table. Then execute the dump transaction command to truncate the active database transaction log, and follow these steps:

1. Quiesce the replication system.
2. Use the alter table command to make changes on the table.
3. Alter the replication definition.
4. Alter the replicate table.
5. Resume activity on the primary database.

Switchover

For short-term transient failures, switchover to standby is not recommended. For these types of failures, you should diagnose the problem and switch over only if it is required. Use switchover for long-term transient failures, such as to perform planned maintenance on the active database or its Adaptive Server, or when the active database may not be available for a longer period.

Planned switchover is usually done for routine maintenance. For these types of switchovers you can gracefully disconnect client connections from the active database, switch over to the standby database using the switch active command, and migrate client connections to the new active database.

For catastrophic failures, you will first need to find unreplicated transactions. Apply these to the new active (old standby), migrate client connections to the new active, drop the physical connection to the old active, rebuild the old active database from the new active database, and then bring up the rebuilt old active as the new standby. If desired, you can switch back as well.

When you issue the switch active command, a number of steps are performed. (The following steps correspond to the numbers in Figure 12-8.)

1. RepAgent and the connection for the failed active is suspended by Replication Server.

2. Replication Server reads and applies all remaining messages on the inbound queue to the standby and forwards any subscription data for normal replication to the outbound queue. Before the switch can be completed, all committed transactions must be processed in the inbound queue.

3. Replication Server suspends DSI connection to standby database.

4. The secondary truncation point and the RepAgent are enabled in the new active database (old standby).

5. Replication Server places a marker in the new active database transaction log to indicate when the standby database became the active database. This marker indicates which transactions in the new active database transaction log should be applied to the new standby and to any replicates.

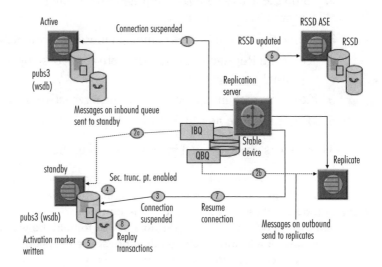

Figure 12-8: Switchover

6. Replication Server updates warm standby data in the RSSD database.

7. You can resume the connection and log transfer for the new active database and start RepAgent for the new active database by issuing sp_start_rep_agent.

8. After completing the above tasks, you may have to resubmit transactions that were committed but not yet reached Replication Server when the active database failed.

   ▶ Keep in mind that RepAgent lags somewhat behind the database transaction log.

   ▶ You must code your application to handle paper trail transactions (those transactions that were applied to the failed database but not yet sent to the new active database).

Switchover steps: To switch from the active database to the standby database:

1. If client applications are still connected to the active database, disconnect them.

2. Stop the active database RepAgent by issuing sp_stop_rep_agent *dbname*.

3. Issue the switch active command in Replication Server.

4. Start the RepAgent for the new active database by issuing sp_start_rep_agent *dbname*.

5. Reconnect client applications to the new active database.

6. Reconnect the new standby database.

These steps are explained in detail following the Note.

Note: If for some reason you cannot bring the new standby database online after switching to the new active, you will need sufficient space in syslogs and stable device to hold the waiting messages. If it is impossible to add more space to syslogs and stable device, you may want to:

- Drop the connection to the standby database.

- Create a new standby connection.

- Reinitialize the standby database from a dump of the new active database.

Step 1. Disconnect client applications: If this is a planned switchover, you can disconnect client applications and then failover. In case of an unplanned switchover, you should disconnect client connections from the old active database as soon as failure is detected. When Adaptive Server fails, client connections are not disconnected automatically; you should develop some procedures or use Sybase OpenSwitch to switch client connections automatically. Once switchover is started, the old active must not be updated by clients, as modifications made during or just before server failure need to be replayed or resubmitted. Once switchover is complete, the client application can update the new active database. If the warm standby application is also a replicate in a regular replication system, then you will need to suspend the connection from the regular primary database also, so that during switchover you do not continue to receive replicated transactions.

Step 2. Stop RepAgent for the active database: If it is a planned switchover, you should wait for all transactions to be read from the active database transaction log before stopping RepAgent. If RepAgent is not stopped, it will eventually be suspended after issuing the switch active command at Replication Server.

Syntax:

```
sp_stop_rep_agent dbname, ['nowait']
```

Example:

```
1> sp_stop_rep_agent pubs3
2> go
The Replication Agent thread for database 'pubs3' is being stopped.
(return status = 0)
```

Step 3. Issue the switch active command: At the Replication Server, issue the switch active command.

Syntax:

```
switch active for logical_ds.logical_db to dataserver_database [with
suspension]
```

The with suspension clause is optional. If used, the DSI connection to the new active database is suspended after the switch is complete. You will need to manually resume the DSI connection to the new active. The with suspension clause should be used if the new active is also a replicate in a regular replication.

You can also use the wait for switch blocking command to get return status information when the switch is complete. This command is very useful in scripting the procedure.

Syntax:

```
wait for switch for logical_ds.logical_db
```

During switchover, the *admin logical_status* command can be used to check the switch status. The *switch active* command returns immediately, but the switch is not complete until *admin logical_status* displays "None" in the State of Operation in Progress field.

Example:

```
1> switch active for PDS.PUBS3 to rds.pubs3
2> go
Switch active to rds.pubs3 for logical connection to PDS.PUBS3 is in
progress

1> admin logical_status
2> go
Logical Connection Name   Active Connection Name   Active Conn State
  Standby Connection Name   Standby Conn State               Controller RS
     Operation In Progress                      State of Operation in Progress
        Spid
------------------------- ------------------------- -------------------
------------------------- -----------------------------------------------
  -------------------------------------------- -------------------------------
     ----
[106] PDS.PUBS3          [108] rds.pubs3        Suspended by Error/
   [107] pds.pubs3          Suspended/Waiting for Enable Marker   [16777317] prs
      Switch Active Connection to rds.pubs3 in progress
```

To finish the failover:

```
1> admin logical_status
2> go
Logical Connection Name   Active Connection Name   Active Conn State
  Standby Connection Name   Standby Conn State   Controller RS   Operation in Progress
    State of Operation in Progress   Spid
------------------------ ------------------------ -------------------
------------------------ -------------------- --------------- ---------------------
-------------------------------- ----
[106] PDS.PUBS3            [108] rds.pubs3          Active/
  [107] pds.pubs3           Active/                 [16777317] prs   None
    None                            0054
```

From the error log:

I. 2007/04/22 16:46:17. **Switch starting : PDS.PUBS3**
I. 2007/04/22 16:46:17. The DSI thread for database 'pds.pubs3' is shutdown.
I. 2007/04/22 16:46:18. **Suspending LogTransfer for pds.pubs3**
I. 2007/04/22 16:46:18. **Suspending LogTransfer for rds.pubs3**
I. 2007/04/22 16:46:18. Switch attempting to Quiesce Dist/DSI for PDS.PUBS3
I. 2007/04/22 16:46:18. The DSI thread for database 'rds.pubs3' is shutdown.
I. 2007/04/22 16:46:22. Setting Replication Agent truncation to 'valid' for rds.
pubs3 log
I. 2007/04/22 16:46:22. **Placing marker in rds.pubs3 log**
I. 2007/04/22 16:46:23. A request to shutdown/suspend the distributor for 106 has been received.
I. 2007/04/22 16:46:23. The distributor for 'PDS.PUBS3' is shutting down
I. 2007/04/22 16:46:24. SQM stopping: 106:1 PDS.PUBS3
I. 2007/04/22 16:46:24. Purging Queue 106:1
I. 2007/04/22 16:46:24. SQM starting: 106:1 PDS.PUBS3
I. 2007/04/22 16:46:24. **Resetting Replication Agent starting log position for rds.pubs3**
I. 2007/04/22 16:46:32. DIST for 'PDS.PUBS3' is Starting
I. 2007/04/22 16:46:32. **Resuming LogTransfer for pds.pubs3**
I. 2007/04/22 16:46:32. **Resuming LogTransfer for rds.pubs3**
I. 2007/04/22 16:46:33. **Switch completed : PDS.PUBS3**

If for some reason you want to abort the switch process after issuing the switch active command, you can do so, but only in the early phases of switchover. If it is too late, you can let the `switch active` command finish, and then issue `switch active` again to switch back.

Syntax to abort the switch process:

```
abort switch for logical_ds.logical_db
```

Step 4. Start RepAgent: After `switch active` is complete, you can start RepAgent for the new active database.

Syntax:

```
sp_start_rep_agent dbname
```

Example:

```
1> sp_start_rep_agent pubs3
2> go
```

RepAgent for the new active database will start reading transactions from the new active database transaction log and will send them to the stable queue for replication to the new standby database.

Step 5. Reconnect client applications: Once the switchover is complete, you can reconnect client applications to the new active database. You can also implement Sybase OpenSwitch for managing client connections. The client application should only update the new active after switchover is complete and RepAgent has been started. Client applications should be coded to check whether their recently submitted modifications were replicated successfully at the standby.

Step 6. Reconnect old active as new standby: After maintenance you can bring the old active database online as the new standby and resume the DSI connection.

Syntax:

```
resume connection to dataserver.database
```

Example:

```
1> resume connection to pds.pubs3
2> go
Connection to 'pds.pubs3' is resumed.
```

If the client application has resubmitted transactions on the new active database, Replication Server will reapply these transactions. You should plan to resolve these conflicts by undoing these transactions on the new standby or create an error class to ignore duplicate rows.

Setting up clients to handle switchover: As mentioned earlier, Replication Server does not switch client connections to the standby automatically. You can use one of the following methods for handling switchover:

▶ **Two interfaces files:** You will need to create two interfaces files — one for Replication Server ($SYBASE/REP-15_0/install/interfaces), which does not change, and one for client applications ($SYBASE/interfaces), in which you can change the port of the new active to the port number of the old active during switchover. Clients always connect to the active Adaptive Server.

Table 12-6

Server	Host	Port	Server	Host	Port
				Before Switch	
PRS	host1	5000	PRS	host1	5000
PDS	host1	5501	PDS	host1	5501
RDS	host2	5502	RDS	host2	5502
				After Switch	
			PRS	host1	5000
			PDS	host1	5502
			RDS	host2	5501

▶ **Using a symbolic data server name:** In this scenario, you can create an interfaces file entry for the data server with a symbolic name for the client application. During switchover, you should edit the interfaces file to change the host name and port number for the symbolic data server to the port number of the new active.

Table 12-7

	Adaptive Server	Host Name	Port Number
Active Database	PDS	Host1	5501
Standby Database	RDS	Host2	5502
Client Application	Client_App	Host1	5501

In this case, after switchover you can edit the interfaces file and change the hostname and port number for Client_App with the new active database, e.g., hostname to Host2 and port number to 5502.

Note that you can implement Sybase OpenSwitch to automatically route clients to the active Adaptive Server.

Switching back to the original active: You can use the following steps for switching back to the original active.

1. Drop the physical connection to the original active database.

    Syntax:

    ```
    drop connection to dataserver.database
    ```

2. Create a physical connection to the original active database (use the original physical connection name).

    Syntax:

    ```
    create connection to data server.database
    set error class [to] error_class
    set function string class [to] function_class
    set username [to] user
    [set password [to] passwd]
    as standby for logical_ds.logical_db
    [use dump marker]]
    ```

Use the as `standby` *for logical_ds.logical_db* and use `dump marker` clauses to recreate the physical connection:

1. Dump the current active database (original standby).
2. Load the original active (current standby).
3. Resume connection to original active.

   Syntax:

   ```
   resume connection to orig_activeDS.orig_activeDB
   ```

4. Issue `switch active` to switch back.

Warm standby application setup is much simpler than regular replication. Check the application's replication requirement to see if a warm standby setup is suitable for your application.

Chapter 13

Multi-Site Availability

The muti-site availability (MSA) feature is available in Replication Server 12.6 and later. MSA requires only one database replication definition and one database subscription for each replicated database. MSA allows replication of data changes from the primary database to multiple replicate databases for warm standby and non-warm standby databases, and allows replication of DDL and system stored procedures to non-warm standby databases. MSA also allows the implementation of a filtering strategy to choose whether or not to replicate individual tables, transactions, functions, system stored procedures, and data filtering based on owner or user and data definition languages. MSA can co-exist with regular replication and warm standby and can be overlaid on top of the existing replication.

Prior to Replication Server 12.6, Replication Server had a number of limitations including the following:

▶ Replication of DDL to non-standby databases was not allowed.

▶ There could not be more than one standby database.

▶ The standby database could not be controlled by a different Replication Server.

▶ No filters were available to filter replication of transactions executed by certain users and owners.

▶ Certain system stored procedures could not be replicated.

MSA in Replication Server 15.x and above supports bidirectional replication by setting the dsi_replication_ddl DSI connection parameter to "on". By default, the dsi_replication_ddl configuration parameter is set to "off". When dsi_replication_ddl is set to "on", DSI sends set replication off to the replicate database, which instructs it to mark the succeeding DDL transactions in the transaction log not to be replicated. These DDL transactions are not replicated back to the original database, which enables the DDL transaction replication in a bidirectional MSA replication setup.

```
alter connection to dataserver.database set dsi_replication_ddl 'on'
```

Before setting dsi_replication_ddl to "on", the maintenance user should be granted the set session authorization privilege.

```
grant set session authorization to maint_user
```

In a mixed Replication Server environment, data features of the higher version are filtered by the primary Replication Server and these incompatible features are not forwarded to the downstream Replication Servers. The Replication Server configuration parameter dist_stop_unsupported_cmd governs whether DIST should ignore incompatible commands or be suspended. When set to "on", DIST is suspended. By default dist_stop_unsupported_cmd is set to "off", which means it ignores incompatible features. Regardless of the parameter setting, an error message is logged by Replication Server when it encounters the first instance of an incompatible command that cannot be forwarded to a lower version of the replicate Replication Servers.

For all connections:

```
configure replication server set 'dist_stop_unsupported_cmd' to ['on |
'off']
```

For an individual connection:

```
alter connection to dataserver.database set 'dist_stop_unsupported_cmd' to
['on' | 'off']
```

For a logical connection:

```
alter logical connection to logicalServer.logicalDatabase set
'dist_stop_unsupported_cmd' to ['on' | 'off']
```

RSSD System Tables Relevant to MSA

The rs_dbreps and rs_dbsubsets tables are replicated to other sites.

▶ rs_dbreps: Stores information about database replication definitions except for name sets. This RSSD system table is replicated to all sites with version number 12.6 or above. It has a unique index on dbrepid, dbid, and dbrepname.

Column	Column Datatype	Column Description
dbrepid	rs_id	ID of database replication definition
dbrepname	varchar(255)	Name of the database replication definition
prsid	int	ID of the primary Replication Server
dbid	int	ID of the primary database
ownerid	rs_id	Replication Server username that created the database replication definition
requestdate	datetime	Creation time for the database replication definition
status	int	Subset content bitmap
minvers	int	Earliest Replication Server version to which this table can be replicated

▶ rs_dbsubsets: This RSSD table stores name sets for database replication definitions. This table is replicated to all sites with a version of 12.6 or above. It has a unique index on dbrepid, type, owner, and name.

Column	Column Datatype	Column Description
dbrepid	rs_id	ID of the database replication definition
prsid	int	ID of the primary Replication Server

Column	Column Datatype	Column Description
type	char	Item type, which is one of the following: T – table name F – function name X – transaction name P – system stored procedure name
owner	varchar(30)	Table or function owner name, or the user name that has executed the transaction or system stored procedure. An * means all owners or users.
name	varchar(255)	Name of the table, function, transaction, or system stored procedure. An * means all tables, functions, transactions, and system stored procedures.

MSA Setup

To replicate DDL and system stored procedures, both the primary and replicate data servers should be Adaptive Server Enterprise and of the same version. For replicating DDL, the login and passwords should be the same on both the primary and replicate data servers. For replicating DDL contained in user-defined transactions, the sp_dboption 'ddl in tran' should be set to "true".

```
sp_dboption dbname, 'ddl in tran', true
```

To replicate the entire database, follow these steps:

1. The primary database should be marked for replication with sp_reptostandby.

   ```
   sp_reptostandby dbname, 'all'
   ```

2. Configure the primary database RepAgent to replicate DDL changes, even if there is no standby database.

   ```
   sp_config_rep_agent dbname, 'send_warm_standby_xacts', 'true'
   ```

You will need to stop and restart RepAgent for the change to take effect.

If you want to replicate stored procedures, you should mark them individually with sp_setrepproc. The stored procedure's owner information is not checked by the database replication definition. Individual tables can be marked with sp_setreptable. When the database is not marked with sp_reptostandby, DDL is not replicated. When table-level replication definitions and subscriptions are used, data can be replicated to both the warm standby and replicate databases by setting the rep_as_standby database parameter to "on".

```
suspend connection to dataserver.database


alter connection to dataserver.database
set rep_as_standby 'on'


resume connection to dataserver.database
```

3. Create the database replication definition. Note that the Replication Server site version must be 12.6 or higher.

Syntax:

```
create database replication definition dbrepdefname
With primary servername.dbname
[[not] replicate DDL]
[[not] replicate setname setcont]
[[not] replicate setname setcont]
[[not] replicate setname setcont]
[[not] replicate setname setcont]


dbrepdefname
```

The database replication definition name

```
servername.dbname
```

The primary data server/database name, e.g., pds.pdb

```
[not] replicate DDL
```

This clause tells Replication Server whether it should or should not replicate DDL to replicate databases. If the replicate DDL clause is omitted or the clause is set to not, then DDL is not replicated to the replicate database.

[not] replicate *setname setcont*

(where *setname* can be tables, functions, transactions, or system procedures and *setcont* can be [in (owner2.lname2 [, [owner2.lname2 [, …]])])

If the system procedures setname is omitted or the not clause is included, Replication Server does not replicate the system procedures. If the tables, functions, or transactions setname is omitted or the not option is included, Replication Server replicates all objects of the setname category. If the primary and replicate databases have different names and system stored procedures are replicated, then the sp_config rep_agent and sp_adduser stored procedures should be filtered out, as database names are used as parameters.

▶ owner: An owner of a table or user who executes a transaction. Owner information for functions and system procedures is not processed by Replication Server. The owner can be replaced with a space surrounded by single quotes (' '), which means no owner, or with an asterisk (*), which indicates all owners.

▶ name: The name of a system procedure, function, transaction, or table. Name information can also be replaced with a space surrounded by single quotes (' '), which indicates no names, or with an asterisk (*), which means all names.

4. Create a database subscription for each replicated database. The Replication Server site version must be 12.6 or higher. Subscriptions can be created with no materialization or bulk materialization. The materialization procedure selected depends on whether or not activities can be suspended on primary tables.

a. Subscription with dump/load coordination: If the primary and replicate databases have identical user IDs, then:

```
define subscription sub_wdb_dl
for database replication definition rep_wdb with primary at
PDS.pdb
```

```
with replicate at RDS.rdb
subscribe to truncate table
use dump marker
```

Dump PDS.pdb and load it to RDS.rdb, and resume the connection to RDS.rdb.

b. Create a database subscription without materialization:

```
create subscription sub_itblA
for database replication definition rep_itbl with primary at
PDS.pdb
with replicate at RDS.rdb
without materialization
```

c. Create a database subscription by simulating atomic materialization:

```
define subscription sub_itblB
for database replication definition rep_itbl with primary at
PDS.pdb
with replicate at RDS.rdb
```

Copy tables and stored procedures out of the primary database (PDS.pdb). Get the subid from the rs_subscriptions table.

```
select subid from rssd..rs_subscriptions where
subname='sub_itblB'
```

```
execute rs_marker 'activate subscription subid with suspension'
```

Copy tables and stored procedures into the replicate database (RDS.rdb), and resume the connection to RDS.rdb.

```
Execute rs_marker 'validate subscription subid'
```

d. Create a database subscription by simulating nonatomic materialization:

```
define subscription sub_itblC
for database replication definition rep_itbl with primary at
PDS.pdb
with replicate at RDS.rdb
```

```
activate subscription sub_itblC
for database replication definition rep_itbl with primary at
PDS.pdb
with replicate at RDS.rdb
with suspension
```

Use dump/load or bcp to copy data from the primary to the replicate and resume the connection to RDS.rdb.

```
select subid from rssd..rs_subscriptions where
subname='sub_itblC'
execute rs_marker 'validate subscription subid'
```

Setting Up Multiple Replicate Databases

MSA can be used to replicate DDL and other database objects to multiple warm standby and replicate databases. Database replication definitions and subscriptions can be created to logical connections. For setting up warm standby, please see Chapter 12.

In the following example we are going to replicate from one primary database (pds.pubs2) to two replicate databases (rds.pubs2 and rds2.pubs2) using one Replication Server (msars15). DDL and system stored procedures can only be replicated by the primary data server (pds) if client connections are switched from pds.pubs2 to rds.pubs2 or rds2.pubs2. DDL and system stored procedures are not replicated. Standby replication is taking place only to and from pds.pubs2.

Basic Steps

The following are the basic steps for using MSA to replicate from one primary database to two replicate databases.

1. Suspend all writes on the pds.pubs2, rds.pubs2, and rds2.pubs2 databases.

2. Execute sp_reptostandby to mark pds.pubs2, rds.pubs2, and rds2.pub2 for replication.

```
1> use pubs2
2> go
```

```
1> sp_reptostandby pubs2, 'all'
2> go
The replication status for database 'pubs2' has been set to 'ALL'.
(return status = 0)
```

3. Configure RepAgent in each of these databases.

```
1> sp_config_rep_agent pubs2, 'send_warm_standby_xacts', 'true'
2> go
Parameter Name              Default    Config Value    Run Value
------------------------    ---------  --------------  ----------
send warm standby xacts     false      true            false
```

```
(1 row affected)
Replication Agent configuration changed for database 'pubs2'. The
changes will take effect the next time the Replication Agent thread is
started.
(return status = 0)
```

Stop and restart the RepAgent:

```
1> sp_stop_rep_agent pubs2
2> go
The Replication Agent thread for database 'pubs2' is being stopped.
(return status = 0)
```

```
1> sp_start_rep_agent pubs2
2> go
Replication Agent thread is started for database 'pubs2'.
(return status = 0)
```

4. At the Replication Server, use alter connection with set
    'dsi_replication' "off" for each connection. dsi_replication
    should be set to "off" at switchover time also to prevent rep-
    lication data in the transaction log from being replicated
    again.

```
1> alter connection to pds.pubs2 set 'dsi_replication' 'off'
2> go
Config parameter 'dsi_replication' is modified. This change will not
take effect until the connection/route is restarted. A connec-
tion/route can be restarted with the suspend and resume commands.
```

```
1> suspend connection to pds.pubs2
2> go
Connection to 'pds.pubs2' is suspended.

1> resume connection to pds.pubs2
2> go
Connection to 'pds.pubs2' is resumed.

1> alter connection to rds.pubs2 set 'dsi_replication' 'off'
2> go
Config parameter 'dsi_replication' is modified. This change will not
take effect until the connection/route is restarted. A connec-
tion/route can be restarted with the suspend and resume commands.

1> suspend connection to rds.pubs2
2> go
Connection to 'rds.pubs2' is suspended.

1> alter connection to rds2.pubs2 set 'dsi_replication' 'off'
2> go
Config parameter 'dsi_replication' is modified. This change will not
take effect until the connection/route is restarted. A connec-
tion/route can be restarted with the suspend and resume commands.

1> suspend connection to rds2.pubs2
2> go
Connection to 'rds2.pubs2' is suspended.

1> resume connection to rds2.pubs2
2> go
Connection to 'rds2.pubs2' is resumed.
```

5. Create a database replication definition for each database, defining each as a primary database.

```
1> create database replication definition pubrep
2> with primary at pds.pubs2
3> replicate DDL
4> replicate system procedures
5> go
Database replication definition 'pubrep' for pds.pubs2 is created.
```

```
1> create database replication definition pubrep
2> with primary at rds.pubs2
3> go
Database replication definition 'pubrep' for rds.pubs2 is created.

1> create database replication definition pubrep
2> with primary at rds2.pubs2
3> go
Database replication definition 'pubrep' for rds2.pubs2 is created.
```

6. Since each database can be primary or standby, create database subscriptions so that each database can subscribe to all the other databases. Different subscription materialization methods can be used for each subscription.

```
1> create subscription rds_sub
2> for database replication definition pubrep
3> with primary at rds.pubs2
4> with replicate at pds.pubs2
5> without materialization
6> subscribe to truncate table
7> go
Subscription 'rds_sub' is in the process of being created.

1> check subscription rds_sub
2> for database replication definition pubrep
3> with primary at rds.pubs2
4> with replicate at pds.pubs2
5> go
Subscription rds_sub is VALID at the replicate.
Subscription rds_sub is VALID at the primary.

1> create subscription rds2_sub
2> for database replication definition pubrep
3> with primary at rds2.pubs2
4> with replicate at pds.pubs2
5> without materialization
6> subscribe to truncate table
7> go
Subscription 'rds2_sub' is in the process of being created.
```

```
1> check subscription rds2_sub
2> for database replication definition pubrep
3> with primary at rds2.pubs2
4> with replicate at pds.pubs2
5> go
Subscription rds2_sub is VALID at the replicate.
Subscription rds2_sub is VALID at the primary.


1> define subscription pds_sub
2> for database replication definition pubrep
3> with primary at pds.pubs2
4> with replicate at rds.pubs2
5> subscribe to truncate table
6> use dump marker
7> go
Subscription 'pds_sub' is in the process of being defined.
```

(There is no need to activate the subscription, as the dump marker clause in the subscription definition automatically activates and validates the subscription(dump/load coordinated materialization.)

```
1> create subscription rds2_sub
2> for database replication definition pubrep
3> with primary at rds2.pubs2
4> with replicate at rds.pubs2
5> without materialization
6> subscribe to truncate table
7> go
Subscription 'rds2_sub' is in the process of being created.

1> check subscription rds2_sub
2> for database replication definition pubrep
3> with primary at rds2.pubs2
4> with replicate at rds.pubs2
5> go
Subscription rds2_sub is VALID at the replicate.
Subscription rds2_sub is VALID at the primary.


1> define subscription pds_sub
2> for database replication definition pubrep
3> with primary at pds.pubs2
4> with replicate at rds2.pubs2
```

```
5> subscribe to truncate table
6> use dump marker
7> go
Subscription 'pds_sub' is in the process of being defined.

1> create subscription rds_sub
2> for database replication definition pubrep
3> with primary at rds.pubs2
4> with replicate at rds2.pubs2
5> without materialization
6> subscribe to truncate table
7> go
Subscription 'rds_sub' is in the process of being created.

1> check subscription rds_sub
2> for database replication definition pubrep
3> with primary at rds.pubs2
4> with replicate at rds2.pubs2
5> go
Subscription rds_sub is VALID at the replicate.
Subscription rds_sub is VALID at the primary.
```

7. Dump the pubs2 database on pds:

```
1> dump database pubs2 to '/tmp/pubdmp'
2> go
```

8. Stop RepAgent on the replicate (rds.pubs2):

```
1> sp_stop_rep_agent pubs2
2> go
The Replication Agent thread for database 'pubs2' is being stopped.
(1 row affected)
```

9. With the DSI connection to rds.pubs2 suspended, load the database on the replicate (rds) and then online it:

```
1> load database pubs2 from '/tmp/pubdmp'
2> go

1> online database pubs2
2> go
```

10. Resume the DSI connection to rds.pubs2:

```
1> resume connection to rds.pubs2
2> go
Connection to 'rds.pubs2' is resumed.
```

11. Since in this case all three data servers are controlled by a single Replication Server, there is no need to disable and enable RepAgent after loading the pubs2 database. Before restarting RepAgent, reset the locater:

```
1> use msars15_RSSD
2> go
1> rs_zeroltm rds, pubs2
2> go
Locater has been reset to zero.
(return status = 0)

1> sp_start_rep_agent pubs2
2> go
Replication Agent thread is started for database 'pubs2'.
(1 row affected)
```

12. With the DSI connection rds2.pubs2 suspended, load the database to rds2.pubs2. If RepAgent is up, stop it before loading the database:

```
1> sp_stop_rep_agent pubs2
2> go
The Replication Agent thread for database 'pubs2' is being stopped.
(1 row affected)

1> load database pubs2 from '/tmp/pubdump'
2> go

1> online database pubs2
2> go
```

13. Resume the DSI connection to rds2.pubs2:

```
1> resume connection to rds2.pubs2
2> go
Connection to 'rds2.pubs2' is resumed.
```

14. Since in this case all three data servers are controlled by a single Replication Server, there is no need to disable and enable RepAgent after loading the pubs2 database. Before restarting RepAgent, reset the locater:

```
1> use msars15_RSSD
2> go
1> rs_zeroltm rds2, pubs2
2> go
Locater has been reset to zero.
(return status = 0)

1> sp_start_rep_agent pubs2
2> go
Replication Agent thread is started for database 'pubs2'.
(1 row affected)
```

15. Resume client activity to these databases.

Switchover

Drain the queues before switching users from the active database (pds.pubs2) to the new active database (could be rds.pubs2 or rds2.pubs). It is best not to block user connections until data in the old active database is replicated to the new active database.

Users can be switched to the new active database by using any of the following methods or your own customized method:

► OpenSwitch

► Switch interfaces file

► Switch IP address

Dropping a Database Subscription

Subscriptions can be dropped with the drop database subscription command:

```
1> drop database subscription pds_sub
2> for database replication definition pubrep
3> with primary at pds.pubs2
4> with replicate at rds.pubs2
```

```
5> without purge
6> go
```

Database subscriptions cannot be altered. To change an existing database subscription, the subscription should be dropped and then recreated. Database subscriptions should be dropped using the without purge clause so that data rows in the replicate databases are not removed by Replication Server. Existing table and function subscriptions are not affected by dropping database subscriptions, and dropping table and function subscriptions doesn't affect database subscriptions.

Dropping Database Replication Definition

Before dropping a database replication definition, the corresponding database subscription should be dropped. The drop database replication definition command will fail if there is a subscription to this database replication definition.

```
1> drop database replication definition pubrep
2> with primary at pds.pubs2
3> go
```

Altering a Database Replication Definition

A database replication definition can be altered using the alter database replication definition command.

```
alter database replication definition db_repdef
with primary at srv.db
{[not] replicate DDL | [not] replicate database setrootl}
[with dsi_suspended]
```

db_repdef

   Name of the database replication definition

srv.db

   Dataserver.database

[not] `replicate_DDL`

Indicates whether or not DDL should be replicated to subscribing databases

[not] `replicate` *setname setcont*

Indicates whether or not Replication Server should replicate
objects listed in setname list. When *setcont* is omitted, Replication Server replicates all objects in the setname list. If the
not keyword is included, those objects are not replicated.

```
setname :: = {tables | functions | transactions | system procedures}
setcont :: = [in ([owner1.] name1 [, [owner2.] name2 [, ...]])
```

owner

Table owner or user who has executed the transaction.
Owner information for functions and system stored procedures is not processed by the Replication Server. The
owner can be replaced with a space surrounded by single
quotes (' ') or with an asterisk (*). A space means there is
no owner. An asterisk means all owners. For example,
*.titles means all tables named "titles" regardless of
owner.

name

The name of the table, function, transaction, or system
stored procedure. The name can be replaced with a space
surrounded by single quotes (' ') or with an asterisk (*). A
space means no name; for example, `fred.' '` means all
unnamed fred user transactions. An asterisk means all
names; for example, `fred.*` means all tables (or transactions) owned by fred.

with `dsi_suspended`

Replication Server suspends the replicate DSI connection,
which can be used to synchronize databases.

Note that the `alter database replication definition` command
doesn't allow changing more than one filter at a time.

To replicate DDL and system procedures at the Replication Server use this syntax:

```
alter database replication definition pubrep
with primary at pds.pubs2
replicate DDL
with dsi_suspended

alter database replication definition pubrep
with primary at pds.pubs2
replicate system procedures
with dsi_suspended
```

At the data server, configure RepAgent to replicate DDL and warm standby transactions:

```
use pubs2
go
sp_reptostandby pubs, 'all'
sp_config_rep_agent pubs2, 'send_warm_standby_xacts', 'true'
```

Stop and restart the RepAgent for the pubs2 database:

```
sp_stop_rep_agent pubs2
sp_start_rep_agent pubs2
```

If no table-level subscriptions exist, the database replication definition should be altered with the dsi_suspended clause, which causes the replicate Replication Server to suspend the replicate DSI when it reads the alter database replication definition marker. When the alter database replication definition command is executed, Replication Server writes an rs_marker to the inbound queue. The alter database replication definition command takes effect only after the marker reaches the DIST (distributor). By then DIST has had enough time to incorporate changes in the database subscription resolution engine (DSRE).

A database can be out of sync after executing the alter database replication definition command. Replicate databases/tables should be resynchronized after this operation. To synchronize:

1. Quiesce the Replication Server and drain the transaction log. Note that the DSI should be suspended since `alter database replication definition` was executed with the `dsi_suspended` clause.
2. Synchronize tables using bulk materialization.
3. Resume the DSI connection.

The `rs_helpdbrep` stored procedure can be executed from the RSSD database to view information about database replication definitions.

To view information about all database replication definitions use this syntax:

```
rs_helpdbrep  [db_repdef [, dataserver[, database]]]
```

Example:

```
1> rs_helpdbrep
2> go
```

```
DB Rep.Def.Name  Primary DS.DB  Primary RS  Rep.DDL  Rep.Sys.  Rep.Table  Rep.Func.
   Rep.Tran.   Creation Date
----------------  -------------  ----------  -------  --------  ---------  ---------
-----------  -------------
pubrep           pds.pubs2      msars15     Yes      All       All        All
   All         Feb 28 2007 9:26AM
pubrep           rds.pubs2      msars15     No       None      All        All
   All         Feb 28 2007 9:27AM
pubrep           rds2.pubs2     msars15     No       None      All        All
   All         Feb 28 2007 9:27AM
(1 row affected)
(return status = 1)
```

To view a specific database replication definition for the data server and database:

```
1> rs_helpdbrep pubrep, pds, pubs2
2> go
```

DB Rep.Def.Name	Primary DS.DB	Primary RS	Rep.DDL	Rep.Sys.	Rep.Table	Rep.Func.	Rep.Tran.	Creation Date
pubrep	pds.pubs2	msars15	Yes	All	All	All	All	Feb 28 2007 9:26AM

(1 row affected)

Name	Rep.Type	Owner

DB Rep.Def.Name	DB Sub.Name	Replicate DS.DB	Replicate RS	Creation Date
pubrep	pds_sub	pds.pubs2	msars15	Feb 28 2007 11:25AM
pubrep	pds_sub	pds.pubs2	msars15	Feb 28 2007 11:30AM

The rs_helpdbsub stored procedure can be executed in the RSSD database to get information about the database subscription for the replicated database:

```
rs_helpdbsub [db_sub [, data_server[, database]]]
```

Example:

```
1> rs_helpdbsub pds_sub, rds, pubs2
2> go
```

DB Sub. Name	Replicate DS.DB	Replicate RS	Status at RRS	DB Rep.Def. Name	Primary DS.DB	Primary RS	Status at PRS	Method	Trunc. Table	Creation Date
pds_sub	rds.pubs2	msars15	Valid	pubrep	pds.pubs2	msars15	Valid	Use Dump Marker	Yes	Feb 28 2007 11:25AM

(return status = 0)

Similar to warm standby, MSA doesn't require table-level replication definitions, although you can do so for performance optimization. Table-level replication definitions can co-exist with database replication definitions. Table replication definitions override database-level replication definitions. You can create a table replication definition to provide a primary key for improved performance. You will also need a table replication definition with the send standby clause to customize function string scope function strings, change the published datatype, replicate minimal columns, and change text columns. When database replication definitions, table/function replication definitions, and database subscriptions exist, and the table/function replication definitions have the send standby clause, then the table/function replication definition is honored by database subscription, and primary key columns and replicate column settings are used to replicate into the replicate database. The send standby all columns clause is treated as send standby replication definition by database subscriptions. But if the table/function replication definition does not have the send standby clause and the table has other replication definitions, then data is replicated by database subscription using the union of all such replication definitions (internal table replication definition). Data is converted to the declared columns/parameters or datatypes and all columns are replicated.

Database subscriptions and table/function subscriptions can co-exist. If both exist, table/function subscriptions override database subscriptions. The where and for new articles clauses are not supported by database subscription. A table/function subscription is required when using the where clause or to replicate a table filtered by database replication definition.

Function strings that are not in the rs_default_function_class function-string class can be customized. rs_default_function_class is used by DSI for functions that do not use table/function replication definition with the send_by clause. Otherwise, the function-string class associated with the connection is used by DSI. For functions with function-string class scope, the function-string class associated with the connection is used by DSI.

rs_dbsubsets: database filters

349

Warm Standby vs. MSA

The following list points out differences between warm standby and MSA.

▶ For warm standby replication, you need to create a logical connection. MSA does not require a logical connection.

▶ MSA supports multiple standby databases, while warm standby can have only one standby.

▶ MSA supports separate handling of system procedure replication.

▶ MSA supports routes, function strings, and split workload/peer-to-peer replication

MSA Limitations

MSA has some limitations, some of which are listed below:

▶ DDL is not replicated by default. To replicate DDL, the database should be marked for replication with sp_reptostandby and the RepAgent parameter send_warm_standby_xacts should be set to "true", even if there is no standby database.

▶ The switch active command is not supported by MSA.

▶ To replicate user stored procedures, mark them with sp_setrepproc.

▶ Table-level replication definitions must be created before customizing replication definition function strings.

▶ Database subscriptions require either no materialization or the bulk method of materialization.

Chapter 14

Performance Monitoring and Tuning

One of the most common problems in administering a Sybase Replication Server is measuring performance and identifying the possible causes of performance issues when they occur. Interestingly enough, in both cases, most Replication Server administrators use the same two techniques that can at best be considered symptoms:

1. Queue disk space consumption for a connection

2. Latency between the primary and replicate — either via attempts to use rs_lastcommit or a separate timing table that is periodically updated

The problem is that while both can be used to identify when there is or isn't a performance issue, neither is very useful beyond simply raising an alert to a possible problem. Unfortunately, the sum total of all the efforts at understanding Replication Server performance for many customers begins and ends with these two — and considerable effort is expended in developing performance monitoring routines. When a problem starts to occur, frequently these two are supplemented by admin who queries, which is unfortunate as not only is most of the output not understood by the administrator, but even the more basic tenets of understanding what is being "queried" is not clearly understood. As a result, many Replication Server administrators don't know how to isolate which components are the true cause of the bottlenecks, how to determine the root cause within those components, and — even

more basic — how to regularly monitor their replication environments to identify patterns of behavior.

The goal of this chapter is to overcome this problem by taking a closer look at:

▶ Common mistakes in performance monitoring/tuning

▶ Tools available for identifying and resolving issues

▶ Detailed analysis of performance metrics

▶ Guidelines for establishing regular performance monitoring

Most of the commands/statistics referenced in this chapter are
based on Replication Server version 15.0.1, as it represents the
state of the technology at the time of this writing.

Common Mistakes

The most common mistakes made by Replication Server administrators in the area of performance monitoring and tuning are
frequently centered on three main areas: using the wrong tools,
improper server configurations, and misdirected focus. Specifically, the most common major mistakes in those categories are:

▶ Using admin who, [sqm | sqt] for performance monitoring or
diagnosis

▶ Overconfiguring the SQT cache while underconfiguring other
server settings

▶ Not monitoring/diagnosing the RDBMS as a cause of the
latency

▶ Not realizing that performance problems may be indicative of
an application design issue and less of a Replication Server
problem

▶ Unrealistic expectations/poor capacity planning

Additionally, there are a few minor common mistakes as well,
including relying on rs_lastcommit to detect latency, measuring
throughput in MB, and reporting latency as queue space in MB.
Some of these minor mistakes are artifacts of the major mistakes

abovc, as we will see when we discuss each and why they are
unreliable.

Monitoring with admin who

The biggest hurdle to overcome in adopting monitor counters and
rs_ticket is to get Replication Server administrators to realize
that admin who is analogous to the ASE sp_who command — its
intention is to tell you who is running and the current state, but
no one would envision monitoring ASE's performance via sp_who.
Yes, sp_who can give you a quick list of who is being blocked, who
is running vs. sleeping, etc., and if stretched to include the CPU
and physical I/O columns of master..sysprocesses, you might be
able to get an idea of resource consumption. While it might be
useful for determining if you may have a problem, it is useless for
actually finding the problem. The same holds true for admin who in
all its variants — sqm, sqt, dist, etc. The goal is to give you status
information that *may* indicate a problem.

The reason that most people make this mistake is due to legacy reasons; prior to Replication Server 12.1, this was the only
means available. The problems with monitoring with the admin
who command are twofold:

▶ admin who represents a single point in time; it's a current snap-
shot if you will.

▶ Each command variant (admin who,sqt and admin who,sqm)
represents the data from a single thread. Most admins don't
realize that "masking" other threads/modules makes output
from the other threads unreliable.

Let's discuss the latter point first as it is the most simple to illus-
trate. Consider the often-used admin who,sqm command with
respect to monitoring latency. A commonly cited statistic is that if
the Next Read output is higher than the Last Seg.Block, then the
Replication Server is caught up, and that by subtracting the two
you can determine the latency in MB. This isn't quite true. For
both the inbound and the outbound queues, the SQT cache will
read from the SQM, which will make it appear that the queue is
fully caught up, whereas in reality it could be as much as

sqt_max_cache_size behind. A quick way to demonstrate this is to suspend a DSI connection (especially in warm standby) and observe the sudden backlog in the queue. In another common situation, since the Next Read represents where the SQMR left off, when Replication Server needs to rescan a large transaction that was removed from SQT cache due to transaction size, the lack of movement in the Next Read is perceived to be a lack of progress. Many times this has resulted in Replication Server admins assuming the thread was "hung" and a variety of unnatural acts are attempted to get it restarted, some of which result in data loss and the need to manually resynchronize the system.

The biggest issue with admin who,sqm is that it really doesn't help identify the problem; instead, it tells the Replication Server administrator something he or she already knew. The most common reason Replication Server admins look at admin who,sqm is because they've already determined there is latency — either by looking at rs_lastcommit (or some other timing mechanism) or intrinsically from data expectations. Knowing that they have latency somewhere, their next step is to execute admin who,sqm, which only tells them something already known — they have latency and, as a result of that latency, a backlog of transactions. Further, it serves as even more of a distraction since the problem will often be reported as they have xMB of latency without knowing whether xMB represents 30 minutes or 30 hours, which is crucial for understanding what the best course of action is (i.e., resynch or let the system catch up).

The admin who,sqt command demonstrates the "single point in time" problem even more than admin who,sqm presents the masking issue. When interpreting admin who,sqt output, most Replication Server admins focus on one of the following metrics:

▶ First Trans: Reports the state and number of commands in the *first* transaction in the queue

▶ Full: Reports when SQT has exhausted memory

The problem with the first one is that admins generally perceive that the first transaction in the queue is the *next* one to be delivered. An easy way to disprove this is to begin a transaction, optionally modify a row (may be needed to force your user log cache to be flushed at primary), and then wait — without committing. Eventually, your transaction will be the first one in the queue. However, other transactions begun later and committed replicate fine. Yet the queue will appear to be "stuck" on an open transaction. A similar "stuck" claim often happens with large transactions and the "closed" (status of "C") state. As the transaction starts being processed, it is too big to fit in the cache, so it gets removed. Later, the commit record is finally read by the SQT from disk or it finally arrives from the RepAgent. The commit has been seen (hence "closed"), yet the SQT needs to go back and rescan significant portions of the disk to reread the commands to send to the DIST, and the DIST is still processing the commands (hence not "read" yet). The result is that some will claim the queue is "stuck" on a "closed" transaction, the DIST isn't processing fast enough, etc. There are other situations in which the output cannot be relied on to report queue processing performance.

The reality is that admin who,sqt tells you so little with respect to queue progress that it is only helpful for spot diagnosis or confirmation of transaction issues. It would have been much more appropriate to have used the Open, Closed, and Read column outputs to track queue progress/throughput, but these (like Full) have another issue.

The Full column actually has two issues. First, it is misleading. The SQT thread is always trying to fill the cache, so it is not necessarily an issue for this column to have a non-zero value. A more appropriate metric would have been the Removed column, which reports the number of transactions actually removed from cache due to exceeding the cache size. Unfortunately, it — along with all the other output from the command — suffers from the problem that it is the *current transient* value, and not a cumulative since last command execution. Effectively, even if you ran the command every 10 minutes, commands could be removed from cache due to size, be fully read and delivered in between sample periods, and you would never realize it as admin who,sqt would only show the current state of 0 transactions removed at each point in time. The fact that the values reported by admin who,sqt are transient make it completely unreliable for troubleshooting as it is likely that you will miss the problem completely or get an inaccurate picture of the severity, duration, and overall impact.

Improper Replication Server Configuration

Another common mistake that Replication Server admins make is configuring the SQT cache too big while ignoring other equally important configuration parameters. Much like finding a DBMS with only basic memory configuration settings changed, finding a Replication Server with a huge sqt_max_cache_size, while parameters such as exec_sqm_request_limit, dsi_cmd_batch_size, and others are still at the defaults is a sure indication of a novice Replication Server administrator — whether they've been using Replication Server for one year or ten. Again, the most common reason this mistake persists is due to historical nature — but in this case not the product's history but the administrator's.

Similar to ASE, the out-of-the-box configuration values for Replication Server are extremely small compared to real-world requirements. At the first sign of latency, adding memory to the SQT cache seems to have an almost magical resolution. So the next time the latency occurs, more memory is added, but this time it doesn't work or it does for a very brief time for warm standby systems. The problem is that on first install, the low memory and resulting low SQT cache settings do contribute to the first brush with latency, and consequently adding memory initially is a good response. Unfortunately, this often begins a cycle of simply trying to throw memory at the problem without understanding that memory being added is dedicated to one purpose while the problem may be caused by something else that should be tuned instead. Some of the more common basic configurations missed are:

▶ Replication Agent tuning (packet size, scan batch size)

▶ RepAgent user (exec_sqm_write_request_limit)

▶ SQM (sqm_recover_seg)

▶ DIST (md_sqm_write_request_limit)

▶ DSI (dsi_cmd_batch_size, dsi_xact_group_size)

Other performance-related configurations such as dsi_serialization_method, dsi_num_threads, dsi_num_large_threads, and dsi_large_xact_size are often missed during initial failed attempts at using parallel DSIs and are a leading cause of failures in those attempts.

Ignoring the Replicate DBMS

Arguably the biggest and most common mistake of all is that most Replication Server admins forget that the final stage of replication is the replicate database itself. The best analogy that can be used is that it is like pushing rope. The faster the receiver is reeling in the rope, the faster you can feed it. However, if the receiver is slow, all that will happen is the rope will pool on the floor until someone trips over it and you get blamed. This is precisely what the vast majority of performance issues that are reported about Replication Server turn out to be. Excessive latency in the outbound queue (inbound queue for warm standby) is blamed not on the replicate database where it belongs but on Replication Server. This is especially true with warm standby implementations and is a frequent problem of an oversized SQT cache. Consider the common vicious cycle that often results:

1. After the first latency issue, when adding memory to the SQT cache helps, the Replication Server admin gains a misconception of Replication Server memory usage and often thinks SQT cache is like data cache to a DBMS and that "more is better."

2. The next time latency occurs, the administrator adds more memory to the SQT cache.

3. The admin does a quick check of the queue "drain" speed by issuing several quick `admin who,sqm` commands.

4. Initially, it appears that it is helping, but within a few minutes, once again things deteriorate.

5. The Replication Server admin adds more memory and the cycle goes back to step 3 — either until the Replication Server admin realizes that memory really isn't helping or the 2 GB limit is reached.

The reason throwing more memory at the problem appears to help is that DSI latency is simply being masked as pending transactions are stuffed into memory. Quick checks using `admin` who,sqm after increasing memory suggest that it is working as the queue is "draining quicker," but only because the command is showing the queue being read faster initially as the cache is being filled. Since admin who,sqm only focuses on the SQM vs. SQT, administrators are unaware of what is happening. Even if they looked at admin who,sqt, they would miss that is really happening since they tend to ignore the Open/Closed/Read columns and focus on the First Trans and Filled columns. Eventually, the newly increased cache is filled as well, at which point even more memory is added — until the 2 GB limit is reached. At this point, it becomes an unproductive discussion with Sybase Technical Support as the customer is arguing that adding memory has helped and the 2 GB limit is impractical in today's 64-bit environments and preventing them from achieving the desired throughput. In reality, the standby database is so slow that the "rope" has pooled up and not only tripped the admin, but has him or her firmly entangled.

Part of the problem is that most sites are not prepared to monitor and diagnose discrete database performance issues. Instead they rely on archaic and legacy system reporting tools such as sp_sysmon in ASE that merely report overall server health and server-level CPU and I/O statistics, which are too gross of metrics to determine that a problem is occurring and, if one is, what is causing it.

Anytime there appears to be latency within Replication Server at the DSI, after tuning the Replication Server parameters referred to above, the first place that should be considered is the replicate database server. To analyze this, you will need to be intimately familiar with detailed performance metrics that your DBMS vendor provides. This can be the MDA tables for Sybase ASE and the V$ tables for Oracle.

Application Design Issues

Another common mistake that contributes to a large number of replication performance issues is directly related to poor application design. It is commonly stated and too often true that the fastest way to find application design problems is to implement replication. Common design problems include:

▶ Bulk SQL statements that affect thousands of rows of data

▶ Inefficient SQL statements with multiple DML operations per row

▶ Sequential key tables

Each of these common design problems may require work-arounds or implementation tricks to avoid huge performance issues. Clearly, the application design needs to consider data replication in the same way that performance and security ought to be considered. Resolving application performance issues caused by poor design is just as costly and laborious as resolving replication performance issues caused by poor design.

Unrealistic Expectations

A final common mistake is unrealistic expectations. You would think this problem is rare, but it is not uncommon to discover that a single Replication Server is being asked to replicate the transaction load of tens of OLTP systems, many of which are hosted on large SMP systems sized to support their OLTP load. It is ludicrous to expect that a single Replication Server running on a few devices can sustain the load of 20 to 30 SMP systems totaling hundreds of CPUs and dozens of different devices to distribute the I/O load. While there is some validity to the claim that reads outnumber the writes even in OLTP systems, the write activity is still fairly high. Additionally, during nightly batch processing, the write volume peaks during very short periods, which accentuates the load. It can't be put any more succinctly than this: OLTP systems that experience high-volume write activity should have dedicated Replication Servers to be able to sustain the replication volume.

Performance Monitoring Tools

When monitoring replication performance, DBAs need to be familiar with three basic tools:

▶ rs_ticket — The primary tool for identifying latency as well as isolating the area where latency is occurring.

▶ RS monitor counters — Highly detailed performance metrics that can be used for configuration tuning as well as determining the precise cause of latency.

▶ DBMS metrics — Detailed DBMS performance metrics that can be used to determine the causes of slow delivery speeds as well as identify application design issues.

Depending on the DBMS vendor, most of these tools are provided either in the form of raw data or as a basic API. Building a monitoring system is often left to the customer, although a number of DBMS vendor partners have developed a variety of third-party tools to assist in monitoring and basic fault isolation. However, for medium to difficult problem identification and resolution, the DBAs still need to know how to make use of the raw tools.

rs_ticket

Over the years, most DBAs have learned the wisdom of implementing a basic "heartbeat" that can be used to identify when latency is occurring. In fact, even Sybase's legacy Replication Server Manager (RSM) implemented a heartbeat table. This common implementation was introduced in Replication Server 12.6 through the rs_ticket feature. Rather than just providing source and replicate timestamps, which only identified that latency was occurring, rs_ticket took it one step further by having threads that needed to inspect the messages as a normal part of their operations add a timestamp of when the ticket record was processed. Threads that normally inspect the message contents are:

▶ Primary database — The timestamp the command is executed

▶ Replication Agent — Converts log records into LTL format

▶ RepAgent user (EXEC) thread — Normalizes the replicated DML

▶ DIST thread (specifically SRE module) — Determines subscription data

▶ DSI thread — Transaction grouping

▶ Replicate database — The timestamp the command is executed at the replicate

The DSI seems a bit out of place as it doesn't require the introspection of the individual commands the way command normalization and subscription resolution do. However, as it needs to determine system commands and other restrictions on grouping, it does need to at least determine the type of command. As it determines grouping rules, when the DSI processes the rs_ticket record, it can simply add its timestamp to the record.

rs_ticket Implementation

rs_ticket is implemented as one of a pair of stored procedures. At the "sender" where the ticket originates, rs_ticket is initiated via a replicated procedure on top of the existing rs_marker payload procedure. The definition for the rs_ticket stored procedure is:

```
create procedure rs_ticket
@head1 varchar(10) = "ticket",
@head2 varchar(10) = null,
@head3 varchar(10) = null,
@head4 varchar(50) = null
as
begin
set nocount on

declare @cmd     varchar(255),
@c_time          datetime

select @cmd = "V=1;H1=" + @head1
if @head2 != null select @cmd = @cmd + ";H2=" + @head2
if @head3 != null select @cmd = @cmd + ";H3=" + @head3
```

```
if @head4 != null select @cmd = @cmd +  ;||4 " * @head4

-- @cmd = "rs_ticket 'V=1;H1=ticket;PDB(name)=hh:mm:ss.ddd'"
select @c_time = getdate()
select @cmd = "rs_ticket '" + @cmd + ";PDB(" + db_name() + ")="
    + convert(varchar(8),@c_time,8) + "." + right("00"
    + convert(varchar(3),datepart(ms,@c_time)),3) + "'"

-- print "exec rs_marker %1!", @cmd
exec rs_marker @cmd
end
go
```

At the replicate, the "receiving" procedure called rs_ticket_
report can be user defined or defined by the Replication Manager
Service (RMS). The RMS replaces the legacy RSM process in
version 15.0 and higher and implements a JMX-based monitoring
capability through the Sybase Unified Agent Framework (UAF).
The RMS version of the procedure can be found in the $SYBASE/
UAF2_0/plugins/com.sybase.rms/scripts/rmsheartbeat.sql script:

```
/* Create the procedure rs_ticket_report. */
create procedure rs_ticket_report
@rs_ticket_param varchar(255)
as
begin
    set nocount on

    declare @n_param varchar(255),
            @c_time datetime

    -- @n_param = "rs_ticket_param;RDB(name)=hh:mm:ss.ddd"
    select @c_time = getdate()
    select @n_param = @rs_ticket_param + ";RDB(" + db_name() + ")="
        + convert(varchar(8), @c_time, 8) + "." + right("00"
        + convert(varchar(3),datepart(ms,@c_time)),3)

    -- print @n_param
    insert rms_ticket_history values (@c_time, @n_param)
end
go
```

Calling it a "report" is a bit of a misnomer as it never actually outputs anything to the user. Typically this is done via a parsing stored procedure that also calculates the different intermodule latencies. Note that the procedure above inserts into a table that RMS also installs. An alternative user-defined procedure that also allows RMS heartbeats would be similar to the following table and procedure definitions:

```
create table rs_ticket_history (
    dsname              varchar(30)           not null,
    dbname              varchar(30)           not null,
    ticket_num          int                   not null,
    ticket_date         datetime              not null,
    ticket_payload      varchar(1024)         null,
        primary key (dsname, dbname, ticket_num)
)
lock datarows
go

create procedure rs_ticket_report
    @rs_ticket_param    varchar(255)
as begin
    set nocount on

    declare   @n_param    varchar(2000),
              @c_time     datetime

    -- @n_param = "@rs_ticket_param;RDB(name)=hh:mm:ss.ddd"
    select @c_time = getdate()
    select @n_param = @rs_ticket_param + ";RDB(" + db_name() + ")="
        + convert(varchar(8), @c_time, 8) + "." + right("00"
        + convert(varchar(3),datepart(ms,@c_time)),3)
    -- for rollovers, add date and see if greater than getdate()
    -- print @n_param


    -- the max()+1 may get a few comments, however,
    -- concurrency on this table shouldn't be a problem...
    -- we'd rather be able to work with the data by exporting
    -- it vs. having to deal with identities, etc.
    insert into rs_ticket_history (dsname, dbname, ticket_num,
        ticket_date, ticket_payload)
        select @@servername, db_name(),
```

```
         isnull(max(ticket_num),0)+1, @c_time,@n_param
      from rs_ticket_history

   -- if RMS support is required, uncomment the next line
   -- insert rms_ticket_history values (@c_time, @n_param)
end
go
```

rs_ticket Calculations

Parsing the tickets can be done by simply substringing the canonical form. During parsing, intermodule latency calculations can be performed. Consider the following example of rs_ticket payloads after insertion into rs_ticket_report.

```
V=1;H1=heartbeat;PDB(MYDB)=12:59:20.296;EXEC(29)=12:59:20.326;B(29)=
2082;DIST(18)=12:59:23.366;DSI(22)=12:59:25.442;RDB(MYDB)=12:59:25.446
```

A quick look at the canonical form is:

▶ V=1 — rs_ticket version number. Currently, this is the first version for rs_ticket. Future versions may have additional data elements, but likely the canonical form will be similar.

▶ H1=heartbeat — This is "header" #1 (@head1). Note that there can be up to four headers for each ticket (@head1-4) with the first three limited to 10 characters and the last one a possible 50 characters. If there is more than one header, the subsequent headers would have the same canonical form (H2=text;H3=text;H4=text).

▶ PDB(MYDB)=12:59:20.296 — This is the time rs_ticket was executed at the primary database (PDB) which in this case is a database named MYDB. This timestamp is created by the rs_ticket procedure before calling rs_marker using concatenation of dateparts to derive the decimal milliseconds vs. the usual ASE format that has a colon between seconds and milliseconds.

▶ EXEC(29)=12:59:20.326 — This is the time the Replication Agent User (EXEC) thread within the Replication Server received the rs_ticket. If you want more process detail information, the process ID, 29, is provided for use with `admin who` or other commands.

▶ B(29)=2082 — This is the number of bytes received by the EXEC thread (note the same process ID). Note also that this counter is shared with the Replication Server monitor counters and can be influenced by their being reset at sample intervals. As a result, this value should only be used to signify data flow and not to monitor throughput.

▶ DIST(18)=12:59:23.366 — This is the time the `rs_ticket` was seen by the PRS distributor (DIST) thread. Various thread modules in between such as the SQM and SQT do not need to inspect the commands, so the DIST is the next `rs_ticket` processing thread along the pathway. Like the EXEC, the process ID (18) is included for reference purposes.

▶ DSI(22)=12:59:25.442 — This is the time the `rs_ticket` was seen by the DSI scheduler thread. Note that the DSI could be in an RRS, and consequently, any latency between the DIST and DSI may be due to routing latency (RSI or RSI user as well as associated queues). Again, the process ID (22) is included for reference purposes.

▶ RDB(MYDB)=12:59:25.446 — This is the time the `rs_ticket` was saved to the replicate database (RDB); in this case it has the same name as the primary: MYDB. This timestamp is created by the `rs_ticket_report` procedure and again uses concatenation of dateparts to achieve a standard decimalization of milliseconds.

Parsing requires some careful consideration as the process IDs can be two to four digits and the database names can be up to 30 characters. A string tokenizer (à la C's `strtok`) in SQL would be handy at this point. In addition, before calculations can be done, the clocks on the PDB host, the Replication Server host, and the RDB host all need to be synchronized.

Calculations can be done within the same `rs_ticket` or between any two `rs_ticket` procedures. For example, consider the following ticket examples:

```
V=1;H1=heartbeat;PDB(TRMASTER)=13:52:34.856;EXEC(26)=13:52:34.905;B(26)=
904;DIST(19)=13:52:36.220;DSI(17)=13:52:40.458;RDB(TRMASTER)=13:52:40.463
```

```
V=1;H1=heartbeat;PDB(TRMASTER)=13:53:35.420;EXEC(26) 13:54:35,542;B(26)=
3709170;DIST(19)=13:54:54.569;DSI(19)=13:58:13.361;RDB(TRMASTER)=
13:58:13.386
```

According to Sybase, there are three types of calculations that are useful in working with rs_ticket procedures:

▶ Horizontal — This is likely the most common as it can be used to find intermodule latency. In this type of calculation, the timestamps between two different modules in the same rs_ticket are compared. For example, looking at the second rs_ticket above, if we compare the EXEC time to the PDB time, we note a difference of ~1 minute. Since the PDB time is when the ticket was executed at the primary and EXEC represents when it got to the RS, any latency here reflects Replication Agent latency, which could be caused by RepAgent performance or Replication Server performance. Further analysis would be needed to determine which is the cause.

▶ Vertical — A vertical calculation comparing the times for the same module between multiple rs_ticket procedures can also be useful to determine how much of a horizontal latency is due to that module. To do so, you need to do several vertical calculations. For example, if we do a vertical calculation of the above EXEC times, we get a difference of ~2:01. If we do the same for the DIST, we get a value of ~2:14, showing a slight 13-second increase in the optimal throughput. By contrast, the horizontal calculation for latency between the EXEC and DIST in the second rs_ticket shows a greater 19-second latency, while the first rs_ticket only shows slightly greater than 1-second latency. We really don't know how much of the 13 seconds is due strictly to the DIST, but we do know there is an additional five to six seconds of latency introduced by the modules between the EXEC and the DIST (SQM and SQT).

▶ Diagonal — A diagonal calculation is done by comparing the timestamp for one module in the first ticket with a later module in the second ticket. This is most useful for describing end-to-end latency for a process. For example, assume that rather than a heartbeat, the above tickets represented the beginning and ending of a particular transaction sequence. A simple vertical calculation for the PDB would show only 1:01 execution time, while the RDB would show execution taking 5:33. However a diagonal calculation between the second RDB and the first PDB shows 5:39, which is the time from the beginning of a process until all the changes are at the replicate. Note that this isn't latency as the horizontal calculation between the RDB and PDB for the second ticket shows a latency of 4:38. But if I was attempting to sequence a process based on the replication status, I'd have to wait the full amount.

rs_ticket Usage

rs_ticket procedures have multiple uses:

▶ Latency heartbeat — As illustrated above, a periodic rs_ticket sent every few minutes can be used as a heartbeat mechanism. In addition to alerting when latency exceeds a desired threshold, historical trend analysis can be performed by plotting the various latency calculations.

▶ Benchmarking — A ticket can be sent at the beginning and end of the benchmark as well as at the boundaries between benchmark phases. This information can then be used to determine how to tune Replication Server to handle the projected load more efficiently.

▶ Quiescent checks — After stopping activity at the primary on a particular table or database, a ticket could be sent. When it arrives at the replicate, all pending changes have been delivered. This can be useful when needing to change a replication definition, subscription, or even a table's schema for a small set of tables without having to block access to the entire database.

▶ Replication setup verification — After setting up replication, a ticket can be sent to verify that the connections have been established, all routes are active, and at least one subscription is active.

The first two are likely the most common uses — in fact, the RMS replaced the legacy RSM heartbeat table with an rs_ticket based implementation. The last one can be equally useful, especially if used with the rs_ticket trace flags:

```
trace "on|off", "EXEC", print_rs_ticket
trace "on|off", DIST, print_rs_ticket
trace "on|off", DSI, print_rs_ticket
```

With these trace flags enabled, you will see the rs_ticket information current at each point printed in the Replication Server error log.

When using rs_ticket, there are a couple of considerations:

▶ Don't use any quotation marks in the header text.

▶ Avoid using punctuation or special characters in the headers if possible. While some may be allowed by RS, they may cause issues when parsing. For example, if you use an equal sign (=) in the header, parsing routines may fail.

▶ RS will not accept a wrongly formatted rs_marker. Do not attempt to call rs_marker directly or modify the ticket format as the only recourse is to skip the log page along with any data on it.

▶ Remember to synchronize the OS system clocks regularly.

Remember, the goal of rs_ticket is to help identify which area of Replication Server to focus on for performance tuning. Latency within one module while previous modules (EXEC) are fine could suggest that the problems are in the intervening modules prior to the ticketed module as well as immediately afterward. For example, latency at the DIST could be due to issues in the inbound SQM or the SQT — or even the outbound SQM. Once the area of concern has been identified, Replication Server monitor counters can be used to further isolate the cause.

RS Monitor Counters

Added in Replication Server 12.1, the monitor counters feature brought the same sort of detailed performance metrics to Replication Server that Monitor Server brought to ASE. The biggest deterrents to their use probably are a combination of usability considerations:

▶ No slick GUI interface with whiz-bang charts to initially attract DBAs

▶ No simple "press here" button that evaluates your system's performance and identifies tuning opportunities or problems

▶ Among the hundreds of available counters, no real documentation about which ones to watch and which ones only apply in special situations.

The monitor counters are organized along the lines of the individual modules as well as internal structures of the Replication Server. A complete list of the available counters for each Replication Server version is maintained in the rs_statcounters table in the RSSD. Each counter is assigned a numeric ID, a 60-character counter name, and a 30-character display name (used for RCL commands). Other details such as the counter description as well as status bits are also available in the rs_statcounters table. Table 14-1 lists the Replication Server modules and their counter ranges:

Table 14-1

Range	Module	Comments
Connection Oriented		
58000	REPAGENT	Counters for the Replication Agent User thread — often referred to as EXEC. As the first thread that data arrives at within RS, these counters will often form the basis for rate comparisons.
6000	SQM	Counters for the SQM writer thread, which writes the replicated commands to the queues/stable devices. When analyzing, you may need to look at SQM counters for the inbound, outbound, and any route queues involved.

Range	Module	Comments
62000	SQMR	The SQM reader module that exists in SQT, DSI, and RSI threads. These counters are extremely useful for identifying rescanning issues as well as comparing rates with previous threads.
24000	SQT	The SQT module that exists in the SQT and DSI threads. One of the more important modules for analysis, these counters can help determine SQT cache sizing as well as transaction profiles.
30000	DIST	The DIST thread that is used in non-warm standby implementations to determine subscribing sites. These counters are useful as they are the first location where the actual type of DML command (insert, update, delete) can be identified.
5000	DSI	The DSI module used by the DSI Scheduler thread for both warm standby and non-warm standby implementations. A crucial set of counters for determining DSI configuration values such as grouping and overall rate information.
57000	DSI EXEC	The DSI EXEC thread that applies the replicated commands to the destination. This set of counters is extremely important — especially the timing metrics — for determining if the latency is really caused by Replication Server or the replicate DBMS, as well as tuning parallel DSI settings.
4000	RSI	The RSI thread that sends replicated commands to the next Replication Server along the route. Obviously only useful in topologies using routes and when latency indicates a routing lag may be the issue, or for initially tuning the route configuration.
59000	RSIUSER	RSIUSER thread that serves as the entry point in the IRS or RRS. Useful in conjunction with RSI counters, but since this is the INC/RRS counters, both sets of counters need to be merged before analysis.
Server Wide and Internal Structures		
13000	CM	Connection Manager — counters that primarily track client connections. Possibly useful in certain debugging situations but otherwise not used.
18000	SERV	Counters that pertain to server-wide resources and processes such as alarms, asynchronous I/O requests, etc. Useful in some debugging situations but not normally analyzed.

Range	Module	Comments
38000	RSH	Counters that pertain to thread internals such as memory, alarms, CPU yields, and internal message queuing operations. Useful in debugging some situations but rarely analyzed.
11000	STS	Counters for the System Table Services module — a common module used by other threads to access the RSSD. Other than analyzing RSSD loading, this set of counters is rarely analyzed.
60000	SYNC	A set of counters that tracks the global pool of synchronization elements — for example, how many are created, etc. Not very useful except in diagnosing certain SMP situations.
61000	SYNCELE	A set of counters for each individual synchronization element. While not normally analyzed, these can be useful to diagnose interthread contention in SMP environments.

The interface to the Replication Server monitor counters is through several RCL commands using the admin statistics routine. These commands are used in a sequence and may differ slightly depending on whether you intend to view the output directly via the Replication Server client program or if you intend to save them to the RSSD for later analysis. Overall, the generic sequence for monitoring Replication Server is the following:

1. Configuring and enabling the statistics collection
2. Defining the sample interval and duration and starting the sampling
3. Viewing the counter statistics (optional if using the client)
4. Stopping the sampling
5. Analyzing the statistics or sample output

The first four steps have corresponding RCL commands, while the last step can be accomplished using SQL, Sybase supplied utilities, or other custom implementations.

It is extremely important to note that there should be only one statistics collection process active at a time. If multiuser access is required, one user should initiate the collection while the others view the data as it is being recorded to the RSSD.

The above steps are discussed in more detail in the following sections.

Statistics Configuration

There are only four possible configuration parameters that need to be adjusted to enable statistics collection. These are listed in Table 14-2.

Table 14-2

Parameter / Values	Comments
stats_reset_rssd [on | off] Default: on Recommended: off	Determines whether statistics previously saved to the RSSD will be truncated when the next statistics collection begins. It is recommended that you set this off and manually truncate the data, especially if planning several short sampling sessions, to avoid losing data. May not be persistent on all platforms, and consequently should be issued at the beginning of each sample collection.
stats_show_zero_counters [on | off] Default: off Recommended: off	Determines whether counters with zero observations will be saved/collected during sampling. Enabling this parameter increases the overhead of saving the samples to the RSSD or increases the volume of statistics output to front-end application. Generally not used; see discussion below.
stats_sampling [on | off] Default: off Recommended: on as needed	Determines whether monitor counter metrics are enabled for collection by Replication Server. While the default is off, this parameter must be enabled before each statistics collection. While most turn it off, it can be left on as enabling statistics is minimal (indiscernible) overhead on Replication Server throughput. In practice, most turn it off when finished collecting statistics.
stats_engineering_counters [on | off] Default: off Recommended: on	This undocumented setting enables additional counters that are used by engineering to diagnose particular performance issues. It is recommended that you enable these as they may be required when interacting with Sybase Technical Support for any performance issues.

The above configuration parameters all are set using the configure replication server command. Most are fairly straightforward, with the exception of stats_show_zero_counters. The explanation for this is based a bit on how the counters work.

Remember, in version 15.0.1, statistics counters are reset for each sample interval (to avoid the nasty delta calculations). The purpose of this counter is to differentiate between counters that had a zero value vs. those that had not recorded any corresponding events.

Consider the following example. Some modules track timing events such as time waiting. The value of the wait time may have been 0 (no wait), but yet the wait event did occur, so we would have a non-zero observation but a zero value. Knowing that the wait event occurred is sometimes as important as knowing how long it occurred. As a result, to save space in the RSSD when saving values, as well as to reduce the overhead in displaying or saving counter values each sample interval, counters with no observations are not displayed or saved. The purpose of the stats_show_zero_counters configuration parameter is to enable counters with zero observations to be displayed or saved. The reason is that if comparing counters between two different threads/modules, one may have observations for a sample interval while the other does not. This can make it difficult to align counter values in tabular spreadsheets or charts as values for some intervals will be "missing." By enabling this parameter, each of the counters being displayed will have a recorded value for each interval. While this may sound handy for monitoring application development, the same effect can be derived using an outer join and the typical isnull(*column*,0) SQL syntax; consequently, it is recommended that this configuration value is set to off simply to avoid the extra overhead.

Starting the Sampling

Statistics sampling, along with the duration and sample interval, is started using the admin stats command. However, before sampling begins, it is always wise to check to see if anyone else is currently sampling statistics (in fact, you should do this prior to changing any of the configuration parameters noted above). This can be accomplished using the following command:

```
admin statistics, status
```

The output from this command will tell you the settings for statistics related configuration values as well as if any statistics sampling is currently underway and when it will complete. Consider the following example outputs:

```
-- no statistics in progress

1> admin stats, status
2> go

Sybase Replication Server Statistics Configuration
=======================================================================


Configuration                     Default    Current
-------------------------------   ---------- ----------
stats_sampling                    off        on
stats_show_zero_counters          off        off
stats_engineering_counters        off        on
stats_reset_rssd                  on         off

-- statistics in progress

1> admin stats, status
2> go
Command in progress, sampling period 00:30:00, time elapsed 00:00:18.

Sybase Replication Server Statistics Configuration
=======================================================================


Configuration                     Default    Current
-------------------------------   ---------- ----------
stats_sampling                    off        on
stats_show_zero_counters          off        off
stats_engineering_counters        off        on
stats_reset_rssd                  on         off
```

The latter output shows that it is currently 18 seconds into a statistics sample of 30 minutes in duration.

In addition to checking if a sample is already in progress, you should also zero any current counter values so that the first sample is normalized rather than skewed by pre-existing data observations. The stats can be reset with the following command:

```
admin statistics, reset
```

The next command actually starts the sampling and can take many different forms. The command syntax is:

```
admin {stats | statistics}
     [, sysmon | "all"
          | module_name [, inbound | outbound] [, display_name]]
     [, server[, database] [instance_id]
     [, display | , save [, obs_interval]]
     [, sample_period]
```

Counters can be enabled for individual modules, module instances, specific connections, or individual counters. While monitoring a specific connection may seem like a good idea and would eliminate a lot of the "noise" of unrelated statistics, this unfortunately presumes a lot from the troubleshooting perspective, leading to assumptions that are rarely accurate. This can be exasperating as the first set of statistics is likely not usable and you will need to wait for the issue to repeat itself and collect statistics again. Therefore, it is recommended that you simply collect all the statistics to the RSSD and use SQL to filter the results. Accordingly, the most commonly used and recommended form is:

```
admin statistics, "all", save, interval, "hh:mm:ss"
```

Where *interval* is in seconds. For example:

```
-- collect stats for 3 hours at 30 sec interval
admin statistics, "all", save, 30, "00:05:00"
```

This will collect statistics every 30 seconds for a total duration of five minutes, which is not very useful as the duration is too short for any real diagnosis. The recommendation is to collect at least 30 minutes worth of statistics at a minimum with one to two hours worth even better. When monitoring for longer periods, the interval can be lengthened to one or two minutes with a upper bound of probably five to ten minutes. The rationale for this is that in order to spot a trend with any assurance, you need 20 to 30 sample intervals to do a reasonable job. Fewer may work, but it would assume that the sample interval is much longer (five to ten minutes) and that the problem is not of such short duration that it might be masked by the longer sample period.

It is also important to note that if collecting statistics to analyze latency, you need to start the statistics collection prior to the latency starting unless the problem is persistent. For example, assume that every night, you encounter latency buildup starting at 8 p.m. and that by 1 a.m., the latency is gone. Collecting statistics during the 11 p.m. to 1 a.m. period is not likely to help, as by that point Replication Server is likely catching up. You would need to start collecting statistics around 7:30 p.m. or so in order for several "normal" samples to be collected prior to the problem developing. However, if the problem is that latency is consistently 30 minutes and does not seem to improve, you could start collecting statistics at any point — although it is likely that Replication Server is not the issue and these stats will merely be used to prove this to the other DBAs, as will be discussed later.

A typical full sampling script would look like the following:

```
-- use admin stats, status to check if any in progress
-- before executing this script
configure replication server set 'stats_sampling' to 'on'
go
configure replication server set 'stats_engineering_counters' to 'on'
go
configure replication server set 'stats_reset_rssd' to 'off'
go
-- outputs the config values and if someone started sampling on us
-- in the meantime from above
admin statistics, status
go

-- zero all the counters that we can
admin statistics, reset
go

-- collect stats for 3 hours at 60 sec interval
admin statistics, "all", save, 60, "03:00:00"
go

-- output the stats to check that the command is in progress
```

```
admin statistics, status
   go
```

Note that statistics collection is not persistent. If you reboot the RS, you will need to restart the statistics collection, although any previously saved statistics will be preserved.

Run-time/Client Statistics Viewing

During the time statistics are being sampled, counter values or performance metrics can be viewed in a variety of ways. First, of course, instead of "saving" the statistics, you can simply have the values output to the display/client application. This will result in a single report at the end of the duration that will resemble the following:

```
1> -- collect stats for 5 minutes at 30 sec interval
2> admin statistics, "all", display, 30, "00:05:00"
Report Time:          10/21/07 07:06:55 PM
Sybase Replication Server Statistics Report
=============================================================================


RepServer Version:      Replication Server/15.0.1/EBF 15041 ESD#2/NT (IX86)/Windows
2000/1/OPT/Mon Sep 17 08:56:12 2007
Open Server Version:    Sybase Server-Library/15.0/P-EBF14617-14616 ESD #9/PC
Intel/BUILD1500-099/OPT/Thu May 24 19:04:48 2007
Open CLient Version:    Sybase Client-Library/15.0/P-EBF14616 ESD #9/PC
Intel/BUILD1500-099/OPT/Thu May 24 19:04:48 2007
RepServer Name:         CHINOOK_RS
=============================================================================


Start Time:          10/21/07 07:06:25 PM
End Time:            10/21/07 07:06:55 PM
Sample Interval (secs):  30


=============================================================================
 Instance                                              Instance ID ModType/InstVal
 ------------------------------------------------------ ----------- ---------------
 DIST, 101 CHINOOK_RS_eRSSD.CHINOOK_RS_eRSSD                101          -1
 Counter                  Obs    Total    Last    Max   Avg ttl/obs Rate x/sec
 ------------------------ ------ -------- ------- ------ ----------- -----------
 #dist_stop_unsupported_cmd    1      0       0      0         0           0
 #SqtMaxCache                  1      0       0      0         0           0
```

(2 rows affected)

```
========================================================================
Instance                                        Instance ID ModType/InstVal
---------------------------------------------- ----------- ---------------
DIST, 103 CHINOOK.pubs2_a                           103           -1
Counter              Obs     Total    Last     Max     Avg ttl/obs Rate x/sec
-------------------- ------- -------- -------- ------- ----------- ----------
#dist_stop_unsupported_cmd   1       0        0        0           0           0
#SqtMaxCache                 1       0        0        0           0           0
```

(2 rows affected)

```
========================================================================
Instance                                        Instance ID ModType/InstVal
---------------------------------------------- ----------- ---------------
REP AGENT, CHINOOK_RS_eRSSD.CHINOOK_RS_eRSSD        101           -1
Observer             Obs         Rate x/sec
-------------------- ----------- -----------
UpdsRslocater             8           0
BuffersReceived          18           0
EmptyPackets             18           0
```

(3 rows affected)

```
Counter              Obs     Total    Last     Max     Avg ttl/obs Rate x/sec
-------------------- ------- -------- -------- ------- ----------- ----------
*BytesReceived            8      431      431     431          53          14
RepAgentRecvTime         27       -1        0       0           0           0
```

...(more)...

Notice this is more of a report format than a result set. As a consequence, it is tougher to build automated analysis or display tools using the display option.

Other commands that can be executed include:

▶ admin statistics, backlog — Reports the current backlog by connection/instance in segments and blocks

▶ admin statistics, bps — Reports the current throughput by connection/instance ID in bytes per second

▶ admin statistics, cps — Reports the current throughput by connection/instance ID in commands per second

▶ admin statistics, tps — Reports the current throughput by connection/instance ID in transactions per second

Like most report formatted outputs, these tend to be difficult to analyze or perform trend analysis with due to parsing requirements. An alternative that may provide a more real-time display of the information is to simply save the data to the RSSD and query the intermediate results periodically.

Stopping the Sample

Statistics sampling can be stopped in two ways. First, of course, the full duration for sampling could simply expire. The second method uses the command:

```
admin statistics, cancel
```

This command is very useful during benchmarking or when you simply want to stop the statistics collection early as the event of concern has already transpired.

Analyzing the Statistics

The easiest way to analyze the statistics is to save the statistics to the RSSD and analyze them in place or extract them to a database created for analysis. When saved to the RSSD, the statistics are recorded to the rs_statruns and rs_statdetail tables.

▶ rs_statruns — This table contains one row for each statistics sample interval with the sample date and time and a run_id. The run_id is an 8-byte binary value composed of the Replication Server site_id for the first 4 bytes and a 4-byte sequential binary number.

▶ rs_statdetail — This table contains the individual counter values collected each sample interval. Each statistic is identified by the run_id, instance_id, and instance_val (in some cases), and reports the observations (counter_obs), the total during the sample period (counter_total), the last value during the sample period (counter_last), and the maximum value during the sample period (counter_max).

The observations counter can be a bit confusing. By definition, it is the number of times that the counter was incremented. For many counters, this will be the same as the total value. However, for counters that report time or other non-incremental values, It represents the number of occurrences — from which an average can be computed by dividing the total by the occurrences.

An ER diagram for these two tables could be depicted as follows:

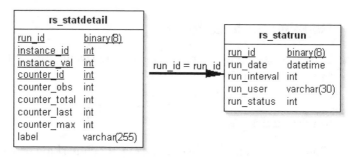

Figure 14-1

The full relationship between these and other connection oriented tables in the RSSD can be illustrated using the following ER diagram:

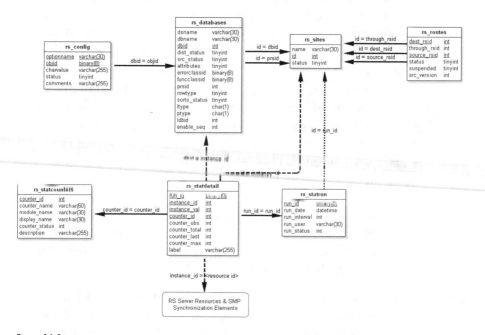

Figure 14-2

This helps to clear up a few relationships between the tables, but some further explanation may be necessary for rs_statdetail with respect to instance_id and instance_val:

▶ instance_id — For database connection counters (i.e., RepAgent), this value is the dbid from rs_databases. For warm standby databases, this could be the ldbid — depending on the module. For route counters (i.e., RSI), this value is the ID from rs_sites for the destination IRS or RRS. For internal resources such as server alarms or SMP synchronization elements, the instance_id is the internal identifier for that resource. For example, SMP synchronization elements are given an ID when created — this is the instance_id that is recorded in rs_statdetail.

▶ instance_val — The value for instance_val depends on the module. See Table 14-3 to determine how to interpret this value for common modules.

Table 14-3

Module	instance_id	instance_val	Interpretation for instance_val
RepAgent	dbid	–1	Not applicable
SQM	1 → ldbid 0 → dbid	{0,1}	0 = outbound queue 1 = inbound queue
SQMR	1 → ldbid 0 → dbid	{10,11,21}	10 = outbound queue DSI SQMR 11 = inbound queue SQT SQMR 21 = inbound queue (warm standby) DSI SQMR
SQT	ldbid	{0,1}	0 = outbound queue 1 = inbound queue
DIST	dbid	–1	Not applicable
DSI	dbid	–1	Not applicable
DSI EXEC	dbid	{1→n}	The DSI EXEC thread number where n is the setting for dsi_num_threads for the connection
RSI	rs_sites.id	–1	Not applicable
SYNCELE	element id	–1	Not applicable
SERV	resource id	–1	Not applicable

Knowing this, you can write queries directly against the rs_statdetail to obtain statistics for a particular counter. Alternatively, there are two different utilities that Sybase has provided via CodeXchange that can also help:

▶ MonCounters-Analysis.zip — This is a Microsoft Excel spreadsheet with macros that charts some of the more common counters within the same module. Uses the output from rs_dump_stats.

▶ M&C Analysis procs — This is a collection of stored procedures that output the counter statistics across the modules for each stage of processing. Best used with Sybase dbIsql or Embarcadero's dbArtisan to allow easy export to Microsoft Excel.

Both are "unsupported" tools in that little documentation is available and Sybase does not provide technical support for improvements or issues with these tools.

DBMS Metrics

In addition to the Replication Server monitor counters, you will likely need to be able to collect detailed DBMS metrics as most (more than 90% of) reported performance issues are directly attributable to replicate database performance. For Oracle, this translates to the V$ tables, while for Sybase ASE, this means collecting MDA data. The key Sybase ASE MDA tables necessary would be:

▶ monOpenObjectActivity — Identifies some of the more common problems such as lack of indexes or inefficient indexing at the replicate, which degrades performance. This table can also be used to identify the DML profile for the transactions (which tables are involved) and help with parallel DSI tuning by identifying tables experiencing contention.

▶ monProcessWaits — This table can be used to identify why the Replication Server maintenance user connection is proceeding so slowly by identifying the major wait events and time for each event.

Other tables could be used in certain situations; however, the above cover the vast majority of requirements.

Third-Party Solutions

In addition to building your own custom solution based on the raw Sybase data structures, some third-party applications also provide Replication Server monitoring capabilities. Many of these focus on monitoring Replication Server health vs. monitoring performance. One notable exception is Bradmark's NORAD Surveillance application, which leverages both rs_ticket as well as Replication Server monitor counters to provide performance monitoring for Sybase Replication Server. This should not be construed as a product endorsement by the authors; however, it should not be ignored, as a prepackaged monitoring solution may provide most of the desired operation performance monitoring functionality needed for the most common performance problems. No tool will meet all requirements, as unexpected performance issues related to rare circumstances are simply too numerous to identify in advance. As a result, such a tool can be extremely useful to meet operational requirements, while rare issues can be analyzed directly via SQL queries.

Analyzing Performance Metrics

Now that we know what not to do and which tools are available to us, and have collected the statistics to help diagnose a problem, we need to analyze these statistics to isolate the problem that is occurring. Also keep in mind the following points:

▶ Multiple different problems could result in the same metrics profiles. For example, insufficient SQT cache and large transactions are two different scenarios that could result in the same sort of metric values.

▶ The key to identifying the likely cause is to look at related metrics that can help isolate the most likely candidate.

▶ It may not be easy to identify the exact cause, especially when the problem is due to Replication Server internals. However, Sybase engineering may be able to identify from the metrics what could be happening and thus suggest configuration changes or product changes.

In this section, we will take a detailed look at each of the main modules involved in the data flow through Replication Server.

Metrics to Focus On

One of the most common complaints of metric-based performance monitoring APIs such as Replication Server monitor counters, ASE MDA, or Oracle V$ is that little is documented to explain the following:

▶ Which are the key metrics to monitor throughput and how do you compare the throughput in the various modules.

▶ Which counters are clear indicators of problem areas.

▶ Which counters should be considered when monitoring resource usage.

▶ Which counters should be considered when determine proper server configuration parameter settings.

The five key areas of commonly used metrics — in order of priority for consideration — are identified in the following paragraphs.

Rate

The very first metric that should always be looked at is rate. Specifically, the rate of one thread's processing should be compared to either historical information (if available) for the same processing load or (more commonly) to the throughput rates of other threads in the processing for the data stream. The very first rate that should be established of course is the Replication Agent User rate, as it is a key reference point. Assuming that all commands are being replicated (vs. empty transactions, subscriptions excluding rows, etc.), any other subsequent thread that is not processing data as fast as the RepAgent User is likely a cause of performance problems.

Rates can be derived by using one of three throughput metrics and dividing by the sample interval. The three metrics are:

▶ Commands — (preferred) This metric refers to the replicated DML, DDL, and Replication Server commands (such as `truncation point management`) that are processed by each module.

▶ Bytes — (SQM and RSI only) This metric refers to the number of bytes processed by each module. Many Replication Server administrators commit the novice mistake of attempting to measure throughput in bytes. The problem is that this is an unreliable method unless the data has extremely consistent data sizes, such as all the tables having the same rowsize. However, the aggregated stable device and route throughputs can be used to see if you are near the edge of practical throughput. (Note "practical," not the highly inflated maximum rating that is rarely achieved, if ever.)

▶ Transactions — (SQT cache only) This metric refers to the number of transactions processed by the modules that measure this (SQT, DSI, DSI EXEC). Because of varying transaction sizes, transactions are useful as a throughput metric for the SQT cache processing.

As you can see, the preferred method of measuring throughput is based on the number of commands. One of the reasons for this is that the number of bytes can vary widely depending on which tables were affected by the DML commands (wide vs. narrow tables), which command (consider the difference between inserts, updates, and deletes and common SQL command sizes), whether or not there are replication definitions, as well as which module is doing the processing. For example, the same command may have one byte length for the RepAgent User thread and a slightly larger byte length for the SQM.

Another common mistake in measuring throughput is trying to establish a maximum, such as 5 MB/sec. This is a mistake because it assumes that the Replication Server throughput is driven by bytes vs. the number of columns in a command, and also does not take into consideration the row sizes, the types of commands (especially the execution of the different types of commands at the replicate), and other factors that distort bytes as a throughput metric. It is not uncommon — especially during batch processing — to see large differences in the throughput as the commands change between inserts, updates, and deletes and the number of columns vary.

The best way to use rate information is not to compare it to a theoretical maximum throughput, but rather to compare the rates between the threads. For example, if the RepAgent User thread is processing 1,000 commands/sec and the SQT is only processing 400 commands/sec, it should be obvious why latency is occurring. If all the threads in the Replication Server are processing commands at the same rate, any latency is likely due to non-Replication Server causes, such as the Replication Agent. Overall, a slow rate at one module can be due to one of three causes: either it is being "starved" by the module ahead of it, internal processing is slow, or the next module is slow. Generally speaking, the threads and modules can be viewed as a series of "stages" or "pipelines" of data flowing through Replication Server, and the throughput rate for each stage is often set by the slowest module. So when comparing the rates, you often need to consider whether the later module is slower or whether a module in between is slower. The stages or pipelines within Replication Server can be thought of as:

▶ RA → SQM — This is the inbound or receiving pipeline composed of the RepAgent User and SQM (writer) for the inbound queue. Performance issues here can impact the Replication Agent throughput. Often the rate in this stage is set by the Replication Agent speed or the rate at which commands can be written to the inbound queue.

▶ SQT → DIST — This is the distribution pipeline composed of the SQT thread (SQMR and SQT modules), the DIST thread, and the SQM (writer) for the outbound queue. Performance issues here are typically configuration related or due to batch processing.

▶ DSI → DSI EXEC — This is the outbound or delivery pipeline composed of the DSI (SQMR, SQT, and DSI modules), the DSI EXEC, and the RDB itself.

▶ WS DSI → WS DSI EXEC — This pipeline is identical to the one above. The only reason it is mentioned separately is because different counter instances are used (i.e., SQMR instance_val=21 vs. 10) and because there is a difference in how the DSI/SQT module needs to be viewed, as it is performing full SQT functions rather than simply being a cache for the DSI EXEC to read from.

▶ PRS RSI → RRS RSIUSER — This is the route pipeline between two RSs that comprise a route — and includes the PRS RSI SQMR, the PRS RSI, the RRS RSIUSER, the RRS DIST, and the RRS SQM (writer). Performance issues here are typically due to one of two causes: simple network speed issues or architectural design when dozens of connections share a common route. While the network itself may not be the limiting factor in this case, the single outbound queue for the route can be.

Rates can also help determine when RSSD interactions might be a contributing factor. For example, the RepAgent's default scan batch size parameter value is 1,000. This sounds like a reasonable number, and people are often unwilling to change this due to fears of the possible impact on the primary database. However, if you are processing 2,000 commands/sec, you quickly realize that you are adding considerable overhead in moving the truncation point twice per second and the half-second recoverability is constraining your overall throughput. This also is true of the Replication Server configuration parameter sqm_recover_seg, which specifies how often Replication Server updates the RSSD with recovery information. The simple explanation is that sqm_recover_seg tells how much of a queue may have to be rescanned during recovery or connection resumption to determine where processing left off. The default of 1 MB again sounds reasonable — until you look at the rate at which recovery information is being written to the RSSD and discover that as a result, the RSSD is acting as an OLTP system and incurring tens of updates/second when all the threads are considered instead of behaving as a metadata catalog with predominately reads. Meanwhile, segment processing of data is occurring at a rate of several thousand per sample interval, meaning that by allowing

Replication Server to obtain sub-second recovery determination, you have made the RSSD an OLTP database.

Time

Time metrics are counters that report the time spent doing a particular task within Replication Server, such as time spent reading packets, converting replicated data into SQL for execution at the replicate, etc. The reason time metrics are so crucial is that once you have identified a thread that is the holdup, it will be the time metrics that tell why that thread is the issue and which particular area needs tuning. A key aspect of time metrics in Replication Server counter data is that the time represents 1/100ths of a second; normalizing to seconds is highly recommended.

Most of the more critical functions within Replication Server — especially where Replication Server interfaces with primary/replicate databases — have timing metrics that detail how much time is spent on the different tasks. The key is to look at each timing metric compared to the sample interval or other timing metrics for the same module to see if an inordinate amount of time is being spent on one task. Unfortunately, the time the thread spent actually running on the CPU during any sample interval is not currently available within RS. As a result, the most useful aspect of the time metrics is to compare the time metrics for the same thread to establish the "worst" offender for the thread. For example, if the batching time for a DSI EXEC was 5 seconds and the result processing time was 30 seconds (of a 1-minute sample), while improving the SQL batching by tuning Replication Server will help, it will not help nearly as much as improving the RDB execution time thereby reducing the result processing time.

Bell Ringers

Within nearly every module, there are certain monitor counters that can be thought of as "bell ringers" that indicate a possible significant problem that is very detrimental to performance. For example, with the RepAgent User, RAWriteWaitsTime (specifically the observations more than the time itself) is a good indicator that the SQM is not able to keep up with write activity. The key to bell ringers is to think about them much like house-hold smoke detectors — the occasional bleep is not a cause for alarm, but if they start screaming constantly, it is time to either fix the problem or get out of the house.

Caches and Queues

As a message store and forwarding system, the absolute ideal configuration for Replication Server is the minimal memory and storage space required. Obviously, in some cases the transaction sizes and rates will dictate how little you can get away with, but the reality of the matter is that the goal of Replication Server is to move a transaction through the system so it remains in memory for as short a time as possible. Contrast this with DBMS's, in which a single data page is read multiple times and large caches are the norm.

This doesn't mean that you may not need 32 MB or even 100 MB for the SQT cache due to large transactions. It does mean that 1 GB or even 2 GB of memory is wasted on Replication Server and would never be effective if Replication Server is prop-erly tuned, and in fact would be detrimental to performance as the increased size of memory pointers, etc., would cause a slight degrade in most systems. As a result, one of the items to watch regularly is how much memory is being used and whether it could be reduced. For example, if the SQT cache for a connection shows a maximum used by the end of the day as 30 MB, and dsi_sqt_max_cache_size is set to 250 MB, 220 MB of memory is being wasted and never used. Adding memory will do nothing.

Similarly, the queue disk space should be minimal. This is the currently used disk space that the SQT cache represents (so why would you want 1 GB of memory for SQT cache when you don't want the corresponding queue size to be 1 GB?).

As a result, the metrics that track cache usage and queue space are high-priority items for monitoring. But while the spe-cific memory/space counters are important, even more important is the associated processing counters that drive the mem-ory/space requirements. For the SQT cache, this is the

Open/Closed/Read transaction counts. For `exec_sqm_write_request_limit`, it is the RAWriteWaitsTime counter_obs metric.

Configuration

The first four of these metrics establish the high-priority types of counters to be looked at, especially during times of latency or poor performance. On the second tier is the set of counters that correspond to Replication Server or connection configuration parameters beyond those discussed. This includes derived counters such as Commands/Packet, which can help tune the Replication Agent, and similar counters. As mentioned, most of these are derived counters, meaning that a relationship with another counter in the same thread is used to derive the expression to calculate the metric.

The reason these are considered second tier when compared to rate, time, cache/space utilization, and the bell ringers is that there are an incredible number of tuning opportunities that can be discovered from monitoring a RS. However, which ones will be meaningful and can possibly contribute to improving performance will only be apparent after the list of possible causes for the performance problem has been narrowed such that the changes to configuration parameters can be effectively measured. The following rules might help in tuning considerations:

1. Use only enough memory to achieve optimal performance. Unlike database servers, messages within any message processing system are perishable and have short time-to-live expectations. Large data caches to hold messages are particularly ineffective and waste resources.

2. Minimize the interactions with the RSSD. The primary offenders here are the updates to rs_locaters (RepAgent and RSI) and rs_oqids (queue space management tracking). Not only do such operations inflict a tiny pause on the Replication Server processing until the RSSD responds, but if you are not careful, the number of updates could push the RSSD from a metadata catalog into an OLTP processing system with larger resource requirements, resulting in resource conflicts.

3. Use separate devices for separate queues. If you think of Replication Server like a message processing system, this is almost a given configuration expectation — you want different "message queues" to use different devices to spread the I/O load so as to avoid bottlenecks. Like DBMS systems, Replication Server manages the space allocations for its stable devices. Consequently, if multiple queue requests are made for the same stable device, Replication Server has to control concurrency for the device via normal thread controls such as mutexes. Contention and normal yield times for mutex processing could be longer than the write operation physically takes.

4. Remove or change any restrictive parameters that are not applicable. A number of configuration parameters in Replication Server were added to throttle particular threads to allow more even distribution of CPU time or were added to cause a specific behavior for a predetermined set of circumstances. In many cases, these are irrelevant and should be configured to remove the limit or make it more appropriate for the current processing load.

5. Understand what you are changing and why you expect any impact, and support the change based on Replication Server monitor counter metrics. There are a lot of sites that establish "standard" configurations for any processing server in their environment. This notion causes several problems. First, it doesn't consider the different load characteristics of different applications. Second, it has resulted in a breed of administrators who don't understand what the parameters that they are changing do, when they should or should not change them (based on metrics), and why they are expecting those parameters to make a difference.

6. Keep the numbers sane. This sounds easier than it is. When configuring memory or buffer sizes, don't overallocate unnecessary space that is unlikely to be used or is impossible to achieve. For example, setting `dsi_cmd_batch_size` to 1 MB assumes that the replicate DBMS can handle a 1 MB command buffer, which is highly improbable. Also, setting delay timers such as `init_sqm_write_delay` below 50 ms is unlikely

to be reasonable as a single write operation could take 20 to 30 ms on slow devices.

7. Keep expectations realistic. Don't expect Replication Server to achieve the same throughput with a single DSI configured as a 60-engine ASE; multiple DSIs will be required in parallel. Along the same lines, if a single source connection is distributing data to multiple destinations, the number of writes it will need to perform and the time to do so will increase proportionately.

Replication Agent User (EXEC)

When analyzing Replication Server performance, it is often best to start at the very beginning of the pipeline; in this case, that is the Replication Agent User (aka EXEC) thread. While it is often referred to as the EXEC thread, especially in Replication Server trace commands, in actuality it is one of several threads in the EXEC class. For the purposes of this chapter, we will try to stick to calling it the "RepAgent User" thread, although careful reading will be needed to distinguish between it and references to the Replication Agent (RepAgent).

The flow of processing within the RepAgent User thread has two main stages. First, the LTL buffer has to be received from the primary. The LTL buffer can be sent in a single packet for small LTL buffers (such as ASE RepAgent) or heterogeneous replication agents may use multiple packets to send larger LTL buffers. Once the full buffer has been received, the RepAgent User then parses the commands, normalizes the columns to match the replication definition, packs the commands into the SQM format, and submits each command as a write request to the SQM via an internal message queue, the write request queue. This flow can be depicted as:

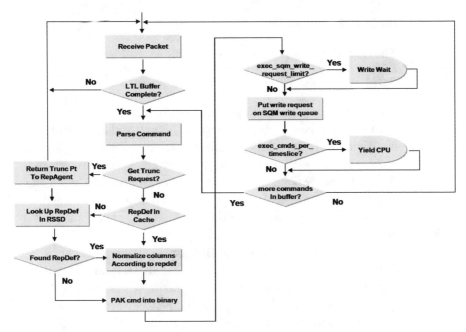

Figure 14-3: Simplified view of RepAgent User thread processing logic

Common Problems

Some of the more common problems with the RepAgent User that occur in replication environments are:

▶ Misconfigured or untuned Replication Agents

▶ Slow SQM writing

▶ Excessive normalization time due to replication definition column ordering not in same sequence as table order

▶ Missing replication definitions

The first two are easily spotted with RepAgent User counters, while the latter two can only be hinted at from using the STS counters and doing a bit of extrapolation.

Metrics to Focus On

The key metrics to focus on for the RepAgent User are:

Rate

For the rate metric, the key metric is Commands/Sec, which is derived from the counter CmdsRecv (58000) and the sample duration. While not all the commands are distributed (e.g., get truncation requests), most likely nearly all of them are. Since this is the entry point into the Replication Server, the command rate from this thread also sets the threshold for all subsequent threads; anything lower than the RepAgent command rate suggests a problem with that thread.

A secondary rate would be Bytes/Sec, which would be derived from the counter BytesReceived (58011) and the sample duration. Note that the byte rate can easily be distorted by the type of command, shortened/normal LTL keywords, and whether compressed syntaxes are used — especially with heterogeneous replication agents or Mirror Activator, as ASE's Replication Agent always uses a compressed syntax for updates. It is extremely important to recognize that you cannot compare byte rates between threads, unlike command rates. The reason for this is that the command sizes fluctuate based on format changes when being written to the queues (i.e., packed binary vs. packed ASCII), the amount of data needed to be written (i.e., if no replication definition, then all the non-BLOB columns are repeated for primary keys), and other differences. However, you can aggregate the byte rates across all the RepAgent User threads plus the DSI EXEC byte rates to see if you are close to the 25% saturation point of most networks.

This leaves us with the following rates:

```
-- Counter:          Counter ID:
-- --------          ------
-- CmdsRecv          58000
-- BytesReceived     58011
-- RepAgentExecTime  58025
-- delta             (sample duration in secs)
CmdsPerSec = CmdsRecv/delta
MbitsPerSec = (BytesReceived*8/1048576)/(RepAgentExecTime/100.0)
```

CmdsPerSec is the key rate to focus on.

Time

The key time counter for RepAgent User is actually not used for time the majority of the time, as you will see in the next section. To understand the counter, you need to recognize that the RepAgent User communicates write requests to the SQM via a write request message queue. If this queue is full, the RepAgent User has to wait for the SQM to write a block to disk to free up space in the write request message queue. The counter RAWriteWaitsTime (58019) tracks how much time the RepAgent User spent waiting on the SQM to write to disk because the write request message queue was full (exec_sqm_write_request_limit) as illustrated by the Write Wait delay in the processing logic illustrated earlier.

The second delay depicted in the processing logic is RepAgentYieldTime (58016), which tracks the amount of time that the RepAgent yielded the CPU when exec_cmds_per_timeslice was reached. This could be a high value if you are using exec_cmds_per_timeslice to throttle the RepAgent input stream to provide more CPU time to other threads within the Replication Server.

Another processing time that is not depicted as a delay is RepAgentRecvTime (58023), which tells how much time the RepAgent User thread spent receiving the packets from the Replication Server. Think of this time as the time spent in the loop depicted in the upper left of Figure 14-3 where the RepAgent User waits for packets to arrive until the full LTL buffer is received. Ideally this should be a higher percentage of all the "times," as this is the one timing metric for RepAgent User that is tracking "working" time.

While any one wait may not be extensive, the total waits could add up to a substantial percentage of the total time the RepAgent User was actually executing. Unlike the other threads that do not have counters yet to tell the execution time, later Replication Server 12.6 and Replication Server 15.0 EBFs added the counter RepAgentExecTime (58025).

Bell Ringers

The key bell ringers for the RepAgent User thread are:

▶ RAWriteWaitsTime (counter_obs and counter_total)

▶ RAYieldTime (counter_obs and counter_total)

Either of these two indicate a disruption in the RepAgent User processing that results in a delay. Note that we focus on the number of observations as much as the total time. The rationale for this is that the timer is based on hundredths of a second; the actual delay time could be less than one one-hundredth, which would get rounded to zero for the delay. The first points to a likely SQM writer bottleneck that needs to be analyzed, while the second suggests that a resource limit configuration parameter (exec_cmds_per_timeslice) should be increased.

Caches and Queues

While the RepAgent User doesn't use any queue space, there are two areas of memory that affect RepAgent User processing. The first affects it only indirectly — the STS cache. As noted in the processing diagram, when the RepAgent User thread is parsing commands from the LTL buffer, it needs to normalize the columns as they are received to the order of the columns in the replication definition. Accordingly, it must first locate the repdef(s) for the physical table in the replicated command. If the repdefs are already in cache, then the processing can continue uninterrupted. However, if not, then the RepAgent User must retrieve the repdefs via the STS interface. An interesting aspect to consider in all of this is that some sites don't like to create repdefs due to maintenance reasons. The result of this thinking should be obvious. With each new table in the LTL stream, the RSSD must be accessed to check for a repdef, for which none exists. Fortunately, Replication Server is intelligent enough to not have to check every time, but it does point out one place where not using repdefs detracts from performance. While a full repdef with all columns is the best choice, a minimal repdef with just the primary key columns and the send standby all columns attribute is much better than no repdef at all.

The second area of memory is `exec_sqm_write_request_limit`. This really isn't memory used by the RepAgent User directly, either. Inside RS, a number of internal message queues are created to allow asynchronous processing between the threads. The `exec_sqm_write_request_limit` parameter refers to the amount of memory that the SQM Write Request message queue can use for each inbound SQM writer thread. By default, this is only 16 K with a maximum of 2 GB (formerly 983,040 bytes); like most memory configurations in RS, oversizing this does not help. The primary function of this message queue — beyond the interthread communications — is to buffer write requests during brief periods when the SQM is busy. If the SQM is frequently delayed due to a slow disk I/O subsystem or device contention, increasing this can help, but eventually this queue will fill regardless of the size.

Tuning for Performance

It is interesting to note that while the RepAgent User thread is rarely a cause for performance issues, the RepAgent feeding it is a common problem area and RepAgent tuning issues can often be identified. Note that both ASE RepAgent and heterogeneous/ Mirror Activator RepAgents have a number of tuning parameters that can affect performance outside of those mentioned in this section. This section will focus on just those that are directly observable using the Replication Server metrics.

RepAgent Packet and Buffer Size

The smaller the packet and buffer sizes used by the RepAgent, the more time the RepAgent User spends waiting on work to arrive. Additionally, the packet overhead is higher, resulting in less network efficiency. The way to determine what tuning should be done is to derive the number of commands received per packet/buffer by formulas such as:

```
-- Counter:          Counter ID:
-- --------          ------
-- CmdsRecv          58000
-- PacketsReceived   58010
-- BuffersReceived   58013
```

```
-- BytesReceived      58011

CmdsPerPacket = CmdsRecv/PacketsReceived
CmdsPerBuffer = CmdsRecv/BuffersReceived
EffPacketSize = BytesReceived/PacketsReceived
EffCmdSize = BytesReceived/CmdsRecv
```

If only a few commands per packet are being received, the packet size should increase until there are at least five to ten commands per packet. Remember that included with the replicated DML commands are the begin transaction and commit transaction records, which are fairly small, so with a typical OLTP system using the default configurations that is receiving two to three commands per packet, only one or two of those commands are likely DML statements; this is horrifically inefficient. For ASE RepAgents, this is the send_buffer_size parameter, which is both the buffer size and packet size. Heterogeneous and Mirror Activator RepAgents have the rs_packet_size parameter. By default, parameters are set to 2048, which is likely not optimal; a setting of 8 K or 16 K may be better.

For heterogeneous or Mirror Activator based-systems, tuning the buffer size is not necessary. For heterogeneous RepAgents, both ltl_batch_size and rs_packet_size parameters exist. While rs_packet_size may need increasing, ltl_batch_size is typically 40,000 bytes. Some slight tuning for matching the packet size may be necessary — such as 40 K (40,960 bytes) for 8 K and 48 K (49,152 bytes) for 16 K — but otherwise the default buffer size is actually fairly optimal, even for high-volume systems.

RepAgent Scan Batch Size

By default the ASE RepAgent's scan_batch_size as well as the heterogeneous RepAgent's max_ops_per_scan are both set to 1,000. Most Replication Server admins are aware that by increasing this, theoretically more transactions are retained in the primary log when truncated by a dump transaction (or similar command), which can affect recoverability. While this is definitely true on low-volume systems that only have a trickle of DML modifications, in most OLTP systems, this default setting of

1,000 corresponds to a few seconds worth of transactions. Interestingly, most ASEs are still running with the default recovery interval setting of 5 minutes, suggesting that increasing this parameter is not likely to have as large of an impact on recovery as most Replication Server admins think. Derived metrics to use for tuning this configuration are:

```
-- Counter:        Counter ID:
-- --------        ------
-- CmdsRecv        58000
-- UpdsRslocater   58009
-- delta           (sample delta in seconds)

ScanBatchSize = CmdsRecv/UpdsRslocater
UpdPerMin = (UpdsRslocater*60)/(delta*1.0) -- decimal(5,2)
```

The first metric should be obvious. Note that as a derived metric, it might not actually read "1,000" each time as the RepAgent may request a new truncation point whenever it hits the end of the log, especially before it goes to sleep. Usually a glance at it will suggest the maximum and the likely setting for the scan batch size.

The second takes a bit of interpolation. First, consider that in many high-volume systems, the RepAgent is capable of processing several thousand commands per second. At a default scan batch size of 1,000, this translates effectively into a 1-second recovery interval for the primary ASE — and a considerable load on the RSSD. Increasing the scan batch size on higher volume systems to 10,000 or even 20,000 still can result in sub-minute recovery intervals from the primary ASE. While allowing the ASE to run for 3 or 5 minutes without moving the truncation point may be a bit long during heavy processing, ideally we would only like to move the truncation point about once per minute. Increasing the scan batch size to achieve this is desirable; however, increases beyond 20,000 are not likely to gain much except in extreme processing environments.

LTL Syntax Compression

There are different types of LTL syntax compression:

▶ Short LTL keywords — LTL keywords are abbreviated to three-character mneumonics (and char and two-char abbreviations). This can reduce the LTL overhead, especially for sites with shorter rows/small transactions.

▶ Structured OQIDs — By default, RepAgents send the full 32-byte OQID length for each replicated command. By enabling structured OQIDs, the RepAgent sends only the applicable OQID portion rather than the full OQID, which includes the recovery pointers.

▶ Column compression — For replicated updates and deletes, normally the full before/after image would be expected to be replicated. For updates, this can be excessive as large character columns (product descriptions, customer names, etc.) are rarely changed. For deletes, this can also contribute significant overhead as non-primary key column values are sent.

The determination to enable compressed syntax and which ones to enable can only be made after looking at the command size as replicated and comparing to the known row size. Usually enabling compressed syntax is not harmful and is typically beneficial, and thus it is recommended. The impact of these settings can be observed by comparing the following metrics from one run to the same metrics from the same transaction mix. While any repeatable transaction mix is usable, a representative mix for peak periods (such as batch processing jobs) will better estimate the actual impact. Note the derived counter formula is the same as one of those used for tuning packet sizes.

```
-- Counter:       Counter ID:
-- --------       ------
-- CmdsRecv       58000
-- BytesReceived  58011

EffCmdSize = BytesReceived/CmdsRecv
```

However, the parameters that need to be adjusted depend on the Replication Agent involved. See Table 14-4.

Table 14-4

Configuration	ASE RepAgents	MRA/RAX
Short LTL keywords	short_ltl_keywords	compress_ltl_syntax
Structured OQIDs	send_structured_oqids	structured_tokens
Column compression	n/a	column_compression and use_rssd

For ASE RepAgents, there are only two parameters: short_ltl_keywords and send_structured_oqids. Both should be enabled. The default settings and behavior for short_ltl_keywords vary depending on the ASE version and can only be verified by tracing the LTL sent to Replication Server via ASE RepAgent LTL trace flags. Some versions of ASE list the default as false, while in reality it is defaulting to using the short_ltl_keywords syntax. On the other hand, send_structured_oqids is fairly consistent in that the default of false seems to be accurate. By default, ASE RepAgent uses a compressed syntax for updates (sending a complete before image and only changed columns for the after image) and a non-compressed syntax for deletes (fewer text/image columns). This reduces the LTL overhead while providing full support for function strings.

For heterogeneous and Mirror Activator Replication Agents, the associated configuration parameters are: compress_ltl_syntax, structured_tokens, and column_compression with use_rssd. While both the former should be enabled by default, care must be taken about the latter, although it generally is recommended. With column_compression enabled, MRA/RAX will send the following:

▶ inserts — Only the columns listed in the repdefs (unless the send standby clause specifies all columns). ASE RepAgent sends all columns regardless.

▶ updates — Full before image and only the changed columns (similar to ASE RepAgent).

▶ deletes — Primary key columns only (ASE RepAgent sends all non-LOB columns).

Note that in order for column_compression to be enabled, the parameter use_rssd must also be enabled as MRA/RAX will use the repdef. The notable difference is in the delete processing as MRA/RAX will only send the primary keys. Consequently, if using custom function strings for deletes, you may not be able to enable column_compression.

Stable Queue Manager (SQM)

For the SQM thread, we are principally focused on the writing. SQM reading is done by the SQMR module within the SQM Reader (the SQT or DSI threads). Overall, the SQM writing logic is pretty simple:

▶ Read a write request from the write request queue.

▶ If a duplicate command (rescanning), discard it.

▶ If not a duplicate, append it to the current block (in memory).

▶ When the block if full or when the timer expires, flush it to disk.

▶ If the segment is full, allocate a new segment.

▶ Update the RSSD recovery and space management information for the queue as each segment is processed.

This can be depicted as follows:

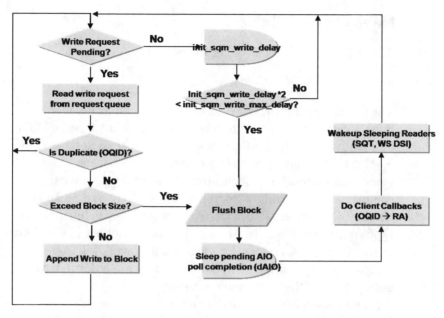

Figure 14-4: SQM write processing (simplified)

Note that when the SQM actually posts the I/O to the physical device, it sleeps until the I/O has completed. This I/O completion is detected by the dAIO daemon, which polls the OS for completed disk I/Os. Having a single dAIO daemon doing the I/O completion polling instead of every SQM thread individually polling for completion reduces the impact on the Replication Server.

Common Problems

The most common problems for the SQM are:

▶ Contention on stable device allocation with other queues

▶ Slow devices

▶ Contention on internal thread resources with queue readers

The first two are quite easily identified. The third can be identified using Replication Server monitor counters; however, Sybase Technical Support and likely engineering assistance will be required to fully diagnose the exact cause. Consequently, the third problem will not be discussed as part of this book.

Metrics to Focus On

The key metrics to focus on for the SQM (writer) are:

Rate

The rate metric for the SQM thread is fairly mundane. If you think about it, once the write request queue is full, it is the SQM rate that will dictate the RepAgent User's processing rate, so the SQM rate and RepAgent User's rate will likely be very close unless there are a lot of duplicates. Since we suggested using commands as the point of reference, there are two command metrics for SQM writers to be aware of: WriteRequests (6040) and CmdsWritten (6000). From a rate standpoint, neither is very illustrative for the reason mentioned above; however, it is useful to compare to the RepAgent CmdsRecv counter in order to have a good picture of the command processing throughput.

This leaves bytes and segments as the next logical choices for observed rate information. The former is a bit misleading as Replication Server writes a full 16 K block each time, so tracking bytes/sec throughput would be an effective rate but not really indicative of the full I/O rate. This leaves segments as the metric of choice — specifically SegsAllocated (6021). Unfortunately, this rate could only be crudely estimated in 12.6 and previous versions of Replication Server due to a lack of a timer for each write. Additionally, remember that the device throughput rate needs to be aggregated across all queues that use that device; it would be a mistake to think that a single queue's 2 MB/sec rate is not being hampered by the device when 10 queues share the device and are all writing one or more segments per second. If you have used disk affinity to separate the queues and you can isolate which queues are using the same device, then a derived I/O throughput rate can be achieved.

```
-- Counter:        Counter ID:
-- --------        ------
-- SegsAllocated   6021
-- SQMWriteTime    6057
QueueWritesMBsec = SegsAllocated/(SQMWriteTime/100.0)
```

The next problem, of course, is that there likely is a mix of writes and reads, so comparing the segment rate in MB/sec is a bit misleading as read activity could influence this dramatically (and does so when rescanning a transaction removed from SQT cache). Comparing SegsAllocated to SegsDeallocated (6022) also can be a bit of an issue as the save interval for Replication Server controls the segment deallocation.

So what should you actually use for rate information? The answer is:

▶ CmdsWritten (6000) — Compare in relative terms to RepAgent User thread's CmdsRecv value. Could be off if there are high numbers of duplicates and will be slightly off due to truncation requests anyhow.

▶ SegsActive (6021) — This indicates a read latency, although not a write problem per se. Ideally, the fewer segments active, the better.

▶ QueueWritesMBsec — As derived above. While precise as noted earlier, if this is approaching several MB/sec, it is likely that device I/O speed could be hampering the throughput.

Time

There are three time metrics for SQM writing activity:

▶ TimeNewSeg (6023) — Time it takes to fully populate a segment. The timer starts when the segment is allocated and ends when the next segment is allocated (essentially when the segment is full).

▶ TimeSeg (6029) — Time it takes to process a segment. This is defined by the time the segment is allocated until the time the segment is deallocated, including save interval time, etc.

▶ SQMWriteTime (6057) — Time it takes per write operation (block writes).

While the first two can be interesting and could be used to establish some relative rate information, the key time metric to watch is SQMWriteTime. In addition to reporting the raw time information, the percentage of time spent writing would also be a good metric to observe:

```
-- Counter:          Counter ID:
-- --------          ------
-- SQMWriteTime      6057
-- BlocksWritten     6002
-- delta             (sample duration in seconds)

WriteTimeSecs = (SQMWriteTime/100.0)
AvgBlockWriteTime = BlocksWritten/(SQMWriteTime*10)
PctWriteTime = (SQMWriteTime)/delta
```

The latter formula needs a bit of explaining. Unlike the RepAgent User, we don't have the total time the SQM was running. Since it sleeps when an I/O is dispatched, the execution time may be useful only to monitor write request processing speed. Consequently, comparing to the full sample delta is likely a bit low. Additionally, percentages are often expressed with a maximum of 100%; normalizing the write time by dividing by 100 is essentially nullified by the need to multiply the numerator by 100 to derive the percentage.

Bell Ringers

The bell ringers for the SQM are:

▶ SegsActive (6020) — Indicates latency in the system.

▶ SleepsWaitSeg (6016) — Indicates stable device contention between queues or possible slow device problems.

▶ Duplicates (6012) — May spike during recovery/RepAgent restart, but high values here could indicate forgetting rs_zeroltm or data loss.

▶ AvgBlockWrite Time (derived) — This reports the average time taken to write a disk block in milliseconds. Generally, 0 to 8 ms per I/O is considered average.

▶ PctWriteTime (derived) — Anytime this exceeds 10 to 20%, it suggests that device response time is slow or Replication Server internal contention.

The most obvious is SegsActive. However, SleepsWaitSeg can also appear and can explain why expected high throughput is not being achieved. Both AvgBlockWriteTime and PctWriteTime can also be a key clue to issues as they may point to slow devices or internal contention. Duplicates should be rare and not as likely to occur.

Caches and Queues

The SQM Writer does not use any configurable memory as cache. Only the block being currently filled is kept in memory. Readers can read this block from memory if it is the next block to be read. To facilitate this, the SQM writer will hold the block in memory if no further write requests are pending for a configurable amount of time. This is controlled by the configuration parameters `init_sqm_write_delay` and `init_sqm_write_max_delay`. The definition for these parameters according to the manuals are:

- ▶ `init_sqm_write_delay` — Write delay for the Stable Queue Manager if queue is being read. Default: 1000 milliseconds.

- ▶ `init_sqm_write_max_delay` — The maximum write delay for the Stable Queue Manager if the queue is not being read. Default: 10,000 milliseconds.

The internal message queue used by the SQM writer has already been discussed. For inbound queues, the `exec_sqm_write_request_limit` parameter controls the amount of memory set aside for each inbound queue for caching write requests from RepAgent User threads. For outbound queues, the configuration parameter is `md_sqm_write_request_limit`. For inbound connections, the size of this cache can be determined by observing the RAWriteWaitsTime metric, which will be incremented when the RepAgent User attempts to submit a write request but cannot due to the write request queue being full. Unfortunately, there is no similar metric for outbound queues, so you will only be able to judge by the write wait activity for outbound queue SQM writers based on the inbound queue write request queue sizing, which is not exactly precise.

The SQM writer is primarily concerned with disk space, so it stands to reason that there are multiple metrics that track disk space, including:

- ▶ BlocksWritten (6002) — The number of 16 K blocks written.
- ▶ SegsActive (6020) — The number of segments that contain undelivered data. Note that the segments could have been

read, but since the commands have not yet been delivered, the space has not been reclaimed yet.

▶ SegsAllocated (6021) — The number of segments that have been allocated.

▶ SegsDeallocated (6022) — The number of segments that have been deallocated.

▶ AffinityHintUsed (6035) — The number of segment allocations that used the disk_affinity hint.

Most of these are fairly self explanatory. Ideally, you want to keep SegsActive as small as possible (preferably 1) and AffinityHintUsed equal to SegsAllocated. If you can achieve this, you will have minimal latency and the desired degree of I/O write concurrency is being achieved.

Tuning for Performance

Tuning the SQM for performance involves mostly minimizing the read activity as much as possible while making the writes as fast as possible and minimizing space management overhead. While writing to a queue is not avoidable (due to preventing data loss), reading from the queue can largely be eliminated by ensuring that:

▶ SQM readers are capable of maintaining the same rate as the SQM writers.

▶ Large transactions that won't fit in the SQM reader's cache are minimized.

How to accomplish that is addressed in the next section on the SQT. The next goal is to make the writes as fast as possible.

disk_affinity

One method for making writes fast is to deconflict the stable queues so that they are not sharing the same devices. This can be accomplished by setting the disk_affinity for the connection. Note that setting it for a connection means that both the inbound and outbound queues for that connection will attempt to use the same physical device; consequently, you may still have contention if a particular connection is both a primary and a replicate.

exec_sqm_write_request_limit and md_sqm_write_request_limit

As mentioned earlier in the discussion about RAWriteWaitsTime, each stable queue has a write request queue to which SQM clients dispatch write requests. The SQM reads the requests from this queue and fills the blocks. For an inbound queue, the only SQM client is the RepAgent User, so there is a 1:1 correlation between non-system commands and write requests. However, for an outbound queue, a single destination may be the target for multiple sources (consider a corporate rollup, for example) in which multiple different threads are attempting to write to the same outbound queue. In this case, each source DIST thread submits a write request to the outbound queue's write request queue. By default, both the exec_sqm_write_request_limit (inbound queue) and md_sqm_write_request_limit (outbound queue) are only 16 KB in size, or about 16 replicated commands. For an inbound queue, this is problematic enough as SQM writer and reader conflicts, space allocation conflicts, write wait time, etc., can all cause intermittent delays in processing the write requests. Ideally, you would like to size the write request queue to be large enough to buffer requests until the SQM can catch up. Typically, it is suggested that this be set to 2 to 4 MB for inbound and outbound queues. However, for outbound queues that are rollups from multiple sources, you might need to set it to 2 MB per source database.

sqm_recover_seg

The space management overhead of the SQM can be larger than realized. By default, the sqm_recover_seg parameter is set to 1, which means that for every segment processed, the RSSD is updated. A sudden influx of activity from the primary can result in multiple updates each second from a single queue. While this is bad enough in a simple warm standby setup with only a single queue for the pair, for MSA or non-warm standby replicates the outbound route or destination queues are likely processing the same volume, which adds to the load. The question is whether this load is really necessary and if it can be reduced without significant harm to the replication environment.

The answer is in understanding what sqm_recover_seg does. The best way to think of it is to picture non-warm standby replication with SQM, SQT, DIST, and other threads. Consider the following ER diagram of this subsection of the RSSD:

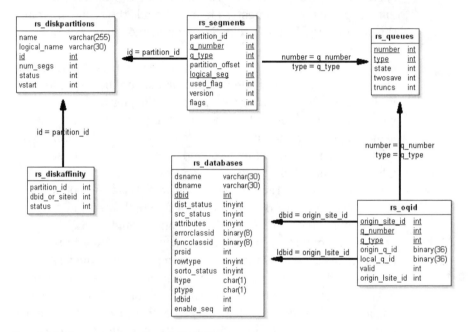

Figure 14-5: Space mangement sub-model for RSSD

As transactions arrive from the primary system, the blocks are written to disk. When that segment is full, a new segment has to allocated. Before assigning the logical segment, Replication Server determines which segment is free by checking internally within its structures to see which other threads are using space on that device, which segments they are using, and the offset for the new segment. Once determined, this allocation is recorded in the rs_segment table and the OQID for the last command for the previous segment is recorded to the rs_oqid table in the RSSD. As the SQT processes each transaction, it builds a list of transactions that can be truncated from the queue. As processing continues, the SQT tells the SQM to truncate those blocks. The

SQM marks the blocks as having been delivered. When the full segment has been processed, the SQM marks the segment as inactive in the rs_segments table and updates the rs_oqid table with the last OQID processed. Note that the rs_oqid table doesn't have a segment; it is only concerned with tracking the last OQID processed from a source database. Asynchronously, the SQM will eventually deallocate the space depending upon any save interval that has been established.

RS recovery works by each thread finding the last OQID that was processed and checking new transactions as they arrive. "Finding" the last OQID typically involves checking with the destination; for example, the DSI checks the rs_lastcommit table. In this case, the DIST would check with the outbound queue SQM, which would look it up in the rs_oqid table for its connection. Transactions or commands with a lower OQID are discarded as duplicates until the desired OQID is reached. The time it takes to find this current OQID is dependent upon how many segments have to be scanned. During recovery, each SQM reader starts scanning from the first "active" segment and begins processing the commands.

So, how does sqm_recover_seg affect this? The answer is that updates to rs_segments and rs_oqid are not recorded, which increases the amount of commands that have to be rescanned/reprocessed during recovery. Consider if sqm_recover_seg is set to 5. Only after every fifth segment allocation would the SQM record its segment allocations and OQID information to the RSSD. Clients (such as the RepAgent) that are moving a truncation point that use the OQID information are only told the last OQID flushed to the RSSD, so they retain the old information. If the Replication Server suddenly crashed after only processing four segments, different parts of the Replication Server might end up reprocessing 4 MB of replicated commands. In many production systems, the size of a replicated command on disk is ~1 K, so this is about 4,000 commands. Interestingly, even ASE's RepAgent is able to process more than 1,000 to 2,000 commands per second, meaning that each segment of commands represents less than one second of reprocessing. Consequently, increasing sqm_recover_seg does not appreciably slow down recovery.

On the flip side, SQM writing to the queue effectively pauses with each RSSD update. So, by default, with `sqm_recover_seg` set to 1, the SQM "pauses" every segment to update the RSSD. This update, while sub-second, could be tens of milliseconds as multiple tables are modified. The response time depends on scheduling with the RSSD, the write-ahead log speed of recording the updates, and the network round-trip time for each command. However, dramatic increases are not necessary. Changing it from 1 to 10, for instance, reduces the impact on the RSSD for a peak load from 1 per second (OLTP-ish rate) to 6 per minute — hardly much of an effort. For tuning purposes, it is suggested that you first try bumping up `sqm_recover_seg` in steps of 3, 5, and finally 10, with 10 being the likely maximum at this stage for Replication Server 15. At each step, roughly aggregate the number of updates to the RSSD for the active connections. If still in the 1 per second range, increase the `sqm_recover_seg` another bump.

sqm_write_flush

By default the `sqm_write_flush` configuration value is turned on. This can be extremely debilitating for Replication Server as all stable devices that are file system based are opened with `dsync`, which forces a flush after each write and on many systems is a synchronous operation. While the `sqm_write_flush` parameter does not apply to raw partitions, the 2000 MB limitation for stable devices in Replication Server versions up through 12.6 often forced system administrators to use file system devices. Additionally, many corporations adopted the use of Veritas File System (VxFS) as the corporate standard for file systems for portability reasons and DBMS performance as VxFS included QuickIO, a method for allowing both asynchronous and unbuffered I/Os to a file system similar to a raw partition. Additionally, in recent years, OS vendors have added support for DirectIO, which allows unbuffered I/Os to the file system, and have modified their I/O drivers to support asynchronous I/O to file system devices. Some of these have taken a further step in supporting file system mounting options that force all writes to the file system to use DirectIO, whether or not the file was opened using DirectIO. Often this was simply accomplished by disabling or bypassing the file system buffer cache for this file system.

Another interesting aspect to consider is how Replication Server works. When this parameter was originally added, the thinking was since writes to (buffered) file systems were not guaranteed (similar to ASE), there was a good chance of data loss occurring in the event of a host OS panic or crash. This certainly was true for ASE — especially in the case of the transaction log. However, for Replication Server, the built-in recovery mechanism as described for sqm_recover_seg greatly reduced this probability, particularly with today's Journaled File System (JFS) implementations. While for ASE, a host OS crash made data loss probable, for Replication Server it was highly unlikely. There still is an element of risk, however, and so the following table should help identify the sqm_recover_seg setting.

Table 14-5

Device Type	sqm_recover_seg	Comments
raw partition	(off)	not applicable
VxFS with QuickIO	off	same as raw partitions (no risk)
NTFS (Windows only)	off	same as raw partitions (no risk)
Mounted with forced DirectIO	off	buffer disabled, eliminates risk
JFS	off?	Depends if journaling can keep within the sqm_recover_seg setting as well as the secondary truncation point/primary log truncation. If willing to issue sysadmin rebuild queues and start the replication agent in recovery mode, off is acceptable.
Buffered UFS	on?	See above, but consider the time span for write destaging to disk from the Unix buffer cache. Typically, this is within a few seconds, so once again the risk can be eliminated if willing to do a sysadmin rebuild queues/ RepAgent recovery.

Consequently, while the default is on, the recommendation for performance reasons is to turn it off. That way if you need to extend a stable queue in a hurry due to an unforeseen problem and you add space via a temporary file system device, you don't compound your problems by causing excessive performance impacts.

init_sqm_write_delay and init_sqm_write_max_delay

Primarily, these timers are considered only when the SQM has a partially filled block and no more write requests are available. In this case, the SQM will wait for the configured time for additional write requests. If none occur, the block is written to disk due to a "timer pop" as is tracked via the counter WritesTimerPop (6038). However, the documentation also says this timer is used while the queue is being read. It is not known whether this refers to the SQMR modules reading the current in-memory block that is waiting to be written, or whether this refers to when the SQMR is physically reading from the queue such as during rescanning activities. The suspicion is the former, and that when a block is full, if the SQMR tries to read the block prior to the block flush happening, the SQM will delay flushing the block to disk until the SQMR has finished reading the block. As a result, it is recommended that you reduce these values to something more in line with today's technology. A good starting point might be 100 ms and 500 ms, respectively.

Stable Queue Transaction (SQT)

The SQT thread is probably the least understood of all the Replication Server threads, yet it remains the most common "tuning" attempt. The best way to think of the SQT thread is to consider the two main modules it uses:

▶ SQMR — This module reads the SQM.

▶ SQT — This module sorts the transactions into commit order.

As a result, we really have two areas to focus on for performance monitoring and tuning within the SQT thread. However, probably the biggest misunderstanding and the key to performance monitoring of the SQT is understanding the SQT cache.

The SQT cache consists of an unordered command cache and four linked lists used for transaction sorting. Each of the four linked lists contains a transaction header and pointers to each of the commands in the SQT cache. These four linked lists are:

▶ Open — Transactions for which the SQT has not yet read the commit. When transactions are first added to the SQT cache, they are added to the Open linked list until the commit has been read. When the commit is read, the transaction header and the command pointers are simply moved to the Closed linked list.

▶ Closed — Transactions for which the SQT has read the commit, but the SQT client (DIST or DSI) has not yet fully processed the *entire* transaction. Once the SQT client has processed the entire transaction, the transaction header and command pointers are moved to the Read linked list.

▶ Read — Transactions stay in the SQT cache after they are read until either the SQT client requests they be deleted or it decides to reread the transactions from a particular point. A good example of the latter is if the DSI suspends. When it resumes, it rereads the transactions by moving the desired reread point and all subsequent read transactions back to the Closed linked list. Once the SQT client has updated the OQID (rs_oqids for outbound queue or rs_lastcommit for replicate database), the SQT client requests the SQT delete the transaction from cache. When the delete is requested, the SQT removes the transaction header and pointer location and frees up the space in the SQT cache used by the commands.

▶ Truncate — As soon as a transaction is added to the Open linked list, it is also added to the Truncate linked list. This list is used by the SQT to know when it can request that the SQM truncate the queue of delivered transactions. Periodically, the SQT reviews the list of transactions in this list to determine the largest contiguous list of blocks for which all the transactions have not only been read, but also deleted from the SQT cache. Note that this is a truncation request to the SQM; the SQM determines whether to actually removed the space depending on other SQM reader locations and the save interval.

Thus, a transaction goes from Open → Closed → Read. Once safely delivered it is then deleted from cache and eventually the disk space is reclaimed. There is a considerable catch, however — *empty transactions*. Empty transactions result from isolation level 3 read activity. While ASE RepAgent filters empty system transactions, empty user transactions still are flushed from ULC to the transaction log. This may not be the case for non-ASE data sources as empty user transactions could be filtered completely — or never logged in the first place. Regardless, once an empty transaction is noted in the SQT cache, it is removed. In Replication Server 12.6, this was removed after the Closed metric was updated. With the changes in Replication Server monitor counters in Replication Server 15, they are now removed before the CloseTranAdd metric is incremented.

From the above you might catch a glimmer why admin who,sqt is unreliable. The status column for admin who,sqt reports the first transaction (in sorted order) that is remaining in the SQT cache. Obviously, the most likely occurrence is that this will be "Read," at least up to the point that either the outbound SQM updates the RSSD (sqm_recover_seg) or the DSI commits the transaction group at the replicate and updates the rs_lastcommit. However, there could be a large transaction that was removed from cache and the SQT could be rescanning, giving the appearance of a "stuck" queue as it could take 10 to 15 minutes to rescan a million row bulk update transaction. Another possibility is that a large number of empty transactions could be occurring. While the empty transactions are being processed and removed, no further transactions are being sent to the destination; thus the queue will give the appearance of being "stuck" until the destination timeout occurs. This situation has resulted in many Replication Server admins thinking there were problems with Replication Server to the point they shut it down and then restart it. At the next observation point, either enough time has transpired that the long transaction has moved, or simply as a result of the shutdown process the queue positions are updated. The Replication Server admin is left with the impression that the queue was "stuck" and a shutdown and restart of Replication Server was required to move past that point. This impression can be hard to unseat as the admin "knows" what was reported via `admin who,sqt`. One advantage of Replication Server monitor counters is that it clearly unmasks such problems and illustrates precisely what is occurring.

Common Problems

Common performance problems with the SQT thread include:

▶ SQT cache size too small, causing frequent removals of transactions from cache and resulting in considerable disk rescanning.

▶ Slow outbound queues restricting the rate at which the DIST (SQT client) can read from the SQT, causing the SQT cache to fill. This may cause some transaction removals, but more importantly, forces the SQMR module to do the initial read from disk vs. the SQM cached block.

▶ Internal contention with the SQM writer for queue access.

▶ SQT cache size too large.

The last point is surprising to many. In fact, in Replication Server 12.5 and 12.6, this often was a leading cause of latency as the SQT prioritized filling the cache ahead of servicing the DIST. Some customers had configured the SQT cache so large that as a result, it would take tens of minutes before the cache filled and the SQT was forced to respond to the DIST requests. While the SQT thread aspect of this has been resolved in Replication Server 15.0.1, the DSI, which has an SQT module (discussed later), can still incur this behavior.

Metrics to Focus On

The key metrics to focus on for the SQT thread are:

Rate

There are three key rate metrics for the SQT thread. The first is the SQMR command rate. Remember, the SQMR module within the SQT thread is responsible for reading the commands from the inbound queue. The goal is that the SQMR command rate is equal to the RepAgent User command rate. If the SQMR is able to keep up, it can read the commands straight out of the SQM's cache for the current block being written to. However, if it gets behind for any reason, the SQMR must then read the commands from disk. Occasionally, the SQMR command rate may appear to be nearly double that of the RepAgent User command rate. This usually happens when a large transaction occurs — so large that the SQT removes the cached commands from the SQT cache. As a result, when the SQT client starts processing the commands, the SQT is forced to reread the commands from disk via the SQMR module. The biggest problem with this is that while the SQT is rescanning a transaction via the SQMR, the SQMR cannot process new commands that are arriving. This means that as soon as it is done rescanning, it will also need to read from disk when it picks up reading from the inbound queue where it left off. Ideally, you would like the SQMR command rate to be sufficient that when this happens it can quickly catch back up and resume reading the transactions from cache.

The second key rate metric is the SQT command rate. Normally, the SQT command rate will be identical to the SQMR command rate. However, when the SQT needs to rescan a transaction from disk, the SQT logic does not need to reprocess (resort) the transaction, so the SQT command rate is not affected by transaction rescanning. As a result, rescanning activity is not only indicated by a much higher SQMR rate than the RepAgent User rate, at the same time the SQT command rate will be much lower (possibly even 0 depending on how long the rescanning takes compared to the sample interval). As a result, this rate is mainly a bell ringer.

The third rate is the Open → Closed → Read latency rate. From a rate perspective, the number of transactions in each list is immaterial. What is important is that as quickly as a transaction is added to the Open linked list, we would like to see the commit read and delete moved to the Closed linked list. Similarly, as quickly as a transaction is added to the Closed linked list, we would like the SQT client to read the transaction and move it to the Read linked list. Consequently, we focus on the difference between the number of transactions *added* to each linked list. Ideally, the numbers should be identical. The latency rate can be best viewed as the lag in transactions being added to the next linked list in order of processing.

▶ Closed lag — This is the lag between transactions being added to the Open linked list and the Closed linked list. Common reasons for lags here are uncommitted transactions at the primary or a large number of empty transactions (as these are not counted in Replication Server 15 since they are removed ahead of the counter being incremented).

▶ Read lag — This is the lag between transactions being added to the Closed linked list and the Read linked list. Common reasons for lags here are SQT client processing rate issues, such as slow outbound queue write rates, poor design architecture with too many outbound queues to maintain a good rate, or STS cache lookups for subscriptions. For DSI/SQT processing, the most common reason is replicate database execution speed as the Closed linked list quickly becomes the buffer to hold transactions while waiting for execution at the replicate (more on this later). For Replication Server 12.6, a lag here could also be attributable to empty transactions that have been removed after Closed incremented.

As a result, the full set of rate counters for the SQT thread are:

```
-- SQMR Module Counters
-- Counter:        Counter ID:
-- --------        ------
-- CmdsRead        62000
--
-- SQT Module Counters
-- CmdsRead        24000
-- OpenTransAdd    24001
-- ClosedTransAdd  24012
-- ReadTransAdd    24013
-- EmptyTransRm    24018
-- delta           (sample duration in seconds)


SQMRCmdsPerSec = SQMR.CmdsRead/delta
SQMRLag = SQMRCmdsRead - SQM.CmdsWritten*
SQTCmdsPerSec = SQT.CmdsRead/delta
```

```
ClosedLag = OpenTransAdd - ClosedTransAdd - EmptyTransRm
ReadLag = ReadTransAdd - ClosedTransAdd
```

Note that SQMRLag could be negative when the SQT needs to rescan a removed transaction.

Time

There are several time counters that track where time is spent within the SQT thread.

▶ SQMRReadTime (62011) — The amount of time taken for SQMR to read a block. Long read times could indicate internal contention. Ideally, you would like this to be a substantial portion of time whenever there is a backlog (SegsActive >1).

▶ SleepForWriteQTime (62015) — The amount of time SQMR should wait for a queue write. This likely will be in multiples of sqt_init_read_delay through sqt_max_read_delay as this counter corresponds to when the SQT wants to read a block that has not yet been written by the SQM.

▶ SQTReadSQMTime (24021) — The time taken by an SQT thread (or the thread running the SQT library functions) to read messages from SQM. This includes SQMRReadTime as well as the time the SQT sleeps waiting for the queue to be written (SQMR.SleepsWriteQ (62006)).

▶ SQTAddCacheTime (24023) — The time taken by an SQT thread (or the thread running the SQT library functions) to add messages to SQT cache. This counter was added in 15.0 in response to the Replication Server 12.5/12.6 SQT DIST starvation scenario.

▶ SQTDelCacheTime (24025) — The time taken by an SQT thread (or the thread running the SQT library functions) to delete messages from SQT cache. This counter was added with SQTAddCacheTime.

Ideally, you want SQTAddCacheTime and SQTDelCacheTime to be close and a very small number (i.e., a few seconds each) proportionate to SQTReadSQMTime, which should account for most of the total time. In addition to the above counters, the following time related metrics can be derived:

```
-- SQMR Module Counters
-- Counter:              Counter ID:
-- --------              ------
-- BlocksRead            62002
-- SleepsWriteQ          62006
-- SQMRReadTime          62011
-- SleepForWriteQTime    62015
--
-- SQT Module Counters
-- SQTReadSQMTime        24021
-- SQTAddCacheTime       24023
-- SQTDelCacheTime       24025
-- delta                 (sample duration in seconds)

-- all times normalized to seconds
AvgBlockReadTime = (SQMRReadTime/100.0)/BlocksRead
SQTTotalTime = (SQTReadSQMTime + SleepForWriteQTime +
     + SQTAddCacheTime + SQTDelCacheTime)/100.0
SQTRunTimePct = (SQTTotalTime*100.0)/delta
SQTSleepQTime = (SQTReadSQMTime - SQMRReadTime)/100.0
SQTReadTimePct = SQMRReadTime/SQTTotalTime
SQTSleepQTimePct = (SQTSleepQTime*100.0)/SQTTotalTime
```

Note that SQTTotalTime, while fairly accurate, is not precise as not all functions are covered by timers. As a result, SQTRun-TimePct may be off slightly. If the sleep time is minimal, the run percentage also can be used to provide a CPU loading factor. However, with SMP off, other threads may simply be using their allotted time, which could make the CPU loading for the SQT appear less than it could be.

Bell Ringers

Because of the two major modules (SQMR and SQT) within the SQT thread, there are plenty of possible bell ringers of performance problems. Some are much more critical as they point to debilitating problems, while others are indications of less severe issues. We will focus on the more critical counters, which are:

```
-- SQMR Module Counters
-- Counter:                           Counter ID:
-- --------                           ------
-- BlocksRead                         62002
-- BlocksReadCached                   62004
-- SleepForWriteQTime (counter_obs)   62015
--
-- SQT Module Counters
-- TransRemoved                       24009
-- CmdsTran (counter_max)             24002
--
-- SQMRLag = SQMR.CmdsRead - SQM.CmdsWritten
-- CmdsRescanned = SQMR.CmdsRead - SQT.CmdsRead
-- ReadLag = ReadTransAdd - ClosedTransAdd
-- BlocksReadCachedPct = (BlocksReadCached*100.0)/BlocksRead
-- SleepsWritePct = (SleepForWriteQTime.counter_obs*100.0)
--                  / BlocksRead
```

The most critical of these is TransRemoved. As transaction commands are read from the SQM they are added to the cache. Obviously, the SQT cache has a limited amount of memory, which raises the question of what happens when the cache is full. If no more transactions are read when the cache is full, a single large transaction could block all further progress. As a result, as a transaction is being read into cache, if it will not fit in cache, the largest *open* transaction will be "removed" from cache, thereby making room. There are several important aspects about this to consider:

▶ "Removed" refers to the commands themselves. The transaction "header" is retained in memory. When the commit for a removed transaction is finally read, the transaction header is what is put on the "Closed" list.

▶ It is the largest transaction on the "Open" list that is removed; no "Closed" or "Read" transactions are removed.

▶ If the current transaction being scanned is the largest, it may be the one removed. This is often the case as large transactions are often the bane of batch processing, which is typically done during low user concurrency or in a bulk operation so the commands for these large transactions are frequently consecutive.

While the occasional large transaction removal is not a problem, transactions regularly being removed cause extreme performance degradation for two reasons:

▶ When the commit is finally seen and the transaction starts to be read by the DIST thread, the SQT will have to rescan the disk segments between the Begin and Commit locations.

▶ During this rescanning of the transaction, the volume of reads obstruct the writes — virtually blocking further RepAgent throughput.

In addition to the TransRemoved counter, another indication of how long the rescanning takes is to watch SQMRLag. Normally, if the SQT is lagging behind the RepAgent and SQM, this will be a positive number. When transactions are rescanned, the SQMR reads the same commands a second time, incrementing the SQMR.CmdsRead counter again — but not incrementing the SQT.CmdsRead counter as the SQT doesn't need to sort or cache the command. As a result, when rescanning is occurring, SQMR CmdsRead will be greater than SQM.CmdsWritten, resulting in a negative number for SQMRLag. However, this could also happen if the SQT was simply lagging behind and the RepAgent slowed to a trickle, allowing the SQT time to catch up. Consequently, a more accurate indication of rescanning is to compare SQM.CmdsRead to SQT.CmdsRead (CmdsRescanned above).

When transactions are removed, typically, they are large transactions, so the CmdsTran counter_max value is a good indication of the largest transaction that was being read. This is particularly interesting as this counter reflects the largest transaction read to date, whether or not the commit has been seen (it is based on SQT.CmdsRead). As a result, a frequently observed occurrence if the counters are presented in a spreadsheet is the following characteristic:

Table 14-6

Sample Period	SQT Cmds Read	Open Trans Add	Closed Trans Add	Trans Removed	SQT CmdsTran (max)
T1	10000	5	4	0	5000
T2	20000	0	0	1	15000
T3	30000	0	0	0	25000
T4	40000	0	0	0	35000
T5	50000	8	9	0	42500
T6	60000	3	3	0	500

The above illustrates a single large transaction of 42,500 commands. During each sample interval, the large transaction has the largest number of commands, so the CmdsTrans counter_max is updated to reflect the number of commands for that transaction read thus far. The proof of this is observing the Closed lag and noting the lag is eliminated at T5 when ClosedTransAdd shows more commits seen than transaction begins for OpenTransAdd.

Besides being used to determine the size of the transaction that was removed from cache and if the SQT cache size could be increased to accommodate it, it generally is a good idea to monitor the largest transactions going through to get an idea of the transaction profile.

In addition to the TransRemoved, CmdsRescanned, and CmdsTransMax counters, the next indication of probable performance issues is when the percentage of BlocksReadCached dips below 80% and especially when it's below 20%. As with Trans-Removed, the occasional dip for a sample interval or two is not significant. However, if it drops and stays down for a considerable stretch, the implication is that the SQT is having trouble keeping up with the rate that transactions are coming in. As a result, rather than being able to read each block as soon as it is written directly from the SQM's buffer for the block, the SQMR must read each block from disk. This, of course, is much slower, which can cause the SQT/SQMR to get even further behind. In addition to BlocksReadCached, a key indicator that the SQT/SQMR is lagging is to look at the SleepForWriteQTime counter_obs value. This counter tells the number of times the SQMR attempted to read from the SQM buffer directly as it was completely caught up and was forced to sleep as the SQM was still writing to the block (filling it with inbound commands). If the SQT/SQMR gets behind, obviously it is not reading from the SQM buffer at all; therefore this counter will be zero. As a result, you would like to see that the SQT/SQMR was caught up enough that it attempted to read from the SQM block buffer two to three or more times at least; effectively you want SleepsWritePct to be 200 to 300%. If SleepsWritePct is extremely high, i.e., greater than 700%, you can safely conclude that the SQT/SQMR is not lagging and any latency in the SQT is due to DIST processing issues.

The final critical bell ringer for the SQT thread is ReadLag. This is important as it is an indication that the DIST thread is not reading from the SQT fast enough, which most likely points to speed issues with the DIST thread's ability to write to the outbound queue. Ideally, you would like to see a transaction get added to the Open list, moved to the Closed list, and then finally moved to the Read list — all within the same sample interval. Obviously small differences are tolerable, but when the difference becomes large, it is time to find out what is holding the DIST up.

A few of the less critical warning metrics include:

▶ SQMRBacklogSeg (62013) — The number of segments yet to be read by the SQMR.

▶ SQMRBacklogBlock (62014) — The number of blocks within a partially read segment that are yet to be read by the SQMR.

▶ ClosedLag (derived) — The number of transactions added to the Open transaction list that have not been added to the Closed transaction list.

The first two taken together are similar to the Next.Read position for admin who,sqm. Earlier we mentioned that SegsActive is a good indication of the backlog. While this is true, it is only an estimate as the active segments include transactions in the Read transaction list that have not yet been truncated as well as those in the Closed list that have been mostly read out. For example, if a 100,000-command transaction is being processed and 99,000 of the commands have been passed to the DIST, SegsActive would still report the full size of the queue. SQMRBacklogSeg/Block would report the number of segments and blocks that have not been read. ClosedLag could indicate a large transaction (or a number of them).

Caches and Queues

The single largest in-memory cache or message queue for the SQT thread is the SQT cache itself. There are a number of counters that help monitor the size of this cache:

```
-- SQT Module Counters
-- Counter:          Counter ID:
-- --------------    -----------
-- CacheMemUsed      24005
-- MemUsedTran       24006
-- SQTCacheLowBnd    24019
-- SQTOpenTrans      24027
-- SQTClosedTrans    24028
-- SQTReadTrans      24029
--
-- CachedTrans = SQTOpenTrans + SQTClosedTrans + SQTReadTrans
```

The first counter reports the total amount of memory used by the SQT cache. Effectively, this is the peak of memory usage by the SQT thread. MemUsedTran is nearly the same, as it reports the amount of memory used by transactions. In Replication Server 12.x, this counter reported average memory per transaction, so it was useful to estimate the amount of memory used by each transaction. But unless the transaction sizes are consistent, knowing the average memory consumption per transaction is not useful for cache sizing. SQTCacheLowBnd is one of the more useful counters, as the counter_max metric indicates the smallest amount of SQT cache that could be configured per sample interval before transactions would start to be removed from cache — assuming TransRemoved=0 already.

The other three counters refer to the number of transactions in cache. For these, the best metric is counter_last, as the actual value will fluctuate during the sample interval. While not as useful for the SQT thread, these counters can be very useful for DSI/SQT processing — particularly SQTClosedTrans as it contains closed transactions that can be grouped. Still, the number of closed transactions in the SQT thread can be a good indication of the number of transactions that are cached and awaiting delivery by the DIST thread.

Tuning for Performance

Most of the tuning for the SQT is in correctly sizing the SQT cache and reducing any unnecessary delays in reading the SQM when writing occurs.

sqt_max_cache_size and dist_sqt_max_cache_size

Tuning the SQT is one place where a very common mistake is made as memory is often just thrown at the SQT cache in an attempt to improve performance. Remember, the concept of Replication Server is to move messages through the system, not to retain them; consequently, the fewer resources used by Replication Server for a single connection's transactions, the more that is available for other connections within the same RS. For example, if sqt_max_cache_size was set to 500 MB (as some users have done), the Replication Server would only be able to manage two to four connections effectively before all memory is exhausted. SQT cache size tuning is best thought of using the following rules:

▶ If TransRemoved=0, increasing sqt_max_cache_size is ineffective and a waste of resources.

▶ Set dist_sqt_max_cache_size to the maximum value reported by SQTCacheLowBnd over a period of time, especially if more than one source connection is managed by the RS.

▶ Set sqt_max_cache_size to the maximum value reported by SQTCacheLowBnd for all connections (including WS DSI/SQT cache).

sqt_init_read_delay and sqt_max_read_delay

Other than tuning the SQT cache size, the only other tuning that can be done to the SQT is to tune the sqt_init_read_delay and sqt_max_read_delay values. By default these are set to 2000 ms and 10,000 ms respectively, which are fairly lengthy times for a sleep period for a modern OLTP environment. It is recommended that these are set much lower with a lower bound of 100 ms and 500 ms, respectively. Testing has shown that values lower than these have no benefit. A word of caution should be noted here: In Replication Server 12.6, it was often suggested to set both of these values to 0. This was an attempt to work around a design implementation that was found to later increase latency. What happened was that in Replication Server 12.6, the SQT was tuned to deliberately favor reading from the SQM over processing DIST or space management tasks. The thinking was that this might reduce the physical reads as more blocks would be read cached. Unfortunately, this tuning often resulted in the DIST requests being starved until the SQT cache was full, which with the often grossly oversized SQT caches that many sites have could be several minutes. This behavior was modified in Replication Server 15.0; consequently it is suggested that you increase these settings above 0 as soon as you upgrade to Replication Server 15.0.

Distributor (DIST)

The DIST thread processing goes through four main stages.

► Read SQT cache — Commands are read from the SQT Closed transaction list in commit order as defined by the SQT.

► Subscription resolution — DIST looks for replication definitions for each replicated command. For each repdef found for the command, it then looks for subscriptions — either a database subscription, a publication subscription, or a basic table/function subscription.

► Routing optimization — If the replicated command is subscribed to by multiple sites, the DIST checks to see if the sites share a common route and, if so, minimizes network traffic by sending only a single message to the route queue.

► Writing to the outbound queue(s) — For each destination queue for which a subscription exists, the command is written to the queue for that destination.

This process is depicted in the following diagram:

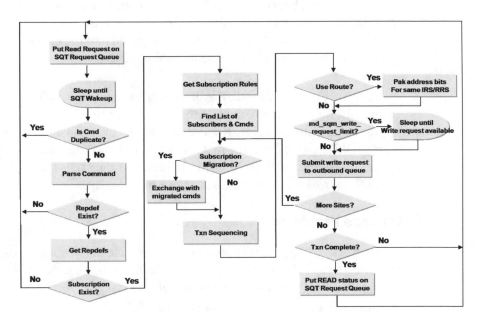

Figure 14-6: Distributor thread processing flow

A few key notes about the processing flow:

▶ The DIST processes one command at a time. There is no cache or queue of requests since the SQT cache is effectively the cache for the DIST. Consequently, each command must be written to the destination queue(s) prior to the next command being read.

▶ Similar to the RepAgent User, the DIST doesn't write directly to the SQM. Instead, it puts write requests on a write request queue. The difference is that while the RepAgent User writes each command to a single write request queue, the DIST may have to write each command to more than one write request queue — one for each subscribing destination.

▶ Transaction sequencing refers to the TD module within the DIST thread. The rationale for this module is that it remembers the transaction information for the current transaction being processed and makes sure the full transaction

information is sent to each subscribing site. This may sound a
bit confusing, but consider a 200-command transaction in
which one site only subscribes to the 199th command — it
needs to have the "begin tran" record injected into the queue
prior to the 199th command being submitted as a write
request.

▶ In the above flow, the DIST is illustrated as telling the SQT
when a transaction is complete to move it from the Closed to
the Read transaction list. Not depicted is that every so often,
the DIST also updates the rs_locater in the RSSD with its processing progress. When this update occurs, it then tells the
SQT to truncate all of the transactions to that point.

Common Problems

In Figure 14-6, two potential problem areas are clearly visible
from the "sleep" steps, and two other problem areas are depicted
in the processing flow that may not be quite as visible:

▶ Slow response from the SQT in processing read requests

▶ Exceeding the md_sqm_write_request_limit (formerly known
as md_source_memory_pool)

▶ Looking up repdef and subscription information

▶ Performing the multiple writes for each command to the subscribing destination queues

The first problem was a common occurrence in Replication
Server 12.5 and 12.6 when users oversized their SQT cache.
Beyond that situation, however, it is not as much of an issue. The
second situation is fairly common as users typically don't tune the
request queues, and even if they tuned exec_sqm_write_request_
limit, they either weren't aware or forgot about md_sqm_write_
request_limit. The third situation is actually not as common, as
most users are aware of the need to tune the STS cache. The last
situation occurs more than you would think. A classic example is
a reference data site that distributes reference information (customers, banking products, etc.) to all the downstream front office,
middle office, and back office systems. Even with routes involved,
if there are 10 destination queues and the RepAgent User is

sustaining 1000 commands per second, the DIST thread would need to sustain 10,000 commands per second — 1000 commands per second to each of the 10 destination queues. Since each command has to be written to all the destinations prior to the next command being processed, a slowdown on even just one of the destinations has the effect of setting the throughput rate for the others. Additionally, with a large number of destinations, it is likely that they share stable devices; any device contention or internal Replication Server contention during segment allocation impacts all of them as well.

Metrics to Focus On

The key metrics to focus on for the DIST thread are:

Rate

In Replication Server processing, there are three threads that typically define the throughput for their respective stages of processing. For inbound processing, the RepAgent User rate defines the throughput. For the inbound to outbound stage (SQT → DIST pipeline), it is the DIST thread that defines the rate, so the DIST rate is one of the more critical rates to observe. For the DIST, there is just a single rate counter:

```
-- Counter          Counter ID
-- -----------      ----------
-- CmdsRead         30000
```

As usual, the rate can be derived by dividing CmdsRead by the sample interval to get the commands per second being processed.

Time

There are only two "time" counters for the DIST thread:

```
-- Counter          Counter ID
-- -----------      ----------
-- DISTReadTime     30028
-- DISTParseTime    30030
```

DISTReadTime is the most critical as it refers to the amount of time it takes for the DIST to get a command from the SQT. DISTParseTime refers to the amount of time it takes for the DIST to parse a command. This is an interesting aspect. The RepAgent User is aware of the individual columns and values, as it receives the commands in LTL format and has to convert them to the binary structure the Replication Server uses internally for the inbound queue. The RepAgent User also performs minimal column processing for update commands since unmodified columns are only recorded once. The DIST needs to perform command introspection for several reasons:

▶ Determining which DML command is involved and for subscription migration purposes

▶ Parsing the columns and values that are used for subscriptions

▶ Converting into the ASCII format used by the outbound queue

While you might think parsing is a intensive process, remember that the SQT reads the command in the binary structure from the inbound queue. So parsing in this sense involves converting the binary structure to the ASCII structure vs. a typical parsing scenario of delimited words. As a result, DISTParseTime tends not to be a significant part of the processing of the DIST thread.

Where significant time *is* spent is writing to the destination queues. Unlike the RepAgent User thread, however, the DIST does not have a counter that signals when the md_write_request_limit has been reached, nor does it have a "timing" counter that tracks the total time spent submitting the write requests to all the queues. It is possible that future versions of Replication Server may include such counters, and if so, they will be some of the more critical counters to observe.

Bell Ringers

The DIST thread really doesn't have any bell ringers that reflect on its own processing performance. However, it does have several that have broader implications for the entire environment. These metrics include:

```
-- Counter            Counter ID
-- ---------------    ----------
-- CmdsNoRepdef       30013
-- SREstmtsInsert     30020
-- SREstmtsUpdate     30021
-- SREstmtsDelete     30022
-- SREstmtsDiscard    30023
--
-- CmdsNoRepdefPct = (CmdsNoRepdef*100.0)/CmdsRead
-- SREDiscardPct = (SREstmtsDiscard*100.0)/CmdsRead
```

The first one, CmdsNoRepdef, is likely the most critical. If this counter has any significant values at all as identified by CmdsNoRepdefPct, this is indicative of one of two possible situations:

▶ A table is marked for replication that was not intended to be replicated.

▶ The database is marked for replication using sp_reptostandby, and a database repdef exists but no table-level repdefs.

Eliminating the first problem not only reduces the workload of the DIST thread, but also has a huge impact on the whole inbound replication stream from the Replication Agent itself (ASE RepAgent or Heterogeneous RepAgent) to the RepAgent User, and SQM and SQT processing overhead.

The second scenario does not appear to be as much of a problem. However, for performance and data integrity reasons, it is always suggested to use replication definitions; at a minimum this scenario is an indicator of a possible need to create repdefs to help performance. In addition, it could point to work tables that are being replicated that are not being excluded in the database repdef or better yet in the Replication Agent (both the mirror Replication Agent and the heterogeneous Replication Agents have the ability to individually exclude tables despite the full database replication).

While not much of a bell ringer to indicate a problem, the subscription resolution counters (SREstmtsInsert, SREstmtsUpdate, and SREstmtsDelete) are the first indication of the transaction profile. This could be useful in identifying when the transaction mix might be a contributing factor, i.e., either from a RepAgent User processing or from a DSI processing perspective.

SREstmtsDiscard is more of a minor indicator. If this is a large number, it indicates that the DIST/SRE is filtering most of the replicated commands (but a repdef does exist!). A common situation in which this could occur is when the destination only subscribes to business data with a particular status, such as order completion, etc. If this is a significant amount, an alternative form of conditional replication using stored procedures or another mechanism could be used to reduce the workload.

Caches and Queues

The only memory cache that has an impact on the DIST thread is the STS cache, which holds the object repdefs and subscriptions. By caching the repdefs and subscriptions and other commonly used object metadata, the Replication Server can avoid RSSD activity, thereby improving performance vs. waiting for an RSSD query response. There are several counters in the STS module that describe interactions with the RSSD. The only indication of any abnormality is to compare the DIST SRE searches to the STS physical selects sent to the RSSD using the following counters:

```
-- Counter              Counter ID
-- -----------          ----------
-- DIST.SREget          30018
-- STS.Selects          11001
-- STS.SelectDistincts  11002
-- STS.Inserts          11003
-- STS.Updates          11004
   STS.Deletes          11006
```

Not all of the selects from the STS are to fetch objects into STS cache. During Replication Server startup as well as when a connection is resumed, configuration parameters are read using individual select statements. In addition, during segment processing, etc., often a select with a holdlock is issued to lock a row while Replication Server prepares to do its internal work and then the update or delete is sent. As a consequence, if STS.Selects is about the same as STS.Updates and STS.Deletes, then it is unlikely that any STS lookups are being done. However, if there is an appreciable difference, the STS may be looking up information.

As imprecise as this sounds, this is not usually a problem for several reasons. First, as mentioned earlier, tuning the STS cache is likely the second thing users try after tuning the SQT cache. Additionally, with Replication Server 12.6, it was easier to just force the STS to fully cache primary tables of concern such as rs_objects and rs_columns using sts_full_cache_*XXX* than to spend the time diagnosing whether the STS cache was impeding performance.

Tuning for Performance

Which brings us to the topic of tuning the DIST thread. In reality, there is very little tuning you can do for the DIST thread itself. Primarily, tuning the DIST thread involves tuning the parameters for related threads/modules. What tuning you can do involves the STS cache.

sts_cachesize

In older Replication Server versions, this parameter used to have to be set a lot higher than the current default of 100. However, with Replication Server 12.6, the introduction of sts_full_cache eliminated the need for the higher settings that were based on the number of rows in the RSSD rs_objects table and other methods used to estimate this. However, it is still suggested to increase this parameter considerably higher than the default, with 1,000 to 2,000 being good starting points. It should only be raised higher than that if you see the "STS cache exceeded" error message in the error log or you determine which table is driving the need for higher STS cache requirements and enable sts_full_cache for that table. One possible consideration for a higher value for sts_cachesize is when using a lot of custom function strings. The function string definitions are stored in rs_systext, along with exception records. Enabling sts_full_cache_rs_systext is not practical; consequently, it is more effective to have sts_cachesize large enough to hold most of the custom function strings used by DSIs local to that RS.

sts_full_cache

By enabling sts_full_cache for particular tables, Replication Server avoids looking up replication metadata from the RSSD. The key is remembering that we are trying to avoid looking up replication metadata. Enabling sts_full_cache for the space management tables is simply a waste of memory as they are primarily the focus of updates, which still must occur. Some of the other tables are likely not used unless certain replication objects are implemented. Table 14-7 shows the sts_full_cache settings:

Table 14-7

sts_full_cache_*	Default	Suggested	Comments
sts_full_cache_rs_articles	off	off	Only enable if articles and publications are used and the number of articles is greater than sts_cachesize
sts_full_cache_rs_classes	off	off	Not likely to ever be higher than sts_cachesize
sts_full_cache_rs_columns	off	on	Cache this unless altering repdefs
sts_full_cache_rs_config	off	off	Not likely to ever be higher than sts_cachesize
sts_full_cache_rs_databases	off	off	Not likely to ever be higher than sts_cachesize
sts_full_cache_rs_datatype	off	off	Not likely to ever be higher than sts_cachesize
sts_full_cache_rs_diskaffinity	off	off	Not likely to ever be higher than sts_cachesize
sts_full_cache_rs_diskpartition	off	off	Space management table
sts_full_cache_rs_erroractions	off	off	Exception processing table; no need to have in cache except common errors that fit within sts_cachesize
sts_full_cache_rs_exceptscmd	off	off	Exception processing table; no need to have in cache

sts_full_cache_*	Default	Suggested	Comments
sts_full_cache_rs_exceptshdr	off	off	Exception processing table; no need to have in cache
sts_full_cache_rs_exceptslast	off	off	Exception processing table; no need to have in cache
sts_full_cache_rs_funcstrings	off	off	Enable if using considerable custom function strings (more than sts_cachesize)
sts_full_cache_rs_functions	off	off	Enable if using considerable custom function strings (more than sts_cachesize)
sts_full_cache_rs_idnames	off	off	Not likely to ever be higher than sts_cachesize
sts_full_cache_rs_ids	off	off	Not likely to ever be higher than sts_cachesize
sts_full_cache_rs_locater	off	off	Space management table
sts_full_cache_rs_maintusers	off	off	Not likely to ever be higher than sts_cachesize
sts_full_cache_rs_objects	off	on	Cache this unless altering repdefs
sts_full_cache_rs_oqid	off	off	Space management table
sts_full_cache_rs_publications	off	off	Only enable if articles and publications are used and the number of publications is greater than sts_cachesize
sts_full_cache_rs_queuemsg	off	off	Exception processing table; no need to have in cache
sts_full_cache_rs_queuemsgtxt	off	off	Exception processing table; no need to have in cache
sts_full_cache_rs_queues	off	off	Space management table
sts_full_cache_rs_recovery	off	off	Not likely to ever be higher than sts_cachesize
sts_full_cache_rs_repdbs	off	off	Not likely to ever be higher than sts_cachesize

sts_full_cache_*	Default	Suggested	Comments
sts_full_cache_rs_repobjs	on	on	Cached by default
sts_full_cache_rs_routes	off	off	Not likely to ever be higher than sts_cachesize
sts_full_cache_rs_routeversion	off	off	Rarely used and typically smaller than the sts_cachesize
sts_full_cache_rs_rules	off	off	Enable if the number of where clauses in table subscriptions exceed sts_cachesize
sts_full_cache_rs_segments	off	off	Space management table
sts_full_cache_rs_sites	off	off	Not likely to ever be higher than sts_cachesize
sts_full_cache_rs_statcounters	off	off	Static table never read by RS
sts_full_cache_rs_statdetail	off	off	Never read by RS
sts_full_cache_rs_statrun	off	off	Never read by RS
sts_full_cache_rs_subscription	off	on?	If you have a number of table subscriptions, you may need this enabled
sts_full_cache_rs_systext	off	off	Impractical, especially if an exception occurs
sts_full_cache_rs_translation	off	off	Enable if you use heterogeneous datatypes and are replicating between different DBMSs
sts_full_cache_rs_users	on	off	Not likely to ever be higher than sts_cachesize
sts_full_cache_rs_version	off	off	Rarely used and typically smaller than the sts_cachesize
sts_full_cache_rs_whereclauses	off	off	Only enable if articles and publications are used and the number of where clauses for articles is greater than sts_cachesize

Data Server Interface (DSI)

The DSI (also known as DSI Scheduler or DSI-S) is one of the more difficult threads to tune as there is no acceptable single setting that works for most situations — unlike the RepAgent User, SQM, SQT, and DIST threads. Much of the DSI tuning depends on the transaction profile, especially if performance requirements require using parallel DSIs. The best way to understand the problems and how to tune the DSI is to understand the functions of the DSI:

▶ Read from the queue (SQMR module) — The DSI reads the replicated commands from the outbound queue for replicate databases and inbound queue for warm standby replication.

▶ Sort transactions (SQT module) — The DSI needs to resort the transactions into commit and origin order if the replicate database is the target for more than one source system. While this may seem to be unnecessary if there is only a single source/target, it is still used for detecting large transactions. Additionally, for warm standby systems, it is the DSI's SQT module that does the transaction sorting as the SQT thread is not used for the standby database.

▶ Group transactions — The DSI groups the transactions into transaction groups to increase replication efficiency. Transaction grouping is accomplished using a variety of rules such as group sizing configuration limits, partitioning rules, origin databases, etc.

▶ Dispatch transaction groups to DSI EXECs — The DSI dispatches the transaction groups to the DSI EXEC thread(s).

The key to tuning the DSI thread is to think of it like the SQT thread, which is no great leap as it is nearly identical (has both SQMR and SQT modules) and its throughput often depends on the ability of the next thread's delivery rate. For the SQT, this was the DIST thread's throughput; for the DSI, it is the throughput of the DSI EXEC thread(s).

Common Problems

The most common problems with the DSI thread can be classified into single DSI and parallel DSI configurations. For single DSI, the most common problems are caused by:

▶ Slow replicate database processing (via DSI EXEC)

▶ Untuned DSI configuration settings (from the defaults)

▶ DSI SQT cache either too small or too large

▶ Not using dynamic SQL or not tuning dynamic SQL for the schema size

All of the above also apply to parallel DSIs, in addition to some problems unique to parallel DSIs including:

▶ Using the default `parallel_dsi='on'` settings, especially `wait_for_commit` serialization

▶ Interthread contention at the replicate database due to inefficient tuning of the DSI grouping and partitioning rules

▶ Interthread contention at the replicate database due to application caused conflicts such as sequential key tables, multiple updates to common rows (i.e., aggregate reporting tables), etc.

▶ DSI EXEC thread execution sequencing when `smp_enable='off'` (due to OS scheduling thread execution)

▶ Too few or too many threads for the transaction profile

While this chapter will touch on monitoring parallel DSI performance (mainly in the next section on the DSI EXEC thread), the topic is too involved to include a lot of guidance about how to optimally configure parallel DSIs within this book.

Metrics to Focus On

The key metrics to focus on for the DSI Scheduler include:

Rate

There are several different counters that measure commands and transactions within the DSI Scheduler.

```
-- Counter:             CounterID
-- ------------------   ----------
-- DSICmdsSucceed       5028
-- DSICmdsRead          5030
-- DSICmdsParsedBySQT   5032
--
-- DSIReadTranGroups    5000
-- DSIReadTransUngrouped 5002
--
-- delta (sample interval in seconds)
-- DSISQMRRate = DSICmdsRead/delta
-- DSICmdsPerSec = DSICmdsSucceed/delta
-- DSIXactsInGroup = (DSIReadTransUngrouped*1.0)
--            / DSIReadTranGroups
--
```

The most critical of these is DSICmdsPerSec. Along with the RepAgent CmdsPerSec and DIST CmdsPerSec, DSI CmdsPerSec is a key throughput metric. A key aspect of DSICmdsSucceed is that it is the total across all DSI EXEC threads, so the DSICmdsPerSec rate represents the aggregated rate for parallel DSI implementations.

The other metrics can be useful to help determine why the rate may not be as high as the other two. The first of these to look at is DSIXactsInGroup, which derives how many transactions are being grouped together on an average basis. With the default dsi_max_xacts_in_group configuration of 20, significantly lower values for the derived metric may indicate tuning possibilities. This will be discussed further in the section on DSI bell ringers.

Time

There are a number of time counters in Replication Server 15.0.1 for the DSI thread. Many of these were added to help detect when the DSI SQT cache was oversized and the DSI was consequently spending more time trying to fill cache rather than dispatching transactions to the DSI EXEC thread(s). The more important time counters include:

```
-- Counter:              CounterID
-- --------------------   ----------
-- DSIFindRGrpTime        5079
-- DSIDisptchRegTime      5083
-- DSIPutToSleepTime      5088
-- DSILoadCacheTime       5090
-- DSIThrdCmmtMsgTime     5093
-- DSIThrdSRlbkMsgTime    5095
-- DSIThrdRlbkMsgTime     5097
```

The first two time metrics relate to how much time the DSI spends grouping cached transactions and dispatching them to the DSI EXEC thread(s). Normally, these are not problem areas, with most observations reporting 0 time used. However, the counter_ obs metric for both are useful to compare to the DSILoadCache-Time counter_obs metric to determine if the SQT cache loading is monopolizing the DSI time.

The second two are more likely to be cause for concern. As one or more DSI EXEC threads are reading from the SQT Closed transaction list in the DSI SQT cache, the DSI puts all DSI EXEC threads that are currently not actively sending commands to the replicate to sleep before it starts to fill the SQT cache. As a result, the total time spent processing SQT cache could be expressed as:

```
DSITotalSQTTime = DSILoadCacheTime + DSIPutToSleepTime
```

However, the time it takes to put a DSI EXEC to sleep is extremely minimal. Here again, it is useful to look at the DSIPutToSleepTime counter_obs metric.

The trick with DSILoadCacheTime is determining whether the time was spent needlessly filling an oversized DSI SQT cache or whether the cause was related to the outbound queue or there is simply a large transaction. This is where it is really helpful to remember that Replication Server monitor counters are on a per module basis rather than per thread. Since the DSI is made up of multiple modules, including the SQMR and SQT modules, previously discussed counters can be used to determine whether or not the DSILoadCacheTime was the fault of outbound queue performance.

442

The last three could indicate when constantly retrying errors or parallel DSI contention is causing a problem. The difference between DSIThrdSRlbkMsgTime and DSIThrdRlbkMsgTime is related to parallel DSIs, with the latter being a key indication of a rollback due to interthread contention with parallel DSIs.

Bell Ringers

Because of the multiple modules within the DSI, there are multiple metrics that could indicate problems. Each one may have additional metrics that might clarify the situation. The first and most obvious set of metrics is the rate metrics. It is highly probable that the DSI cmd/sec rate is much lower than the RepAgent User or DIST thread rates, and as a result, a backlog will exist in the outbound queue:

```
-- Counter:                  CounterID
-- ---------------------     ----------
-- DSICmdsSucceed            5028
-- DSIReadTranGroups         5000
-- DSIReadTransUngrouped     5002
-- SQMRBacklogSeg            62013
-- DSICmdsPerSec = DSICmdsSucceed/delta
-- DSIXactsInGroup = (DSIReadTransUngrouped*1.0)
--                    / DSIReadTranGroups
```

If the rate is but a small fraction of the RepAgent User or DIST rate, it is likely the replicate database, which can be confirmed by looking at the DSI EXEC metrics.

However, if the rate is fairly close but still lagging, and DSIXactsInGroup is considerably less than the dsi_max_xacts_in_group setting, you will need to next check the grouping-specific metrics to determine if the transaction grouping is as efficient as desired.

```
-- Counter:                    CounterID
-- ------------------------    ----------
-- GroupsClosedBytes           5042
-- GroupsClosedNoneOrig        5043
-- GroupsClosedMixedUser       5044
-- GroupsClosedMixedMode       5045
-- GroupsClosedTranPartRule    5049
```

```
-- GroupsClosedTrans      5063
-- GroupsClosedLarge      5068
-- GroupsClosedWSBSpec    5069
-- GroupsClosedResume     5070
-- GroupsClosedSpecial    5071
```

High values for some of these can't necessarily be avoided. However, there are a couple of common ones that can be resolved.

► GroupsClosedBytes — This metric is by far the most common. It refers to the number of transaction groups that were closed due to exceeding the configuration parameter dsi_xact_group_size. Often the problem here is that dsi_xact_group_size was left at the default of 64 KB (65,536 bytes), which for most environments is ~60 replicated commands. Depending on the number of commands per transaction, it is highly unlikely that the DSI grouping rule came close to the dsi_max_xacts_in_group limit as a result.

► GroupsClosedLarge — This metric is similar to Groups-ClosedBytes, except that it refers to the configuration parameter dsi_large_xact_size, which defaults to 100. While a 100-command transaction is fairly big for an OLTP system, many such systems have batch processes that update thousands to millions of rows in a transaction.

► GroupsCloseTranPartRule — Is only of concern when using parallel DSIs and using a partitioning rule to reduce contention between the threads. As a result, this may be naturally high. However, if using a compound partitioning rule, such as origin_sessid, time, a high value for this metric may be an indication that a singleton rule might be more efficient.

► GroupsClosedTrans — Refers to the number of transaction groups that were closed due to reaching the dsi_max_xacts_in_group setting. Ideally, you would like this to be the predominant reason for transaction groups to be closed.

► GroupsClosedNoneOrig — Interestingly, you may also see a high value for this metric. Although it can refer to the fact that different origin databases are involved, it more often simply refers to the fact that no transaction group for that origin was available as the scheduler forced a flush. This happens

frequently enough that most of the time you will see
GroupsClosedTrans and GroupsClosedNoneOrig as the primary causes when the DSI is maximizing the transaction
grouping.

The other values refer to DDL replication, asynchronous request
functions, and other likely minor reasons that likely cannot be
tuned as they are application dependent.

The replicate database usually accounts for 90% of the performance problems with Replication Server, so the first discussion is
particularly applicable. Of the other 10%, most of these are due to
configuration issues such as grouping for the DSI or SQT cache
sizing for both the DSI and SQT thread. Attacking the 90% problem often requires using parallel DSIs, which is an extremely
misunderstood Replication Server feature and a victim of a lot of
FUD about data loss, missing transactions, etc., spread mostly by
people who have never really used it. One of the biggest problems for those who do is failing to understand that the transaction
grouping that works well for a single DSI more than likely contributes to problems with parallel DSIs. The large transaction
groups hold locks longer and as a result extend the window during which contention can occur. If using parallel DSIs, it is then
highly important that the interthread contention can be easily
spotted. Replication Server includes several different metrics that
focus on parallel DSI and in particular interthread contention with
parallel DSIs.

```
-- Counter:                CounterID
-- --------------------    ----------
-- TrueCheckThrdLock        5060
-- CommitChecksExceeded     5062
-- DSIThrdRlbkMsgTime       5097
-- PartitioningWaits        5050
-- DSIReadTranGroups        5000
--
-- PartitionWaitsPct = (DSIReadTranGroups*100.)
--                     /PartitioningWaits
```

The first two are applicable only when DSI commit control is
enabled (the default) rather than using rs_threads. If using

commit control, the first counter, TrueCheck ThrdLock, is the number of times Replication Server detected that a DSI was blocking another user and rolled back the transactions for subsequent threads to allow the others to finish. The second counter, CommitChecksExceeded, reports the number of times that a DSI finished its transaction group and was waiting for a previous thread to complete, and the previous thread did not complete within a given time period so the DSI decided to roll back in case an undetected issue was blocking the earlier thread. The section on DSI EXEC will have a discussion on tuning these; for now, the point is to recognize that any appreciable number of these is a problem. That is, if more than one TrueCheckThrdLock or CommitChecksExceeded are happening within a 10-second interval, then it is probable that the number of rollbacks due to contention is restricting Replication Server throughput.

Likewise, the counter_obs metric for DSIThrdRlbkMsgTime reports the number of parallel DSI rollbacks when using rs_threads vs. commit control. As with commit control, several failures per minute is not a big issue, but several within a few seconds is. However, this needs to be analyzed across the full daily load. A large number of failures over a short time frame but greater throughput during the rest of the day may be acceptable.

One way that contention can be controlled is through using the DSI partitioning feature. However, if set up incorrectly, it could have the net effect of reducing the parallel DSIs to essentially a single DSI, but with a lot of extra overhead so it could be lower throughput than even a single DSI. PartitioningWaits is a metric that reports the number of times a parallel DSI was told to send its transaction group in serial based on the partitioning rules. While a high number of waits could occur depending on the rule (such as origin_sessid during batch processing), if the percentage of waits is very high compared to the number of transaction groups, then the partitioning rule is obstructing throughput and a less restrictive rule should be used.

Caches and Queues

The DSI has one main cache — the DSI SQT cache — and a message queue for dispatching messages to the DSI EXEC threads. The latter, while similar to the SQM write request queues, is unlike them in that it cannot be tuned by adjusting the size. This actually isn't as much of a problem since the commands themselves are read directly out of the SQT cache by the DSI EXEC threads, so the only messages being sent/received on the DSI message queue are workload dispatch messages.

The DSI SQT cache is identical in every way and operation to the SQT cache that is within the SQT thread. There is a difference though in how it is tuned, especially the lower bounds of the SQT cache size. If the DSI EXEC metrics don't show performance is being limited by the replicate database, then it is likely that the DSI is limiting the throughput — either due to configuration such as grouping or due to the SQT cache "starvation" problem mentioned earlier. This problem first manifested itself when Replication Server switched from internal OpenServer threads that it could schedule as tasks required to native OS threads that are scheduled by the operating system. (In a bit of a twist on being careful what you ask for, both customers and industry analysts insisted that Sybase should use native POSIX threads rather than SMP engines or OpenServer threading. The result of this has shown that in sequential pipeline processes such as RS, the operating system scheduling of threads can cause erratic performance and starvation of different pipeline processes.) On top of this, the SQT tuning that was done to improve the cache reads resulted in SQT readers practically being starved until the SQT cache filled and the SQT was forced to yield the CPU to other processes and service reader requests more often. In the case of the DSI SQT, a large SQT cache could result in low throughput to the DSI EXEC threads. A caveat here is that a warm standby DSI may require the same amount of SQT cache as the SQT thread itself. The following metrics can be used to determine when the DSI SQT cache may be either too large or too small.

```
-- Counter:             CounterID
-- --------------------- ----------
-- SQT cache metrics:
-- CacheMemUsed         24005
-- TransRemoved         24009
-- SQTCacheLowBnd       24019
-- SQTClosedTrans       24028
--
-- DSI metrics:
-- DSIReadTranGroups    5000
-- DSIReadTransUngrouped 5002
-- DSILoadCacheTime     5090
--
-- derived metrics:
-- DSIXactsInGroups = (DSIReadTranGroups*1.0)
--                  / DSIReadTransUngrouped
-- MaxCachedGroups = SQTClosedTrans  / dsi_max_xacts_in_group
-- AvgCachedGroups = SQTClosedTrans  / DSIXactsInGroups
-- GroupsPerThread = AvgCachedGroups / dsi_num_threads
```

The obvious metric for determining if the SQT cache is too small is TransRemoved. Additionally, the derived metrics GroupsPer-Thread, AvgCachedGroups, and MaxCachedGroups can be used to determine appropriate DSI SQT cache sizing. The key is that DSI dispatches full transaction groups to each DSI EXEC thread. If there are not enough cached groups, then a DSI EXEC will have to wait for additional transactions to be read into cache; hence the cache is too small. Minimally, you need at least twice the number of transaction groups as DSI EXEC threads. The DSI EXEC is currently working on one group; when it finishes, it needs another group to be available immediately to continue working. However, too many cached groups are a sign that the DSI SQT cache is too large. For example, if the number of cached transaction groups is more than five times the number of threads, the SQT cache is likely too large. This is true whether the DSI is a warm standby or a standard replicate database; as long as TransRemoved is minimized to the occasionally excessively large transaction, having more than five transaction groups in cache is not effective.

Tuning for Performance

Tuning the DSI for performance can be a bit tricky for the following reasons:

▶ Most of the performance problems are in the replicate database. Unless you are familiar with ASE MDA or Oracle V$ tables, it will be difficult to isolate the exact cause.

▶ Tuning for single vs. parallel DSIs are frequently the opposite; consequently settings that worked well for a single DSI typically perform poorly for parallel DSIs.

▶ Tuning the DSI often involves changing multiple related configuration parameters at the same time. This requirement is counter to the common practice of only changing one parameter at a time.

With that in mind, consider the following:

dsi_sqt_max_cache_size

In the "Caches and Queues" section earlier, we describe how to determine the right size for the DSI SQT cache. The goal is pretty simple: Have three to five transaction groups in cache. Less than three could lead to DSI EXEC threads waiting on the SQT cache to fill, while more than five is a waste of memory as it is ineffective.

dsi_max_xacts_in_group and dsi_xact_group_size

Generally speaking, you want to control the number of transactions in a group using dsi_max_xacts_group but prevent the groups from being excessively large using dsi_xact_group_size as a limiter. If using a single DSI, the default dsi_max_xacts_in_group of 20 may be fine or you could increase it. Certainly, the default for dsi_xact_group_size of 64 KB is too small. While a common approach is to "unlimit" it by setting it to 2 billion, this could be detrimental for large transactions if an error occurs and also could be problematic with parallel DSIs when large transactions are involved. As a result, it is recommended that you set dsi_xact_group_size to 2,097,152 (2 MB) to start and monitor the GroupsClosedBytes metric. If GroupsClosedBytes is more than

GroupsClosedTrans and using a single DSI, consider increasing it
until most groups are closed due to hitting the `dsi_max_xacts_`
`in_group` limit.

DSI Executor (DSI EXEC)

As 90% of the latency for Replication Server is due to replicate
database throughput, monitoring the DSI EXEC is key to determining if the cause is the replicate database and if Replication
Server tuning could help. DSI EXEC processing can be described
using the following flow diagram.

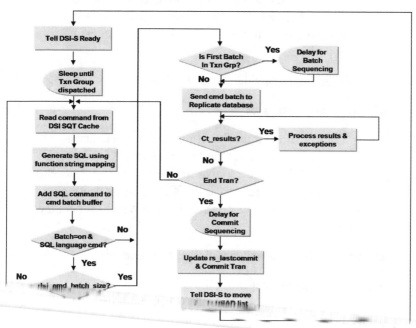

Figure 14-7: DSI EXEC processing flow

The key processing steps depicted above are:

1. DSI EXEC waits for a transaction group to be dispatched to it
    by the DSI-S thread. The dispatch message contains the
    transaction IDs and whether the transaction group is to be
    sent in serial or parallel.

2. DSI EXEC reads each command from the DSI SQT cache. If the transaction has been removed from cache, the DSI EXEC reads the command from disk.

3. As each command is read, it maps the replicated command to a SQL language or RPC call according to the function string specification.

4. Each command is added to the DSI EXEC's command batch buffer.

5. If batching is on and if the command was a language command (vs. an RPC or dynamic SQL statement), check the command buffer size to see if dsi_cmd_batch_size would be exceeded when the command is added to the batch. If so, send the current batch.

6. RPC commands, dynamic SQL statements (which use RPC calls), and text pointer commands cannot be batched with other commands; consequently each command is sent as a separate batch.

7. Before the batch is sent, if parallel DSIs are being used, check to see if the DSI EXEC is supposed to wait for batch sequencing. If not, send the batch immediately; otherwise, wait for the batch sequencing condition (defined by dsi_serialization_method).

8. DSI EXEC needs to process the results for each command in the batch. For text pointer initialization, the command result is used for subsequent text commands. For other commands, the results are discarded. If any exceptions occurred for the command, they are processed according to the error action mapping.

9. If this was not the last batch in the transaction, repeat from step 2.

10. If parallel DSIs are in use, check the commit sequencing. This happens regardless of dsi_serialization_method.

11. Once able to commit, update the rs_lastcommit table and commit the transaction group.

12. Tell the DSI-S that the transaction group completed and that it can move it to the Read list in the SQT cache. Then tell the DSI-S that DSI EXEC is ready for another transaction group.

A quick summary of these steps is as follows:

▶ Read a command from SQT cache.

▶ Convert to SQL using function strings.

▶ Add command to command batch.

▶ When batch is full, send to replicate database.

▶ For each command, process the results/exceptions.

▶ Repeat until transaction is complete.

▶ Update rs_lastcommit, commit the transaction, and get ready for the next one.

Common Problems

Much like with the DSI-S, the most common problems with DSI EXEC fall into single and parallel DSI categories. In general, the most common problems are:

▶ Replicate database performance too slow, especially if triggers exist and are enabled (`dsi_keep_triggers`)

▶ `dsi_cmd_batch_size` too small

▶ `db_packet_size` too small

▶ Dynamic SQL not configured correctly (or enabled)

In addition, parallel DSIs often fail to achieve the desired effect due to:

▶ `dsi_serialization_method` left at wait_for_commit

▶ `dsi_num_large_xact_threads` preserving DSI EXEC threads reduce parallelism

▶ `dsi_commit_check_locks_intrvl` too long (left at the default of 1 second)

▶ `dsi_partitioning_rule` too restrictive

▶ Only used the default of `parallel_dsi=on`, which leads to all the above

- ▶ Transaction grouping (dsi_max_xacts_in_group) too large, leading to interthread contention
- ▶ Interthread contention due to application causes
- ▶ Too many threads (dsi_num_threads) for the degree of contention

For single DSI connections, some fairly quick fixes will help improve the throughput. For parallel DSIs, some careful tuning by observing the application behavior will be required in order to achieve optimal results. As evident by the list of common problems specific to parallel DSIs, it takes careful tuning of a wide range of parameters. Database administrators who think that simply flipping the switch produces miraculous results will only suffer disappointment, as it will take considerable monitoring and tweaking over time.

Metrics to Focus On

The key metrics to focus on for the DSI EXEC threads include:

Rate

Much like with every other module/thread, the key rate metric is the commands per second each DSI EXEC is processing. In addition to the command rate, it is often helpful to know which type of command is being processed. For example, if you notice that throughput is slower during updates, it can be a clue that minimal column replication is not enabled. Additionally, the update trigger at the replicate or the lack of an unique index on the primary key may be causing the performance degradation. Believe it or not, the single most common reason for performance problems at the replicate database in recent years has been the lack of primary keys. Consequently, updates and deletes typically show the slowest rates as each update or delete will result in a table scan or partial table scan when using a non-unique index. Consider the following counters:

```
-- Counter:             CounterID
-- ----------------     ----------
-- DSIECmdsSucceed      57147
--
-- DML/DDL commands:
-- InsertsRead          57010
-- UpdatesRead          57011
-- DeletesRead          57012
-- ExecsWritetext       57013
-- ExecsGetTextPtr      57014
-- CmdsSQLDDLRead       57120
--
-- Dynamic SQL usage:
-- DSIEDsqlPrepared     57149
-- DSIEDsqlDealloc      57150
-- DSIEDsqlExecuted     57151
--
-- Derived metrics:
-- DSIECmdsSec = DSIECmdsSucceed/delta
-- DynamicSQLPct = (DSIEDsqlExecuted*100.0)/DSIECmdsSucceed
```

As mentioned in the section on DSI, the sum of DSIECmdsSucceed will be the same as DSI.DSICmdsSucceed.

Time

As mentioned multiple times, the most common replication performance problem is the replicate database. The time metrics for the DSI EXEC thread are the metrics that will show whether this is the cause or whether tuning can help, and if so, how much tuning will help. The key time metrics are:

```
-- Counter:              CounterID
-- ------------------    ----------
-- In processing sequence order:
-- DSIEReadTime          57130
-- DSIEWaitSQT           57132
-- DSIEParseTime         57139
-- DSIEFSMapTime         57096
-- DSIEBatchTime         57070
-- SendTime              57037
-- SendRPCTime           57051
-- SendDTTime            57057
```

```
-- DSIEResultTime         57063
--
-- Parallel DSI coordination:
-- DSIESCBTime            57108
-- DSIESCCTime            57102
--
-- Aggregated times:
-- DSIEPrepareTime        57141
-- DSIEExecCmdTime        57143
-- DSIEExecWrtxtCmdTime   57145
-- DSIETranTime           57114
```

A bit more obvious in this list is that most of the DSI EXEC metrics begin with "DSIE", similar to the DSI counters that use "DSI" as a common prefix.

If the SQT cache is too small or a really large transaction is removed from cache, the first two time values will be higher than normal. If using custom function-string classes, DSIEFSMapTime will be higher than with the default function class. This may seem a bit odd, but for the default class, Replication Server doesn't have to parse the function string definition to determine the SQL format. This should not discourage you from using custom function strings when necessary as likely this time will not be significant.

The next time parameter, DSIEBatchTime, is fairly important as it does indicate a possible tuning issue. Surprisingly, the larger the command batches, the less time seems to be spent on batching, which is counterintuitive.

SendTime reports the time spent sending the normal language commands to the replicate database, SendRPCTime reports time spent sending RPC calls, and SendDTTime reports time spent sending text/image data. Note that sending the commands does not necessarily include execution time. Effectively, it is timing for the ct_send() CT-Lib function call, which includes the network time and the time the replicate server spends parsing the commands to determine if there is a syntax error prior to execution. Due to the tremendous overhead of parsing, this likely will be one of the higher time values.

DSIEResultTime is probably the most critical of all the time metrics. This reports the time spent processing results, which includes query optimization and command execution as well as network time to return the result set to Replication Server; this typically is just a "1 Row Affected" type message. Of all the time metrics, this typically will be the largest as most performance problems are due to replicate database processing. The reason for this is that most RDBMS engines are tuned for multiple concurrent users, consequently a single user's process is often put to sleep when I/O is pending while the RDBMS looks for other work.

If parallel DSIs are in use, DSIESCBTime and DSIESCCTime are important metrics to watch. DSIESCBTime reports the time spent while sequencing the beginning of the first batch in each transaction for each thread. This is applicable when dsi_serialization_method is wait_for_commit, wait_for_start, or the legacy none, but not applicable for no_wait. If dsi_serialization_method is wait_for_commit, these times will be fairly large as each thread must wait for the previous thread to commit or at least be at the commit stage. Depending on the number of threads, this could be a significant period. For dsi_serialization_method=wait_for_start, there will be a slight lag as each subsequent thread waits for the previous thread to begin. This delay might be marginally longer depending on the batch_begin setting, which may include the begin in the first batch, however, the delay should be hardly noticeable. In any case, a large value for DSIESCBTime typically indicates that dsi_serialization_method is wait_for_commit, or it could be the result of dsi_partitioning.

DSIESCCTime is the time spent waiting for the previous thread to commit. A common misconception is that the dsi_serialization_method of none bypasses commit sequencing, while in reality all serialization methods adhere to strict commit sequencing. In any serialization method, a large DSIESCCTime could be an indication of contention or that one of the threads had an uneven workload. As a result, DSIESCCTime is one of the more critical metrics for parallel DSI threads.

The last four metrics above are aggregates in that they include one or more of the individual time metrics. For example, DSIETranTime includes all of the time spent processing the entire transaction group. Large values here are likely directly traceable to one of the other metrics. However, an interesting aspect is that the aggregates may be slightly higher than the components due to being inclusive of the clock granularity. In other words, several individual time metrics may report 0 hundredths of a second each, yet obviously some time was spent. By including the time from the very beginning, some of the optimistic tendencies of the clock granularity are corrected for.

Bell Ringers

The most critical bell ringers for the DSI EXEC threads are all time related, specifically:

```
-- Counter:            CounterID
-- ----------------    ----------
-- DSIEReadTime        57130
-- DSIEWaitSQT         57132
-- DSIEBatchTime       57070
-- SendTime            57037
-- DSIEResultTime      57063
```

These are often used in conjunction with the command/DML counters, which may give an indication of the probable cause:

```
-- Counter:            CounterID
-- ----------------    ----------
-- DSIECmdsSucceed     57147
--
-- DML/DDL commands:
-- InsertsRead         57010
-- UpdatesRead         57011
-- DeletesRead         57012
-- ExecsWritetext      57013
-- ExecsGetTextPtr     57014
```

If parallel DSIs are in use, there are additional bell ringers in the begin/commit sequencing times as well as the DSI metrics for the number of rollbacks due to contention or exceeding the commit control checks.

```
-- Counter:            CounterID
-- ----------------    ----------
-- DSIESCBTime         57108
-- DSIESCCTime         57102
```

Caches and Queues

The only cache that is configurable for the DSI EXEC thread is the command batch buffer via the dsi_cmd_batch_size parameter. The efficiency of this buffer can be observed through a multitude of counters that report the number of commands per batch as well as why the batch was "closed" and sent to the replicate database. All of the metrics related to this last situation are prefixed with "DSIEBF".

```
-- Counter:            CounterID
-- ----------------    ----------
-- DSIEBatchSize       57076
-- DSIEOCmdCount       57079
-- DSIEICmdCount       57082
--
-- Batch flush reasons:
-- DSIEBatchSize       57076
-- DSIEBFResultsProc   57085
-- DSIEBFCommitNext    57086
-- DSIEBFMaxCmds       57087
-- DSIEBFRowRslts      57088
-- DSIEBFRPCNext       57089
-- DSIEBFGetTextDesc   57090
-- DSIEBFBatchOff      57091
-- DSIEBFMaxBytes      57092
-- DSIEBFBegin         57093
-- DSIEBFSysTran       57094
-- DSIEBFForced        57095
```

DSIEBatchSize not only reports the size of the batches that have been sent, but the counter_obs metric reports the number of command batches that have been sent, which is useful when comparing the various batch flush reasons to see which makes up the higher percentage.

The difference between DSIEICmdCount and DSIEOCmd-Count is that the former is the number of replicated commands input into the DSI EXEC function string mapping process, while the latter is the number of commands output as a result of the function string. Normally, this should be a one-for-one process, but in the case of identity columns (need to send set identity_insert first) as well as custom function strings containing more than one command, there could be more than one command as a result of a single input command. The maximum number of commands in a batch that Replication Server will allow is 50 as measured by DSIEICmdCount.

The rest of the metrics are all related to the reason the batch was forced to be flushed to the replicate database. Most of these are informational as the replicated commands themselves are dictating that the batch be flushed. Ideally, you would like the most common reason to be DSIEBFMaxCmds since it would indicate that the batch reached the internally controlled maximum number of commands in a batch. Metrics that might indicate a configuration issue are:

▶ DSIEBatchSize — This is fairly common as most DBAs have not tuned dsi_cmd_batch_size from its pathetic default of 8192 bytes, which is about enough to hold five to six replicated commands. A much better starting point is 64 KB (65536).

▶ DSIEBFBatchOff — This configuration is usually not that common unless batching is turned off, which is likely for heterogeneous connections. If not a heterogeneous connection, this should be explored as to why batching is disabled.

▶ DSIEBFBegin — This metric reports the number of times the batch was flushed as the batch contained begin tran. This is controlled by the batch_begin connection configuration parameter.

▶ DSIEBFCommitNext — Normally, because of the group sizing, you expect to see multiple batches sent per grouped transaction. However, if this metric is a significant number, it may indicate that either the transaction grouping is not efficient (set too low) or there are a lot of atomic transactions being replicated in which the transaction group is filled quickly. Check dsi_xact_group_size and dsi_max_xacts_in_group.

Several of the metrics are due to different situations in which the replicated command is expected to return a result set that will then be used for subsequent queries. These metrics include DSIEBFResultsProc, DSIEBFRowRslts, and DSIEBFGetText-Desc. The first two are extremely rare as most replicated commands are DML commands, while the last one is common in systems containing text/image data that is replicated.

Tuning for Performance

As most DSI EXEC performance issues are related to the replicate database, this section will include some tips to consider for the replicate server from the perspective that the replicate server is Sybase ASE. Heterogeneous systems may have similar features that can be used or alternative implementations. In addition, some aspects of parallel DSI tuning will be covered in this section.

Replication Definitions and Unique Indexing

Beyond a doubt, one of the biggest performance drags on a system is the lack of a replication definition and especially the lack of a unique index on the columns defined to be the primary key in the repdef. What is surprising to many is the performance impact that a replication definition can have. The reason for this is fairly simple: If I have a repdef that specifies the primary key and a unique index on it, the DBMS can locate the row simply by traversing the index. Without the repdef, Replication Server must use all non-LOB (non text/image) columns in the where clause. Even if a unique index exists, the DBMS must still apply all the other search conditions to the row to make sure all where clause conditions match. This typically includes doing string comparison on long varchar fields such as names, comments, descriptions, etc., as well as tens of comparisons that otherwise would not be necessary. The lack of replication definitions can lead to database inconsistencies as well if the replicate table contains approximate numerics (float, real, double), columns populated by a trigger, different sort orders/character sets, and other similar problems.

One of the more surprising recent developments has been a regression in some schemas to forget unique indexes. The result on replication throughput can be extremely profound for updates and deletes. Inserts do not escape indexing issues either. A clustered index on a nonunique set of columns can result in inserts scanning to find the insertion point. The less unique the cluster index, the worse the problem becomes.

Disabling or Optimizing Triggers

Other than a lack of unique indexing, probably the second biggest drag on replication throughput is the presence of triggers on replicated tables. The problem is that triggers typically involve a huge overhead in that each trigger firing involves a log scan to materialize the inserted/deleted virtual tables of changes. Worse yet, the impact of the trigger firing is multiplied at the replicate system. At the primary system, the trigger is fired for each statement that is executed. The problem is that the transaction logs contain only the before and after images of the row modifications. Consequently, Replication Server constructs a statement for each row that was modified. As a result, a single statement at the primary that affects 100 rows is replicated as 100 statements — and consequently 100 separate firings of the trigger — and 100 log scans. Additionally, many of the statements within the trigger contain joins or other statements that are optimized for the trigger firing on bulk operations rather than single rows. Consider the following guidance for triggers in a replicate database:

▶ Disable triggers — In RS, configure the dsi_keep_triggers to "off". While this is the default for warm standby, it is not the default for MSA or any other replicate database.

▶ Test for maint user — If you can't disable the triggers as not supported by the DBMS, at least test for the maintenance user and exit the trigger early. While this may not avoid the log scan, it does eliminate the overhead of the rest of the processing.

▶ Optimize for single row — If the triggers are required, add logic to optimize the trigger code for single row modifications. For example, select the modified values into variables to eliminate joins between inserted/deleted tables, etc. Add if update() logic to reduce the execution path within the trigger.

461

Do NOT use triggers as a means of populating reporting tables or denormalized schema components. If only a few tables are being maintained, it would be much faster to customize the function strings to perform the multiple DML statements. If the tables are contained in a separate database, use a separate connection and associated subscriptions.

Replication Definitions and Minimal Column Replication

Another reason for using replication definitions is the ability to leverage minimal column replication. This can have a considerable impact for updates at the replicate. Because of the extra overhead it would take, most DBMS engines do not compare the current row values to the values specified in the set clause to see if they differ. As a result, without minimal column replication enabled, a typical Replication Server update statement will update every column in the row — *every* column, primary keys, static values, indexed columns, etc. The result is that not only does the row itself get modified, but the index values do as well. This latter result is particularly nasty as indexes are considered as an ordered list of values. Consequently, a change in the values is often similar to a deferred update — the current row is deleted and the modified row is inserted in the new location. If the actual values never were modified, this could lead to some interesting performance considerations since space reclamation (page shrinkages, etc.) when the row is deleted and re-expansion (page splits, row forwarding, etc.) all add considerable overhead to the index maintenance, possibly making the index maintenance more expensive than the update to the data row itself.

Increase ULC and Enable Delayed Commit

The default ULC size of 2 KB will likely not contain many rows, especially with transaction grouping in effect. As a result, the typical maintenance user connection will have multiple ULC flushes per grouped transaction. Each of these ULC flushes must grab the log semaphore for the transaction log and then wait for the physical writes to disk. A larger ULC size will help reduce the effort needed to get the log semaphore. In addition, as of ASE 15.0, ASE has the ability to enable delayed commits, which allows a transaction to commit without waiting for the last page of the log to be fully written to disk. As this can be enabled at the session level, one option is to modify class-level function strings, or alternatively, use a login trigger and export the setting if possible.

One word of caution about this recommendation: As the ULC size is server-wide, it could have far-reaching implications for standby systems as it could increase the memory requirements for each connection. Prior to increasing the ULC or enabling delayed commit, monitor the maintenance processes to see if they have a noticeable indication that they are waiting for the log semaphore or log writes. For ASE, this can be accomplished via the MDA table monProcessWaits and looking for waits on WaitEventID's 54 and 55.

Use Dynamic SQL/Prepared Statements

RS 15.0.1 introduced the ability for Replication Server to issue fully prepared SQL statements to a replicate DBMS, thus bypassing the language parsing and optimization overhead. This can be significant as test applications have shown that the language parsing and optimization overhead can be significant — from a low of 2x to a high of 10x performance drag on applications. Sybase's Enterprise Connect Data Access components generally support dynamic SQL when using an ODBC driver; consequently this feature should work with heterogeneous targets as well. The performance gains of using dynamic SQL may be enough to eliminate the need for parallel DSIs or may improve the throughput with fewer parallel threads and consequently reduce contention. There are three configuration parameters that need to be changed to enable dynamic SQL:

► `dynamic_sql` — Turns the dynamic SQL feature on or off for a connection. The default is "off", but you should try "on" and monitor the situation.

► `dynamic_sql_cache_size` — Specifies the maximum number of tables for which dynamic SQL statements will exist at any given time. Note that a single table could have three possible statements — insert, update, and delete. With a default of 20 (100 in 15.0.1 ESD #2), this allows the specified number of tables to have dynamic SQL statements for each — for a total

of 60 statements (or 300 for 15.0.1 ESD #2). It is recommended that the minimum setting be the greater of 100 or the
number of commonly modified tables in the schema — and the
maximum be the total number of tables in the schema. For
larger schemas, an initial setting between 250 and 500 may be
more effective than the default.

▶ dynamic_sql_cache_management — Specifies whether the
dynamic SQL cache uses a LRU/MRU management strategy
or remains fixed once fully allocated. The original default of
"mru" resulted in a lot of cache thrashing at the default cache
size as statements were constantly being deallocated and new
ones created. In Replication Server 15.0.1 ESD #2, the default
was changed to "fixed" as a result.

Dynamic SQL usage can be monitored using the following
metrics:

```
-- Counter:             CounterID
-- ------------------   ----------
-- DSIECmdsSucceed      57147
-- DSIEGiveUpConnTime   57128
-- InsertsRead          57010
-- UpdatesRead          57011
-- DeletesRead          57012
--
-- DSIEDsqlPrepared     57149
-- DSIEDsqlDealloc      57150
-- DSIEDsqlExecuted     57151
--
   TotalDML = InsertsRead + UpdatesRead + DeletesRead
-- DsqlUsagePct = (DSIEDsqlExecuted*100.0)/TotalDML
-- ConnFadeOuts = DSIEGiveUpConnTime.counter_obs
```

If memory restrictions or an extremely large schema with wide-
spread modifications prevent using a "fixed" cache strategy and
larger dynamic SQL caches, you can try using "mru" and monitor
the DSIEDsqlDealloc counter as it will indicate deallocations that
signify possible dynamic SQL cache thrashing. Remember,
dynamic SQL statements exist at both the client and the server
(for ASE, this is in the form of a lightweight procedure); consequently if the connection fades out or is suspended, the dynamic

SQL statements will need to be recreated. Thus, after a resumption the number of prepared dynamic SQL statements (DSIEDsqlPrepared) may spike. Otherwise, ideally you would like to see the number of prepared and deallocated statements be a trickle when compared to the number of DML statements executed.

Enable Statement Cache with Literal Parameterization

An alternative to using the dynamic SQL feature is to enable the server's statement cache. However, this will only be effective if literal parameterization is also enabled since replicated commands rarely if ever contain the same literal values. With ASE, both of these can be controlled at the session level; consequently, modifying a class scope function string (i.e., rs_usedb) or using a login trigger and exporting the settings are both possibilities if enabling globally is not desired.

Of the two, dynamic SQL will have the greatest benefit as the language parsing and statement hashing is completely avoided. However, enabling statement cache along with dynamic SQL can have benefits for customized function strings and text pointer selects, as well as supplementing a smaller dynamic SQL cache.

Parallel DSI Contention and Group Sizing/Partitioning

When discussing parallel DSIs, mainly what is being referred to is connection configurations in which `dsi_serialization_method` is anything other than `wait_for_commit`. Because `wait_for_commit` sequences the transactions, forcing each thread to wait until the previous has committed, little if any real parallelism results. Consequently, the following configuration parameters are suggested for parallel DSI effectiveness:

- `dsi_serialization_method` — Set to `wait_for_start` or `no_wait`.
- `dsi_isolation_level` — Set to 3 if updates or deletes could affect rows also being modified within `dsi_num_threads` * `dsi_max_xacts_in_groups` transactions. If predominantly inserts or if it is known that the updates/deletes only affect older data rows, a setting of 1 is more desirable.

Parallel DSIs can introduce contention at the replicate where none existed at the primary due to four situations:

▶ By default, the same user's transactions could use different parallel threads. For example, let's say a user inserted a row and then shortly after updated it in separate transactions. At the primary, this was done on the same connection, so the sequencing prevented any contention. At the replicate, however, it is possible that the insert and update transactions may use different threads, thus causing contention.

▶ The transaction grouping increases the lock duration beyond the scope of the original transaction. Given the above scenario, for example, the insert could be at the beginning of one group and would have its locks held for another 19 unrelated transactions by default. Even if the update was executed at a later time on a separate thread, contention could result if the grouped transaction containing the insert was still uncommitted.

▶ If dsi_isolation_level=3, inserts may cause "next key" (aka "infinity") locks and updates could cause range locks to ensure repeatable reads as required under isolation level 3. Additionally, any selects embedded in triggers or replicated procedures will hold locks.

▶ Tables containing commonly updated values such as sequential key tables or aggregates such as bank balances, etc., are sequenced at the primary due to blocking. At the replicate, the sequencing may be different, leading to deadlocks between transaction groups.

As should be evident, the amount of contention — and therefore the tuning — for parallel DSIs is extremely application dependent. If the contention is so bad that either the parallel DSIs are rarely executing due to blocking on replicate tables or causing excessive deadlocks (more than one every two or three seconds), some tuning may be required to regain the throughput required. Some common techniques are:

▶ Use datarows locking — This should be the absolute first thing attempted. Unless datarows locking is enabled, the index contention, especially for inserts, will practically prevent any attempt to use parallel DSIs. If even one commonly modified table does not have datarows locking, the result can be much worse performance than a single DSI as every transaction will be tried, rolled back, and retried serially. This not only incurs the huge overhead of the rollback, but each statement has to be parsed, compiled, and optimized twice, etc.

▶ Add `noholdlock` or `at isolation level` clause — For selects embedded in triggers or procedures invoked by replicated commands, add the `noholdlock` keyword (ASE) or the `at isolation level` clause (supported by most heterogeneous DBMSs) to avoid holding locks where not desired. Note that this is only applicable if using `dsi_isolation_level=3` or the legacy (deprecated in Replication Server 15.0) `dsi_serialization_method` of `isolation_level_3`.

▶ Reduce the group size — If contention appears to be due to the larger group sizes, reducing `dsi_max_xacts_in_group` to 5 or fewer may resolve much of the contention.

▶ Reduce the number of parallel threads — Applications with little contention due to a profile that avoids contention can leverage more threads at the replicate. This includes applications that are predominantly insert intensive (85%+) or where it is known that the updates affect different rows. Otherwise, reducing the number of threads could reduce the contention for update-intensive applications or others whose profile lends it toward contention.

▶ Use DSI partitioning — This can be particularly effective if it is known that the contention is due to transactions from the same primary session being applied at the replicate with parallel threads, or with light to medium contention on common data rows such as sequential key tables or aggregates.

▶ Collapse repeated row modifications — This technique is especially effective for high-volume sequential key tables. A discussion on how to achieve this follows the discussion on DSI partitioning.

The first four are fairly self explanatory, but the last two could use some explanation.

DSI partitioning can be a bit mystifying at first. The simple way to explain it is to consider that with the exception of the "time" rule, anytime the value for a transaction and the subsequent transaction differ, they will be sent in parallel. This means that:

▶ If two transactions have the same value for the rule, they can be grouped together and sent as a grouped transaction.

▶ If two transactions have different values for the rule, it is assumed that do not conflict and therefore can be applied in parallel. As a result, the first transaction group is closed and a new transaction group opened with the second transaction and the transaction groups are dispatched as parallel.

▶ If two transactions have the same value but the transaction grouping limits requires that they be in separate groups, the grouping limits have precedence, so the first transaction group will be closed and a new transaction group opened. The assumption is that there could be conflicts and therefore the transaction groups are dispatched in serial.

The time rule is similar, but it uses the origin begin and commit times (rs_origin_begin_time and rs_origin_commit_time) to determine if the transactions can be sent in parallel or serial. If the two subsequent transactions have overlapping begin/commit times, it is assumed that there was either no contention at the primary or minimal blocking, and they can be submitted in parallel at the replicate. However, if the second transaction's begin time is after the first transaction's commit time, they are sent in serial.

The method for controlling parallel or serial execution of the transaction groups is by using the begin sequencing. Transactions that can be submitted in parallel use the begin sequencing as allowed by dsi_serialization_method. Transactions that must be submitted in serial ignore dsi_serialization_method, as the second transaction waits until the previous transaction has committed before sending its first batch. Another way to think of it is that the dsi_serialization_method of wait_for_commit is implemented by every transaction group being dispatched as serial. Consequently, using DSI partitioning with dsi_serialization_method of wait_for_commit is a moot point.

The default DSI partitioning rule is "none". A common recommendation is to use the combination origin_sessid, time, which would only allow transactions to be executed in parallel at the replicate if different SPIDs executed the transactions at the primary and the transactions overlapped for at least part of the time. This can be extremely restrictive but is likely to resolve most contention issues. It also is a bit redundant as the time rule also forces different transactions by the same session to be applied serially as they physically cannot overlap. Unfortunately, it is likely to prevent any parallelism during nightly batch processing in which a single session at the origin database may insert, update, or delete millions of rows using batches of a few hundred or thousand to avoid transaction log space issues or locking contention. The problem is that the most noticeable periods of latency within Replication Server occur during this period (batch processing) so using either origin_sessid or time as partitioning rules could effectively limit the Replication Server to a single DSI during batch processing, which leaves the latency. The following table lists the partitioning rules in order from most restrictive to least restrictive.

Table 14-7

Partitioning Rule	Comment
time	Most restrictive as transactions must overlap. Implicitly, this means that transactions from the same session cannot be applied in parallel, so it is redundant with origin_sessid.
name	Transactions with different names can be applied in parallel. This is likely not all that effective as few developers use transaction names.
user	Transactions from the same user cannot be applied in parallel even if different origin sessions.
origin_sessid	Transactions from different origin sessions can be applied in parallel irrespective of transaction name or user name.
none	(Default)

Realistically, then, there will be only three real partitioning rules in use — origin_sessid, user, or time. You can choose to start with the most restrictive and see what impact it has on contention and gradually shift to less restrictive partitioning rules if performance requires, or you can start with the least restrictive (`origin_sessid`) and go more restrictive if contention requires. If contention is due to the same rows (i.e., sequential key table or aggregate columns), it is likely that you will need to use `time` as a starting point.

The impact of partitioning rules and the degree of parallelism can be monitored using the following metrics:

```
-- Counter:                CounterID
-- ---------------------   ----------
-- UserRuleMatchGroup       5051
-- UserRuleMatchDist        5052
-- TimeRuleMatchGroup       5053
-- TimeRuleMatchDist        5054
-- NameRuleMatchGroup       5055
-- NameRuleMatchDist        5056
-- OriginRuleMatchGroup     5072
-- OriginRuleMatchDist      5073
-- OSessIDRuleMatchGroup    5074
-- OSessIDRuleMatchDist     5075
-- IgOrigRuleMatchGroup     5076
-- IgOrigRuleMatchDist      5077
```

At first, the suffix of "MatchGroup" or "MatchDist" can look confusing. Essentially, the DSI has to make both a grouping and a distribution decision; that is, whether the two transactions can be grouped together and whether the transaction groups must be sent in serial or parallel. If the partitioning rule causes the current transaction group to be closed and a new one started (due to being able to apply in parallel), then a MatchGroup decision occurred, i.e., the partition rule applied and two different groups were created to be submitted in parallel. Remember, though, that a transaction group can be closed due to grouping limits. So if a transaction can be grouped together, no rule applies, and therefore no MatchGroup. However, if the transactions must be grouped due to the grouping limit, then the new transaction group must be sent in serial since the partitioning rule has already been checked for parallelism. This is a distribution decision vs. a grouping decision. So to simplify the suffixes:

▶ MatchGroup — Transactions split into separate groups to allow parallelism.

▶ MatchDist — Transactions exceed grouping limit and must be distributed serially.

Ideally, then, you would like the MatchGroup metric to be higher than the MatchDist if parallelism is required, although if only a slight latency needs to be overcome, then a predominantly serial execution is acceptable as long as the throughput rate (cmds/sec) matches the input rate (RA cmds/sec).

Parallel DSIs and "Collapsing Updates"

The last suggestion regarding parallel thread contention allows transaction grouping and parallel threads to work effectively when sequential key tables or frequently updated aggregate columns are involved. Consider a typical high-volume order entry system that uses sequential keys assigned from a typical key table using logic similar to:

```
begin tran
update key_table set next_key=next_key+1
select @next_key=next_key from key_table
insert into orders (...) values (@next_key, ...)
commit tran
```

While not a great design (considering alternatives), at the primary server the result is that users are essentially single-threaded through the table. The problem is replicating such transactions, especially if they make up most of the DML activity as is common in such systems. The problems start as soon as you attempt to use parallel DSIs with any serialization method other than wait_for_commit. Because sequential transactions are grouped and groups are executed in parallel, the parallel threads will immediately suffer blocking. In the best scenario, it will simply behave as wait_for_commit if the threads each start in sequence. In other cases, deadlocking and rollbacks will result. While this contention can be relieved by using dsi_partitioning_rule=time, the net result of this is similar to wait_for_commit. If replicating to a reporting system, the simplest solution to this problem is to not

bother replicating the key_table, as it likely is not even necessary. The same trick could be used for standby systems, provided
that during failover scenarios the table could be simply set via a
select max() on the tables that use the key. Some DBAs don't
want manual processes during a failover and prefer to replicate
the key tables anyhow.

This doesn't work for common aggregates. Consider a trading
system in which a small number of risk metrics or trading volumes are maintained for dashboard type displays. Again,
applications at the primary become serialized for those that are
updating the same aggregate. At the replicate, we are effectively
limited again to a single DSI or a lot of contention, neither of
which is ideal.

A trick that works in these cases is to "collapse" these
updates into a single update at the end of the transaction group. In
order for this to work, the following restrictions have to be met:

▶ All the updates to the key or aggregate tables must strictly
  update the key/aggregate value(s). If other columns exist in
  the tables, they must remain static.

▶ The connection must not be a warm standby as you will be
  altering a function string.

The logic for the collapsing is similar to:

```
rs_begin            → declare variable to hold aggregate/key
key_table.rs_update → increment variable
rs_commit           → update key_table with variable
```

Since the commits are serialized, this effectively eliminates the
contention. Some may be quick to point out that T-SQL variables
expire at the end of a batch, and without a begin batch function,
the variable and its value will both be lost.

The trick is to use the ACF features of ASE:
set_appcontext(), rm_appcontext(), and get_appcontext(). Consider the following pseudocode implementation:

```
alter function string rs_begin
  for my_connection_function_class
  output language
  '
```

```
      begin transaction t_?rs_origin_xact_name!sys_raw?;
      select rm_appcontext('repserver','aggregate_name');
      select set_appcontext'repserver','aggregate_name',
            convert(varchar(30),0));
        ı


alter function string key_table_rd.rs_update
   for my_connection_function_class
   output language
     ı
   select rm_appcontext('repserver','aggregate_name');
   select set_appcontext'repserver','aggregate_name',
         convert(varchar(30),?next_key!new?));
     ı


alter function string rs_commit
   for my_connection_function_class
   output language
     ı
update key_table
   set next_key= convert(int, get_appcontext('repserver',
       'aggregate_name'));
execute rs_update_lastcommit
   @origin = ?rs_origin!sys?,
   @origin_qid = ?rs_origin_qid!sys?,
   @secondary_qid = ?rs_secondary_qid!sys?,
   @origin_time = ?rs_origin_commit_time!sys?;
commit transaction
  ı
```

It may seem odd that both rm_appcontext() and set_appcontext() are called together during the update and initialization. However, application contexts cannot be overwritten or modified once set, so they must be removed and then reset.

The net effect of the above is that the actual update to the key table doesn't happen until the commit is actually set, which is serialized by the commit control mechanism. It is important that the update to the key table or aggregate occur ahead of the actual commit in order to ensure proper rollback handling.

Replication Server Interface (RSI) and RSI User

The RSI thread is probably one of the simplest within the Replication Server directly involved in command replication. Its job is to simply read the replicated commands from the outbound queue for the route, translate them into Replication Transfer Language (RTL), and send them to the next Replication Server along the route. Remember, for a route, you really have two different threads in two different RSs involved. At the PRS, you have the RSI thread — the "sender," and the RRS, you have the RSI User — the "receiver." In a sense, the RSI at the PRS works much like a Replication Agent, while the RSI User at the RRS functions much like the RepAgent User (less normalization).

Common Problems

Usually, any difficulty the RSI has in keeping up is due to the outbound queue, either the local one at the PRS or the remote RRSs outbound queue(s). Sometimes the problem is architecture related, and in other cases it is simply a lack of CPU or Replication Server internal contention. This may be surprising, as most people tend to focus on the WAN links between the servers as a likely source of problems in global systems. Most problems are actually the result of the two queues. WAN link speeds and stability do play a part, especially during batch processing when the volume of data changes may exceed the link capacity. The most common problems associated with an RSI include:

▶ Poor architecture with too many high-volume sources sharing a common route, consequently bottlenecking on the route's outbound queue

▶ Slow outbound queue writes at the replicate, possibly due to the number of distributions that need to be made at the RRS

▶ Slow RSI read times due to outbound queue contention with writers

▶ Slow/low WAN link speed and protocol transmission times

▶ Untuned route connection configuration parameters

The first two may become obvious by taking a step back and looking at the broader picture, but certainly can be detected by looking at the SQM Writer metrics for the PRS or RRS queues. The latter three, however, are likely only noticeable by looking at the RSI metrics.

Metrics to Focus On

Other than the SQM Writer metrics for the queues involved, the key RSI and RSI User metrics to focus on are discussed in the following sections. However, if focusing on just the RSI and RSI User metrics, there is a lot of overlap as illustrated in the following table:

Table 14-8

Counter ID	RSI Counter Name	Counter ID	RSI User Counter Name
4000	BytesSent	59016	RSIUBytsRcvd
4002	PacketsSent	59012	RSIUPcktsRcvd
		59014	RSIUEmptyPckts
		59015	RSIUConnPcktSz
4004	MsgsSent	59001	RSIUMsgRecv
		59000	RSIUCmdsRecv
		59005	RSIUCmdLen
4005	MsgsGetTrunc	59002	RSIUGetTRecv
		59004	RSIUSetTRecv
		59006	RSIUSendGetT
		59008	RSIUSendSetT
4006	FadeOuts		
4007	BlockReads		
4009	SendPTTime	59010	RSIURecvPckt
4015	RSIReadSQMTime		
		59003	RSIURebldQRecv
		59013	RSIUBuffsRcvd

While the RSI User metrics have a bit more detail about the time spent processing synchronization points (truncation requests) and packet processing (empty packets as well as the back size), the result is that a route's throughput could be measure equally from either side. Most of the differences though are either minor or could be computed, such as the PacketSize (~BytesSent/PacketsSent) and the number of CmdsSent (MsgsSent/Msgs-GetTrunc), leaving the only real advantage for the RSI User metrics in tracking the time spent processing truncation requests during the synchronization intervals. However, since the RSI metrics from the PRS also include such information as time reading from the SQM and blocking reads, the PRS might be the logical choice.

Additionally, remember that at the RRS, the data is being written into one or more outbound queues by the MD module of a DIST. While most of the modules are bypassed and therefore their counters are not available, the SQM counters are available, but these would be the SQM counters for the destination queues rather than the route itself.

Rate

There are two main rate aspects to the RSI thread. The first is how many commands it is processing across the link, i.e., commands per second. This is the most useful of the rates as it can be used to directly compare with the RepAgent rate as well as the DIST rate to determine if the route is lagging. A second rate — bytes per second (or better yet Mbit/sec or Kbit/sec) — is useful in determining if the network capacity is restricting the RS. Both of these rates, along with some other useful rate related metrics, can be calculated using the following counters and formulas.

```
-- Counter:           CounterID
-- ----------------   ----------
-- BytesSent          4000
-- PacketsSent        4002
-- MsgsSent           4004
-- MsgsGetTrunc       4005
--
-- Derived Metrics:
-- CmdsPerSec = (MsgsSent-MsgsGetTrunc)/delta
```

476

```
-- MbitPerSec = (BytesSent*8.0)/(1024*1204*delta)
-- PacketSize = BytesSent/PacketsSent
-- RSIBatchSize = MsgsSent/MsgsGetTrunc
-- TruncPerMin = (MsgsGetTrunc*60/delta)
```

In addition to the two rates we discussed above, the other derived metrics can be useful for tuning purposes. The PacketSize metric should help in adjusting `rsi_packet_size` from its default of 2048 as necessary. Similarly, RSIBatchSize can help determine when `rsi_batch_size` or `rsi_sync_interval` need to be tuned due to RSI's synchronizing too frequently. While a handful per minute is likely acceptable, more than one every few seconds is likely too many. With the default `rs_batch_size` of 256 K, the RSIs for some high-volume systems could be trying to synchronize several times per second, which is far too frequently and would definitely be a drag on network performance. After Replication Server 12.6 ESD #7, this setting could be raised to something more practical; similar to setting `sqm_recover_seg`, 5 to 10 MB would be more appropriate.

Time

There are a couple of time counters that can signal where an RSI thread is spending its time:

```
-- Counter:           CounterID
-- ----------------   ----------
-- SendPTTime         4009
-- RSIReadSQMTime     4015
```

The first refers to the amount of time in hundredths of a second that the Replication Server spent sending packets on the route, while the second is the amount of time spent reading the commands from the RSI outbound queue. Because WAN speeds vary greatly, it isn't possible to specify a desired ratio between the two; however, they do help to rule out certain tuning aspects. For example, if most of the time is spent reading from the queue, actions such as changing the packet size, changing `rsi_batch_size`, and modifying other RSI tuning parameters are not likely to help. Even if most of the time is spent sending packets, changing those parameters is not likely to help unless you can obtain the time spent writing to the outbound queue(s) at the RRS.

On the RRS side, we can track the amount of time spent receiving the packets as well as processing the truncation requests via these counters:

```
-- Counter:            CounterID
-- ------------        ---------
-- RSIUSendGetT        59006
-- RSIUSendSetT        59008
-- RSIURecvPckt        59010
```

While the latter tracks the amount of time spent receiving a packet — and was illustrated as overlapping with RSI SendPTTime — there could be differences, so the values might not match exactly.

The first two track how much time was spent responding to get truncation and set truncation requests. RSIUSendGetT should be common, as it overlaps with the get truncation request from the PRS during the synchronization points. RSIUSendSetT is much rarer and likely only used during recovery operations.

Bell Ringers

Unlike the other modules, the RSI and RSIUSER modules don't have clear bell ringers such as RAWriteWaitsTime, SleepsWait-Seg, and other examples in the other modules. As a result, the only real warning signs for route performance is the message/command throughput rates and the message synchronization rate. What to use for a warning, however, depends on what the norm is. For instance, if the rate of SQM CmdsWritten into the route queue is 500/second and RSI MsgsSent/second is only 250/second, this could be an issue, but if the WAN speed for the route prohibits higher throughput, then the real warning point may be when MsgsSent/second drops below 150/second when SQM CmdsWritten/second is higher.

Caches and Queues

The RSI and RSIUser threads are also unique in that there really isn't a cache or interthread message queue that can be adjusted for the threads themselves. However, the RRS DIST thread does have `md_sqm_write_request_limit` (and remember, it is the MD module within the DIST that the RRS uses). Now this is where it gets interesting. You can configure or alter a database connection's setting for this parameter pretty easily via the following command:

```
alter connection DS.DB
    set md_sqm_write_request_limit to '######'
```

You can also adjust many of the route configuration settings at the PRS via the alter/configure route commands. However, what is not possible is directly tuning the DIST settings at the RRS. Note the word "directly". You can indirectly tune this setting by changing the RRS's server-level default for the configuration value via the following:

```
-- max for Replication Server 12.6 pre ESD #7 is 983040
configure replication server
    set md_sqm_write_request_limit to '4194304'
go
```

This is interesting for two reasons. First, it sets the server-wide default for `md_sqm_write_request_limit` to 4 MB. The second is that while this does take effect and is viewable in the rs_config table within the RSSD afterward, this technique of setting server-wide defaults for connection level settings is not documented! This is likely an oversight as empirical evidence has shown that using this to set `exec_sqm_write_request_limit` server wide does indeed work. Using this to set `md_sqm_write_request_limit` can't be verified as there is no metric in the DIST that corresponds to the RepAgent User's RAWriteWaitsTime metric (at least as of this writing).

Tuning for Performance

Tuning a route for performance is fairly simple as there aren't too many options available.

disk_affinity

Although this is probably one of the most forgotten, it will be the one most likely to help in larger scale system environments. Consider a typical "fan-out" situation in which data from a single primary source is replicated to half a dozen destinations, each via a separate route. This means that the DIST thread for the primary connection has to write the same insert/update/delete replicated command into six outbound queues — one for each route. In most systems, all six of those route queues are likely all on the same physical stable device, and the consequence is rather predictable. For instance, assume that the primary is high volume and is writing 1,000 commands/sec to the inbound queue. If all the route queues were on the same device, that device would have to sustain 6,000 commands/sec, and likely more as that device is often the very device that the inbound queue resides on as well. A key metric to look for to indicate when this is necessary is to look at the SQM counter SleepsWaitSeg. More than likely the lack of using disk_affinity is a problem, as each of the route queues is likely to be requesting segment allocations at the same time (as the same commands are written to them in order).

rsi_batch_size

Prior to Replication Server 12.6 ESD #7 and Replication Server 15.0 ESD #1, this setting was limited to 256 KB. After these releases, the parameter can be between 256 KB and 128 MB. 128 MB is likely too large. A good starting point might be to use a value no higher than sqm_recover_seg, but no lower than a single segment (1 MB). You could also start in the 2 to 4 MB range and then monitor the rate of MsgsGetTrunc sent per minute. If more than 10, you might want to look at increasing this.

rsi_sync_interval

Generally the default of 60 seconds is fine. The `rsi_batch_size` setting is more likely to drive when synchronization occurs than `rsi_sync_interval`. You could increase this, but it is not recommended to go much above the default — certainly 5 minutes (300 seconds) ought to be the maximum considered. However, years of monitoring have proved that increasing this has almost no effect due to `rsi_batch_size`. Think of this parameter as regulating the synchronization intervals during lulls in activity. For example, during high-volume situations, `rsi_batch_size` will likely drive the truncation requests. Assuming we set it to 4 MB and we are sending 75 MB/min (10 Mbit/sec), we will have ~19 sync points, or one every 3 seconds (and likely an increase in `rsi_batch_size` is called for). However, when the rate drops to low volume during off-hours processing, without this setting it could be a long time before route synchronization occurs and space is freed in the route outbound queue. For instance if `rsi_batch_size` is set to 4 MB and we have a lull in which activity drops to 100 KB/min, it would take 40 minutes before a sync point occurred without `rsi_sync_interval`. Even during low-volume periods, however, 60 seconds is likely sufficient, so decreasing this parameter is not likely to help much either.

rsi_packet_size

With a 2 KB default, as with the RepAgent itself, this likely is contributing to lower network efficiency and RSI processing. A good starting point for this parameter might be 8192 or 16384 (the maximum value). Note that unlike ASE, you do not have to configure the Replication Server to allocate extra memory for large packet sizes. You can monitor this either from the RRS via the RSI User's RSIUConnPcktSz metric, or you can compute it at the PRS by using the RSI BytesSent/PacketsSent formula and then rounding to the nearest packet size likely used.

Monitoring Performance

Having discussed the common mistakes made while monitoring (i.e., using admin who, sqm, etc.) and reviewed the metrics in detail, the final discussion for this chapter is how to best monitor for performance.

Establishing a Heartbeat

The first step is to establish a heartbeat. While most long-time users of Sybase Replication Server often developed their own, they had a number of shortcomings in that they could only show the primary and replicate database times but nothing to indicate where the latency was. RS's rs_ticket feature is likely the best place to start as it not only indicates the primary/replicate times, but also enough internal timestamps that a good indication of where the problem is can be determined. Establishing a heartbeat mechanism is fairly simple; you can use RMS (Replication Monitoring Services) and leverage its heartbeat capability, or cron, or some other scheduling mechanism. A good heartbeat would be every 5 to 15 minutes, as longer times could result in performance problems that are resolved without any indication other than user complaints about data currency.

Collecting Replication Server Monitor Counters

The second step is to collect the counters. By this we are not talking about the ability of admin statistics to save the statistics to the RSSD — although this is critical. What we are referring to is:

▶ Setting up periodic sampling of statistics; i.e., collecting statistics at one- to five-minute sample intervals during peak processing periods.

▶ Exporting the statistics to a centralized repository where trend analysis and day-over-day comparisons can be made as well as cross database analysis involving routes.

While this latter is fairly crucial for analyzing Replication Server performance, it also can be used to track business activity since you will have a record of the number of transactions as well as a good idea of the transaction profiles for the applications from the metrics.

Primary and Replicate DBMS

Lastly, when researching potential Replication Server problems, it is very important that you monitor the primary and replicate databases as well, especially the replicate database. As mentioned earlier, for ASE, this would mean collecting monOpenObjectActivity and monProcessWaits (for maintenance users) metrics to isolate when Replication Server latency is due to slow replicate execution of the commands due to missing indexes or other problems (blocking, log contention, etc.). Similar to the Replication Server metrics, this information should be exported from the individual servers and added either to the Replication Server repository or at least a repository within the same server so that joins for particular time ranges can be facilitated.

Chapter 15

Disaster and Recovery

In this chapter we will discuss types of failures, procedures for recovering from failures, and how to prevent and plan for recoverability.

Types of Failures

There are several types of failures. These can be short duration transient or long duration transient. Additionally, they can cause data loss, and one or more Replication Server components may suffer disk failures causing data loss.

Short Duration Transient Failures

Replication Server's store and forward protocol ensures that after its component or thread is restarted, Replication Server picks up where it left off without any data loss. These include:

► Host machine reboot

► Adaptive Server Enterprise or Replication Server error or shutting down the server

► DSI connection thread being suspended due to permission error

► Network failures

Long Duration Transient Failures

Replication Server's stable queue or database transaction log may fill up if a Replication Server component is inactive or down for a prolonged period of time. If the database transaction log is full, the database administrator may stop replication by ignoring the secondary truncation point and truncating the transaction log. If those records are not yet sent to Replication Server and the queues have been purged, then the transient failure can become a more serious data loss failure.

Failures Causing Data Loss

There are two types of failure that can lead to a loss of data:

▶ Database corruption due to software errors

▶ Hardware crash/errors resulting in disk failures

The following situations can result in data loss:

▶ The database's transaction log gets corrupted or the disk it is on fails. In this case, you can recover the database from the last full database dump and transaction log dump.

▶ Replication Server's stable queue can get corrupted or the disk it is on fails.

▶ RSSD database can get corrupted or the disk it is using for its data and log segment can fail.

Disaster Recovery Fundamentals

In order to recover from Replication Server system disasters, you should understand the following concepts:

▶ Functionality of the Adaptive Server Enterprise transaction log

▶ Secondary truncation point issues

▶ Backup and recovery

▶ Sybase HA failover

- ▶ Save interval
- ▶ Generation ID and the origin queue ID
- ▶ rs_subcmp

Functionality of Adaptive Server Enterprise Transaction Log

Every Adaptive Server Enterprise database has the syslogs system table that contains the transaction log. Every data modification operation (DML) is logged in syslogs. It is used by Adaptive Server for recovery and roll forward, transaction recovery from a rollback, database recovery from server crash, incremental backups, and replication.

The transaction log is comprised of several sections, as discussed below.

Inactive section: This section of the database transaction log starts at the beginning of the transaction log and ends at the beginning of the oldest active/open transaction. This section contains all the committed transactions and can be truncated by transaction log truncation.

Active section: This section of the database transaction log starts at the oldest active transaction and ends at the most recent transaction log record. This section contains both committed and uncommitted transaction log records. Committed transactions cannot be truncated unless preceding transactions have been committed.

Empty section: This section of the database transaction log starts at the most recent transaction log record in the transaction log (end of the transaction log). Last Chance Threshold (LCT) space is reserved in this section, which prevents the transaction log from getting full. Once the LCT is crossed, all activity in the database is suspended or aborted.

The Adaptive Server Enterprise database transaction log can be truncated with any of the following methods:

- ▶ database option "truncate log on checkpoint" is set
- ▶ dump transaction *database* with truncate_only
- ▶ dump transaction *database* to '*filename*'

▶ dump transaction *database* with no_log

For complete details on the dump transaction command, please check the Adaptive Server Enterprise system administration guide.

All of these dump transaction commands will truncate the log to the end of the inactive section of the transaction log. If replication is not enabled, the primary truncation point is the oldest active transaction in a database and it is the first page not to be deallocated with dump transaction.

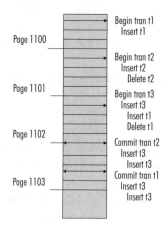

Figure 15-1

In the above figure, if a dump transaction command is run for this database, dump transaction will deallocate pages 1100 and 1101.

Secondary Truncation Point Issues

When RepAgent is added to the primary database, the secondary truncation point is created in the database transaction log. The secondary truncation point points to the transaction log record that contains the begin transaction for the oldest open transaction not yet fully sent to the Replication Server. RepAgent scans the transaction log and sends both committed and uncommitted log records marked for replication to Replication Server.

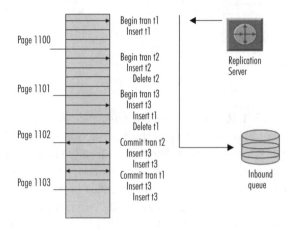

Figure 15-2

In Figure 15-2, RepAgent has processed transaction log records from the beginning of the log until insert t3 on page 1103. Because transaction t1 is still open at this point, the secondary truncation point will remain the same. If dump transaction is run on this database, it will dump up to the page holding the begin tran t3 on page 1102, but will deallocate only up to a previous page holding the secondary truncation point. Since the secondary truncation point is set on the first log page, dump transaction will not deallocate any page.

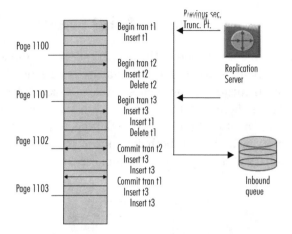

Figure 15-3

In Figure 15-3, Replication Agent has processed transaction log records from the beginning of the transaction log until insert t3 on page 1103. Since transaction t1 is already closed at that point but transaction t3 is still open, the secondary truncation point will move to page 1102. If dump transaction is now run on this database, it will dump the page holding the begin tran t3 on page 1102 and will deallocate pages 1100 and 1101 because the secondary truncation point is now set on page 1102.

You can find the location of the secondary truncation point by using the following methods:

```
1> select logptr from master..sysdatabases where dbid=7
2> go
logptr
-----------
     13144

(1 row affected)

1> select * from master..syslogshold where dbid=7
2> go
```

```
dbid   reserved    spid   page         xactid          masterxactid
  starttime               name                         xloid
------ ----------- ------ ----------- --------------- --------------
-------------------- ------------------------------- ----------
7      0           0      13144        0x000000000000 0x000000000000
  Sep 30 2007 12:31PM   $replication_truncation_point  0

(1 row affected)

1> sp_help_rep_agent pubs3, 'scan'
2> go
Replication Agent Scan status
database   start_marker   end_marker    current_marker  log_recs_scanned oldest_transaction
---------  -------------- ------------- --------------- ---------------- ------------------
pubs3      (13144,32)     (13144,35)    (13144,35)      0                (-1,0)
(return status = 0)

1> dbcc gettrunc
2> go
secondary trunc page   secondary trunc state  dbrepstat  generation id  database id
  database name                         ltl version
--------------------   ---------------------- ---------- -------------- -----------
----------------------------- -----------
13144                  1                      495        0              7
  pubs3                                700
```

The primary truncation point stops moving if the client has not yet committed an open transaction or a large batch job is running that will only commit at the end of the job.

The secondary truncation point will also stop moving because the secondary truncation point cannot go past the primary truncation point. The transaction log cannot be truncated, but transactions are still being applied in the database. Eventually the database will cross Last Chance Threshold for transaction log and all activity in the database will be suspended.

If the secondary truncation point stops moving either because the primary truncation point cannot move or because one of Replication Server's components is down or the inbound queue is full, the transaction will fill because it cannot be truncated. However, transactions are still being applied in the primary database. Eventually the database will cross Last Chance Threshold and all activity in the database will be suspended. If the inbound queue is full, you should add more stable devices to the Replication Server so that it can hold messages until the primary database issue is resolved.

Backup and Recovery

You should always take a full dump of the RSSD/ERSSD database following any replication DDL changes, creating routes, or adding replication definitions, subscriptions, publications, and/or articles. Recovery of the RSSD/ERSSD database will depend on how much activity there has been since the last full database dump.

Replication Server provides a method of coordinated dumps and transaction log dumps to ensure consistency after a restore on multiple data servers at all sites in the replication system. A coordinated dump can be used on databases that are either primary or replicate databases but not both. A database dump is initiated from the primary database. RepAgent retrieves and sends a dump record from the transaction log to Replication Server. Replication Server distributes the dump request to the replicate sites, ensuring that all of the data can be restored to a known point of consistency.

Creating a Coordinated Dump

Each function-string class assigned to the databases involved in replication at each site of the Replication Server system creates function strings for the rs_dumpdb and rs_dumptran system functions. rs_dumpdb and rs_dumptran function strings should be created at the Replication Server that is the primary site for the class. These function strings should call stored procedures that execute dump database and dump transaction and update rs_lastcommit. The following example of a function string works best if you have only one replicate database or the databases using the function-string class have the same dump device names.

```
create function string rs_dumpdb
for sqlserver_derived_class
output language
```

```
'dump database ?rs_destination_db!sys_raw?
to pubs3_dmpdb;
execute rs_update_lastcommit
? rs_update_lastcommit
?rs_origin!sys?,
?rs_origin_qid!sys?,
?rs_secondary_qid!sys?,
?rs_origin_commit_time!sys?'
```

The following example calls dbdump_proc, which manages the dump devices at the replicate sites. Make sure that this stored procedure selects the dump device to use and then marks it as "used" so that subsequent database dumps do not overwrite the previous dumps.

```
alter function string rs_dumpdb
for sqlserver_derived_class
output rpc
'execute dbdump_proc
?rs_dump_database!sys?,
?rs_dump_label!sys?,
?rs_dump_timestamp!sys?,
?rs_destination_db !sys ?,
?rs_origin !sys ?,
?rs_origin_qid!sys?,
?rs_secondary_qid!sys?,
?rs_origin_commit_time!sys?'
```

rs_origin, rs_origin_qid, and rs_secondary_qid are used by this stored procedure to execute rs_update_lastcommit. If Replication Server fails after the dump has been completed but before the rs_lastcommit system table has been updated, the database dump is restarted when Replication Server is restarted.

```
create proc dbproc_proc
@dump_database varchar(30),
@dump_label varchar(30),
@dump_timestamp varbinary(16),
@destination_database varchar(30),
@origin int,
@origin_qid binary(36),
@secondary_qid binary(36),
@origin_time datetime
```

493

```
as
print 'Received a dump database command from Application Server:'
declare @message varchar(255)
select @message = 'dump database ' + @dump_database
     + '. Label= '' + @dump_label
     + ''. Dest.db = '' + @destination_database
     + ''''
print @message
if @destination_database = 'pubs3'
begin
print 'issuing ''dump database pubs3.'''
dump database pubs3 to pubs3_dmp
update dmp_count set d_count = d_count + 1
exec pubs3.dbo.rs_update_lastcommit
@origin, @origin_qid, @secondary_qid,
@origin_time
end
else if @destination_database = 'pix2'
begin
    print 'issuing ''dump database pix2.'''
    dump database pix2 to pix2_dmp
    update dmp_count set d_count = d_count + 1
    exec pix2.dbo.rs_update_lastcommit
        @origin, @origin_qid, @secondary_qid,
        @origin_time
end
```

Follow these steps to create a coordinated dump:

1. At each replicate site, use the alter connection command to enable a coordinated dump:

```
suspend connection to rrs1.pubs3
alter connection to rrs1.pubs3
set dump_load to 'on'
resume connection to rrs1.pubs3
```

2. When the database dump is started at the primary database, dump record of dump database and/or dump transaction is transferred by RepAgent to Replication Server.

3. The rs_dumpdb or rs_dumptran function class is then distributed to all replicate sites by Replication Server.

4. At each replicate site, a customized stored procedure is executed by rs_dumpdb or rs_dumptran.

Up-to-the-Minute Recovery

If Adaptive Server is up and running and the database transaction log is not corrupted or damaged but the database is damaged and cannot be repaired, you can do the following to recover the database:

1. Stop activity in the database. There should not be any user connection in the database because their transactions will be lost.

2. Dump the database transaction log with no truncation:

   ```
   dump transaction pdb to "/tmp/pdbdmp" with no_truncate
   ```

   This up-to-the-minute backup will capture all the committed transactions since the last transaction log dump.

3. If you don't have a create database script, extract the DDL for creating a database with the DDLGen utility.

4. If database physical devices are damaged, replace them if necessary.

5. Drop and recreate database devices with the disk init command if necessary.

   ```
   disk init name='logical name', physname='physical name', size='size'
   ```

   For the complete syntax of the disk init command, refer to the Adaptive Server reference manual.

6. If necessary, drop and recreate the database.

7. Load the database dump.

8. Load transaction log dumps using the same sequence in which they were dumped.

9. Load the last up-to-the-minute dump of the transaction log dump.

10. Online the database.

If all these operations succeed, the primary database should be up to date and you should be able to resume replication.

Sybase HA Failover

Adaptive Server 12.0 and above and Replication Server 12.0 and above support the Sybase HA failover licensed feature. This feature allows you to configure two Adaptive Servers as companions. When the primary server fails, the secondary server takes over the failed primary server's devices, databases, and connections.

Sybase HA failover can be configured as asymmetric or symmetric. In both configurations, both host machines are configured for dual access so that disks are visible and accessible to both servers.

In an asymmetric configuration, one companion server acts as a secondary companion for another primary companion. Only a primary companion can failover to a secondary server. The secondary server only acts as "hot standby" and doesn't perform any activity until failover occurs. In this configuration, both Adaptive Servers are on two separate machines, but they share the same system disks, system and user databases, and user connections.

In a symmetric configuration, both servers on each node perform as secondary companions for each other. In this configuration, both Adaptive Servers are on two separate machines, but each Adaptive Server has its own system devices, system and user databases, and connections. In case of failover, the other server will take the workload of the failed server.

For detailed information on Sybase HA failover, please see "Using Sybase Failover in High Availability" in the Sybase documentation.

Configuring Replication Server for HA Failover

The HA failover feature is not a substitute for warm standby. Warm standby keeps a copy of a primary database, while HA failover allows accessing the same database from a different host machine. HA failover support works the same for connections from Replication Server to warm standby databases.

Adaptive Server must be configured to support HA failover, only then can you configure Replication Server to support HA failover. The HA failover feature can be enabled for an RSSD database connection and then for all user database connections.

You cannot enable or disable the HA failover feature for individual connections except the RSSD database connection.

In failover mode, when the primary companion fails and the workload is taken by the secondary companion, incomplete transactions or operations that require updates to the RSSD database will fail. But internal operations such as update to locater, disk segment, and so on should not fail. Existing connections are retried by Replication Server, but new connections are failed over.

RSSD database and user database failover is configured directly through Adaptive Server. RepAgent failover and reconnection to Replication Server after failover/failback is handled by Adaptive Server. Replication Server failover is not supported.

You can enable HA failover support at the time of Replication Server installation with rs_init. After installation, you can edit the Replication Server configuration file and change RSSD_ha_failover to "yes":

```
RSSD_ha_failover=yes
```

To disable HA failover support for RSSD, change RSSD_ha_failover to "no":

```
RSSD_ha_failover=no
```

These changes are dynamic, so you don't need to restart Replication Server.

To enable HA failover support for user databases, log in to Replication Server with a login that has administrative privileges:

```
configure replication server set ha_failover to 'on'
```

Save Interval and Recovery

The save interval is the number of minutes that the Replication Server saves messages after they have been successfully passed to the destination Replication Server or data server. Failures can occur anytime, anywhere in the replication system. When this parameter is configured, Replication Server will retain messages in their queues for that period of time after the next site has acknowledged the receipt of messages. When deletes are performed, the delete time of the segment is set. The time when a segment would be deallocated is calculated by adding the current time to the two save interval set. For persistent purposes, the two save interval is stored in the rs_segments table. After a failure, when a replicate Replication Server restarts the route, all the segments whose deletion is marked for a future time would be resent.

The save interval can be set with the following:

```
alter connection to rds.rdb
set save_interval to '60'                        --(database connection)
alter route to rrs set save_interval to '60'    --(Route)
```

A strict save interval specifies how long Replication Server is to retain messages in the DSI queue for a logical connection (warm standby). This configuration parameter should be set to "strict", unless your stable device is full and you don't have disk space; in that case, you can set it to "0" minutes.

The materialization_save_interval configuration parameter for logical connection should be set to "strict" too, meaning the data from materialization queues will not be deleted until they are applied to the standby database.

You should never set these parameters to anything other than "strict" or "0". Setting them to something else can result in serious losses that Replication Server won't be able to detect, and it will be extremely hard to locate and correct such issues.

The following RCL command can be used to restore backlogged transactions:

```
sysadmin restore_dsi_saved_segments, dataserver, database
```

You will need to suspend DSI thread connection before this command can be used to restore saved segments. rs_get_lastcommit is used by Replication Server to decide which transactions to filter.

The Origin Queue ID and the Generation ID

Each command scanned by RepAgent is assigned a unique OQID. It is a monotonically increasing binary 36 number (see Appendix A for OQID contents). This OQID is used by the Replication Server for duplicate and loss detection. OQID is stored in the rs_lastcommit table in the replicate database. There is one row per source database in the rs_lastcommit table, and that row contains the source OQID. OQID is also stored as the last locater field received by stable queues from each of their senders in the rs_locater table in the RSSD database. The OQID value saved in the rs_lastcommit table will sometimes but not always match its corresponding locater values. If the incoming OQID is lower than the last OQID saved in the rs_lastcommit table, then Replication Server assumes that it has already been applied and is a duplicate row. If the incoming OQID is higher than the last OQID saved in the rs_lastcommit table, then Replication Server assumes it is a new transaction.

Duplicate Detection

The rs_locater table in RSSD/ERSSD is not updated with every single transaction; instead, it is updated only after a batch of transactions has been applied. There is a big window between the time a transaction is committed at the data server and the time the command is actually deleted from the outbound queue. If Replication Server crashes or is stopped and restarted, DSI would reapply the transactions already applied at the data server. Already applied transactions need to be ignored. Replication Server executes the rs_update_lastcommit stored procedure to update the rs_lastcommit table before it commits the transaction. rs_lastcommit stores the last transaction (OQID) from a given origin to the database. If the transaction fails to commit at the data server, it is logged in the exception log. When Replication Server is restarted, DSI continues after taking a retryable exception.

Both OQID and GENID are stored in the database dump, but only OQID is stored in the transaction log dump. For up-to-the-minute recovery, the database timestamp is restored to the value it held at the time of the database crash; otherwise, the database timestamp will only be restored to the value at last backup. In this case, the next OQID generated by RepAgent will be lower than the last OQID received by Replication Server. This will cause Replication Server to discard transactions as duplicates until the database timestamp value catches up to the last replicated value of the OQID. However, error messages are not logged in the Replication Server error log, but the duplicate count in admin who, sqm will increment. Replication Server will continue discarding transactions as duplicate until the OQID in the primary database catches up to the OQID of the replicate database or the generation ID is incremented.

Incrementing Generation ID

To increment the GENID at the Replication Server:

```
admin get_generation, primarydataserver, primarydatabase
```

To increment the GENID at the primary database:

```
sp_stop_rep_agent database
dbcc settrunc(ltm, 'gen_id', new gen_id)
```

new gen_id should be incremented by 1. For example, if gen_id is 100, then new gen_id should be set to 101.

```
sp_start_rep_agent database
```

After incrementing the generation ID, replicated transactions will not be discarded by Replication Server because now they have a higher OQID.

rs_subcmp to Reconcile Data and Schema

rs_subcmp is a standalone executable program run from the operating system for comparing data from the replicate table to the primary version of the table. rs_subcmp can compare schemas between replicate and primary tables, and can find missing, inconsistent, and orphaned rows and optionally can reconcile too.

rs_subcmp can be used to reconcile inconsistencies between primary and replicate tables rather than resubscribing to the data.

SYBASE and library path environment variables must be set before executing rs_subcmp. For comparing schema, the DDLGENLOC and SYBROOT environment variables should also be set. The DDLGENLOC environment variable should be set to $SYBASE/ASEP/bin/ddlgen, and the SYBROOT environment variable should be set to $SYBASE.

rs_subcmp compares data in replicate and primary tables by executing a supplied select command in both primary and replicate databases and verifies that the select command returns the same columns, based on the name and the datatype of each column. If the returned columns match, rs_subcmp categorizes the differences as:

▶ Orphan rows — Rows exist at the replicate, but not at the primary

▶ Missing rows — Rows exist at the primary, but not at the replicate

▶ Inconsistent rows — Rows exist at both primary and replicate with the same primary key but have different values in other columns

After these lists are compiled, rs_subcmp verifies inconsistencies again by iterating for the specified number of times and checking:

▶ If orphaned rows disappear from the replicate

▶ If missing rows appear at the replicate

▶ If inconsistent rows match

▶ If the new replicate row value matches the primary row value from the previous iterations

After iterating for the specified number of times, the contents of three lists are printed to standard output if the -V option was specified. rs_subcmp has three types of return codes:

▶ 0 — Both replicated and primary tables are the same.

▶ 1 — An error occurred while executing rs_subcmp.

▶ 2 — The replicated and primary tables are different.

It is best to run rs_subcmp when the primary is not being updated; otherwise, rs_subcmp will detect false differences and latency can be large. rs_subcmp can impact Adaptive Server performance because the select used by rs_subcmp can do a tablescan and the order by clause may cause a sort, which creates internal worktables in the tempdb.

Replication Server 15.0.1 rs_subcmp uses a hash algorithm to improve performance. The hash algorithm compresses the data in primary and replicated tables. The compressed data is then fetched by rs_subcmp, meaning instead of taking the entire row of data during comparison between the primary table and the replicated table, rs_subcmp transfers only the compressed data for each data row from the primary and replicate tables, and then verifies or reconciles inconsistencies between them. A fast comparison with the hash algorithm can only be used with Adaptive Server 15.0.2 and above. Note that a fast comparison with hash algorithm does not support text, image, or unitext datatypes. For complete details, please see the Replication Server 15.0.1 Reference Guide in the Sybase documentation.

Below is the command-line syntax:

```
rs_subcmp [-R | -r] [-v] [-V] [-z[1 | 2]]
[-f config_file] [-F]
-S primary_ds [-D primary_db]
-s replicate_ds [-d replicate_db]
-t table_name [-T primary_table_name]
-c select_command [-C primary_select_command]
-u user [-U primary_user]
[-p passwd] [-P primary_passwd]
[-B primary_init_batch]
[-b replicate_init_batch]
[-n num_iterations] [-w wait_interval]
[-e float_precision] [-E real_precision]
[-k primary_key_column [-k primary_key_column]...]
[-i identity_column]
[-l text_image_column_name
[-l text_image_column_name]...]
[-L text_image_length_in_kilobytes]
[-N text_image_column_name
[-N text_image_column_name]...]
[-Z language]
[-o sort_order]
[-O sort_order]
[-J rs_subcmp_charset]
```

```
[-j rep_charset]
[-a replicate_column_name primary_column_name
[-a replicate_column_name primary_column_name]...]
[-q unicode_sort_order]
[-Q unicode_sort_order]
[-x schema_flag]
[-X filter_flag]
[-I interface_file]
[-g reconciliation file]
[-h fast comparison]
[-H normatlization option]
```

rs_subcmp uses the following flags:

-R — Reconciles the replicate data with the primary data. Before inserting a missing row or deleting an orphan row, rs_subcmp reverifies the inconsistency by logging into the primary database and verifies that the missing row in the replicate table still exists in the primary table. In the case of an orphan row in the replicate table, rs_subcmp verifies that it doesn't exist on the primary table. Values are Y or N.

-r — Reconciles the replicate data with the primary data by inserting if the row is missing on the replicate table, deleting if the row exists on the replicate but not on the primary, and updating if data in replicate columns doesn't match the column data on the primary. No final verification of data inconsistencies at the primary database is done. Values are Y or N.

-v — Prints version information.

-V — Prints results of comparison on the display. Text and image values are not displayed.

-z1, -z2 — Provides trace information.

-f — Name of configuration file if one is used.

-F — Display configuration file format.

-S — Primary data server name with the primary data for the subscription.

-D — Primary database name with the primary data for the subscription.

-s — Replicate data server name with the replicate copy of the data.

-d — Replicate database name with the replicate copy of the data.

-t — The name of the table in primary and replicate databases.

-T — Primary table name in the primary database. You can use this flag to make sure primary and replicate table names are different. You can also qualify the table name with the owner.

-c/-C — Select commands that retrieve subscription data. -c retrieves data from both primary and replicate tables, and -C retrieves data only from primary table. Columns specified by -c and -C must return columns with the same name and same datatype from both primary and replicate tables. A select command must order rows based on the primary key. You must have a clustered index on primary key columns or an order by clause in the select statement; otherwise, if rows are not received in the correct order, rs_subcmp may delete rows in the replicate table. Columns with text, image, and unitext datatypes cannot be part of the primary key and these columns should be listed in the end of the column list. If columns with text, image, or unitext datatypes allow nulls, then you should use the -N flag with rs_subcmp to indicate that these column do allow null, because by default the replicate table doesn't allow null values for these columns. Inconsistencies for columns with text/image/unitext datatypes are not stored in a list. rs_subcmp logs back into the primary database and re-executes the select command to reconcile missing or inconsistent rows that contain text/image/unitext values. If an inconsistent or missing row is found, the replicate table is modified by rs_subcmp by inserting or updating the row. If inconsistent or missing rows are not found on the primary table, then rs_subcmp deletes the inconsistent row from the replicate and does not take any action for the missing row. Columns with the rs_address datatype should not be specified in the select command (-c and -C), because data in these columns may not be identical for both primary and replicate. Updates to these columns are filtered out by Replication Server so as not to replicate them unnecessarily. rs_subcmp reconciles inconsistent values for the identity column in rows by deleting the row from the replicate table and then inserting the row from the primary table.

> **Note:** Instead of comparing the entire table, you can specify a where clause that might check key ranges.

-u — The primary user login name used to log in to the primary and replicate data servers.

-U — The primary user login name used to log in to the primary data server. This flag can be used if you have different login names for the primary and replicate data servers.

-p — The password for the primary user login. If this flag is omitted, the null password is used by rs_subcmp for logging in to the primary and replicate data servers.

-P — The password to be used for user login specified with -U.

-B — rs_subcmp logs into the primary database and executes the command batch (for example, set isolation level) specified with this flag.

-b — rs_subcmp logs into the replicate database and executes the command batch (for example, disable triggers) specified by this flag.

-n — This parameter governs how many times rs_subcmp will reverify inconsistent rows it finds in the first iteration. Inconsistency found in the first iteration might be due to lag in the replication. Default: 10.

-w — The number of seconds rs_subcmp should wait before beginning another iteration. Default: 5 seconds.

-e — This flag is used to set the number of decimal places in exponential notation that floating-point values are expected to have. The default is set to the maximum precision supported by the platform.

-E — This flag sets the number of decimal places in exponential notation that real values are expected to have. The default is set to the maximum precision supported by the platform.

-k — Column name that is part of the primary key for the table. If column names are different for the primary and replicate tables, then the column name specified by the -k flag is the replicate column name. You will need to use the -k flag for each column in the primary key. The primary key must be unique and cannot have columns with text, image, or unitext datatypes.

-i — Identity column name in the replicate table.

-l — Text, image, or unitext column name. This flag turns off logging of updates to text, image, or unitext columns.

-L — You can specify the longest value the data server returns for text, image, or unitext columns. For example, if you want to specify 49152 bytes (48 KB) for text or image column size, then -L=48.

-N — This flag indicates that text, image, or unitext columns of the replicate table allow null values. By default nulls are not allowed for text, image, or unitext columns of the replicate tables.

-7 — rs_subcmp uses the language specified with this flag for generating error and other messages. By default rs_subcmp uses the default locale entry for your platform.

-o — The name of the non-Unicode sort order used by your replication system. The sort order specified by this flag is used by rs_subcmp for comparing primary key columns. When this flag is specified, rs_subcmp does a binary comparison of the primary key columns. If the primary keys match, binary comparison of the remaining columns is done by rs_subcmp. If they don't match, the inconsistent row is reported. If the primary keys do not match, rs_subcmp compares them with the specified sort order. If the primary keys columns match, the inconsistent row is reported. If the primary keys do not match, the missing or orphan row is reported.

If you do not specify any sort order, rs_subcmp does a simple binary comparison of each column of the primary and the replicate row. If you have a different sort order for the primary and the replicate data servers and the where clause of the select statement includes character or text datatypes, the results may be confusing. To avoid this confusion, you should run rs_subcmp first without using reconciling flags (-R, -r) and with the visual (-V) flag to review the potential effects of the data.

-0 — The name of the non-Unicode sort order used by your replication system. The sort order specified by this flag is used by rs_subcmp for comparing all columns of types char, varchar, and text. With this flag, rs_subcmp doesn't do any binary comparison.

-J — The character set name used by rs_subcmp error and informational messages and in all configuration parameters and command-line options. The default character set is the character set specified in the locale entry of your platform.

-j — The character set name used by the replicate data server. This character set is used by rs_subcmp for comparing and reconciling replicate and primary copies of a table. The default is to use the character set specified with -J (rs_subcmp_charset).

If your primary and replicate data servers have different character sets, then the replicate data server's character set must be loaded into the primary data server. This enables the primary data server to do necessary character set conversion. If the primary and replicate data servers' character sets are incompatible, no data conversion is done. If the character sets are incompatible, but a single character from the primary data server has no representation in the replicate data server's character set, then that character is replaced with a "?" and processing continues.

-a — With this flag you can specify the primary column name associated with a replicate column name if the primary column name is different than that for the replicate column name. The replicate column name must be specified before the primary column name.

-q — The Unicode sort order used by rs_subcmp for comparing Unicode primary key columns. When the flag is used, rs_subcmp does a binary comparison of the Unicode primary key columns. If the primary key columns match, then binary comparisons of the remaining columns are done by rs_subcmp; if they do not match, the inconsistent row is reported by rs_subcmp. However, if the primary key columns do not match, then rs_subcmp compares them by using the specified sort order. If the Unicode primary key columns match, the inconsistent row is reported. If the primary key columns do not match, the orphan or missing row is reported by rs_subcmp.

-Q — The Unicode sort order used by rs_subcmp for comparing all Unicode columns. No binary comparison is performed by rs_subcmp.

-x — This schema flag specifies the rs_subcmp comparison types. See Table 15-1 for valid values.

Table 15-1: Schema flag values

Schema Flag Value	Description
0	Default: data comparison
1	Database schema between two databases is compared.
2	Table schema between two tables is compared.

-X — This filter specifies the schema types and subtypes included or excluded from the comparison. If the value starts with a "+", only the schema types are selected for comparison and subtypes are ignored. Otherwise, both schema types and subtypes are unselected and not used for comparison.

See Table 15-2 for a list of schema types and Table 15-3 for a list of subtypes.

Table 15-2: Schema types

Schema Type	Description
A	All aliases in the database
D	All defaults in the database
E	All user-defined user types in the database
G	All groups in the database
P	All stored procedures in the database
R	All rules in the database
T	All user tables, indexes, keys, constraints, and triggers in the database
U	All users in the database
V	All views in the database

Table 15-3: Schema subtypes

Schema Subtype	Description
c	Constraint
d	Bind default
f	Foreign key
g	Grant
i	Index
m	Stored procedure mode
p	Primary key
r	Bind rule
t	Trigger

-I — Interfaces file location.

-g — A reconciliation file is created for inconsistent data; however, SQL statements in this file cannot have text, image, or unitext data. This file is created in the current working directory. The default filename is *reconcile_file_PROCID*.sql.

For every schema comparison, rs_subcmp creates a report file. The report file details the schema inconsistencies between two databases or two tables. This file is also created in the current working directory and the default filename is *reportPROCID*.txt.

-h — rs_subcmp performs fast comparison.

-H — This normalization option specifies how to normalize the data when performing fast comparison. The options are listed in Table 15-4.

Table 15-4: Normalization options

Normalization Option	Description
lsb	All data is normalized to little endian byte order.
msb	All data is normalized to big endian byte order.
unicode	All data is normalized to Unicode (utf-16).
unicode_lsb	All data is normalized lsb in conjunction with Unicode for platform independence.
unicode_msb	All data is normalized msb in conjunction with Unicode for platform independence.

You can also use a configuration file containing all rs_subcmp configuration parameters and specify it on the command line using the -f flag. This can reduce the complexity of the command lines and consequent errors. If both the configuration file and the command-line options are specified, the command-line values override the values in the configuration file. Table 15-5 summarizes the command-line options and configuration parameters.

Table 15-5: Command-line options and configuration file parameters

Command Line Option	Configuration Parameter	Value
-a	REP_PRI_COLNAME	Replicate-primary column name pair
-b	RINITBATCH	Replicate database initialization command batch. Batch can span multiple lines if newline characters are preceded by "\" (backslash). Up to 1024 characters per line and 64 K total characters are allowed.

Command Line Option	Configuration Parameter	Value
-B	PINITBATCH	Primary database initialization command batch. Batch can span multiple lines if newline characters are preceded by "\" (backslash). Up to 1024 characters per line and 64 K total characters are allowed.
-c	RSELECT	Replicate select command. This command can span multiple lines if newline characters are preceded by "\" (backslash). Up to 1024 characters per line and 64 K total characters are allowed.
-C	PSELECT	Primary select command. This command can span multiple lines if newline characters are preceded by "\"(backslash). Up to 1024 characters per line and 64 K total characters are allowed.
-d	RDB	Replicate database name
-D	PDB	Primary database name
-e	FPRECISION	Expected floating-point precision (integer; platform dependent)
-E	RPRECISION	Expected real precision (integer; platform dependent)
-g	RECONCILE_FILE	Indicates whether a reconciliation file should be created. Values: "Y", "N". Default: "N"
-h	FASTCMP	Indicates whether or not fast comparison should be performed. Values: "Y", "N". Default: "N"
-H	HASH_OPTION	Indicates the normalization option used for fast comparision. If this configuration parameter is not in the configuration file, then the native byte order and character set is used by rs_subcmp for normalization. See Table 15-4 for supported rs_subcmp normalization options.
-i	IDENTITY	Identity column name in replicate table
-I	IFILE	The interfaces file location

Command Line Option	Configuration Parameter	Value
-i	SCHARSET	rs_subcmp's character set
-J	RCHARSET	Replicate data server's character set
-k	KEY	Primary key column in replicate table
-l	NO_LOG	Turns off logging of updates to a text, image, or unitext column
-L	TXT_IMG_LEN	Longest value of text, image, or text column data server returns
-n	NUM_TRIES	Number of comparisons (integer). Default: 10
-N	NULLABLE	The text, image, or unitext column accepts nulls in the replicate table.
-o	SORT_ORDER	Use specified sort order to compare primary key columns
-O	SORT_ORDER_ALL_COLS	Use specified sort order to compare all columns
-P	PPWD	Primary user password
-q	UNICODE_SORT_ORDER	The Unicode sort order used by rs_subcmp to compare Unicode primary key columns
-Q	UNICODE_SORT_ORDER_ALL_COLS	The Unicode sort order used by rs_subcmp to compare all Unicode columns
-r	RECONCILE	Reconciles differences ("Y", "N")
-R	RPWD	Replicate user password
-R	RECONCILE_CHECK	Reconciles differences with verification ("Y", "N")
-s	RDS	Replicate data server name
-S	PDS	Primary data server name
-t	RTABLE	Replicate table name
-T	PTABLE	Primary table name
-u	RUSER	Replicate user name
-U	PUSER	Primary user name
-V	VISUAL	Prints comparison results on the display.

Command Line Option	Configuration Parameter	Value
-w	WAIT	Interval in seconds rs_subcmp waits before beginning another iteration. Default: 5 seconds
-x	SCHEMAFLAG	The rs_subcmp comparison type
-X	FILTER	The filter used to indicate the schema subtype included or excluded in the schema. See Tables 15-2 and 15-3 for schema types and subtypes supported by rs_subcmp.
-z	TRACE	Enable trace information (z1, z2)
-Z	LANGUAGE	Language of rs_subcmp error and informational messages

Example 1:

```
rs_subcmp -f titleauthor.cfg
```

The configuration file consists of the following:

```
# titleauthor.cfg - Reconcile
# PDS.pubs2.dbo.titleauthor with
# RDS.pubs2.dbo.titleauthor.
#
PDS       = PDS
RDS       = RDS
PDB       = pubs2
RDB       = pubs2
PTABLE    = titleauthor
RTABLE    = titleauthor
PSELECT   = select au_id, title_id, au_ord from titleauthor order by au_id
RSELECT   = select au_id, title_id, au_ord from titleauthor order by au_id
PUSER     = sa
RUSER     = sa
PPWD      = reppass
RPWD      = reppass
KEY       = au_id
RECONCILE = Y
VISUAL    = Y
NUM_TRIES = 3
WAIT      = 10
```

513

```
FASTCMP    = Y
HASH_OPTION = [lsb | msb | unicode | unicode_lsb | unicode_msb]
```

Example 2: Compare all schemas between two databases using the authors.cfg file:

```
rs_subcmp -f authors.cfg
```

The configuration file contains the following:

```
PDS = PDS
RDS = RDS
PDB = pubs2
PTABLE = authors
RTABLE = authors
PUSER = sa
RUSER = sa
PPWD = reppwd
RPWD = reppwd
SCHEMAFLAG = 1
```

Example 3: Compare schemas between two databases without a configuration file:

```
rs_subcmp -Spds -srds -Dpdb -drdb -Usa -usa -Preppwd -preppwd -x1
```

Example 4: Compare schemas of two databases excluding index, trigger, and datatype:

```
rs_subcmp -Spds -srds -Dpdb -drdb -Usa -usa -Preppwd -preppwd -x1 -XitD
```

Example 5: Compare all table schemas and user schemas:

```
rs_subcmp -Spds -srds -Dpdb -drdb -Usa -usa -Preppwd -preppwd -x1 -X+TU
```

Recovering the Primary Database

A primary database is a database that contains all the tables and stored procedures and is a source of transactions to be replicated. The primary database can encounter problems due to database corruption or disk failure, host crash, or user error. In some of these cases, the primary database may recover without losing any committed transactions after you fix the problem, but if it fails to recover all committed transactions, you might have to restore it to the previous state from backups and then follow the recovery procedure to restore inconsistencies at replicate sites. You can recover from a failed primary database in two ways: with coordinated dumps or by loading a primary database from dumps.

Recovery with Coordinated Dumps

If you have a coordinated database dump of both primary and replicate databases, you can follow the steps listed below to load all databases in the replication system to a consistent state.

1. Execute the `admin_get_generation` RCL command from the primary Replication Server and note the generation number for the primary database:

   ```
   admin get_generation, primarydataserver, primarydatabase
   ```

2. Execute the `sp_stop_rep_agent` system stored procedure to stop RepAgent for the primary database:

   ```
   sp_stop_rep_agent database
   ```

3. Suspend the DSI connection to the primary database so that you load the backup:

   ```
   suspend connection to dataserver.database
   ```

4. Load the database from the backups. If you have transaction log dumps, they should be loaded in the same sequence in which they were dumped.

   ```
   load database database from 'dumpfile'
   go
   load transaction database from 'trandmp'
   go
   ```

   For complete `load database` and `load transaction` syntax, see Sybase's Adaptive Server Enterprise System Administration Guide volume 2.

5. Bring the database online by executing the `online database` command from the primary data server:

   ```
   online database database
   ```

6. Dump the primary database transaction log:

```
use database
go
dbcc settrunc(ltm, 'ignore') -> Disable secondary truncation point
go
dump transaction database with truncate_only
go
dbcc settrunc(ltm, valid)  -> Enable secondary truncation point
go
```

7. Increment the generation number by adding 1 to the old generation number (from step 1) for the restored primary database:

```
use database
go
dbcc setttrunc(ltm, 'gen_id', new_gen_id)
```

For example, if gen_id was 100, then new_gen_id should be set to 101.

8. Replication Server keeps track of the location of the secondary truncation point in the RSSD..rs_locater table. Since we have moved the secondary truncation point without updating the RSSD database, we must reset the locater by executing following command:

```
use rssddb
go
rs_zeroltm dataserver, database
```

9. Start the database RepAgent by executing the sp_start_rep_ agent system stored procedure:

```
sp_start_rep_agent database
```

10. Resume a DSI connection:

```
resume connection to dataserver.database
```

11. Suspend database connections to all replicate databases in the replication system. You will need to execute the suspend connection RCL command for each replicate database by logging in to its managing Replication Server.

```
suspend connection to dataserver.database
```

12. Load all replicate databases from the coordinated dumps that correspond to the restored primary database state.

13. Set the generation number for all replicated databases by logging in to its managing Replication Server. Execute the `sysadmin set_dsi_generation` RCL command to set the generation number for the replicated database to the same generation number used in step 7.

```
sysadmin set_dsi_generation, gen_number, primary_dataserver, -
primary_database, replicate_dataserver, replicate_database
```

14. Execute `resume connection` for each replicate database from its managing Replication Server:

```
resume connection to dataserver.database
```

15. Restart the primary Replication Server.

16. Stop and restart the primary database RepAgent:

```
sp_stop_rep_agent database
sp_start_rep_agent database
```

If some of the subscriptions were materializing when database failure occurred, you will need to drop and recreate those subscriptions.

Loading Primary Database from Dumps

If you do not have coordinated dumps, follow the steps listed below to recover the primary database in the replication system.

1. Execute the `admin get_generation` RCL command at the primary Replication Server to get the primary database generation number and note the number:

```
admin get_generation, primary_dataserver, primary_database
```

2. If you have transaction log dumps for the database, you can do up-to-the-minute backup with the steps listed in the section titled "Up-to-the-Minute Recovery" earlier in this chapter.

If you were not performing regular transaction log dumps, but instead you have enabled `trunc log on chkpt` on the database or you have run some minimally logged commands (`fast bcp`, `select into`, `dump tran database with truncate_only`, or `dump tran database with no_log`), then you will not be able to perform up-to-the-minute database recovery.

517

3. If the database is available, shut down its RepAgent.

```
sp_stop_rep_agent database
```

4. Suspend the DSI connection for the database:

```
suspend connection to dataserver, database
```

5. If your database is corrupted, you may have to drop and recreate it. Before dropping the database, make sure you have
create database scripts; otherwise you can extract create
database ddl with the ddlgen utility (documented in the Adaptive Server Enterprise utility guide).

To drop the database:

```
sp_configure 'allow updates to system tables', 1
go
begin tran
update sysdatabases set status=320 where name=database
commit tran
go
checkpoint
go
dbcc dbrepair(database, dropdb)
go
```

6. Recreate the database for load. (For create database syntax,
see the Adaptive Server Enterprise reference guide.)

7. Restore the database by loading the database dump and transaction log dumps in sequence (if you were performing
transaction log dumps).

8. Online the database:

```
online database database
```

9. Dump the primary database transaction log to remove old
transactions:

```
use database
go
dbcc settrunc(ltm, 'ignore')  -> Disable secondary truncation point
go
dump transaction database with truncate_only
go
dbcc settrunc(ltm, 'valid')  -> Enable secondary truncation point
go
```

10. Increment the generation number by adding 1 to the old generation number (from step 1) for the restored primary database.

```
use database
go
dbcc setttrunc(ltm, 'gen_id', new_gen_id)
```

For example, if gen_id was 100, then new_gen_id should be set to 101.

11. Replication Server keeps track of the location of the secondary truncation point in the RSSD..rs_locater table. Since we have moved the secondary truncation without updating the RSSD database, we must reset the locater entry in the RSSD database by executing the following command:

```
use rssddb
go
rs_zeroltm dataserver, database
```

12. Start the database RepAgent by executing the sp_start_rep_agent system stored procedure:

```
sp_start_rep_agent database
```

13. Resume the DSI connection:

```
resume connection to dataserver.database
```

To reconcile replicate data with the restored primary database, you can run the rs_subcmp program for each subscription at the replicate, or you can drop and recreate subscriptions.

Recovering from Truncated Primary Database Transaction Log

In some scenarios, such as if one of the Replication Server components is down or network issues cause the stable queue to fill up and the secondary truncation point cannot be moved, Adaptive Server Enterprise will not be able to truncate the log, causing the primary database log to fill up. Log in to Replication Server and check if any component is down:

```
admin who_is_down
```

If the DSI connection thread is down, check Replication Server error logs for problems that can be fixed quickly. For example, the DSI connection thread may be down due to permission issues or deadlock. You can fix the problem and resume the DSI connection thread, and replication will catch up. But if you have a small number of known bad transactions, you can resume the DSI connection with skip transaction, and synchronize the replicate data with primary later.

```
resume connection to dataserver.database skip transaction
```

Check the exceptions log in the RSSD database:

```
rs_helpexception
```

Display detailed information on transaction number tran_id including the text of the transaction:

```
rs_helpexception tran_id, v
```

To delete transactions in the exception log:

```
rs_delexception tran_id
```

If replication is suspended for a longer period, the primary database log can fill up. You can stop RepAgent, remove the secondary truncation point, and truncate the database transaction log.

```
use database
go
sp_stop_rep_agent database
go
dbcc settrunc(ltm, 'ignore')
go
dump transaction database to "dbtrandump"
go
```

You can keep truncating the database transaction log with the dump transaction command. The primary database will stay up and production will not be impacted. After all replication system issues are resolved, you will need to resynchronize replicate data with primary. You can either use rs_subcmp or replay database dump and transaction log dumps through the replication system.

In order to recover from a truncated database log, you will need to create a temporary database, load it with a primary database dump and transaction log dumps, and then start RepAgent in recovery mode. Follow these steps:

1. Restrict activity on the primary database before dumping and truncating the primary database transaction log.

2. Create a temporary database with the same size and segmap order as the primary database.

3. Shut down Replication Server.

4. Start Replication Server in standalone mode by booting with the -M flag.

5. Log in to the Replication Server and execute the set log recovery command for each primary database whose transactions are to be recovered from offline dumps:

   ```
   set log recovery for dataserver.database
   ```

   The set log recovery command puts Replication Server in loss detection mode for the specified databases. DSI checks to see if it has detected loss and prints those messages to the Replication Server error log.

6. Execute the allow connections command after set log recovery to set Replication Server to recovery mode. Replication Server accepts connect requests only from other Replication Servers and RepAgent started in recovery mode for the specified databases. This ensures that old transaction log records are replayed before new transaction log records are accepted.

   ```
   allow connections
   ```

7. Load the temporary database from the primary database dump.

8. Load the first or next transaction log dumps (transaction log dumps should be loaded in the same sequence as they were dumped).

9. Start the temporary database's RepAgent in recovery mode:

```
sp_start_rep_agent temp_database, recovery,
  'original_dataserver',
  'original_database',' repserver_name',
  'repserver_username',
  'repserver_ password'
```

RepAgent will transfer data in the transaction log of the temporary database to the original primary database. RepAgent will shut down after every load. Check Adaptive Server's error log to verify that RepAgent has replayed the transaction log of temp_database. You should see this message:

```
Recovery or transaction log is complete. Please load the next transac-
tion log dump and then start up the RepAgent with sp_start_rep_agent
with 'recovery' specified
```

Or you can check admin who_is_down at Replication Server:

```
admin who_is_down
go
```

If the temporary database's RepAgent is down, you can start loading the next transaction log dump.

10. Repeat steps 8 and 9 until all transaction log dumps have been processed. You can now resume normal replication from the original primary database.

11. Check Replication Server error log for loss detected messages.

12. If no loss was detected, shut down Replication Server which is still in standalone mode.

13. Reestablish a secondary truncation point for the primary database:

```
use database
go
dbcc settrunc(ltm, 'ignore')
go
dbcc settrunc(ltm, 'valid')
go
```

14. Reset rs_locater from the RSSD of the primary database to clear the locater information:

    `rs_locater dataserver, database`

15. Restart Replication Server in normal mode.

16. Restart RepAgent for both primary and RSSD databases.

    `sp_start_rep_agent database`

17. Drop the temporary database.

18. Use rs_subcmp to verify that the replicate and primary databases are synchronized.

Recovering the RSSD Database

The RSSD database is a vital component of the replication system, as all replication system information is stored here. This database stores schema information such as routes, replication definitions, articles, publications, subscriptions, and function strings. It also holds operations information such as the state of stable queues, queue pointers describing queue allocations, locations within partitions, and the state for other RSSDs in the replication system. Routine database dumps and transaction log dumps (after any schema changes such as creating routes, replication definitions, articles, publications, subscriptions, or function strings) are crucial for RSSD database recovery. If you have up-to-the-minute backup of RSSD databases, you should be able to recover the RSSD database very easily. If, on the other hand, any of the following were occurring at the time of database failure, you will need to perform different procedures for recovering an RSSD database:

▶ No DDL changes (creating, altering, or dropping, routes, replication definitions, subscriptions, function strings, functions, function-string classes, error classes, articles, or publications) had been done.

▶ Minor DDL activity was going on, but no new subscriptions or routes had been created.

▶ New subscriptions had been created.

▶ New routes were being created.

Recovering the RSSD Database with Up-to-the-Minute Backup

1. Stop all RepAgents that are connecting to the Replication Server of that RSSD:

   ```
   sp_stop_rep_agent database
   ```

2. If Replication Server is still up, log in to Replication Server and issue the shutdown command to shut it down:

   ```
   shutdown
   ```

3. Drop the RSSD database. If it is marked suspect, then drop it with the dbcc dbrepair command. Before dropping it, extract the DDL to create the RSSD database with ddlgen.

   ```
   dbcc dbrepair(rssddb, dropdb)
   ```

4. Drop RSSD database devices, if necessary:

   ```
   sp_dropdevice devicename
   ```

5. Create RSSD database devices if they were dropped:

   ```
   disk init
   name = "device_name" ,
   physname = "physicalname" ,
   [vdevno = virtual_device_number ,]
   size = number_of_blocks
   [, vstart = virtual_address
   , cntrltype = controller_number]
   [, dsync = {true | false}]
   [, directio = {true | false}]
   ```

6. Create RSSD database for load:

   ```
   create database rssddb on rssddat='100M'
       log on rssdlog='50M'
       for load
   ```

7. Load the RSSD database from the database dump.

8. Load transaction log dumps in the same sequence in which they were dumped.

9. Load the up-to-the-minute backup (transaction log dump).

10. Bring the RSSD database online:

    ```
    online database rssddb
    ```

11. If the RSSD database has RepAgent, then re-establish the secondary truncation point:

    ```
    dbcc settrunc(ltm, 'ignore')
    dump tran RSSD with truncate_only
    dbcc settrunc(ltm, 'valid')
    ```

12. Restart Replication Agent:

    ```
    sp_start_rep_agent rssddb
    ```

13. Resume replication.

Basic Recovery of an RSSD Database

The basic recovery procedure described here should be used if no DDL changes had been done since the last backup of the RSSD database. No DDL command should be executed until you have finished all these recovery steps.

1. Shut down all RepAgents that connect to the Replication Server of this RSSD database:

    ```
    sp_stop_rep_agent database
    ```

2. Replication Server might be down due to RSSD database failure. If it is not down, you should log in to Replication Server and then issue the shutdown command:

    ```
    shutdown
    ```

Note: Data in the queues at the time of shutdown may be lost when the queues are rebuilt.

3. Drop the RSSD database. If it is marked suspect, drop it with the dbcc dbrepair command. Extract a script to create the RSSD database with ddlgen or dbartisan.

    ```
    dbcc dbrepair(rssddb, dropdb)
    ```

4. If necessary, drop and recreate RSSD database devices.

5. Create the RSSD database for load:

    ```
    create rssddb on rssddat='100m'
    log on rssdlog='50M'
    for load
    ```

6. Load the RSSD database from the database dump.

7. Load the RSSD database transaction log dumps in the same order in which they were dumped.

8. Bring the RSSD database online:

    ```
    online database rssddb
    ```

9. Restart Replication Server in standalone mode by adding the -M flag to the repserver command line.

10. Log in to Replication Server and get the generation number for the RSSD database:

    ```
    admin get_generation, primary_dataserver, primary_database
    ```

11. Issue the rebuild queues command to rebuild the queues:

    ```
    rebuild queues
    ```

12. Restart all RepAgents except for the RSSD database RepAgent that connects to the Replication Server of this RSSD database:

    ```
    sp_start_rep_agent database, recovery
    ```

    The RepAgent scans the database transaction log and prints a message in the error log indicating that it is finished with the current log.

13. Check the current Replication Server error log as well as the error logs of all downstream Replication Servers (the current Replication Server has a direct route to these Replication Servers) for loss detection messages. If loss is detected, then issue the ignore loss command:

    ```
    ignore loss from dataserver.pdb to dataserver.rdb
    ```

    (where pdb is the primary database and rdb is the replicate database).

    Compare the primary and replicate databases with rs_subcmp and resynchronize the data.

    If routes were active at the time of RSSD database failure, you probably will not experience any real data loss. You can have real data loss if the primary database transaction log were truncated and the `rebuild queues` command did not have enough information to recover. If you have real data loss, you should load the database transaction log dump from the old dumps. See the section titled "Recovering from Truncated Primary Database Transaction Log" earlier in this chapter.

14. Shut down all RepAgents connected to this Replication Server:

```
sp_stop_rep_agent database
```

15. Disable the secondary truncation point for the restored RSSD database and move the secondary truncation point to a new page:

```
use rssddb
go
dbcc settrunc(ltm, 'ignore')
go
```

16. Truncate the RSSD database transaction log:

```
dump tran rssddb with truncate_only
go
begin tran
commit tran
go 40
```

17. Re-establish the secondary truncation point:

```
dbcc settrunc(ltm, 'valid')
```

18. Increment the generation number by adding 1 to the generation number retrieved in step 10. For example, if the old generation number was 0, then the new generation number will be 1.

```
dbcc settrunc(ltm, 'gen_id', 1)
```

19. Clear locater information in the RSSD database:

```
rs_zeroltm rssd_dataserver, rssd_database
```

20. Back up the RSSD database:

```
dump database rssddb to 'rssddmp'
```

21. Shut down Replication Server:

```
shutdown
```

22. Remove the -M flag from Replication Server's runserver file and restart Replication Server in normal mode.

23. Restart RepAgents for the RSSD database and for user databases in normal mode:

`sp_start_rep_agent` *database*

Subscription Comparison Procedure for Failed RSSD Database

This procedure should be followed for recovering an RSSD database if some DDL commands were executed but no new changes were done to subscriptions and routes since the last RSSD database dump was taken. This procedure will not work if you have different versions (mixed version) of Replication Servers in the replication system. No DDL commands should be executed until you have completed this recovery procedure. The where and orderby clauses of the rs_subcmp `select` statement must select all rows to be replicated.

1. Shut down all RepAgents that connect to the Replication Server of this RSSD database:

`sp_stop_rep_agent` *database*

2. Replication Server might be down due to RSSD database failure. If it is not down, you should log in to Replication Server and issue the `shutdown` command:

`shutdown`

Note: Data in the queues at the time of shutdown may be lost when the queues are rebuilt.

3. Drop the RSSD database. If it is marked suspect, drop it with the `dbcc dbrepair` command. Extract a script to create an RSSD database with ddlgen or dbartisan:

`dbcc dbrepair(rssddb, dropdb)`

4. If necessary, drop and recreate RSSD database devices.

5. Create the RSSD database for load:

    ```
    create rssddb on rssddat='100m'
    log on rssdlog='50M'
    for load
    ```

6. Load the RSSD database from the database dump.

7. Load the RSSD database transaction log dumps in the same order in which they were dumped.

8. Bring the RSSD database online:

    ```
    online database rssddb
    ```

9. Restart Replication Server in standalone mode by adding the -M flag to the repserver command line.

10. Execute the `admin quiesce_force_rsi` command sequentially at each upstream replication server, starting with the Replication Server that is farthest upstream from the current Replication Server. This command will ensure that all committed messages from the recovering replication server have been applied before executing rs_subcmp for comparing subscriptions. Make sure the RSSD outbound queues are empty; that is, all the messages have been applied.

    ```
    admin quiesce_force_rsi
    ```

11. Execute the `admin quiesce_force_rsi` command sequentially at each downstream replication server starting with the Replication Server that is directly downstream from the recovering Replication Server. This will ensure that all committed messages bound for the recovering Replication Server have been applied before executing rs_subcmp for comparing subscriptions. Make sure the RSSD outbound queues are empty; that is, all messages have been applied.

    ```
    admin quiesce_force_rsi
    ```

12. First run rs_subcmp without reconciliation to check for inconsistencies. Once you are ready to reconcile, run rs_subcmp as the maintenance user with the -r option using the failed RSSD database as replicate and each upstream RSSD databases as primary, starting with the farthest upstream Replication Server and proceeding downstream for all other Replication Servers with a direct or indirect route to the recovering Replication Server. You will need to reconcile

each of these RSSD system tables with rs_subcmp: rs_articles, rs_classes, rs_columns, rs_databases, rs_erroractions, rs_functions, rs_funcstrings, rs_objects, rs_publications, rs_systext, and rs_whereclauses. The failed RSSD database should be fully recovered now.

13. Run rs_subcmp again without reconciliation to check for inconsistencies. When you are ready to reconcile, run rs_subcmp as the maintenance user again with the -r option using the failed RSSD database as primary and each downstream RSSD database as replicate, starting with Replication Servers that are immediately downstream and proceeding downstream for all other Replication Servers with routes (direct or indirect) from the failed Replication Server. You will need to reconcile each of these RSSD system tables with rs_subcmp: rs_articles, rs_classes, rs_columns, rs_databases, rs_erroractions, rs_functions, rs_funcstrings, rs_objects, rs_publications, rs_systext, and rs_whereclauses. All downstream RSSDs should be fully recovered now.

14. If the failed RSSD is for the Replication Server that is the ID Server, you will need to restore the IDs of all the Replication Servers and databases in its RSSD. Check the rs_databases and rs_sites RSSD system tables for their IDs and insert the appropriate row into the rs_idnames system table if they are missing. To ensure that the rs_ids RSSD system table is consistent, execute the rs_mk_rsids_consistent stored procedure in the RSSD of the recovering Replication Server.

15. If the recovering Replication Server is not an ID Server and a new database connection was added after the last database dump (if no transaction log dumps) or the last transaction log dump, you will need to delete the corresponding row for that database from the rs_idnames system table in the RSSD of ID Server.

16. Perform steps 10 through 23 in the "Basic Recovery of an RSSD Database" section of this chapter.

17. Apply all the DDL changes to the RSSD database that were executed after the last transaction log dump.

Sample rs_subcmp Select Statements

Suppose you have the following Replication Server sites in your replication system, and site rrs1 is the failed site.

Table 15-6: Replication Server and Site IDs

Replication Server	Site ID
prs	1
rrs1	2
rrs2	3
rrs3	4

You have the following direct routes:

> prs → rrs1
> rrs2 → rrs1
> rrs1 → rrs3

To bring RSSD into a consistent state, you will need to perform the following tasks on the rs_classes, rs_columns, rs_databases, rs_erroractions, rs_funcstrings, rs_functions, rs_objects, and rs_systext system tables:

1. **Select statement for reconciling upstream RSSDs**: Run rs_subcmp against the above listed RSSD tables, specifying rrs1 as the replicate and prs as the primary with prsid=1 in the where clause. For rs_columns, rs_databases, rs_funcstrings, rs_functions, and rs_objects RSSD system tables, if rowtype=1, then it is the replicated row and we need to compare only replicated rows with rs_subcmp.

   rs_classes

   ```
   select * from rs_classes where prsid in
   (select source_rsid from rs_routes
   where (through_rsid=1 or through_rsid=2)
   and dest_rsid=2)
   order by classname, classtype
   ```

   rs_columns

   ```
   select * from rs_columns where prsid in
   (select source_rsid from rs_routes
   ```

```
where (through_rsid=1 or through_rsid=2)
and dest_rsid=2)
and rowtype=1
order by objid, colname
```

rs_databases

```
select * from rs_databases where prsid in
(select source_rsid from rs_routes
where (through_rsid=1 or through_rsid=2)
and dest_rsid=2)
and rowtype = 1
order by dataserver, database, ltype
```

rs_erroractions

```
select * from rs_erroractions where prsid in
(select source_rsid from rs_routes
where (through_rsid=1 or through_rsid=2)
and dest_rsid=2)
order by ds_errorid, errorclassid
```

rs_functions

```
select * from rs_functions where prsid in
(select source_rsid from rs_routes
where (through_rsid=1 or through_rsid=2)
and dest_rsid=2)
and rowtype=1
order by objid, funcname
```

rs_funcstrings

```
select * from rs_funcstrings where prsid in
(select source_rsid from rs_routes
where (through_rsid=1 or through_rsid=2)
and dest_rsid=2)
and rowtype=1
order by classid, funcid, name
```

rs_objects

```
select * from rs_objects where prsid in
(select source_rsid from rs_routes
where (through_rsid=1 or through_rsid=2)
and dest_rsid=2)
```

```
and rowtype=1
order by objid, dbid
```

rs_systext

```
select * from rs_systext where prsid in
(select source_rsid from rs_routes
where (through_rsid=1 or through_rsid=2)
and dest_rsid=2)
and texttype in ('O','S')
order by parentid, texttype, sequence
```

2. **Select statement for reconciling upstream RSSDs**: Run rs_subcmp against all the above listed RSSD tables, specifying rrs1 as the replicate and rrs2 as the primary with prsid=3 in the where clause. For rs_columns, rs_databases, rs_funcstrings, rs_functions, and rs_objects RSSD system tables, if rowtype=1, then it is a replicated row and we need to compare only replicated rows with rs_subcmp.

rs_classes

```
select * from rs_classes where prsid in
(select source_rsid from rs_routes
where (through_rsid=3 or through_rsid=2)
and dest_rsid=2)
order by classname, classtype
```

rs_columns

```
select * from rs_columns where prsid in
(select source_rsid from rs_routes
where (through_rsid=3 or through_rsid=2)
and dest_rsid=2)
and rowtype=1
order by objid, colname
```

rs_databases

```
select * from rs_databases where prsid in
(select source_rsid from rs_routes
where (through_rsid=3 or through_rsid=2)
and dest_rsid=2)
and rowtype=1
order by dataserver, database, ltype
```

rs_erroractions

```
select * from rs_erroractions where prsid in
(select source_rsid from rs_routes
where (through_rsid=3 or through_rsid=2)
and dest_rsid=2)
order by ds_errorid, errorclassid
```

rs_funcstrings

```
select * from rs_funcstrings where prsid in
(select source_rsid from rs_routes
where (through_rsid=3 or through_rsid=2)
and dest_rsid=2)
and rowtype=1
order by classid, funcid, name
```

rs_functions

```
select * from rs_functions where prsid in
(select source_rsid from rs_routes
where (through_rsid=3 or through_rsid=2)
and dest_rsid=2)
and rowtype=1
order by objid, funcname
```

rs_objects

```
select * from rs_objects where prsid in
(select source_rsid from rs_routes
where (through_rsid=3 or through_rsid=2)
and dest_rsid=2)
and rowtype=1
order by objid, dbid
```

rs_systext

```
select * from rs_systext where prsid in
(select source_rsid from rs_routes
where (through_rsid=3 or through_rsid=2)
and dest_rsid=2)
and texttype in ('O','S')
order by parentid, texttype, sequence
```

Note: Initially, system-provided function-string and error classes do not have a designated primary site, meaning their site ID is 0. Since rs_default_error_class and rs_db2_function_class cannot be modified, they can never have a designated site ID. rs_sqlserver_function_class and rs_sqlserver_error_class can be modified, so they may have a designated primary site. Parent and derived function-string classes have the same primary site. If Replication Server was made the primary site for a function-string class after recovery, then while reconciling RSSD system tables (rs_erroractions, rs_classes, and rs_funcstrings) rs_subcmp may find orphaned rows in downstream RSSDs. In that case, run rs_subcmp again on these RSSD system tables (rs_erroractions, rs_classes, and rs_funcstrings) using prsid=0 in the select statement, which will repopulate these tables with the default settings.

For example:

rs_classes

```
select * from rs_classes where prsid = 0
order by classname and classtype
```

rs_funcstrings

```
select * from rs_funcstrings where prsid = 0
order by classid, funcid, name
```

rs_erroractions

```
select * from rs_erroractions where prsid = 0
order by ds_errorid, errorclassid
```

3. **Select statement for reconciling downstream RSSDs:** Run rs_subcmp against all the above listed RSSD tables in the same order, specifying rrs1 as the primary and rrs3 as the replicate with prsid=2 in the where clause. For rs_columns, rs_databases, rs_funcstrings, rs_functions, and rs_objects RSSD system tables, if rowtype=1, then it is a replicated row and we need to compare only replicated rows with rs_subcmp.

rs_classes

```
select * from rs_classes where prsid in
(select source_rsid from rs_routes
```

```
where (through_rsid=2 or through_rsid=4)
and dest_rsid=4)
order by classname, classtype
```

rs_columns

```
select * from rs_columns where prsid in
(select source_rsid from rs_routes
where (through_rsid=2 or through_rsid=4)
and dest_rsid=4)
and rowtype=1
order by objid, colname
```

rs_databases

```
select * from rs_databases where prsid in
(select source_rsid from rs_routes
where (through_rsid=2 or through_rsid=4)
and dest_rsid=4)
and rowtype=1
order by dataserver, database, ltype
```

rs_erroractions

```
select * from rs_erroractions where prsid in
(select source_rsid from rs_routes
where (through_rsid=2 or through_rsid=4)
and dest_rsid=4)
order by ds_errorid, errorclassid
```

rs_funcstrings

```
select * from rs_funcstrings where prsid in
(select source_rsid from rs_routes
where (through_rsid=2 or through_rsid=4)
and dest_rsid=4)
and rowtype=1
order by classid, funcid, name
```

rs_functions

```
select * from rs_functions where prsid in
(select source_rsid from rs_routes
where (through_rsid=2 or through_rsid=4)
and dest_rsid=4)
and rowtype=1
order by objid, funcname
```

rs_objects

```
select * from rs_objects where prsid in
(select source_rsid from rs_routes
where (through_rsid=2 or through_rsid=4)
and dest_rsid=4)
and rowtype=1
order by objid, dbid
```

rs_systext

```
select * from rs_systext where prsid in
(select source_rsid from rs_routes
where (through_rsid=2 or through_rsid=4)
and dest_rsid=4)
and texttype in ('O','S')
order by parentid, texttype, sequence
```

Subscription Recreation for a Failed RSSD

The steps listed in this procedure should be followed for recovering the RSSD database if some new subscriptions were created and other DDL commands were executed since the last backup of the RSSD database but no new routes were created. You should not execute any new DDL commands until you have restored the failed RSSD database. In this procedure, the failed RSSD is first made consistent with upstream RSSDs or restored by loading with the most recent database dump and transaction log dumps if there is no upstream Replication Server. Then downstream RSSDs are made consistent with the failed RSSD.

1. Shut down all RepAgents that connect to the Replication Server of this RSSD database:

    ```
    sp_stop_rep_agent database
    ```

2. Replication Server might be down due to RSSD database failure. If it is not down, log in to Replication Server and then issue the shutdown command:

    ```
    shutdown
    ```

Note: Data in the queues at the time of shutdown may be lost when the queues are rebuilt.

3. Drop the RSSD database. If it is marked suspect, then drop it with the dbcc dbrepair command. Extract a script to create RSSD database with ddlgen or dbartisan.

   ```
   dbcc dbrepair(rssddb, dropdb)
   ```

4. If necessary, drop and recreate RSSD database devices.

5. Create the RSSD database for load:

   ```
   create rssddb on rssddat='100m'
   log on rssdlog='50M'
   for load
   ```

6. Load the RSSD database from the database dump.

7. Load the RSSD database transacton log dumps in the same order in which they were dumped.

8. Bring the RSSD database online:

   ```
   online database rssddb
   ```

9. Restart Replication Server in standalone mode by adding the -M flag to the repserver command line.

10. Execute the admin quiesce_force_rsi command sequentially at each upstream Replication Server, starting with the Replication Server farthest upstream from the current Replication Server. This command will ensure that all committed messages from the recovering replication server have been applied before executing rs_subcmp for comparing subscriptions. Make sure RSSD outbound queues are empty; that is, all the messages have been applied.

    ```
    admin quiesce_force_rsi
    ```

11. Execute the admin quiesce_force_rsi command sequentially at each downstream Replication Server, starting with Replication Servers that are directly downstream from the recovering Replication Server. This will ensure that all committed messages bound for the recovering Replication Server have been applied before executing rs_subcmp for comparing subscriptions. Make sure RSSD outbound queues are empty; that is, all messages have been applied.

```
admin quiesce_force_rsi
```

12. Shut down all upstream and downstream Replication Servers using the `shutdown` command:

```
shutdown
```

13. Restart all upstream and downstream Replication Servers in standalone mode by adding the -M flag to the runserver file.

14. First run `rs_subcmp` without reconciliation to check for inconsistencies. Once you are ready to reconcile, run `rs_subcmp` as the maintenance user with the -r option using the failed RSSD database as replicate and each upstream RSSD database as primary, starting with the Replication Server that is farthest upstream and proceeding downstream for all other Replication Servers with direct or indirect routes to the recovering Replication Server. You will need to reconcile each of these RSSD system tables with `rs_subcmp`: rs_articles, rs_classes, rs_columns, rs_databases, rs_erroractions, rs_functions, rs_funcstrings, rs_objects, rs_publications, rs_systext, and rs_whereclauses. The failed RSSD database should be fully recovered now.

15. Run `rs_subcmp` again without reconciliation to check for inconsistencies. Once you are ready to reconcile, run `rs_subcmp` as the maintenance user with the -r option using the failed RSSD database as primary and each downstream RSSD database as replicate, starting with Replication Servers that are immediately downstream and proceeding downstream for all other Replication Servers with routes (direct or indirect) from the failed Replication Server. You will need to reconcile each of these RSSD system tables with `rs_subcmp`: rs_articles, rs_classes, rs_columns, rs_databases, rs_erroractions, rs_functions, rs_funcstrings, rs_objects, rs_publications, rs_systext, and rs_whereclauses. All downstream RSSDs should be fully recovered now.

16. If the failed RSSD is for the Replication Server that is the ID Server, you will need to restore the IDs of all the Replication Servers and databases in its RSSD. Check the rs_databases and rs_sites RSSD system tables for their IDs and insert the appropriate row into the rs_idnames system table if they are missing. To ensure that the rs_ids RSSD system table is

consistent, execute the rs_mk_rsids_consistent stored procedure in the RSSD of the recovering Replication Server.

17. If the recovering Replication Server is not an ID Server and the new database connection was added after the last database dump (if there are no transaction log dumps) or the last transaction log dump, then you will need to delete the corresponding row for that database from the rs_idnames system table in the RSSD of the ID Server.

18. Query the rs_subscriptions RSSD system table of the recovering Replication Server for names of subscriptions (subname), replication definitions, or publications and their associated databases.

    You will need to query the rs_subscriptions RSSD system table on the RSSD of all Replication Servers that have primary or replicate subscriptions.

    You can query rs_subscriptions by using the rs_helpsub stored procedure:

```
1> rs_helpsub
2> go
```

```
** This Site is 'rrs1' **
```

				Status at	
Subscription Name	Rep. Def. Name	Replicate DS.DB	A/C	RRS	PRS
mysub	myrep	rds16k.rdb	0	Valid	Unknown
testsub	testrep	rds16k.rdb	0	Valid	Unknown
textsub	textrep	rds16k.rdb	0	Valid	Unknown

19. You can also run check subscription on each subscription on the recovering Replication Server and on all other Replication Servers that have primary or replicate subscriptions.

20. Shut down both primary and replicate Replication Servers that have non-valid subscriptions in the rs_subscriptions RSSD system table:

    shutdown

21. For each replicate Replication Server that has a non-valid subscription with the recovering Replication Server as the primary, perform the following:

    a. Note the subid of the non-valid subscription from the rs_subscriptions RSSD system table and use that subid to query rs_rules (rs_rules has one row for each term in a subscription clause, such as the where clause). Delete these rows from both the rs_subscriptions and rs_rules RSSD system tables.

    b. Query the rs_subscriptions and rs_rules RSSD system tables on each RSSD of replicate Replication Servers and recovering Replication Server as primary. If a subscription exists on the rs_subscriptions and rs_rules system tables on the primary RSSD but not in the replicate rs_subscriptions and rs_rules (because it was dropped), delete that subscription from rs_subscriptions and rs_rules of the primary RSSD and then follow steps 29 through 31 of the procedure to recreate a subscription.

    c. If a subscription exists on the rs_subscriptions and rs_rules RSSD system tables on the replicate RSSD but not in the rs_subscriptions and rs_rules system tables on the primary RSSD, delete that subscription from the rs_subscriptions and rs_rules system tables of the replicate RSSD.

    d. If a subscription exists on RSSDs of both primary and replicate but is not valid at one of the sites, you should delete that subscription from both primary and replicate RSSDs, and then follow steps 29 through 31 of the procedure to recreate a subscription.

22. For each primary Replication Server that has a non-valid subscription with the recovering Replication Server as the replicate, resolve subscriptions by doing the following:

    a. If a subscription is in the rs_subscriptions and rs_rules system tables in the primary RSSD and not in the rs_subscriptions and rs_rules system tables in the replicate RSSD, delete it from both tables in the primary

RSSD and follow steps 29 through 31 of the procedure to recreate a subscription.

b. If a subscription is in the rs_subscriptions and rs_rules system tables in the replicate RSSD and not in the rs_subscriptions and rs_rules system tables in the primary RSSD, delete it from both tables in the replicate RSSD.

c. If a subscription is in the rs_subscriptions and rs_rules system tables on both the primary and replicate RSSD, but it is not valid at one of the sites, delete it from both sites and follow steps 29 through 31 of the procedure to recreate a subscription.

23. Restart the primary and replicate Replication Servers in standalone mode by adding the -M flag to the runserver file.

24. At both the primary and replicate Replication Servers, drop materializing queues with the `sysadmin drop_queue` command for subscriptions deleted in steps 21 and 22.

```
sysadmin drop_queue, queuenumber, queuetype
```

25. Shut down the primary replicate Replication Servers:

```
shutdown
```

26. Restart the primary and replicate Replication Servers in normal mode.

27. Perform steps 10 through 23 in the "Basic Recovery of an RSSD Database" section.

28. Re-execute all DDL commands that were executed at the recovering Replication Servers since the last backup.

29. Turn on autocorrection for each replication definition and replicate database:

```
set autocorrection on
for repdef_name
with replicate at dataserver.database
```

30. Recreate missing subscriptions using bulk materialization (`define subscription`, `activate subscription`, and `validate subscription`) or no materialization.

31. Run `rs_subcmp` with the -r flag to reconcile both replicate and primary subscription data.

Deintegration/Reintegration Procedure

If routes were created after the last backup of the RSSD database, you should remove the Replication Server with failed RSSD from the replication system, reinstall it, and then create routes and subscriptions.

Removing Replication Server from the Replication System

To remove Replication Server if it is not running, follow the steps listed below:

1. Drop the route to the Replication Server (we will call it bad_rs) of the failed RSSD. Execute the drop route command with the "with nowait" option at each Replication Server that has a route to this Replication Server (bad_rs). This command deletes the information about the subscriptions created at bad_rs for data management by this Replication Server.

   ```
   drop route to bad_rs with nowait
   ```

2. If bad_rs was primary for any customized function-string classes or error classes other than rs_default_function_class and/or rs_sqlserver_error_class, which are the system defaults, you should create a new class for each original customized class (as on old_rs) at the new primary Replication Server. The new primary Replication Server should have a route to all other Replication Servers that will use this new class. (See Chapter 11 for creating function-string classes.) Alter each database connection that was using the original class to use the new class.

   ```
   suspend connection to dataserver.database
   alter connection to dataserver.database
   set function string class to new_function_class
   set error class to new_error_class
   resume connection to dataserver.database
   ```

3. Purge the route at each Replication Server that bad_rs has a route to. The sysadmin_purge_route_at_replicate command

will remove all subscriptions and route information originating from the bad_rs (primary Replication Server) after the route is dropped from it.

```
sysadmin drop_route_at_replicate, bad_rs
```

4. Execute the sysadmin droprs command at the ID Server to drop this Replication Server (bad_rs) from the ID Server.

```
sysadmin droprs, bad_rs
```

5. Execute the sysadmin dropdb command at the ID Server to drop all databases including the RSSD database managed by this Replication Server (bad_rs) from the ID Server:

```
sysadmin dropdb, dataserver, database
```

There might be some replicate data that is not deleted from replicated Replication Servers, because subscriptions from bad_rs (Replication Server) did not go through dematerialization.

See Appendix B for information on removing the active Replication Server from the replication system.

Reinstall a new Replication Server. (See Chapter 4 for instructions if necessary.) Recreate Replication Server routes, replication definitions, and subscriptions.

Recovering from a Damaged Partition

Messages destined for other replication servers or data servers are stored on partitions by Replication Server. Each stable queue holds messages to be delivered to another data server or replication server. Replication Server allocates space in partitions to stable queues and operates in 1 MB segments. A segment is allocated to only one queue, which means different queues cannot be shared by the same segment. Each segment has 64 blocks (the size of each block is 16 K). A block is a unit of transfer between cache and disk. A block may contain one or more messages. A segment cannot be deallocated until all blocks are deleted. If the destination data server or Replication Server is down, the stable device can fill up. You can add or drop partitions dynamically.

To add a 20 MB partition:

```
create partition q1 on '/dev/rsdev1' with size 20
```

Note: Replication Server 15.0.1 and above support 1 TB of partition size. For recoverability purposes, raw devices should be used for stable queue partitions. Because operating systems buffer file I/O, you may not be able to recover stable queues completely.

To drop a partition:

```
drop partition q1
```

You can also specify how Replication Server should allocate queue segments to the partition instead of using the default mechanism. The default mechanism is to assign queue segments to the next partition in an ordered list. You can use alter connection or alter route to change the segment allocation mechanism.

```
suspend connection to dataserver.database
alter connection to dataserver.database
set disk_affinity to ['partition' | 'off']
resume connection to dataserver.database

suspend route to replication_server
alter route to replication_server
set disk_affinity to ['partition' | 'off']
resume route to replication_server
```

Where *partition* is the logical name of the partition to which you want to allocate a segment for the connection or the route. See Chapter 14 for information on performance and tuning.

RSSD System Tables that Store Partition Information

There are several system tables that store partition information: rs_diskpartitions, rs_segments, and rs_queues.

rs_diskpartitions: This RSSD system table stores information about the disk partitions that Replication Server uses for stable queue messages. For example:

```
1> select * from rs_diskpartitions
2> go
name              logical_name     id            num_segs     status    vstart
----------------  ---------------  -----------   -----------  --------  ------
/dev/mydev/q1     q1               101           20           1         0
/dev/mydev/q4     q4               102           20           1         0
```

name — Operating system name for the disk device

logical_name — User-defined name for the partition

id — Partition ID assigned by Replication Server

num_segs — Total size of the partition in segments

status — Status of disk partitions:

    1 — Online

    2 — Partition is being dropped

vstart — Offset at which Replication Server starts writing to the partition (in MB)

rs_segments: This RSSD system table stores information about segment allocation.

```
1> select * from rs_segments
2> go
partition_id  q_number    q_type   partition_offset  logical_seg  used_flag  version  flags
--------      ----------  -------   ----------------  -----------  ---------  -------  -----
   101        16777318       0             0              0            1        112      0
   101        16777320       0             1              0            1         31      0
   101        101            1             2          10499            1       5098      0
   101        0              0             3              0            0       5067      0
   101        0              0             4              0            0         13      0
```

partition_id — Unique partition ID

q_number — The queue this partition belongs to

q_type — Queue type, which is one of the following:

    1 — Inbound

    0 — Outbound

partition offset — Segment offset within partition

logical_seg — Segment offset within queue

used_flag — Stores the current status of the segment:

    0 — Inactive

    1 — Active

    n — save interval; n indicates the actual time (measured in seconds from the base date) when this segment can be deleted

version — Stores the current version of the segment; the version number increases after each use.

flags — Set to 1 on the last segment of the DSI queue after switch active

rs_queues: This RSSD system table is used by Replication Server Stable Queue Manager and guaranteed delivery system. This table stores information that allows site recovery.

```
1> select * from rs_queues
2> go
number       type        state       twosave      truncs
-----------  ----------- ----------- ------------ -----------
        101            0           1            0           1
        101            1           1            0           1
        106            0           1           -1           1
        106            1           1            0           2
   16777318            0           1            0           1
   16777320            0           1            0           1
```

number — Queue ID. The number in this column represents the source database for the inbound queue and the destination database or Replication Server for the outbound queue. Value in this column correspond to database entries in the dbid column of the rs_databases RSSD system table and to the entries for the Replication Servers in the id columns in the rs_sites RSSD system table.

type — Queue type:

0 — Outbound queue

1 — Inbound queue

large negative number — A subscription materialization queue

state — Current state of the queue:

0 — Failure

1 — Active

2 — Delete

twosave — The number of seconds the Replication Server maintains the SQM segment after all messages in the segment have been acknowledged by destinations. –1 indicates a strict setting.

truncs — The number of truncation points

```
1> select * from rs_sites
2> go
name                               id          status
------------------------------ ----------- ------
prs                             16777317      0
rrs1                            16777318      0
rrs2                            16777319      0
rrs3                            16777320      0
```

```
1> select * from rs_databases
2> go
dataserver  database  dbid  dist_status  src_status  attributes  errorclassid
  funcclassid          prsid     rowtype sorto_status ltype ptype ldbid      enable_seq
----------- --------- ----- ------------ ----------- ----------- -------------
  ------------------ --------- ------- ------------ ----- ------ -------- ----------
PDS         PUBS3     106   65             1           0           0x0000000000000000
  0x0000000000000000 16777317  1       0            L     L      106      0
pds         prs_RSSD  101   1              1           0           0x0000000001000002
  0x0000000001000001 16777317  0       0            P     A      101      0
```

pds	pubs3	107	1		1		0		0x0000000001000002
0x0000000001000001	16777317	1		0		P	A	106	0	
rds	pubs3	108	3		1		0		0x0000000001000002
0x0000000001000001	16777317	1		0		P	S	106	0	

From the above select, we can see that 101 and 106 values in the rs_queues..number column corresponds to databases with dbid 101 and 106 in rs_databases, and 16777318 and 16777320 values in the rs_queues..number column correspond to site id 16777318 and 16777320 in the rs_sites system table.

When a stable device becomes inaccessible due to a failed or missing partition, Replication Server shuts down the stable queues that are using that partition and logs a message about the failure in the Replication Server error log. Simply restarting Replication Server does not correct the problem. You must drop the failed or missing partition with the drop partition command:

```
drop partition partition_logicalname
drop partition q1
```

Use the create partition command to replace the lost partition:

```
create partition partition_logicalname
on 'physical_name' with size size
[starting at vstart]

create partition q1 on '/dev/q1' with size 20
```

Rebuild stable queues with the rebuild queues command. Check the Replication Server error log for loss detected messages. Issue the ignore loss command and then reconcile the replicate data with primary data and if necessary recover lost messages.

If recovery procedures are performed immediately after failure, then chances of recovering without data loss or with minimal data loss are greater. If you have minimal latency in your replication system, only the most recent messages are lost when its queues are rebuilt.

If the destination replication server or data server is not available for some period of time or the route or database connections are down or suspended for some period of time, then messages are stored and reapplied when the destination site/route/database connection becomes available. The save interval specifies how long data can be kept in the outbound database/RSI queues before it is deleted. If the save interval is not configured high enough to handle a backlog of messages, your chances of recovering these transactions decreases with time. Keep in mind that a higher save interval will require larger stable devices.

If you have partition failure on the primary Replication Server, you can perform recovery by recovering messages from the offline database transaction log, but if partition failure is on the replicate Replication Server, recovery will be done from stable queues of the upstream Replication Server.

Recovering from a Failed or Lost Partition

You can perform the steps listed below to recover from a failed or lost partition:

1. Log into Replication Server and issue the drop partition command to drop the failed partition.

    ```
    drop partition partition_name
    ```

2. If the partition is still in use and is undamaged, it won't get dropped. The partition is only dropped after all of the messages from that partition are delivered to replication sites and deleted.

3. Add a new partition to replace the failed partition:

    ```
    create partition partition_logicalname
    on 'physical_name' with size size
    [starting at vstart]
    ```

> **Note:** In Unix or raw files the partition must already exist. For operating system files, you can create the file with the touch command. The create partition command extends the file to the specified size.

4. Check the partition status with the admin disk_space command:

    ```
    admin disk_space
    ```

A failed partition should have a status of DROPPED, and a newly added partition should have a status of ONLINE.

5. Execute the `rebuild queues` command at Replication Server to rebuild queues:

```
rebuild queues
```

The `rebuild queues` command instructs Replication Server to ignore messages in the queues and sends a signal to upstream Replication Servers and primary RepAgents to resend every message they have available. After removing all of the stable queues from the partition, the failed/damaged partition is dropped from the system and queues are rebuilt using the remaining partitions.

6. The queues in this Replication Server and downstream Replication Servers also go into loss detection mode, meaning the first message they receive has a larger origin_quid (OQID) than the last message they have (loss exists). When loss is detected, the queue stops accepting messages from the origin and a loss detected message is written to the Replication Server error log. You can either perform message recovery from the offline database transaction log or issue the `ignore loss` command for the database on the Replication Server where the loss was detected to allow replication to continue through that queue.

```
ignore loss from dataserver.pdb to dataserver.rdb
```

In this case you must reconcile the primary and replicate database with rs_subcmp with the -r flag or recreate the subscriptions at the destination.

Message Recovery from the Online Database Transaction Log

If messages still exist in the online transaction log at the primary database, you can perform the following steps to recover them:

1. Stop all writes to the primary database.

2. Execute the `sp_stop_rep_agent` command to stop RepAgent for the primary database:

   sp_stop_rep_agent *database*

3. Restart RepAgent for the primary database in recovery mode:

   sp_start_rep_agent *database*, for_recovery

   The for_recovery clause will tell RepAgent to scan the transaction log from the beginning so that all the messages can be retrieved.

Message Recovery from the Offline Database Transaction Log

If all the messages cannot be recovered from the online database transaction log because it does not have all the messages needed to recover, you must load an earlier database and transaction log dump of the primary database into a temporary database and restart RepAgent in recovery mode. (You can use date and time from loss detected messages in the Replication Server error log. The date in the loss detected message is the date and time of the oldest open transaction in the database transaction log when the last message received by the Replication Server was generated by the origin queue. You must load the transaction log dump with timestamp before the timestamp in the loss detected message and database dump taken before that transaction log dump.)

1. If Replication Server is still up and running, issue the shutdown command:

   shutdown

2. Restart Replication Server in single user mode by adding the -M flag in the Replication Server runserver file.

3. Log into Replication Server and issue the rebuild queues command:

   rebuild queues

4. Create a temporary database with the same size and segmap order as the primary database.

5. Load the temporary database from the primary database dump.

6. Load the first or next transaction log dumps (transaction log dumps should be loaded in the same sequence in which they were dumped).

7. Start RepAgent for the temporary database in recovery mode:

```
sp_start_rep_agent temp_database, recovery,
'original_dataserver',
'original_database', 'repserver_name',
'repserver_username',
'repserver_password'
```

RepAgent will transfer data in the transaction log of the temp_database to the original primary database, and will shut down after every load. Check the Adaptive Server error log to verify that RepAgent has replayed the transaction log of temp_database.

You should see this message in the Adaptive Server error log:

```
Recovery or transaction log is complete. Please load the next transac-
tion log dump and then start up the RepAgent with sp_start_rep_agent
with 'recovery' specified.
```

Or you can check `admin who_is_down` at the Replication Server:

```
admin who_is_down
go
```

If temp_database RepAgent is down, you start loading the next transaction log dump.

8. Repeat steps 6 and 7 until all transaction log dumps have been processed. You can now resume normal replication from the original primary database.

9. Check the Replication Server error log for loss detected messages.

10. If no loss was detected, shut down Replication Server, which is still in standalone mode.

11. Re-establish a secondary truncation point for the primary database:

```
use database
go
```

```
dbcc settrunc(1tm, ignore)
go
dbcc settrunc(1tm, valid)
go
```

12. Execute rs_locater from RSSD of the primary database to clear the locater information:

    ```
    rs_locater dataserver, database
    ```

13. Restart Replication Server in normal mode.

14. Restart RepAgent for both primary and RSSD database:

    ```
    sp_start_rep_agent database
    ```

15. Drop the temporary database.

16. Use rs_subcmp to verify that the replicate and primary databases are synchronized.

Summary Plan for Recovery

The following list summarizes the necessary steps when planning for recovery.

1. Always keep current backups of RSSD/ERSSD and the primary databases. If the replicate databases are not the same as the primary database, you should keep current backups of replicate databases as well.

2. Perform transaction log dumps for your RSSD, primary database, and replicate database for up-to-the-minute recovery.

3. Mirror RSSD/ERSSD, primary, and replicate database devices. You can do Sybase or OS mirroring.

4. Make sure RSSD, primary, and replicate database devices are not shared by other databases. You should always put them on separate disk drives.

5. Put data and log segments of RSSD, primary, and replicate databases on separate devices; if possible, put them on separate disk drives.

6. Keep all DDL scripts (e.g., create database, create replication definitions, subscriptions, articles, publications, route, function strings, error classes).

7. Always back up RSSD after all DDL changes including alter, create, and drop routes.

8. Document topology and all the components of your replication system.

9. Create rs_subcmp configuration parameter files for every subscription you have in your replication system.

10. Run rs_subcmp on a regular basis on primary and replicate tables and for comparing DDL to ensure that they are synchronized.

11. Use OS mirroring for mirroring stable devices.

12. Make sure that stable devices are big enough to hold messages in case of replication failure.

Chapter 16

Replicating Oracle Data

Sybase Replication System for Non-Sybase Data Servers

Sybase Replication Server supports replicating transactions to and from non-Sybase data servers (Oracle, IBM DB2, and Microsoft SQL Server). These non-Sybase data servers may act as both primary and replicate while using Sybase Replication Server technology as the central distribution mechanism in providing near real-time updates. For replicating to and from non-Sybase data servers, you will need two additional components, which are bundled with Replication Server Options:

▶ A Replication Agent

▶ Sybase Enterprise Connect Data Access (formerly DirectConnect)

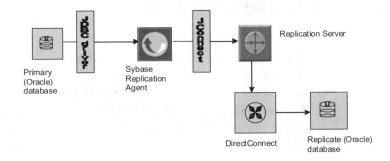

Figure 16-1: Sybase replication system for non-Sybase data servers

Replication Agent

The Replication Agent reads the primary database transaction log and transfers log records for replicated tables and replicated stored procedures to the Replication Server that manages that primary database. Replication Agent does this by generating Log Transfer Language (LTL) output. LTL is used by Replication Server to process and distribute transactions throughout a replication system. These transactions are reconstructed by Replication Server and then forwarded to the sites that have subscriptions for the data. Replication Agent is needed by each primary database that contains primary data or in which replicated stored procedures are executed. It consists of four components, all of which work together in reading and transferring transactions from the primary database for replication to Replication Server.

▶ Log Reader: Reads the primary database transaction log to retrieve transactions for replication.

▶ Log Transfer Interface (LTI): Generates Log Transfer Language and forwards it to the primary Replication Server.

▶ Log Administrator: Manages the Replication Agent transaction log and transaction log records.

▶ Log Transfer Manager: Manages all other components and their operations and interactions.

Types of Replication Agents

Sybase supports two types of Replication Agents.

▶ **Log-based replication agents:** The native transaction log is used by Adaptive Server Enterprise Replication Agent, Replication Agent for DB2 UDB for OS/390, Replication Agent for Microsoft 15.1, and Replication Agent for Oracle. Replication Agent retrieves information required for transaction replication from the native transaction log. This type of transaction log is maintained by the primary database itself. Log-based replication agents should be installed on the same OS host machine that has access to the primary database transaction log.

▶ **Trigger-based replication agents:** Triggers are created by Replication Agent in the primary database when a table or stored procedure is marked for replication. These triggers are automatically removed by Replication Agent when the table or stored procedure is unmarked for replication. Triggers capture data involved in replication and also keep track of other information required to replicate the transaction such as the transaction ID, which is used by Replication Agent to identify each operation associated with a transaction. When triggers are fired, they record the data to be replicated in one or more Replication Agent system tables in the primary database. These Replication Agent system tables are user tables maintained by Replication Agent. A trigger-based replication agent can reside on the same host machine as the primary database or on any host machine that has network access to the primary database.

Replication Agent for Oracle release 12.6 and above read data directly from the Oracle redo logs. Before 12.6, triggers were added to the Oracle database to capture required data.

Sybase Enterprise Connect Data Access

Sybase Enterprise Connect Data Access (ECDA) is a set of gateway applications that use OpenServer, DB-Library, CT-Library, Java Database Connectivity (JDBC), and Open Database Connectivity (OBDC) routines. These middleware connectivity protocols allow a connection to Replication Server and the processing of Replication Server requests. They forward the request to non-Sybase data servers with the replicated data and return the status of the request to Replication Server through OpenServer library routines.

Installation Steps

Make sure the required OS patches are installed to support Java 1.4.2 (depending on the ECDA option release version). ECDA for Oracle and Replication Agent are installed in the same base directory ($SYBASE), which is defined by the SYBASE environment variable. DirectConnect for Oracle 15.0 and above doesn't require any Oracle software on the machine where it is installed, because it is already linked with Oracle libraries. However, the tnsnames.ora file must be accessible to DirectConnect for Oracle. The tnsnames.ora file is similar to Sybase interfaces/sql.ini. The configuration process copies this file to $SYBASE/DCO-15_0/ network/admin directory.

Follow these steps:

1. Install Oracle.

2. Download Replication Server Options for Oracle 15.0 and Enterprise Connect Data Access 15.0 for your platform from https://sybase.subscribenet.com/.

   Replication Server Options for Oracle 15.0 has four components:

   ▶ Enterprise Connect Data Access 12.6.1 Options *platform* (Instead of 12.6.1 Enterprise Connect Data Access, you can also install Enterprise Connect Data Access 15.0)

   ▶ DirectConnect Client 12.6.1

   ▶ Replication Server Options 15.0 Sybooks

   ▶ Replication Agent 15.0 *platform*

   The current name for DirectConnect for Oracle is Enterprise Connect Data Access for Oracle.

3. Before installing DirectConnect for Oracle, you should set up Oracle users with the correct permissions, as follows:

   ▶ DCO administrator: This user will be responsible for configuring, starting up, and shutting down DCO. It is usually the system account name.

   ▶ DCO administrator password: The password for the DCO administrator. This password is not logged in the DCO configuration file, but if DCOConfig is invoked with the "-trace" argument, then the password is written in the config.log file.

   ▶ Replication Server maintenance user: This user will apply transactions to the replicate database.

4. Enter the location of tnsnames.ora, which is usually in the $ORACLE_HOME/admin/network directory and should be accessible to DCO. If it is not accessible, tnsnames.ora should be copied to the local location before configuring DCO.

5. Enter the Oracle server connection string. This is usually oracle SID.

6. Enter the DirectConnect server name and port number.

   For complete installation instructions, please refer to the DirectConnect installation guide (http://sybooks.sybase.com/nav/base.do). From the directory where you have downloaded and extracted the DirectConnect software, you can launch Installshield by executing the setup routine.

7. Select **custom install** and **ECDA Option for Oracle**. By default, DirectConnect for Oracle can be configured during the installation. DirectConnect for Oracle can be installed in one of the following ways:

   ▶ GUI interface (./setup) — The setup program needs at least 100 MB of temporary disk space. If setup fails with a "not enough temporary disk space" error message, use the following command to specify another directory, which can be used to set up temporary disk space:

   ```
   ./setup -is:tempdir tempdirectory
   ```

   Sybase recommends that you install DirectConnect for Oracle using GUI mode.

   ▶ If you don't have access to Xwindows or can't do a remote install, you can run installation in components in command-line mode:

   ```
   ./setup -console
   ```

   ▶ You can also install DirectConnect for Oracle using a response file in one of two ways:

      ▶ Silent: Silent mode allows you to install DirectConnect for Oracle without any interaction. This method can be used if you are going to install identical installations on multiple host machines.

▶ Interactive: Interactive mode allows you to install interactively but with all the responses already filled in so that you can accept all the default values and install DCO according to the responses in the response file. This method is useful for standard installation of DirectConnect for Oracle at several sites.

8. On the Welcome window, click **Next**.

9. Select a geographic location, read the license and copyright information, select **I agree**, and click **Next**.

(If DirectConnect is installed with other Sybase products, you may be prompted to indicate whether the installer should overwrite earlier versions of files with newer versions. If so, select to overwrite.)

10. Click **Next** to select the installation directory. If the directory you have selected doesn't exist, the installer prompts:

   `The directory does not exist. Do you want to create it?`

   If the directory already exists, the installer prompts:

   `You have chosen to install into an existing directory. Any older versions of the products you choose to install that are detected in this directory will be replaced.`

   If you are prompted to overwrite any files, select **Yes** *only* if the version of the new file is later than the one it is attempting to overwrite.

11. In the next window, you are prompted for the type of installation. There are two types of installations: full and custom. Sybase recommends that you use custom install and select **ECDA for Oracle** from the option list. Then click **Next**.

12. When a custom installation is selected, the installer in the next window displays all the ECDA options "unchecked" (not selected) and all the components "checked" (selected). You must select the ECDA Option for Oracle and uncheck or deselect the components that you do not want installed. Note that if an unchecked component is required to run selected

components, the unchecked component is automatically installed. Click **Next**.

13. Before proceeding to the next window, the installer verifies the selection, and checks for dependencies and free disk space. If there is not enough disk space available, the installer stops the installation and the available free space and free space required for installation is displayed. You should verify that you have enough space and have selected the correct type of installation to complete the process. Click **Next**.

14. The installer uploads all the components from the software installation CD and a progress indicator is displayed. When the installer displays a message indicating that installation is complete, click **Next** to configure the server and select servers you want to configure or deselect all servers to configure later with the DCOConfig utility.

15. In the configuration option window, you are prompted for the following:

   ▶ Servername: DCO server name

   ▶ Port Number: Port number for the DCO server to listen on

   ▶ DCO Admin Account Name: Valid Oracle user, usually the system account

   ▶ Oracle Connect String: Name of the Oracle instance in the tnsnames.ora file

   ▶ Location of Oracle tnsnames.ora file: Installer copies the existing tnsnames.ora file to $SYBASE/$SYBASE_DCO/ network/admin directory

   The installer displays a message indicating that DCO configuration and startup was successful.

16. After this you can enter the Software Asset Management certificate by running:

   `$SYBASE/$SYBASE-SYSAM/bin/lmgr`

   If you choose not to configure DirectConnect Server at this time, you can configure it by using /DCOconfig. Before

invoking DCOConfig, source $SYBASE/DCO-15_0/DCO_
SYBASE.csh to set up all your environment variables.

```
$SYBASE/$SYBASE-DCO/install/DCOConfig

% ./DCOConfig


-------------------------------------------------------
Setting environment variables for configuration...
-------------------------------------------------------



Enter DirectConnect for Oracle Server Name:
DCO150


Enter DirectConnect for Oracle Server Port Number:
8601


Enter DirectConnect for Oracle Administrator Name:
system


Enter the Oracle Server Connection String:
orcl


Enter the path (including file name) to a valid Oracle tnsnames.ora
file so it can be copied to the local DCO environment;
/var/h1/oracleiog/network/admin/tnsnames.ora


-------------------------------------------------------------
Creating DirectConnect for Oracle configuration file
DCO150.cfg.
-------------------------------------------------------------



-------------------------------------------------------------
Creating DirectConnect for Oracle run file
RUN_DCO150.
```

```
------------------------------------------------------------

------------------------------------------------------------
Adding DCO150 to /work1/ecda1500/DCO-15_0/connectivity/interfaces
file.
------------------------------------------------------------

------------------------------------------------------------
Copying tnsnames.ora file.
------------------------------------------------------------


------------------------------------------------------------
An existing /work1/ecda1500/DCO-15_0/connectivity/../net-
work/admin/tnsnames.ora
was found, renaming to tnsnames.ora.bak prior to
copying of /work1/oracle10g/network/admin/tnsnames.ora.
------------------------------------------------------------


------------------------------------------------------------
Starting DirectConnect for Oracle.
------------------------------------------------------------


DirectConnect-Oracle/15.0/P/sun_svr4/OS 5.8/9/OPT/28-Jul-2007 20:50:31

Confidential property of Sybase, Inc.
Copyright 1995, 2007
Sybase, Inc. All rights reserved.
Unpublished rights reserved under U.S. copyright laws.

This software contains confidential and trade secret information of
Sybase, Inc.  Use, duplication or disclosure of the software and docu-
mentation by the U.S. Government is subject to restrictions set forth
in a license agreement between the Government and Sybase, Inc. or
other written agreement specifying the Government's rights to use the
software and any applicable FAR provisions, for example, FAR
52.227-19. Sybase, Inc. One Sybase Drive, Dublin, CA 94568, USA

Language is us_english.
Character set is iso_1.

Option [traceflags] not found in configuration file
'/work1/ecda1500/DCO-15_0/connectivity/../install/DCO150.cfg'.
```

```
Generating new configuration file.

Startup complete.
```

DirectConnect configuration can fail for the following reasons:

▶ DirectConnect Admin user name is not a valid Oracle user.

▶ DirectConnect Admin user password is incorrect.

▶ Oracle connect string is incorrect.

▶ tnsnames.ora doesn't have correct Oracle connect string.

▶ If DirectConnect Server fails to start, check $SYBASE/log.txt for error messages.

Verify that you can connect to Oracle (isql to Oracle via DirectConnect):

```
isql -Usystem -Psybase -SDCO150
1> select banner from v$version
2> go
BANNER
-----------------------------------------------------------------
Oracle Database 10g Enterprise Edition Release 10.2.0.1.0 - 64bi PL/SQL
Release 10.2.0.1.0 - Production
CORE   10.2.0.1.0      Production
TNS for Solaris: Version 10.2.0.1.0 - Production
NLSRTL Version 10.2.0.1.0 - Production
```

DCO can be uninstalled with the uninstall program. Before uninstalling DCO, SySAM service should be stopped; otherwise some of the files and directories will not be deleted. To uninstall on Solaris, use the following:

```
cd $SYBASE/uninstall/FCOASuite/uninstall
```

Replication Agent Installation

For complete installation steps, please see the Replication Agent installation guide. Replication Agent must be installed in the same release directory ($SYBASE) as DirectConnect for Oracle, and on the same host machine as the Oracle redo logs or on a host (same OS and platform) with shared access to the same devices. As mentioned earlier, Replication Agent should be installed after the DirectConnect software.

1. From the directory where you have downloaded, uncompressed, and extracted the Replication Agent software, launch Installshield by executing the setup routine appropriate for the desired platform:

   ./setup*platform*

   The following platforms are valid:

   ▶ Solaris: /setupsolaris
   ▶ HP-UX: /setuphp11x
   ▶ IBM AIX: ./setupaix
   ▶ Linux: ./setuplinux
   ▶ Windows: ./setupwin32

2. As mentioned earlier, you can run the installer in GUI or console mode or by using a response file. GUI mode is the recommended method to run Installshield. Select a typical installation. When the installer displays a summary of what is to be installed, click **Next**.

3. You will get a message about replacing files. Click **No to all**. When you receive a message that the installation was successful, click **Next**.

4. The SySAM License Server window opens and displays the message "Will license be obtained from the License Server?" Select **Yes** to use a pre-existing SySAM network and click **Next**.

5. The SySAM notification window prompts you to configure your server for email notification. When configuration is enabled, you will receive information about license management events that require attention. You can accept default values that are supplied or enter values for the following:

   ▶ SMTP server host name
   ▶ SMTP server port number
   ▶ Email return address

567

▶ Recipients of the notification

▶ Message severity level of an event that will trigger email. Your choices are Informational, Warning, and Error.

6. If you don't want to have email alerts or severity messages logged, you should click **No**, click **Next**, and click **Finish** to complete installation and close Installshield.

To uninstall Replication Agent software, shut down all Sybase Replication Agent instances and other components you want to uninstall, and invoke the uninstall program by executing $SYBASE/uninstall/RAX-15_0/uninstaller. The uninstaller program opens the window and lists all installed products and features. You can select the products and features you want to uninstall. The default is to uninstall all the products. You may be prompted by the uninstaller to decide whether to remove shared files; Sybase recommends that you do not remove shared files.

The assumption is that you have already installed Replication Server and have identified primary and replication data servers.

Configuring DirectConnect for Oracle

Before using DirectConnect for Oracle and Adaptive Server Enterprise to access remote data, you should add DirectConnect as a remote server to sysservers in Adaptive Server Enterprise:

```
1> sp_addserver DCO150, direct_connect, DCO150
1> go
Adding server 'DCO150', physical name 'DCO150'
Server added.
```

You can modify DirectConnect configuration parameters with the sp_configure stored procedure. For more information on DirectConnect administration and DirectConnect Manager, see Sybase's ECDA documentation.

Creating Maintenance User in Oracle

The maintenance user is a valid Oracle user used by Replication Server for applying commands to the replicate Oracle database. The maintenance user name should not be the same as the DCO admin account name used in DCO configuration.

Using SQLPLUS (in the replicate database):

```
SQL> create user maintuser identified by password;

User created.

Grant dba and create session permissions to the maintenance user

SQL> grant dba to maintuser;

Grant succeeded.

SQL> grant create session to maintuser;

Grant succeeded.
```

Creating DDL User in Oracle

A user who is going to apply DDL on the primary database should be added to the replicate database as well, because DDL is applied by the user who has applied DDL on the primary database. You can only replicate DDL from an Oracle database to another Oracle database. DDL commands cannot be replicated from an Oracle database to a non-Oracle database. The pdb_setrepddl Replication Agent for Oracle configuration parameter must be enabled, and ddl_username and ddl_password must be set. The name of the DDL user should not be the same as the maintenance user name defined in Replication Server for the replicate database connection. Objects owned by the SYS user are not replicated. The default list of owners whose objects will not be replicated is provided by Sybase. You can edit that list using the pdb_ownerfilter command, and can remove or add any user except for the SYS user.

```
SQL> create user DDLuser identified by password;

User created.
```

You can grant permissions to the DDL user to perform DDL activities including creating a user, and creating, altering, and dropping a procedure, index, and table. This user must have authority in the replicate database to issue ALTER SESSION SET CURRENT_SCHEMA= user for any user that can create DDL in the primary database.

```
SQL> grant alter session to DDLuser;

Grant succeeded.

SQL> grant create user to DDLuser;

Grant succeeded.

SQL> grant create procedure to DDLuser;

Grant succeeded.

SQL> grant create table to DDLuser;

Grant succeeded.
```

Creating Objects and Public Synonyms in Oracle SID

Log in to Oracle through DCO as the maintenance user (assuming that the maintenance user has the resource role to create tables):

```
isql -Umaintuser -Ppassword -SDCO150
-i/work2/rel150_rs/REP-15_0/scripts/hds_oracle_setup_for_replicate.sql
Msg 942, Level 16, State 0:
Server 'DCO150':
ORA-00942: table or view does not exist
```

You can ignore the "ORA-00942: table or view does not exist" message.

Log in to Oracle through DCO and verify the installed objects:

```
isql -Umaintuser -Ppassword -SDCO150
1> select * from rs_info
2> go
RSKEY                RSVAL
-------------------- --------------------
charset_name         iso_1
sortorder_name       bin_iso_1
```

To verify that the rs_lastcommit table has been successfully created, do the following:

```
1> select * from rs_lastcommit
2> go
ORIGIN              ORIGIN_QID                SECONDARY_QID
  ORIGIN_TIME                 DEST_COMMIT_TIME
------------------- ------------------------- -------------------------
  ------------------------- -------------------------
(0 rows affected)
```

Before configuring Replication Agent, Oracle SID (primary database) must be configured for replication:

▶ Archiving of redo logs should be enabled.

▶ "Automatic" archiving must be disabled.

▶ Supplemental logging of primary key data must be enabled.

Oracle should be configured to use an additional directory for archive log files, which should be used exclusively for replication, and Replication Agent should be configured to use the directory path where archive logs are located. Sybase recommends that Replication Agent instances should be configured to remove archive logs only if an additional directory is used; otherwise it can interfere with other archive file processes. When the pdb_include_archives Replication Agent configuration parameter is set to "true", which is the default setting, then redo logs are not archived by Replication Agent. Sybase recommends configuring Oracle to do automatic archiving for redo logs. When the pdb_include_archives Replication Agent configuration parameter is set to "false", archiving of redo logs is done by Replication

Agent for Oracle; in that case, automatic archiving of Oracle redo logs must be disabled. The Replication Agent instance administrator user who will start the Replication Agent instance for Oracle should have read permission to the Oracle redo log files and the Oracle archive directory that contains archive log files to be accessed for replication. If old archive log files will be removed by a Replication Agent instance, then the Replication Agent administrator user must have update authority to the archive log directory and the archive log files.

Checking Current Archiving Settings of Redo Logs

Using SQLPLUS, connect to Oracle SID as a system administrator and run the following command:

```
SQL> select log_mode from v$database;

LOG_MODE
------------
NOARCHIVELOG
```

To turn on log archiving:

```
SQL> shutdown immediate;
  Database closed.
  Database dismounted.
  ORACLE instance shut down.
  SQL> startup mount;
ORACLE instance started.

Total System Global Area  293601280 bytes
Fixed Size                  1978176 bytes
Variable Size             125833408 bytes
Database Buffers          163577856 bytes
Redo Buffers                2211840 bytes
Database mounted.
SQL> alter database archivelog;

Database altered.

SQL> alter database open;
```

```
Database altered.

SQL> select log_mode from v$database;

LOG_MODE
------------
ARCHIVELOG        -----> log archiving is enabled.
```

Replication Agent for Oracle requires that automatic archiving of Oracle redo logs be disabled. Replication Agent performs automatic archiving as data in the redo log files is replicated.

Note: For Oracle, the RAC Replication Agent configuration parameter pdb_include_archives **should be set to "true", which is the default, and** log_mode **should be automatic.**

Disabling Automatic Archiving

To disable automatic archiving, do the following:

```
 SQL> shutdown immediate;
Database closed.
Database dismounted.
ORACLE instance shut down.
SQL> startup mount;
ORACLE instance started.

Total System Global Area   293601280 bytes
Fixed Size                   1978176 bytes
Variable Size              113250496 bytes
Database Buffers           176160768 bytes
Redo Buffers                 2211840 bytes
Database mounted.
SQL> alter database ARCHIVELOG MANUAL;

Database altered.

SQL> alter database open;

Database altered.
SQL> select log_mode from v$database;
```

```
LOG_MODE
------------

MANUAL              --------->automatic log archiving is disabled
```

Forced Logging of All Database Changes

Forced logging of all database changes to Oracle redo logs should
be enabled to ensure that all data that should be replicated is
logged. To enable this setting, execute the following command on
the Oracle SID (primary database):

```
SQL> alter database FORCE LOGGING;

Database altered.
```

To verify that forced logging of all database changes has been
enabled:

```
SQL> select force_logging from v$database;

FOR
---
YES
```

To check if supplemental logging of primary key data is enabled,
log in to Oracle SID as system administrator using SQLPLUS and
run the following command:

```
SQL> SELECT SUPPLEMENTAL_LOG_DATA_PK, SUPPLEMENTAL_LOG_DATA_UI FROM
V$DATABASE;

SUP SUP
--- ---
NO NO
```

By default, supplemental logging of primary keys and unique
indexes to the redo log is not enabled. You must enable logging of
these values for a successful replication of all table values.

To enable supplemental logging of primary key data:

```
SQL> ALTER DATABASE ADD SUPPLEMENTAL LOG DATA (PRIMARY KEY, UNIQUE
INDEX) COLUMNS;
```

```
Database altered.


 SQL> ALTER DATABASE ADD SUPPLEMENTAL LOG DATA;

Database altered.

SQL> SELECT SUPPLEMENTAL_LOG_DATA_PK, SUPPLEMENTAL_LOG_DATA_UI FROM
V$DATABASE;

SUP SUP
--- ---
YES YES  -→supplemental logging of primary key data is enabled
```

Sybase Replication Agent for Oracle requires that one user must be defined with the following permissions:

▶ Create session

▶ Select_catalog_role

▶ Alter system

▶ Execute on DBMS_FLASHBACK

Replication Agent for Oracle does not support the flashback feature available in Oracle version 10g. You should disable the recycle bin by logging in to Oracle SID with sysdba privileges.

To view the current configuration of the recycle bin:

```
SQL> select inst_id, value from v$parameter;
```

To view the contents of dba_recyclebin:

```
SQL> select * from dba_recyclebin;
```

To disable dba_recyclebin:

```
SQL> purge dba_recyclebin;

DBA Recyclebin purged.

SQL> ALTER SYSTEM SET recyclebin = OFF;

System altered.
```

Permissions

> **Note:** In Oracle RAC with Replication Agent 15.1 for Oracle, all `alter system` commands should be issued with "scope=both sid='*';."
> SQL> ALTER SYSTEM SET recyclebin = OFF scope=both sid='*';

To determine whether the Replication Agent user contains 'resource' and 'select_catalog_role', log in to Oracle SID (primary database) with Replication Agent user login:

```
select GRANTED_ROLE from USER_ROLE_PRIV
where GRANTED_ROLE='RESOURCE'
OR GRANTED_ROLE='SELECT_CATALOG_ROLE';
```

To determine whether the Replication Agent user contains 'alter system' and 'alter session' system privileges, log in to Oracle SID (primary database) with Replication Agent user login:

```
select PRIVILEGE from USER_SYS_PRIVS
where PRIVILEGE='ALTER SYSTEM'
OR PRIVILEGE='ALTER SESSION';
```

You must install TNS listener service and Oracle JDBC driver on the Replication Agent host machine for Replication Agent Connectivity and the Oracle data server. The Oracle JDBC driver must be in the CLASSPATH environment variable.

You must grant the Oracle permissions in Table 16-1 to pds username (user used by Replication Agent for Oracle to connect to Oracle SID):

Table 16-1: Oracle permissions

Permissions	Required to
create session	Connect to Oracle
select_catalog_role	Select from the DBA_*views
alter system	Perform redo log archive operations
execute on DBMS_FLASHBACK	Execute DBMS_FLASHBACK.get_system_change_number

Permissions	Required to
alter any procedure	Instrument procedures for replication
create table	Create tables in the primary database
create procedure	Create rs_marker and rs_dump procedures
create public synonym	Create synonyms for created tables in the primary database
drop public synonym	Drop created synonyms
select on SYS.OBJ$	Process procedure DDL commands
select on SYS.LOB$	Support LOB replication
select on SYS.COLLECTIONS$	Support table replication
select on SYS.COL$	Support table replication
select on SYS.CON$	Support table replication
select on SYS.CDEF$	Support replication
select on SYS.USER$	Support replication
select on SYS.SEQ$	Support sequence replication

In addition to the above grants, the user who will start the Replication Agent for Oracle instance must have read permission on redo log files and the archive logs in Oracle's archive directory. If you are planning to configure a Replication Agent instance to remove old archive logs, pds_username must be granted update authority to the Oracle archive directory and the archive log files.

Configuring Replication Server

For information on installing and configuring Replication Server, see Chapter 4. For replicating data from non-Sybase primary to Sybase Adaptive Server Enterprise, you must apply $SYBASE/REP-15_0/scripts/hds_clt_*xxx*_to_ase.sql to RSSD of the replicate Replication Server to provide automatic translation of the primary database datatypes to Adaptive Server native datatypes. Edit the hds_oracle_udds.sql, hds_clt_*xxx*_to_ase.sql, and hds_oracle_funcstrings.sql scripts and add the name of your RSSD database.

The following list contains the scripts that need to be loaded for replicating data from/to non-Sybase data servers:

```
$SYBASE/REP-15_0/scripts: ls
hds_oracle_funcstrings.sql
hds_oracle_new_setup_for_replicate.sql
hds_oracle_new_udds.sql
hds_clt_asa_to_oracle.sql          hds_clt_oracle_to_informix.sql
hds_clt_ase_to_oracle.sql          hds_clt_oracle_to_msss.sql
hds_clt_db2_to_oracle.sql          hds_clt_oracle_to_udb.sql
hds_clt_informix_to_oracle.sql     hds_clt_udb_to_oracle.sql
hds_clt_msss_to_oracle.sql         hds_oracle_udds.sql
hds_clt_oracle_to_asa.sql
hds_clt_oracle_to_ase.sql
hds_clt_oracle_to_db2.sql
```

Load these scripts in RSSD/ERSSD, either as primary user or SA:

```
isql -Usa -P -Spds -Dprs_RSSD -i$SYBASE/REP-15_0/scripts/hds_clt_oracle_
to_ase.sql
isql -Usa -P -Spds -Dprs_RSSD -i$SYBASE/REP-15_0/scripts/hds_oracle_
udds.sql
isql -Usa -P -Spds -Dprs_RSSD -i$SYBASE/REP-15_0/scripts/hds_oracle_
funcstrings.sql
isql -Usa -P -Spds -Dprs_RSSD -i hds_oracle_new_udds.sql
isql -Usa -P -Spds -Dprs_RSSD -i hds_clt_ase_to_oracle.sql
```

After installing these scripts, log in to Replication Server, issue the shutdown command, and restart the Replication Server.

To replicate data from Oracle to Oracle, you must perform the steps listed below:

1. Enter cd to $SYBASE/rel150_rs_options/RAX-15_0/scripts.

2. Create an Oracle class by executing the following scripts:

   Execute oracle_create_error_class_1_rs.sql and oracle_create_error_class_3_rs.sql to the Replication Server and oracle_create_error_class_2_rssd.sql to the RSSD/ERSSD.

   ```
   isql -Usa -P -Sprs -i oracle_create_error_class_1_rs.sql
   isql -Usa -P -Sprs -i oracle_create_error_class_3_rs.sql
   ```

For heterogeneous datatype support, apply hds_oracle_new_setup_for_replicate.sql to Oracle SID (replicate data server). This script should be executed via DirectConnect by the maintenance user.

```
isql -Umaintuser -Ppassword -SDC0150 -i hds_oracle_new_setup_for_rep-
licate.sql
```

3. Create a table in the primary database:

```
SQL> create table rax_text
        (charcol char(255) default null,
        decimalfixedcol decimal(32,16) default null,
        floatcol float(14) default null,
        integercol int default null,
        serialcol number primary key,
        varcharcol varchar2(255) default null
        );
```

```
Table created.
```

4. Create a table in the replicate database:

```
SQL> create table rax_rtest
        (charcol char(255) default null,
         decimalfixedcol decimal(32,16) default null,
         floatcol float(14) default null,
         integercol int default null,
         serialcol number primary key,
         varcharcol varchar2(255) default null
         );
```

```
Table created.
```

5. Create a connection for the Oracle SID (primary database) by making a copy of $SYBASE/rel150_rs_options/RAX-15_0/scripts/oracle_create_rs_primary_connection.sql:

```
cd $SYBASE/rel150_rs_options/RAX-15_0/scripts
cp oracle_create_rs_primary_connection.sql
oracle_create_rs_primary_connection.sql.cpy
```

Before executing this script in Replication Server, change references to pds.pdb where pds is the primary data server name used for the rs_source_ds Replication Agent configuration property and pdb is the primary database name used for the rs_source_db Replication Agent configuration property. Also change sys and sys_pwd to the Oracle user and password of the Oracle user who would have permissions to apply DML operations against all user tables to be replicated.

```
create connection to myrao.orcl
    set error class rs_sqlserver_error_class
    set function string class rs_oracle_function_class
    set username sys
    set password sybase
    with log transfer on, dsi_suspended
    go
```

```
isql -Usa- P -Sprs -i oracle_create_rs_primary_connection.sql.cpy
```

6. Create a connection for the replicate database by making a copy of $SYBASE/rel150_rs_options/RAX-15_0/scripts/ oracle_create_rs_standby_connection.sql:

```
cd $SYBASE/rel150_rs_options/RAX-15_0/scripts
cp oracle_create_rs_standby_connection.sql
oracle_create_rs_standby_connection.sql.cpy
```

Edit the oracle_create_rs_standby_connection.sql.cpy script, changing the value for rds.rdb, and execute the modified script against Replication Server, where rds is the DirectConnect server name and rdb can be any valid identifier. Sybase recommends setting these to Oracle SID. rs_maint_user and rs_maint_user_pwd are the maintenance user name and password created earlier in DirectConnect for Oracle. For example:

```
create connection to DCO150.orcl2
    set error class oracle_error_class
    set function string class rs_oracle_function_class
    set username maintuser
    set password "password"
    set batch to "off"
```

```
isql -Usa -P -Sprs -i oracle_create_rs_standby_connection.sql.cpy
Connection to 'DCO150.orcl' is created.
```

To verify the Replication Server connection to the replicate database, log in to prs (Replication Server):

```
isql -Usa -P -Sprs
1> admin who
2> go
 Spid Name         State                    Info
 ---- ----------   --------------------     ------------------------
   40 DIST          Awaiting Wakeup          106 PDS.PUBS3
   44 SQT           Awaiting Wakeup          106:1  DIST PDS.PUBS3
   31 SQM           Awaiting Message         106:1 PDS.PUBS3
   30 SQM           Awaiting Message         106:0 PDS.PUBS3
   55 DSI EXEC      Awaiting Command         109(1) DCO150.orcl
   54 DSI           Awaiting Message         109 DCO150.orcl
   53 SQM           Awaiting Message         109:0 DCO150.orcl
```

From the above output you can see that the status for the DSI connection for DCO150.orcl is "Awaiting Message."

7. Create a replication definition in the primary Replication Server:

```
1> create replication definition raxtestrep
2> with primary at myrao.orcl
3> with all tables named 'rax_test'
4> (charcol char(255),
5> decimalfixedcol decimal,
6> floatcol float,
7> integercol int,
8> serialcol int,
9> varcharcol varchar(255) )
10> primary key (serialcol)
11> searchable columns (serialcol)
12>
13> go
Replication definition 'raxtestrep' is created.
```

8. Create a subscription in the replicate Replication Server:

```
1> create subscription rax_rtest_sub
2> for raxtestrep
3> with replicate at DCO150.orcl2
4> without materialization
5> go
```

```
Subscription 'rax_rtest_sub' is in the process of being created.

1> check subscription rax_rtest_sub
2> for raxtestrep
3> with replicate at DC0150.orcl
4> go
Subscription rax_rtest_sub is VALID at the replicate.
Subscription rax_rtest_sub is VALID at the primary.
```

9. To replicate DDL, you must create a database replication definition. You can edit the sample create database replication definition script oracle_create_rs_db_repdef.sql in the $SYBASE/RAX-15_0/scripts directory:

```
create database replication definition {pds}_repdef1
    with primary at {pds}.{pdb}
    replicate DDL
```

where pds.pdb is the Replication Server connection used by the Replication Agent instance. For example:

```
create database replication definition myrao_repdef1
    with primary at myrao.orcl
    replicate DDL
```

10. To create a database replication subscription, you can edit the sample create database subscription script oracle_create_rs_db_sub.sql in the $SYBASE/RAX-15_0/scripts directory:

```
create subscription {pds}_sub1
    for database replication definition {pds}_repdef1
    with primary at {pds}.{pdb}
    with replicate at {rds}.{rdb}
    without materialization
```

Change all occurrences of pds.pdb to the Replication Server connection used by Replication Agent and rds.rdb to the Replication Server connection used to connect to Oracle.

```
create subscription myrao_sub1
    for database replication definition myrao_repdef1
    with primary at myrao.orclpdb}
    with replicate at DC0150.orcl2
    without materialization
```

Configuring a Replication Agent Instance

You must create the Replication Agent instance for each Oracle SID for which you want to replicate transactions. Each Replication Agent instance will have its own configuration and log files, administration port, and connections to the primary database and primary Replication Server.

In the following tables, replace the example values in the Value column with your values.

In Table 16-2, you will need to fill out all the relevant administration information about your instance typ, which can be Oracle, ibmudb (IBM DB2 universal database), or mssql (Microsoft SQL Server).

Table 16-2: Replication Agent administration information

Configuration Parameter	Description	Value
Instance Type	Primary database type the Replication Agent works with.	Oracle
Replication Agent Instance Name	Replication Agent instance name must be unique among all Replication Agent instances.	myrao
admin_port (Replication Agent Port Number)	Replication Agent for Oracle requires two port numbers; the second port is for RASD (Replication Agent System Database). By default RASD is assigned admin port + 1.	9000
Interfaces file location	Specify interfaces file location, if you are planning to use isql or Replication Server Manager for administering Replication Agent instance.	$SYBASE/ interfaces
admin_user (Replication Agent admin user name)	Administrative user login used to log in to Replication Agent. Default: sa	admin_user
admin_pw (Replication Agent admin password)	Administrative user password. Default: empty string("")	admin_pwd

In Table 16-3, fill out the values of the connection parameters for Replication Server. These values are used by Replication Server for creating the primary database connection.

Table 16-3: Replication Server configuration parameter values for primary database connection

Configuration Parameter	Description	Value
rs_source_ds	Primary data server name to which Replication Server connects. rs_source_ds value can be the name of the Replication Agent and this value is used in the Replication Server `create connection` command used to create Replication Agent connection.	myrao
rs_source_db	Primary database name to which Replication Server connects. rs_source_db can be set to Oracle database SID or any name that you can identify as primary database; this value is used in the Replication Server `create connection` command to create the Replication Agent connection in the primary Replication Server.	orcl
Maintenance user	Maintenance user ID must be valid at the primary database. The maintenance user ID is required by Replication Server for each database connection.	maintuser
Maintenance user password	Maintenance user password.	password

The parameters in Table 16-4 are used with the Replication Agent configuration command `ra_config` when you configure a Replication Agent instance.

Table 16-4: Replication Agent configuration parameter values for Replication Server

Configuration Parameter	Description	Value
rs_host_name	Replication Server host name.	myrshost
rs_port_number	Replication Server port number.	7221
rs_username	Replication Server user name, used by Replication Agent to log in to primary Replication Server. It shouldn't be the same as the maintenance user (Table 16-3). This user must have connect source permission in the Replication Server.	ra_rs_user
rs_password	Replication Server user password.	ra_rs_user_ps
rs_charset	The character set specified with rs_charset is used by Replication Agent for creating LTL commands for Replication Server; it must match the Replication Server character set. If it is not the same as the primary Replication Server, incorrect character set conversion of LTL commands is done by Replication Server. If the rs_charset value is different from the RA_JAVA_DFLT_CHARSET value (which should match the character set of the primary database), then character set conversion on the character data being replicated will be done by Replication Agent. Character set conversion impacts performance.	iso_1

Log in to the primary Replication Server with a login that has sa permissions and create a Replication Server user login for a Replication Agent instance. This login will be used by Replication Agent to send replicated transactions to Replication Server:

```
1> create user ra_rs_user set password to ra_rs_user_ps
2> go
User 'ra_rs_user' is created.
```

Where:

ra_rs_user

Replication Agent user login name

ra_rs_user_ps

Password for the Replication Agent user login

```
1> grant connect source to ra_rs_user
2> go
Permission granted to user 'ra_rs_user'.
```

In Table 16-5, you will need to fill out configuration parameters for RSSD/ERSSD (Embedded RSSD) for the primary Replication Server. There is no difference in configuration parameters for RSSD/ERSSD. Connection to either RSSD/ERSSD is supported by the Replication Agent.

Table 16-5: Replication Agent configuration parameter values for the RSSD

Configuration Parameter	Description	Value
rssd_host_name	Host name on which the RSSD of the primary Replication Server resides.	ase_host
rssd_port_number	Port number for the RSSD data server.	7100
rssd_database_name	Name of the RSSD database of the primary Replication Server.	prs_RSSD
rssd_username	Name of the RSSD user used by Replication Agent to access the RSSD of the primary Replication Server.	ra_rssd_user
rssd_password	RSSD user password.	ra_rssd_user_ps

Log in to the Adaptive Server Enterprise managing the RSSD database with system administration user role and add rssd user login and rssd user to the RSSD database:

```
1> use master
2> go
```

```
1> sp_addlogin ra_rssd_user, ra_rssd_user_ps, prs_RSSD
2> go
Password correctly set.
Account unlocked.
New login created.
(return status = 0)
```

```
ra_rssd_user
```

Name of Replication Agent RSSD user login

```
ra_rssd_user_ps
```

Password for the Replication Agent RSSD user

```
prs_RSSD
```

Name of the RSSD database

Add the rssd user in the RSSD database as a member of the rs_systabgroup, so that the user has read permission on Replication Server system tables:

```
1> use prs_RSSD
2> go
1> sp_adduser ra_rssd_user, ra_rssd_user, rs_systabgroup
2> go
New user added.
(return status = 0)
```

If you are using an Embedded RSSD database instead of an RSSD database, you can use the following steps to add Replication Agent RSSD user login to ERSSD.

1. Log in to ERSSD database as primary user and add Replication Agent ERSSD user login:

    ```
    grant connect to ra_rssd_user
    identified by ra_rssd_user_ps
    ```

2. Grant read permission on Replication Server system tables to Replication Agent ERSSD user:

    ```
    grant membership in group rs_systabgroup to ra_rssd_user
    ```

In Table 16-6, you will need to fill out relevant values for the primary data server, which can be oracle, mssql, or ibmudb.

Table 16-6: Replication Agent configuration parameter values for the primary data server

Configuration Parameter	Description	Value
pds_host_name	Host name on which the primary data server resides.	ora_pds
pds_port_number	Port number for primary data server.	1521
pds_database_name	Primary database name (oracle database SID). This should be the same as rs_source_db (Table 16-3).	orcl
pds_username	Username used by Replication Agent to log in to primary database.	ra_user
pds_password	pds user password.	ra_user_ps
Primary database character set	If the system default character set is different than the character set of the primary database, you will need to specify the Java-equivalent of the primary database character set in the Replication Agent runserver file by setting RA_JAVA_DFLT_CHARSET.	ISO8859-1

3. Create pds.username in the primary data server and grant required permissions:

```
./sqlplus system/sybase@orcl;

SQL*Plus: Release 10.2.0.1.0 - Production on Wed Dec 19 15:26:04 2007

Copyright (c) 1982, 2005, Oracle. All rights reserved.



Connected to:
Oracle Database 10g Enterprise Edition Release 10.2.0.1.0 - 64bit
Production
With the Partitioning, OLAP and Data Mining options

SQL> create user ra_user profile "DEFAULT" identified by ra_user_ps default
tabl
espace "USERS" account unlock;
```

```
User created.
SQL> grant "CONNECT" to ra_user;

Grant succeeded.

SQL> grant "RESOURCE" to ra_user;

Grant succeeded.

SQL> grant "SELECT_CATALOG_ROLE" to ra_user;

Grant succeeded.

SQL> grant alter session to ra_user;

Grant succeeded.

SQL> grant alter system to ra_user;

Grant succeeded.

SQL> grant execute on "SYS"."DBMS_FLASHBACK" to ra_user;

Grant succeeded.

SQL> grant alter any procedure to ra_user;

Grant succeeded.

SQL> grant create table to ra_user;

Grant succeeded.

SQL> grant create procedure to ra_user;

Grant succeeded.

SQL> grant create public synonym to ra_user;

Grant succeeded.
```

```
SQL> grant drop public synonym to ra_user;

Grant succeeded.

SQL> SQL> grant select on SYS.OBJ$ to ra_user;

Grant succeeded.

SQL> grant select on SYS.LOB$ to ra_user;

Grant succeeded.

SQL> grant select on SYS.COLLECTION$ to ra_user;

Grant succeeded.

SQL> grant create sequence to ra_user;

Grant succeeded.

SQL> grant select on SYS.CON$ to ra_user;

Grant succeeded.

SQL> grant select on SYS.COLTYPE$ to ra_user;

Grant succeeded.

SQL> grant select on SYS.COL$ to ra_user;

Grant succeeded.

SQL> grant select on SYS.CDEF$ to ra_user;

Grant succeeded.

SQL> grant select on SYS.USER$ to ra_user;

Grant succeeded.

SQL> grant select on SYS.SEQ$ to ra_user;
```

```
Grant succeeded.

SQL> grant select on SYS.IND$ to ra_user;

Grant succeeded.
```

To verify Oracle user roles have been granted to the Replication Agent user, log in to Oracle SID as the newly created Replication Agent user:

```
%./sqlplus ra_user/ra_user_ps@orcl

SQL> select granted_role from user_role_privs;

GRANTED_ROLE
-------------------------------
CONNECT
RESOURCE
SELECT_CATALOG_ROLE
```

In Table 16-7, you will need to fill out values for the replicate data server to be used for materialization.

Table 16-7: Replication Server configuration parameters for the replicate data server

Configuration Parameter	Description	Value
Replicate hostname	Host name on which the replicate data server resides.	ora_rds
Replicate database name	Replicate database name (oracle database SID).	orcl2
ddl_username	ddl_username value must not be the same as the maintenance username defined in Replication Server for replicate database connection. ddl_username is used by Replication Server to apply DDL commands at the replicate database. This user should be granted permissions to create any schema or issue any DDL command replicated from the primary database.	DDLuser
ddl_password	DDL user password.	"password"

Creating a Replication Agent Instance

A Replication Agent instance can be created using the command-line utility ra_admin.sh or the GUI utility administrator.sh. You can have more than one Replication Agent instance on a single host machine, but each Replication Agent instance should have a unique name and unique administration port number. Each Replication Agent instance creates its own instance directory, under which it has an instance configuration file, RUN_*instancename* (script to start instance), log files, and script files. Some tables and stored procedures are also created in the primary database by the Replication Agent instance. Connections to the primary data server, primary Replication Server, and RSSD database are managed by their own Replication Agent instances. Before creating a Replication Agent instance, navigate to the $SYBASE release directory and set Sybase environment variables by sourcing the SYBASE.csh/.sh script in UNIX and SYBASE.bat in Windows:

```
% cd /work1/rel150_rs_options
% ls
DC-12_6                  SYBASE.env           config
DCM_install_log.txt      SYBASE.sh            installed
DCManager-12.6           SYBASE.sh.orig       interfaces
DCO-15_0                 SYBCENT.csh          interfaces.org
EBF14310_Buglist.txt     SYBCENT.sh           locales
EBF14310_Filelist.txt    SYSAM-1_0            log.txt
EBF14310_README.html     SYSAM-2_0            runSybaseCentral.sh
EBF14310_README.txt      _jvm_ECDA_Solaris    shared
OCS-12_5                 _jvmrax              shared-1_0
RAX-15_0                 uninstall.sh         uninstall
SYBASE.csh               charsets             vpd.properties
collate

% source SYBASE.csh
```

Navigate to the $SYBASE/RAX-15_0/bin directory and use the ra_admin utility to create a new Replication Agent instance:

```
% cd /work1/rel150_rs_options/RAX-15_0/bin
% ls
administrator.sh                 ra.sh
```

```
gen_RAO_migrate.ksh              ra_admin.sh
gen_RAO_migrate_with_parms.ksh  ra_debug.sh
```

The ra_admin.sh utility (ra_admin.bat on Windows) is the command-line utility and can be used for creating, copying, deleting, verifying, and listing Replication Agent instances.

Syntax:

```
% ra_admin.sh
```

Usage:

```
ra_admin -options
```

A command option is required; options include:

```
-c instance -p port {-t type | -f exist_inst}
```

```
-c instance
```

Creates a Replication Agent instance with name *instance*

```
-p port
```

The socket port for the administration connection

```
-t type
```

The type of database Replication Agent will connect to: oracle, ibmudb, or mssql. If you are not copying an instance, then you must provide the -t *type* option.

```
-f exist_inst
```

The existing instance from which to copy a configuration file. PDS parameters and port number are not duplicated.

```
-v instance
```

Verifies a Replication Agent instance with name *instance*.

```
-d instance
```

Deletes a Replication Agent instance with name *instance* if not currently running

-u *src_dir*

    Upgrades all verifiable Replication Agent instances

-l

    Lists all Replication Agent instances and if they are running

-b

    Displays the Replication Agent base directory

-h[elp]

    Displays this usage message

Use this command to create, list, verify, and delete Replication Agent instances. Then use the ra command to start a Replication Agent instance that has been created by ra_admin.

```
% ./ra_admin.sh -c myrao -p 9000 -t oracle
```

-c

    Replication Agent instance name

-p

    Administration port number of the new Replication Agent instance

-t

    Data server type that contains the primary database

```
Waiting for ASA's dbinit process to complete...
Executing ASA utility: dbinit -c -e -p 2048 -o
/work1/rel150_rs_options/RAX-15_0
/myrao/repository/trace.log -t
/work1/rel150_rs_options/RAX-15_0/myrao/repository/myrao.log
/work1/rel150_rs_options/RAX-15_0/myrao/repository/myrao.db
Waiting for ASA <dbinit> process to complete.
ASA <dbinit> process succeeded.
Processing...
```

```
Executing ASA utility: dbspawn -f -p -q dbeng9 -sb 0 -ti 0 -ga -ud -x
tcpip{PORT=9001} -o /work1/rel150_rs_options/RAX-15_0/myrao/repository/
trace.log /work1/rel150_rs_options/RAX-15_0/myrao/repository/myrao.db
Waiting for ASA <dbspawn> process to complete.
ASA <dbspawn> process succeeded.
Processing...
Processing...
Repository database </work1/rel150_rs_options/RAX-15_0/myrao/repository/
myrao.db> successfully created.
Successfully created instance <myrao>.
The log file for this session is:
/work1/rel150_rs_options/RAX-15_0/admin_logs/admin122008_14259.log
%
```

You can verify that the Replication Agent instance was created properly by invoking ra_admin.sh with -v and the newly created Replication Agent instance name. This utility checks for the Replication Agent instance directory with the instance name under Sybase Replication Agent base and subdirectories under the Replication Agent instance directory.

Note: In Replication Agent 15.1, you can set Replication Agent configuration parameters in the Oracle.rs resource file and create a Replication Agent instance after verifying the resource file:

```
ra_admin.sh  -vr oracle.rs      (resource file is validating)
```

To create a Replication Agent instance:

```
ra_admin.sh  -r oracle.rs
```

```
start_instance=USE_DEFAULT
initialize_instance=USE_DEFAULT
```

When the Replication Agent parameters start_instance and initialize_instance are set to "true", then Replication Agent is created, started, and automatically initialized.

```
% ra_admin.sh -v myrao

Replication Agent Instance: myrao (Oracle)
    Instance working directory: /work1/rel150_rs_options/RAX-15_0/myrao
    Log directory: /work1/rel150_rs_options/RAX-15_0/myrao/log
```

```
Script directory: /work1/rel150_rs_options/RAX-15_0/myrao/scripts
Configuration file: /work1/rel150_rs_options/RAX-15_0/myrao/myrao.cfg
Repository directory: /work1/rel150_rs_options/RAX-15_0/myrao/repository
Repository database file: /work1/rel150_rs_options/RAX-15_0/myrao/
repository/myrao.db
```

The log file for this session is /work1/rel150_rs_options/
RAX-15_0/admin_logs/admin122008_144128.log.

```
% cd /work1/rel150_rs_options/RAX-15_0

% ls
ASA-9_0          admin_logs       config           scripts
JRE-1_4_2        bin              lib              sysam
ThirdPartyLegal  classes          myrao
```

 Note: myrao is the new replication instance directory.

```
% cd myrao
% pwd
/work1/rel150_rs_options/RAX-15_0/myrao
% ls
RUN_myrao    log         myrao.cfg    repository   scripts
```

The Replication Agent system and trace logs will reside in the log
directory, and the Replication Agent System Database (RASD) db
file and logs are stored in the repository directory. RASD is an
Embedded Adaptive Server Anywhere database that is used for
persistent storage of schema information to limit access needs to
the Oracle instance.

You can also list all Replication Agent instances running on
the Replication Agent host machine by executing rs_admin.sh
with the -l (lowercase L) option:

```
% ra_admin.sh -l
```

```
The following Replication Agent instances were found:
    NAME      TYPE      PORT    RUNNING
    myrao     oracle    9000    no
```

A new Replication Agent instance can also be created using the existing Replication Agent configuration file.

Syntax:

```
ra_admin.sh -c new_instance -p port_number -f old_instance
```

Where:

new_instance

New Replication Agent instance name

port_number

Administration port number for new Replication Agent instance

old_instance

Existing Replication Agent instance name, whose configuration you want to copy for the new Replication Agent instance

As mentioned above, you can verify whether the Replication Agent is created by executing rs_admin.sh -v. List all Replication Agent instances on the Replication Agent host, execute ra_admin.sh -l (lowercase L). The values of the configuration parameters are not copied from the configuration file of an existing Replication Agent instance because those values are relevant only to that Replication Agent instance. Below is the list of configuration parameters that are not copied:

```
admin_port
log_directory
pds_database_name
pds_datasource_name
pds_host_name
pds_password
pds_port_number
pds_retry_count
pds_retry_timeout
pds_server_name
pds_username
rs_source_db
```

```
rs_source_ds
rasd_backup_dir
rasd_database
rasd_trace_log_dir
rasd_tran_log
asa_port
```

You can also create a new Replication Agent instance with the administrator.sh utility in GUI (use administrator.bat for Windows). As with ra_admin.sh, you will need to first set your SYBASE environment variables by sourcing SYBASE.csh (or SYBASE.bat on Windows) and then invoke the administrator.sh utility.

```
% xhost +
```

Access control disabled, clients can connect from any host

```
xhost
```

Must be on local machine to enable or disable access control

```
% cd /work1/rel150_rs_options
% source SYBASE.csh
% cd RAX*/bin
% pwd
/work1/rel150_rs_options/RAX-15_0/bin
% ls
administrator.sh              ra_admin.sh
gen_RAO_migrate.ksh           ra_debug.sh
gen_RAO_migrate_with_parms.ksh  rax
ra.sh
% administrator.sh
```

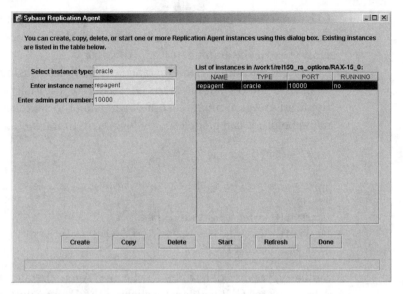

Figure 16-2: Administrator GUI window

Provide the following information for each Replication Agent in the Administrator GUI window:

▶ Type: Replication Agent instance type; select from the drop-down list:

oracle — Oracle

ibmudb — DB2 Universal Database

mssql — Microsoft SQL Server

▶ Name: Replication Agent instance name (default name is Replication Agent)

▶ Port: Administrator port number assigned to the Replication Agent instance (default port is 10000)

▶ Running: Indicates whether or not the Replication Agent instance is running

Click on the **Create** button to create a Replication Agent instance, and then the **Start** button to start the instance. Click **Done** to exit the Administrator GUI window.

The Replication Agent instance can be deleted using the command line (ra_admin.sh) or GUI (administrator.sh) utility. Replication Agent must be shut down using the shutdown command before it can be deleted by logging in to the instance.

```
% ./ra_admin.sh -d myrao

Are you sure you wish to delete Replication Agent instance <myrao>? [y/n]
y
Successfully deleted instance <myrao>.
The log file for this session is: /work1/rel150_rs_options/RAX-15_0/
admin_logs/admin122008_191042.log
```

Similarly, you can delete the Replication Agent instance using the Administrator GUI window by clicking the **Delete** button and then **Done** to exit the GUI.

Starting a Replication Agent Instance

Once the Replication Agent instance is created, it can be started using the ra.sh utility, RUN_*instance*, or the administrator.sh utility.

```
% /work1/rel150_rs_options/RAX-15_0/bin
administrator.sh                    ra_admin.sh
gen_RAO_migrate.ksh                 ra_debug.sh
gen_RAO_migrate_with_parms.ksh
ra.sh
```

The ra.sh and administrator.sh utilities can be invoked from the $SYBASE/RAX-15_0/bin directory. RUN_*instance* resides in the $SYBASE/RAX-15_0/*instance* directory. Before starting the Replication Agent instance, set up the CLASSPATH environment variable. It should be pointing to the JDBC driver location for the primary database.

Syntax:

```
setenv CLASSPATH /oracle_reldirectory/jdbc/lib/classes12.zip
```

Example:

```
setenv CLASSPATH /work1/oracle10g/jdbc/lib/classes12.zip
```

The Replication Agent default character set should be the same as the primary database default character set. If it is different from the primary database character set or the system character set, you will need to set the RA_JAVA_DFLT_CHARSET environment variable. This is because by default the JVM (Java virtual machine) under which the Replication Agent instance is running gets the default character set of the Replication Agent host machine. Sybase recommends keeping the same character set on all platforms and servers in a Sybase Replication Agent. If the character sets are incompatible, there will be data inconsistencies between the primary and replicate databases. The RA_JAVA_DFLT_CHARSET environment variable can be set to valid Java supported encoding in the ra.sh, RUN_*instance*, and administrator.sh utility scripts. The valid values of Java character sets for supported encodings on the internationalization page are listed for J2SE 1.4.1 JDK at http://java.sun.com/javase/technologies/core/basic/intl.

If your Replication Server is replicating a number of different character sets, the default character set for Replication Server and RA_JAVA_DFLT_CHARSET should be set to UTF8:

```
setenv  RA_JAVA_DFLT_CHARSET  UTF8
```

The GUI screen displays all the Replication Agent instances available on that Replication Agent host. Select the instance you want to start and then click **Start**. On the Windows platform, the console window is opened for the Replication Agent that is started. On UNIX, the Replication Agent instance is started in the background. All startup messages and errors are logged in *instance*.log file in $SYBASE/RAX-15_0/*instance*/log directory.

When the Replication Agent instance is started, it opens a network connection to the primary Replication Server (and to the RSSD database, if it is configured) and to the Oracle SID (primary database). Its internal thread, the Log Reader, scans the primary database transaction log and generates and distributes LTL (Log

Transfer Language) to the Replication Server. Replication Agent goes from the admin state to the replicate state.

To start a Replication Agent instance by executing $SYBASE/RAX-15_0/bin/ra.sh:

```
cd $SYBASE/RAX-15_0/bin
ra.sh -i instance -state
```

where *instance* is the name of your Replication Agent instance and state can be admin or replicate. The default is admin.

▶ admin: The Replication Agent instance goes to the admin state when it is started in the default state, started with the ra utility -admin option, when the quiesce or suspend command is executed, when Replication Agent encounters an unrecoverable error, or the connection to the primary database or primary Replication Server or primary RSSD/ERSSD is dropped due to network failures when it was in the replicating state. In admin state, the Replication Agent instance is still up and running but it doesn't have any connection to the primary Replication Server, primary RSSD/ERSSD database, or primary database. The Replication Agent instance can still open a connection to the primary database and can execute configuration related tasks, but data cannot be replicated. All administrative tasks should be done while the Replication Agent instance is in the admin state.

▶ replicate: As the name suggests, Replication Agent is started in the replicating state with the ra utility -replication option or the Replication Agent resume command is executed. Replication Agent will not go into the replicate state if the primary database connection has not been created. In the replicate state, the Replication Agent instance maintains connections to the primary database, primary Replication Server, and primary RSSD/ERSSD database. The Log Reader component of the Replication Agent instance scans the primary database transaction log for transactions to replicate. If the Replication Agent instance has no more records to scan or it has finished scanning the primary database transaction log, its state continues to appear as replicating. When the Replication Agent instance reaches the end of the log, the Log Reader component of the

Replication Agent instance will sleep depending on the configured values of `scan_sleep_increment` and `scan_sleep_max`. After the LTI component of Replication Agent has processed all the transaction log records it has received from the Log Reader and sent all the LTL to the Replication Server, no replication will occur until the new replicated transaction log records appear in the transaction log and Log Reader scans them. The Replication Agent instance remains in the replicating state until some error causes it to go to the admin state.

The preferred method to start a Replication Agent instance is to execute the RUN_*instance* file from the Replication Agent instance directory:

```
cd $SYBASE/RAX-15_0/instance_name
cd $SYBASE/RAX-15_0/myrao
./RUN_myrao &
```

Stopping a Replication Agent Instance

To shut down a Replication Agent instance, log in to the instance as the administrative user and issue the `shutdown` command. The shutdown and startup of a Replication Agent instance is independent of all other components in the replication system. You can shut down a Replication Agent instance using one of the following two options:

▶ Normal shutdown: The Replication Agent instance is quiesced, i.e., the Log Reader component stops reading the primary database transaction log and the connection to the primary database is dropped. Transactions that are already in inbound queues are processed, and then the connection and the instance shut down.

Log in to the Replication Agent instance as administrator login:

```
shutdown
```

▶ Immediate shutdown: The Replication Agent instance shuts down without quiescing and terminates its process immediately. The normal `shutdown` command is ignored by the

Replication Agent instance when it is moving from one state to another, but the `immediate shutdown` command is not ignored.

Log in to the Replication Agent instance as administrator login:

```
immediate shutdown
```

Quiescing a Replication Agent Instance

A Replication Agent instance can be quiesced by logging in as administrator to the Replication Agent instance port and issuing the `quiesce` command. The `quiesce` command causes Replication Agent to stop the replication processing and ensure that all replicated transaction log records from the primary database transaction log have been read and sent to the primary Replication Server. If the primary database is still receiving new replicated transactions and internal queues are full, the `quiesce` command may take some time to take effect. After Replication Agent is quiesced, its state is changed to admin.

Log in to the Replication Agent instance and issue the `quiesce` command:

```
quiesce
```

Check the Replication Agent instance state with `ra_status`. It should change from replicating to admin state.

```
ra_status
```

Initializing a Replication Agent Instance

While initializing a Replication Agent instance, you should stop all activity that would change schema in the primary database. To quiesce the primary database log into the primary database and execute:

```
SQL> alter system quiesce restricted;

System altered.
```

Log in to the Replication Agent instance as administrator user login and execute the pdb_xlog command. This command will check that the primary database already has a transaction log associated to the Replication Agent instance. If no transaction log exists, this command will return no information about transaction log objects and it continues to create a transaction log in the primary database. pdb_xlog verifies transaction log objects based on the pdb_xlog_prefix Replication Agent configuration parameter. If the value of the pdb_xlog_prefix parameter is changed after the transaction log is created, the pdb_xlog command will not find the transaction log objects created previously. If the primary database has a Replication Agent transaction log, the pdb_xlog command returns a list of transaction log objects. If replication for a Replication Agent instance for Oracle has been initialized, the Oracle database instance name is returned. In that case, you don't need to complete this procedure. You can use a particular string for the primary database object name prefix of the transaction log objects by executing:

```
ra_config pdb_xlog_prefix, xxx
```

Where "*xxx*" is a one- to three-character new prefix value of the pdb_xlog_prefix Replication Agent configuration parameter. The new prefix will be used in the primary database names of the transaction log objects when the transaction log is created. The default pdb_xlog_prefix is ra_.

```
ra_config pdb_xlog_prefix
```

The above command can be executed to determine the current value of the pdb_xlog_prefix Replication Agent configuration parameter.

Execute the pdb_xlog init command to initialize the Replication Agent transaction log. This command verifies that the primary Oracle database is correctly configured to provide supplemental logging and archived logging. This command will cause Replication Agent to load metadata from the primary database to the Replication Agent System database (RASD), also known as the repository, and redo log location information from the primary Oracle database. For Oracle, the partinit.sql script is saved in

$SYBASE/RAX-15_0/instance_name/scripts/xlog/installed directory. This script is informational only; you cannot execute it manually.

```
% isql -Uadmin_user -Padmin_pwd -Smyrao
    1> pdb_xlog init
    2> go
    Msg 0, Level 20, State 0:
    Server 'myrao', Procedure 'pdb_xlog init', Line 1:
Successful
```

You can resume replication by executing the resume command:

```
    1> resume
    2> go
    State       Action
    ------------ --------------------------
    REPLICATING  Ready to replicate data.
```

Execute the ra_status command to check the replication status of Replication Agent. If the returned state is admin, check the Replication Agent system log for errors, fix the errors, and issue resume again to check the status of Replication Agent.

Suspending a Replication Agent Instance

A Replication Agent instance can be suspended by issuing the suspend command. When a Replication Agent instance is suspended, it immediately stops replication processing by stopping the process of reading the primary database transaction log, and the LTI (Log Transfer Interface) component of Replication Agent stops sending LTI commands to Replication Server. Data in inbound and outbound queues of the Log Reader and Log Transfer Interface components of Replication Agent is also flushed without any further processing, and connections to Replication Server, RSSD/ERSSD, and the primary database are released. The Replication Agent instance state is changed from replicating to admin.

Log in to the Replication Agent instance with administrator user login and issue the suspend command:

suspend

Check the Replication Agent instance state with the `ra_status` command. It should change from replicating to admin:

ra_status

Creating Administrator User Login

You can log in to the Replication Agent instance using isql or sqladvantage (both require the interfaces file) or jConnect Isql or IsqlApp. Use the default login sa and null password and then create a new administrator login and password (see Table 16-2).

```
% isql -Usa -P -Smyrao
1> ra_set_login admin_user, admin_pwd
2> go
```

Where:

admin_user

New administrator login for new Replication Agent instance

admin_pwd

Password for admin_user (new administrator login)

Configuring Replication Agent Connection Configuration Parameters

Log in to the Replication Agent with the new administrator login and configure the Replication Agent connection parameters. The Replication Agent instance should be in admin state for setting up connection parameters. The Replication Agent instance is available for executing administrative commands in admin state, but it does not have any connections established to other replication system components.

Configuring Connection Parameters for Oracle SID (Primary Data Server)

```
% isql -Uadmin_user -Padmin_pwd -Smyrao
```

1. Check Replication Agent instance status:

```
1> ra_status
2> go
State   Action
------  ------------------------------
ADMIN   Waiting for operator command.
```

If the Replication Agent instance state is not admin, you can issue the suspend command to change it to admin state.

2. Configure the primary data server host name (see Table 16-6):

```
1> ra_config pds_host_name, ora_pds
2> go
Parameter Name  Parameter Type   Current Value  Pending Value  Default Value
  Legal Values  Category           Restart  Description
--------------- ---------------- -------------- -------------- -----------------
------------- ----------------- -------- ---------------------------------------
pds_host_name   String           ora_pds        NULL           <not_configured>
  N/A           PDS Connectivity           0 Name of the host on which PDB resides.
```

3. Configure the primary data server user login for the Replication Agent instance (see Table 16-6):

```
1> ra_config pds_username, ra_user
2> go
Parameter Name  Parameter Type   Current Value  Pending Value  Default Value
  Legal Values  Category           Restart  Description
--------------- ---------------- -------------- -------------- -----------------
------------- ----------------- -------- ---------------------------------------
pds_username    String           ra_user        NULL           <not_configured>
  N/A           PDS User                   0 User ID with DBA privileges for the primary
                                             database.
```

4. Configure the primary data server port number (see Table 16-6):

```
1> ra_config pds_port_number, 1521
2> go
Parameter Name  Parameter Type  Current Value  Pending Value  Default Value
  Legal Values    Category          Restart  Description
--------------- ---------------- --------------- --------------- ------------------
--------------- ----------------- -------- -----------------------------------------
pds_port_number int            1521           NULL          1111
  range: 1,65535  PDS Connectivity        0 Port number for the primary data server.
```

5. Configure the primary database name (see Table 16-6):

```
1> ra_config pds_database_name, orcl
2> go
Parameter Name    Parameter Type  Current Value  Pending Value  Default Value
  Legal Values    Category      Restart  Description
------------------ ---------------- --------------- --------------- ------------------
--------------- ------------- -------- -----------------------------------------
pds_database_name  String          orcl           NULL          <not_configured>
  N/A             PDS Database          0 Name of the primary database to connect to.
```

6. Configure the primary data server user login used by Replication Agent for logging in to the primary data server (see Table 16-6):

```
1> ra_config pds_username, ra_user
2> go
Parameter Name  Parameter Type  Current Value  Pending Value  Default Value
  Legal Values  Category  Restart  Description
--------------- ---------------- --------------- --------------- ------------------
------------- --------- -------- -----------------------------------------
pds_username    String          ra_user        NULL          <not_configured>
  N/A           PDS User              0 User ID with DBA privileges for the primary
                                        database.
```

7. Configure the password for the Replication Agent instance user for the primary data server (see Table 16-6):

```
1> ra_config pds_password, ra_user_ps
2> go
Parameter Name  Parameter Type  Current Value  Pending Value  Default Value
  Legal Values  Category  Restart  Description
--------------- --------------- -------------- -------------- -----------------
------------- --------- -------- ----------------------------------------------
pds_password    password        ******         NULL           <not_configured>
  N/A           PDS User         0 Password for the user name with DBA privileges.
```

8. Configure DDLuser for replicating DDL.

```
1> ra_config ddl_username, DDLuser
2> go
Parameter Name  Parameter Type  Current Value  Pending Value  Default Value
  Legal Values  Category         Restart  Description
--------------- --------------- -------------- -------------- -----------------
------------- --------------- -------- --------------------------------------
ddl_username    String          DDLuser        NULL           <not_configured>
  N/A           DDL Replication  0 The User ID used to apply DDL at the
                                   replicate database.
```

9. Configure password for DDLuser:

```
1> ra_config ddl_password, password
2> go
Parameter Name  Parameter Type  Current Value  Pending Value  Default Value
  Legal Values  Category         Restart  Description
--------------- --------------- -------------- -------------- -----------------
------------- --------------- -------- --------------------------------------
ddl_password    password        ******         NULL           <not_configured>
  N/A           DDL Replication  0 The Password for the User ID used to apply
                                   DDL at the replicate database.
```

10. Test the Replication Agent instance's connectivity to the primary data server:

```
    1> test_connection PDS
    2> go
    Type Connection
    ---- ----------
    PDS  succeeded
```

11. Configure the location for archived Oracle redo logs. If the pdb_include_archives Replication Agent configuration parameter is set to "true", then pdb_archive_path must be set to the valid directory path for the Oracle redo log before Replication Agent can be put into the replicating state.

```
1> ra_config pdb_archive_path, /work1/oradata/orcl
2> go
Parameter Name   Parameter Type  Current Value      Pending Value  Default Value
  Legal Values   Category        Restart Description
---------------- --------------- ------------------ -------------- ------------------
 -------------- --------------- -------- ---------------------------------------------
pdb_archive_path String          /work1/oradata/orcl NULL           <not_configured>
  N/A            LR archive logs      0 Specifies the directory path to search for
                                       archived redo log files.
```

New Replication Agent Configuration Parameters for Oracle RAC in Replication Agent 15.1

Replication Agent 15.1 supports Oracle ASM features. Archive log files and online redo log files managed by Oracle ASM can be used for replication. ASM disk groups can be changed with replication without any interference. Replication Agent recognizes when disks are added or dropped from the ASM disk group and automatically updates its device information for affected disk log devices. Multiple disk failures within the same disk group can be supported by Replication Agent without affecting replication. Replication Agent automatically discovers the ASM online redo log destinations. To configure Replication Agent to replicate redo logs, the following new Replication Agent configuration parameters should be configured:

```
asm_tns_filename=work1/oracle10g/network/admin/tnsnames.ora
asm_tns_connection=ASM
asm_username="sys as sysdba" (asm_username must have sysdba permissions)
asm_password=password
```

Replication Agent must be configured to manage archive log files. To do so, log in to Oracle SID and run the following SQL to determine the ASM disk group in Oracle:

```
select dest_id, destination from v$archive_dest;
```

Log in to Replication Agent instance with administrator login:

```
pdb_archive_path=+DATz
```

`pdb_archive_path` must be set to the ASM disk group preceded by the plus sign (+).

For Oracle RAC, in place of the `pds_hostname`, `pds_port_number`, and `pds_database` configuration parameters, you will need to set the new Replication Agent connectivity configuration parameters `pds_tns_filename` and `pds_tns_connection`:

```
pds_tns_filename=work1/oracle10g/network/admin/tnsnames.ora
pds_tns_connection=clusterdb
```

(Primary database connection in Oracle)

Note: In Replication Agent 15.1 you can set Replication Agent configuration parameters in the Oracle.rs resource file and create a Replication Agent instance after verifying the resource file:

```
ra_admin.sh  -vr oracle.rs      (resource file is validating)
```

To create a Replication Agent instance:

```
ra_admin.sh -r oracle.rs
```

```
start_instance=USE_DEFAULT
initialize_instance=USE_DEFAULT
```

When the Replication Agent parameters `start_instance` and `initialize_instance` are set to true, then Replication Agent is created, started, and automatically initialized.

Configuring Connection Parameters for the Replication Server

Log in to the Replication Agent with the new administrator login and configure the Replication Agent connection parameters. The Replication Agent instance should be in admin state for setting up connection parameters. The Replication Agent instance is available for executing administrative commands in admin state, but it does not have any connections established to other replication system components

```
% isql -Uadmin_user -Padmin_pwd -Smyrao
```

1. Check replication instance status:

```
1> ra_status
2> go
State   Action
------  ------------------------------
ADMIN   Waiting for operator command.
```

If the Replication Agent instance status is not admin, you can issue the suspend command to change it to admin state.

2. Configure the Replication Server host name for the Replication Agent instance (see Table 16-4):

```
1> ra_config rs_host_name, myrshost
2> go
Parameter Name   Parameter Type  Current Value         Pending Value  Default Value
   Legal Values  Category        Restart  Description
----------------  ---------------  --------------------  --------------  ------------------
   -------------  ---------------  --------  ------------------------------
rs_host_name     String           myrshost              NULL           <not_configured>
   N/A           RS Connectivity          0 Replication Server host name.
```

3. Configure the Replication Server port number for the Replication Agent instance (see Table 16-4):

```
1> ra_config rs_port_number, 7221
2> go
Parameter Name  Parameter Type  Current Value      Pending Value  Default Value
  Legal Values    Category          Restart  Description
---------------- --------------- -------------------- -------------- ------------------
---------------- --------------- -------- --------------------------------
rs_port_number   int               7221               NULL           1111
  range: 1,65535  RS Connectivity     0 Replication Server port number.
```

4. Configure the Replication Server character set for the Replication Agent instance (see Table 16-4). The character set should be Replication Server's default character set and listed in the configuration file of Replication Server.

```
1> ra_config rs_charset, iso_1
2> go
Parameter Name  Parameter Type  Current Value      Pending Value  Default Value
  Legal Values    Category          Restart  Description
---------------- --------------- -------------------- -------------- ------------------
---------------- --------------- -------- --------------------------------
rs_charset       String            iso_1              NULL           NULL
  N/A             RS Connectivity     0 The character set name to use to connect
                                        to Replication Server. If not set, the
                                        default is the ASCII_7 charset.
```

5. Configure the Replication Server user name for the Replication Agent instance (see Table 16-4):

```
1> ra_config rs_username, ra_rs_user
2> go
Parameter Name  Parameter Type  Current Value  Pending Value  Default Value
  Legal Values  Category  Restart  Description
---------------- --------------- -------------- -------------- ------------------
-------------- --------- -------- ------------------------------------
rs_username      String            ra_rs_user     NULL           <not_configured>
  N/A             RS User             0 Replication Server login user name.
```

6. Configure the password for the Replication Server user login for the Replication Agent instance (see Table 16-4):

```
1> ra_config rs_password, ra_rs_user_ps
2> go
Parameter Name   Parameter Type  Current Value  Pending Value  Default Value
  Legal Values   Category  Restart  Description
---------------- ---------------- -------------- -------------- ------------------
-------------- ---------- -------- ------------------------------------
rs_password      password        ******         NULL           <not_configured>
  N/A            RS User         0 Replication Server login password.
```

7. Configure the primary data server name for the Replication Server primary database connection. The primary data server name is used by the Replication Agent instance in the LTL connect source command (see Table 16-3).

```
1> ra_config rs_source_ds, myrao
2> go
Parameter Name   Parameter Type  Current Value  Pending Value  Default Value
  Legal Values   Category  Restart  Description
---------------- ---------------- -------------- -------------- ------------------
-------------- ---------- -------- ------------------------------------
rs_source_ds     String          myrao          NULL           <not_configured>
  N/A            RS Source       0 The primary database server name used in the
                                   Replication Server connection definition.
```

8. Configure the primary database name for the Replication Server primary database connection. The primary database name is used by the Replication Agent instance in the LTL connect source command (see Table 16-3).

```
1> ra_config rs_source_db, orcl
2> go
Parameter Name   Parameter Type  Current Value  Pending Value  Default Value
  Legal Values   Category  Restart  Description
---------------- ---------------- -------------- -------------- -----------------
-------------- ---------- -------- ------------------------------------------------
rs_source_db     String          orcl           NULL           <not_configured>
  N/A            RS Source       0 The primary database name used in the Replication
                                   Server connection definition.
```

Configuring Replication Agent Instance Connection Parameters for the RSSD (or ERSSD)

Log in to the Replication Agent with the new administrator login and configure the Replication Agent connection parameters. The Replication Agent instance should be in admin state for setting up connection parameters. The Replication Agent instance is available for executing administrative commands in admin state, but it does not have any connections established to other replication system components.

```
% isql -Uadmin_user -Padmin_pwd -Smyrao
```

1. Check replication instance status:

    ```
    1> ra_status
    2> go
    State  Action
    ------ -----------------------------
    ADMIN  Waiting for operator command.
    ```

    If the Replication Agent instance status is not admin, you can issue the suspend command to change it to admin state.

2. Configure the host name of the RSSD/ERSSD database on which Adaptive Server Enterprise resides (see Table 16-5):

```
1> ra_config rssd_host_name, ase_host
2> go
```

| Parameter Name | Parameter Type | Current Value | Pending Value | Default Value |
Legal Values	Category	Restart	Description	
-------------	-------------------	--------	-----------------------------------	
rssd_host_name	String	ase_host	NULL	<not_configured>
N/A	RSSD Connectivity	0	Replication Server System Database host name.	

3. Configure the port number for the ERSSD or Adaptive Server Enterprise on which the RSSD database resides (see Table 16-5):

```
1> ra_config rssd_port_number, 7100
2> go
Parameter Name    Parameter Type  Current Value  Pending Value  Default Value
  Legal Values    Category          Restart  Description
----------------- --------------- -------------- -------------- -----------------
----------------- --------------- -------- ------------------------------------
rssd_port_number  int              7100            NULL           1111
  range: 1,65535  RSSD Connectivity      0 Replication Server System Database
                                          port number.
```

4. Configure the RSSD/ERSSD database name (see Table 16-5):

```
1> ra_config rssd_database_name, prs_RSSD
2> go
Parameter Name      Parameter Type  Current Value  Pending Value  Default Value
  Legal Values  Category            Restart  Description
------------------- --------------- -------------- -------------- -----------------
------------- ----------------- -------- ------------------------------------------
rssd_database_name  String          prs_RSSD        NULL           <not_configured>
  N/A           RSSD Connectivity      0 Replication Server System Database name.
```

5. Configure the RSSD/ERSSD user login for the Replication Agent instance (see Table 16-5):

```
1> ra_config rssd_username, ra_rssd_user
2> go
Parameter Name    Parameter Type  Current Value  Pending Value  Default Value
  Legal Values  Category    Restart  Description
---------------- --------------- -------------- -------------- -----------------
------------- ---------- -------- -----------------------------------------------------
rssd_username    String          ra_rssd_user    NULL           <not_configured>
  N/A           RSSD User           0 Replication Server System Database login user name.
```

6. Configure the password for RSSD/ERSSD user login for the Replication Agent instance (see Table 16-5):

```
1> ra_config rssd_password, ra_rssd_user_ps
2> go
Parameter Name   Parameter Type  Current Value  Pending Value  Default Value
  Legal Values  Category   Restart  Description
---------------- ---------------- --------------- -------------- -----------------
------------- ---------- -------- -------------------------------------------------
rssd_password    password       ******         NULL           <not_configured>
  N/A            RSSD User       0 Replication Server System Database login password.
```

7. After setting connection parameters for the primary Replication Server and RSSD database, test connectivity between Replication Agent, Replication Server, and the RSSD database:

```
1> test_connection RS
2> go
Type Connection
---- ----------
RS   succeeded
```

The test_connection command should only be executed when the Replication Agent instance is in admin state. When test_connection is executed without any parameters, it checks network connectivity between the Replication Agent instance, primary database, Replication Server, and RSSD database. If the use_rssd Replication Agent configuration parameter is set to "true", then test_connection tests connectivity to the RSSD database and Replication Server.

```
1> test connection
2> go
Type Connection
---- ----------
PDS  succeeded
RS   succeeded
```

The test_connection command can fail with a failure message if any of the Replication Agent connection configuration parameters (data server name, port number, user login, user login password, host name) have incorrect values. The connection to the data server can also fail due to network issues or the data server being down. The test_connection command does not validate Replication Agent user permissions in the primary database; it only validates the user login name and password. All connection failure messages are logged in the Replication Agent instance log ($SYBASE/ RAX-15_0/*instance*/log/*instance*.log). *instance*.log contains Informational (I), Warning (W), Trace (T), and Error (E) messages.

Replication Agent Transaction Log Management

The native Oracle log is used by Replication Agent for Oracle to capture replicated transactions. It creates transaction log objects in the primary database, which facilitate stored procedure replication. No routine maintenance is required for these database objects. After processing all the replicated log records in redo and archive logs, Replication Agent for Oracle issues the archive log command to the Oracle primary database.

Primary database backup utilities should be used to back up Replication Agent instance transaction log objects in the primary database.

Removing the Replication Agent Transaction Log

To remove the Replication Agent transaction log, the Replication Agent instance must be up and running in admin state. The Replication Agent instance can be determined by executing the ra_status command.

Log in to the Replication Agent instance as administrator user login and execute the pds_xlog command to determine which transaction log is associated with this Replication Agent instance.

```
pdb_xlog
```

This command will check whether the primary database already has a transaction log associated with the Replication Agent instance. If no transaction log exists, this command will return no information about transaction log objects and continues to create a transaction log in the primary database. `pdb_xlog` verifies transaction log objects based on the `pdb_xlog_prefix` Replication Agent configuration parameter. If the value of `pdb_xlog_prefix` is changed after the transaction log is created, the `pdb_xlog` command will not find the transaction log objects created previously. If the primary database has a Replication Agent transaction log, the `pdb_xlog` command returns a list of transaction log objects.

Replication for all marked tables and stored procedures should be disabled, and tables and stored procedures should be unmarked for replication.

1. Execute the `pdb_setreptable` command with the `all` and `disable` keywords to disable replication for all marked tables in the primary database:

   ```
   pdb_setreptable all, disable
   ```

2. Execute the `pdb_setrepproc` command with the `all` and `disable` keywords to disable replication for all marked stored procedures in the primary database:

   ```
   pdb_setrepproc all, disable
   ```

3. Execute the `pdb_setreptable` command with the `all` and `unmark` keywords to remove replication for all marked tables in the primary database:

   ```
   pdb_setreptable all, unmark
   ```

The `pdb_setreptable` command may return an error message if there are any pending transactions for trigger-based tables. In that case, use the `force` keyword to remove replication for marked tables:

   ```
   pdb_setreptable all, unmark, force
   ```

4. Execute the `pdb_setrepproc` command with the `all` and `unmark` keywords to remove replication for all marked stored procedures in the primary database:

    ```
    pdb_setrepproc all, unmark
    ```

    The `pdb_setrepproc` command may return an error message if there are any pending transactions for trigger-based stored procedures. In that case, use the `force` keyword to remove replication for all marked stored procedures:

    ```
    pdb_setrepproc all, unmark, force
    ```

5. Execute the `pdb_xlog` command with the `remove` keyword to remove the Replication Agent transaction log. If the Replication Agent transaction log doesn't exist, this command will fail with an error message.

    ```
    pdb_xlog remove
    ```

When the `pdb_auto_run_scripts` Replication Agent configuration parameter is set to "false", the `pdb_xlog remove` command just builds the script so you can execute this script manually to remove the Replication Agent transaction log. If the Replication Agent transaction log was successfully removed by the log removal script, the removal script is stored in the $SYBASE/ RAX-15_0/*instance_name*/scripts/xlog/installed directory.

If the Replication Agent transaction log removal script does not execute successfully, the log removal script is stored in $SYBASE/RAX-15_0/*instance_name*/scripts/xlog directory. Even if you check the Replication Agent instance log and the primary database log for the errors, fix them, and execute the log removal script to remove the transaction log, it will immediately fail because some of the transaction log components are missing. To avoid this issue, the `pdb_xlog` command should be executed with the `remove` and `force` keywords.

```
pdb_xlog remove, force
```

Truncating the Replication Agent Transaction Log

You can truncate the Replication Agent transaction log manually or enable automatic log truncation. The transaction log can be truncated manually at any time, even if automatic log truncation is enabled. When the Replication Agent log is truncated, its truncation point is determined by the most recent LTM locater received from the primary Replication Server. By default, automatic truncation is enabled.

When the Replication Agent configuration parameter `pdb_include_archives` is set to "true" and `pdb_remove_archives` is set to "false", then online or archived transaction log truncation is not done by Replication Agent. When the Replication Agent configuration parameters `pdb_include_archives` and `pdb_remove_archives` are set to "true", then archived log records that have already been processed are deleted from the location defined by `pdb_archive_path`. Sybase recommends configuring Replication Agent to remove archive log files only if an additional archive log directory is used.

When the Replication Agent configuration parameter `pdb_include_archives` is set to "false", online redo transaction log truncation (both automatic and manual) is performed by Replication Agent by issuing the `alter system` command with archive log sequence number. This command is only issued by Replication Agent when the redo log file whose contents it is processing has current status.

Automatic Truncation

A Replication Agent instance can be configured for automatic log truncation using `locater_update` or at a specified time interval:

▶ Log in to the Replication Agent instance as administrator user login and execute `ra_config` to set the truncation type to `locater_update`. Replication Agent will truncate the log whenever it receives a new locater value from the primary Replication Server.

```
1> ra_config truncation_type, locator_update
2> go
Parameter Name    Parameter Type  Current Value  Pending Value Default Value
  Legal Values                             Category          Restart
    Description
---------------- ---------------- --------------- -------------- ----------------
 ---------------------------------------- ---------------- --------
  -------------------------------------------------
truncation_type  String          LOCATOR_UPDATE NULL          LOCATOR_UPDATE
   list: COMMAND,INTERVAL,LOCATOR_UPDATE  LR Log Truncator      0
   Determines which Log Truncation algorithm to use.
```

▶ Log in to the Replication Agent instance as administrator user
login and execute ra_config to set the truncation type to a
time interval in seconds. The truncation_interval value can
be from 0 to 720 minutes.

```
ra_config truncation_type, interval
ra_config truncation_interval, ss
```

```
1> ra_config truncation_interval, 60
2> go
Parameter Name       Parameter Type  Current Value  Pending Value Default Value
  Legal Values  Category          Restart  Description
-------------------- ---------------- -------------- -------------- -----------------
 ------------- ------------------ -------- -------------------------------------------
truncation_interval  int             60             NULL           0
   range: 0,720  LR Log Truncator        0 Determines the frequency (minutes), to
                                           perform Transaction Log Truncation.
                                           Valid if Interval Truncator is used.
```

ss is the number of seconds between automatic transaction
log truncations.

To disable automatic log truncation, log in to the Replication Agent instance with administrator login and set
truncation_interval to 0.

```
ra_config truncation_type, interval
ra_config truncation_interval, 0
```

```
1> ra_config truncation_interval, 0
2> go
```

Parameter Name	Parameter Type	Current Value	Pending Value	Default Value
Legal Values	Category	Restart	Description	
truncation_interval	int	0	NULL	0
range: 0,720	LR Log Truncator		0 Determines the frequency (minutes), to perform Transaction Log Truncation. Valid if Interval Truncator is used.	

Manual Truncation

The Replication Agent instance transaction log should be truncated manually periodically if automatic truncation is disabled.

1. Log in to the Replication Agent instance with administrator login and execute the ra_statistics command:

    ```
    ra_statistics
    ```

2. Execute the pdb_truncate_xlog command. Since this command is asynchronous, no success or failure message is returned, unless it encounters some immediate error.

    ```
    1> pdb_truncate_xlog
    2> go
    Msg 0, Level 20, State 0:
    Server 'myrao', Procedure 'pdb_truncate_xlog', Line 1:
    successful
    (0 rows affected)
    ```

3. Execute the ra_statistics command again and compare the truncated value:

    ```
    ra_statistics
    ```

624

Marking Objects for Replication in the Primary Database

Tables, stored procedures, and sequences must be marked and enabled for replication. Stored procedure replication is not available for the DB2 Universal database. Large-object column (LOB) and DDL must be marked and enabled for replication. DDL replication is only available for Oracle.

Enabling and Disabling Replication for User Objects

To check if an object is enabled and marked for replication:

```
1> pdb_setreptable rax_test
2> go
Owner Name      Marked    Enabled   Replicate Send Owner Shadow Table
   Shadow Row Proc  Blob Shadow Table  Blob Row Proc
----- --------- --------- --------- --------- ---------- ------------
     ---------------- ------------------ -------------
SYS   RAX_TEST unmarked  disabled            disabled   N/A
   N/A              N/A                N/A
```

where rax_test is the name of the primary table.

```
1> pdb_setreptable rax_test, mark
2> go
Msg 0, Level 20, State 0:
Server 'myrao', Procedure 'pdb_setreptable rax_test,mark', Line 1:
successful
(0 rows affected)
1> pdb_setreptable rax_test
2> go
Owner Name      Marked Enabled Replicate     Send Owner Shadow Table
   Shadow Row Proc  Blob Shadow Table  Blob Row Proc
----- --------- ------- -------- ------------- ---------- ------------
     ---------------- ------------------ -------------
SYS   RAX_TEST marked  enabled SYS.RAX_TEST  disabled   N/A
   N/A              N/A                N/A
(1 row affected)
```

pdb_setreptable all, {mark|enable} can be used to mark or enable all tables for replication at once. You can also mark a table for replication with the owner clause, so that Replication Agent can pass the owner name along with the object name in the LTL.

```
pdb_setreptable rax_test, mark, owner
```

If the Replication Agent configuration parameter pdb_dflt_object_repl is set to "true", then the table is ready for replication after marking it with pdb_setreptable. If pdb_dflt_object_repl is set to "false", then replication must be enabled by executing the following:

```
pdb_setreptable object_name, enable
```

After the objects are marked and enabled for replication, you can begin replicating transactions that affect data in these objects by executing the resume command.

Enabling and Disabling DDL Replication

For Oracle only, DDL replication can be enabled by executing the pdb_setrepddl command. To replicate DDL, you will need to create a database replication definition with the replicate ddl clause set in the replication definition (see Chapter 13).

```
1> pdb_setrepddl enable
2> go
Status

enabled
```

DDL replication can be disabled by executing:

```
pdb_setrepddl disable
```

DDL replication is disabled by default.

Enabling and Disabling Stored Procedure Replication

pdb_setrepproc can be executed for marking or unmarking stored procedures for replication. Before marking or unmarking stored procedures for replication in Oracle, you must disable DDL replication and re-enable it after marking or unmarking stored procedure replication.

To mark, unmark, enable, or disable replication for stored procedures:

```
pdb_setrepproc proc_name, {mark | unmark[, force] |enable | disable}
```

To unmark, enable, or disable replication for all marked stored procedures:

```
pdb_setrepproc all, {unmark[, force] | enable | disable}
```

To get the marking status of stored procedure replication:

```
pdb_setrepproc [proc_name | mark | unmark | enable | disable]
```

Enabling and Disabling Sequence Replication

pdb_setrepseq can be used to mark, unmark, enable, or disable replication for user sequences in the primary database. This command is only applicable to Oracle databases.

To get the replication marking status of a sequence:

```
pdb_setrepseq [sequence_name | mark | unmark | enable | disable]
```

To unmark, enable, or disable the replication status of marked sequences:

```
pdb_setrepseq all, {unmark [, force] | enable | disable}
```

To mark, unmark, enable, or disable the replication status of a specified user sequence:

```
pdb_setrepseq sequence_name, {mark | unmark [, force] | enable | disable}
```

To mark a specified sequence for replication with a replicated name (sequence name at replicate, which is different from sequence name at primary):

```
pdb_setrepseq sequence_name, rep_name, mark
```

pdb_setrepcol can be used to enable or disable replication for LOB (large columns) within marked tables. If the pdb_dflt_column_repl Replication Agent configuration parameter is set to "true", then LOB column replication is automatically enabled when a table is marked for replication with pdb_setreptable. The default of pdb_dflt_column_repl is "false".

To check the replication status of all columns in all tables or all columns in a specified table:

```
pdb_setrepcol [table_name | enable | disable]
```

To check the replication status for a specific column in a specified table:

```
pdb_setrepcol table_name, col_name
```

To enable or disable replication of all LOB columns in all marked tables:

```
pdb_setrepcol all, {enable | disable [, force]}
```

To enable or disable replication of a specified LOB column in a specified table:

```
pdb_setrepcol table_name, col_name, {enable | disable [, force]}
```

After the objects are marked and enabled for replication, you can begin replicating transactions that affect data in these objects by executing the resume command.

To start replication, log in to the Replication Agent instance with administrator login and use resume to start replication.

```
1> resume
2> go
State          Action
------------   -------------------------
REPLICATING    Ready to replicate data.
```

Execute the `ra_status` command to verify that the Replication Agent instance is in the replicating state.

Oracle Database Specific Issues

In this section we will address a number of issues specific to the Oracle database that are necessary to understand for successful replication.

Character Case of Database Object Names

In Oracle, by default all database object names are stored in uppercase. Primary database object names must be sent to the primary Replication Server in the same character case as they are specified in the replication definition; otherwise, replication will fail because the object name couldn't be found. The Replication Agent configuration parameter `ltl_character_case` can be configured to control character case in the LTL it sends to the primary Replication Server. The `ltl_character_case` configuration parameter can be set to one of these values:

▶ upper: All database object names are delivered to the primary Replication Server in uppercase, regardless of the character case in which they are stored in the primary database.

▶ asis: asis is the default value for the `ltl_character_case` configuration parameter. All database object names are delivered to the primary Replication Server in the same character case in which they are stored in the primary database.

▶ lower: All database object names are delivered to the primary Replication Server in lowercase regardless of the character case in which they are stored in the primary database.

To set ltl_character_case to lowercase:

```
1> ra_config ltl_character_case, lower
2> go
Parameter Name      Parameter Type  Current Value  Pending Value  Default Value
  Legal Values             Category       Restart  Description
------------------- --------------- -------------- -------------- -----------------
  ----------------------- --------------- --------
  ----------------------------------------------------------------------------------
ltl_character_case  String             lower          NULL           asis
  list: asis,lower,upper  LTL Formatting        0
    Configures the LTI to generate object and column/parameter names in LTL using the
    specified character case: asis, upper, lower.
```

Datatype Compatibility Issues

Oracle transactions are processed by Replication Agent for Oracle and passed to the primary Replication Server. If Oracle or another non-Sybase primary table has columns with Sybase unsupported datatypes, data can be replicated by creating a replication definition with a compatible Sybase supported datatype.

The following table lists Oracle datatypes and the equivalent in Sybase.

Table 16-8: Oracle datatype conversion to Sybase datatype

Oracle Datatype	Sybase Datatype	Oracle Datatype Length/Range	Sybase Datatype Length/ Range	Comments
CHAR	char	255 bytes	32 K	
VARCHAR2	varchar	2000 bytes	32 K	
NCHAR	char/unichar	255 bytes, multibyte characters	32 K	
NVARCHAR2	varchar/ univarchar	2000 bytes, variable-length multibyte characters	32 K	

Oracle Datatype	Sybase Datatype	Oracle Datatype Length/Range	Sybase Datatype Length/Range	Comments
NUMBER(p,s)	number, decimal, int, float, real, rs_oracle_decimal	21 bytes, variable-length numeric data	Number and decimal: 2 to 17 bytes, integer: 4 bytes, float: 4 to 8 bytes, real: 4 bytes	Decimal and number datatypes are truncated if the range is greater than -10^{38} to $10^{38}-1$. Integer datatypes are truncated if the range is greater than 2,147,483,647 to $-2,147,483,648\text{-}1$ If the float datatype range is exceeded, it is converted to scientific notation. Oracle precision: 1 to 38 digits, default: 18 digits. Oracle scale: 84 to 127, default: 0
DATE	datetime or rs_oracle_datatype	8 fixed-length bytes	8 bytes	Sybase Replication Server Date datatype support: January 1, 1753 to December 31, 9999 Oracle Date datatype support: January 1, 4712 BC to December 31, 4712 AD If the Replication Agent configuration parameter pdb_convert_datetime is set to "true", then Sybase datetime is used and the replicate datetime format is YYYYMMDD HH:MM:SS.sss. If the pdb_convert_datetime parameter is set to "false", then rs_oracle_datatype is used and the replicate datetime format is MM/DD/YYYY HH:MI:SS

Oracle Datatype	Sybase Datatype	Oracle Datatype Length/Range	Sybase Datatype Length/ Range	Comments
TIMESTAMP(n)	Datetime or rs_oracle_ timestamp9	21 to 31 variable-length bytes	8 bytes	Sybase Replication Server Date datatype support: January 1, 1753 to December 31, 9999 Oracle Date datatype support: January 1, 4712 BC to December 31, 4712 AD If the Replication Agent configuration parameter pdb_convert_datetime is set to "true", then the Sybase datatype datetime is used. If pdb_convert_datetime is set to "false", then the Sybase datatype rs_oracle_ timestamp9 is used.
TIMESTAMP(n) with (LOCAL) TIME ZONE	rs_oracle_ timestamptz	variable-length		When the timestamp with local time zone datatype is replicated, the timestamp information is not replicated but is used to resolve to the local time zone, and that resolved value is replicated. For example, if in the primary Oracle database the timestamp with time zone value is "-02-Feb-08 09:00:00:000000AM -8:00" and the local time zone is -6:00, then the difference between the Oracle recorded time zone of -8:00 and the local time zone of -6:00 will be adjusted and resolved, and the value "02-Feb-08 11:00:00:000000" will be replicated.
INTERVAL YEAR(n) TO MONTH	rs_oracle_ interval	variable-length		
INTERVAL DAY(n) TO SECOND(n)	rs_oracle_ interval	variable-length		
BLOB	image	4 GB binary variable-length	2 GB	
CLOB	text	4 GB character variable-length	2 GB	

Oracle Datatype	Sybase Datatype	Oracle Datatype Length/Range	Sybase Datatype Length/ Range	Comments
NCLOB	unitext/text	4 GB multibyte variable-length	2 GB	Prior to Replication Server 15.x, NCLOB datatype maps to Sybase text datatype. Replication Server 15.x NCLOB datatype maps to unitext.
BFILE	image	4 GB, locater pointing to large binary file	2 GB	
LONG	text	2 GB character variable-length		
LONG RAW	image	2 GB binary variable-length		
RAW	rs_oracle_ binary	2000 bytes binary variable-length		
UDD object type	rs_rs_char_raw	character variable-length		Details are in the "Oracle User-Defined Datatypes" section later in this chapter.
BINARY_FLOAT	rs_oracle_float	5 bytes, 32-bit single-precision floating-point number data-type	4 to 8 bytes depending on precision	Maximum positive finite: 3.40262E+38F Minimum positive finite: 1.17549E-38F
BINARY_ DOUBLE	double	9 bytes, 64-bit single-precision floating-point number datatype	8 bytes	Maximum positive finite: 1.79769313486231E+308 Minimum positive finite: 2.22507485850720-308
MLSLABEL		5 bytes binary variable-length OS label		
ROWID	rs_oracle_ rowid	6 bytes binary data representing row addresses	32 K	

Unsigned integer datatypes are supported by Replication Server 15.x and above. These unsigned datatypes can be specified in the replication definitions. For Replication Server versions prior to 15.x, you cannot use unsigned integer datatypes; instead you must use the following datatypes in replication definitions.

633

Table 16-9: Unsigned integer datatype mapping

Replication Server 15.x Unsigned Datatype	Replication Definition Datatype
Unsigned int	Numeric(10)
Unsigned bigint	Numeric(20)
Unsigned tinyint	tinyint
Unsigned smallint	int

The following Oracle datatypes are unsupported:

▶ Oracle NESTED TABLE type

▶ Oracle VARRAY type

▶ Oracle REF type

▶ Oracle-supplied types

Oracle Large Object (LOB) Datatype Support

In Oracle, Large Object datatypes can be in character or binary formats. LONG, CLOB, and NCLOB are character LOB datatypes, and LONG RAW, BLOB, and BFILE are binary LOB datatypes. Data in all LOB datatypes except for BFILE is stored in the database. The content of LOB data is recorded in redo logs and read by Replication Agent and is submitted for replication. Data in BFILE format is stored outside the Oracle database, so its contents are not logged in the redo log. For replicating data in BFILE format, Replication Agent connects to the primary Oracle database and issues a query to select BFILE format data. Since BFILE data is selected independent of other data in the redo logs it can be temporarily out of sync if the BFILE contents are changed multiple times. Replication Agent can only replicate the last change to the BFILE.

The BLOB, CLOB, and NCLOB datatypes can be defined to be stored with "disable storage in row" characteristics. "Disable storage in row" characteristics indicate that LOB data should always be recorded in redo logs separate from the rest of the data in the row to which LOB data belongs, and updates to LOB data are handled in a special way. Unlike non-LOB data, changes to the LOB data row are not logged in the redo logs; only changes to the index holding LOB data are recorded in the redo logs.

Example:

```
update Oratab set CLOBCOL to 'clob data' where nonlobcol1=1
```

In this example, the value for nonlobcol1 in the where clause is not logged in the redo logs, as there is not enough information for Replication Agent for Oracle to build a correct where clause that can be used to apply changes at the replicate. To get around this issue, Replication Agent for Oracle requires that modification to the LOB column defined with "disable storage in row" must be immediately preceded or followed by an insert or update to the same row in the table to which the LOB column belongs, which helps Replication Agent in building a correct where clause to support replication.

Example:

```
begin
update Oratab set CLOBCOL to 'clob data' where nonlobcol1=1 ;
update Oratab set updated = sysdate() where nonlobcol1=1 ;
commit
```

or

```
begin
update Oratab set updated = sysdate() where nonlobcol1=1 ;
update Oratab set CLOBCOL to 'clob data' where nonlobcol1=1 ;
commit
```

To determine which LOB columns have been defined with "disable storage in row" characteristics, execute the following query in the primary database:

```
select owner, table_name, column_name from db_lobs where in_row = 'NO';
```

Oracle User-Defined Datatypes

Oracle built-in datatypes and other user-defined datatypes are used by user-defined datatypes to model the structure and behavior of Oracle data in applications. Replication of Oracle user-defined object types is supported by Replication Agent for Oracle. To replicate the Oracle user-defined datatype, you must specify the rs_rs_char_raw datatype in the replication definition. To install this datatype in the RSSD database, execute the hds_oracle_new_udds.sql script located in $SYBASE/RAX_ *release_dir*/scripts in the RSSD database. This script will install user-defined datatypes in the RSSD..rs_datatypes table.

```
isql -Usa -P -Spds -Dpds_RSSD -i /work1/rel150_rs_options/RAX-15_0/
scripts/hds_oracle_new_udds.sql
```

Replication Server must be restarted after adding user-defined datatypes.

To test the rs_rs_char_raw datatype, log in to Replication Server and execute the admin translate command:

```
1> admin translate, 'testing new user-defined datatype', 'char(50)'
,'rs_rs_char_raw'
2> go
Delimiter Prefix  Translated Value                    Delimiter Postfix
----------------  ----------------------------------  -----------------
NULL              testing new user-defined datatype   NULL
```

Excerpt from hds_oracle_new_udds.sql:

```
NOTE: rs_oracle_timestamp9 in hds_oracle_new_udds.sql has issue in accept-
ing 4 digit year with loss of precision. Below is modified rs_oracle_
timestamp9 datatype to accept 4 digit year to prevent loss of precision


/*
 ****************************************************************
 *
 * Name: rs_oracle_timestamptz
 * ID # 0x00010211
 *
 * Defines an Oracle TIMESTAMP WITH TIME ZONE.
 * Assuming the maximum length of a time zone name is 35, the maximum
 * length of a timestamp with time zone would be 60.
 * '2005-01-01 11:00:00.000000 ' + 'up to 28 char name'
 *
 */
delete from rs_datatype where dtid = 0x0000000000010211
insert into rs_datatype
```

```
values(
    0,                          /* primary rep server ID */
    0x0000000001000008,         /* classid */
    'rs_oracle_timestamptz',    /* name */
    0x0000000000010211,         /* datatype id */
    0x00,                       /* base_dtid - char*/
    60,                         /* length */
    0,                          /* status */
    4,                          /* length_err_act - truncate right */
    'CHAR',                     /* mask */
    0,                          /* scale */
    31,                         /* default_len */
    '01-JAN-00 12.00.00.000000000 AM',    /* default_val */
    10,                         /* delim_pre_len */
    'TIMESTAMP''',              /* delim_pre */
    1,                          /* delim_post_len */
    '''',                       /* delim_post */
    0,                          /* min_boundary_len */
    '',                         /* min_boundary */
    1,                          /* min_boundary_err_act */
    0,                          /* max_boundary_len */
    '',                         /* max_boundary */
    1,                          /* max_boundary_err_act */
    0                           /* rowtype */
)

go


/*
************************************************************************
* Name: rs_rs_char_raw
* ID # 0x0000011d
*
* Defines a character field but does not wrap it with delimiters.
* Used when supplying a function call to a column value (wrapping the
* value with delimiters would result in the function name, instead of
* the function execution, being replicated).
*
* admin translate, 'MAX(col1)', 'char(255)', 'rs_rs_char_raw'
*
************************************************************************
*/
delete from rs_datatype where dtid =   0x000000000000011d
```

```
        insert into rs_datatype
        values(
            0,                          /* prsid */
            0x0000000001000013,         /* classid */
            'rs_rs_char_raw',           /* name */
            0x000000000000011d,         /* dtid */
            0,                          /* base_coltype */
            255,                        /* length */
            0,                          /* status */
            1,                          /* length_err_act */
            'CHAR',                     /* mask */
            0,                          /* scale */
            0,                          /* default_len */
            '',                         /* default_val */
            0,                          /*-delim_pre_len-*/
            '',                         /* delim_pre */
            0,                          /*-delim_post_len-*/
            '',                         /* delim_post */
            0,                          /* min_boundary_len */
            '',                         /* min_boundary */
            3,                          /* min_boundary_err_act */
            0,                          /* max_boundary_len */
            '',                         /* max_boundary */
            4,                          /* max_boundary_err_act */
            0                           /* rowtype */
        )
        go


        /*
        **************************************************************************
        * Name: rs_oracle_binary
        * ID # 0x00010202
        *
        * Maps to the Oracle RAW (binary) datatype.
        * The hexadecimal format for Oracle does not contain a delimiter
        * (No '0x' in front of binary values as ASE does).
        * Changed to wrap the value in HEX_TO_RAW function
        *
        * admin translate, '696e626c6f62', 'char(40)', rs_oracle_binary
        *
        **************************************************************************
        */
        delete from rs_datatype where dtid =   0x0000000000010202
```

```
insert into rs_datatype
values(
    0,                          /* primary rep server ID */
    0x0000000001000008,         /* classid */
    'rs_oracle_binary',         /* name */
    0x0000000000010202,         /* datatype id */
    0x01,                       /* base_dtid - binary */
    0,                          /* length */
    0,                          /* status */
    4,                          /* length_err_act - truncate right */
    'CHAR',                     /* mask */
    0,                          /* scale */
    0,                          /* default_len */
    0x0,                        /* default_val */
    10,                         /* delim_pre_len */
    'HEXTORAW(''',              /* delim_pre */
    2,                          /* delim_post_len */
    ''')',                      /* delim_post */
    0,                          /* min_boundary_len */
    '',                         /* min_boundary */
    2,                          /* min_boundary_err_act */
    0,                          /* max_boundary_len */
    0x0,                        /* max_boundary */
    2,                          /* max_boundary_err_act */
    0                           /* rowtype */
)
go


/*
*************************************************************************
* Name: rs_oracle_rowid
* ID # 0x00010212
*
* Defines an Oracle rowid, replicated as an 18 bytes base 64 representation
* admin translate, 'CDFGHCBFED', 'char(40)', rs_oracle_rowid
*
*************************************************************************/
delete from rs_datatype where dtid =  0x0000000000010212
insert into rs_datatype
values(
    0,                          /* primary rep server ID */
    0x0000000001000008,         /* classid */
    'rs_oracle_rowid',          /* name */
```

```
        0x0000000000010212,        /* datatype id */
        0x00,                      /* base_dtid - char*/
        20,                        /* length */
        0,                         /* status */
        4,                         /* length_err_act - truncate right */
        'CHAR',                    /* mask */
        0,                         /* scale */
        0,                         /* default_len */
        0x0,                       /* default_val */
        1,                         /* delim_pre_len */
        '''',                      /* delim_pre */
        1,                         /* delim_post_len */
        '''',                      /* delim_post */
        0,                         /* min_boundary_len */
        '',                        /* min_boundary */
        1,                         /* min_boundary_err_act */
        0,                         /* max_boundary_len */
        '',                        /* max_boundary */
        1,                         /* max_boundary_err_act */
        0                          /* rowtype */
)

go


/*
************************************************************************
* Name: rs_oracle_interval
* ID # 0x00010213
*
* Defines an Oracle interval type.  Supports both month to day and
* day to second types.
* admin translate, '+0000000005 01:01:01.000000000 ', 'char(40)',
* rs_oracle_interval
*
************************************************************************
*/
delete from rs_datatype where dtid =  0x0000000000010213
insert into rs_datatype
values(
    0,                         /* primary rep server ID */
    0x0000000001000008,        /* classid */
    'rs_oracle_interval',      /* name */
    0x0000000000010213,        /* datatype id */
```

```
    0x00,                         /* base_dtid - char*/
    40,                           /* length */
    0,                            /* status */
    4,                            /* length_err_act - truncate right */
    'CHAR',                       /* mask */
    0,                            /* scale */
    0,                            /* default_len */
    0x0,                          /* default_val */
    1,                            /* delim_pre_len */
    '''',                         /* delim_pre */
    1,                            /* delim_post_len */
    '''',                         /* delim_post */
    0,                            /* min_boundary_len */
    '',                           /* min_boundary */
    1,                            /* min_boundary_err_act */
    0,                            /* max_boundary_len */
    '',                           /* max_boundary */
    1,                            /* max_boundary_err_act */
    0                             /* rowtype */
)

go


/*
*************************************************************************
* Name: rs_oracle_timestamp9
* ID # 0x0001020f
*
* Defines an Oracle TIMESTAMP or TIMESTAMP(9) with Oracle default format.
*
* Note: HDS will follow the convention, a two-digit year less than 50 will
be interpreted as next century; greater than or equal to 50 will be inter-
preted as this century.
*
* Note that Oracle TIMESTAMP does support BC dates, too, but this UDD does
not support them.
*
* admin translate, '02/25/2006 13.35.41.123456789', 'char(29)', rs_ora-
cle_timestamp9
*
*************************************************************************
*/
delete from rs_datatype where dtid =  0x000000000001020f
```

```
insert into rs_datatype
values(

    0,                               /* primary rep server ID */
    0x0000000001000008,              /* classid */
    'rs_oracle_timestamp9',          /* name */
    0x000000000001020f,              /* data type id */
    0x00,                            /* base_dtid - char*/
    29,                              /* length */
    0,                               /* status */
    4,                               /* length_err_act */
    'CHAR',                          /* mask */
    0,                               /* scale */
    29,                              /* default_len */
    '01/01/2000 12.00.00.000000000', /* default_val */
    14,                              /* delim_pre_len */
    'TO_TIMESTAMP(''',               /* delim_pre */
    29,                              /* delim_post_len */
    ''',''MM/DD/YYYY HH24.MI.SS.FF'')', /* delim_post */
    29,                              /* min_boundary_len */
    '01/01/0000 00.00.00.000000000', /* min_boundary */
    1,                               /* min_boundary_err_act */
    29,                              /* max_boundary_len */
    '12/31/2099 11.59.59.999999999 PM', /* max_boundary */
    1,                               /* max_boundary_err_act */
    0                                /* rowtype */
)

go
```

Configuring and Tuning Replication Agent for Oracle

Replication Agent for Oracle can be optimized by tuning some of its parameters. The configuration file of Replication Agent should not be directly updated. Instead, the ra_config command should be used to modify configuration parameters. Replication Agent configuration parameters should be modified only when the Replication Agent instance is in admin state. Modifications made to these parameters with ra_config are recorded in the Replication Agent instance configuration file, but changes to some of them do not take effect until Replication Agent is shut down and restarted. When ra_config is invoked without any parameters, it lists all Replication Agent configuration values:

```
isql -Uadmin_user -Padmin_pwd -Smyrao
1> ra_config
2> go
Parameter Name        Parameter Type  Current Value  Pending Value  Default Value
  Legal Values        Category         Restart  Description
--------------------- ---------------- -------------- -------------- ----------------
------------------- ----------------- -------- ---------------------------------------

admin_port            int             9000           NULL           10000
  range: 1,65535      Admin                    1 The client socket port number.
column_compression    boolean         true           NULL           true
  list: false,true    LTL Formatting           0 Configures the LTI to generate LTL
                                                   commands using compressed syntax if
                                                   possible.

compress_ltl_syntax   boolean         true           NULL           true
  list: false,true    LTL Formatting           0 Configures the LTI to generate LTL
                                                   commands using the compressed form of
                                                   LTL keywords.

connect_to_rs         boolean         true           NULL           true
  list: false,true    RS Connectivity          0 Configures the LTI to generate LTL
                                                   commands without sending them to
                                                   Replication Server. Use in conjunction
                                                   with the LTITRACELTL trace flag.
ddl_password          password        ******         NULL           <not_configured>
  N/A                 DDL Replication          0 The password for the user ID used to
                                                   apply DDL at the replicate database.
ddl_username          String          DDLuser        NULL           <not_configured>
  N/A                 DDL Replication          0 The user ID used to apply DDL at the
                                                   replicate database.
dump_batch_timeout    int             5              NULL           5
  range: 1,60         LTL Buffering            0 If batching, configure the amount of
                                                   time to allow for a batch to fill
                                                   before flushing the batch to
                                                   Replication Server.

filter_maint_userid   boolean         true           NULL           true
  list: true, false   LR Log Scan              0 If true, Replication Agent filters all
                                                   maintenance user transactions at the
                                                   primary database.
```

function_password	password	******	NULL	NULL
N/A	PDS Function Replication	0	Password for user replicating PDB Function executions.	
function_username	String	sa	NULL	sa
N/A	PDS Function Replication	0	Username to be used for replicating PDB Function executions.	
log_backup_files	int	3	NULL	3
range: 1,2147483647	Logging	0	Number of wrapped log files to maintain.	
log_directory	String	/work1/rel150_rs_options/RAX-15_0/myrao/log		
			NULL	work1/rel150_rs_options/ RAX-15_0/myrao/log
N/A	Logging	0	Directory for system log files.	
log_trace_verbose	boolean	true	NULL	false
list: false,true	Logging	0	Enable or disable more verbose trace message content.	
log_wrap	int	500	NULL	1000
range: 500,2097151	Logging	0	Number of 1k blocks before wrapping files.	
lti_batch_mode	boolean	true	NULL	true
list: false,true	LTL Buffering	0	Configures the LTI to send multiple LTL commands to Replication Server in a batch.	
lti_max_buffer_size	int	5000	NULL	5000
range: 1000,100000	LTL Buffering	0	Configures the maximum number of commands stored in the LTI's inbound and outbound queues during processing.	
lti_update_trunc_point	int	1000	NULL	1000
range: 1,100000	LTL Buffering	0	Configures the number of LTL commands the LTI sends to Replication Server before synchronizing the replication truncation point.	
ltl_batch size	int	40000	NULL	40000
range: 16384,1048576U	LTL Buffering	0	If batching, configure the size of the LTL batch buffer to send to Replication Server.	
ltl_character_case	String	lower	NULL	asis
list: asis,lower,upper	LTL Formatting	0	Configures the LTI to generate object and column/parameter names in LTL using the specified character case: asis, upper, lower.	

ltl_origin_time_required boolean   false   NULL   false
     list: false,true   LTL Formatting   0 Configures the LTI to generate LTL commands including the origin timestamp of the database operation.

max_ops_per_scan   int   1000   NULL   1000
     range: 25,2147483647 LR Log Scan   0 Maximum number of logged operations to replicate in a single log scan.

pdb_archive_path   String   /work1/oradata/orcl NULL   <not_configured>
     N/A   LR archive logs   0 Specifies the directory path to search for archived redo log files.

pdb_archive_remove   boolean   false   NULL   false
     list: false,true   LR archive logs   0 If true, Replication Agent automatically removes archived redo log files when they are no longer needed for replication.

pdb_auto_create_repdefs boolean   false   NULL   false
     list: false,true   Category   0 If true, during replication, Replication Agent will automatically generate table replication definitions if they are missing.

pdb_auto_run_scripts   boolean   true   NULL   true
     list: false,true   PDB   0 If true, Replication Agent automatically runs marking/unmarking scripts at the PDB.

pdb_automark_tables   boolean   true   NULL   false
     list: false,true   PDB   0 If true, user tables are automatically marked for replication during initialization and DDL replication.

pdb_convert_datetime   boolean   false   NULL   false
     list: false,true   PDB   0 If true, Replication Agent converts the primary database DATETIME format to Sybase format.

pdb_dflt_column_repl   boolean   false   NULL   false
     list: false,true   PDB   0 If true, LOB column replication is enabled at the time a table is marked.

pdb_dflt_object_repl   boolean   true   NULL   true
     list: false,true   PDB   0 If true, replication is enabled at the time an object is marked.

pdb_exception_handling boolean   false   NULL   false
     list: false,true   PDB   0 If true, Replication Agent writes trigger errors to the XLog exception table.

645

pdb_include_archives   boolean   true   NULL   true
    list: false,true   Category   0 If true, archive log files are accessed if needed. When false, only online redo logs are accessed and the Rep Agent is responsible for performing redo log archiving.

pdb_support_large_identifier   boolean   false   NULL   false
    list: false,true   PDB   0 If true, objects containing large identifiers may be marked.

pdb_timezone_file   String   <not_configured>   NULL   <not_configured>
    N/A   PDS Database   0 Specifies the file to be read at initialization to obtain Oracle time zone information.

pdb_xlog_device   String   NULL   NULL   NULL
    N/A   PDB   0 Primary database device where XLog components will be created. An empty entry will default to the database default.

pdb_xlog_prefix   String   RA_   NULL   ra_
    N/A   PDB   0 Prefix used in generating PDB-object names in the transaction log.

pdb_xlog_prefix_chars   String   _#$ NULL   _
    N/A   PDB   0 Valid prefix characters, in addition to a-z.

pds_connection_type   String   ORAJDBC   NULL   ORAJDBC
    list: ORAJDBC   PDS Connectivity   0 Type of connection to use to connect to PDS.

pds_database_name   String   orcl   NULL   <not_configured>
    N/A   PDS Database   0 Name of the primary database to connect to.

pds_datasource_name   String   <not_configured>   NULL   <not_configured>
    N/A   PDS Database   0 Name of the ODBC data source.

pds_host_name   String   myhost   NULL   <not_configured>
    N/A   PDS Connectivity   0 Name of the host on which PDB resides.

pds_password   password   ******   NULL   <not_configured>
    N/A   PDS User   0 Password for the user name with DBA privileges.

pds_port_number   int   1521   NULL   1111
    range: 1,65535   PDS Connectivity   0 Port number for the primary data server.

pds_retry_count int 5 NULL 5
 range: 0,2147483647 PDS Connection 0 Number of times to retry establishing a connection to the PDB.

pds_retry_timeout int 10 NULL 10
 range: 0,3600 PDS Connection 0 Number of seconds to wait between retries to establish a connection to PDB.

pds_server_name String <not_configured> NULL <not_configured>
 N/A PDS Connectivity 0 Server name of the primary data server.

pds_username String ra_user NULL <not_configured>
 N/A PDS User 0 User ID with DBA privileges for the primary database.

ra_retry_count int 2 NULL 2
 range: 1 RS Connectivity 0 The number of times LTM attempts to re-establish replication after a connection failure.

ra_retry_timeout int 10 NULL 10
 range: 1 RS Connectivity 0 The number of seconds LTM waits between replication retries.

rasd_backup_dir String
 /work1/rel150_rs_options/RAX-15_0/myrao/repository/backup
  NULL /work1/rel150_rs_options/ RAX-15_0/asa/backup
 N/A Repository 0 Replication Agent System Data Repository backup directory.

rasd_database String
 /work1/rel150_rs_options/RAX-15_0/myrao/repository/myrao.db
  NULL /work1/rel150_rs_options/ RAX-15_0/asa/asa.db
 N/A Repository 0 Replication Agent System Data Repository database file.

rasd_mirror_tran_log boolean false NULL false
 N/A Repository 0 If true, the Replication Agent System Data Repository log is mirrored.

rasd_trace_log_dir String /work1/rel150_rs_options/RAX-15_0/myrao/ repository
  NULL work1/rel150_rs_options/ RAX-15_0/asa/
 N/A Repository 1 Replication Agent System Data Repository trace log directory.

rasd_tran_log	String		/work1/rel150_rs_options/RAX-15_0/myrao/ repository/myrao.log		
				NULL	/work1/rel150_rs_options/ RAX-15_0/asa/asa.log
N/A	Repository		0 Replication Agent System Data Repository database transaction log file.		
rasd_tran_log_mirror	String		/work1/rel150_rs_options/RAX-15_0/myrao/ repository/tran_log_mirror/myrao.log		
				NULL	/work1/rel150_rs_options/ RAX-15_0/asa/tran_log_ mirror/asa.log
N/A	Repository		0 Replication Agent System Data Repository transaction log mirror file.		
rs_charset	String	iso_1	NULL	NULL	
N/A	RS Connectivity		0 The character set name to use to connect to Replication Server. If not set, the default is the ASCII_7 charset.		
rs_host_name	String	myhost	NULL	<not_configured>	
N/A	RS Connectivity		0 Replication Server host name.		
rs_packet_size	int	2048	NULL	2048	
range: 512,8192	RS Connectivity		0 Replication Server connection network I/O packet size in bytes.		
rs_password	password	******	NULL	<not_configured>	
N/A	RS User		0 Replication Server login password.		
rs_port_number	int	7221	NULL	1111	
range: 1,65535	RS Connectivity		0 Replication Server port number.		
rs_retry_count	int	5	NULL	5	
range: 1	RS Connectivity		0 The number of times Replication Agent attempts to retry a connection to RepServer.		
rs_retry_timeout	int	10	NULL	10	
range: 1	RS Connectivity		0 The number of seconds Replication Agent waits between RepServer connection retries.		
rs_source_db	String	orcl	NULL	<not_configured>	
N/A	RS Source		0 The primary database name used in the Replication Server connection definition.		

rs_source_ds	String	myrao	NULL	<not_configured>
N/A	RS Source		0 The primary database server name used in the Replication Server connection definition.	
rs_username	String	ra_rs_user	NULL	<not_configured>
N/A	RS User		0 Replication Server login user name.	
rssd_charset	String	NULL	NULL	NULL
N/A	RSSD Connectivity		0 The character set name to use to connect to Replication Server System Database. If not set, the default is the ASCII_7 charset.	
rssd_database_name	String	prs_RSSD	NULL	<not_configured>
N/A	RSSD Connectivity		0 Replication Server System Database name.	
rssd_host_name	String	myhost	NULL	<not_configured>
N/A	RSSD Connectivity		0 Replication Server System Database host name.	
rssd_password	password	******	NULL	<not_configured>
N/A	RSSD User		0 Replication Server System Database login password.	
rssd_port_number	int	7100	NULL	1111
range: 1,65535	RSSD Connectivity		0 Replication Server System Database port number.	
rssd_username	String	ra_rssd_user	NULL	<not_configured>
N/A	RSSD User		0 Replication Server System Database login user name.	
scan_sleep_increment	int	5	NULL	5
range: 0,300	LR Log Scan		0 Number of seconds to increment wait time between checking log for transactions to be replicated.	
scan_sleep_max	int	60	NULL	60
range: 5,3600	LR Log Scan		0 Maximum number of seconds between scan operations.	
skip_ltl_errors	boolean	false	NULL	false
list: false,true	LTL Handling		0 Configures the LTI to ignore LTL errors from Replication Server.	

structured_tokens	boolean	true	NULL	true
list: false,true	LTL Formatting		0 Configures the LTI to generate LTL using structured tokens. Structured tokens can significantly improve performance because they generally reduce the size of the LTL, and they allow the LTL to be parsed much more efficiently.	
truncation_interval	int	0	NULL	0
range: 0,720	LR Log Truncator		0 Determines the frequency (minutes) to perform transaction log truncation. Valid if Interval Truncator is used.	
truncation_type	String	LOCATOR_UPDATE	NULL	LOCATOR_UPDATE
list: COMMAND, INTERVAL, LOCATOR_UPDATE				
	LR Log Truncator		0 Determines which log truncation algorithm to use.	
use_rssd	boolean	false	NULL	true
list: false,true	LTL Formatting		0 Configures the LTI to use the RSSD replication definitions for generating LTL commands. Using RepDefs allows LTL to be optimized by limiting columns sent to those defined in the RepDef, and maps datatypes according to the type declared in the RepDef.	

To get information about a specified configuration parameter:

```
1> ra_config pdb_automark_tables
2> go
Parameter Name      Parameter Type  Current Value  Pending Value  Default Value
  Legal Values        Category  Restart  Description
------------------- --------------- --------------- ---------- --------
------------------- --------- -------- -----------------------------------------------
pdb_automark_tables boolean          true           NULL           false
  list: false, true PDB            0 If true, user tables are automatically marked
                                     for replication during initialization and DDL
                                     replication.
```

To change the value of a specific configuration parameter, execute the ra_config command with the configuration parameter and its value:

```
1> ra_config pdb_automark_tables, false
2> go
Parameter Name          Parameter Type  Current Value  Pending Value  Default Value
  Legal Values          Category  Restart  Description
--------------------    ---------------  --------------  --------------  -----------------
--------------------    ---------  --------  -------------------------------------------
pdb_automark_tables     boolean         false          NULL           false
  list: false,true      PDB              0 If true, user tables are automatically marked
                                           for replication during initialization and DDL
                                           replication.
```

To reset a configuration parameter value to the default, execute the ra_config command with the configuration parameter and the default keyword:

```
1> ra_config use_rssd, default
2> go
Parameter Name          Parameter Type  Current Value  Pending Value  Default Value
  Legal Values          Category     Restart  Description
--------------------    ---------------  --------------  --------------  -----------------
--------------------    ---------------  --------  -------------------------------------------
use_rssd                boolean         true           NULL           true
  list: false,true      LTL Formatting   0 Configures the LTI to use the RSSD
                                           replication definitions for generating LTL
                                           commands. Using RepDefs allows LTL to be
                                           optimized by limiting columns sent to
                                           those defined in the RepDef, and maps
                                           datatypes according to the type declared
                                           in the RepDef.
```

Parameters for Tuning Replication Agent Throughput

The following configuration parameters can be tuned for improving Replication Agent throughput.

▶ **RA_JAVA_MAX_MEM**: Maximum Java memory (can be specified as m for megabytes or g for gigabytes) with the default being 128m. You can edit the Replication Agent instance startup script (RUN_*instance*) and set it to the desired number. Maximum Java memory is limited by available system memory. As memory statistics can change from

time to time, you can monitor memory usage with
ra_statistics.

▶ **lti_max_buffer_size**: Governs the maximum number of operations that can be stored in the Log Transfer Interface (LTI)
component's inbound and outbound queues.

Unit: Int

Values: 1000 to 100000

Default: 5000

▶ **max_ops_per_scan**: Maximum number of primary database
operations the Log Reader (LR) component of Replication
Agent reads during each transaction log scan. LR always reads
at least one transaction from the log, regardless of the number
of operations in that transaction. For example, if max_ops_per_
scan is set to 2000 and the transaction has 1400 operations, LR
will read all 1400 operations in one scan when it reads the
transaction.

Unit: Int

Values: 25 to 214,748,3647

Default: 1000

Tip: lti_max_buffer_size * 2 + (max_ops_per_scan * 2 * average row size) + ~10m < VM allocated memory

---

▶ **column_compression**: Set this parameter to "true" to
improve Replication Agent throughput. When this parameter
is set to "True", columns in which data is changed as a result of
updates are sent in LTL by the LTI component. Columns in
which data is not modified as a result of updates is not sent in
LTL.

Unit: Boolen

Values: True, False

Default: True

▶ **compress_ltl_syntax**: Set this parameter to "true" to
improve Replication Agent throughput. When this parameter

is set to "true", LTL commands are compressed by LTI using appreviated LTL syntax.

Unit: Boolen

Values: True, False

Default: True

▶ **lti_batch_mode**: Set this parameter to "true" to get better throughput with Replication Agent. When this parameter is set to "true", LTI will fit as many LTL commands in its buffer as possible, then send the buffer. In Replication Server 12.5 and above, ltl_batch_size can be configured to set the size of the LTI component's LTL batch mode buffer. When lti_batch_mode is set to "false", LTI will send one LTL command to Replication Server.

Unit: Boolen

Values: True, False

Default: True

▶ **lti_batch_size**: This parameter sets the size of the LTI component's LTL batch mode buffer.

Unit: Int

Values: 16384 to 10485760

Default: 40000

▶ **lti_origin_time_required**: Set this parameter to "false" to improve throughput. When this parameter is set to "true", the origin_time command tag is included in the LTL generated by LTI. Origin_time specified in datetime is the time the transaction was recorded in the transaction log at the primary database; it is not the time when it was scanned and processed by the Log Reader component. Set this parameter to "true" if using Replication Server Manager to report latency.

Unit: Boolen

Values: True, False

Default: False

▶ **structured_tokens**: This parameter should be set to "true". It improves overall Replication Server performance specifically when replicate non-Sybase datatypes in the primary database must be translated by the Replication Server. When this parameter is set to "true", the LTI component of Replication Agent uses structured tokens to generate LTL commands.

Unit: Boolen

Values: True, False

Default: True

▶ **rs_packet_size**: Maximum size in bytes of the network packet used by Replication Agent for sending to the primary Replication Server. The Replication Agent configuration parameter rs_packet_size is equivalent to the Replication Server configuration parameter rs_packet_size. If it is configured too small, Replication Agent will send more packets to the primary Replication Server; if it is configured too large, more system resources will be used to process a larger packet size. This parameter should be configured on the basis of the type of data being replicated. If your typical data operation is very large, then throughput will improve by configuring rs_packet_size to a large size.

Unit: Int

Values: 512 to 8192

Default: 2048

Parameters for Tuning Replication Agent Latency

Replication Agent latency can be minimized by tuning the following Replication Agent configuration parameters.

▶ **scan_sleep_max and scan_sleep_increment**: scan_sleep_increment governs the number of seconds to increase Log Reader's wait before the next scan after finding no operations to replicate, and scan_sleep_max governs the maximum number of seconds for Log Reader to wait before the next scan after finding no operations to replicate. scan_sleep_increment cannot be set higher than scan_sleep_max. These two configuration parameters specify how long Replication Agent should wait when it reaches the end of the log before starting to rescan the log if there are no records to replicate. If you notice latency with the default setting of 60 seconds for scan_sleep_ max, you can reduce this parameter with the ra_config command. Lowering the value of scan_sleep_max makes Replication Agent scan the log more frequently. On the other hand, if a higher percentage of CPU utilization is a concern, you may want to increase the scan_sleep_max configuration parameter.

```
ra_config scan_sleep_max, ss
```

where *ss* is number of seconds

▶ **dump_batch_timeout**: This parameter governs the maximum time in seconds to wait before sending the LTL command contents to the Replication Server. If set to a higher value, it delays sending the contents of the LTL command but allows full batches. When set to a lower value, it sends data sooner but with smaller batches. If ltl_batch_mode is set to "false", then dump_batch_timeout does not have any effect.

Unit: Int

Values: 1 to 60

Default: 5

▶ **lti_update_trunc_pt**: This parameter governs the maximum number of LTL commands sent to the Replication Server before requesting a secondary truncation point update. Higher values of lti_update_trunc_pt improve replication system performance but may increase the time it takes to recover from replication failure. Lower values of lti_update_trunc_pt decrease the time it takes to recover from replication failure but can have an adverse affect on overall replication system performance. When the truncation_type configuration parameter is set to locater_update, a lower value of lti_update_ trunc_pt will cause automatic log truncation more frequently.

Unit: Int

Values: 1 to 100000

Default: 1000

Tuning the Size of the Replication Agent Instance System Log

▶ **log_wrap:** By default the Replication Agent instance system log wraps after 1000 KB are written to it. The size of the Replication Agent instance system log can be adjusted with the log_wrap configuration parameter. To save disk space, you can decrease the size of log_wrap. To save log data for longer periods, increase the size of log_wrap. Before modifying the log_wrap configuration parameter, verify by executing the ra_status command that the Replication Agent is in admin state.

```
ra_config log_wrap, nnnn
```

where *nnnn* is the size in kilobytes.

▶ **log_backup_files:** log_backup_files can be modified to increase or decrease the number of backup log files in the log directory. The default value is 3. Before modifying the log_backup_files configuration parameter, verify by executing the ra_status command that the Replication Agent is in admin state.

```
ra_config log_backup_files, nn
```

where *nn* is the number of log backup files.

Troubleshooting Replication Agent

The Replication Agent instance log resides in $SYBASE/RAX-15_0/*instance_name*/log/*instance*/log. This log can have various types of messages logged:

▶ Informational (I) messages:

```
I.     2008/01/28 15:23:04.763        INFORMATION
com.sybase.ra.conn.RAConnectionMgr              close
14              Closed connection to <jdbc:oracle:thin:@myhost:1521:orcl>.
```

▶ Warning (W) messages:

```
W.      2008/01/28 15:23:11.576        WARNING
com.sybase.ra.conn.RAConnectionMgr              addConnection
14              Connection reported database access warning: 010UF: Attempt
to execute use database command failed. Error message: Line 1, character 1:
Incorrect syntax with the keyword 'use'.
```

▶ Error (E) messages:

```
E.      2008/01/28 15:24:03.940        ERROR
com.sybase.ra.lr.oracle.
RAOLogReader            setValidArchiveLogPath        30
The specified archive redo log path <<not_configured>> is not a valid
directory.
```

All Replication Agent logs are instance specific. When a Replication Agent instance is started, it creates a new log and the old log is backed up. The size of the log file is limited by the log_wrap configuration property. The default value of log_wrap is 1000 K. The maximum number of backed-up files is governed by log_backup_files. When the maximum number of backup files is reached, the oldest backup log file is deleted. The default value of log_backup_files is 3.

1. When traces are enabled, trace output of Replication Agent traces is also logged to the *instance*.log. For debug flags, you will need to run the debug build of the Replication Agent binary. You can turn on trace flags to get additional information.

    Trace *traceflag*, true|false

    The following trace flags can be used:

    ▶ **LTITRACELTL:** When this trace flag is enabled, all LTI in the trace is written in LTITRACELTL.log. LTITRACELTL logs commands and data sent to Replication Server.

    ```
    1> trace LTITRACELTL, true
    2> go
    ```

```
T.      2008/03/23 17:01:53.106        LTITRACE
com.sybase.ra.lti.rs.LTL
Session                rs_get_truncation              12
RepServer get truncation results:
0000000000000000000000000000000000000000000000000000000000000000
T.      2008/03/23 17:01:53.113        LTITRACE
com.sybase.ra.lti.LTI                  fireMaintenanceUserUpdated     12
LTI maintenance user updated event.
```

▶ **LTITRACE**: When this trace flag is enabled, it traces the general execution of the Log Transfer Interface component. This trace flag is useful for diagnosing problems between the Replication Agent instance and the primary Replication Server.

```
1> trace LTITRACE, true
2> go
```

▶ **LRTRACE**: When this trace flag is enabled, it traces the general execution of the Log Reader component. This trace flag is useful for identifying replication problems.

```
1> trace LRTRACE, true
2> go
```

▶ **RACONTRC**: When this trace flag is enabled, it traces connection and query execution.

```
1> trace RACONTRC, true
2> go
```

▶ **RACONTRCSQL**: When this trace flag is enabled, it traces SQL statements to be executed. This trace flag is useful for identifying problems with SQL commands to Replication Server, Replication Agent System Database (RASD), or the primary data server (PDS).

```
1> trace RACONTRCSQL, true
2> go
```

If you don't get enough information using these trace flags, you can also enable all the trace flags by executing the trace all command:

```
1> trace all, true
2> go
```

To disable tracing:

```
1> trace all, off
2> go
```

The quality of the trace information captured by Replication Agent can also be tuned by setting these Replication Agent configuration parameters:

▶ **log_trace_verbose**: When this Replication Agent configuration parameter is set to "true", trace flags provide a more verbose description of traced components.

```
1> ra_config log_trace_verbose, true
2> go
Parameter Name     Parameter Type  Current Value  Pending Value  Default Value
  Legal Values      Category  Restart  Description
------------------ --------------- -------------- -------------- ----------------
------------------ --------- -------- ---------------------------------------------
log_trace_verbose  boolean         true           NULL           false
  list: false,true  Logging          0 Enable or disable more verbose trace message
                                       content.
```

▶ **compress_ltl_syntax**: This Replication Agent configuration parameter should be set to "false" to get a more verbose description of LTL commands:

```
1> ra_config compress_ltl_syntax, false
2> go
Parameter Name      Parameter Type  Current Value  Pending Value  Default Value
  Legal Values       Category  Restart  Description
------------------- --------------- -------------- -------------- ----------------
------------------ --------------- -------- ---------------------------------------------
compress_ltl_syntax  boolean         false          NULL           true
  list: false,true  LTL Formatting         0 Configures the LTI to generate LTL
                                           commands using the compressed form of
                                           LTL keywords.
```

▶ **connect_to_rs**: Setting this Replication Agent configuration parameter to "false" will allow LTL to be generated

without an actual connection to or sending information to
the Replication Server.

```
1> ra_config connect_to_rs, false
2> go
Parameter Name  Parameter Type  Current Value  Pending Value  Default Value
  Legal Values     Category         Restart  Description
---------------  ---------------  ---------------  --------------  -----------------
-----------------  ---------------  --------  ---------------------------------------
connect_to_rs   boolean          false           NULL            true
  list: false,true  RS Connectivity         0 Configures the LTI to generate LTL
                                              commands without sending them to
                                              Replication Server. Use in conjunction
                                              with the LTITRACELTL trace flag.
```

▶ **use_rssd**: Setting this Replication Agent configuration
parameter to "false" will provide a complete generation of
LTL commands without modification for replication definition information.

```
1> ra_config use_rssd, false
2> go
Parameter Name  Parameter Type  Current Value  Pending Value  Default Value
  Legal Values     Category         Restart  Description
---------------  ---------------  ---------------  --------------  -----------------
-----------------  ---------------  --------  ---------------------------------------
use_rssd        boolean          false           NULL            true
  list: false,true  LTL Formatting          0 Configures the LTI to use the RSSD
                                              replication definitions for generating
                                              LTL commands. Using RepDefs allows LTL to
                                              be optimized by limiting columns sent to
                                              those defined in the RepDef, and maps
                                              datatypes according to the type declared
                                              in the RepDef.
```

▶ **column_compression**: When this Replication Agent configuration parameter is set to "false", Replication Agent
sends complete column information in the generated LTL
for update operations.

```
1> ra_config column_compression, false
2> go
Parameter Name    Parameter Type  Current Value  Pending Value  Default Value
  Legal Values    Category        Restart  Description
------------------ ---------------- -------------- -------------- ----------------
------------------ ---------------- -------- ---------------------------------------
column_compression boolean          false          NULL              true
  list: false,true LTL Formatting           0 Configures the LTI to generate LTL
                                             commands using compressed syntax if
                                             possible.
```

2. To verify connections, log in to the Replication Agent instance and execute test_connection. The test_connection command verifies that logins can connect; it doesn't verify a user's permissions. Connection results for Replication Server (RS) include a connection to RSSD:

```
1> test_connection
2> go
Type Connection
---- ----------
PDS  succeeded
RS   succeeded
```

If test_connection fails, the cause of the failure is logged in the instance.log.

```
1> test_connection
2> go
Type Connection
---- ----------
PDS  failed
RS   succeeded

E.    2008/03/23 21:31:26.297        ERROR
com.sybase.ra.conn.RAConnectionMgr              testConnect
15           Could not connect to <ORAJDBC(@host:port:databaseSID):
'@myhost:1521:orcl'>: Io exception: Connection reset
```

3. The character set of the Replication Agent instance should match the character set of Replication Server, and the Replication Server character set should match the character set of the primary database. If these are not the same, you can run into replication issues. The RA_JAVA_DFLT_CHARSET

environment variable can be set to the primary data server character set in the Replication Agent instance runserver file:

```
RA_JAVA_DFLT_CHARSET=charset
```

Verify the replication charset setting in the Replication Server configuration file:

```
RS_CHARSET=charset
```

Verify the rs_charset property set in the Replication Agent instance:

```
1> ra_config  rs_charset
```

If it is not set the same as Replication Server RS_CHARSET, then configure it:

```
1>ra_config rs_charset, RS_CHARSET
```

Replication Agent uses rs_charset for communicating with Replication Server. If it does not match, then data is not replicated to the replicate.

    4.   To check the version of all the replication components:

```
1> ra_version_all
2> go
Component
  Version
--------------------
  ------------------------------------------------------------------------------
Instance:
  myrao - Oracle


Replication Agent:
  Sybase Replication Agent for Unix & windows/15.0.0.5401P1/P/generic/JDK
  1.4.2/rax150sustain/5401P1/VM: Sun Microsystems Inc. 1.4.2_12/OPT/Thu Jan 25 18:25:52
  MST 2007

JRE:
  Sun Microsystems Inc. Java(TM) 2 Runtime Environment, Standard Edition/1.4.2_12-b03/
  SunOS 5.10/sparc/32

RASD:
  Adaptive Server Anywhere/9.0.2.3300/UNIX
```

```
Primary Data Server:
  Oracle Oracle Database 10g Enterprise Edition Release 10.2.0.1.0 - 64bit Production
  With the Partitioning, OLAP and Data Mining options

PDS JDBC Driver:
  Oracle JDBC driver 10.2.0.1.0

RepServer:
  Replication Server/15.0.1/P/Sun_svr4/OS 5.8/1/OPT/Wed Jan 24 17:16:58 2007

RSSD:
  Adaptive Server Enterprise/15.0.2/EBF 14328/P/Sun_svr4/OS 5.8/ase1502/2486/64-bit/
  FBO/Thu May 24 12:18:26 2007

Sybase JDBC Driver:
  jConnect (TM) for JDBC(TM)/6.05(Build 25828)/P/EBF13044/JDK14/Fri Sep 30 1:05:16 2005
```

5. Test if Replication Agent is ready to replicate:

```
1> ra_status
2> go
State          Action
------------   -------------------------
REPLICATING    Ready to replicate data.
```

6. Verify if primary object is marked for replication:

```
1> pdb_setreptable rax_test
2> go
Owner Name       Marked  Enabled  Replicate      Send Owner Shadow Table
     Shadow Row Proc Blob Shadow Table Blob Row Proc
----- ---------  -------  --------  -------------  ---------- ------------
     --------------- ----------------- -------------
SYS   RAX_TEST   marked   enabled  SYS.RAX_TEST   disabled   N/A
     N/A             N/A               N/A
```

7. The ra_statistics command can be used to monitor memory usage and performance of Replication Agent components such as how many transactions have been processed, whether it is scanning the transaction log, and whether it is sending LTL to the Replication Server and the Java Virtual Machine. If ra_statistics is executed with the reset keyword, all the statistics are reset except the following:

Log Transfer Manager statistics:

▶ Time statistics obtained

▶ Time replication last started

▶ Time statistics last reset

Log Transfer Interface statistics:

▶ Last OID send

▶ Last Transaction ID sent

Statistics for all Java Virtual Machines are reset when the ra_statistics command is invoked.

```
1> ra_statistics
2> go
Component Statistic
    Value
--------- -------------------------------------
    --------------------------------------------------------------------
LTM      Time statistics obtained
    Sun Mar 23 17:15:14 EDT 2008
LTM      Time replication last started
    Sun Mar 23 17:03:00 EDT 2008
LTM      Time statistics last reset
    Sun Mar 23 17:01:46 EDT 2008
LTM      Items held in Global LRUCache
    12
VM       VM maximum memory
    132907008
VM       VM total memory allocated
    14450000
VM       VM free memory
    6675144
VM       VM memory usage
    7783736
VM       VM % max memory used
    5.86
LR       Current operation queue size
    0
LR       Log reposition point locator
0x000000000000002baf960000002b000000000000000000002b0000000000000000
LR       Last processed operation locator
0x000000000000002baf960000002b000000000000000000002b0000000000000000
```

```
LR        Avg xlog operation wait time (ms)
   0.0
LTI       Number of LTL commands sent
   0.0
LTI       Avg LTL command size
   0.0
LTI       Avg LTL commands/sec
   0.0
 LTI        Total bytes sent
   0.0
LTI       Avg Bytes/second during transmission
   0.0
LTI       Avg LTL buffer cache time
   0.0
LTI       Avg Rep Server turnaround time
   0.0
LTI       Avg data arrival time
   67.797
LTI       Avg time to create distributes
   0.0
LTI       Avg LTL buffer size
   0.0
LTI       Avg LTM buffer utilization (%)
   0.0
LTI       Avg LTL commands/buffer
   0.0
LTI       Input queue size
   0.0
LTI       Output queue size
   0.0
LTI       Last QID sent
   None
LTI       Last transaction ID sent
   None
```

If the number in "LTI number of LTL commands sent" is increasing, that indicates Replication Agent is sending LTL to Replication Server. To verify whether Replication Agent is scanning the transaction log, check "LR Total operations scanned"; this counter should be increasing.

Memory usage by the Replication Agent instance should be monitored with the ra_statistics command. When you see java.lang.OutOfMemoryError in the Replication Agent

665

instance log, the Replication Agent instance stops replicating and the state is changed to admin. You can give more memory to the Replication Agent instance by adjusting the RA_JAVA_MAX_MEM environment variable in the RUN_*instance* script and restarting the Replication Agent instance.

a. Verify if the secondary truncation point is moving. Execute ra_locator to get the current locator value:

```
1> ra_locator
2> go
Locator
------------------------------------------------------------------
000000000000002baf960000002b000000000000000002b0000000000000000
```

Execute ra_helplocator *locator_value*. This command returns information about fields in the specifed LTM locator value. ra_helplocator is only applicable to Replication Agent for Oracle.

```
ra_helplocator
000000000000002baf960000002b000000000000000002b0000000000000000
2> go
Field          Hex Value            Decimal Value
-------------  -------------------  -------------
GENID          0x0000               0
SCN            0x00000000002baf96   2862998
LSN            0x0000002b           43
BLKNUM         0x00000000           0
BLKOFFSET      0x0000               0
OATLSN         0x0000000b           43
OATBLKNUM      0x00000000           0
OATBLKOFFSET   0x0000               0
UNIQUE         0x0000               0
```

To get a new locator value from Replication Server, invoke ra_locator with the update keyword. This command only takes effect if the Replication Agent instance is in the replicating state.

```
1> ra_locator update
```

To set the locator value of the Replication Agent instance to zero, invoke ra_locator with the zero keyword:

```
1> ra_locator zero
```

b. Since Replication Agent for Oracle is using RASD (embedded ASA database that keeps track of DDL changes), it is important to know what is missed between the point where the Replication Agent for Oracle is currently reading and where you want it to start up.

To move the truncation/start point of where Replication Agent for Oracle reads, log in to the Replication Agent instance using administrator login and get values for rs_zeroltm from the Replication Agent instance:

```
ra_config rs_source_ds
ra_config rs_source_db
```

Note the values for rs_source_ds and rs_source_db.

```
pdb_init move_truncpt
pdb_xlog init, force
```

The pdb_init move_truncpt command will move the start point to the end of the Oracle transaction log. The pdb_xlog init, force command will refresh the RASD (Replication Agent System Database) if DDL changes were made between where the Replication Agent for Oracle left off and where you are going to start it up. Replication Agent for Oracle has not processed the DDL changes into the RASD; hence this command must also be run to get the correct structure of all the tables marked for replication.

The pdb_init and pdb_xlog commands can be executed in any order. Log in to Adaptive Server Enterprise, where RSSD resides:

```
use rssd
go
rs_zeroltm dataserver, database
```

dataserver: Use rs_source_ds value

database: Use rs_source_db value

To move the start point to the beginning of the log, log in to Replication Agent instance with administrator login and get values for rs_zeroltm:

```
ra_config rs_source_ds
ra_config rs_source_db
```

Note the values for rs_source_ds and rs_source_db.

```
ra_locator zero
```

Log in to Adaptive Server Enterprise, where RSSD resides:

```
use rssd
go
rs_zeroltm dataserver, database
```

dataserver: Use rs_source_ds value

database: Use rs_source_db value

In this case, since you are moving the locater back in the transaction log, the RASD will contain correct information for each of the "versions" of the table. Therefore it is not necessary to repopulate the RASD.

8. Chapter 20 describes troubleshooting tasks for Replication Server, such as debugging failures with Data Server Interfaces (DSI) and routes, diagnosing and correcting issues with replication definitions and subscriptions, and dumping queues. In this section, we will talk about basic checks that can be performed when data is not replicating.

   a. Primary database inbound queue not moving: Execute the admin who,sqm RCL command at the primary Replication Server to determine if the number of blocks being written for the specific connection's inbound queue at the primary Replication Server is not changing and the number in the Duplicates column is also not increasing.

```
1> admin who,sqm
2> go
Spid State              Info             Duplicates  Writes  Reads  Bytes
  B Writes  B Filled  B Reads  B Cache  Save_Int:Seg  First Seg.Block  Last Seg.Block
    Next Read  Readers  Truncs
---- ----------------- ------------------ ----------- ------- ------ -----
   --------- --------- -------- -------- ------------- ---------------- --------------
     ---------- -------- -------
36   Awaiting Message  111:1 myrao.orcl  0           0       7      0
   0         0         7        0        0:0           0.7              0.7
     0.8.0      1        1
```

In that case, perform the following steps:

  i. Verify if the Replication Agent instance for the primary database connection is up and running by executing admin who at the primary replication server. Connection information (primary data server and primary database) can also be verified by executing the admin show_connections and admin who,dsi RCL commands. If status is Down, restart the Replication Agent instance (follow the steps listed in the "Starting a Replication Agent Instance" section earlier in this chapter).

```
1> admin who
2> go
Spid Name       State                Info
---- ---------- -------------------- --------------------
     DSI EXEC   Down                 109(1) DC01261.orcl
     DSI        Down                 109 DC01261.orcl
  34 SQM        Awaiting Message     109:0 DC01261.orcl
     DSI EXEC   Down                 112(1) DC0150.orcl
  43 DSI        Sleeping             112 DC0150.orcl
  37 SQM        Awaiting Message     112:0 DC0150.orcl
     .
     .
     .
     REP AGENT  Down                 myrao.orcl
```

If admin who doesn't show connection information for the Replication Agent instance for a particular connection, then the connection was not created with the with log transfer on clause. Alter the primary database connection to turn on log transfer:

```
Alter connection myrao.orcl
    with log transfer on
```

ii. Verify that the Replication Agent instance was configured with the correct rs_source_ds and rs_source_db configuration parameters. These parameters should match exactly, even the case, of the *dataserver.database* defined in the create connection command.

In Replication Agent instance:

```
a. ra_config rs_source_ds, myrao
1> ra_config rs_source_db, orcl
```

In Replication Server:

```
create connection to myrao.orcl
set error class rs_sqlserver_error_class
set function string class rs_oracle_function_class
set username sys
set password sybase
with log transfer on, dsi_suspended
```

iii. Verify that primary database objects are marked for replication. Log in to the Replication Agent instance and execute appropriate commands:

▶ Verify if the user table is marked for replication:

```
pdb_setreptable tab_name
```

where *tab_name* is the name of a table you want to verify is marked for replication.

▶ Verify if a specific stored procedure is marked for replication:

```
pdb_setrepproc proc_name
```

where *proc_name* is the name of the stored procedure you want to verify is marked for replication.

▶ Verify if LOB is marked for replication:

```
pdb_setrepcol tab_name, lob_col
```

where *tab_name* is the name of a marked user table that contains an LOB column.

If the objects are marked and/or replication is not enabled, see the section titled "Marking Objects for Replication in the Primary Database" earlier in this chapter. If objects are marked and replication is enabled for replication, then turn on Replication Agent tracing (see the sections on LTITRACE and LTITRACELTL), update the primary table, and verify Replication Agent is sending data to the primary Replication Server by using admin who,sqm and checking the inbound queue.

b. Replicate database outbound queue not moving: If the outbound queue for the replicate database doesn't get updated when you have issued admin who,sqm, check the admin who,sqm output to verify if the number of blocks written in the outbound queue for a specific replicate database is changing and the number of duplicate messages being detected is not increasing.

```
1> admin who,sqm
2> go
Spid State           Info              Duplicates  Writes Reads  Bytes
  B Writes  B Filled  B Reads  B Cache  Save_Int:Seg  First Seg.Block  Last Seg.Block
    Next Read  Readers  Truncs
---- ----------------- ------------------ ----------- ------- ------ -----
   --------- --------- -------- -------- ------------- ---------------- ---------------
   ---------- -------- -------
37   Awaiting Message  112:0 DC0150.orcl 0           0      0      0
   0        0         0        0        0:0           0.1              0.2
     0.1.0     1        1
```

Most of the time, issues with inbound and outbound queues are related to naming problems. Execute the admin who_is_down RCL command at the Replication Server to determine whether the DSI thread for a specific connection is down. If it is down, review the

Replication Server error log for errors, fix the error, and resume the DSI connection.

c. Check primary replication definition: The primary Replication Server inbound queue is receiving the data, but data is not being applied to any replication definition. This can happen when the name of the replication definition does not match the name in LTL created by the Replication Agent. You can encounter this issue when the default character case of the primary database is different. Processing of Replication Server commands by Replication Server is case sensitive. You will need to make sure that Replication Server connection names and primary replication definition object names match the LTL generated by Replication Agent. The Replication Agent configuration parameter `lti_character_case` can be configured to specify a character set. The best practice is to use one case (either upper or lower) consistently with all Replication Server connection names, primary replication definitions, and subscriptions (see the section in this chapter titled "Character Case of Database Object Names").

Turn on LTL trace in the Replication Agent (see the beginning of this section) and execute the `rs_helprep` command to verify the primary replication definition name. Be sure the name provided in LTL matches the character case and spelling. If the replication definition was misspelled, drop and recreate the replication definition; if the character case is incorrect, configure it correctly with `ra_config ltl_character_case`.

d. Replicate database is not updated: If the outbound queue is receiving data, but it is not being applied at the replicate database, execute `rs_helpsub` *subname* to verify the text of the subscription. If the subscription has a where clause, verify that transaction data will qualify any where clause in the subscription. Check the replicate Replication Server error log and the replicate database server error log for errors. If there are any errors, fix them and resume replication. To check that the maintenance login has correct permissions to the replicate table/stored procedure, log in as maintenance user to the replicate data server or DirectConnect and verify that you have update authority for modifying data at the replicate database.

Log in to the replicate Replication Server and enable DSI trace:

```
1> trace "on", DSI,"DSI_BUF_DUMP"
```

Review the transactions logged into the replicate Replication Server error log, which is being sent to the replicate database. Alternatively, enable tracing in the DirectConnect configuration file:

```
traceflags: 1,2,3,4,5,6,10
```

If after performing all these diagnostics and analysis, you cannot determine the cause for the replicate database not being applied, contact Sybase Technical Support.

9. Skipping problem records: In some cases, you might have to skip one or more problem records in order to resume replication without reinitializing the Replication Agent. Skipped records are logged in the instance error log as warning messages. To skip problem records, you will need to put the Replication Agent instance in admin state.

Execute ra_status to check the replication status of Replication Agent.

Step 1. Check the Replication Agent instance status:

```
1> ra_status
2> go
State  Action
------ ------------------------------
ADMIN  Waiting for operator command.
```

If the Replication Agent instance status is not admin, you can issue the suspend command to change it to admin state.

Step 2. Use the pdb_skip_op command to add or remove an identifier or all identifiers from a list of records to skip.

Syntax:

```
pdb_skip_op [[add, identifier] | [remove, all | identifier]]
```

add

> Specified ID is added to the list of identifiers of records to skip

remove

> Specified ID is removed from the list of identifiers of records to skip

all

> Add or remove all IDs in the list of identifiers to skip

identifier

> ID of the record to skip; identifier syntax is database specific

In Oracle, the identifier is the value of LSN.BLKNUM.BLK-OFFSET in hex or decimal format.

LSN: Log Sequence Number

BLKNUM: Block Number of the record

BLKOFFSET: Offset into the block to locate the record

Use the rs_helplocator command to get values of the above parameters:

```
1> ra_helplocator
000000000000002baf960000002b00000000000000000002b0000000000000000
2> go
Field          Hex Value              Decimal Value
-------------  ---------------------  -------------
GENID          0x0000                 0
SCN            0x00000000002baf96      2862998
LSN            0x0000002b              43
BLKNUM         0x00000000             0
BLKOFFSET      0x0000                 0
OATLSN         0x0000002b              43
OATBLKNUM      0x00000000             0
OATBLKOFFSET   0x0000                 0
UNIQUE         0x0000                 0
```

When `pdb_skip_op` is invoked without any parameter, it returns the list of record identifiers to be skipped.

To add the identifier of the record to the list:

```
1> pdb_skip_op add, 0x0000002b, 0x00000000, 0x0000
```

To remove the identifier of the record from the list:

```
1>pdb_skip_op remove, 0x0000002b, 0x00000000, 0x0000
```

To remove all the identifiers of the records from the list:

```
1>pdb_skip_op, remove, all
```

When replication is resumed, the Replication Agent instance will skip the records specified in the skip list.

10. The Replication Server `set autocorrection` command prevents the DSI thread from getting suspended because of missing or duplicate rows in a replicated table.

   In order to use the `set autocorrection` command in Replication Agent for Oracle 15.0, the `use_rssd` Replication Agent configuration parameter should be set to "false". In Replication Agent for Oracle 15.1, you can set the Replication Agent configuration parameters `column_compression` and `ltl_send_only_primary_keys` to "false".

   Syntax:

```
set autocorrection {on | off}
for replication_definition
with replicate at dataserver.database
```

11. If the expected datatype translation is not occurring correctly, use the steps listed below to validate your install:

   a. Reboot the replication servers. The Replication Server caches all function string information at startup. Subsequent changes to the function strings stored in the RSSD will not take effect until the Replication Server is restarted.

   b. Verify that user-defined datatypes have been defined. The Replication Server script hds_oracle_new_udds.sql provides the SQL statements necessary to apply predefined user-defined datatypes to the Replication Server's

RSSD for a specific non-ASE replicate database. The scripts issue a delete followed by an insert command for each datatype. You can rerun these scripts without failure. These scripts need to be executed at each Replication Server where the non-ASE data server is a replicate database and the non-ASE data server's primary replication definition refers to a UDD using the map_to clause. Verify your copy of the scripts has been updated with the correct "use" statement for your RSSD name.

c. Verify that class-level translations have been applied to the replicate Replication Server. Replication Server scripts hds_clt_*xxx*_to_*xxx*.sql (e.g., hds_clt_ase_to _oracle.sql provides the class-level translations going from ASE to Oracle) provide the SQL statements necessary to apply predefined class-level translations to the replicate Replication Server's RSSD for a specific combination of primary database vendors to non-ASE replicates. (Note: The hds_clt_ase_to_*xxx*.sql script is required for any non-ASE replicate database.) You can rerun these scripts without failure. Verify your copy of the scripts has been updated with the correct "use" statement for your RSSD name. (Note: Translations adversely affect performance. You should not apply translations that are not required for your replication environment.)

d. Verify your replicate database's Replication Server connection is for the desired function-string class. In order to take advantage of class-level translations, your replicate Replication Server connection must use the correct predefined non-ASE function-string class. To see what function-string class is defined, use the Replication Server rs_helpdb command. Available classes are:

▶ Adaptive Server Enterprise — rs_sqlserver_function_class

▶ DB2 — rs_db2_function_class

▶ Microsoft SQL Server — rs_msss_function_class

▶ Oracle — rs_oracle_function_class

You can display a list of active function-string classes using the Replication Server command admin show_function_classes.

You can use the Replication Server alter connection command to change the function-string class of an existing connection.

e. Verify the non-ASE function-string classes have been updated with appropriate non-ASE function strings. The Replication Server script hds_oracle_funcstrings.sql provides the SQL statements necessary to apply predefined function strings to the replicate Replication Server's RSSD for a specific non-ASE replicate database. The scripts issue a delete followed by an insert command for each function string. You can rerun these scripts without failure. Verify your copy of the scripts has been updated with the correct use statement for your RSSD name.

f. Use the Replication Server command admin translate. This command allows you to verify the results of a specific translation. Use this command to verify the translation engine is providing the translation results you expect. Refer to the Replication Server Administration guide for more information on heterogeneous datatype support (HDS) and the admin translate command.

Troubleshooting Replication Agent System Database (RASD)

For Replication Agent for Oracle, critical metadata of the primary database is stored in the database managed by Embedded Adaptive Server Anywhere. RASD is automatically created when Replication Agent is created and is populated when a Replication Agent instance is initialized. When Replication Agent is initialized, it queries the primary database for information about log devices, users, datatypes, articles (tables and stored procedures), fields (table columns and stored procedures), truncation point, generation ID, schema changes, etc. Metadata is stored as binary in image columns and is identified by ID or owner-qualified name. The following commands can be used to view metadata:

▶ Execute ra_helpdb to view the primary database name.

Syntax:

```
ra_helpdb
```

```
1> ra_helpdb
2> go
ID          Database
----------- --------
1147999488  ORCL
```

▶ Execute ra_helpdevice to view information about log device metadata.

Syntax:

```
ra_helpdevice [device_id]
```

device_id

The device ID of the primary database log device

```
1> ra_helpdevice
2> go
ID Database Device Name Server Path                     Disk Mirror Path  Mirror Status
-- -------- ----------- ------------------------------- ----------------- -------------
1  orcl     redo01.log  /work1/oradata/orcl/redo01.log  DEFAULT           ACCESSIBLE
2  orcl     redo02.log  /work1/oradata/orcl/redo02.log  DEFAULT           ACCESSIBLE
3  orcl     redo03.log  /work1/oradata/orcl/redo03.log  DEFAULT           ACCESSIBLE

1> ra_helpdevice 1
2> go
ID Database Device Name Server Path                     Disk Mirror Path  Mirror Status
-- -------- ----------- ------------------------------- ----------------- -------------
1  orcl     redo01.log  /work1/oradata/orcl/redo01.log  DEFAULT           ACCESSIBLE
```

▶ Execute ra_helpuser to view information about primary database users.

Syntax:

```
ra_helpuser [user [, version]]

user
```

User name or user ID of a user in the primary database

```
version
```

The version number of the database user in the RASD
(Replication Agent System Database)

```
1> ra_helpuser
2> go
ID  Name                       Status Version
--- -------------------------- ------ -------
0   SYS                        NULL   NULL
1   PUBLIC                     NULL   NULL
2   CONNECT                    NULL   NULL
3   RESOURCE                   NULL   NULL
4   DBA                        NULL   NULL
5   SYSTEM                     NULL   NULL
.
.
.
62  MAINTUSER                  NULL   NULL
63  DDLUSER                    NULL   NULL
65  RA_USER                    NULL   NULL
66  _NEXT_USER                 NULL   NULL

1> ra_helpuser RA_USER
2> go
ID  Name      Status Version
--- --------- ------ -------
65  RA_USER   NULL   NULL
```

▶ Execute ra_helparticle to view information about articles.

Syntax:

```
ra_helparticle [[owner.]article [, version]]
```

article

> The object name or object ID of the article (table or stored procedure) in the primary database. Article names can be qualified with the owner name.

version

> Locator value in hexadecimal that identifies the version of the article specified in the *article* option

```
1> ra_helparticle
2> go
ID     Database Owner      Name             Type         Status
   Version
------ -------- ---------- ---------------- ------------ ----------
-----------------------------------------------------------------
4       orcl    SYS        TAB$             TABLE        Current
   00000000000000000000000000000000000000000000000000000000000000

.

.   <output removed>

.

54016  orcl    MAINTUSER  RS_INFO          TABLE        Current
   00000000000000000000000000000000000000000000000000000000000000
54017  orcl    MAINTUSER  RS_LASTCOMMIT    TABLE        Current
   00000000000000000000000000000000000000000000000000000000000000
54026  orcl    SYS        RAX_TEST         TABLE        Current
   000000000000002d80c700000030000000000000000000300000000000000000
54036  orcl    RA_USER    RA_PCALL_        SEQUENCE     Current
   00000000000000000000000000000000000000000000000000000000000000
54038  orcl    RA_USER    RA_PROCACTIVE    TABLE        Current
   000000000000002bb0c30000002b00000000000000000002b00000000000000000
54040  orcl    RA_USER    RA_DUMPSH_       TABLE        Current
   000000000000002bb0c40000002b00000000000000000002b0000000000000000
54042  orcl    RA_USER    RS_DUMP          PROCEDURE    Current
   000000000000002bb0c40000002b00000000000000000002b0000000000000000
54045  orcl    RA_USER    RA_MARKERSH_     TABLE        Current
   000000000000002bb0c30000002b00000000000000000002b0000000000000000
54047  orcl    RA_USER    RS_MARKER        PROCEDURE    Current
   000000000000002bb0c30000002b00000000000000000002b0000000000000000
```

```
1> ra_helparticle 54047
2> go
ID      Database Owner      Name             Type          Status
   Version
------  -------- ----------  ---------------  ------------  ----------
        ----------------------------------------------------------------
54047  orcl     RA_USER     RS_MARKER        PROCEDURE     Current
   000000000000002bb0c30000002b000000000000000002b0000000000000000
```

▶ Execute ra_helpfield to view information about primary database fields.

Syntax:

```
ra_helpfield [[owner.]article [, version[, field]]
```

article

> The object name or object ID of the article (table or stored procedure) in the primary database. Article names can be qualified with the owner name.

version

> Locator value in hexadecimal that identifies the version of the article specified in the *article* option

field

> Name or ID of the field (column name of the table or input parameter of stored procedure) in the specified article

```
1> ra_helpfield RAX_TEST
2> go
```

ID	Name	Type ID	Type	Precision	Length	Scale	Nullable	Identity	Primary Key
1	CHARCOL	96	CHAR	0	255	0	true	false	false
2	DECIMALFIXEDCOL	2	NUMBER	32	22	16	true	false	false
3	FLOATCOL	2	NUMBER	14	22	0	true	false	false
4	INTEGERCOL	2	NUMBER	0	22	0	true	false	false
5	SERIALCOL	2	NUMBER	0	22	0	false	false	true
6	VARCHARCOL	1	VARCHAR2	0	255	0	true	false	false

Backing up RASD

You should always back up the RASD database like any other database to prevent data loss in case of device failure. If you are replicating DDL, you should periodically back up the RASD database and truncate the log. Without maintenance, the RASD database and log will grow indefinitely. If you are not replicating DDL, you should back up the database and truncate the log as necessary. Only the secondary truncation point changes in the RASD database, so database size is static, but the log grows slowly. Maintenance commands for RASD can be executed when Replication Agent is in the replicating state. To back up the RASD database and log files and truncate the database log, log in to the Replication Agent instance with administrator login:

```
1> rasd_backup
2> go
Msg 0, Level 20, State 0:
Server 'myrao', Procedure 'rasd_backup', Line 1: successful
```

If there are permissions problems or the backup directory listed in 'rasd_backup_dir' does not exist, Replication Agent returns an error. You must fix the problem and reissue the rasd_backup command.

Use the ra_truncatearticles command to truncate all archived and dropped articles in the repository up to the specified locator. This command truncates prior versions of all articles with versions less than the LTM Locator values specified. If the most recent article version is older than the version identified by the LTM locator value, it is not truncated. The RASD database should be backed up before executing ra_truncatearticles. This command can be executed when the Replication Agent instance is in either the admin or the replicating state.

Syntax:

```
ra_truncatearticles locator
```

locator

LTM Locator value

```
1> ra_truncatearticles
000000000000002baf960000002b00000000000000000002b000000000
0000000
2> go
Msg 0, Level 20, State 0:
Server 'myrao', Procedure 'ra_truncatearticles
000000000000002baf960000002b00000000000000000002b0000000000000000',
Line 1: successful
```

Use the ra_truncateusers command to truncate all archived and dropped users. The RASD database should be backed up before executing ra_truncateusers. This command can be executed when the Replication Agent instance is in either the admin or the replicating state.

```
1> ra_truncateusers
00000000000000000000000000000000000000000000000000000000000000
0000
2> go
Msg 0, Level 20, State 0:
Server 'myrao', Procedure 'ra_truncateusers
00000000000000000000000000000000000000000000000000000000000000000',
Line 1: successful
```

Updating the Log Device Repository in RASD

Whenever a log device is added, dropped, or extended, its information must be updated in the RASD database with the ra_updatedevices command. You should always coordinate log devices changed at the primary database by updating the log device repository in RASD with ra_updatedevices. When ra_updatedevices is executed, the following actions occur in the Replication Agent instance:

▶ Archive log information is refreshed.

▶ All the data in the log device repository is deleted.

▶ The log device location is not overwritten if it is already set.

▶ The primary database is checked for information about its log devices.

▶ The log device repository in RASD is repopulated with current information about log devices returned by the primary data server.

You cannot update the log device repository in RASD; instead you have to quiesce the primary database. Log in to the Replication Agent instance with administrator login and put the Replication Agent instance in admin state.

1. Execute the ra_status command to check the replication status of Replication Agent.

```
1> ra_status
2> go
State   Action

------  ------------------------------

ADMIN   Waiting for operator command.
```

If the Replication Agent instance status is not admin, you can issue the suspend command to change it to admin state.

2. Use the ra_updatedevices command to update the log device repository in the RASD.

```
1> ra_updatedevices
```

3. Since the entire log device repository is recreated with the ra_updatedevices command, any log device path that was modified earlier (with ra_devicepath) is overwritten with current log device information from the primary database. If you want to change from the default path, you can use ra_devicepath to update disk device path information for each log device.

Syntax:

```
ra_devicepath device, dev_dirpath
```

device

Device ID is the Oracle redo log "group number"

dev_dirpath

Disk device path, pointing to the disk log device for the device specified in the device option

```
1> ra_devicepath 3, /work/oradata/orcl/redo3.log
```

Recovering from Corrupted RASD

Normal replication activity updates the RASD. If you suspect a corrupted RASD, contact Sybase Technical Support and follow the steps listed below for updating RASD with their recommendation. Log in to the Replication Agent instance with the administrator login and put the instance in admin state if it is in replicate state.

1. Check the Replication Agent instance status:

    ```
    1> ra_status
    2> go
    State  Action
    ------ -----------------------------
    ADMIN  Waiting for operator command.
    ```

    If the Replication Agent instance status is not admin, you can issue the suspend command to change it to admin state.

2. Use the pdb_xlog init, force command to reinitialize the Replication Agent instance and force it to update its RASD by creating or reloading any required xlog-based components. This command checks the redo group number, redo name, and redo path for each log device and the redo log identified in the RASD. If any of these do not match the information returned from the primary data server (Oracle), this command will overwrite the record in RASD for that log device or redo log with the information returned by the primary data server.

    ```
    1> pdb_xlog init, force
    ```

3. Resume replication by executing the resume command:

    ```
    1> resume
    2> go
    State        Action
    ------------ -------------------------
    REPLICATING  Ready to replicate data.
    ```

685

Use the ra_status command to check the replication status of the Replication Agent instance. If the returned state is admin, check the Replication Agent system log for errors, fix the errors, issue resume again, and check the status of Replication Agent.

Restoring RASD from Backup

If the RASD database became corrupted due to hardware issues such as a lost device or device failure, you can restore it from backups. Before restoring RASD from backup, verify that the Replication Agent instance is in admin state. Log in to the Replication Agent instance with administrator login.

1. Execute the ra_status command to check the replication status of Replication Agent:

    ```
    1> ra_status
    2> go
    State  Action
    ------ ------------------------------
    ADMIN  Waiting for operator command.
    ```

    If the Replication Agent instance state is not admin, you can issue the suspend command to change it to admin state.

2. Use the rasd_restore command for restoring RASD. When this command is invoked, it looks for the most recent dump in the backup directory specified by the rasd_backup_dir Replication Agent configuration parameter. If there are permissions problems or the backup directory listed in rasd_backup_dir does not exist, Replication Agent returns an error. You must fix the problem and reissue the rasd_restore command. After restoring RASD, you will need to restart the Replication Agent instance

    ```
    1> rasd_restore
    ```

3. After restoring RASD, you can resume replication by executing the resume command:

```
1> resume
2> go
State        Action
------------ ------------------------
REPLICATING  Ready to replicate data.
```

4. Execute the ra_status command to check the replication status of Replication Agent.

5. Shut down and restart the Replication Agent instance.

Typical Topology of Heterogeneous Replication

In this section we will discuss guidelines and drawbacks for setting up heterogeneous replication for the following:

▶ One-way replication from Oracle to Sybase Adaptive Server Enterprise

▶ Replicating from Sybase Adaptive Server Enterprise to Oracle database

▶ Replicating from non-Sybase primary to non-Sybase replicate database

▶ Bidirectional replication with non-Sybase primary and replicate databases

One-way Replication from Oracle to Sybase Adaptive Server Enterprise

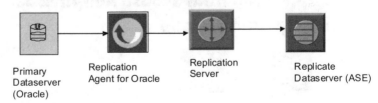

Primary Dataserver (Oracle) Replication Agent for Oracle Replication Server Replicate Dataserver (ASE)

Figure 16-3: One-way replication from Oracle to Sybase ASE

This is the simplest heterogeneous replication scenario for replicating one way from Oracle (or MSSQL/DB2) to Sybase Adaptive Server Enterprise. The only unique requirement is that a Replication Agent is used to extract transaction data from Oracle SID (primary database).

Basic components:

▶ Primary Oracle database

▶ Replication Agent for Oracle

▶ Replication Server

▶ Adaptive Server Enterprise replicate database

Considerations:

▶ The Replication Server primary database connection must include a valid user and password for the primary Oracle database, even though this ID will not be used, in this scenario, to apply transactions to the primary Oracle database.

```
create connection to myrao.orcl
set error class rs_sqlserver_error_class
set function string class rs_oracle_function_class
set username sys
set password sybase
with log transfer on, dsi_suspended
go
```

▶ The hds_clt_oracle_to_ase.sql script must be applied to the replicate Replication Server's RSSD to provide automatic translation of the primary's native datatypes to ASE.

Replicating from Sybase Adaptive Server Enterprise to Oracle

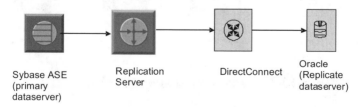

Sybase ASE
(primary
dataserver)

Replication
Server

DirectConnect

Oracle
(Replicate
dataserver)

Figure 16-4: Replicating from Sybase ASE to Oracle

This is another simple heterogeneous scenario of replicating one way from Sybase Adaptive Server Enterprise to a non-Sybase (Oracle) data server. The unique requirement in this scenario is the use of DirectConnect to apply transaction data to the replicate database.

Basic components:

▶ Sybase Adaptive Server Enterprise primary database

▶ Replication Server

▶ DirectConnect for Oracle (Enterprise Connect Data Access)

▶ Non-Sybase replicate database (e.g., Oracle)

Considerations:

▶ The Replication Server replicate connection must include a valid user and password for the replicate non-Sybase database:

```
create connection to DCO150.orcl2
set error class oracle_error_class
set function string class rs_oracle_function_class
set username maintuser
set password "password"
set batch to "off"
```

▶ The hds_oracle_setup_for_replicate.sql script must be executed against the replicate database to create rs_info and rs_lastcommit tables in the replicate database.

▶ The Replication Server connection must be created referencing the correct function-string class designed for this particular non-Sybase (Oracle) database (rs_oracle_function_class).

```
create connection to DCO150.orcl2
set error class oracle_error_class
set function string class rs_oracle_function_class
set username maintuser
set password "password"
set batch to "off"
```

▶ The hds_oracle_funcstrings.sql script must have been applied to the replicate Replication Server's RSSD.

▶ The hds_clt_ase_to_oracle.sql script must be applied to the replicate Replication Server's RSSD to provide automatic translation of the Adaptive Server Enterprise native datatypes to the replicate non-Sybase (Oracle) database's native datatypes.

Replicating from Non-Sybase Primary to Non-Sybase Replicate Database

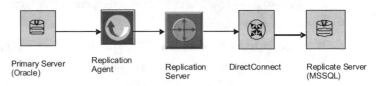

| Primary Server (Oracle) | Replication Agent | | Replication Server | DirectConnect | Replicate Server (MSSQL) |

Figure 16-5: Replicating from Oracle to Microsoft SQL database

Replicating from a non-Sybase primary database to a non-Sybase replicate database can be a little complex depending on the mix of non-Sybase databases. If the primary and replicate databases are the same non-Sybase databases (e.g., Oracle to Oracle), then fewer default class-level translations will be required (Sybase does not have to "translate" an Oracle date to another Oracle date datatype). If the primary and replicate database are not the same non-Sybase databases, the additional default class-level translations must be applied.

Basic components:

▶ Primary Oracle database

▶ Replication Agent for Oracle

▶ Replication Server

▶ DirectConnect for MSSQL (Enterprise Connect Data Access)

▶ Replicate MSSQL (MicroSoft SQL Server) database

Considerations:

▶ The Replication Server primary connection must include a valid user and password for the primary Oracle database:

```
create connection to myrao.orcl
set error class rs_sqlserver_error_class
set function string class rs_oracle_function_class
```

Chapter 17

Security

This chapter discusses Replication Server security issues including creating and modifying logins, authentication, passwords, and permissions. Replication Server includes many components, and managing the login names and passwords is part of managing Replication Server security. For example, depending on your security requirements, you can encrypt all the passwords at the Replication Server system level and manage the encrypted passwords, or you can decrypt some of the passwords and manage them as cleartext passwords. Replication Server security includes issues related to third-party network-based authentication.

Login Names and Password Management

In general, different Replication Server components have different login names. The user and password information is available in the rs_users and rs_maintusers system tables. The rs_init program can be used to encrypt passwords for all of the login names after installing the Replication Server. As shown in the following example output from the rs_users table, the password encryption option and encrypted password are also saved in the table.

```
1> select * from rs_users
2> go
username          uid                  password   permissions   use_enc_password
enc_password
---------------   --------------------  ----------  -------------  -----------------
-------------------------------------------------------------------
NYRS_RSSD_prim  0x0100006502000065  NULL         10            1
   0x02db8993c1283702389c39bb85a3a16033ee76a9561bad5a2948d127213b6cdf
NYRS_id_user    0x0100006502000068  NULL         0             1
   0x02c494a43192096fb901d87c509bb638a343d62ebf77677fa278bfd278d2cac6
NYRS_ra         0x0100006502000067  NULL         2             1
   0x02c044e57c283e84a9dd7ab2eccd8e3afc8f86f0cbcd437287d7b4f10ef3f622
NYRS_rsi        0x0100006502000066  NULL         2             1
   0x02c1efacc6564cb08f2a2eea1438c8841a9b38dce934285e17e11a2c1d9d1aff
sa              0x0000000002000001  NULL         1             1
   0x02cd394ba6f311474a8f06bf00679e1c1261e9811d1aff8383b34e335eec0e50
```

The maintenance user information is saved in the rs_maintusers system table.

```
1> select * from rs_maintusers
2> go
destid   username              password   use_enc_password
  enc_password
--------  --------------------  ----------  -----------------
-------------------------------------------------------------------
101       NYRS_RSSD_maint      NULL        1
   0x02d8f05b148d9a7057ddfce3a48812fc5351aa6ba21bae5e9feac0941551ca64
103       reptest_db1_maint    NULL        1
   0x02de2e9f943f77b2b32163a30af09abff0456490b676afeac324aabb45bdf407
105       reptest_db1_maint    NULL        1
   0x02de2e9f943f77b2b32163a30af09abff0456490b676afeac324aabb45bdf407
```

User names and login names of the Replication Server components include the primary, maintenance, and RepAgent user and the ID Server, Replication Server Interface, and Adaptive Server maintenance user logins.

Primary User and Maintenance User

Setup and Function

During installation, rs_init adds the primary user login and the maintenance user login. Replication Server uses the primary user login to modify the RSSD system tables for the primary Replication Server. Modifications to the system tables include changes to routes, replication definitions, subscription definitions, exception handling, and any other information that needs to be saved persistently in the system tables. Password changes are also saved in the RSSD tables.

The maintenance user login is used to modify the user tables in the replicated databases. Transactions applied by the maintenance user are normally not replicated back to the primary Replication Server to avoid circular replication. The maintenance user is also set up using rs_init.

Password Management

▶ If you change the login name or password for either the primary or maintenance user logins, be sure to apply the same changes to the Replication Server configuration file. A typical configuration entry for an RSSD user and password is shown below:

```
RSSD_server=LONDON_DS
RSSD_database=R1250RRS_RSSD
RSSD_primary_user=R1250RRS_RSSD_prim
RSSD_primary_pw=R1250RRS_RSSD_prim_ps
RSSD_maint_user=R1250RRS_RSSD_maint
RSSD_maint_pw=R1250RRS_RSSD_maint_ps
```

▶ Never change the passwords of the primary user while a route is being created. Replication Server uses the same login and password both at the primary and replicate to create the route.

▶ Use the same login name and password for the primary user at both the primary and replicate sites.

▶ If you have to change both the login name and the password for these users, you must use drop user and then create user.

If only the password needs to be changed, you may use the `alter user` command with the `set password` clause. Be sure to update the changed password in the configuration file. If the password is encrypted, you may need to use rs_init, which updates the configuration file as well.

▶ For changes to take effect, restart the Replication Server.

RepAgent User

Setup and Function

The RepAgent user needs a login to connect to the RSSD and to each of the user databases.

Password Management

The RepAgent logins are added with rs_init. The default password is set to the RepAgent login name appended with "_ps".

▶ If you want to change the password, use the `alter user` command with the `set password` option.

▶ If you have to change the login name and password, you must use `drop user` and `create user`.

▶ You can also use `sp_config_rep_agent` to change the login name and the password. Restart the Replication Server for the changes to take effect.

```
sp_config_rep_agent [dbname
  [, {'enable', 'repserver_name',
     'repserver_username', 'repserver password'}
... < more syntax ..>
```

Where:

repserver_name

The Replication Server for which the RepAgent login name and password are being changed

repserver_username

The RepAgent login name

repserver_password

> The RepAgent password to connect to the Replication Server

Please refer to Chapter 6 for more information on Replication Agent configuration management.

ID Server Login and Password

The ID Server is a Replication Server that registers the Replication Servers and objects in a domain. The ID Server can be the first Replication Server that you start in a replication system domain. Replication Server uses the ID Server login and password to connect to the ID Server. If the ID Server login name or password is changed, then it should be changed in the configuration files of all of the Replication Servers associated with that ID Server as well. The login name and password are initially set by rs_init. The ID Server must be accessible when a new Replication Server is installed within the domain, a new database connection is created or dropped, or a new route is added to a replication system.

Replication Server Interface (RSI) Login and Password

Replication Server uses a login to connect to the other Replication Servers via the route. This login is called the RSI user. This login and password can be created by rs_init. Use the alter route command to change the password. Please refer to Chapter 8 for information on creating and managing routes.

Syntax:

```
alter route to dest_replication_server {
    set next site [to] thru_replication_server |
    set username [to] 'user' set password [to] 'passwd' |
    set password [to] 'passwd' |
    set route_param [to] 'value' |
```

```
set security_param [to] 'value' |
set security_services [to] 'default'}
```

Example to change route user and password:

```
alter route to R1250RRS
        set username R1250RRS_rsi
        set password R1250RRS_rsi_passwd
```

Adaptive Server Maintenance User Login and Password

Replication Server uses the maintenance user login name to access the Adaptive Server to make changes to either an RSSD database or a user database. The maintenance user is an Adaptive Server user. The maintenance user must have the replication_ role and also needs privileges to be able to execute DML changes and stored procedures to perform function replication.

Use the alter connection command to change the maintenance user password. Note that the maintenance user will not execute the truncate table command unless the maintenance user either is the database owner or is given sa_role.

Client Connections and Encrypted Passwords

It is possible to configure Replication Server to use encrypted passwords over the network. The isql command provides the -X option, which initiates a connection to the server with client-side password encryption over the network. The client specifies to the server that a password encryption is desired. The server sends an encryption key to the client, which the client uses to encrypt the password. If isql crashes, the core will include the encrypted password. If the encryption was not used, the core will have a cleartext password. The Replication Server can be configured with the send_enc_password or RS_send_enc_pwd options to establish client connections with encrypted passwords. The send_enc_ password option ensures all the connections including the first connection to the RSSD are with encrypted passwords, whereas the RS_send_enc_pwd option ensures all the client connections are with encrypted passwords except the first connection to the RSSD. send_enc_password overrides RS_send_enc_pwd.

```
configure replication server
set send_enc_password to 'on'
```

The password encryption option is recorded in the configuration file, and in the rs_users and rs_maintusers tables.

Encrypting Existing Passwords

It is possible to encrypt an existing cleartext Replication Server password.

First, use the configure replication server command to enable future password encryption:

```
configure replication server
set password_encryption to '1'
```

Use the alter user command to reset the password, which will be encrypted:

```
alter user user set password password
```

Where:

user

The Replication Server user for which the password is to be encrypted

password

The existing password that needs to be encrypted

To encrypt a maintenance user password:

```
alter connection to data_server.database set password to password
```

Where:

data_server.database

> The connection for which the maintenance user password is being encrypted

password

> The existing maintenance user password that needs to be encrypted

To encrypt the existing route user password:

```
alter route to dest_replication_server set password to password
```

dest_replication_server

> The destination Replication Server for which the route user (RSI) password is to be encrypted

password

> The existing password to be encrypted

For all users, rs_init can be used to encrypt passwords in the RSSD and configuration file. If you use the interactive commands listed above, you need to make sure the passwords are encrypted in the configuration file using rs_init.

Disabling Password Encryption

You can disable password encryption for all future passwords. To do so, use the `configure replication server` command:

```
configure replication server
set password_encryption to '0'
```

This will only disable password encryption for any future passwords.

To change already encrypted passwords to cleartext, use the `alter user` command after making the configuration change with the `configure replication server` command.

```
alter user user
set password to new password
```

To change password encryption to cleartext, use the alter connection command for the maintenance user, and use the alter route command to change route password encryption to cleartext.

Manually edit the Replication Server configuration file and enter the cleartext passwords to match the passwords used in the alter user command.

The RepAgent password is always encrypted in the system tables.

Be sure to restart the Replication Server for the new configuration to take effect.

RSSD System Tables and Password Encryption

Use the rs_helpuser stored procedure to display any Replication Server user information including user name and password. You can also directly query the rs_maintusers and rs_users system tables. Do not attempt to directly update these system tables to change passwords. Use the alter user command instead as described in this chapter.

```
1> rs_helpuser
2> go

Users and Privileges Known at Site JDBCD05A_REP

Primary Users

User Name                        Permission(s) Name
-----------------------------    -----------------------------
R1250RRS_RSSD_prim               no grants
sa                               sa
JDBCD05A_REP_ra                  connect source
JDBCD05A_REP_rsi                 connect source
JDBCD05A_REP_RSSD_prim           connect source, primary subscr
```

```
Maintenance Users

User name                          Destination DS.DB
------------------------------     ------------------------------
JDBCD05A_REP_RSSD_main             JDBCD05A_SYB.JDBCD05A_REP_RSSD
pubs2_maint                        JDBCD05A_SYB.pubs2
(return status = 0)
```

Select from the rs_users system table to find out whether password encryption is turned on. The use_enc_password column will be non-zero if the passwords are encrypted, and the enc_password column will be non-null.

```
1> select convert(varchar(25),username),password, use_enc_password, convert(varchar(5),
enc_password) enc_password from rs_users
2> go
username                  password                  use_enc_password  enc_password
----------------------    ----------------------    ----------------  ------------
R1250RRS_REP_RSSD_prim    R1250RRS_REP_RSSD_prim_ps 0                 NULL
R1250RRS_REP_ra           R1250RRS_REP_ra_ps        0                 NULL
R1250RRS_REP_rsi          R1250RRS_REP_rsi_ps       0                 NULL
R1250RRS_RSSD_prim        R1250RRS_RSSD_prim_ps     0                 NULL
sa                        reptest                   0                 NULL

(5 rows affected)

1> select convert(varchar(25), username) username, use_enc_password, enc_password from
rs_users
2> go
username              use_enc_password   enc_password
--------------------  -----------------  --------------------------------
LONDON_RS_RSSD_prim   1                  0x02d18G3db4G0af6591c1fd2b9979+
LONDON_RS_id_user     1                  0x02d2d4febe6b8782e325017a3c154
LONDON_RS_ra          1                  0x02d0f63caf46e5394f6cha2dad319
LONDON_RS_rsi         1                  0x02df3528e0c0943a8d6e1bfc4072aa688
LONDON_RS_RSSD_prim   1                  0x02d17f213a883df79bd5fe73c6bc179c
sa                    1                  0x02c23faf7ca930745c4a744eec300

(8 rows affected)
```

Similar information can be obtained from the rs_maintusers table for the maintenance user.

Network-based Security

In a networked client-server environment, it is important to
ensure a secure pathway is established between the client and
the server. Both client and server must agree upon a common
security protocol in transferring and manipulating data. Replication Server 12 and above support industry standard network-
based security mechanisms such as CyberSafe Kerberos version
5 security server and Transarc DCE version 1.1 security server.
The features of these security mechanisms can include unified
login, confidentiality, origin verification, and out of sequence
validation.

Replication Server can be a client or server or both, depending on the implementation design. When it is a server,
Replication Server authenticates incoming connections. Standard
authentication protocols will be followed based on the security
mechanism chosen. Similarly, when Replication Server is a client,
Replication Server will adhere to the standard message protection techniques in establishing a secure pathway.

Note that all clients and servers that the Replication Server
connects to or accepts connections from must support the
selected security mechanism. Additionally, user names must be
unique throughout the replication system, including Replication
Servers, data servers, and other heterogeneous data sources. If
multiple security mechanisms are supported in the Replication
Server environment and unique user names are possible, request
stored procedures may need to be turned off.

You can turn off request stored procedures to the primary
data server by using the alter connection command:

```
alter connection to data_server.database
    set dsi_exec_request_sproc 'off'
```

Setting Up Network-based Security

Assuming one of the supported security mechanisms is installed on all of the hosts, setting up a network-based security mechanism for Replication Server includes:

▶ Changing the configuration parameters

▶ Identifying the Replication Server principal user. A principal user may be the Replication Server name itself.

▶ Activating the security mechanism

Changing the Configuration Parameters

Depending on the network-based security mechanism selected, one or more of the following security configurations may need to be updated.

▶ libctl.cfg: This is a template file that will help establish an interface with the selected security mechanism and includes configuration information for the selected security mechanism drivers. It is located in the $SYBASE/SYBASE_REP/config directory (UNIX) or the %SYBASE%\ini directory (Windows 2000 or 2003). This file provides the initialization string for the selected security mechanism.

```
Provider=driver initialization_string
```

Where:

```
Provider
```

The local name for the security mechanism provider such as Kerberos or DCE. If the provider is Kerberos, the local name is csfkrb5. If the provider is DCE, the local name is dce.

An example entry for the DCE security driver:

```
[SECURITY]
dce=libsdce.so secbase=/.:/cell_name
```

Where:

```
dce
```

Provider name

```
libsdce.so
```

The driver

```
secbase=/.:/cell_name
```

The initialization string

An example entry for the Kerberos driver:

```
[SECURITY]
csfkr5=libsybkrb.so secbase=@ASElibgss=/krb5/lib/libgss.so
```

Where:

```
csfkr5
```

The provider name

```
libsybkrb.so
```

The driver file

```
secbase=@ASElibgss=/krb5/lib/libgss.so
```

The initialization string

▶ objectid.dat: You need to edit this file only if you change the name of the security mechanism to a different local name. You edit this file to map global object identifiers to the local name in the libctl.cfg file.

Part of the objectid.dat file:

```
; comment character is a semicolon
;
; OBJECTID.DAT
;
; Flat-file database for mapping global object identifiers to local names.
;

<Some of the file is deleted intentionally>
```

```
[secmech]
1.3.6.1.4.1.897.4.6.1   = dce
1.3.6.1.4.1.897.4.6.2   = nds
1.3.6.1.4.1.897.4.6.3   = NTLM
1.3.6.1.4.1.897.4.6.6   = csfkrb5
```

▶ interfaces: The interfaces file, which is located in the $SYBASE directory. When a security mechanism like DCE or Kerberos is configured, the interfaces file entry needs to include the security information.

A sample interfaces file entry for a Kerberos security mechanism:

```
#
server_principal_user_name
query tcp ether plum 1050
master tcp ether plum 1050
secmech 1.3.6.1.4.1.897.4.6.6
```

Where:

secmech

The section of the objectid.dat file

1.3.6.1.4.1.897.4.6.6

The security identifier mapped to Kerberos name csfkrb5

server_principal_user_name

The principal user identified by the Replication Server system administrator

Identifying the Replication Server Principal User

First, the system administrator defines the Replication Server principal user name to the security mechanism. Consult the security mechanism documentation for further details on how to create the security mechanism principal user. The server principal user must be unique for Replication Server and the servers the Replication Server is to connect to.

Typically the server_principal_user_name is the name of the Replication Server. In the absence of network-based security, Replication Server logs in to other servers as any one of the logins defined for the purpose. For example, Replication Server will log in to replicate Adaptive Server Enterprise as maintenance user to apply data modification statements. But when any network-based security is activated, Replication Server will log in to the other clients or servers as the server principal user as defined by the system administrator. The server principal user can be defined in the rs_users table, or the Replication Server name can serve as the server principal user.

Each of the security mechanisms may need global environment variables. For example, the CSFC5KTNAME global environment variable is required for Kerberos setup.

Activating Network-based Security

Before configuring the Replication Server to use network-based security, network-based security must be turned on. Additionally, you need the key table location for the security mechanism, which can be found in the security mechanism documentation. Network-based security can be turned on by following these steps:

1. Log in to the Replication Server and use the following command to turn on the network-based security:

   ```
   configure replication server
   set use_security_services to 'on'
   ```

2. Include the -K option to specify the security mechanism key table location in the RUN SERVER for DCE security mechanism. Use the CSFC5KTNAME global environment variable for specifying the key table location for Kerberos security.

3. Restart the Replication Server.

For the proper functioning of network-based security, all clients and servers must be started after the host is started with proper security mechanism credentials. For example, when using Kerberos, all clients and servers must be started after issuing the kinit command and acquiring a Kerberos ticket. A similar startup procedure is followed for the DCE security mechanism on UNIX and on Windows. Please refer to the security mechanism documentation for more information.

Chapter 18

Internationalization

In today's global environment, we need to understand how character set, language, and sort order settings can impact our replication system and the design. Replication Server, Sybase Central, and Replication Server Manager support a global environment by providing support for all Sybase supported character sets, with character set conversion between replication sites, localization of messages into Sybase supported languages, and non-binary sort orders. RepAgent uses the same character set, sort order, and language as Adaptive Server Enterprise.

Message Language

Although "us_english" is the default language setting and is compatible with all Sybase supported character sets, Replication Server can be configured to print messages to the Replication Server error log and client logs in languages other than English. Be aware that languages selected for Replication Server should be compatible with the Replication Server default character set. Unlike Adaptive Server Enterprise and RepAgent, Replication Server does not check for the client's language; instead it sends messages to clients in their own language, which can result in a mixed language error log. To avoid this, replication servers and clients should be configured with the same language. The default language for Replication Server can be configured at installation time with rs_init.

```
rs_init menu:

REPLICATION SERVER INFORMATION

1.  Is this Replication Server the ID Server? no
2.  Replication Server error log:
        /opt/sybase/rel150_rs/REP-15_0/install/prs.log
3.  Replication Server configuration file:
        /opt/sybase/rel150_rs/REP-15_0/install/prs.cfg
4.  Replication Server password encryption: no
5.  Replication Server character set: iso_1
6.  Replication Server language: us_english
7.  Replication Server sort order: binary
8.  Replication Server Interfaces Information          Incomplete
9.  Use SSL Service:  no


Ctrl-a Accept and Continue, Ctrl-x Exit Screen, ? Help.
```

You can also set the language after Replication Server installation by editing the Replication Server's configuration file and changing the value of the RS_language configuration parameter:

1. Shut down Replication Server.

2. Change the value of RS_language in Replication Server's configuration file.

3. Restart Replication Server.

```
# Configuration file for Replication Server 'prs' created by rs_init.
#
RSSD_embedded=no
RSSD_server=pds
RSSD_database=prs_RSSD
RSSD_primary_user=prs_RSSD_prim
RSSD_primary_pw=prs_RSSD_prim_ps
RSSD_maint_user=prs_RSSD_maint
RSSD_maint_pw=prs_RSSD_maint_ps
RSSD_ha_failover=no
ID_server=prs
ID_user=prs_id_user
ID_pw=prs_id_passwd
RS_charset=iso_1
```

```
RS_language=us_english
RS_sortorder=binary
```

Character Set

The character set is the language in which the server sends and receives the data from client-servers. All servers in the replication system should have the same or compatible character sets. Sybase doesn't support conversion between single-byte and multibyte character sets. Replication Server's default character set is influenced by the Replication Server's default language. All Sybase supported character sets are supersets of ASCII-7. All characters support at least two languages: English and one other language.

Table 18-1 lists the Sybase supported character sets and languages.

Table 18-1: Sybase supported character sets and languages

Language Group	Languages	Character Set
Group 1	Western European	ASCII 8, cp 437, cp 850, cp 860, cp 863, cp 1252, iso 8859-1, iso 8859-15, macintosh, roman, roman8, roman9, iso-15, cp 858
Group 2	Eastern European (and English)	cp 852, cp 1250, iso 8859-2, macintosh central european
Group 4	Baltic (and English)	cp 1257
Group 5	Cyrillic (and English)	cp 855, cp 866, cp 1251, iso 8869-5, koi8, macintosh cyrillic
Group 6	Arabic (and English)	cp 864, cp 1256, iso 8859-6
Group 7	Greek (and English)	cp 869, cp 1253, greek8, iso 8859-7, macintosh greek
Group 8	Hebrew (and English)	cp 1255, iso 8859-8
Group 9	Turkish (and English)	cp 857, cp 1254, iso 8859-9, macintosh turkish, turkish 8
Group 101	Japanese (and English)	cp 932 dec kanji, euc-jis, shift-jis

Language Group	Languages	Character Set
Group 102	Simplified Chinese (PRC) (and English)	cp 936, euc-gb, gb18030
Group 103	Traditional Chinese (ROC) (and English)	big 5, cp 950, euc-cns, big 5 hkscs
Group 104	Korean (and English)	euc-ksc, cp 949
Group 105	Tahi (and English)	cp 874, tis 620
Group 106	Vietnamese (and English)	cp 1258
Unicode	Over 650 languages	UTF-8

Replication Server's default character set can be configured at installation time with rs_init.

```
Rs_init menu:

REPLICATION SERVER INFORMATION

1.  Is this Replication Server the ID Server? no
2.  Replication Server error log:
         /opt/sybase/rel150_rs/REP-15_0/install/prs.log
3.  Replication Server configuration file:
         /opt/sybase/rel150_rs/REP-15_0/install/prs.cfg
4.  Replication Server password encryption: no
5.  Replication Server character set: iso_1
6.  Replication Server language: us_english
7.  Replication Server sort order: binary
8.  Replication Server Interfaces Information         Incomplete
9.  Use SSL Services: no


Ctrl-a Accept and Continue, Ctrl-x Exit Screen, ? Help
```

Replication Server's default character set can also be configured by editing Replication Server's configuration file and changing the value of the RS_charset configuration parameter. Be sure not to change the CONFIG_charset parameter; this parameter tells Replication Server to decode using the given character set, which is commonly the default character set for that OS. Steps to change the default character set and sort order are listed at the end of this chapter.

```
# Configuration file for Replication Server 'prs'. Created by rs_init.
#
RSSD_embedded=no
RSSD_server=pds
RSSD_database=prs_RSSD
RSSD_primary_user=prs_RSSD_prim
RSSD_primary_pw=prs_RSSD_prim_ps
RSSD_maint_user=prs_RSSD_maint
RSSD_maint_pw=prs_RSSD_maint_ps
RSSD_ha_failover=no
ID_server=prs
ID_user=prs_id_user
ID_pw=prs_id_passwd
RS_charset=UTF8
CONFIG_charset=iso_1
RS_language=us_english
RS_sortorder=binary
```

When a subscription is materialized, Replication Server copies the requested data from the primary database to the replicate database. During the materialization phase, the primary data server converts character data to the replicate data server's character set. If the replicate data server character set is different from the primary data server, the replicate data server's character set should be installed at the primary data server. Similarly, when a route is created, the replicate Replication Server's character set should be installed at the data server of the primary Replication Server's RSSD (Replication Server System Database).

The Replication Server configuration parameter dsi_charset_ convert can be used to specify whether Replication Server should do character set conversion. For details on this parameter, please see Chapter 5.

Character set conversion is done at the replicate (destination) Replication Server. All messages packed for RSI include the name of the primary (source) Replication Server's character set, which is used by the replicate Replication Server for character set conversion and to identify its own character set. At character set conversion time, the replicate Replication Server checks to see whether both source and destination character sets are compatible; if they are not, then no conversion occurs. When both source and destination character sets are compatible, the characters that do not exist in the destination replicate data server are replaced by a question mark (?). In order to avoid this, make sure object names and character data do not include any characters that are not common to both character sets.

Unicode

Unicode is an international character set that supports almost all the languages of the world. The Unicode standard assigns each character a unique numeric value and name. Unicode design is based on ASCII, but it goes far beyond ASCII's limited ability to encode only the Latin alphabet. Unicode uses three types of encode forms that allow data to be transmitted in byte, word, or double word (8, 16, and 32 bits per code unit). These three encode forms can be efficiently converted to one another without losing data. Currently Sybase supports UTF-8 and UTF-16 encoding.

Replication Server 12.5 and above support UTF-8 as the default character set. Replication Server supports three Unicode datatypes — unichar, univarchar, and unitext. In order to use unichar and univarchar datatypes, the site version must be set to 12.5 or later. The unitext datatype is introduced in Replication Server 15. To use unitext, the site version and route version must be set to 15.0 or later and the ltl version must be set to 700. If at connect-source time the ltl version is less than 700, RepAgent will convert unitext columns to image. Unichar, univarchar, and unitext datatypes use UTF-16 encoding.

▶ Unichar — Unicode fixed-width character datatype

▶ Univarchar — Unicode variable-width character datatype

▶ Unitext — Unicode variable-width text datatype that can hold up to $2^{30}-1$ (1,073,741,823) Unicode characters. This equals $2\wedge31-1$ (2,147,483,647) bytes. Unitext columns can be replicated to replicate and standby databases.

UTF-8

HTML and similar protocols, Adaptive Server Enterprise, Oracle, IBM UDB, and Microsoft support UTF-8 encoding. UTF-8 transforms all Unicode characters into variable-length encoding of bytes (1 to 4 bytes). UTF-8 supports all ASCII code values as well as values from many other languages. In UTF-8 ASCII characters are stored as 1 byte, accented latin-1 characters (used in European languages) are stored in 2 bytes, and Japanese, Chinese, and Korean ideographs are stored in 3 bytes. Code values beyond the basic multilingual plane (BMP) require surrogate pairs and 4 bytes.

UTF-16

UTF-16 encoding is used in environments that need to balance efficient access to characters with economical use of storage. All characters take 2 to 4 bytes of space. This encoding is more space efficient and slightly faster than UTF-8, because UTF-8 data must be converted to UTF-16 to be processed internally. All characters take 2 bytes of storage, except for values beyond BMP, which are represented using surrogate pairs and take 4 bytes.

UTF-32

UTF-32 encoding is fixed length and is used where memory space is not a concern. When using this encoding, each character is encoded in a single 32-bit code unit. Currently Sybase does not support UTF-32.

Sort Order

The same characters are sorted differently in different languages. Each character set comes with one or more sort orders that is supported by the server. The sort orders available for a particular character set are located in sort order definition files (*.srt) in the character set directory.

For example:

```
/opt/sybase/charsets/iso_1
```

avt.xlt	cit50.xlt	**espnocs.srt**	**nocase.srt**	vt100.xlt
binary.srt	**dictiona.srt**	hds200_7.xlt	**nocasepr.srt**	vt200.xlt
charset.loc	**dictionary.srt**	iso_1.cfg	**nocasepref.srt**	vt330.xlt
cit101e.xlt	**espdict.srt**	**noaccent.srt**	sun.xlt	wyse50.xlt
cit101xl.xlt	**espnoac.srt**	**noaccents.srt**	UTF8.ctb	

Replication Server supports all Sybase supported sort orders including non-binary sort orders. European languages need non-binary sort order to correctly order character data and identifiers. Non-binary sort should also be used when primary and replicate data servers have different character sets (8-bit character data) and you want to include columns with this data in the where clause of a subscription or query the database with an order by clause involving the columns with this data.

All Replication Server components (primary and replicate data servers, Replication Servers) should be configured with the same sort order. Replication Server's default sort order can be set at installation time with rs_init.

```
rs_init menu:

REPLICATION SERVER INFORMATION

1.   Is this Replication Server the ID Server? no
2.   Replication Server error log:
        /opt/sybase/rel150_rs/REP-15_0/install/prs.log
3.   Replication Server configuration file:
        /opt/sybase/rel150_rs/REP-15_0/install/prs.cfg
4.   Replication Server password encryption: no
5.   Replication Server character set: iso_1
6.   Replication Server language: us_english
7.   Replication Server sort order: binary
8.   Replication Server Interfaces Information          Incomplete
9.   Use SSL Service:  no


Ctrl-a Accept and Continue, Ctrl-x Exit Screen, ? Help.
```

You can also edit the Replication Server configuration file. Steps to change the default character set and sort order are provided at the end of this chapter.

```
# Configuration file for Replication Server 'prs'. Created by rs_init.
#
RSSD_embedded=no
RSSD_server=pds
RSSD_database=prs_RSSD
RSSD_primary_user=prs_RSSD_prim
RSSD_primary_pw=prs_RSSD_prim_ps
RSSD_maint_user=prs_RSSD_maint
RSSD_maint_pw=prs_RSSD_maint_ps
RSSD_ha_failover=no
ID_server=prs
ID_user=prs_id_user
ID_pw=prs_id_passwd
RS_charset=UTF8
CONFIG_charset=iso_1
RS_language=us_english
RS_sortorder=binary
```

Subscriptions compare data at materialization. During this process, the replicate Replication Server retrieves data from the primary data server by issuing a select statement. All character data is converted by the primary data server to the replicate Replication Server's character set, and then data is inserted at the replicate data server by the replicate Replication Server. It is very important that the replicate Replication Server's character set be installed at the primary data server if it is different from the primary data server's.

If a subscription is initialized using bulk materialization, you should make sure the sort order is the same on Replication Server components and the character set is compatible and data is converted correctly to the replicate data server's character set.

During subscription resolution, the primary transaction log for updates is scanned by RepAgent, the primary Replication Server uses its sort order to qualify log records for this subscription, and RSI messages are packed with the primary replication server's character set. Data is then converted if necessary by the replicate Replication Server and applied to the replicate data server.

For subscription reconciliation, rs_subcmp uses the replicate data server's character set to select data from both the primary and replicate data servers. All character sets at the primary data server are converted to the replicate data server by the primary data server. Sort order should be the same on both primary and replicate data servers.

For subscription dematerialization, the replicate Replication Server selects data from the replicate data server, using the replicate data server's sort order to construct the dematerialization queue.

Unicode Sort Order

The default Unicode sort order is different from the sort order of Replication Server's default character set. This parameter can be set by editing Replication Server's configuration file.

```
# Configuration file for Replication Server 'prs'. Created by rs_init.
#
RSSD_embedded=no
RSSD_server=pds
RSSD_database=prs_RSSD
RSSD_primary_user=prs_RSSD_prim
RSSD_primary_pw=prs_RSSD_prim_ps
RSSD_maint_user=prs_RSSD_maint
RSSD_maint_pw=prs_RSSD_maint_ps
RSSD_ha_failover=no
ID_server=prs
ID_user=prs_id_user
ID_pw=prs_id_passwd
RS_charset=UTF8
CONFIG_charset=iso_1
RS_language=us_english
RS_sortorder=binary
RS_unicode_sort_order=binary
```

To change RS_unicode_sort_order:

1. Stop Replication Server.

2. Edit Replication Server and change RS_unicode_sort_order.

3. Restart Replication Server.

Changing the Character Set and Sort Order

These steps explain how to change Replication Server's character set and sort order. To change the Adaptive Server Enterprise character set and sort order, please follow instructions from the Adaptive Server Enterprise System Administration Guide.

1. All Replication Server components should be identified, including primary Replication Servers, replicate Replication Servers, primary and replicate data servers, and Adaptive Server Enterprises hosting RSSD (Replication Server System Database).

2. Drain primary database transaction logs to make sure Replication Server has processed all the transactions.

3. Quiesce all Replication Servers involved in the replication system.

   a. Execute the suspend log transfer from all command at each Replication Server.

   b. Execute admin quiesce_force_rsi at each Replication Server.

   c. Execute admin quiesce_check at each Replication Server to make sure Replication Server is quiesced.

   d. Repeat steps b and c until all Replication Servers are quiesced.

   e. After all Replication Servers are quiesced, execute admin quiesce_force_rsi followed by admin quiesce_check.

4. Shut down Replication Servers and Replication Agents.

5. Change the Adaptive Server Enterprise's default character set and/or sort order and recycle Adaptive Server Enterprise.

6. Start Adaptive Server Enterprise and make sure there is no activity on the primary and replicate data servers. If there is activity, start Adaptive Server Enterprise in single-user mode.

7. Remove the secondary truncation point. From each Adaptive Server Enterprise:

   ```
   use dbname
   go
   dbcc settrunc(ltm, ignore)
   ```

8. Truncate the database transaction log:

   ```
   dump transaction db_name with truncate only
   ```

9. Validate the secondary truncation point:

   ```
   dbcc settrunc(ltm, valid)
   ```

10. Reset the locater value for the primary database:

    ```
    use rssd_db
    go
    rs_zeroltm data_server, db_name
    ```

11. Shut down and restart Adaptive Server Enterprise in multi-user mode if it was booted in single-user mode, and resume activity.

12. Restart Replication Servers.

13. Resume log transfer. From each Replication Server:

```
resume log transfer from data_server.db_name
```

14. Start RepAgents. From each Adaptive Server Enterprise:

```
sp_start_rep_agent db_name
```

15. Resume replication.

If the character set is changed from a single-byte to a multi-byte character set or vice versa, then stored procedure messages of all databases controlled by Replication Server should be loaded. If the character set is changed to UTF-8, then both $SYBASE/$SYBASE_REP/scripts/rsspmsg1.sql and $SYBASE/$SYBASE_REP/scripts/rsspmsg2.sql should be loaded to the RSSD database.

If the character set is changed from single byte to multibyte:

```
isql -Usa -P<password> -S<RSSD_Server> -D<RSSD_DB> -i
$SYBASE/$SYBASE_REP/scripts/rsspmsg2.sql -Jeucjis
```

If the character set is changed from multibyte:

```
isql -Usa -P<password> -S<RSSD_Server> -D<RSSD_DB> -i
$SYBASE/$SYBASE_REP/scripts/rsspmsg1.sql -Jiso_1
```

In a replication system, all the component servers should have the same or compatible character sets in order to keep from having to do character set conversion. Character set conversions can affect performance. Similarly, sort orders should be compatible with the character sets selected and should be the same across the replication domain.

Chapter 19

ERSSD

Replication Server requires a system database just like an Adaptive Server Enterprise needs a system database. Replication Server 12.6 and above support Embedded Replication Server System Database (ERSSD). ERSSD is an alternative to RSSD. RSSD needs an Adaptive Server Enterprise running, whereas ERSSD uses an Adaptive Server Anywhere. An Adaptive Server Anywhere is a minimally managed server. When ERSSD is selected during Replication Server installation, there is no additional installation and configuration requirement. ERSSD is automatically installed, configured, and started in the background if you specify that you want to use it. Backup procedures are automatic and preconfigured.

You can choose ERSSD during the Replication Server installation process. During rs_init an option is provided to select to install ERSSD. ERSSD is an ASA database with low or no maintenance. The Replication Server software distribution medium includes all the necessary software to install a minimally configured ASA. You will notice the subdirectory ASA9 under the Replication Server install directory with ASA files. Please make sure you have this directory included in the $PATH and the $LD_LIBRARY_PATH variables.

ERSSD uses the following files to manage the system database:

► A database root file
► A transaction log file
► A transaction log mirror file

For recoverability and performance, the database root files and the transaction log files should be placed on different physical devices.

ERSSD installation includes installing an ASA 9.0.1 or above. rs_init gives the opportunity to select the ERSSD during Replication Server installation. When you choose this option, rs_init also provides additional menus to specify the directory path names to create the files required for ERSSD management.

Installing ERSSD Using rs_init

```
REPLICATION SERVER SYSTEM DATABASE CHOICE

1.  Do you want Replication Server System Database embedded: no


2.  Replication Server System Database on ASE              Incomplete




Ctrl-a Accept and Continue, Ctrl-x Exit Screen, ? Help.

Enter the number of your choice and press return: 1
```

When you choose option 1 in the above screen during the rs_init process, the switch will toggle to "yes". Choosing option 2 presents additional screens to install the system database in an Adaptive Server Enterprise. You will need to complete inputs related to directory paths for the files to locate ERSSD data files, log files, and backup files, and you will need to specify an interfaces entry for the ASA. Be sure to pre-populate the interface entries for the Replication Server and the ERSSD prior to starting the installation process. If the interfaces file is not accessible to rs_init, it may signal something is not correct in your host-level global variable definitions (for example, the $PATH) or you may need to define additional symbolic links from the Replication Server install directory to the actual interfaces file. If you are using one interfaces file for both data servers and Replication Servers, define symbolic links from the actual interfaces file location to the Replication Server installation directory or subdirectories.

Upon entering all the information required to install the ERSSD as part of the Replication Server installation process, the rs_init screen will look like the following:

```
EMBEDDED REPLICATION SERVER SYSTEM DATABASE

1.  ERSSD database directory:  /db/dumps/rep_erssd/REP-15_0/data
2.  ERSSD transaction log directory:  /data/rep_tranlogs
3.  ERSSD backup directory:  /db/dumps/rep_erssd/REP-15_0/backup
4.  ERSSD error log directory:  /usr/sybase/logs
5.  ERSSD Interfaces Information                          Complete




Ctrl-a Accept and Continue, Ctrl-x Exit Screen, ? Help.

Enter the number of your choice and press return: Ctrl-a
```

When **Ctrl-a** is entered, this menu will be accepted as part of the Replication Server installation.

Special Features of ERSSD and Replication Server 15.0 Enhancements

The following list points out features and enhancements in ERSSD.

▶ The ASA network server acts as an Open Server to the Replication Server.

▶ The startup and shutdown processes of the ASA are controlled and coordinated with the startup and shutdown of the Replication Server and are managed by the Replication Server.

▶ The backups are configured automatically. Make sure there is enough disk space in the backup directory path for full backups.

▶ The transaction logs for the ERSSD are mirrored. Store the transaction log mirror file on a disk separate from the primary transaction log file.

▶ In Replication Server 15.0 and above, a route can be initiated from the Replication Server with an ERSSD. In prior Replication Server releases, routes could not be initiated for the Replication Server with an ERSSD, although this Replication Server could still receive a route. This limitation no longer exists. Replication Server 15.0 and above with ERSSD can participate in a two-way route. Routes can exist between a Replication Server with ERSSD and a Replication Server with ERSSD or with ASE RSSD.

▶ In Replication Server 15.0, all limitations and differences between ASE RSSD and ERSSD are removed.

▶ In Replication Server 15.0, support for ASA 9.0.1 is added.

▶ No maintenance is required to manage the ASA or the ERSSD. However, the ASA can be stopped and started using the dbspawn and the dbstop commands.

▶ If a previous installation included an ASE-based RSSD, it can be migrated to an ERSSD. A migration from the ERSSD to the RSSD is not supported.

ERSSD Files

The following table lists files related to the management of ERSSD.

Table 19-1: ERSSD files

ERSSD File	Description
Database file	Default name: erssd_name.db
	During the installation you cannot change this name, as you will not enter the file name. You can only enter the directory name.
	Location: The directory path that you enter during the installation.
	Make sure there is enough space for growth even though the ERSSD is not that large of a database.
Transaction log file	Default name: erssd_name.log
	The file name cannot be changed during the installation, as only the directory name can be entered.
	Location: The directory path that you enter during installation.
	Cleanup: Truncated after the backup
Transaction log mirror file	Default name: erssd_name.mlg
	Location: The directory path that you enter during the installation.
	Cleanup: Same as transaction log file.
Error log file	Name: erssd_name.out
	Location: The error log directory entered during installation.

ERSSD Maintenance

ERSSD is hosted on a mostly self-managed ASA. The memory, user connections, and other run-time configurations are self tuned. The disk space is self adjusted as long as there is disk space available to the ASA. The ASA starts and shuts down along with the Replication Server. The mirrored transaction logs provide maximum recoverability.

ERSSD Backup

The ERSSD backups are also automatic, occurring at 1:00 a.m. every day by default. Note that the time is configurable. At backup time, both the database and the transaction logs are backed up.

The sysadmin command with erssd as the argument can be used to print the ERSSD file names. The output also shows the default ERSSD backup start time and the backup interval.

```
1> sysadmin erssd
2> go
ERSSD Name    ERSSD Database File
 ERSSD Transaction Log              ERSSD Transaction Log Mirror
  ERSSD Backup Start Time    ERSSD Backup Start Date   ERSSD Backup Interval
  ERSSD Backup Location
------------ --------------------------------------------------
 ------------------------------- ---------------------------------------------------------
  ------------------------ ------------------------ ---------------------
   -----------------------------------
BLRRS_ERSSD  /db/dumps/rep_erssd/REP-15_0/data/BLRRS_ERSSD.db
 /data/rep_tranlogs/BLRRS_ERSSD.log /db/dumps/rep_erssd/REP-15_0/backup/BLRRS_ERSSD.mlg
   1:00AM                2007-03-03              24 hours
    /db/dumps/rep_erssd/REP-15_0/backup
```

You can also get the backup-related file names from the configuration file:

```
sybase@host:/usr/sybase/REP_150_1/REP-15_0/install> cat BLRRS.cfg
#
# Configuration file for Replication Server 'BLRRS', created by rs_init.
#
#
# Do not edit the following ERSSD lines.
#
erssd_dbfile=/db/dumps/rep_erssd/alt_data/BLRRS_ERSSD.db
erssd_translog=/data/rep_tranlogs/BLRRS_ERSSD.log
erssd_logmirror=/db/dumps/rep_erssd/REP-15_0/backup/BLRRS_ERSSD.mlg
erssd_backup_dir=/db/dumps/rep_erssd/REP-15_0/new_dump_dir/
```

To perform a backup manually, execute the sysadmin erssd, backup Replication Server command:

730

```
1> sysadmin erssd, backup
2> go
Backup completed.
```

If you want to back up to a directory other than the configured directories, the full syntax is:

```
sysadmin erssd, backup, [dbfile_dir | logfile_dir | logfile_mirror_dir],
PATH
```

Here is an example to back up the data to a different directory:

```
1> sysadmin erssd, backup, 'dbfile_dir',
'/db/dumps/rep_erssd/REP-15_0/alt_backup/data'
2> go
Backup completed.
```

Similarly, it is possible to take frequent transaction log dumps of the ERSSD using the option 'logfile_dir'.

The transaction log file and the transaction log mirror file are truncated after a successful backup. The previous copy of the backup files is saved for safe recovery with the file name extension ".pre".

```
sybase@host:/db/dumps/rep_erssd/REP-15_0/backup> ls -lrt
-rw-r-----  1 sybase sybase    4096 Mar  7 20:47 BLRRS_ERSSD.log.pre
-rw-r-----  1 sybase sybase 2983936 Mar  7 20:47 BLRRS_ERSSD.db.pre
-rw-r-----  1 sybase sybase  131072 Mar  7 20:55 BLRRS_ERSSD.mlg
-rw-r-----  1 sybase sybase    4096 Mar  7 20:55 BLRRS_ERSSD.log
-rw-r-----  1 sybase sybase 2983936 Mar  7 20:55 BLRRS_ERSSD.db
```

Reconfiguring the ERSSD Backup Settings

It is possible to reset the ERSSD backup configuration parameters. However, do not use rs_configure and do not directly update the rs_config system table. Instead, use the configure replication server command.

The backup parameters that can be altered are:

▶ erssd_backup_dir

▶ erssd_backup_start_time

▶ erssd_backup_start_date

▶ erssd_backup_interval

```
1> configure replication server set erssd_backup_dir to
"/db/dumps/rep_erssd/REP-15_0/new_dump_dir/"
2> go
Config parameter 'erssd_backup_dir' is modified.
1>
```

The configuration change is saved in the Replication Server configuration file. However, do not update the configuration file directly. Please use the `configure replication server` command as detailed above.

```
sybase@host:/usr/sybase/REP_150_1/REP-15_0/install> cat BLRRS.cfg
#
# Configuration file for Replication Server 'BLRRS'. Created by rs_init.
#
<Some information intentionally deleted>

erssd_dbfile=/db/dumps/rep_erssd/REP-15_0/data/BLRRS_ERSSD.db
erssd_translog=/data/rep_tranlogs/BLRRS_ERSSD.log
erssd_logmirror=/db/dumps/rep_erssd/REP-15_0/backup/BLRRS_ERSSD.mlg
erssd_backup_dir=/db/dumps/rep_erssd/REP-15_0/new_dump_dir/
```

Relocating the ERSSD Backup Files

Use the `sysadmin` command to relocate backup-related files. Moving the data file and the transaction log file to different locations is an expensive operation. Use this option only if you must relocate the files. During the process of relocating the files, ERSSD will become unavailable.

ERSSD will shut down to facilitate the move of the files, and then will update the configuration files. Be sure to restart the ERSSD.

Always check `sysadmin erssd` to find out the current backup file locations:

```
1> sysadmin erssd
2> go
```

```
ERSSD Name    ERSSD Database File
 ERSSD Transaction Log              ERSSD Transaction Log Mirror
  ERSSD Backup Start Time   ERSSD Backup Start Date  ERSSD Backup Interval
   ERSSD Backup Location
------------ --------------------------------------------------
 ---------------------------------- --------------------------------------------------------
  ----------------------- ----------------------- --------------------
   ------------------------------------------
BLRRS_ERSSD  /db/dumps/rep_erssd/REP-15_0/data/BLRRS_ERSSD.db
 /data/rep_tranlogs/BLRRS_ERSSD.log /db/dumps/rep_erssd/REP-15_0/backup/BLRRS_ERSSD.mlg
  1:00AM                  2007-03-03              24 hours
   /db/dumps/rep_erssd/REP-15_0/new_dump_dir/
```

To relocate the database dump directory from the current directory /db/dumps/rep_erssd/REP-15_0/data to /db/dumps/rep_erssd/REP-15_0/alt_data, execute:

```
sysadmin erssd, dbfile_dir, "/db/dumps/rep_erssd/REP-15_0/alt_data"
```

When any backup file directory is relocated to a different directory, a series of messages is printed to the error log:

```
I. 2007/03/08 20:28:55. Executing command: /bin/cp
/usr/sybase/REP_150_1/REP-15_0/install/BLRRS.cfg
/usr/sybase/REP_150_1/REP-15_0/install/BLRRS.001
I. 2007/03/08 20:28:55. Executing command: /bin/mv -f
/usr/sybase/REP_150_1/REP-15_0/install/BLRRS.002
/usr/sybase/REP_150_1/REP-15_0/install/BLRRS.cfg
I. 2007/03/08 21:10:32. Executing command: /bin/cp
/usr/sybase/REP_150_1/REP-15_0/install/BLRRS.cfg
/usr/sybase/REP_150_1/REP-15_0/install/BLRRS.002
I. 2007/03/08 21:10:32. Moving embedded RSSD database file from
'/db/dumps/rep_erssd/REP-15_0/data/BLRRS_ERSSD.db' to
'/db/dumps/rep_erssd/alt_data//BLRRS_ERSSD.db'.
I. 2007/03/08 21:10:32. Stopping embedded RSSD: dbstop -q -y -c
"uid=BLRRS_RSSD_prim;pwd=****;eng=BLRRS_ERSSD;LINKS=tcpip(HOST=
localhost;PORT=3204;DOBROAD=NONE)"
I. 2007/03/08 21:10:32. Executing command: /bin/cp
/db/dumps/rep_erssd/REP-15_0/data/BLRRS_ERSSD.db
/db/dumps/rep_erssd/alt_data//BLRRS_ERSSD.db
I. 2007/03/08 21:10:32. Executing command: /bin/mv -f
/usr/sybase/REP_150_1/REP-15_0/install/BLRRS.003
/usr/sybase/REP_150_1/REP-15_0/install/BLRRS.cfg
```

```
I. 2007/03/08 21:10:32. Starting embedded RSSD:
/usr/sybase/REP_150_1/REP-15_0/ASA9/bin/dbspawn -f -q
/usr/sybase/REP_150_1/REP-15_0/ASA9/bin/dbsrv9 -ti 0 -x
"tcpip(PORT=3204;DOBROAD=NO;BLISTENER=NO)" -o
/usr/sybase/logs/BLRRS_ERSSD.out
/db/dumps/rep_erssd/alt_data//BLRRS_ERSSD.db
I. 2007/03/08 21:10:34. Executing command: /bin/rm -f
/db/dumps/rep_erssd/REP-15_0/data/BLRRS_ERSSD.db
I. 2007/03/08 21:10:35. Embedded RSSD database file is moved to
/db/dumps/rep_erssd/alt_data//BLRRS_ERSSD.db.
```

ERSSD Users

There are only two users in the ERSSD — the primary user and the maintenance user. These two users are automatically added to the ERSSD as part of the rs_init. The primary user is also the system administrator. The names of these users can be seen in the configuration file:

```
#
# Configuration file for Replication Server 'BLRRS'. Created by rs_init.
#
RSSD_embedded=yes
RSSD_server=BLRRS_ERSSD
RSSD_database=BLRRS_ERSSD
RSSD_primary_user=BLRRS_RSSD_prim
RSSD_primary_pw_
enc=0x02d8bc59952dba1d8468b28824c05002ce03031c2a0c28c5020dc0757204101d
RSSD_maint_user=BLRRS_RSSD_maint
RSSD_maint_pw_
enc=0x02d975429b814286f74156b58f343e9ee52d4f264d32404561e8d67966a6e12
```

To add new users or to change any user, you need to log in to the ERSSD database as the primary user.

The sa user account password for the ERSSD server can be reset if you log in as the ERSSD primary user:

```
1> sp_password BLRRS_RSSD_prim_ps, reptest, sa
2> go
(return status = 0)
```

Any new users added to the ERSSD need to be granted dba authority to be able to select from system tables.

To add a new user to the ERSSD:

1. Log in as the ERSSD primary user to the ERSSD database.
2. Use the grant command to create the user and password.
3. To grant permission to read system tables, add the user to the rs_systabgroup group.

```
sybase@host:/home/sybase> isql -UBLRRS_RSSD_prim -SBLRRS_ERSSD >
Password:
1> grant connect to myrep_user identified by test321
2> go
1> grant dba to myrep_user
2> go
1> grant membership in group rs_systabgroup to myrep_user
2> go
1>
```

The only other user that is automatically added to the ERSSD database is the maintenance user:

```
sybase@host:/home/sybase> isql -UBLRRS_RSSD_maint -SBLRRS_ER >
Password:
1> select user_name()
2> go
user_name(*)
--------------------------------------------------------------------------
BLRRS_RSSD_maint

(1 row affected)
1>
```

The Replication Server configuration file should not be edited directly to change a user's password. Do not use rs_init for updating a configuration file, even if using password encryption.

To change an ERSSD primary user password, use the alter user command as follows in the Replication Server:

```
alter user username set password new passwd
```

The alter user command will change the password at the Replication Server and the ERSSD, and the ERSSD tables and the

Replication Server configuration file will be updated. Similarly, to change the maintenance user password, use the alter connection command. Please refer to Chapter 7 for more information on alter connection.

ERSSD and Routes

You can create routes from Replication Server 15.x with ERSSD if both source and destination Replication Server versions are 15.0 or above. Before creating the route, the RepAgent name should be added to the interfaces file. The RepAgent connection entry name in the interfaces file will be *ERSSD_name*_ra. Be sure to use an unused port number for the RepAgent connection interfaces entry. Routes can be created using the create route command (no syntax change is required).

When the create route command is executed at the Replication Server, it:

▶ Validates the RepAgent entry in the interfaces file

▶ Configures RepAgent

▶ Starts RepAgent

▶ Turns on log transfer

▶ Changes the ERSSD backup method from transaction log truncate to transaction log rename

ERSSD RepAgent is the dbltm process, which is an open server. The default RepAgent name, *ERSSD_name*_ra, can be renamed using the configure replication server command:

```
configure replication server set erssd_ra to 'new value'
```

The dbltm (RepAgent) error log is located in the same directory as the Replication Server error log.

ERSSD Recovery

The ERSSD is hosted on an Adaptive Server Anywhere, which is a self-managed and self-recovered product. The ERSSD recovers from most OS-related database crashes. In the case of media failures, however, it is necessary to recover it manually.

ERSSD recovery involves either log recovery or data recovery.

Before attempting the ERSSD recovery process, make sure the environment variables $PATH and $LD_LIBRARY_PATH are set to include ASA9 directories:

```
export PATH=/usr/sybase/REP_150_1/REP-15_0/ASA9/bin:$PATH
export LD_LIBRARY_PATH=/usr/sybase/REP_150_1/REP-15_0/ASA9/
lib:$LD_LIBRARY_PATH
```

ERSSD Log Recovery

Run the ASA log translation utility to generate the SQL file:

```
Sybase@host:/db/dumps/rep_erssd/REP-15_0/new_dump_dir>dbtran
BLRRS_ERSSD.log
Adaptive Server Anywhere Log Translation Utility Version 9.0.1.1989
Transaction log "BLRRS_ERSSD.log" starts at offset 0001257753
100% complete
Transaction log ends at offset 0001261070
```

Run the log translation utility on the online transaction log file and the backup transaction log. If the transaction log file is fine, it will generate a SQL file. If the transaction log file is corrupted, dbtran will report errors. After finding the uncorrupted transaction log, copy that file over the corrupted log file, and restart the Replication Server.

ERSSD Data Recovery

Log in to the Replication Server and find out the current backup directory by executing the `sysadmin erssd` command:

```
1> sysadmin erssd
2> go
ERSSD Name    ERSSD Database File
 ERSSD Transaction Log              ERSSD Transaction Log Mirror
  ERSSD Backup Start Time   ERSSD Backup Start Date  ERSSD Backup Interval
   ERSSD Backup Location
------------ ----------------------------------------------
----------------------------------- -----------------------------------------------------
----------------------- ------------------------ --------------------
------------------------------------------
BLRRS_ERSSD  /db/dumps/rep_erssd/alt_data//BLRRS_ERSSD.db
 /data/rep_tranlogs/BLRRS_ERSSD.log /db/dumps/rep_erssd/REP-15_0/backup/BLRRS_ERSSD.mlg
  1:00AM                   2007-03-03              24 hours
   /db/dumps/rep_erssd/REP-15_0/new_dump_dir/
```

The /db/dumps/rep_erssd/REP-15_0/new_dump_dir/ directory is the last successful backup directory. You will copy the data and the log files from the last successful backup directory during the ERSSD data recovery process.

1. Before attempting the recovery of data files, copy the online transaction log file to a different name:

```
sybase@host:/data/rep_tranlogs> cp BLRRS_ERSSD.log BLRRS_ERSSD.log.copy
```

2. Make a new directory named "recovery" to keep the recovery related files.

```
sybase@host:/db/dumps/rep_erssd/REP-15_0> mkdir recovery
```

3. Copy the dbfile and transaction log file from the *last successful backup directory*:

```
sybase@host:/db/dumps/rep_erssd/REP-15_0/new_dump_dir> cp BLRRS_ERSSD.db ../recovery
sybase@host:/db/dumps/rep_erssd/REP-15_0/new_dump_dir> cp BLRRS_ERSSD.log ../recovery
```

4. Apply the backup transaction log to the database file using the dbsrv9 command.

```
sybase@host:/db/dumps/rep_erssd/REP-15_0/recovery> dbsrv9 BLRRS_ERSSD.db -a
BLRRS_ERSSD.log

Adaptive Server Anywhere Network Server Version 9.0.1.1989

Copyright (c) 1989-2004 Sybase, Inc.
Portions Copyright (c) 2002-2004, iAnywhere Solutions, Inc.
All rights reserved. All unpublished rights reserved.

This software contains confidential and trade secret information of
iAnywhere Solutions, Inc.
Use, duplication or disclosure of the software and documentation
by the U.S. Government is subject to restrictions set forth in a license
agreement between the Government and iAnywhere Solutions, Inc. or
other written agreement specifying the Government's rights to use the
software and any applicable FAR provisions, for example, FAR 52.227-19.

iAnywhere Solutions, Inc., One Sybase Drive, Dublin, CA 94568, USA

Per-processor licensing model. The server is limited to use 10 proces-
sor(s).
This server is licensed to:
    "sybase"
    "Sybase, Inc."
Running on Linux 2.6.9-42.0.2.Elsmp #1 SMP Thu Aug 17 17:57:31 EDT 2006 x
8192K of memory used for caching
Minimum cache size: 8192K, maximum cache size: 262016K
Using a maximum page size of 2048 bytes
Starting database "BLRRS_ERSSD" (/db/dumps/rep_erssd/REP-15_0/recov-
ery/BLRRS_ERSSD.db) at Sat Mar 10 2007 18:53
Database recovery in progress
    Last checkpoint at Fri Mar 09 2007 17:55
    Checkpoint log...
    Transaction log: BLRRS_ERSSD.log...
    Rollback log...
    Checkpointing...
Starting checkpoint of "BLRRS_ERSSD" (BLRRS_ERSSD.db) at Sat Mar 10 2007
18:53
Finished checkpoint of "BLRRS_ERSSD" (BLRRS_ERSSD.db) at Sat Mar 10 2007
18:53
```

```
Recovery complete
Database server stopped at Sat Mar 10 2007 18:53
```

5. Copy the online transaction log file to the recovery directory. You may have to delete the previous transaction log files, if any, in the recovery directory before copying the online transaction log file. If you do not manually delete the previous transaction log files in the recovery directory, the copy operation may fail.

```
sybase@host:/db/dumps/rep_erssd/REP-15_0/recovery> cp /data/rep_tranlogs/
BLRRS_ERSSD.log
```

6. Apply the online transaction log file to the database file using the dbsrv9 command.

```
sybase@host:/db/dumps/rep_erssd/REP-15_0/recovery>dbsrv9 BLRRS_ERSSD.db -a
BLRRS_ERSSD.log
```

```
Adaptive Server Anywhere Network Server Version 9.0.1.1989

Copyright (c) 1989-2004 Sybase, Inc.
Portions Copyright (c) 2002-2004, iAnywhere Solutions, Inc.
All rights reserved. All unpublished rights reserved.

This software contains confidential and trade secret information of
iAnywhere Solutions, Inc.
Use, duplication or disclosure of the software and documentation
by the U.S. Government is subject to restrictions set forth in a license
agreement between the Government and iAnywhere Solutions, Inc. or
other written agreement specifying the Government's rights to use the
software and any applicable FAR provisions, for example, FAR 52.227-19.

iAnywhere Solutions, Inc., One Sybase Drive, Dublin, CA 94568, USA

Per-processor licensing model. The server is limited to use 10 proces-
sor(s).
This server is licensed to:
    "sybase"
    "Sybase, Inc."
Running on Linux 2.6.9-42.0.2.Elsmp #1 SMP Thu Aug 17 17:57:31 EDT 2006 x
8192K of memory used for caching
```

```
Minimum cache size: 8192K, maximum cache size: 262016K
Using a maximum page size of 2048 bytes
Starting database "BLRRS_ERSSD" (/db/dumps/rep_erssd/REP-15_0/
recovery/BLRRS_ERSSD.db) at Sat Mar 10 2007 19:20
Database recovery in progress
    Last checkpoint at Sat Mar 10 2007 19:18
    Checkpoint log...
    Transaction log: BLRRS_ERSSD.log...
    Rollback log...
    Checkpointing...
Starting checkpoint of "BLRRS_ERSSD" (BLRRS_ERSSD.db) at Sat Mar 10 2007
19:20
Finished checkpoint of "BLRRS_ERSSD" (BLRRS_ERSSD.db) at Sat Mar 10 2007
19:20
Recovery complete
Database server stopped at Sat Mar 10 2007 19:20
```

7. Copy the updated database file to the actual database
   directory:

```
sybase@host:/db/dumps/rep_erssd/alt_data>cp /db/dumps/rep_erssd/REP-15_0/
recovery/BLRRS_ERSSD.db actual database file location noted earlier using
sysadmin erssd command
```

This updated database file will be used later with the dbspawn
command.

8. Start the ERSSD from the Replication Server install directory. The best method to start the ERSSD is to copy and
   execute the dbspawn command from the Replication Server
   error log. Simply cut and paste the command as it appears in
   the Replication Server error log.

```
sybase@host:/usr/sybase/REP_150_1/REP-15_0/install>
/usr/sybase/REP_150_1/REP-15_0/ASA9/bin/dbspawn -f -q
/usr/sybase/REP_150_1/REP-15_0/ASA9/bin/dbsrv9 -ti 0 -x
"tcpip(PORT=3204;DOBROAD=NO;BLISTENER=NO)" -o
/usr/sybase/logs/BLRRS_ERSSD.out
/db/dumps/rep_erssd/alt_data//BLRRS_ERSSD.db
```

The dbspawn command will error out or finish starting the
ERSSD successfully. Start the Replication Server and check
the error log to make sure all the components are up and

running. If errors occur, correct the errors and restart using dbspawn.

9. Log in to the ERSSD and verify that the ERSSD is accessible:

```
sybase@host:/usr/sybase/REP_150_1/REP-15_0/install> isql -UBLRRS_RSSD_prim
-SBLRRS_ERSSD -w899
Password:
1> select db_name()
2> go
 db_name(*)
 ---------------------------------------------------------------------------
 BLRRS_ERSSD

(1 row affected)
1> select @@servername
2> go
 @@servername
 ---------------------------------------------------------------------------
 BLRRS_ERSSD

(1 row affected)
```

10. Log in to the Replication Server and check the Replication Server components:

```
sybase@host:/home/sybase> isql -Usa -SBLRRS -w899
Password:
1> admin who
2> go
 Spid Name        State              Info
 ---- ----------- ------------------ ------------------------------------
   14 DSI EXEC     Awaiting Command   106(1) BLRRS_ERSSD.BLRRS_ERSSD
   10 DSI          Awaiting Message   106 BLRRS_ERSSD.BLRRS_ERSSD
    9 SQM          Awaiting Message   106:0 BLRRS_ERSSD.BLRRS_ERSSD
   11 dSUB         Sleeping
    6 dCM          Awaiting Message
    8 dAIO         Awaiting Message
   12 dREC         Sleeping           dREC
   15 USER         Active             sa
    5 dALARM       Awaiting Wakeup
   13 dSYSAM       Sleeping
1>
```

If for any reason the stable queue partition is not added, then log in to the newly created Replication Server and create a new stable queue partition. First check if the disk partition is created with the `admin disk_space` command:

```
1> admin disk_space
2> go
Partition
  Logical                         Part.Id   Total Segs  Used Segs  State
---------------------------------------------------------------------------
-------------------------- --------- ----------- ---------- -----------
```

If the disk partition is not created, use the `create partition` command to create a new partition. `create partition` is similar to `add partition` except `add partition` is likely to be deprecated in the future.

```
1> create partition q4
2> on '/db/dumps/devices/sybase/q4' with size 20
3> go
Partition 'q4' is added.
1> admin disk_space
2> go
Partition
  Logical                         Part.Id   Total Segs  Used Segs  State
---------------------------------------------------------------------------
-------------------------- --------- ----------- ---------- -----------
/db/dumps/devices/sybase/q4
  q4                              101       20          0          ON-LINE//
1>
```

The ERSSD is an Adaptive Server Anywhere database. As described in this chapter, the ASA is a self-managed and self-recovered database product. Make sure the ASA directories are included in the $PATH and $LD_LIBRARY_PATH variables. In a high-transaction replication system, you must make sure enough disk space is available for the ERSSD to expand. Even though the backups are automatic, it is possible to make manual backups or change the default backup schedule.

Chapter 20

Troubleshooting

In this chapter we will discuss common problems encountered with replication, including issues with Replication Agent, DSI, stable queues, data not replicating, and data latency.

Replication Agent

Replication Agent scans the transaction log of the primary database, converts log records directly into LTL commands, and forwards them to the Replication Server in batches. After sending records to the inbound queue, Replication Agent requests a new secondary truncation point for the transaction log. The primary Replication Server returns a cached locator and writes this locator to the rs_locater table in the RSSD database.

Replication Agent reports and logs error messages that can be caused by Adaptive Server, Replication Server, and Replication Agent.

Invalid Login

```
Error: 9214, Severity: 16, State 0
02:00000:00013:2007/08/09 18:41:57.39 server Replication Agent(4): Failed
to connect to Replication Server. Please check the Replication Server,
username, and password specified to sp_config_rep_agent. RepSvr = prs, user
= sa).
```

To fix this error:

1. Execute use database.

2. Disable the secondary truncation point:

    ```
    sp_config_rep_agent database, 'disable',
    ['preserve secondary truncpt']
    ```

3. Enable the secondary truncation point with correct configuration parameter values:

    ```
    sp_config_rep_agent database, 'enable', 'RSName', 'RSName_ra',
    'RSName_ra_ps'
    ```

4. Reset locator information in RSSD database:

    ```
    use rssddb
    go
    rs_zeroltm dataserver, database
    go
    ```

5. Start Database Replication Agent with sp_start_rep_agent:

    ```
    sp_start_rep_agent database
    ```

Missing Replication Server Name in Interfaces

```
00:00000:00023:2007/08/14 19:19:02.19 server Rep Agent Thread for database
'pubs2' (dbid = 4) terminated abnormally with error. (major 92, minor 61)
01:00000:00032:2007/08/14 19:19:02.44 server Replication Agent(4): Received
the following communications error message: Msg 06080503: ct_connect():
directory service layer: Internal directory control layer error: Requested
server name not found.
01:00000:00032:2007/08/14 19:19:02.44 server Error: 9214, Severity: 16,
State:0
01:00000:00032:2007/08/14 19:19:02.44 server Replication Agent(4): Failed
to connect to Replication Server. Please check the Replication Server,
username, and password specified to sp_config_rep_agent. RepSvr = prs, user
= prs_ra).
01:00000:00032:2007/08/14 19:19:02.44 server Error: 9261, Severity: 20,
State:0
```

Check the interfaces file for the Replication Server entry; it should be the same interfaces file with which Adaptive Server was booted (check the interfaces location in the Adaptive Server runserver file).

Permission Issue

```
Error: 9261, Severity: 20, State: 0
CONNECT SOURCE permission is required to execute command.
```

Replication Agent/Replication Server user should be granted connect source permission. Connect source permission is required to log in to Replication Server.

```
grant connect source to prs_ra
```

Misconfigured Replication Agent

```
Replication Agent(6): Received the following error message from the Repli-
cation Server: Msg 14029. Replication Agent connection for 'rds.rdb' is not
allowed because the stable queue for this source is not active.
```

After loading the replicate database with the primary database dump, the Replication Agent for the replicate database should be disabled and enabled with correct configuration values, as follows:

1. Execute use database.
2. Disable Replication Agent for the database:

   ```
   sp_config_rep_agent database, 'disable',
   ```

3. Enable Replication Agent with correct configuration parameter values:

   ```
   sp_config_rep_agent database, 'enable', 'RSName', 'RSName_ra',
   'RSName_ra_ps'
   ```

4. Start Database Replication Agent with sp_start_rep_agent:

   ```
   sp_start_rep_agent database
   go
   ```

Invalid Truncation Page

```
01:00000:00003:2007/08/06 14:51:33.40 server Error: 691, Severity: 20,
State: 1
01:00000:00003:2007/08/06 14:51:33.40 server Encountered invalid logical
page '0' while accessing object '8' in database '4'. This is an internal
system error. Please contact Sybase Technical Support.
```

After using dbcc settrunc, you must use the rs_zeroltm stored
procedure to reset the locator value for a database to 0. Otherwise, the log page stored in the rs_locater system table may
become invalid. Starting the Replication Agent may then cause
Adaptive Server Enterprise to register data corruption and to pro-
duce errors such as 691, 605, and 813.

1. Execute use database.

2. Disable the secondary truncation point:

   ```
   dbcc settrunc(ltm, ignore)
   ```

3. Reset the secondary truncation point:

   ```
   dbcc settrunc(ltm, valid)
   ```

4. Reset locator in RSSD database:

   ```
   use rssddb
   go
   rs_zeroltm dataserver, database
   ```

5. Start Replication Agent for the database:

   ```
   sp_start_rep_agent database
   ```

Syslogs Corruption

```
00:00000:00014:2007/07/30 17:14:48.91 server Error: 3474, Severity: 21,
State: 1
00:00000:00014:2007/07/30 17:14:48.91 server during redo the page timestamp
value is less than old timestamp from log. Page #=2793145, object id =
768002736, page timestamp=0000 2b02c610be. Log old timestamp=0000 02c615cb.
Log record marker = (4456371, 11).
00:00000:00014:2007/07/30 17:14:48.91 server Error: 21, Severity: 21,
State: 1
```

```
00:00000:00014:2007/07/30 17:14:48.91 server WARNING — Fatal Error 3414
occurred at Jul 30 2007 5:14PM. Please note the error and time, and contact
a user with System Administrator (SA) authorization.
00:00000:00014:2007/07/30 17:14:48.92 server Error: 3414, Severity: 21,
State: 1
00:00000:00014:2007/07/30 17:14:48.92 server Database 'pubs2' (dbid 4):
Recovery failed. Check the SQL
```

These steps should be followed under the supervision of Sybase Technical Support.

1. Enable updates to the system table in Adaptive Server:

   ```
   sp_configure 'allow updates to system tables', 1
   go
   ```

2. Set database status to bypass recovery in sysdatabases:

   ```
   begin tran
   update sysdatabases set status=-32768 where dbid =dbid
   go
   select name, dbid, status from sysdatabases where dbid=dbid
   go
   ```

   Make sure you are updating the status for the correct database. If it is correct and you see the "1 row affected" message, then commit; otherwise rollback.

   ```
   commit tran
   go
   ```

3. Issue checkpoint in the master database:

   ```
   checkpoint
   go
   ```

4. Shut down Adaptive Server with nowait:

   ```
   shutdown with nowait
   ```

5. Restart Adaptive Server.

6. Log in to Adaptive Server and disable the secondary truncation point for the database:

   ```
   use database
   go
   ```

```
dbcc settrunc(ltm, ignore)
go
```

7. Truncate the database log with no_log:

```
use master
go
dump tran database with no_log
go
```

8. Reset the database status back to the original status:

```
update sysdatabases set status=original status
go
```

9. Issue checkpoint in the master database:

```
checkpoint
go
```

10. Shut down Adaptive Server:

```
shutdown with nowait
go
```

11. Restart Adaptive Server.

12. isql to Adaptive Server and put the database in single-user mode:

```
sp_dboption database, 'single user', true
go
```

There is no need to run checkpoint if the server is 12.5.1 or above. Otherwise, execute use database and run checkpoint.

13. Since we have truncated the database log with no_log, run dbcc tablealloc with the full and fix options on syslogs:

```
use database
go
dbcc traceon(3604)
go
dbcc tablealloc(8, full, fix)
go
```

14. Put the database in multiuser mode:

```
use master
go
sp_dboption database, 'single user', false
go
```

15. Reset the secondary truncation point:

```
use database
go
dbcc settrunc(ltm, valid)
go
```

16. Reset locator in RSSD database:

```
use rssddb
go
rs_zeroltm dataserver, database
go
```

17. Start database Replication Agent:

```
sp_start_rep_agent database
go
```

18. Disable updates to system tables in Adaptive Server:

```
sp_configure 'allow updates to system tables', 0
go
```

You should reconcile the database after suiciding the log since the database might be inconsistent.

Primary Database Transaction Log Full

Execute sp_who in Adaptive Server to see if any process is in log suspend. If the database is in log suspend, you will not be able to execute any transactions in that database.

1. Query syslogshold for long-running transactions:

```
select * from syslogshold where dbid=dbid
```

2. If there are no long-running transactions, check Replication Server:

    a. To see if any component is down, execute:

        ```
        admin who_is_down
        ```

    b. If Replication Agent is down, check for error messages in the Adaptive Server error log and try to resolve the error. If Replication Agent is up, shut down Replication Agent with sp_stop_rep_agent. If you are not able to shut down Replication Agent, you can shut down Replication Server and then stop Replication Agent with sp_stop_rep_agent. Then follow the steps listed below to free up space in the transaction log.

        i.   Execute use database.

             ```
             go
             ```

        ii. Disable the secondary truncation point:

             ```
             dbcc settrunc(ltm, ignore)
             go
             ```

        iii. Truncate the database transaction log:

             ```
             dump tran database to 'dumptranfile'
             ```

Note: If you have the database option 'trunc. log on chkpt' you can truncate the log with truncate_only.

---

        iv. Enable the secondary truncation point:

             ```
             dbcc settrunc(ltm, valid)
             go
             ```

        v.   Reset the locator in RSSD database:

             ```
             use rssddb
             go
             rs_zeroltm dataserver, database
             go
             ```

vi. Start Replication Agent for the database:

```
sp_start_rep_agent database
go
```

Follow the procedure for recovering from primary database truncated log in Chapter 15 or add more space to the transaction log with the alter database command. (For alter database syntax, see the Adaptive Server Enterprise Reference Manual.)

3. If the DSI thread is down, check the Replication Server error log for the error that caused the DSI connection to go down, resolve the error, and resume the connection:

```
resume connection to dataserver.database
```

4. If no component is down but the stable queue is still filling up, check for an aborted open transaction by executing:

```
admin who,sqt
```

```
Spid State                  Info          Closed  Read  Open  Trunc   Removed  Full
 SQM Blocked  First Trans                  Parsed  SQM Reader  Change Oqids
  Detect Orphans
---- ---------------------- --------------- ------- ----- ----- ------ -------- ----
------------ --------------------------- ------- ----------- ------------
 --------------
21  Awaiting Wakeup 1517:1  DIST pds.pubs2  0       0     1     1       0        0
 1           st:0,cmds:1,qid:11977:16:12  0       0           0
  0
```

The above output has an open transaction. Before purging the open transaction, check the Replicate Adaptive Server error log to make sure the replicate database doesn't have a full log or any other error. If there is an error, fix it. If there are no errors, dump the queue and identify the open transaction.

```
sysadmin dump_file,'/work2/qdmp'
sysadmin dump_queue, 1517, 1,11977,12,16
```

Identify uncommitted transactions from the queue dump, purge open tran, and then reapply the purged transaction. The `sysadmin purge_first_open` RCL command can only be used with the inbound queue. It needs enough space to purge the first open transaction from the stable queue. If there is not enough space, you will be required to open another isql session and add disk space to the Replication Server.

```
sysadmin purge_first_open, 1517,1
```

If no component is down and the secondary truncation point is not moving, stop and restart Replication Agent and recycle Replication Server.

Standby Database Transaction Log Full

If the standby database transaction log gets full after loading the dump from the active database, you should disable the secondary truncation point for the standby database:

```
use standbydb
go
1> dbcc gettrunc
2> go
secondary trunc page  secondary trunc state  dbrepstat  generation id  database id
  database name  ltl version
--------------------- ---------------------- ---------- -------------- -----------
-------------- -----------
13080                 1                      173        0              5
  standbydb      700
```

From the above dbcc gettrunc command output we see that the truncation state is 1 (secondary truncation point is valid). We can ignore it with dbcc settrunc:

```
dbcc settrunc(ltm, ignore)
go
```

Error 9209

Error 9209, Severity: 20, State: 0

01:00000:01418:2007/08/03 12:28:29.30 server Replication Agent(4): Missing datarow in TEXT/IMAGE insert log record. Transaction log may be corrupt. Please contact Sybase Technical Support. (Current marker = (1223239, 1)).

For this error you can move the secondary truncation point to the next page:

1. ```
   use database
   go
   ```

2. Move the secondary truncation point to the next page:

   ```
   dbcc settrunc(ltm, pageid, 1223240)
   go
   ```

3. Reset the locator:

   ```
   use rssddb
   go
   rs_zeroltm dataserver, database
   go
   ```

4. Start Replication Agent for the database:

   ```
   sp_start_rep_agent database
   go
   ```

Or you can reset the secondary truncation point for this database and resynchronize the databases:

1. ```
   use database
   go
   ```

2. Disable the secondary truncation point:

   ```
   dbcc settrunc(ltm, ignore)
   go
   ```

3. Truncate the database transaction log:

   ```
   dump tran database with truncate_only
   ```

4. Enable the secondary truncation point:

```
dbcc settrunc(ltm, valid)
go
```

5. Reset the locator in the RSSD database:

```
use rssddb
go
rs_zeroltm dataserver, database
go
```

6. Start Replication Agent for the database:

```
sp_start_rep_agent database
```

Replication Status Inconsistency of text, unitext, or image Columns

E. 2007/08/11 09:10:24. ERROR #32046 DSI EXEC(104(1) rds.pubs2) -
/nrm/nrm.c(2576)
Column 'blurbs.'copy' status 'always_replicate' in replication definition
does not match database status 'replicate_if_changed'. Use 'alter replication definition' to set 'replicate_if_changed' status, at least until
existing transactions have been processed. (Refer to the troubleshooting
guide for recovery procedures.)

If the status of a text, unitext, or image column is not the same in
both the Adaptive Server database and in the replication definition, inconsistency is detected by the Replication Server when
the modification is replicated, and the Replication Agent shuts
down.

When text, unitext, or image columns are included in the replication definition and the replication status of this column is set
to do_not_replicate at the Adaptive Server database, Replication
Server sends the modification to the replicate database without
the text, unitext, or image data, but the warning is recorded in the
Adaptive Server error log and replication continues.

To fix this error, you can either change the replication status
for text, unitext, or image columns in the Adaptive Server database to always_replicate or execute alter replication

definition at the primary Replication Server to set the status of these columns to `replicate_if_changed`.

To set the replication status to `replicate_if_changed` for text, unitext, or image columns in the replication definition at the primary Replication Server:

1. Alter the replication definition *repdef* `replicate_if_changed` *colname*. Wait for the modified replication definition to arrive at replicate sites.

2. Execute `sp_start_rep_agent` *database* at the primary Adaptive Server.

There can be other scenarios, which are described below.

To set the replication status to `always_replicate` for text, unitext, or image columns in the Adaptive Server database:

1. Quiesce the replication system by draining queues, so that all transactions with a status of `replicate_if_changed` are processed.

2. Execute `sp_setrepcol` to change the status of the column in the Adaptive Server database to `always_replicate`:

   ```
   sp_setrepcol tabname, colname, 'always_replicate'
   ```

3. Execute `alter replication definition` to change the status of the column to `always_replicate`:

   ```
   alter replication definition repdef always_replicate colname
   go
   ```

To set the status to `do_not_replicate` when the replication definition text, unitext, or image status is set to `always_replicate` or `replicate_if_changed`:

1. Stop activity to the primary table.

2. Drop subscriptions to the replication definition.

3. Drop the replication definition.

4. Recreate the replication definition without including text, unitext, or image columns.

5. Recreate subscriptions to the replication definition.

6. Resume activity to the primary table.

To set status to `always_replicate` or `replicate_if_changed` when the replication status for text, unitext, or image columns is set to `do_not_replicate` in the Adaptive Server database:

1. At the Adaptive Server database, execute `sp_setrepcol` to change the status for text, unitext, or image columns to `always_replicate` or `replicate_if_changed`.

2. Wait for subsequent transactions that modify the text, unitext, or image columns to be processed by the Replication Server.

After resolving inconsistencies in any of the above scenarios, you will need to reconcile the primary and replicate with rs_subcmp or with any other method.

Error 2033

```
ERROR: 2033 REP AGENT
(pds.pubs2) - s/prsobj.c(367)
Tag 'origin_time' is expecting datatype 'datetime'.
```

Replication Agent shuts down itself with this message when the database transaction log is not truncated before upgrading Adaptive Server.

1. ```
   use database
   go
   ```

2. Disable the secondary truncation point:

   ```
   dbcc settrunc(ltm, ignore)
   go
   ```

3. Move the secondary truncation to the next page:

   ```
   begin tran
   commit tran
   go 40
   ```

4. Truncate the transaction log:

   ```
   dump tran database with truncate_only
   go
   ```
   ```

5. Reset locator in RSSD database:

```
use rssddb
go
rs_zeroltm dataserver, database
go
```

6. Enable the secondary truncation point

```
use database
go
dbcc settrunc(ltm, valid)
go
```

7. Start Replication Agent for the database:

```
sp_start_rep_agent database
go
```

Replication Agent shuts down with the "message empty" message when installmaster is not run after upgrading Adaptive Server with new EBF.

Load installmaster and the instmsgs.ebf scripts into Adaptive Server Enterprise and then restart Replication Agent.

Error 9202

```
Error 9202: %S_REPAGNT: Nested replicated stored procedure detected. Trans-
action log may be corrupt.
```

Nested stored procedure replication is not allowed. Only the outer stored procedure call is forwarded by Replication Agent to the Replication Server. To restart Replication Agent, you will need to skip the nested stored procedure transaction, as shown below.

1. Find the secondary truncation point page:

```
use database
go
dbcc gettrunc
go
```

2. Find the valid page after the nested stored procedure:

```
select object_id('nested_procname')
go
dbcc traceon(3604)
go
dbcc log(dbid, object_id of proc from above)
go
dbcc pglinkage(dbid, lastpage_listed, 0, 2, 0, 1)
go
```

3. Set a new secondary truncation point on a valid page after the nested stored procedure transaction:

```
dbcc settrunc('ltm', 'pageid', page number)
```

Where *page number* is the page number for a page after the current page you retried in dbcc pglinkage in step 2.

4. Reset locator in the RSSD:

```
use rssddb
go
rs_zeroltm dataserver, database
go
```

5. Start Replication Agent:

```
sp_start_rep_agent database
```

Errors 9204 and 9254

Error 9204: %S_REPAGNT. Could not locate a schema for object with id = (%d) current marker (%d, %d)

Error 9254: %S_REPAGNT: Could not locate schema version for object id '%d' in the transaction log.

Errors 9204 and 9254 are raised together when Replication Agent encounters an EXECBEGIN log record of the stored procedure belonging to a different database if the schema is not logged. To fix this:

1. bcp out the sysobjects table from that database.
2. sp_configure 'allow update', 1

3.  ```
    begin tran
    update sysobjects set version_ts=NULL where version_ts is not
    NULL and type = 'U'
    commit tran
    ```

4.  ```
    sp_configure 'allow update', 0
    ```

Error 9205

Error 9205: %S_REPAGNT: A replicated end stored procedure execution log record was found without a Begin. Transaction log may be corrupt.

This error is raised when Replication Agent encounters XREC_EXECEMD without a corresponding XREC_EXECBEGIN. To fix this, enable replication of the stored procedure and set it to replicate with the 'function' option:

```
sp_setrepproc sprocname, 'function'
```

Error 9240

Error 9240: %S_REPAGNT: Could not allocate an alarm. Try restarting this Rep Agent Thread after freeing up some alarms, or restart the server with more alarms allocated.

This error is caused when Adaptive Server runs out of alarm resources. To correct this, increase the 'number of alarms' configuration parameter:

```
sp_configure 'number of alarms', nnn
```

Error 9255

Error 9255: %S_REPAGNT: Rewrite of PREPARE log record failed at (%d, %d).
0:00000:00294:2006/10/05 06:30:46.08 server Error: 9255, Severity: 20,
State: 0
00:00000:00294:2006/10/05 06:30:46.10 server Replication Agent(4): Rewrite
of PREPARE log record failed at (413996, 17).
00:00000:00294:2006/10/05 06:30:46.11 server Rep Agent Thread for database
'pubs2' (dbid = 4) terminated abnormally with error. (major 92, minor 55)

The PREPARE is rewritten as COMMIT or ABORT. Basically, Replication Agent will sleep until it is woken up. In this case, it looks like the Replication Agent was woken up for a reason other than the the ENDXACT being rewritten. For instance, maybe it was killed. In this case, Replication Agent does not know how to proceed, so it issues the error message and exits. You might want to do a dbcc log to see if that ENDXACT is still in PREPARE. If it is in COMMIT or ABORT, restarting the Replication Agent will go smoothly. If it is still in PREPARE, Replication Agent will wait again for the rewrite.

```
dbcc traceon(3604)
go
dbcc log(dbid, -1, page, row, 10, -1, 0)
```

For example:

```
dbcc log(4, -1, 413996, 17, 10, -1, 0)
```

Error 9261

Error 9261: %S_REPAGNT: This Rep Agent Thread is aborting due to an unre-coverable communications or Replication Server error.

This is a communication error with the Replication Server. Ensure that the Adaptive Server interface file entry for Replication Server is not missing or incorrect.

Errors 9278 and 9279

Error 9278: %S_REPAGNT: Encountered a feature that cannot be supported by the current Replication Server version. Upgrade the Replication Server version to a higher level, or use sp_config_rep_agent to set the 'skip unsupported features' option.

Error 9279: %S_REPAGNT: Connecting to a Replication Server that supports a lower LTL version. Features that are not supported by the lower LTL version may cause the Replication Agent to shutdown. Set the 'skip unsupported fea-tures' configuration option to prevent shutdown.

Error 9278 and 9279 are informational messages. The 'skip unsupported features' option instructs Replication Agent to skip log records for Adaptive Server features unsupported by the Replication Server. This option is normally used if Replication Server is a lower version than Adaptive Server. The default is "false". To set this to "true", execute:

```
use database
go
sp_config_rep_agent database, 'skip unsupported features'
go
```

Then stop and restart Replication Agent:

```
sp_stop_rep_agent database
go
sp_start_rep_agent database
```

Error 9286

```
Error 9286: %S_REPAGNT: The data or object identifier at (%d, %d) is too
wide for the Replication Server, '%.*s', to handle. Check the 'data limits
filter mode' configuration parameter.
```

Adaptive Server 12.5 and above have support for wider columns. Replication Server prior to 12.5 doesn't support wider column (>2048 bytes). The 'data limits filter mode' option specifies how Replication Agent should handle log records containing new wider columns and parameters or larger column and parameter counts before attempting to send them to Replication Server. Valid values for 'data limits filter mode' are "off", "stop", "skip", and "truncate".

▶ off: Replication Agent allows all log records to pass through.

▶ stop: Replication Agent shuts down if it encounters log records containing wide data.

▶ skip: Replication Agent skips log records containing wide data and logs a message to the error log.

▶ truncate: Replication Agent truncates wide data to the maximum the Replication Server can allow.

Sybase recommends not using the `'data_limits_filter_mode'` "off" setting with Replication 12.1 or earlier, as this may cause Replication Agent to skip or truncate wide data or to stop.

The default value of this parameter depends on the Replication Server version number. For 12.1 and earlier, the default is "stop". For 12.5 and later, it is "off".

DSI Issues

Data Server Interface (DSI) executes transactions from Replication Server outbound SQM queues to the data server, which can be Adaptive Server Enterprise or a non-Sybase data server. DSI provides mapping of data server errors into Replication Server errors and error actions, and logs failed and orphan transactions in the exception log. Additionally, DSI detects duplicates. To detect duplicates, the commit function string executes the stored procedure rs_update_lastcommit to update the rs_lastcommit table before it commits the transaction. rs_lastcommit stores the last transaction from a given origin to the database. DSI also does loss detection, which is the opposite of duplicate detection. To verify that there is no loss from a given source, the next transaction received from that site is checked to see if it is a duplicate transaction. If it is, no loss is detected from that source; otherwise, a potential for loss exists and Replication Server flags that a loss has been detected and a message is logged in the Replication Server.

```
msars15.log:I. 2007/00/17 08:49:10. Checking loss for pds.msars15_RSSD from
rds2.msarrs215_RSSD Date: Aug 17 2007 8:47:52:326AM
qid=000000000001ba5a00004685000d00004685000a0000008d0090fc020000000000000003
msars15.log:I. 2007/08/17 08:49:10. No loss for pds.msars15_RSSD from
rds2.msarrs215_RSSD
```

If loss is detected, the following message is printed in the Replication Server error log:

```
Loss detected for pds.prs126_RSSD from rds.rrs126_RSSD
```

As mentioned in Chapter 2, the DSI thread is composed of the DSI Scheduler (DSI) thread and *n* DSI Executor (DSI EXEC) threads. If the DSI thread is suspended when Replication Server starts up, the output of `admin who` will show only one DSI EXEC thread, even if additional DSI Executor threads (parallel DSI) are configured. The RCL commands `admin who` and `admin who,dsi` show states of DSI and DSI EXEC threads. (For a complete description of `admin who,dsi` output, please see the Sybase Replication Server Reference Manual.)

```
1> admin who
2> go
Spid Name        State                 Info
---- ----------  --------------------  ------------------------
  41 DIST        Awaiting Wakeup       106 PDS.PUBS3
  44 SQT         Awaiting Wakeup       106:1  DIST PDS.PUBS3
  31 SQM         Awaiting Message      106:1 PDS.PUBS3
  30 SQM         Awaiting Message      106:0 PDS.PUBS3
  46 DSI EXEC    Awaiting Command      101(1) pds.prs_RSSD
  36 DSI         Awaiting Message      101 pds.prs_RSSD
  40 DIST        Awaiting Wakeup       101 pds.prs_RSSD
   .
   .

   .
  37 DSI         Awaiting Message      107 pds.pubs3
  48 DSI EXEC    Awaiting Command      108(1) rds.pubs3
  38 DSI         Awaiting Message      108 rds.pubs3
   .
   .

   .
1> admin who,dsi
2> go
```

```
Spid State              Info              Maintenance User  Xact_retry_times  Batch
Cmd_batch_size  Xact_group_size  Dump_load  Max_cmds_to_log  Xacts_read  Xacts_ignored
Xacts_skipped  Xacts_succeeded  Xacts_failed  Xacts_retried  Current Origin DB
Current Origin QID
 Subscription Name  Sub Command  Current Secondary QID  Cmds_read
 Cmds_parsed_by_sqt  IgnoringStatus  Xacts_Sec_ignored  GroupingStatus
  TriggerStatus  ReplStatus  NumThreads  NumLargeThreads  LargeThreshold  CacheSize
  Serialization   Max_Xacts_in_group  Xacts_retried_blk  CommitControl
   CommitMaxChecks  CommitLogChecks  CommitCheckIntvl  IsolationLevel
---- ------------------ -------------------- ----------------- ----------------- ------
---------------- ---------------- ---------- ---------------- ----------- ------------
--------------- ---------------- -------------- -------------- ----------------
------------------------------------------------------------------------------
------------------ ------------ ---------------------- ----------
------------------ -------------- ----------------- ---------------
--------------- ----------- ----------- ---------------- ---------------- --------
---------------- ------------------- ------------------ --------------
---------------- ---------------- ----------------- --------------
37  Awaiting Message    107 pds.pubs3    pubs3_maint    3                on
8192         65536        off     -1          0          0
 0           0           0         0         0
    0x0000000000000000000000000000000000000000000000000000000000000000000000000
  NULL           NULL       NULL            0
   0              Applying     0             on
    on          on      1        0          100        0
     wait_for_commit  20              0            on
      400         200        1000          default
36  Awaiting Message    101 pds.prs_RSSD  prs_RSSD_maint  3              on
8192         65536        off     -1          0          0
 0           0           0         0         0
    0x0000000000000000000000000000000000000000000000000000000000000000000000000
  NULL           NULL       NULL            0
   0              Applying     0             on
    on          on      1        0          100        0
     wait_for_commit  20              0            on
      400         200        1000          default
```

States of DSI Scheduler Thread

The RCL commands `admin who` and `admin who,dsi` will show the DSI Scheduler thread in one of the following states:

▶ **Active:** The DSI thread is starting or restarting after logging an exception to the RSSD/ERSSD database or an internal error.

▶ **Awaiting Command:** There are no complete transactions in the stable queue and the DSI thread is waiting for a transaction to become available in the stable queue.

▶ **Awaiting Wakeup:** After receiving a data server error that can be retried, the DSI Scheduler thread sleeps for 2 minutes. If the error is fixed during this interval, the DSI thread wakes up and retries the command. A failed transaction is retried when the error action assigned to the data server error is the `retry_stop` or `retry_log` option with the `assign action` command. When `assign action` is set to `retry_stop`, this tells Replication Server to roll back the transaction log record and retry it. The number of retry attempts is governed by the `'command_retry'` configuration parameter set with `alter connection`. If the error continues after retrying n times, the DSI thread is suspended for the database.

▶ **Awaiting Message:** The DSI Scheduler is waiting for transactions to complete after dispatching them to DSI Executor threads.

▶ **Suspended:** This state is only reported by the `admin who` RCL command when the DSI connection is suspended by a data server error, a user command, the `activate subscription with suspension` clause, or the `drop subscription` command.

▶ **Down:** This state is only reported by the `admin who` RCL command. It indicates that the DSI Scheduler thread has not been started.

States of DSI Executor Thread

The DSI Executor states are only listed by the admin who RCL command. These are:

▶ **Active:** The DSI EXEC thread is starting or restarting after logging an exception to the RSSD/ERSSD database or an internal error.

▶ **Awaiting Message:** The DSI EXEC thread is processing a transaction and is waiting for another thread to complete processing its transaction, or the DSI EXEC thread is waiting to receive another statement from the Stable Queue Transaction (SQT) interface.

▶ **Awaiting Command:** The DSI EXEC thread is waiting to receive another transaction from the DSI Scheduler thread.

▶ **Suspended:** This state is only reported by the admin who RCL command when the DSI connection is suspended by a data server error, a user command, the activate subscription with suspension clause, or the drop subscription command.

▶ **Down:** The DSI EXEC thread down status depends on the DSI Scheduler thread status:

  ▶ If the DSI Scheduler thread is down, the DSI Executer thread connection was suspended when the Replication Server started and the connection has been resumed.

  ▶ If the DSI Scheduler thread is Active or Awaiting Wakeup, the DSI Executor thread connection is recovering from a retryable error and is either starting or restarting.

The DSI thread connection can be suspended or down due to an incorrect login or password, permissions issues, connectivity errors, data server errors, or Replication Server errors. For some data server errors, you can create error classes and assign actions. These topics are covered in the following section.

Creating an Error Class for Duplicate Key

rs_sqlserver_error_class is the default error class. The default action can be altered. Error actions must be assigned on the same Replication Server where the error class is created. Follow these steps:

1. At replicate Replication Server:

   ```
   create error class duplicate_error_class
   ```

2. At RSSD database:

   ```
   rs_init_erroractions duplicate_error_class
   ```

3. View errorclass:

   ```
   rs_helpclass duplicate_error_class
   ```

4. At replicate Replication Server:

   ```
   assign action ignore
   for duplicate_error_class
   to 2601,3621

   alter connection to dataserver.database
   set error class to duplicate_error_class

   suspend connection to dataserver.database
   resume connection to dataserver.database
   ```

Turning On DSI Trace Flags

To resolve data-specific problems, you will need to turn on DSI trace flags.

At the replicate Replication Server:

```
trace "on", dsi, dsi_buf_dump

suspend connection to dataserver.database
resume connection to dataserver.database
```

Note: The `dsi_buf_dump` trace flag doesn't need the debug Replication Server binary, but in order to use the `dsi_cmd_dump` trace flag you will need to boot Replication Server with the repserver.diag binary.

Turning Off DSI Trace Flags

To turn DSI trace flags off:

```
trace "off", dsi, dsi_buf_dump

suspend connection to dataserver.database
resume connection to dataserver.database
```

For example:

```
1> trace "on", dsi, dsi_buf_dump
2> go
1> admin version
2> go
Version
 --------------------------------------------------------------------------------
 -----------------------------------
 Replication Server/15.0.1/EBF 14804 ESD#1/Linux Intel/Linux 2.4.21-20.ELsmp
 i686/1/OPT/Mon Jul 16 12:42:11 2007
```

Output from the error log with the `dsi_buf_dump` trace flag:

```
I. 2007/10/18 06:49:58. Trace enabled 'dsi', 'dsi_buf_dump'.
T. 2007/10/18 06:51:51. (25): Command(s) to 'rds16k.rdb':
T. 2007/10/18 06:51:51. (25): 'use rdb'
T. 2007/10/18 06:51:51. (25): Command(s) to 'rds16k.rdb':
I. 2007/10/18 06:51:51. (25): 'set ciphertext on'
T. 2007/10/18 06:51:51. (25): Command(s) to 'rds16k.rdb':
T. 2007/10/18 06:51:51. (25): 'set dml_on_computed on'
I. 2007/10/18 06:51:51. ...... connected to server 'rds16k' as user 'rdb_maint'.
T. 2007/10/18 06:51:52. (25): Command(s) to 'rds16k.rdb':
T. 2007/10/18 06:51:52. (25): 'begin transaction [0a] insert into test (a, b)
values ('a', 2) '
T. 2007/10/18 06:51:52. (25): Command(s) to 'rds16k.rdb':
T. 2007/10/18 06:51:52. (25): 'execute rs_update_lastcommit @origin = 103, @ori-
gin_qid = x0000000000bd1f750005b58b007f0005b58b007d000099cb007111da0000000000000
```

001, @secondary_qid = x00000000000000000000000000000000000000000000000000000000
0000000000000000, @origin_time = '20071018 06:51:40:460'[0a] commit transaction

Output from the error log with the dsi_cmd_dump trace flag:

```
1> admin version
2> go
Version
 --------------------------------------------------------------------------------
------------------------------------
 Replication Server/15.0.1/EBF 14804 ESD#1/Linux Intel/Linux 2.4.21-20.ELsmp
i686/1/DEBUG/Mon Jul 16 12:40:00 2007    -> repserver debug binary

1> trace "on", dsi, dsi_cmd_dump
2> go
1> T. 2007/10/18 07:35:19. (27): Command sent to 'rds16k.rdb':
T. 2007/10/18 07:35:19. (27): 'use rdb'
T. 2007/10/18 07:35:19. (27): Command sent to 'rds16k.rdb':
T. 2007/10/18 07:35:19. (27): 'set ciphertext on'
T. 2007/10/18 07:35:19. (27): Command sent to 'rds16k.rdb':
T. 2007/10/18 07:35:19. (27): 'set dml_on_computed on'
T. 2007/10/18 07:35:19. (27): Command sent to 'rds16k.rdb':
T. 2007/10/18 07:35:19. (27): 'begin transaction'
T. 2007/10/18 07:35:19. (27): Command sent to 'rds16k.rdb':
T. 2007/10/18 07:35:19. (27): 'insert into test (a, b) values ('b', 3) '
T. 2007/10/18 07:35:19. (27): Command sent to 'rds16k.rdb':
T. 2007/10/18 07:35:19. (27): 'execute rs_update_lastcommit @origin = 103, @ori-
gin_qid =0x0000000000bd1f750005b58b00850005b58b0083000099cb007d0b610000000000000
001, @secondary_qid = x00000000000000000000000000000000000000000000000000000000
0000000000000000, @origin_time = '20071018 07:35:16:376''
T. 2007/10/18 07:35:20. (27): Command sent to 'rds16k.rdb':
T. 2007/10/18 07:35:20. (27): ' commit transaction'
```

Connectivity Issues

Verify that the data server entry is listed in the interfaces file, and the data server is up and running.

Incorrect Login/Password

```
E. 2007/06/13 07:58:21. ERROR #1028 DSI (193 rds.rdb) - seful/cm.c(2681)
Message from server: Message: 4002, State 1, Severity 14 -- 'Login
failed.'.
E. 2007/06/13 07:58:21. ERROR #1027 DSI (193 rds.rdb) - seful/cm.c(2681)
Open Client Client-Library error: Error: 67175468, Severity 4 -- 'ct_con-
nect(): protocol specific layer: external error: The attempt to connect to
the server failed.'.
E. 200706/13 07:58:21. ERROR #13045 DSI (193 rds.rdb) - seful/cm.c(2685)
Failed to connect to server 'rds' as user 'rdb_maint'. See CT-Lib and/or
server error messages for more information.
```

The maintenance user password is incorrect. Use the alter connection command to change the maintenance user password and
resume the connection:

```
alter connection to rds.rdb set password to rdb_maint_ps
resume connection to rds.rdb
```

Permission Issues

```
Message from server: Message: 10330, State 1, Severity 14 -- 'EXECUTE per-
mission denied on object rs_update_lastcommit, database rdb, owner dbo'.
E. 2007/06/13 11:41:58. ERROR #5046 DSI(193 rds.rdb) - /dsioqid.c(1951)
```

When executing the rs_get_lastcommit function in database rdb,
this indicates that Replication Server received data server errors.
See logged data server errors for more information.

The DSI thread can be suspended if the maintenance user
does not have correct permissions to apply transactions at the
replicate database.

```
use rdb
grant exec on rs_update_lastcommit to rdb_maint
```

At the replicate Replication Server:

```
resume connection to rds.rdb
```

SUID Mismatch

```
E. 2007/04/19 16:21:46. ERROR #1028 DSI(228 rds.rdb) - /dsiexec.c(392)
Message from server: Message: 10351, State 1, Severity 14 -- 'Server user
id 12 is not a valid user in database 'rdb'
I. 2007/04/19 16:21:46. Message from server: Message: 5701, State 1, Sever-
ity 10 -- 'Changed database context to 'master'.
'.
E. 2007/04/19 16:21:46. ERROR #5051 DSI(228 rds.rdb) - /dsiexec.c(409)
Received errors from database 'rds.rdb'. See logged ct-lib and data server
messages for more information.
```

DSI can shut itself down with the above message when the replicate database is initialized with a dump from the primary database
and the SUIDs (Server User IDs) between these two servers
don't match.

```
use rdb
go
sp_dropuser rdb_maint
go
```

Add the user to the database and grant necessary permissions:

```
sp_adduser rdb_maint
```

Connection Failures with Asynchronous Transaction and DDL Replication

To replicate asynchronous stored procedures at the primary Replication Server, the DSI uses the original user login and password
to connect to the primary data server. The maintenance user
login is not used. Similarly, for DDL replication the original user
login and password are used to connect to the replicate data
server, and the maintenance user login is used for DML replication. If the DSI thread connection goes down with a login failure
message, then use:

```
sysadmin log_first_tran, dataserver, database
```

This logs the failed transaction in the exception log. The app_user and app_pwd columns in the rssd..rs_exceptshdr system table contain the login and password used by DSI to log in to the primary data server (for asynchronous transactions) and the replicate data server (for DDL replication).

To view the logged exception, execute rs_helpexception in the RSSD database:

```
rs_helpexception
```

To display detailed information on specific transactions including the text of the transaction:

```
rs_helpexception tran_id, v
```

To delete transactions in the exceptions log:

```
rs_delexception tran_id
```

Whenever a transaction is skipped, either as a result of a log action assigned to data server errors or explicitly skipped with resume connection to *dataserver.database* skip transaction, that skipped transaction is written to the exception log. The exception log is made up of the rs_exceptscmd, rs_systext, and rs_exceptshdr RSSD system tables. rs_exceptscmd stores the information used to retrieve the text of transactions from the exception log, rs_exceptshdr stores information about failed transactions, and rs_systext stores the text of all commands. Orphan transactions and transactions logged by the sysadmin log_first_tran RCL command are also logged in the exception log.

Before skipping transactions, you should make sure that the data and log segments of the RSSD database have enough space. And you should regularly clean exceptions logged in the exception log with rs_delexception.

The following query can be executed to view information source commands and corresponding output commands for each transaction logged in the exceptions log.

```
select hdr.sys_trans_id, cmd_type, textval
from rs_exceptshdr hdr,
```

```
      rs_exceptscmd cmd,
      rs_systext
where error_site = data_server
      and error_db = database
      and hdr.sys_trans_id = cmd.sys_trans_id
      and cmd_id = parentid
order by log_time, src_cmd_line,
      output_cmd_index, sequence
```

Data Server Errors

Data server errors (such as mismatched datatypes, login/password/permissions problems, unique and foreign key constraint violations, and data corruption) are logged in the replicate Replication Server error log. The DSI thread connection can be resumed after fixing data server errors. If the error cannot be fixed, then the DSI thread connection can be resumed using skip transaction:

```
resume connection to rds.rdb skip transaction
```

The skip transaction option of resume connection should be used as a last resort, because it can cause inconsistent data on the replicate and can fill up the RSSD transaction log as well. In this case, you will need to clean up the RSSD exception log with rs_delexception. Subsequent transactions that depend on the skipped transaction will cause more errors. Since materialization or dematerialization requests are special types of transactions, if such a transaction is skipped, the subscription is invalidated and must be dropped. To avoid unique key violations during nonatomic materialization, you can use the set autocorrection on command to turn on automatic error correction before you resume the connection.

```
set autocorrection on
for myrep
with replicate at rds.rdb
```

When autocorrection is turned on, Replication Server converts the insert to a delete followed by an insert so that the insert cannot fail because of an existing row. Autocorrection cannot be turned on if the replication definition uses the replicate minimal columns option or the replication status for text, image, or unitext columns is set to replicate_if_changed.

You can also create error classes and assign actions for customized handling of data server errors. The default error action is "stop_replication" or "retry_log". The error action can be "ignore", "warn", "retry_log", "log", "retry_stop", or "stop_replication".

```
assign action warn
for duplicate_error_class
to rds.rdb
```

▶ **ignore:** The error is ignored by Replication Server and processing continues. This error action should only be used when the data server error code indicates a successful execution or an inconsequential warning.

▶ **warn:** Replication Server logs a warning message in the Replication Server error log without rolling back the transaction or retrying the command.

▶ **retry_log:** The transaction is rolled back by Replication Server and retried. The number of times Replication Server should retry can be set with alter connection or configure connection. If the error continues even after retrying, the transaction is logged in the exception log and the next transaction is executed by Replication Server.

```
suspend connection to rds.rdb
alter connection to rds.rdb set command_retry to '5'
resume connection to rds.rdb
```

▶ **log:** The current transaction is rolled back and logged in the exception log and the next transaction is executed by Replication Server.

▶ **retry_stop:** The transaction is rolled back and retried by Replication Server. The number of times Replication Server should retry can be set with alter connection or configure connection. If the error continues after retrying, the connection is suspended by Replication Server.

▶ **stop_replication:** Replication Server rolls back the current transaction and suspends the connection to the replicated database.

Unique Key Violation

```
I. 2007/04/04 15:12:27. The first transaction for database 'rds.rdb' has
been logged into the exceptions log and skipped.
E. 2007/04/04 15:12:27. ERROR #1028 DSI EXEC(106(1) rds.rdb) -
dsiqmint.c(2892)
Message from server: Message: 2601, State 3, Severity 14 -- 'Attempt to
insert duplicate key row in object 'Titles' with unique index 'ititles'
I. 2007/04/04 15:12:27. Message from server: Message: 3621, State 0,
Severity 10
-- 'Command has been aborted.
```

To fix this error, you can set autocorrection on or create an error class for duplicates and assign an appropriate action:

```
set autocorrection on for my rep
with replicate at rds.rdb

resume connection to rds.rdb
```

To create an error class for a duplicate key, follow these steps:

1. At the replicate Replication Server:

    ```
    create error class duplicate_error_class
    ```

2. At the RSSD database:

    ```
    rs_init_erroractions duplicate_error_class
    ```

3. View error class:

    ```
    rs_helpclass duplicate_error_class
    ```

4. At the replicate Replication Server:

    ```
    assign action ignore
        for duplicate_error_class
        to 2601,3621
    ```

```
alter connection to dataserver.database
set error class to duplicate_error_class

suspend connection to dataserver.database
resume connection to dataserver.database
```

Datatype Issue

E. 2007/06/05 10:27:55. ERROR #1028 DSI EXEC(112(1) rds.rdb) -
dsiqmint.c(2968)
Message from server: Message: 584, State 1, Severity 16 -- 'Explicit value
specified for identity field in table 'mytab' when 'SET IDENTITY_INSERT' is
OFF.
'.
H. 2007/03/05 10:27:55. THREAD FATAL ERROR #5049 DSI EXEC(112(1) rds.rdb) -
dsiqmint.c(2975)
The DSI thread for database 'rds.rdb' is being shutdown. DSI received data
server error #584 which is mapped to STOP_REPLICATION. See logged data
server errors for more information. The data server error was caused by
output command #1 mapped from input command #2 of the failed transaction.

The identity column in the replication definition should be defined
with the identity datatype, not numeric or integer. Use alter
replication definition to change the column datatype or drop
and create the replication definition:

```
1> alter replication definition myrep
2> alter columns with b as identity
3> go
```

Replication definition 'myrep' is altered.

resume connection to rds.rdb

To replicate identity columns, Replication Server turns on iden-
tity_insert:

```
set identity_insert table_name on
```

In the replicate database, before sending an insert command after
applying an insert to the replicated table, Replication Server turns
off identity_insert:

```
set identity_insert table_name off
```

Since all DML commands are executed by the maintenance user at the replicate database, the maintenance user must be aliased to dbo or the owner of the table at the replicate database in order to use the TSQL `identity_insert` option.

text/image Column Replication Status and the Null Property

```
W. 2007/08/22 17:59:13. WARNING #5065 DSI(124 rds.rdb) - /dsiutil.c(3092)
When writing a transaction for database 'rds.rdb' into the exceptions log,
received parser error 'Function 'rs_writetext' is not defined for table
'myrep'.' when parsing command '1'. The command is logged in its original
format."
```

This error is raised when the replication status and/or null property of a text/image column in a replication definition is not the same as was defined in the table. If the replication status for the text/image column in the table is set to `replicate_if_changed` with `sp_setrepcol` and the text/image column allows nulls, the text/image column should be defined as null in the replication definition, and the replication status for text/image columns should be set to `replicate_if_changed` in the replication definition. For existing replication definitions, you can use `alter replication definition` to change the replication status of the text/image column:

```
1> alter replication definition myrep replicate_if_changed b
2> go
Replication definition 'myrep' is altered.
```

```
1> alter replication definition myrep
2> alter columns with b text null
3> go
Replication definition 'myrep' is altered.
```

Missing Column in Replication Definition

```
E. 2007/08/27 13:39:47. ERROR #1028 DSI EXEC(126(1) rds.rdb) -
dsiqmint.c(2361)
Message from server: Message: 233, State 2, Severity 16 -- 'The column
emplname in table Employee does not allow null values.'.
H. 2007/08/27 13:39:47. THREAD FATAL ERROR #5049 DSI EXEC(126(1) rds.rdb) -
dsiqmint.c(2368)
The DSI thread for database 'rds.rdb is being shutdown. DSI received data
server error #233 which is mapped to STOP_REPLICATION. See logged data
server errors for more information. The data server error was caused by
output command #1 mapped from input command #3 of the failed transaction.
I. 2007/08/27 13:39:47. The DSI thread for database 'rds.rdb' is shutdown.
```

Most probably column names that appear in error message 233 are missing in the replication definition for that table. Replication Server generates an insert statement that consists of columns defined in the replication definition, and when DSI tries to apply that insert statement on the replicate database, Adaptive Server Enterprise raises error 233, since it will try to insert nulls in the missing columns in the replication definition.

You will need to add missing columns in the replication definition with alter replication. If this column is part of the primary key or where clause in the subscription, you will need to drop and recreate the subscription as well and then resynchronize replicate data.

Corruption Errors

```
E. 2007/00/22 10.33.30. ERROR #1020 DSI EXEC (126 (1) rds.rdb) -
dsiqmint.c(2968)
Message from server: Message: 21, State 1, Severity 21 -- 'WARNING - Fatal
Error 605 occurred at Aug 22 2007 6:33PM. Please note the error and time,
and contact a user with System Administrator (SA) authorization.
'.
H. 2007/08/22 18:33:38. THREAD FATAL ERROR #5049 DSI EXEC (126 (1) rds.rdb)
- dsiqmint.c(2975)
The DSI thread for database 'rds.rdb' is being shutdown. DSI received data
server error #21 which is mapped to STOP_REPLICATION. See logged data
server errors for more information. The data server error was caused by
output command #1 mapped from input command #3 of the failed transaction.
```

I. 2007/089/22 18:33:38. The DSI thread for database 'rds.rdb' is shutdown.

Review the replicated Adaptive Server Enterprise error log:

```
02:00000:00886:2007/08/22 18:33:38.19 server Error: 605, Severity: 21,
State: 1
02:00000:00886:2007/08/22 18:33:38.19 server An attempt was made to fetch
logical page '10544649' in database 'rdb' from cache 'default data cache'.
Page belongs to object with id '181252629510', not to object 'titles'
```

The problem here is that the server has requested a page for object titles; however, the page data indicates that this page really belongs to object ID 181252629510. This may or may not be hard corruption depending on whether the reference page used for the read is permanent or found incorrectly in cache. Run dbcc tablealloc on the objects listed involved in error 605. To resolve this error, please check the Adaptive Server Troubleshooting Guide and contact Sybase Technical Support.

Replication Server Errors

Replication Server errors are logged to the Replication Server error log. These errors can include "function string not found" or "Error 29094: no matching function string found" or issues with subscriptions.

The "function string not found" error can be due to incorrect use of variables in customized function strings used to replicate changes. Below are the restrictions:

▶ Only rs_insert and rs_update function strings can use new column values.

▶ Only rs_delete and rs_update function strings can use old column values.

▶ Only rs_select and rs_select_with_lock function strings can have input templates and can use user-defined variables.

▶ Only function strings for user-defined functions can use parameter values of functions. The parameter value of a function consists of the parameters passed to a replicated stored procedure.

WARNING #32020

W. 2007/10/18 08:48:17. WARNING #32020 DIST (103 pds16k.pdb) - xec/dist.c (3088) Table 'test2' is not defined.

This warning is raised when a table is marked for replication with sp_setreptable, but no replication definition has been created on this table. To fix this error, unmark the table for replication:

sp_setreptable test2, false

Stable Queues

The stable device is used to hold transactions in flight. Stable queues are message queues with the following features, which guarantee delivery of messages:

▶ Queues are written to disk so that messages added to them are non-volatile.

▶ Duplicate messages from an origin by OQID are recognized and ignored.

▶ Messages read from the queue are not automatically deleted. Deletion is done only when SQM (Stable Queue Manager) is requested to delete messages.

▶ Messages can be reread from the first undeleted message in the queue.

There are four types of queues:

▶ **Inbound queue:** Log records for objects marked for replication are forwarded by Replication Agent into the inbound queue of Replication Server. Transactions are ordered strictly in the order of occurrence of the commands. These log records are stored in the inbound queue of the stable queue until the transactions are complete. Transactions finish with either a commit or a rollback. Rollback transactions are discarded from the inbound queue. Committed transactions undergo subscription resolution at the primary Replication Server. Replication Server queries RSSD/ERSSD to determine which inbound queue transactions have subscriptions. Transactions that don't have subscriptions are discarded.

▶ **Outbound queue:** Transactions that have subscriptions in the inbound queue are forwarded to the appropriate outbound queue in commit order. Depending on the destination for these transactions, these queues are named as:

    ▶ **DSI queue:** If the destination is a database, the queue is named DSI queue. DSI thread (reader) treats this queue as a FIFO (first in, first out) transaction queue.

    ▶ **RSI queue:** All transactions being sent to another Replication Server are stored in the RSI (route) queue. The RSI thread treats this queue as a FIFO (first, in first out) transaction queue, with transactions from different sources physically interspersed with each other.

▶ **Materialization queue:** Messages that are part of a data materialization process of a subscription are stored in this queue.

▶ **Dematerialization queue:** The queue where dematerialization messages are stored.

Queues Are Full, They Are Not Getting Truncated

You may have set save_interval to a very high interval.

Replication Server retains messages in their queues for the period of time (configured with save_interval) after the next site (destination Replication Server) acknowledges receipt of the messages. The default save_interval is 0 (minutes), which may be an acceptable setting for recovery for low volume. Messages are not deleted immediately after receiving acknowledgement from destination; instead, messages are deleted in chunks. You can check the save_interval configured value by executing:

```
1> admin who,sqm
2> go
Spid State                 Info            Duplicates  Writes  Reads  Bytes
  B Writes  B Filled  B Reads  B Cache  Save_Int:Seg  First Seg.Block  Last Seg.Block
  Next Read  Readers  Truncs
---- -------------------- --------------- ----------- ------- ------ ------
--------- --------- -------- -------- ------------- ---------------- --------------
---------- -------- ------
29   Awaiting Message      101:0 rds.rdb  0            0       21     0
  0         0         7        0        120:7873      7873.7           7873.7
  7873.8.0  1         1
```

In the above example, Save_Int has been set to 120 minutes.
Replication Server will retain messages in the queue for 120 minutes after messages have been forwarded. If the replicate data
server rds that is connected to the the replicate repserver rrs
experiences a failure, rds can obtain the messages saved in the
DSI queue at rrs to resynchronize the replicate database rdb after
it has been restored. To change save_interval for a database connection or route:

```
suspend connection to rds.rdb
alter connection to rds.rdb set save_interval to '60'
resume connection to rds.rdb

suspend route to rrs
alter  route to rrs set save_interval to '60'
resume route to rrs
```

One or more components may be down. Check with admin
who_is_down. If SQM is down, then recycle Replication Server. If
distributor is down:

```
1> resume distributor pds.prs_RSSD
2> go
Distributor for 'pds.prs_RSSD' has been resumed.
```

If the DSI connection thread is down, then check the Replication
Server error log for error messages, resolve the error, and
resume the DSI connection.

Open Transaction in the Inbound Queue

Open transactions can impact the replication system badly, even stalling replication. If you have an open transaction:

▶ You won't be able to truncate the primary database transaction log because Database Replication Agent maintains information about the oldest open transaction in the transaction log. The secondary truncation point maintained by the Replication Agent would not allow truncation of the transaction log until the ENDXACT record is seen for the transaction. This will cause the primary database to get full, while other processes in that database can go to the LOG SUSPEND state.

▶ The stable device of the Replication Server can grow and eventually run out of space, causing replication to stop from or to other Replication Servers or databases.

▶ Stopped replication could cause an increase in latency.

You can have an open transaction due to:

▶ Transaction is not committed or rolled back in the primary database.

▶ Replication Agent has not yet scanned the database transaction log segment where the ENDXACT record has been written.

▶ The stable device doesn't have any free space available for SQM to write into stable devices.

▶ The secondary truncation point has been ignored and the transaction log has been truncated before the commit/rollback record is read by the Replication Agent.

▶ The replication component may not be available.

To identify an open transaction, you can query the master..syslogshold table in Adaptive Server Enterprise:

```
1> select * from master..syslogshold where dbid=4
2> go
dbid  reserved  spid page   xactid         masterxactid    starttime
  name              xloid
----- --------- ----- ------- --------------- --------------- --------------------
-------------------- -----
4     0         34    374155  0x8bb505006600  0x000000000000  Sep 30 2007  9:48AM
  $user_transaction  0
```

To query Replication Server:

```
1> admin who,sqt
2> go
Spid State           Info               Closed  Read  Open  Trunc  Removed  Full
  SQM Blocked                   First Trans  Parsed  SQM Reader  Change Oqids Detect Orphans
---- ---------------- ---------------------- ------- ----- ----- ------ -------- -----
------------------------ ------------ ------- ----------- ------------ --------------
21   Awaiting Wakeup  103:1 DIST pds16k.pdb 0      0     1     1      0        0
  1 st:0,cmds:5,qid:0:30:0  0               0           0            0
```

You can see that here we have one open transaction in the pdb database's inbound queue. This transaction has about five commands. The BEGIN TRANSACTION record for the transaction is located at segment 0 and block 30 in queue 103:1.

To find out what this transaction consists of, you will need to dump the queue using the sysadmin dump_queue command. This command can be used to dump queue contents to the RSSD database, the Replication Server error log, or a file. For complete syntax, please check the Sybase Replication Server Reference Manual.

In this example, we will dump the queue contents to file:

```
1> sysadmin dump_file,'/tmp/qdmp'
2> sysadmin dump_queue, 103, 1, 0, 30, -1
3> go

QUEUE DUMP FOR 103:1
BLOCK BEGIN q_number=103 q_type=1 blk=0:30 cnt=5
    Begin Transaction Origin User=sa Tran Name=_user_transaction
        ENTRY ver=1100 len=224 orig=103 lorig=0
oqid=0000000000bd1f750005b58b00660005b58b0066000099b900a1bbec0000000000000000
lqid=0:30:0 st=4 tr= '0000000000bd1f' u '00' fpds16kpdb comlen=104 begin
transaction
```

```
    ENTRY ver=1100 len=316 orig=103 lorig=0
oqid=0000000000bd1f750005b58b00670005b58b0066000099b900a1bbec0000000000000000
lqid=0:30:1 st=2097152 tr= '0000000000bd1f' u '00' fpds16kpdb comlen=197 insert
into dbo.test (a, b) values ('a', 1)

    ENTRY ver=1100 len=316 orig=103 lorig=0
oqid=0000000000bd1f750005b58b00680005b58b0066000099b900a1bbec0000000000000000
lqid=0:30:2 st=2097152 tr= '0000000000bd1f' u '00' fpds16kpdb comlen=197 insert
into dbo.test (a, b) values ('b', 2)

    ENTRY ver=1100 len=316 orig=103 lorig=0
oqid=0000000000bd1f750005b58b00690005b58b0066000099b900a1bbec0000000000000000
lqid=0:30:3 st=2097152 tr= '0000000000bd1f' u '00' fpds16kpdb comlen=197 insert
into dbo.test (a, b) values ('c', 3)

    ENTRY ver=1100 len=316 orig=103 lorig=0
oqid=0000000000bd1f750005b58b006a0005b58b0066000099b900a1bbec0000000000000000
lqid=0:30:4 st=2097152 tr= '0000000000bd1f' u '00' fpds16kpdb comlen=197 insert
into dbo.test (a, b) values ('d', 4)

END QUEUE DUMP FOR 103:1
```

The Origin Queue ID

Each command scanned by Replication Agent is assigned a unique OQID. It is a monotonically increasing binary 36 number (see Appendix A for OQID contents). This OQID is used by the Replication Server for duplicate and loss detection. OQID is stored in the rs_lastcommit table in the replicate database. There is one row per source database in the rs_lastcommit table, and that row contains the source OQID. OQID is also stored as the last locator field received by stable queues from each of their senders in the rs_locater table in the RSSD database. The OQID value saved in the rs_lastcommit table will sometimes but not always match its corresponding locator values. If an incoming OQID is lower than the last OQID saved in the rs_lastcommit table, Replication Server assumes that it has already been applied and is a duplicate row. If an incoming OQID is higher than the last OQID saved in the rs_lastcommit table, Replication Server assumes it is new and it is applied to the transaction.

Replication Agent has its own format for the origin queue ID. For complete details, see the Sybase Replication Agent Primary Database Guide.

From the queue dump in the "Open Transaction in the Inbound Queue" section, we see that the transaction is at segment 0 block 30. This transaction is attempting to insert into the test table. Now we need to identify why this transaction is open with the dbcc log command in conjunction with the OQID entry from sysadmin dump_queue.

15 to 20 bytes of the OQID contains begin record information for the oldest open transaction. The begin record (6 bytes) is a combination of page (4 bytes) and rowid (2 bytes) in the transaction log.

From this queue dump, OQID is:

```
oqid=0000000000bd1f750005b58b00660005b58b0066000099b900a1bbec000000000000000000

RID of begin transaction (15-20bytes): 0005b58b0066

Page number: 0005b58 (374155 decimal)
Row ID: 0066 (102 decimal)
```

To find the state of transaction 374155,102 we will use the dbcc log command to dump all the records associated with this transaction:

```
dbcc traceon(3604)
go
dbcc log(4,1,374155,102,0,-1,1)
go

    LOG RECORDS:
        BEGINXACT              (374155,102)   sessionid=374155,102
        attcnt=1 rno=102 op=0 padlen=1 sessionid=374155,102 len=144
        odc_stat=0x0000 (0x0000)
        loh_status: 0x0 (0x00000000)
        masterxsid=(invalid sessionid)
        xstat=XBEG_ENDXACT,XBEG_USERINFO_EXT,
        spid=34 suid=1 uid=1 masterdbid=0 dtmcord=0
        name=$user_transaction   time=Sep 30 2007  9:48:51:346AM
```

```
xversion=0 xextension.encrypt_method=2 xextension.encrypt_area_len=62
xextension.encrypt_area:
0x1562c2840 (    0):  9d9dee8f dcb9c9e9 daeacaf8 c8f8cfef  ...............
0x1562c2850 (   16):  cff6ccf8 c081cc9f fa8aaa99 a989bb8b  ...............
0x1562c2860 (   32):  bb8cac8c b58fbb83 c28fdcb9 c9e9daea  ...............
0x1562c2870 (   48):  caf8c8f8 cfefcff6 ccf8c081 cc9f      .............
```

```
INSERT                   (374155,103)   sessionid=374155,102 [REPLICATE]
attcnt=1 rno=103 op=4 padlen=5 sessionid=374155,102 len=64
odc_stat=0x0008 (0x0008 (LHSC_REPLICATE))
loh_status: 0x8 (0x00000008 (LHSC_REPLICATE))
objid=1136004047  ptnid=1136004047 pageno=145753 offset=32 status=
0x800(0x0800(XSTAT_EXPAGE))
```

This is the BEGINXACT record for transaction 374155,102. Now we can attempt to print the ENDXACT record for this same transaction by using 30 for log record type ENDXACT:

```
dbcc traceon(3604)
go
dbcc log(4,1,374155,102,0,30,1)
go
```

```
LOG SCAN DEFINITION:
        Database id : 4
        Forward scan: starting at beginning of log
        Log records for session id 374155,102
        Log operation type ENDXACT (30)


LOG RECORDS:

Total number of log records 0
```

From the dbcc log output we don't have an ENDXACT log record for this transaction, meaning this transaction is open. Most probably it is open at the database level and will require administration assistance.

There are other reasons a transaction could be open. You can do the following to avoid an open transaction:

1. Make sure Replication Agent is running without any issues since Replication Agent can go down after it has passed the begin record.

2. Make sure the stable queue has adequate free space for the SQM to write the messages coming from Replication Agent.

3. Make sure the `sqt_max_cache_size` is large enough to hold the largest transaction. To tune this parameter, you need to estimate the transaction sizes and overheads. To size `sqt_max_cache_size`, review the monitor counter 24019-SQTCacheLowBnd.

4. After determining the status of the open transaction in the Adaptive Server Enterprise, you can purge it from the inbound queue:

```
sysadmin purge_first_open, queueno, queuetype
```

or

```
sysadmin purge_all_open, queueno, queuetype
```

5. You can also use `sysadmin sqm_zap_command` to zap the open transaction:

```
1> sysadmin hibernate_on
2> go
The Replication Server has now entered hibernation mode.

1> sysadmin sqm_zap_command, 103,1,0,30,0
2> go
1> sysadmin hibernate_off
2> go
The Replication Server has now finished hibernation mode.
```

Data Not Being Replicated

If you have rebuilt queues or have replayed the transaction log in recovery mode, you should check the Replication Server error log for loss detected messages and query the rssd..rs_oqid and rssd..rs_exceptslast tables:

```
select * from rs_oqid where valid >0
select * from rs_exceptslast where status >0
```

Sybase recommends using the RCL `ignore loss` command, which will allow Replication Server to accept messages after it detects a loss:

```
ignore loss from data_server.database [to {data_server.database | replication_server}]
```

For warm standby databases, use the logical connection name for `data_server.database` except for losses detected by Replication Server between the active database and the standby database. To ignore those losses, use the physical `data_server.database`.

If you are using routes, check both Replication Server error logs for loss detected messages. For direct routes, the destination Replication Server detects message losses from the source Replication Server. Replication Server detects message losses on connection to the replicate database it manages.

After executing the `ignore loss` command, you will need to reconcile replicate databases.

Duplicates Being Ignored

The DSI connection thread will start ignoring transactions as duplicates after restoring from dumps. To fix this you will need to increase the `gen_id` of the database:

```
admin get_generation, prim_dataserver, prim_database
```

Increase the `gen_id` by executing the Adaptive Server Enterprise command `dbcc settrunc`:

```
use database
sp_stop_rep_agent database
dbcc settrunc(ltm, 'gen_id', db_generation)
sp_start_rep_agent database
```

db_generation

Should be one greater than the old generation ID you got by executing the `admin get_generation` command from Replication Server.

Error 6025

This error is issued because of block inconsistency caused by hardware/OS problems. Replication Server tries to read a block from the stable device for a given queue and then checks if the read block is the one it has requested; if not, error 6025 is raised.

Sometimes recycling Replication Server resolves this error. If the problem persists after rebooting, follow these steps:

1. Dump the queue using `sysadmin dump_queue` (explained in the "Open Transaction in the Inbound Queue" section):

    `sysadmin dump_queue, queueno, queuetype, segment, block, -1`

2. Suspend the connection to `replicateds.replicatedb`.

3. Shut down Replication Server.

4. Restart Replication Server in standalone mode by adding the -M flag to the runserver file.

5. Purge the queue with the `sysadmin sqm_purge_queue` command:

    `sysadmin sqm_purge_queue, queueno, queuetype`

6. Shut down Replication Server:

    `shutdown`

7. Restart Replication Server in normal mode.

8. Reconcile the replicate database.

In some cases, you won't be able to dump the queue because the `sysadmin dump_queue` command will hang. In that case, follow this procedure:

1. Restart Replication Server in standalone mode by adding the -M flag to the runserver file.

2. Purge the queue with the `sysadmin sqm_purge_queue` command:

    `sysadmin sqm_purge_queue, queueno, queuetype`

3. Shut down Replication Server:

   ```
   shutdown
   ```

4. Restart Replication Server in normal mode.

5. Reconcile the replicate database with the primary.

Corruption in the Queue

Corruption in the stable queues can cause DSI to be suspended.

```
W. 2007/08/09 13:23:38. WARNING #5065 DSI (103 rds.rdb) - /dsiutil.c(2508)
When writing a transaction for database 'rds.rdb' into the exceptions log,
received parser error 'Line 1, character 2651: Incorrect syntax with
'g73'.' when parsing command '1'. The command is logged in its original
format.
```

The first step is to dump the queue using the `sysadmin` `dump_queue` command.

Here is a section of the queue dump:

```
BAD ENTRY len=2900 orig=104 oqid=0000000167983b8900403f1a000500403f150003
000092dd00d1edc80000000000000002 lqid=547795:60:0 st=0 tr= '00000001' g
'98' ;w'0003' pds.pdb comlen=2769 A0110 05iso_1_ds 0,~"!,...
   .
   .
   .

734065617274686c696e6b2e6e65651800351009500d3008000017274d6963726g73,103945
5851, 831595422,4279,0,~":Fwd: Fw: strange injuries,0,NTLL,NULL ...
```

From this dump we see that one bit is added at one place (g73, probably should be f73) and then one bit is reduced (NTLL should have been NULL). This is quite possibly due to some issues on the network, since it is one bit that is getting bad. You should investigate network issues.

Data Latency

Replication Agent may not be reading transactions quickly. You will need to monitor Replication Agent performance, tune the primary database transaction log by binding it to its own cache, and use large logiosize. DSI may not be applying transactions to the replicate database fast enough. To tune the replication system, please refer to Chapter 14.

Appendix A

Origin Queue ID

Each record in the transaction log is identified by the origin queue ID. The format of the origin queue ID is determined by the primary database type and the Replication Agent instance.

The origin queue ID (OQID) for Sybase Adaptive Server Replication Agent is 36 bytes and contains the following fields:

Bytes	Contents
1-2 (2)	Generation number
3-8 (6)	Log page timestamp
9-14 (6)	Rowid of this tran
15-20 (6)	Rowid of begin tran
21-28 (8)	Datetime of begin tran
29-30 (2)	Reserved for RepAgent to delete orphans
31-32 (2)	Unused
33-34 (2)	Appended by TD (Transaction Delivery module) for uniqueness
35-36 (2)	Appended by MD (Message Delivery module)

The origin queue ID for Replication Agent 15.0 is 32 bytes, or 64 hexadecimal characters:

Character	Bytes	Description
0-3	2	Database generation ID
4-19	8	System change number
20-27	4	Log sequence number
28-35	4	Block number
36-39	2	Block offset, relative to the start of the block
40-47	4	Oldest active transaction begin log sequence number
48-55	4	Oldest active transaction begin block number
56-59	2	Oldest active transaction block offset
60-63	2	Available for specifying uniqueness

The origin queue ID for Replication Agent 15.1 contains the following fields:

Character	Bytes	Description
0-3	2	Generation ID of the database
4-15	6	System Change Number (SCN)
16-19	2	Redo log thread
20-23	2	System Change Number Subindex
24-43	10	Redo log record block address
44-55	6	System Change Number of the oldest active transaction
56-63	4	Locator ID

Appendix B

Removing the Active Replication Server from the Replication System

To remove an active Replication Server from the replication system, follow these steps:

1. Execute the rs_helprep stored procedure in the RSSD database to determine which replication definitions defined at the Replication Server are to be removed from the replication system. rs_helprep without any parameters displays information about all the replication definitions. rs_helprep *repdef* displays information about the replication definition and corresponding subscriptions. The rs_helpdbrep stored procedure should be executed to display information about database replication definitions.

2. For each replication definition/database replication definition defined at the primary Replication Server, execute drop subscription for each subscription on all replicate Replication Servers that manage subscribing data:

```
drop subscription mysub
for myrep
with replicate at rds.rdb
without purge
```

Note: To retain data in the replicate database, you should drop the subscription using the `without purge` clause. To delete data, use the `with purge` clause. When a subscription is dropped with the `with purge` clause, Replication Server logs in to the replication database as maintenance user and selects and evaluates sets of rows that could be deleted against subscriptions. The delete is done in a single transaction, performed by an `rs_select_with_lock` function string in the replicate database. You can also drop subscriptions using `incrementally with purge`; this tells Replication Server to delete 10 rows at a time. It is best to drop a subscription using `without purge` and then manually delete subscription data. Database subscriptions should be dropped with `without purge`, but table subscriptions or publications can be dropped using either `with purge` or `without purge`. Execute `check subscription` to make sure subscriptions are dropped:

```
check subscription mysub
for myrep
with primary at rds.rdb
```

For complete details, see Chapter 10.

After dropping the subscription, drop each table replication definition or database replication definition at the primary Replication Server:

```
drop replication definition myrep
```

To drop the database replication definition:

```
drop database replication definition mydbrep
with primary at pds.pdb
```

Execute rs_helprep/rs_helpdbrep in RSSD again to make sure all table replication definitions/database replication definitions are dropped from all the Replication Servers to which this Replication Server has routes.

If the Replication Server to be removed has subscriptions for replication definitions to other Replication Servers, you should drop them using the `without purge` clause if you want to retain subscription data and `with purge` if you want to delete subscription data. Then drop the corresponding replication definition at each Replication Server.

3. If this Replication Server is primary for any customized func-
    tion-string class or error class, then execute move primary at
    the new primary Replication Server to change the primary
    Replication Server for the function-string class or error class.
    You must have a route from the Replication Server (to be
    removed) to the new primary Replication Server, and this
    new primary Replication Server should also have a route to
    all the same Replication Servers as the old primary Replica-
    tion Server. Execute the following command at the new
    primary Replication Server (*new_prim*):

    ```
    move primary of
        error class dup_err
    new_prim
    ```

4. Stop RepAgent commected to this Replication Server, using
    the sp_stop_rep_agent system stored procedure at Adaptive
    Server Enterprise:

    ```
    sp_stop_rep_agent database
    ```

5. Execute sp_config_rep_agent to disable the RepAgent con-
    nected to this Replication Server at Adaptive Server
    Enterprise:

    ```
    use database
    go
    sp_config_rep_agent database, 'disable'
    ```

6. Drop database connections to all databases managed by this
    Replication Server:

    ```
    drop connection to dataserver.database
    ```

 Note: If you want to replicate data in databases managed by
the Replication Server that is to be removed, you must create
new database connections to other Replication Servers and create new subscriptions.

---

7. If this Replication Server is an intermediate site for indirect
    routes, execute alter route so that this Replication Server is

no longer an intermediate site for an indirect route. See Chapter 8 for more information about routes.

8. Drop all routes from this Replication Server by executing the drop route command for each route from this Replication Server to another Replication Server:

```
drop route to repserver_name
```

9. Drop all routes to this Replication Server from each Replication Server by executing the drop route command from each Replication Server from which you have a route to this Replication Server:

```
drop route to old_rs
```

10. Execute the sysadmin droprs command at the ID Server to drop this Replication Server from the ID Server:

```
sysadmin droprs, old_rs
```

11. Execute the sysadmin dropdb command at the ID Server to drop all databases including the RSSD database managed by this Replication Server from the ID Server:

```
sysadmin dropdb, dataserver, database
```

Appendix C

Useful Queries

The queries presented here can be used by the Replication Server DBA to get information directly from RSSD system tables.

▶ Find databases controlled by a particular Replication Server:

```
select dsname, dbname from rs_databases, rs_sites
where prsid = id and name = replication_server
```

▶ Check header information for all logged transactions intended for a particular query:

```
select * from rs_exceptshdr
where error_site = data_server
and error_db = database
order by log_time
```

▶ View complete information about a transaction in the exception log:

```
select h.sys_trans_id, cmd_type, textval
from rs_exceptshdr h, rs_exceptscmd c, rs_systext
where error_site = data_server
and error_db = database
and h.sys_trans_id = c.sys_trans_id
and cmd_id = parent_id
order by log_time, src_cmd_line
output_cmd_index, sequence
```

▶ Find maintenance user name and password:

```
select username, password from rs_maintusers, rs_databases
where destid = dbid
and dsname = dataserver
and dbname = database
```

► Find total segments used by each inbound Replication Agent queue:

```
select dsname, dbname, sum(used_flag) 'usedsegs'
from rs_segments s, rs_databases d
where d.dbid=s.q_number
and s.q_type=1
group by dsname, dbname
```

► Find total segmens used by each DSI queue:

```
select dbname, dbname, sum(used_flag) 'usedsegs'
from rs_segments s, rs_databases d
where d.dbid=s.q_number
and s.q_type=0
group by dsname, dbname
```

► Find total segments used by each RSI queue:

```
select name, sum(used_flag) 'usedsegs'
from rs_segments sg, rs_sites st
where st.id=sg.q_number
group by name
```

► To find out origin queue IDs stored in the stable queue (note that the OQID is refreshed constantly):

```
select origin_q_id, valid, dsname, dbname
from rs_databases d, rs_oqid o
where d.dbid=o.origin_site_id
and o.q_number=queue number
and o.q_type=queue type
```

Example:

```
select origin_q_id, valid, dsname, dbname
from rs_databases d, rs_oqid o
where d.dbid=o.origin_site_id
and o.q_number=101
and o.q_type=1
```

► To find out RSI locator received by the Replication Server:

```
select name, locater
from rs_sites s, rs_locater 1
where s.id=1.sender
```

```
and 1.type="R"
```

▶ To list all the replication definitions for a given primary database and data server (execute this query in the primary RSSD database):

```
select objname, dsname, dbname
from rs_databases d, rs_objects o
where d.dbid=o.dbid
and d.dsname='primary_dataserver'
and d.dbname='primary_database'
```

Example:

```
select objname, dsname, dbname
from rs_databases d, rs_objects o
where d.dbid=o.dbid
and d.dsname='pds'
and d.dbname='prs_RSSD'
```

▶ To list replication definitions that have subscriptions for a given replicate database:

```
select distinct (objname), subname
from rs_subscriptions s, rs_objects o, rs_databases d
where s.dbid=d.dbid
and s.objid=o.objid
```

▶ To list the primary data server and database name for a particular subscription (execute this query from the replicate RSSD/ERSSD):

```
select distinct d.dsname, d.dbname, s.subname
from rs_subscriptions s, rs_objects o, rs_databases d
where o.dbid=d.dbid
and s.objid=o.objid
and s.subname='subname'
```

▶ To get a database replication definition for a given data server and database:

```
select dbrepname
from rs_databases, rs_dbreps
where rs_databases.dbid=rs_dbreps.dbid
and rs_databases.dsname='primary_dataserver'
and rs_databases.dbname='primary_database'
```

Example:

```
select dbrepname
from rs_databases, rs_dbreps
where rs_databases.dbid=rs_dbreps.dbid
and rs_databases.dsname='pds'
and rs_databases.dbname='pubs2'
```

▶ To list a database that has a database subscription for a given database replication definition:

```
select distinct (r.dsname + '.'+r.dbname)
from rs_subscriptions s, rs_repdbs r, rs_dbreps d
where s.objid=d.dbrepid
and s.dbid=r.dbid
and d.dbrepname='dbrepdefname'
```

Example:

```
select distinct (r.dsname + '.'+r.dbname)
from rs_subscriptions s, rs_repdbs r, rs_dbreps d
where s.objid=d.dbrepid
and s.dbid=r.dbid
and d.dbrepname='pubrep'
```

Index